Doris Berger-Grabner
Strategic Retail Management and Brand Management

Doris Berger-Grabner

Strategic Retail Management and Brand Management

Trends, Tactics, and Examples

DE GRUYTER
OLDENBOURG

ISBN 978-3-11-054383-4
e-ISBN (PDF) 978-3-11-054382-7
e-ISBN (EPUB) 978-3-11-054395-7

Library of Congress Control Number: 2021938689

Bibliographic information published by the Deutsche Nationalbibliothek
The Deutsche Nationalbibliothek lists this publication in the Deutsche Nationalbibliografie;
detailed bibliographic data are available on the internet at http://dnb.dnb.de.

© 2021 Walter de Gruyter GmbH, Berlin/Boston
Cover image: Ekkasit919/iStock/Getty Images Plus
Typesetting: Integra Software Services Pvt. Ltd.
Printing and binding: CPI books GmbH, Leck

www.degruyter.com

Preface

The traditional retail industry and associated business models have gone through a significant phase of disruption. The rapid emergence of new technologies, digital business models, and the evolution of social media platforms as a new sales channel continue to influence the retail sector. Key contextual or external trends that will affect and shape the retail landscape in the years to come are mainly the changing face of the consumer and new patterns of personal consumption, evolving geopolitical dynamics, technological advancements, and structural industry shifts. Each of these trends will have a different level of impact in the retail industry. It is important that retailers use these trends, adapt their retail strategies and tactics, and come up with innovative, new ways of doing business.

When a crisis occurs, it is usually unforeseeable and an exceptional situation. No company is protected from crises, but it is necessary to prepare for them. With an efficient crisis management, appropriate concepts should be developed, which also consider the company-specific conditions. Crises present us all with new challenges. The coronavirus pandemic has shown how health crises quickly turn into economic crises and what drastic effects such a global pandemic has on all of us. In particular, the retail landscape, and especially the food trade, was in the spotlight as a system-relevant industry. However, it also became clear how important it is to switch to new and digital business models and to adapt to changes in consumer behaviour quickly and in line with the situation. And the retail sector has once again demonstrated how innovative and flexible it can be in responding to crisis situations. It was also the retail sector that gave people security in uncertain times. Security that the supply of everyday goods is guaranteed and that no one must worry that they will run out of goods for daily needs.

Moreover, online retailing has also allowed an enormous upswing. Many consumers who had previously never or hardly ever shopped on the internet have taken advantage of this sales channel. These new sales channels are likely to remain with us in the future, so they should be seen as an opportunity.

There are great opportunities for integrating digital technologies in-store, particularly since they can support the consumer showrooming behaviour, especially in the apparel sector. So today, we are observing yet another technological shift in the retail experience. Mobile inspired customers are on the go make easy online transactions. These technology shifts have caused great disruption but have also led to innovation.

Today we are living in a challenging time for retail. The changes that digital technologies and innovations have created are providing retailers with opportunities to know their customers, create deeper relationships and lower the friction of the connection through a seamless omnichannel experience.

https://doi.org/10.1515/9783110543827-202

And what can also be said with a fair amount of certainty is that humans are social creatures and need physical contact. The retail employee will therefore always be important, perhaps in the future no longer to perform manual work but to advise the customer and to have an open ear. They will continue to have an important role in offering the customer a shopping experience and meeting the desire for individualization and simplification in times of oversupply.

To conclude, consumer engagement with the retail sector and retailers is constantly evolving and is being strongly influenced by technology. But one thing will remain constant—strong retail brands have survived disruptive changes in the past and will continue to do so. Continuous investment in building a brand identity and image, staying close to its purpose, moving with times, and establishing a core equity of the brand, are some of the key characteristics of a strong retail branding strategy.

Finally, the "Wheel of Retailing" will continue to turn and will change the trading landscape even further. However, a city without places of trade, without stores or marketplaces, would be possible, but we will not see this in the future, this will indeed remain only science fiction!

Prof. (FH) Dr. Doris Berger-Grabner, MA

Contents

Part One: **Strategic retail management**

An overview of strategic retail management

Alibaba Group Holding Limited is the leading online commerce provider in China, offering a broad spectrum of business-to-business (B2B), business-to-consumer (B2C), and consumer-to-consumer (C2C) e-commerce services as well as mobile payments. The stand-alone B2B e-commerce portal Alibaba.com was established in 1999 as a B2B portal connecting Chinese manufacturers to overseas buyers, essentially making it easy to do business anywhere. Now the group is the leading e-commerce provider in Asia as its C2C online marketplace Taobao (https://world.taobao.com/) and B2C online retail platform Tmall (http://about.tmall.com/) are also the market leaders in their respective business segments.

The Alibaba Group has since then grown to become the largest e-commerce company in the world with a gross merchandise volume of US$0.43 trillion in 2017 and US$454 million annual active buyers on its various marketplaces.

The vision is "to become a truly global company, providing solutions to real world problems and using e-commerce to help globalization by making retail more inclusive."

The philosophy is "to build long-term strategic value and drive synergies for its global business through organic growth and strategic acquisitions."

Technology has been the driving force behind the phenomenal growth of the Figure Alibaba group. Since its founding in 1999 the company has also moved into new business areas such as digital entertainment and local services. Core commerce still refers to a combination of retail and wholesale commerce business. There have been two notable shifts in Alibaba's retail commerce platforms: first, from its origins as a marketplace to becoming a social commerce platform, allowing consumers to have fun exploring, and second, Alibaba's move from online to offline, providing consumers with an omnichannel experience (Weinswig, August 2017).

Gather more useful information on the Alibaba Group Holding Limited by using the links: https://www.alibaba.com/ and https://www.weforum.org/agenda/2017/01/factbox-alibaba/

- **Chapter 1 Strategic Retail Management introduces** retailing in general and shows why this field is so essential to be studied. Furthermore, the strategic planning process in retailing will be discussed. In detail, it will be explained how to develop an appropriate retail strategy and how to target different types of consumers. Retail branding and positioning and sustainable retailing, with a special focus on ethical performance in retailing, will also be discussed in Chapter 1.
- **Chapter 2 Marketing Mix in Retailing** explains the retail marketing mix and refers to the 7Ps in retailing: Product, Price, Place, Promotion, Presentation, People, and Process. There is an emphasis on essential strategic marketing management issues, especially merchandise management, category management, and customer relationship management (CRM).
- **Chapter 3 E-Commerce, E-Tailing, and Digitalization** looks at trends and developments within the retail sector and defines the most important terms in the digital age. Furthermore, this chapter illustrates innovative technologies and instruments in the retail sector and their challenges and opportunities for retailers and customers.

https://doi.org/10.1515/9783110543827-001

1 Strategic retail management

1.1 Introduction to retailing

Changing consumer behaviour in general and changing shopping tastes and expectations are quietly transforming the international retail landscape. Today's consumers increasingly demand instant gratification, personalized goods and services and go further towards the direction of borrowing goods instead of buying them. As a result, the retail business model of the future is expected to look different than just a decade ago, and retailers that do not keep pace with changing consumer tastes will not survive in the long run. In an environment of heightened competition and saturated markets retail companies constantly must evaluate and rethink their business models and focus on what makes them different from competitors. The retail stores of the future will focus on selling experiences, lifestyles, and lifestyle products, instead of offering "just" physical products and therefore provide an added value in the customer's daily life.

In saturated markets where products and services are becoming increasingly indistinguishable it is essential for every retailer to redefine its key strategies and to focus on strong, mainly emotional, attributes but also on entering new markets and targeting new consumer groups. Retailers constantly experiment with various marketing techniques to make their products more appealing to consumers, to be in the customer's relevant set (i.e., a group of products or brands in the mind of the customer that limit external search and alternative limitation) and to increase the purchase probability in their sales channels, online and offline. Studies have shown that most of the consumers still make their final purchase decisions directly in a store, at the so-called point of sale (POS). The importance of the POS is still undisputable as more than 70% of customers' buying decisions are made directly in a store at the POS (POPAI, 2016). When analysing consumers' buying behaviour and trying to find out which factors influence in-store buying decisions, several in-store attention-based factors can be identified – above all product presentation in general, the shelf position of the product, the number of facings (i.e., the number of products that are placed next to each other on a shelving unit) (Chandon, Hutchinson, Bradlow, & Young, 2007) and the packaging of the product (Clement, 2007). Nevertheless, most of the in-store purchase decisions are based on unconscious processes (Häusel, 2006). Therefore, for marketers and retailers it is very important to understand not only the visible and conscious processes, but also those unconscious processes, to make their products and brands more visual, to increase product sales and to generate customer satisfaction and long-term relationships with their customers.

Since the last few years, more and more retailers start experiencing with new, innovative technologies to make shopping more interactive and to achieve customer engagement. Customer engagement is especially important for every retailer as it is the emotional connection between a customer and a product. Highly engaged

https://doi.org/10.1515/9783110543827-002

customers usually buy more, promote their favourite products through word of mouth, are less price-sensitive and demonstrate more loyalty. Creating holistic, high-quality shopping experiences is an important component in a retailer's customer engagement strategy. The box below provides an illustrative example how a retailer can create a holistic shopping experience for the customers.

> **Alibaba, the market leader in China's booming e-tailing business, experiences with innovative ways of shopping for creating holistic shopping experiences**
> Virtual reality (VR) shopping is no longer science fiction and is already very popular among certain consumer groups, especially Generation Y and Z. Alibaba, the Chinese internet conglomerate, is constantly experimenting with new ways of shopping. One way is the Buy+ VR experience. For engaging in this shopping experience, customers must use a VR headset or a cardboard VR headset, slip their smartphones into the headset, and then are able to walk virtually, for example, through the streets of New York City. There they can take a yellow cab to a department store, where they can stroll around the store and browse a broad range of products, examine them virtually, and purchase goods instantly. VR shopping gives online shoppers a more interactive and holistic shopping experience.
>
> Another new shopping concept tested and used by Alibaba applies augmented reality (AR) technology and gamification elements. This particular technology, similar to the technology behind the popular game Pokemon Go, is provided to create holistic shopping experiences when shopping online. Like Pokemon Go, the so-called Tmall game (http://about.tmall.com/) has a virtual map that players can explore. Using a game within the Tmall app, shoppers "capture" Tmall's cat mascot at participating shops and restaurants to unlock and win "red packets." Users must tap on their phones to capture Tmall's cat mascot. Gamifying shopping, where customers must make repeat visits to win rewards, can help to increase customer loyalty (BBC, November 2016) and customer engagement.
>
> These examples of new ways of shopping create new opportunities for retailers to engage and communicate with their customers and improve customer relations. By using VR and AR retailers can fulfill the customers' preferences for personalization and individualization. They can customize, for example, their storefronts, their product and service offerings, and also their marketing materials so that every consumer sees personalized search results, recommendations and offerings, when they accept and use these new technologies (BBC, 2016) and new ways of shopping.

The following chapters go into more detail and will point out essential issues and provide knowledge, which are important for making strategic retail decisions.

1.1.1 "Wheel of Retailing" and further developments

The literature contains various approaches to explaining the dynamic development of forms of business. The displacement theory approach is one of the most discussed theories by scientists, which assumes that the emergence and rise of forms of business are based on a uniform basic pattern.

McNair (1931), with his observation of the empirical phenomenon "Wheel of Retailing," made the first attempts to legally formulate the development process of forms of business and, based on this, Nieschlag (1954) developed the "Law of the Dynamics of Forms of Business."

Nieschlag (1954) coined the term "dynamics of the forms of trade." In his explanations he tries to elaborate those regularities in the market-structural developments, according to which new forms of business arise in trade. In doing so, he takes up the basic idea of the closely related "Wheel of Retailing" by McNair (1931). During this period, Nieschlag (1954) attempted to divide the development of business forms into three phases, preferring to divide them into two:
– emergence and rise
– maturity and assimilation

Both approaches to displacement theory take the view that new, price-aggressive forms of business initially appear on the market and try to attract consumers' attention and open the market through price. The attractiveness of these forms of business (innovators) decreases over time, partly because this form of business is copied by other companies.

In the second phase, the innovators change their business policy. The use of additional competitive instruments, such as expanding the product range, improving quality, or offering additional services, begins. This transition from price to nonprice competition is known as "trading up" and leads to new, price-aggressive entrants in the market attacking the former innovators, for whom price activity is weakening due to increased costs. McNair (1931, 39) formulates this strategy of trading up as follows: "After they (the retailing institutions) had traded up the quality of the merchandise handled, and some of the price advantage has been lost in the process, distributive enterprises develop into a third stage, characterised by competition in services of all kinds."

In the subsequent assimilation phase, the former innovators gradually adapt to the already established, traditional forms of business and thus offer a promising starting point for the emergence of new, price-aggressive innovators.

The "Wheel of Retailing" model describes a regular development pattern of business forms in retailing, a certain empirical regularity. Some experts state that this displacement-theoretical explanatory approach is a phenomenon that can often be observed in western industrial nations, whereas in emerging and developing countries there is a particularly large number of so-called nonconforming examples. The development of the forms of enterprise described by these theories can therefore neither be described as legally nor interculturally valid. Therefore, experts have tried to expand the model with three further evolutionary patterns of operational structure (Köhler, 1990):
– high-level trading strategy: sales policy instruments other than price policy dominate a type of business
– trading-down strategy: besides high-price business forms, there are also those with a low-price policy
– low-level trading strategy: forms of business maintain a low-price policy

High-end strategy
- High prices
- Excellent facilities and services
- Upscale consumers

Medium strategy
- Moderate prices
- Improved facilities
- Broader base of value - and service-conscious consumers

Low-end strategy
- Low prices
- Limited facilities
- Price-sensitive consumers

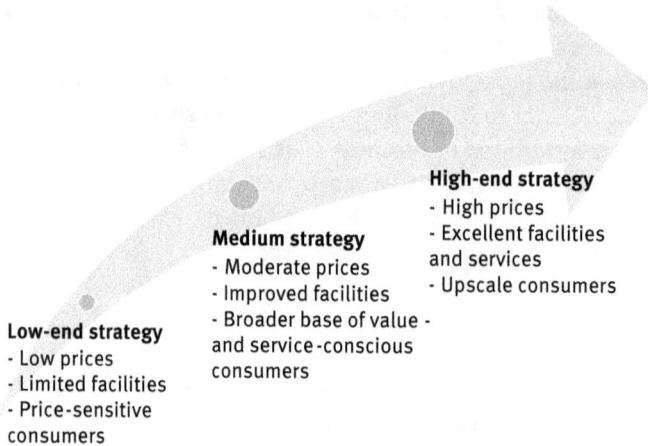

Figure 1.1: Expansion of the Wheel of Retailing.
Source: Own elaboration based on Köhler, 1990

According to Köhler (1990, 64), this extended "dynamic of the forms of retailing" can be used as a starting point for strategic planning in retail.

In summary, it can be stated that the justification for the success of new forms of business using a single sales policy instrument, price policy, is insufficient, since counterexamples partially refute the theses of McNair (1931) and Nieschlag (1956). A variation or innovation of business forms can also take place through the combination of other characteristics, such as product range, service or performance, location, and/or communication policy. Due to this versatility of market access and development possibilities, it is advisable to supplement the concepts of the "Wheel of Retailing" and the "Law of the Dynamics of Form of Business." To this end, Köhler (1990) offers the expansion proposal just outlined. The existing explanatory approaches offer suggestions for analysing and explaining the dynamic development processes of business forms in retail.

1.1.2 Facts and figures of the largest retailers in the world

This chapter points out the largest retailers in the world, analyses their performance across geographies, sectors and channels, and illustrates why the global retail sector has such a huge impact on the world's economy.

The economic environment for retailers continues to be challenging. Reasons are slow economic growth in major developed economies, high levels of debt in emerging countries, deflation or low inflation in rich countries, troubled credit markets in some countries, and superannuation of the population in developed countries.

Nevertheless, and luckily for all retailers, consumers still need to shop. Therefore, the outlook for many retailers, especially the largest retailers in the word, is positive.

Table 1.1 ranks the 15th largest retailers in the world by their retail sales. Above all, the US retail corporation Walmart, that operates a chain of hypermarkets, discount department stores and grocery stores, leads the ranking, followed by the US supermarket giant Kroger and the US warehouse club operator Costco. The Home Depot, an American home improvement supplies retailing company that sells tools, construction products and services, is ranked fourth and Walgreens Boots Alliance, consisting of several pharmaceutical manufacturing, wholesale, and distribution companies is the fifth largest retailer in the world (National Retail Federation, 2016). Table 1.1 lists the 15th largest retailers in the world, also including Amazon.com, which is ranked eighth. Most of the retailers are based in the United States and therefore are less well-known in Europe. For that reason, it seems to be reasonable to describe some of these US-based retailers in more detail.

The Kroger Co. is an American retailing company founded by Bernard Kroger in 1883 in Cincinnati, Ohio. It is the United States' largest supermarket chain by revenue and the second-largest general retailer behind Walmart. Kroger is also the third-largest retailer in the world and the third largest private employer in the United States. Kroger operates 2,778 supermarkets and multidepartment stores with store formats that include hypermarkets, supermarkets, superstores, department stores, and 326 jewellery stores. Kroger-branded grocery stores are in the Midwestern and Southern United States. Kroger operates 37 food processing or manufacturing facilities, 1,360 supermarket fuel centres, and 2,122 pharmacies (Kroger, 2018).

Costco is an American multinational corporation, which operates a chain of membership-only warehouse clubs. As of July 2018, Costco had a total of 751 warehouses, mainly in the United States and Canada but also in Asia, Australia, and Europe. The retailer focuses on selling products at low prices at extremely high volume. These goods are usually bulk packaged, allowing further reductions in price and marketing costs. A typical Costco warehouse carries only 4,000 distinct products, while a typical Walmart Supercentre carries approximately 140,000 products.

Costco also saves money by not stocking extra bags or packing materials; to carry out their goods, customers must use a shopping cart, bring their own bags, or use empty merchandise shipping boxes from the company's vendors. Lighting costs are reduced on sunny days, as most Costco locations have several skylights. During the day, electronic light meters measure how much light is coming in the skylights and turn off an appropriate percentage of the interior lights. Most products are delivered to the warehouse on shipping pallets and these pallets are used to display products for sale on the warehouse floor. Costco's annual membership fees account for 80% of Costco's gross margin and 70% of its operating income (Gabler, 2016).

Target Corporation is an upscale discount retailer that provides high-quality, on-trend merchandise at attractive prices in spacious and guest-friendly stores. Target has 1,835 stores in the United States, 39 distribution centres in the United States,

350,000-plus team members worldwide, and operates an online business at target.com. Target is recognized as a leader in innovation across the retail industry, from pioneering the concept of designer partnerships to consistently being best in class in store design. Target continually reinvents its stores, including layout, presentation, and merchandise assortment, to create an engaging shopping experience.

Albertsons operates as a banner of Albertsons Companies, one of the largest food and drug retailers in the United States. With both a strong local presence and national scale, the company operates stores across 35 states and the District of Columbia under 19 well-known banners. Albertsons Companies is dedicated to helping people across the country live better lives. In 2015 alone, with the help of generous customers, Albertsons Companies and the Albertsons Companies Foundation gave more than $270 million in food and financial support to the more than 2,300 communities they serve (Albertsons, 2018).

Publix Super Markets is also ranked as one of the largest US regional grocery chains. Publix is an employee-owned, American supermarket chain headquartered in Lakeland, Florida. It is a private corporation that is wholly owned by present and past employees and members of the founder family Jenkins. As of July 2018, Publix employs about 193,000 people at its 1,187 retail locations, cooking schools, corporate offices, nine grocery distribution centres, and 11 manufacturing facilities. The manufacturing facilities produce its dairy, deli, bakery, and other food products. Publix is among Fortune magazine's list of 100 Best Companies to Work for 2018 (Publix, 2018).

Best Buy is a US-based multinational consumer electronics retailer headquartered in Minnesota. The US retailer puts its emphasis on consumer electronics and a variety of related merchandise, including software, video games, music, mobile phones, digital cameras, and video cameras, in addition to home appliances. The retailer offers products and services to the customers visiting its stores, engaging with Geek Squad agents, or using its Websites or mobile applications. It has operations in the United States, Canada, and Mexico. The company operates through two segments: domestic and international. The domestic segment consists of the operations in all states, districts, and territories of the United States, under various brand names, including Best Buy, bestbuy.com, Best Buy Mobile, Best Buy Direct, Best Buy Express, Geek Squad, Magnolia Home Theater, and Pacific Kitchen and Home. The international segment consists of all operations in Canada and Mexico under the brand names, Best Buy, bestbuy.com.ca, bestbuy.com.mx, Best Buy Express, Best Buy Mobile, and Geek Squad. As of 2016 the company operated 1,200 large-format and 400 small-format stores. It has a global sourcing operation to design, develop, test, and contract-manufacture its brand products (Reuters, 2018).

The world's largest retailer Walmart usually leads the retail rankings. The success behind the retailer is its business model with a strong focus on "everyday low prices" possible through operational excellence and efficient supply chain management serving a mass market. Walmart operates over 11,500 retail units under scores

Table 1.1: The largest retailers in the world by retail sales 2015 (Source: National Retail Federation, 2016).

Rank	Company	Retail Sales 2015
1	Walmart Stores	$353,108,000
2	The Kroger Co.	$103,878,000
3	Costco	$83,545,000
4	The Home Depot	$79,297,000
5	Walgreens Boots Alliance	$76,604,000
6	Target	$73,226,000
7	CVS Health	$72,151,000
8	Amazon.com	$61,619,000
9	Albertsons	$58,443,000
10	Lowe's Companies	$57,486,000
11	McDonald's	$35,837,000
12	Best Buy	$35,148,000
13	Apple Stores/iTunes	$34,949,000
14	Publix Super Markets	$32,633,000
15	Macy's	$27,002,000

of banners in an increasing number of countries and has several e-commerce websites. It employs millions of associates around the world, with over a million of these residing in the United States. It reportedly grossed 485 billion dollars in the fiscal year ending January 2017, which was up from 408 billion in the fiscal year of 2010. It's also been noted that Walmart's revenue is 2% of the US economy alone.

Walmart was founded by Sam Walton, who opened his first five-and-dime store in 1950 with a business model that was focused on keeping prices as low as possible. Walmart continues to offer "everyday low prices," which is possible due to Hyde (2018):
– its huge volume of sales that's possible due to the spread of its operation and its wide customer base
– a supply chain management system that maximizes efficiencies and reduces outlays
– minimization of overhead and operational costs
– leveraging of its bargaining power to force suppliers to lower prices

Sales volume: Walmart has been able to capture a huge market share of the retail sector by selling almost everything and being almost everywhere in the United States. There is a so-called omnipresence to the Walmart store, which allows the retailer to increase its penetration in customers' lives and to increase the probability of a purchase at one of the Walmart stores. It meets the demand of various consumer segments mainly by selling the goods through four types of stores: discount stores, Walmart Supercentres, Sam's Club warehouses, and neighbourhood markets. Its large sales volume enables it to make substantial profits although margins on single items may be slimmer than those of its competitors (Hyde, 2018).

Supply chain management: Walmart has a supply chain system that is regarded as one of the most technologically advanced and efficient. Whether in the case of barcodes or RFID tags (radio frequency identification technology), Walmart is always a pioneer. The retailer gets detailed product information electronically attached to products so that such information could inform its inventory management system.

Another key strategy by Walmart has been its move to deal directly with manufacturers. Suppliers become responsible for managing inventory in its warehouses. This shift in responsibility for inventory management from Walmart to the suppliers creates a smoother flow of inventory, with less irregularities, and helps to ensure that products requested by customers are available on the shelves.

Information such as point-of-sales data, as well as warehouse inventory and real-time sales are all sent to and stored in a centralized database that is shared with suppliers who know when to ship more products. Also key to the cost-effectiveness of Walmart's supply chain strategy and distribution network is the positioning of its 160 distribution centres, which are all within 130 miles of the stores they supply. With the usage of cross-docking at their warehouses (i.e., a process in which products are taken from a truck upon its arrival and packed in a truck headed to a store without spending time in the warehouse), Walmart reduced costs for inventory storage and has lowered transportation costs (Hyde, 2018).

Minimization of overhead and operational costs: Continuing the model Walton established for a low-cost operation, Walmart keeps its overhead low. Its executives reportedly fly coach and share hotel rooms with colleagues. Its meager wages and low-benefit healthcare plans that are offered to rank-and-file employees have been publicized and protested, although it should be noted that the company announced in January 2018 that it would be raising the starting wage. Researchers at some policy institutes have speculated that each Walmart associate does the job of 1.5 to 1.75 competitive employees. Costs are kept at a minimum, even for heating and cooling of the buildings.

Leveraging of its bargaining power to force suppliers to lower prices: Many well-known companies rely on Walmart for more than 20% of their revenue. Walmart, as the number one supplier-retailer of most of our consumer goods, wields considerable power over their bottom line and in fact wields this power over almost all the consumer goods industries in the United States. In adhering to a strategy of keeping prices low (experts estimate that Walmart saves shoppers at least 15% on a typical cart of groceries), Walmart is constantly pushing its suppliers to cut prices. (Hyde, 2018).

To summarize the situation in the worldwide retail sector, we see that the largest retailers in the world all rethink the role of their brick-and-mortar (physical) stores. With online growth outpacing overall growth of retail sales in their physical stores, retailers are rationalizing their physical footprint and intensifying their e-commerce presence. Given the negative impact of e-commerce on store productivity, many have concluded that their existing store base is simply too big. This is resulting in store closures, a move to smaller and more flexible store formats, and new roles for their physical stores (Deloitte, 2017). In 2017 alone, there were more than 7,000 store closures across the US retail sector, unable to withstand consumers' rapid migration to e-commerce, the explosive growth of direct-to-consumer brands, and the glut of retail square footage in the heavily over-stored US market. Retail space per capita in the United States is 15 to 20 times that of other major developed markets. Customer traffic at malls has been steadily decreasing. Margins are declining in almost every retail category. Given these trends, it's becoming harder to justify keeping expensive brick-and-mortar stores open if they don't meet sales expectations. Already, in the first few months of 2018, retailers have announced plans to shutter an additional 3,800-plus US stores (Podreciks, Uhlenbrock, & Ungerman, 2018).

Nevertheless, physical retail stores still have a great importance. It is estimated that in-store sales will still make up 75% to 85% of retail sales by 2025. The physical store will play several possible roles (Podreciks, Uhlenbrock, & Ungerman, 2018):
- it might serve as an experiential showroom for products as well as a brand-building and customer acquisition channel
- a cross-channel fulfillment centre (i.e., use of one channel, such as store, to support or promote another channel) for online orders, serving as pickup stations or a place for returning or exchanging online purchases
- a hangout where friends can try things on and take selfies that they then post on social media
- a destination for those seeking ideas and inspiration

It is entirely possible for a physical store to have weak sales and profits but still be a strong contributor to the retailer's overall performance. Therefore, retailers must measure the total cross-channel value of a retail store; in detail how a store's existence influences the performance of the retailer's other sales channels. With the help of sophisticated data analytics using internal and external data, geospatial data could help to identify the factors that have the greatest positive or negative effect on a physical store's total sales (Podreciks, Uhlenbrock, & Ungerman, 2018). With the abundance of location data generated from smart phones and connected devices, the potential of geospatial data has expanded dramatically, especially in the retail industry. Geospatial data better enables retail organizations to focus marketing activities on target customers and to evaluate which of the retail outlets are accessible for these customers.

Without knowing anything other than addresses, ages, and survey results, it is often difficult to answer important questions. Leading retailers, for instance Walmart, has already realized the benefits of location-based data to achieve growth and digital transformation (Qian, 2017), like measuring the total cross-channel value of a physical retail store or to focus marketing activities on target customers.

Other omnipresent retailers, like Lowe's and Target, see potential in urban areas with smaller, more flexible format stores whose size and assortment will be customized according to the demographics of the neighbourhood. They develop new urban concepts about one-quarter the size of the retailers' typical big-box stores.

Many retailers start with experiments to integrate e-tailing with brick-and-mortar stores, and introduce so-called cloud stores. These stores feature a category mix tailored to the population and consumption characteristics. To enhance the product line-up, about half the store is devoted to an area where customers can see, touch, and try products that can then be ordered online for home delivery. Lowe's, for example, is using 3D imaging where shoppers can view life-size products such as appliances and see what they look like inside. High-tech touchscreens throughout the stores let shoppers browse Lowe's complete assortment and place orders for delivery (Deloitte, 2017).

Retailers worldwide know technology is no longer supplemental to the shopping experience, it is fundamental. But technology alone is not enough. Customers are constantly seeking new and surprising products and experiences. Therefore, retailers are challenged to find ways to delight and engage their customers and strengthen customer loyalty (Deloitte, 2017). There are many more trends and developments in the worldwide retail sector. Retail companies that want to be successful have to study emerging trends and begin to prepare for them. The following chapter explains the most influential trends and the main forces shaping the future retail landscape.

1.1.3 Trends in the retail landscape

The key contextual or external trends that will affect and shape the retail landscape in the years to come can be grouped into five main areas (McKinsey & Company, 2015):
– the changing face of the consumer
– evolving geopolitical dynamics
– new patterns of personal consumption
– technological advancements
– structural industry shifts

Table 1.2 illustrates these five areas and points out the key aspects to describe and understand these dominate forces and underlying trends.

Table 1.2: Five dominant forces and underlying trends (Source: Own elaboration based on McKinsey &Company, 2015).

Changing face of consumer	Evolving geopolitical dynamics	New patterns of personal consumption	Technological advancements	Structural industry shifts
– Middle class explosion – Aging population – Women in workplace – Urbanization – Rich becoming richer – Millennials taking over – Shrinking household size	– Rising labour and commodity costs – Economic power shifts – Climate change	– Increase in convenience – Focus on health and wellness – Demand for personalization and customization – Sharing economy – Focus on shopping experience – Buying local – Simplification of choice	– Mobile world – internet of things – Smart Data – 3D printing – Advanced robotics – Social media driven consumption – Virtual, augmented, and mixed realities	– Direct-to-consumers models – Continued consolidation – Talent shift

One of the main forces shaping the future retail landscape is the *changing face of the consumers*. Changing demographics, such as the shift in global population, urbanisation, and cross-border migration, but also the explosion of the middle-class, the shrinking household size and the growth among aging populations, especially in developed countries, will challenge retail companies. In an era of fast-changing consumer behaviours, companies must understand what consumers want and need. Millennials, the generation born from the early 1980s to late 1990s, will have the biggest purchasing power, therefore, retailers will have to meet their demands. Millennials have grown up during a time of technological change, globalisation, and economic disruption. These factors have given them a distinctive set of behaviours and experiences. Millennials want customer-centric experiences, not only in-store but also through social media channels. Millennials have grown up with mobile devices and smart technology. Therefore, it is expected that this consumer segment will also use these devices for shopping purposes.

The next major force are the *evolving geopolitical dynamics* economic power shifts, including the reshuffling of the world's top economies, the growing gap between industrialised and developing countries, as well as a focus on social responsibility among the more developed countries. In addition, ecological issues, including energy and fuel scarcity and efficiency, sustainability, and waste management, are main issues that will gain importance in the years to come. Rising labour and commodity costs will also influence the worldwide geopolitical situation, especially the supply chain issue, like sourcing of raw materials, manufacturing, and production.

New patterns of personal consumption is another complex trend, which has a huge influence on the retail landscape. This trend consists of various aspects: an increase in convenience, the focus on health and wellness, a demand for personalization and customization, a focus on shopping experience, buying their products locally, and the simplification of choice. Another key driver is the movement towards collaborative consumption (i.e., the shared usage of goods or services by a group of consumers) and the rise of sharing economy organizations and business models. The term "sharing economy" originates from the English language and is based on the terms "sharing," "exchanging," "giving," and "benefitting" from goods and services. The sharing economy describes the entirety of alternative forms of consumption. Sharing may be regarded as the most elemental form of economic distribution within societies. Nowadays sharing has developed from the former community practise to a commercial business model of sharing resources between individuals primarily through peer-to-peer services. There exist different forms of sharing concepts depending on the involved parties: peer-to-peer (P2P), business-to-consumer (B2C), consumer-to-business (C2B) and, on whether the sharing of the products and services is free of charge or a fee must be paid. There are many shareable resources (Fraunhofer IAO, 2014, 14):

- products and services: cars, consumer goods, real estate, human resources
- equipment and facilities: means of production, manufacturing equipment, and infrastructure

- infrastructure: transportation and mobility, logistics, telecommunications
- information: knowledge, data, ideas, and experiences

Changes in the social, environmental, and economic sphere force companies to analyse and consider customers' needs in their retail strategies and tactics. Therefore, it is essential for companies to rethink production and consumption possibilities and to search for new business models, like the concept of "sharing."

The next major force that will affect and shape the retail landscape are *technological advancements* and new technologies, such as virtual reality (VR) and augmented reality (AR), the internet of things (IoT), and information networks. They all have the potential to make data, people, and objects accessible everywhere and immediately. Artificial intelligence (AI) and advanced robotics, 3D printing, wearable devices (a technology that is worn on the human body, e.g., a smart watch) and social media driven consumption are new technologies that will have an important influence on retailers in general and their business models. Lowe's, for example, is already experimenting with retail service robots in its stores. The robot greets customers in English and Spanish, scans products to determine whether the store has the item in stock, and guides customers to products through store navigation capabilities. Another example, eBay, has created the world's first VR department store (for video, see https://www.youtube.com/watch?v=UAeJB7d4jh0). Consumers can explore over 12,500 products from Myer, an upmarket Australian department store chain, access real-time price, and product information, and add selected items to their shopping basket.

Technological advancements will change how we live and how we will shop. Consider the arrival of driverless cars and the potential impacts on shopping behaviour. Driverless cars will allow smaller or local retailers to afford personal, same-day deliveries. Imagine being able to program your car to run errands to multiple stores and pick up everything on your shopping list. The impacts to the customer journey from self-driving cars are endless. The same huge impacts can be expected from the wide-scale adoption of AR, 3D printing, and hologram kiosks that show 3D customization options using a smartphone (for video, see https://www.youtube.com/watch?v=SX9lVYJa5bU), and other technologies (Deloitte, 2017).

Structural industry shifts include the rise of direct-to-consumer models (DTC). Manufacturers no longer need the help of larger intermediaries or established brands to connect with their customers. Selling directly to consumers represents a favourable opportunity for manufacturers. However, the DTC model bears many risks, for example, skills, culture, processes, insights, etc. Companies without the ability to build by acquisition, must choose their sales partners and platforms carefully to bring the expertise, agility, and innovation required to be profitable. Amazon, for example, is a threat to nearly every retailer and consumer packaged goods company that exists today. The online retailer accounted for 43% of all e-commerce sales in the United States during 2016. It is estimated that 52% of consumers start their online shopping by going to Amazon. Consequently, many manufacturers are facing the options between selling through Amazon in order to maintain access to consumers, in the full knowledge that Amazon is entering many product categories itself, or developing a DTC model to build stronger customer understanding and loyalty (knexus, 2017).

Furthermore, consolidation in the retail landscape will continue, resulting in the fact that the largest retailers will get even larger and more powerful and smaller retailers, especially those who are "stuck in the middle" (i.e., when a retailer does not have a competitive strategy), will have to shut down their stores.

Talent shift is another development that is likely to occur in years to come. Retailers using multichannel strategies will face a shift in their talent (employee) requirements. Issues around talents are one the biggest challenges retailers will face in years to come. Given the demand for employees with specific skill sets, specifically in technology and at the store level, larger retailers will be more able to attract, retain, and engage talents they need to advance their business strategies.

To summarize, each of these five trends will have a different level of impact on the consumer packaged goods and retail industry. Still, it is essential to have a basic understanding of which trends and developments could influence retail businesses and learn ways to adapt the retail strategy and tactics (see Chapter 1.2 for more information on Implementing a retail strategy). The following example box provides illustrative information on how retailers use those trends to adapt their retail strategies and come up with innovative, new ways of doing business.

The world's most innovative companies according to the Forbes ranking (Forbes, 2017)
Top 3 is Amazon and Top 5 is Netflix
Amazon.com
Amazon.com provides online retail shopping services and offers its services to four primary customer sets: consumers, sellers, enterprises, and content creators. The company also provides additional promotional services, for instance, online advertising and co-branded credit card agreements. It serves consumers through its retail websites with a focus on three basic elements: product selection, price, and convenience.

It designs its websites to enable its products to be sold by the company and by third parties across various product categories. The company also serves developers and enterprises of all sizes through Amazon Web Services (AWS), which provides access to technology infrastructure that enables virtually any type of business. The company operates through three segments: North America, International, and AWS. The North American segment includes retail sales of consumer products and subscriptions through North America-focused websites such as www. amazon.com and www.amazon.ca. The International segment includes retail sales of consumer products and subscriptions through internationally focused websites. The AWS segment includes global sales of computer, storage, database, and other AWS service offerings for start-ups, enterprises, government agencies, and academic institutions.

Market Cap as of May 2017: $427 Billion
Industry: Internet & Catalog Retail
Founded: 1994
Country: United States
Chief Executive Officer: Jeffrey P. Bezos

Website: http://www.amazon.com
Employees: 341,400
Headquarters: Seattle, Washington

Netflix

Netflix operates as an internet subscription service company, which provides subscription service streaming movies and TV episodes over the internet and sending DVDs by mail. The company operates its business through three different segments: domestic streaming, international streaming, and domestic DVD. Netflix obtains content from various studios and other content providers through fixed-fee licenses, revenue sharing agreements and direct purchases. It markets its service through various channels, including online advertising, broad-based media, such as television and radio, as well as various partnerships.

Market Cap as of May 2017: $61.6 Billion
Industry: Internet & Catalog Retail
Founded: 1997
Country: United States
Chief Executive Officer: Reed Hastings Jr.
Website: http://www.netflix.com
Employees: 4,700
Headquarters: Los Gatos, California

Netflix illustrates a design principle that any company aspiring to succeed at disruptive innovation must adopt. It has four parts (Forbes, 2017): Think Big, Start Small, Fail Quickly, and Scale Fast.

Think big: CEO Hastings pursued his big idea, streaming video, even though it would render obsolete his successful, mail-based system for distributing DVDs. By contrast, most companies think small and try to protect their existing business even if they can see a long-term threat from the internet or other technological disrupter.

Start small: Though CEO Hastings had a big idea that he believed in, he started with lots of small projects. On the contrary, companies with big ideas tend to fall in love with them and rush into making them real before doing a pilot project or introducing a prototype.

Fail quickly: When early efforts at streaming video were doubtful, Hastings saved his money for the right day to come, although he hoped that his idea would be successful. By contrast, most companies keep following their ideas far too long, partly because those involved know that a failure will tarnish them.

Scale fast: Netflix is now scaling streaming video fast, maintaining the lead it worked so hard to build over competitors. In many companies great innovations are successfully developed but never are rolled out to the market, unlike the Netflix example because those companies are not willing to attack their core business.

1.2 Implementing a retail strategy

A retail strategy is the plan or framework of action that guides a retail company. This strategy covers everything from what retail channels a product or service will be available to what the price should be and how to communicate effectively with customers and how to display the product in the store and on the shelf. It influences the company's business activities and the company's response to market forces. It outlines a retailer's mission and goals, it allows a retailer to determine how to differentiate itself from competitors, and to develop a product or service offering that appeals to a certain group of customers. In addition, the retail strategy has to offer an analysis of the legal, economic, and competitive environment of the retailer and therefore encourages anticipation and avoidance of crises. Finally, but most importantly it provides an overall long-term plan and sets long-term and short-term objectives for the coordination of the retailer's total efforts.

Strategic retail planning offers a retailer several benefits. According to Berman and Evans (2013) these benefits are listed below. A strategic retail plan:
- provides thorough analysis of the requirements for doing business with different types of retailers
- outlines retailer goals
- allows the retailer to determine how to differentiate itself from competitors
- allows the retailer to develop an offering that appeals to a group of customers
- offers an analysis of the legal, economic, and competitive environment
- provides for the coordination of the firm's total efforts
- encourages anticipation and avoidance of crises

Literature (Berman & Evans, 2013) defines six major steps in strategic retail planning:
- define the type of business
- set long-term and short-term objectives
- determine the customer market
- devise an overall long-term plan
- implement an integrated strategy
- evaluate and correct

All these steps will be described in further detail in the subchapters below.

Define the type of business
Retail business is a very diverse business. Retailers range from street vendors, traditional supermarkets, neighbourhood stores, discount stores, convenience stores like petrol station shops, to multichannel retailers that have a physical store presence and offer online channels (see Table 1.3). Each retailer fulfills certain customer needs and offers benefits, ideally more effectively than competitors can. As consumer needs and wants, but also the entire market situation, changes over time, new retail formats are created.

Types of retailers

There are many different types of retailers. They can be categorized in two main criteria: the size of their business and the way in which they sell their products (e.g., location, atmosphere, merchandise, price, promotion).

The seven main types of retailers are (The Reseller Network, 2018):

Department store: This type of retailer is the most complex retailer. It offers an extensive width and depth of assortment and can appear as a collection of smaller retail stores managed by one company. The department store retailers offer products at various pricing levels from average to above average. This type of retailer adds high levels of customer service by providing a pleasant atmosphere and adding convenience enabled by a large variety of products to be purchased from one retailer.

Supermarkets: Range from traditional medium-sized supermarkets to larger formats, like hypermarkets or superstores. Generally, this type of retailer concentrates on supplying a range of food and beverages and provides a full assortment of supermarket items. Many supermarkets, especially the larger formats, now have diversified and supply products from health and beauty, and from home, fashion, and electrical products. Supermarkets have significant buying power and unusually high competition and often sell their products at lower prices.

Warehouse retailers: This type of retailer is usually situated in a retail or business park where rents are lower. This enables this type of retailer to stock, display, and retail a large variety of goods at extremely competitive prices.

Specialty retailers: Specialising in specific industries or products, this type of retailer can offer the customer expert knowledge and a high level of service. They also add value by offering accessories and additional related products at the same outlet.

E-tailer: This type of retailer enables customers to shop online via the internet and buy products that are delivered to them. This type of retailer is very convenient and can supply a wider geographic customer base. E-tailers often have lower rent and ovehead so they offer competitive pricing.

Convenience retailer: Usually located in residential areas, this type of retailer offers a limited range of products at premium prices due to the added value of convenience.

Discount retailer: This type of retailer offers a variety of discounted products. They offer lower prices on less fashionable products from a range of suppliers by reselling end of line and returned goods at discounted prices (The Reseller Network, 2018).

Experts often use the term "retailization" for the changing, creating, and evolving of new retail formats. The sharing economy, the "multioptional" consumer, advances in technology, economic conditions, and various other factors have made it increasingly difficult to define what a retailer is and does. In years past, a retailer's main business was to buy and sell products, either in a brick-and-mortar stores or through an online shop. Market fragmentation in the retail industry will also continue in years to come. There is an explosive growth of nontraditional retailers developing new models to better serve customer needs and wants.

Table 1.3: Overview of the benefits of individual store formats and channels (Source: Sonneck & Ott, 2010).

Store formats/channels	Individual benefit
Discounter	Fast orientation with the central focus on food items and products for daily requirements. This entails a standardized product choice with a limited range. There are dis- count prices on high-quality products. Special products are also offered at extremely low prices.
Supermarket	Neighbourhood retailer (proximity) for food and products for daily requirements. Includes an extensive range of fresh products. Satisfies consumer purchasing requirements for brand names: consumers find products that have been advertised in the media.
Self-service warehouse/ shopping mall	A comprehensive range of private label and branded products in the food and nonfood segments with additional customer service.
Department store	A wide range of products offered in a large space (almost) everything under one roof with additional customer service.
Franchise specialist store	Specialist product range offered in a large space at attractive prices, comprehensive brand-name articles.
Specialist store	Specialist product range with a high degree of customer service and personal advice.
Dispatcher/sender	Shopping after normal opening hours. Offers branded products as well as private labels from a wide range of products and specialist products.
Newspaper stand	Close proximity shop focused on food and snacks without waiting time.
Service station	Impulse shopping and convenience shopping for quick purchases without long waiting times.
Tele-shopping	Shopping from the living room chair. Products are presented live and replace personal service in stores.
Internet	Offers comprehensive information and products 24 hours a day and 7 days a week. Allows the highest levels of personal freedom and price comparison.

In China, for example, e-commerce power-players Alibaba and Tmall get serious competition from the leading online discount retailer for brands in China Vipshop (https://www.vip.com/), which has grown by popularizing the so-called flash-sale model. It sells mid-market clothing and accessory brands, using a time-limited discount model. It offers high quality and popular branded products to consumers throughout China at a significant discount from retail prices (Deloitte, 2017).

In developing economies where customers are gaining purchasing power, there is a greater willingness to rely on less traditional retail models for more purchases.

Whereas, in established markets, there is less dramatic market penetration from alternative formats. Low barriers to entry have led to the pop-up of new "retailers" like subscription services (see the box below).

The "power of surprise"
Nowadays, products are largely similar and oftentimes identical products are offered by a range of suppliers. Various tools and strategies are used for differentiation, like pricing, packaging, or shopping experience (Ebster & Garaus, 2011). Many companies decide to use innovative and creative ways to offer a more appealing shopping experience to their customers. Subscription boxes could be a way to do this. Here, customers do not buy individual products, but an assortment of products of a certain category. Which products they will receive is unknown to them beforehand with a certain risk to receive products they do not like or can not use. This risk has to be compensated by perceived values of such a box, for example the elements of anticipation and surprise (Kaufman, 2012).

Subscription boxes enjoy growing popularity among all age groups. Choosing from a big variety of different product fields, customers sign up to receive boxes with an unknown content. The aim of this study was to find out which value customers perceive from subscription boxes, causing them to prefer the risk of unknown content over buying the exact products they desire or need elsewhere. This is done by identifying influencing factors on the perceived value and the subscription behaviour, as well as by identifying a possible relation between the knowledge level about a product category and the respective subscription behaviour. Three exemplary subscription boxes are discussed and compared to point out examples for the various different business models.

Table 1.4: Examples of subscription boxes (Source: Own elaboration).

	Glossybox	Outfittery	BioBox
Segment	Beauty care & cosmetics	Fashion	Food & drink; beauty care & cosmetics
Pricing	→ €12.50–€17.95 → Varying for special editions → Depending on contract length	Depends on products which are kept	→ €14–€18 → Separate pricing for special editions → Depending on contract length
Periodicity	One-time or monthly; flexible; 3, 6, or 12 months	Upon order	One-time or monthly; 3, 6, or 12 months
Return Policy	No returns	Returns possible	No returns
Assortment	Online profile	→ Online profile → Individual curation	Generic
Specials	→ Limited editions for separate orders → Goodies and vouchers	Personal consultation via phone or Whatsapp	→ Limited editions for separate orders → Rotatory is possible
Value	Product value > box price	Retail prices for items kept	Product value ~ box price

The Glossybox (https://www.glossybox.com/) is a subscription box company for beauty care products. The main product is the Beauty Box that is delivered monthly to more than 200,000 customers, mainly in European countries.

The Outfittery (https://www.outfittery.com/) shopping box contains men's clothing and operates in eight countries. Outfittery combines online shopping with personal consultation, based on a detailed questionnaire about preferred clothing.

The third box is the so-called biobox (http://www.biobox.at/). The box contains a selection of products with natural ingredients and ecological and sustainable production processes.

The feeling that the products in the box were chosen specifically according to the individual preferences raises the perceived value of a subscription box. Subscription boxes are considered a luxury extra expenditure, which has to be deducted from consumers' disposable income. Therefore, subscribers want to be as flexible as possible, instead of being obliged to pay regularly. Other important reasons for subscribing are the appeal of receiving a box with unknown content as a self-reward and the desire to try and get to know new and possibly exclusive products, as well as to receive information about the products themselves and how to use them. Moreover, the perception of saving money plays a big role. Others subscribe for convenience reasons.

Finally, the "power of surprise" is important. Subscribers like the experience of receiving something to their doorstep, unwrapping it, and seeing the product presentation. Subscribers normally show a very high involvement towards the subscribed product category and want to experience it with all their senses. Here, the excitement of applying a new and innovative way of shopping plays a big role.

As disruption and alternative business models persist, retailers will need to reinvent themselves (Deloitte, 2017) and rethink their business model to stay competitive and up to date.

Set long-term and short-term objectives

The second important step when planning a retail strategy is defining long-term and short-term objectives. *Long-term objectives* are performance goals of a company that are intended to be achieved over a period of five years or more. These objectives can include specific improvements of the retailer's sales and profit, market share, competitive position, technology leadership, stakeholder relations, productivity, and/or the retailer's image. These goals must be carefully considered, as they usually mean major changes for the company and are often very cost intensive. In addition, these goals and their realization mean a drastic change for the entire company and often also for the corporate culture. It therefore makes sense to involve all key departments and employees in a so-called strategy process. This to a large extent ensures that these changes are supported by the employees.

Short-term objectives are smaller, intermediate goals to be achieved over a shorter period when moving towards a long-term objective. An example for a long-term objective would be to double revenue by the end of the current fiscal year. To achieve this goal supporting short-term objectives have to be defined. A short-term objective example is to spend the next four weeks to analyse key competitors and conduct a brainstorming workshop on what product features could have an added value for the customers. These findings could then be used to design a new advertising campaign that highlights these product features. Short-term objectives are less cost intensive and time consuming than long-term objectives but equally important because without them it would not be possible to achieve the long-term goals.

Determine the customer market

The third step when planning a retail strategy is determining the customer market. In general, customer markets can be classified into several types. For retailers, the three customer markets are the most important markets and therefore seem essential to be defined and explained: consumer market, reseller market, and international market.

Consumer market: Consists of individuals and households that buy goods and services for personal consumption. Within this market several sub-types exist. The most important type of consumer market is the fast-moving consumer goods (FMCGs) market. This market is characterised by high volume, low unit value products that have a fast repurchase cycle, like fruits and vegetables, toothpaste, toilet paper, newspapers, etc. Another important type are the durable goods. They are characterised by low volume, high unit value products, for instance, electronic items, like a washing machine or a TV.

A consumer market is normally a highly competitive market with lots of competition. Consumers tend to be disloyal to brands and can easily switch from one brand to another, when competitors offer cheaper or more innovative products or offer an attractive benefit (added value) for its customers.

Reseller market: In a reseller market, a company buys goods and services from other companies to sell them at a profit. The retail industry is a good example of a reseller market. It consists of several types of business, like supermarket chains, hypermarkets, discount or specialty stores, convenience stores, etc. The main functions of a retail market are accessibility and affordability. A retail market usually generates low profit margins but has high growth potential. To make use of this growth potential, companies must rethink their business strategy and modify it in accordance with the changing market situation and consumption trends of the customers.

International market: An international market can be defined geographically as a market outside the national borders of a company's home country. The opposite of an international market is the company's domestic market, which is the geographic region within the national boundaries of a company's home country. An international

market consists of buyers in other countries, including consumers, producers, re-
sellers, and/or governments. For more information related to international marketing
management, refer to subject-related literature (e.g., Glowik, M., Smyczek, S., 2012:
International Marketing Management – Strategies, Concepts and Cases in Europe;
Oldenbourg).

In saturated markets, it is essential to determine the customer market and to
have a well-defined target market. Smaller retailers can effectively compete with large,
more powerful retailers by targeting a specific customer market, a so-called niche market. Targeting a specific market does not mean that consumer groups are excluded, but
it allows focusing business and marketing activities on distinctive consumer groups
that are more likely to buy the offered goods or services. A company must figure out
not only who has a need for the product or service, but also who is most likely to buy
it. Demographic factors must be considered, like age, gender, education level, occupation, family status, and location. In addition, psychographics (personal characteristics
of a person) is relevant when targeting a specific market, including personality, interests, opinions, values, attitudes, behaviour, and activities.

Chapter 1.3 goes into more detail and explains the so-called STP marketing
strategy – a useful strategy for targeting the right customers with a suitable marketing strategy.

Devise an overall long-term plan

An overall, long-term plan gives a retailer and its stakeholder, especially the employees, a general direction and guides a retailer. The process of devising a long-
term plan has several advantages. First, it provides a comprehensive analysis of the
requirements for doing business and outlines the retailer's goals. Second, the external and internal environmental factors must be studied and ways of differentiation
from competitors are determined. Customers are analysed from their point of view.
Finally, yet importantly, the retailer's total efforts are coordinated.

Retailers who do not define an overall, long-term plan, together with the implementation of an integrated strategy, can be unable to cope with the dynamic market
and developments in consumer behaviour and will be overtaken by competitors.

Implement an integrated strategy

As mentioned above, a retailer must set long-term and short-term objectives, determine
the customer market, devise an overall, long-term plan and general decisions must be
made about managing the business, store location, merchandise management and
pricing, etc. All these decisions and elements must be coordinated to implement a consistent *integrated strategy*.

The implementation of an integrated strategy involves two components:
- controllable variables: business aspects a retailer can directly affect
- uncontrollable variables: factors a retailer can not control and to which a retailer must adapt

The *controllable variables* of a strategy consist of store location, merchandise management, managing the business, pricing, and communicating with the customers. The *uncontrollable variables* are composed of the following factors: consumers, competition, technology, economic conditions, seasonality, and legal restrictions (Berman & Evans, 2013).

After an integrated strategy is determined, the retailer implements short-term objectives for each controllable variable of this strategy. These short-term objectives (tactis) must respond to the internal and external environment of the retailer. Each step in implementing an integrated strategy must be coordinated to have a consistent, unified strategy.

To summarize, an integrated strategy is a document that spells out a retailer's programs to achieve success in the market and determines the long-term goals of a retailer and the tactical program to reach these goals. For doing so, retail management considers the internal conditions, including funds and employee talent available, and the external market situation in which the retailer operates, including competitors, demographic developments, environmental factors, government policy, etc.

In addition to the two variables described above (i.e., controllable and uncontrollable), implementing an integrated strategy involves two major processes: the strategy formulation and the strategy implementation.

Strategy formulation involves, first, a study of the external environment of a company and the preparation of a game plan to face its competitors. Several questions about the external and internal environments of the company need to be answered in formulating the strategy. Some of the most important questions that must be asked are: Who is the target customer? Which products should the company produce or not produce? How do customers see the company and its products/services in relation to its competitors?

Strategy implementation, the second major process, considers how the company will harness its resources to meet objectives. More detailed, strategy implementation are all the activities within a company or organization designed to manage the activities associated with the fulfilment of a strategic plan. It is a critical process to a company's success, addressing the who, where, when, and how of reaching the desired goals and objectives, like structure, culture, resources, people, and the control system. It focuses on the entire organization. Figure 1.5 illustrates the strategic management process in which strategy implementation is the fourth stage. The other three stages are the determination of the strategic mission, vision, and objectives, the environmental and organizational analysis, and formulating the strategy. The strategy implementation is followed by the strategic evaluation and control.

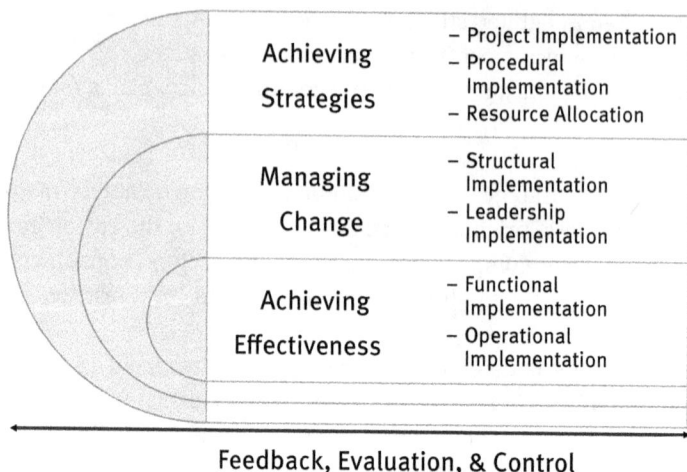

Feedback, Evaluation, & Control

Figure 1.2: Strategy implementation model
Source: Own elaboration based on McKinsey, 2016.

As shown in Figure 1.2 strategy implementation is the third phase after environmental scanning and strategy formulation. Environmental scanning, consisting of external and internal scanning, helps to identify strategic issues and objectives. The most important and useful tools for environmental scanning and corporate development are the following:
- SWOT analysis
- PEST analysis
- Porter's Five-Forces analysis
- BCG matrix
- Balanced scorecard
- Blue ocean strategy

SWOT analysis

A SWOT analysis is a strategic planning tool that can be used to help a company identify its strengths, weaknesses, opportunities, and threats related to competitors. It is intended to specify the objectives of the company and identify the internal and external factors that are favourable and unfavourable to achieving these objectives. A SWOT analysis indicates to the users and decision-makers the chances of a company reaching its objectives by overcoming hurdles and helps to improve their strategy.

Table 1.5: SWOT analysis examples (Source: Obfuscata, 2019).

	Positive	Negative
Internal	**Strengths**	**Weaknesses**
	→ Advantages (financial reserves, like returns; accreditations, qualifications, certifications; competitive advantages) → Capabilities (location and geography; innovative aspects) → Resources, assets, people (processes, systems, IT; culture, attitudes, behaviours; management cover; experience, knowledge, data; patents; strong brand names) → Marketing reach, distribution, awareness (USPs; price, value, quality)	→ Lack of competitive strengths (gaps in capabilities; disadvantages of proposition; weak brand name) → Financials (cash flow, high-cost structure) → Vulnerabilities → Timescales, deadlines, and pressures (reliability of data, plan predictability) → Continuity, supply chain robustness → Process and systems (management cover, succession; morale, commitment, leadership)
External	**Opportunities**	**Threats**
	→ Market developments (competitors, vulnerabilities; niche target markets; new markets; unfilled customer needs; new technologies; loosening of regulations; changing of international trade barriers) → Business and product development (seasonal, weather, fashion influences; technology development and innovation; industry or lifestyle trends)	→ Environmental effects (seasonal, weather effects; national and international economy; political effects; legislative effects) → Market demand (new technologies, services, ideas; IT developments, shifts in consumer tastes) → Obstacles (new regulations; increased trade barriers; competitor intentions, sustainable financial backing)

Users of a SWOT analysis often ask and answer questions to generate meaningful information for each category to make the tool useful and identify their competitive advantage.

When identifying the *strengths (internal factors)* of a company the following questions can be asked:

- What are we really good at?
- What are our best and unique skills?
- What internal talents do we have (staff)?
- What other resources do we have (funds)?
- What are our advantages over our competitors?

When identifying the *weaknesses (internal factors)* of a company the following questions can be asked:
- What does our company lack (staff, funds, location, products/services)?
- What departments or sections within the company are lagging?
- Where are we losing time and money?
- What skills aren't up to the mark?

The *opportunities (external factors)* of a company can be identified with the following questions:
- What are the market opportunities that we have?
- What are the changes in our external environment that we can take advantage of (changing competitor situation, changing laws, changing customer preferences)?
- Can we enter new customer markets or categories?
- Are there related businesses (products or services) that we can get into?

The *threats (external factors)* can be identified with the following questions:
- What expertise do we lack to make use of our opportunities?
- What are key factors in which our competitors are performing better than us?
- Are there any economic factors or market factors that can affect us?
- What are our biggest obstacles?

A SWOT analysis can be used at any stage in the life of a company. It can be used at the start, when a company or a product is being launched, or later, when the company is implementing a new plan or evaluating plans. It can also be helpful in a crisis to find solutions, but it should never be used to justify a past decision or strategy.

A SWOT analysis can be used in conjunction with a PEST (political, economic, social, and technological) analysis described next.

PEST analysis

Another strategic management tool is the so-called PEST analysis. This tool analysis is a company's environment to find out the PEST factors that may facilitate or disrupt efforts to achieve the objectives of a company.

The main difference between a SWOT analysis and a PEST analysis is that while SWOT identifies the overall feasibility of a business proposition or idea at a point in time, a PEST analysis evaluates the market a company wants to enter. A company's future developments are mainly influenced by the quality of leadership and extent of financial resources, but also by macro-environmental factors.

Therefore, the PEST factors listed in Table 1.6 also greatly influence a company's future efforts. It must be mentioned that a company normally has no control over these factors and can only manage them and adjust to them as best it can.

Table 1.6: PEST factors (Source: Own elaboration based on Kotler & Bliemel, 2001).

Political factors	Economic factors	Social factors	Technological factors
– Political ideology of the government – Pricing regulations – Level of political stability – Taxation of a country – Trade laws – Safety regulations – Anti-trust laws – Labour law – Wage legislation	– Type of economic system in countries of operation – Rate of economic growth – Rate of inflation – Exchange rates – Interest rates – Economic stability – Employment policy – Efficiency of financial markets – Unemployment rate – Inflation rate – Infrastructure in the country	– Demographics – Average age and income of the population – Level of education – Leisure interests – Lifestyle trends – Consumer attitudes and opinions – Culture – Class structure – General outlook on life (liberal, conservative, etc.) – Lifestyle preferences	– Technological developments – Rate of technological diffusion – Maturity of technology – Information and communication technology – Impact of technology on product offering – Impact on cost structure – Competing technologies

The PEST factors described above may affect companies differently. For example, the policies of the government of the country where the company is operating has a strict health and safety policy. These regulations would require a restaurant business to invest more in systems to ensure hygiene and safety regulations.

Another example, the higher the inflation of the country where the company is operating, the higher the staff wages and the higher the business expenditure of a company. One more example, a garment retailer will be more affected by social factors such as lifestyle and customer preferences than a defense equipment manufacturer.

Porter's Five-Forces analysis

Porter's Five-Forces analysis is a strategic tool that helps analyze the level of competition within a particular market. The Five-Forces model was created by Michael

Porter in 1979 to understand how five key competitive forces are affecting an industry. The state of competition in an industry depends on the following five forces:
- threat of new entrants
- bargaining power of suppliers
- bargaining power of buyers/customers
- threat of substitute products or services
- competition: existing industry rivalry

These five forces determine an industry structure and the level of competition in that industry. The stronger competitive forces are in the industry, the less profitable they are. An industry with low barriers to enter, having few buyers and suppliers but many substitute products and competitors, will be very competitive and thus, not so attractive due to its low profitability (Jurevicius, 2013). Table 1.7 illustrates the differences between attractive and unattractive industries and their profit potential.

Table 1.7: Level of competition (Source: Jurevicius, 2013).

Attractive industry	Unattractive industry
- High barriers to enter	- Low barriers to enter
- Weak suppliers bargaining power	- Strong suppliers bargaining power
- Weak buyers bargaining power	- Strong buyers bargaining power
- Few substitute products or services	- Many substitute products or services
- Low competition	- Intense competition

This strategic analysis tool is especially useful for retailers when it comes to formulating a retailer's dependency on how powerful each of the five key forces in a particular market is.

Threat of new entrants. This force determines how easy it is to enter a certain market. If a market is profitable and there are very few barriers to enter the market, competition intensifies. When more retailers compete for the same market share, sales volume and profits start to fall. Therefore, existing retailers must create high entry barriers.

Threat of new entrants is high when (Jurevicius, 2013):
- low amount of capital is required to enter a market
- existing firms do not possess patents, trademarks, or have established brand reputation
- there is no government regulation
- customer switching costs (i.e., the costs a customer must pay when switching to a different brand or retailer) are low
- there is low customer loyalty
- products are very similar
- economies of scale can be easily achieved

Bargaining power of suppliers. A strong bargaining power means that suppliers can sell their raw materials or products at a higher price or with a lower quality. This force directly affects the buyers because they must pay more for their raw materials or products. Suppliers have strong bargaining power when (Jurevicius, 2013):
– there are many buyers but only a few suppliers,
– suppliers are large and threaten to forward integrate (forward integration is a form of vertical integration in which a company expands its role to fulfill tasks formerly completed by businesses down the supply chain, mainly to include control of the direct distribution or supply of a company's products)
– few substitute raw materials or products exist
– suppliers hold necessary or desired resources
– cost of switching raw materials is high

Bargaining power of buyers. This force means that buyers have the power to demand lower prices for raw materials or products or higher product quality from their suppliers due to the situation that they have strong bargaining power. Lower price means lower revenues for the suppliers, while higher quality products usually raise production costs. Buyers have strong bargaining power when (Jurevicius, 2013):
– only few buyers exist
– switching costs to another supplier are low.
– they threaten to backward integrate (backward integration is a form of vertical integration in which a company expands its role to fulfill tasks formerly completed by businesses up the supply chain)
– there are many substitute products
– buyers are price sensitive

Threat of substitutes. This force is especially threatening when buyers can easily find substitute products with attractive prices or better quality and when buyers can switch from one product or service to another with little cost. For example, to switch from strawberries to raspberries doesn't cost anything, unlike switching from train to car.

Rivalry among existing competitors. This force shows how competitive and how profitable a particular market is. In competitive markets, companies compete aggressively for a market share. This strong competition results in low profit margins. Rivalry among competitors is strong when (Jurevicius, 2013):
– there are many competitors
– exit barriers are high
– industry of growth is slow or negative
– products can be easily substituted
– competitors are of equal size
– there is low customer loyalty

Figure 1.3 illustrates Porter's framework to analyse the collective strength of these five forces described above that determine the profit potential of a market and its attractiveness and help retailers to set their expectations of profitability. The figure also provides a list of the Five-Forces factors, which help to describe and analyse each of these forces.

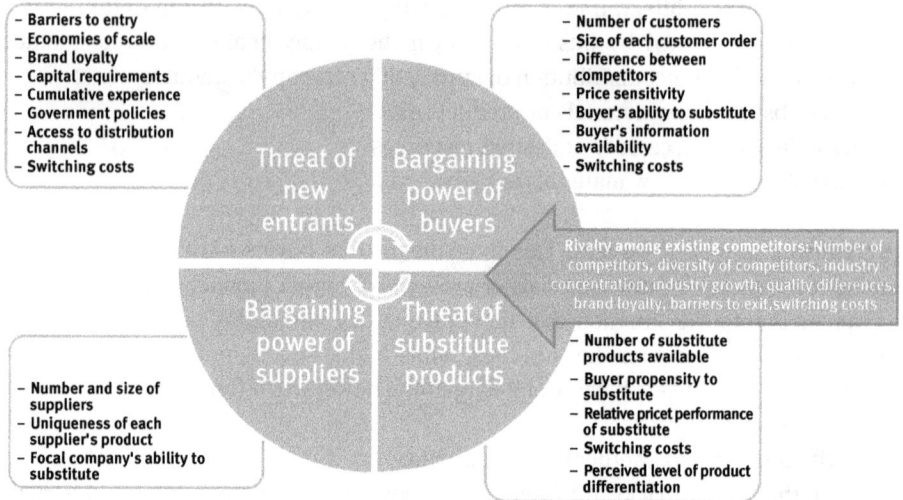

– Barriers to entry
– Economies of scale
– Brand loyalty
– Capital requirements
– Cumulative experience
– Government policies
– Access to distribution channels
– Switching costs

– Number of customers
– Size of each customer order
– Difference between competitors
– Price sensitivity
– Buyer's ability to substitute
– Buyer's information availability
– Switching costs

Threat of new entrants

Bargaining power of buyers

Bargaining power of suppliers

Threat of substitute products

Rivalry among existing competitors: Number of competitors, diversity of competitors, industry concentration, industry growth, quality differences, brand loyalty, barriers to exit, switching costs

– Number and size of suppliers
– Uniqueness of each supplier's product
– Focal company's ability to substitute

– Number of substitute products available
– Buyer propensity to substitute
– Relative pricet performance of substitute
– Switching costs
– Perceived level of product differentiation

Figure 1.3: Porter's Five-Forces analysis.
Source: Business-to-you, 2018

Airline industry and Porter's Five-Forces analysis
When looking at the airline industry in the German market, we see that the whole sector is extremely competitive because of several reasons. The mean reasons are the entry of low-cost carriers like German wings or Air Berlin, the tight regulation of the industry wherein safety becomes paramount leading to high fixed costs and high barriers to exit, and the fact that the industry is very stagnant in terms of growth. The switching costs for customers are also very low and many other airlines in the industry (competitors) are similar in size leading to fierce competition between those companies. Taken altogether, when analysing the collective strength of these five forces to determine the market attractiveness and profitability, it can be said that rivalry among existing competitors in the German airline sector is very high and the market attractiveness is low.

BCG matrix

The BCG matrix is a framework created by the Boston Consulting Group to evaluate the strategic position of the business brand portfolio and its potential. It classifies a business portfolio into four categories based on market attractiveness (growth rate of that market) and competitive position (relative market share). The matrix tags business units (like products, product categories, brands, etc.) as "stars," "questions marks," "cash cows," and "dogs" based on their cash consumption and their share of market growth. The general purpose of the analysis is to help understand which brands the company should invest in and which ones should be divested (Strategic management insight, 2013). Figure 1.4 illustrates an example of a BCG matrix.

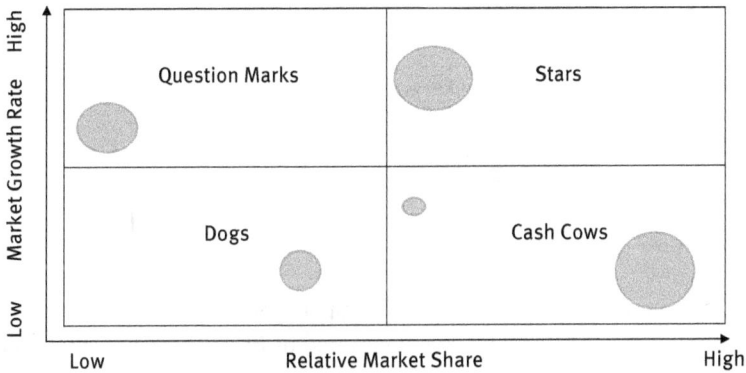

Figure 1.4: Example of a BCG matrix.
Source: Strategic management insight, 2013

For a better understanding two terms must be defined: relative market share and market growth rate.

– **Relative market share.** One of the dimensions used to evaluate business portfolio is relative market share. Higher corporate's market share results in higher cash returns. This is because a firm that produces more, benefits from higher economies of scale and experience curve, which results in higher profits. Nonetheless, it is worth noting that some firms may experience the same benefits with lower production outputs and lower market share.

– **Market growth rate.** High market growth rate means higher earnings and sometimes profits but it also consumes lots of cash, which is used as investment to stimulate further growth. Therefore, business units that operate in rapid growth industries are cash users and are worth investing in only when they are expected to grow or maintain market share in the future (Strategic management insight, 2013).

In Table 1.8 we see four quadrants into which a company's brands, products, product categories, etc., can be classified.

Table 1.8: Characteristics of the four BCG matrix quadrants.

Star	Question Mark
High market growth	High market growth
High market share	Low market share
Cash neutral	Cash absorbing
Hold	Build
Cash Cow	**Dog**
Low market growth	Low market growth
High market share	Low market share
Cash generating	Cash neutral
Harvest	Divest

Dogs: Dogs hold low market share compared to competitors and operate in a slowly growing market. In general, SKUs (stock keeping units) or BUs (business units) that are classified as dogs are not worth investing in because they generate low cash returns. Moreover, some dogs may be profitable for a long period of time and may provide synergies for other brands or products or they are of strategic importance, like so-called flagship products (i.e., an important product of a company, which is typically why the company was founded or what made the company or brand well-known). Therefore, it is always important to perform analysis of each brand, SKU, or BU to make sure they are not worth investing in or must be divested.

Cash cows: Cash cows are the most profitable brands or products of the company that should be "milked" to provide as much cash as possible. The cash gained from these "cows" should be invested into the so-called stars to support their further growth. Cash cows are generally large corporations; BUs or SKUs that have the potential to generate new and innovative products or processes, which may become new stars in the near future. Therefore, cash cows also need support to be capable of such innovations.

Stars: Stars normally operate in high growth industries and maintain high market share. Stars can be cash generators and/or cash users. They are the primary BUs or SKUs in which a company should invest because stars are expected to become cash cows and generate cash. In rapidly changing industries it can also happen that a star instead of becoming a cash cow, becomes a dog due to new technological advancements of competitors.

Question marks: Question marks are BUs or SKUs that require much closer consideration. They hold low market share in fast growing markets while they consume large amounts of cash. But they have the potential to gain market share and become a star, and this star could later become a cash cow. Question marks do not always succeed and even after large number of investments they eventually become dogs. Therefore, they require remarkably close consideration to decide if they are worth investing in.

GE-McKinsey matrix

The GE-McKinsey matrix is a strategic management tool that maps a company's business units in a nine-cell grid, based on two factors:

– industry attractiveness
– strengths of business units

The GE-McKinsey is a framework that evaluates a business portfolio, provides further strategic implications, and helps to prioritize the investment needed for each business unit (Jurevicius, 2014). Going back to history, in the 1970s, General Electric was managing a complex portfolio of unrelated products and was unsatisfied with the returns from its investments in the products. Therefore, the company consulted the external consulting company McKinsey & Company and they developed together this nine-cell grid. This grid or matrix plots the company's business units in these nine cells that indicate whether the company should invest in a product, harvest, or invest in it. The business units, as already mentioned above, are evaluated according to two factors (x- and y-axis): industry attractiveness and a competitive strength of a unit.

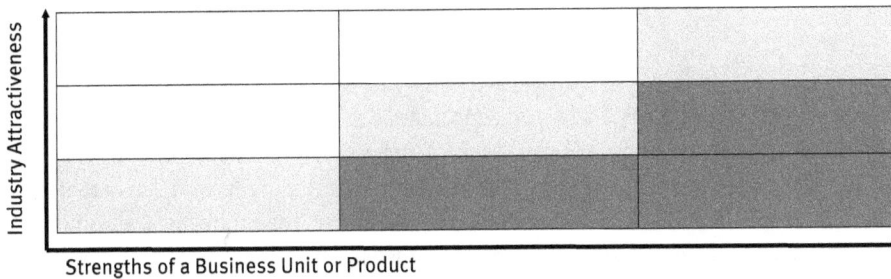

Figure 1.5: GE-McKinsey matrix.
Source: Jurevicius, 2014

Industry attractiveness indicates how hard it will be for a company to compete in the market and be profitable. The more profitable the industry is, the more attractive it becomes. When evaluating the industry attractiveness, it is essential to predict how the industry will change in the long run, because the investments needed for the product usually require a long-lasting commitment. The following list provides the most common factors that can be used to rate the industry attractiveness: long-term growth rate, industry size, industry profitability (e.g., entry barriers, exit barriers, supplier power, buyer power, threat of substitutes, and available complements), product life cycle changes, demand changes, price trend, macro environment factors, availability of labour, market segmentation, seasonality, etc. (Jurevicius, 2014).

Competitive strength of a business unit or a product describes how strong, in terms of competition, a particular business unit is against its competitors. The competitive strength of a business unit can be determined by the following factors: total market share, market share growth, profitability of the company, customer satisfaction and loyalty, brand value, strength of a value chain, level of product differentiation, flexibility of production, etc. (Jurevicius, 2014).

The advantage of the usage of this strategic management tool is that it helps to prioritize the limited resources of a company in relation to the profitability. Moreover, management of the company becomes aware of how their products or business units perform, also in relation to competitors' products or brands. But there are also some disadvantages. It requires a highly experienced person to determine an industry's attractiveness and business unit strength as accurately as possible. Moreover, it doesn't consider the synergies that could exist between business units.

The GE-McKinsey matrix is a very similar to the BCG matrix described above. Both pursue the same objective: they are used to analyse a company's product or business unit portfolio and help to facilitate strategic decisions, mainly investment decisions. The main difference is that the nine-cell matrix provides a better visualization and is more comprehensive than the BCG four cell matrix and therefore gives a more complete picture when it comes to investment decisions.

Balanced scorecard

The balanced scorecard is a strategy performance management tool that can be used by managers and retailers to keep track of the execution of activities by the staff within their control and to monitor the consequences arising from these activities. It provides executives with a comprehensive framework that translates a company's strategic objectives into a set of performance measures. It is not only a measurement tool, it is a management system that can bring forward improvements in areas as product, process, customer, and market development. The scorecard presents managers with four different perspectives from which to choose measures. It complements traditional financial indicators with measures of performance for customers, internal processes, and innovation and improvement activities. It must be mentioned that a balanced scorecard is not a template that can be applied to all businesses or retailers in general. Different market situations, product strategies, and competitive markets or situations require different balanced scorecards. Scorecards have to be customized to fit a company's vision, mission, strategy, technology, and culture.

So, to summarize a balanced scorecard focuses on the strategic agenda of the company, concentrates on a selection of a small number of data items to monitor, and provides a mix of financial and nonfinancial information.

The balanced scorecard in Figure 1.6 provides a very simple example of a scorecard from a furniture retailer. It shows the four perspectives financial, customer, internal process, and organizational capacity, the strategic objectives for each of these perspectives and the performance measurement indicators, as well as the targets of the retailers.

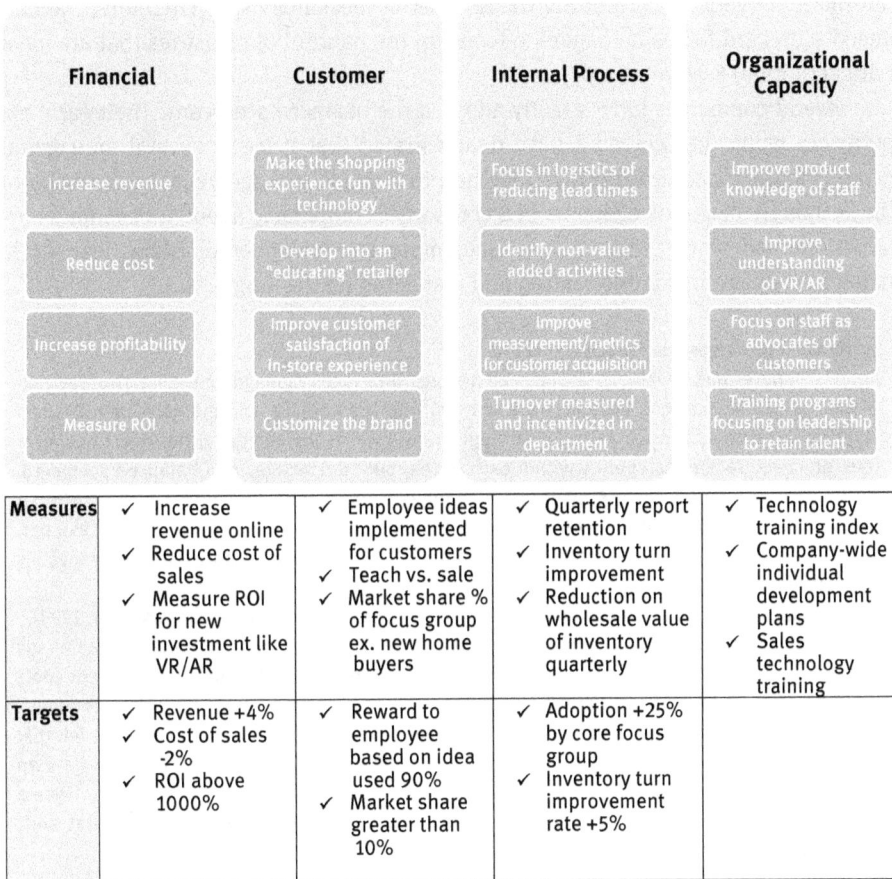

Financial	Customer	Internal Process	Organizational Capacity
Increase revenue	Make the shopping experience fun with technology	Focus in logistics of reducing lead times	Improve product knowledge of staff
Reduce cost	Develop into an "educating" retailer	Identify non-value added activities	Improve understanding of VR/AR
Increase profitability	Improve customer satisfaction of in-store experience	Improve measurement/metrics for customer acquisition	Focus on staff as advocates of customers
Measure ROI	Customize the brand	Turnover measured and incentivized in department	Training programs focusing on leadership to retain talent

	Financial	Customer	Internal Process	Organizational Capacity
Measures	✓ Increase revenue online ✓ Reduce cost of sales ✓ Measure ROI for new investment like VR/AR	✓ Employee ideas implemented for customers ✓ Teach vs. sale ✓ Market share % of focus group ex. new home buyers	✓ Quarterly report retention ✓ Inventory turn improvement ✓ Reduction on wholesale value of inventory quarterly	✓ Technology training index ✓ Company-wide individual development plans ✓ Sales technology training
Targets	✓ Revenue +4% ✓ Cost of sales -2% ✓ ROI above 1000%	✓ Reward to employee based on idea used 90% ✓ Market share greater than 10%	✓ Adoption +25% by core focus group ✓ Inventory turn improvement rate +5%	

Figure 1.6: Example of a balanced scorecard of a furniture retailer.
Source: Home Delivery, 2019

What we see in Figure 1.6 the balanced scorecard links performance measures for all four perspectives (Kaplan & Norton, 1992):
–   Customer perspective: How do customers see us?
–   Internal perspective: What must we excel at?
–   Innovation and learning perspective: Can we continue to improve and create value?
–   Financial perspective: How do we look to shareholders?

The main advantage of this strategic management tool is that while giving managers information from four different perspectives, the balanced scorecard minimizes information overload by limiting the number of measures used. Therefore, the balanced scorecard forces managers to focus on the handful of measures that are most critical (Kaplan & Norton, 1992).

Several companies have already adopted the balanced scorecard. Their early experiences using the scorecard have demonstrated that it meets several managerial needs. First, the scorecard brings together, in a single management report, many of the seemingly disparate elements of a company's competitive agenda: becoming customer-oriented, shortening response time, improving quality, emphasizing teamwork, reducing new product launch times, and managing for the long term.

Apple Computer uses a balanced scorecard
Apple Computer has developed a balanced scorecard to focus management on a strategy that would expand discussions beyond gross margin, return on equity, and market share. A small steering committee, familiar with the strategic objectives of the company, decided to concentrate on measurement categories within each of the four perspectives of a balanced scorecard. For the financial perspective, Apple puts an emphasis on shareholder value. For the customer perspective, the focus is on market share and customer satisfaction. The internal process perspective concentrates on core competencies and the innovation and improvement perspective concentrates on employee attitudes.

Below these five performance indicators are described in more detail (Kaplan & Norton, 1993):
–   **Customer satisfaction:** Apple has always been a technology- and product-focused company that competed by designing better computers. Customer satisfaction measurement tools are just being introduced to orient employees towards becoming a customer-driven company. However, because it recognized that its customer base was not homogeneous, Apple felt that it had to go beyond using an external customer-survey company and develop its own independent surveys in order to track its key market segments around the world. Once a technology- and product-focused company, Apple has introduced measures that shift the emphasis towards their customers.
–   **Core competencies:** Company executives wanted employees to be highly focused on a few key competencies like user-friendly interfaces, powerful software architectures, or effective distribution systems. Management recognized that measuring performance along these competency dimensions could be difficult. Therefore, Apple started experimenting with obtaining quantitative measures of these hard-to-measure competencies.
–   **Employee commitment and alignment:** Apple conducts a comprehensive employee survey in each of its organizations every two years, surveys of randomly selected employees are performed more frequently. Survey questions are concerned with how well employees understand the company's strategy as well as whether they are asked to deliver results

that are consistent with that strategy. The results of the survey are displayed in terms of both the actual level of employee responses and the overall trend of responses.

- **Market share:** Achieving a critical threshold of market share was important to management not only for the obvious sales growth benefits but also to attract and retain software developers to Apple platforms.
- **Shareholder value:** Shareholder value as a measurement tool was included to offset the previous emphasis on gross margin and sales growth, measures that ignored the investments required today to generate growth for tomorrow. In contrast, the shareholder value quantifies the impact of proposed investments for business creation and development. The majority of Apple's business is organized on a functional basis – sales, product design, and worldwide manufacturing and operations – so shareholder value can be calculated only for the entire company instead of at a decentralized level. This measurement tool helps management in each major organizational unit assess the impact of their activities on the entire company's valuation and evaluate new business ventures.

These five performance indicators have helped Apple's management to focus their strategy in a number of ways. First, the balanced scorecard at Apple serves primarily as a planning device, instead of as a control device. Moreover, these indicators, except for shareholder value, can be driven both horizontally and vertically into each functional organization. Considered vertically, each individual measure can be broken down into its component parts to evaluate how each part contributes to the functioning of the whole. Thought of horizontally, the measures can identify how, for example, design and manufacturing contribute to an area such as customer satisfaction. In addition, Apple has found that its balanced scorecard has helped develop a language of measurable outputs for how to launch and leverage programs (Kaplan & Norton, 1993).

Apple uses the scorecard as a device to plan long-term performance, not as a device to drive operating changes.

The five performance indicators at Apple are benchmarked against best-in-class organizations. Today they are used to build business plans and are incorporated into senior executives' compensation plans (Kaplan & Norton, 1993).

Blue ocean strategy

Based on strategy initiatives of corporations over 30 years, researchers came up with the theory that companies can grow by creating new and unexplored markets (blue oceans) rather than by competing in already saturated markets (red oceans). Blue ocean strategy is the simultaneous pursuit of differentiation and low cost to open a new market space and create new demand in a particular market. It empowers companies by providing a set of analytical tools and frameworks that any company can apply to reshape market boundaries which gives the company a competitive advantage. Kim and Mauborgne (Kim & Mauborgne, 2019) have created a comprehensive set of analytic tools and frameworks to create blue oceans of new market space. Most frequently used tools and frameworks are:

- blue versus red ocean strategy
- strategy canvas
- four actions framework
- ERRC grid

Blue versus red ocean strategy

Blue and red ocean strategies use the terms red and blue oceans to denote a particular market. Red oceans are all the existing markets, where boundaries are defined and companies try to outperform their competitors to gain a bigger share of a particular market. Blue oceans stand for all the industries not in existence today, a so-called unknown market space, unexplored and untainted by competition, offering opportunities and profitable growth.

Table 1.9 summarizes the distinct characteristics of competing in red oceans (Red Ocean Strategy) versus creating a blue ocean (Blue Ocean Strategy).

Table 1.9: Blue Ocean Strategy versus Red Ocean Strategy (Source: Kim & Mauborgne, 2019).

Blue Ocean Strategy	Red Ocean Strategy
Create uncontested market space	Compete in existing market space
Make the competition irrelevant	Beat the competition
Create and capture new demand	Exploit existing demand
Break the value-cost trade-off	Make the value-cost trade-off
Align the whole system of a companies' activities in pursuit of differentiation and low cost	Align the whole system of a companies' activities with its strategic choice of differentiation or low cost

Apple uses Blue Ocean Strategy – The example of iTunes
With the launch of iTunes, Apple unlocked a blue ocean of new market space in digital music that it has now dominated for more than a decade.

Apple observed the flood of illegal music file sharing that began in the late 1990s, enabled by several file sharing programs, for example, Napster or Kazaa. By 2003 more than two billion illegal music files were being traded every month. While the recording industry fought to stop the cannibalization of physical CDs, illegal digital music downloading continued to grow. This trend was intensified by the fast-growing demand for MP3 players that played mobile digital music (e.g., Apple's iPod).

In agreement with five major music companies – BMG, EMI Group, Sony, Universal Music Group, and Warner Brothers Records – iTunes offered legal, easy-to-use, and flexible song downloads. By allowing people to buy individual songs and strategically pricing them far more reasonably, iTunes broke a key customer annoyance factor: the need to purchase an entire CD when they wanted only one or two songs on it. iTunes also provided a leap in value beyond free downloading services via sound quality as well as intuitive navigation, search and browsing functions.

The unprecedented value iTunes offered triggered customers the world over to flock to iTunes with recording companies and artists also winning. Under iTunes they receive some 70% of the purchase price of digitally downloaded songs, at last financially benefiting from the digital downloading craze. In addition, Apple further protected recording companies by devising copyright protection that would not inconvenience users – who had grown accustomed to the freedom of digital music in the post-Napster world – but would satisfy the music industry.

Today iTunes offers more than 37 million songs as well as movies, TV shows, books, and podcasts. It has now sold more than 25 billion songs, with users downloading on average 15,000 songs per minute. iTunes is estimated to account for more than 60% of the global digital music download market. While Apple has dominated this blue ocean for more than a decade, as other online stores zoom in on this market, the challenge for Apple will be to keep its sights on the evolving mass market and not to fall into competitive benchmarking or high-end niche marketing (Kim & Mauborgne, 2019).

Strategy canvas

Strategy canvas is a central diagnostic tool and an action framework that graphically captures the current strategic landscape and the prospects for a company. The horizontal axis on the strategy canvas (see Figure 1.7) captures the range of factors that an industry competes on and invests in, while the vertical axis captures the offering level that buyers receive across all these key competing factors (Kim & Mauborgne, 2019).

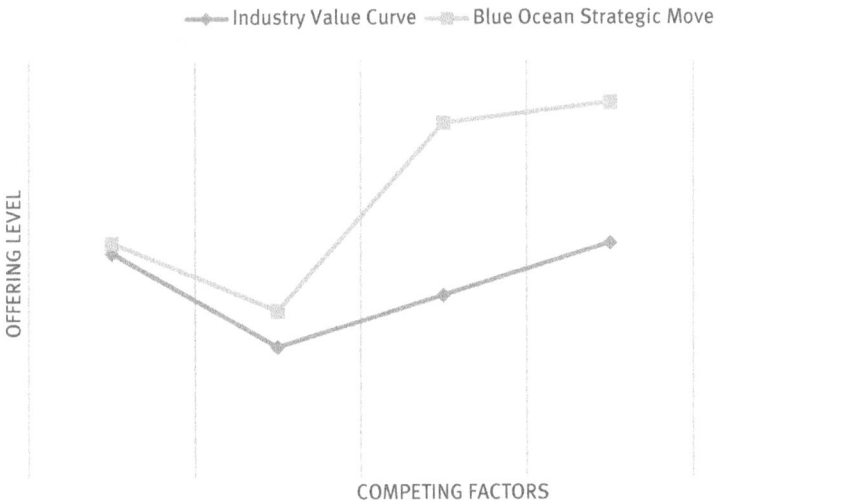

Figure 1.7: **Strategy Canvas.**
Source: Kim & Mauborgne, 2019

A strategy canvas allows a company to see in one figure all the factors a company competes on and invests in, what buyers receive, and what the strategic profiles of the major players are. It exposes just how similar the players' strategies look to buyers and reveals how they drive the industry towards the red ocean. It creates a commonly owned baseline for change (Kim & Mauborgne, 2019).

The strategy canvas follows two objectives (Kim & Mauborgne, 2019):

– It captures the current situation in a known market, which allows users to clearly see the factors that an industry competes on and invests in, what buyers receive, and what the strategic profiles of the major players are.

– It propels users to action by reorienting their focus from competitors to alternatives and from customers to noncustomers and allows to visualize how a blue ocean strategic move would be possible.

Four Actions Framework

Another Blue Ocean Strategy tool is the Four Actions Framework. This strategic tool is mainly used to add new values to the strategic canvas value curve. Moreover, it can be used to reconstruct buyer value elements in crafting a new value curve or strategic profile. To break the trade-off between differentiation and low cost in creating a new value curve, the framework poses four key questions a company must ask itself:

– Which factors should be eliminated that the industry has long competed on?
– Which factors should be reduced well below the industry's standard?
– Which factors should be raised well above the industry's standard?
– Which factors should be created that the industry has never offered?

Figure 1.8 illustrates the Four Actions Framework.

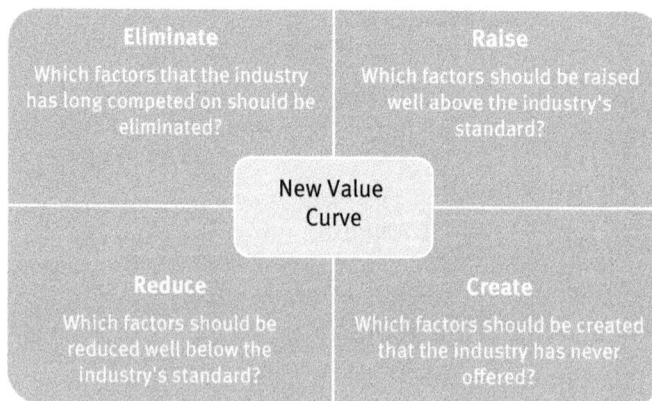

Eliminate
Which factors that the industry has long competed on should be eliminated?

Raise
Which factors should be raised well above the industry's standard?

New Value Curve

Reduce
Which factors should be reduced well below the industry's standard?

Create
Which factors should be created that the industry has never offered?

Figure 1.8: Four Actions Framework.
Source: Kim & Mauborgne, 2019

ERRC Grid

The ERRC Grid (i.e., Eliminate-Reduce-Raise-Create Grid) is an analytic tool that complements the Four Actions Framework described above (see Table 10). It is a simple matrix that drives companies to focus simultaneously on eliminating and reducing, as well as raising and creating while unlocking a new blue ocean. It pushes companies not only to ask the questions posed in the Four Actions Framework but also to act on all four to create a new value curve (or strategic profile), which is essential to unlocking a new blue ocean. The grid gives companies four immediate benefits (Kim & Mauborgne, 2019):

- It pushes companies to simultaneously pursue differentiation and low cost to break the value-cost trade off.
- It immediately flags companies that are focused only on raising and creating, thereby lifting the cost structure and often over-engineering products and services—a common plight for many companies.
- It is easily understood by managers at any level, creating a high degree of engagement in its application.
- It drives companies to thoroughly scrutinize every factor the industry competes on, helping them discover the range of implicit assumptions they unconsciously make in competing.

Table 10: ERRC Grid (Source: Kim & Mauborgne, 2019).

Eliminiate	Raise
Which factors should be eliminated that the industry has long competed on?	Which factors should be raised well above the industry's stand-ard?
Reduce	**Create**
Which factors should be reduced well below the industry's standard?	Which factors should be created that the industry has never of-fered?

Evaluate and correct

The last phase in the strategic retail planning process is the evaluation and correction process. A retailer constantly must evaluate its performance and correct weaknesses or problems when observed. A retail audit systematically reviews a strategy and its execution on a regular basis. Utilizing a retail audit is essential for a retailer to capture critical field data that affects the health of the company and its products. By analysing longitudinal data (e.g., sales volume, stock levels, promotional activities, competitor analysis, pricing, merchandising, etc.) retailers can make more informed decisions and adjustments to their retail plan. A retail audit is carried out on a certain number of retail outlets to measure the effectiveness, sales trends, sales volume, etc., of a brand or product in the retail outlet. Technology is one of the key tools being used by companies to carry out a retail audit. The technology can be used to obtain product information (e.g., sales, brand value, etc.), evaluate competitors, getting real time data and improving performance trends. A retail audit should be carried out at real time because it gives an accurate picture of the events at a retail outlet and helps to carry out corrective or improving measures at that time. In-store merchandising (e.g., placement of products) constitutes an important part of a retail audit. Moreover, strengths are emphasised and weaknesses are minimized, corrected, or eliminated. On an annual basis, it is important to reevaluate the retailer's priorities and strategic planning to ensure that the company is competitive and profitable in the long run. Over time, the retailer may also find that its mission and vision is not up to date anymore and needs to be changed or corrected. An annual evaluation is recommended to consider certain changes or corrections and revise the plan before it is implemented again.

How to react during a crisis – On the example of the coronavirus crisis
The food-retail industry plays a critical role in uncertain times. Here is an example of a worldwide crisis, the COVID-19 pandemic. The impact of this crisis was quite different for every retailer, depending on country, category, and customer mix. McKinsey (Aull, Kuijpers, Sawaya, & Vallöf, 2020) recommends six actions that food retailers can take to continue serving as reliable sources of food and essential items for customers worldwide:

1. Protect your employees and customers
Food retailers must step up frontline hygiene and limit human contact as much as possible, using as much technology as possible, for example, by encouraging self-checkout, minimizing cash payments, stocking shelves only before or after store hours, and having drivers drop off deliveries at doorsteps.

   Beyond workplace and store safety, it is crucial to create an environment that fosters social distancing or isolation to protect the vulnerable. We have seen retailers implement paid sick leave for affected employees, free testing, and stay-at-home policies for employees who have colds or are feeling ill. Food retailers must also prepare for worst-case scenarios by, for instance, proactively creating backup plans for the most crucial staff, working in A/B teams, and moving quickly to hire additional flexible capacity. Grocery chains are setting aside certain store hours to serve the elderly exclusively (to lessen elderly customers' risk of infection). Other retailers are donating food and essential items to the needy in their communities or offering free meals to healthcare workers and first responders.

2. Secure business continuity
Food retailers must keep stores and distribution centres open, employees must continue to work, home deliveries must be made, and customers must be served. This has proven challenging, especially when schools and childcare facilities are closed. Equally challenging is meeting the enormous (700% or more) spikes in demand on e-commerce with the associated struggles of getting enough delivery drivers, giving customers accurate delivery time slots, and keeping the IT systems running.

   Food retailers must take the time to listen to customers' most acute needs, and then use those insights for solutions. For example, some retailers have switched selected stores entirely to click-and-collect formats to protect both customers and employees. Companies must work with local governments, suppliers, employees, and service providers to develop a set of minimum norms for operating during a crisis.

3. Get a granular view of the local reality

The pace of recovery from COVID-19 – and, consequently, the patterns in consumer demand – vary across countries and categories. Some retailers are facing spikes in demand of up to 800% in over-the-counter cold and flu medicines and between 25% and 50% in food items. Within food categories, we've seen consumers in some areas buying fruit over beer – but, after a few days, returning to beer and snacks as they find themselves having to stay home for extended periods of time. Certain store formats (e.g., convenience stores) are seeing steep declines in sales, while others (such as the aforementioned e-commerce players experiencing a 700% increase in demand) are unable to fulfill customer orders.

Continually staying abreast of what is happening at a detailed, local level will enable food retailers to act appropriately and act fast. Many retailers are setting up some form of a virtual nerve centre to control, plan, stabilize stakeholder management, address primary threats rapidly, and mitigate threats' root causes. Financial stress testing and a cash control tower are critical in any crisis. Some retailers are offering shorter payment terms to keep their suppliers afloat.

4. Simultaneously manage supply and demand

The crisis has changed what an average grocery basket looks like and the supply chain is struggling to keep up. This is not just a matter of paying close attention to critical steps in the supply chain – such as providing supplier credits, finding alternative sources of supply, pulling in extra shifts, and safeguarding in-store replenishment, warehouses, truck drivers, and last-mile delivery. It is not just a matter of paying extra wages to secure flexible capacity to cover the peaks. These actions are, of course, important to ensure that retailers can fulfill peak demand. But it's just as important to manage consumer demand proactively.

On this front, we have seen both positive actions (CEOs and governments advising consumers to avoid panic buying and hoarding) and abhorrent behaviour (online sellers charging exorbitant prices for hand sanitizer and thermometers). We suggest taking a "cleansheet" look at your marketing and promotional calendar and adjusting, such as reducing promotion intensity in select categories, to smooth out unexpected peaks in the supply chain – not just today but also as a regular practice going forward.

5. Transform your business model to ensure that it is tech enabled and future proof

The crisis has accelerated many societal trends that were already under way: remote working, online shopping, tech-enabled retail, and localized supply chains. Even as food retailers address today's short-term challenges, they should take the time to rethink their business models to become more efficient – and, therefore, less exposed to shocks:

Stores. Can you make your store model cashless or virtually cashless? Can you replace the cashier-based model with a seamless no-checkout model? Are you using data to measure on-shelf availability in real time? Are you automating replenishment?

Supply chain. Are you embracing technology sufficiently in warehousing and transportation to reduce the burden on labour? Have you adopted machine learning in your forecasting so that you can spot abnormalities fast and adjust immediately?

Merchandising. Are your merchants equipped with the technological tools to run their categories "customer back" and remotely? Have you diversified sourcing sufficiently to derisk future shocks? Are there reasons for you to pursue more vertical integration or more strategic partnerships? In light of the latest consumer trends, are you striking the right balance between local and international partnerships? Should you expand your position in private labels in the face of potential gross domestic product (GDP) adversity and customers' quest for value? Or, put another way, should you introduce more private labels with a diversified but primarily local supplier mix?

E-commerce. Can you accelerate investments in a seamless online-to-offline experience and proactively shift spending to your online channel, in a model that serves the customer better and is sustainable over the long term? Do you have a scalable technological backbone and delivery network to flex up and down as needed?

Head office. Can you transform your head office into a flexible, remote-working team supported by tech and data? Are your systems able to handle the increased load and cybersecurity issues that come with distributed remote work?

6. Boldly reshape your ecosystem, including through mergers and acquisitions
Experience teaches us that crises typically trigger new avenues for growth and mergers and acquisitions (M&A). What moves can you make now to serve your customers, your employees, and your stakeholders better for the longer term? Which growth avenues could you pursue?

Are there companies you could potentially partner with to keep them afloat while providing yourself with an opportunity to grow into adjacencies (such as food service)? Is there room to expand your footprint and find new franchise models in the aftermath of the crisis? Are there moves along the value chain and ecosystem, such as vertical integration, services, or payments, that have become more attractive? What partnerships or acquisitions, such as tech companies and tech talent, could you pursue now that were perhaps more difficult before?

1.2.1 Total retail experience

In times of saturated markets, when many retailers are fighting for market shares, rough competition, and times when the internet is becoming dominant as a favourable marketplace, retailers are attempting to speak to the customers by developing new and innovating retail strategies and techniques on how to engage with them more efficiently and effectively. Nowadays, many customers, especially the younger consumers (Generation X, Y, and Z), are fed up with ordinary shopping environment. They want something more, something new that will get their attention, help them to relate and engage with the brand. Finally, yet importantly, they want something memorable and engaging that will make them visit the store again and create customer loyalty.

During the past decades, the type of products and services that retailers offer have remarkably changed, but so has the needs, desires, and lifestyles of consumers. Several changes in the retail environment in addition to the speed of consumption have made todays customers appreciate the hedonic part of shopping and consumption. Nowadays customers are not only looking for functional and high-quality products, but they also desire products that can be associated and related to fun or entertainment and reflect their own individuality and their way of life. Consumers want experience, entertainment, and are also looking for emotional stimulation while they are shopping. They do not only want to buy products, but they also want to experience something exciting (Kim, Sullivan, & Forney, 2007, 12).

1.2.1.1 Experiential retailing

One way how to solve all the issues described above and offer customers inimitable experience is the retailing concept called *experiential retailing*. The main concept of the experiential retailing is to: "Create a retail environment that offers unique and memorable sensory experience to convert shopping into an interactive, enjoyable and exciting experience" (Zentes, Morschett, & Schramm-Klein, 2011, 279). Furthermore, experiential retailing should also have an emotional impact on the customer. The emotional impact should be related to how they perceive the store and what image the store has in the customer's eyes. Experiential retailing is all about following the latest consumer's trends and additionally organizing some thrilling events for the customers. The key is to provide an overall pleasant and memorable experience. Make the customers spend more and more of their leisure time doing the shopping and, in the end, enjoy the whole process of shopping. That is the reason why experiential retailing is truly often also labeled as "entertailing" or "shoppertainment" (Zentes, Morschett, & Schramm-Klein, 2011, 279–280).

Mascarenhas et al. (2006) state that since the mid-2000s customers' emotional attachment with a brand, mainly through customer experience, gained more and more importance in the marketing literature. Companies and marketing managers have shifted their emphasis from a strict focus on the physical aspects of a product or service to delivering a total customer experience (TCE) by creating engaging and lasting experiences for their customers that provide an added value and strengthen customer loyalty (Mascarenhas et al., 2006).

Research has shown that pleasant customer experiences are able to improve customer satisfaction and customer loyalty, word of mouth communication, and a positive image formation (Verhoef et al., 2009).

Verhoef et al. (2009) proposes a theory-based conceptual model (see Figure 1.9) in which the antecedents to and moderators of customer experience are discussed. Figure 1.9 illustrates that customer experience is a holistic construct that involves distinctive responses to elements, which the retailer can control (e.g., retail atmosphere, assortment, price, etc.), and elements that are outside the retailer's control (e.g., competition, social environment, economic factors, climate, etc.). Determinants of customer experience, drawn from prior research, are the social environment, service interface, retail atmosphere, assortment, price, and customer experiences in other channels, for example, online channels or events.

The customer experience creation process is a dynamic process because a current customer experience (t) is affected by past customer experiences ($t-1$). Consumer moderators (e.g., consumers' goals, attitudes, or sociodemography) and situation moderators (e.g., location, culture, season, competition, etc.) are influencing factors on the delivered customer experience. The interaction between the retail brand and the customer experience is also part of this conceptual model.

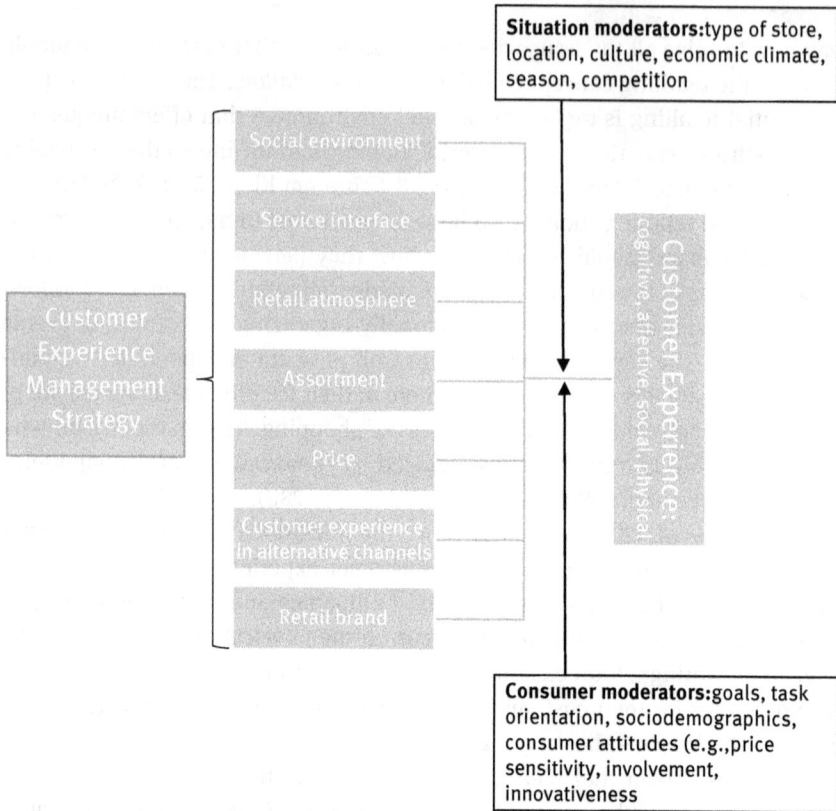

Figure 1.9: Conceptual model of customer experience creation.
Source: Verhoef et al., 2009

This conceptualization of customer experience is a holistic approach and therefore differs from most other customer experience models in the retailing literature. Most conceptualizations of customer experience focus on elements of the retail environment that are under the control of the retailer and examine how these elements influence specific customer responses.

Even though experiential retailing became popular all over the world, there are still some areas of retail where this concept might not be the most suitable. Retailers must keep in mind the customers' initial goals and attitudes towards shopping. For instance, if the shopping goal of most customers is task oriented, then the retailers should focus on store environment and not sidetrack the customer from their shopping task. This might be the case of grocery shoppers because grocery shopping is quite often labeled as an unpleasant activity. Conversely, apparel shopping is mostly related with fun and joy, especially with female and younger consumers, and customers will most likely prefer and appreciate a unique and thrilling shopping environment.

However, nowadays retailers also differ in the level of experience within the store, based on the product categories and customers' shopping attitudes towards them. (Zentes, Morschett, & Schramm-Klein, 2011, 279–280)

Events also play a role in creating a memorable and pleasant experience within a store. However, the result of various events vastly depends on how extraordinary and sophisticated the events are and how they are related to the store's or brand's image and character. Commonly used types of events within a store usually include fashion shows, cooking lessons, tastings, cosmetics treatments, and sport or artist performance. (Zentes, Morschett, & Schramm-Klein, 2011, 279–280) A perfect and suitable example where experiential retailing is used is, for instance, Apple stores. Apple, the leading technology lifestyle brand has opened stores with an iconic, minimalistic store design, with materials like aluminum, glass, and wood. The stores are designed entirely around the consumer, where service, learning, and products are combined. In the stores, customers have the opportunity and are encouraged to try out the Apple products. Apple products are available around the store specifically for the purpose of trial.

A new experientially-oriented approach in terms of luxury fashion brand interaction is pop-up retailing. Pop-up stores are physical retail setting often linked to other events, for example, fashion weeks for luxury fashion brands. Theses temporary brand stores last from a few days to an entire year and have a promotional and experiential emphasis (Taube & Warnaby, 2017). Experientially-oriented fashion events, such as pop-up stores or fashion shows, are aimed at attracting their key customers but also the so-called *new* luxury consumers.

The key characteristics of the "new" luxury consumer: young (millennials) and female, single, well-educated, and single, fashionable, and urban, individualistic, morally conscious, high levels of brand awareness, technology-savvy, hedonic motivations, and those interested in unique and meaningful experiences (Taube & Warnaby, 2017). Unique target-group oriented events, like luxury fashion pop-up activities, pop-up stores, or fashion shows, give the visitors exactly what they are looking for: these events offer a certain element of surprise, entertainment and fun, and bring like-minded customers together. Furthermore, these events with an experiential emphasis facilitate the contact with brand representatives (Taube & Warnaby, 2017), which might help to transform the customer's relationship with the promoted brand.

To conclude, the main purpose of such brand interaction events is not to sell many products, but rather to stimulate positive word of mouth to enlarge the brand reach in existing and new target groups and create customer engagement (Taube & Warnaby, 2017).

Customer experience in times of crisis

McKinsey (Diebner, Silliman, Ungerman, & Vancauwenberghe, 2020) has done some research on how to adapt customer experience in times of a crisis, like the coronavirus pandemic, and how to address customers in a post-crisis era. Particularly in times of crises, customer interaction with a company can trigger an immediate and lingering effect on their sense of trust and loyalty to the company. A basic expectation of customer experience will be how the businesses they frequent and depend upon deliver experiences which meet their needs with empathy, care, and concern. A company must consider the changing customer preferences and redesign customer journeys.

McKinsey (Diebner et al., 2020) suggests four customer experience practices that can frame short-term responses, build resilience, and prepare customer-forward companies for success in the days following the crisis. These are (see Figure 1.10 in the example of the COVID-19 pandemic):

- focusing on care and connection
  meeting customers where they are today
- reimagining customer experience for a post-crisis world
- building capabilities for a fast-changing environment

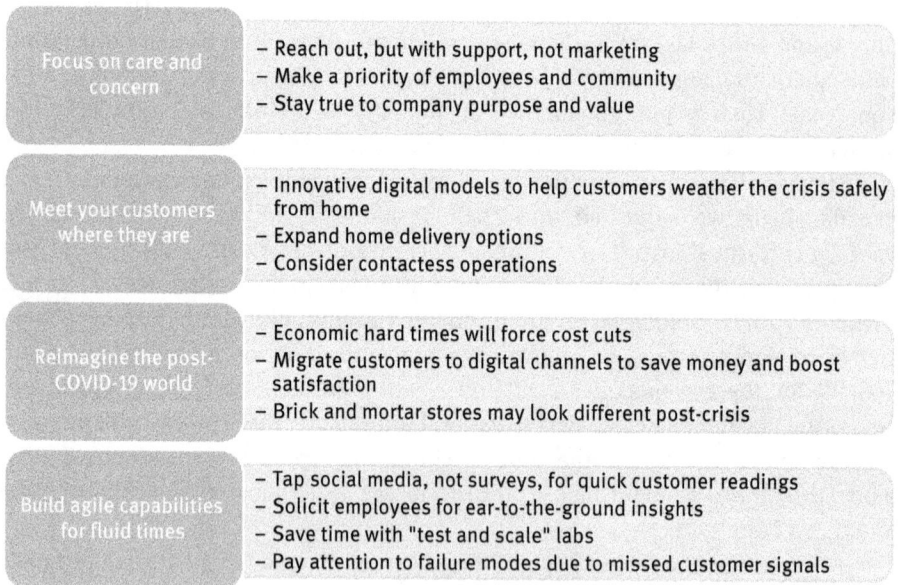

Focus on care and concern	– Reach out, but with support, not marketing – Make a priority of employees and community – Stay true to company purpose and value
Meet your customers where they are	– Innovative digital models to help customers weather the crisis safely from home – Expand home delivery options – Consider contactess operations
Reimagine the post-COVID-19 world	– Economic hard times will force cost cuts – Migrate customers to digital channels to save money and boost satisfaction – Brick and mortar stores may look different post-crisis
Build agile capabilities for fluid times	– Tap social media, not surveys, for quick customer readings – Solicit employees for ear-to-the-ground insights – Save time with "test and scale" labs – Pay attention to failure modes due to missed customer signals

Figure 1.10: Adapting customer experience in the time of coronavirus.
Source: Diebner, Silliman, Ungerman, & Vancauwenberghe, 2020

Focus on fundamentals: Care and connection

In times of a crisis, customers need trustworthy information, guidance, and support to cope with challenges, from keeping their families safe to helping their kids learn when schools are shut down. They want a resource they can trust and that offers support, for example, payment relief, credit support, and supporting aid organisations with money and food. These actions are critical for customers in the short term, and the impact will build positive relationships that are bound to last long after a crisis has ended. In times of crisis, caring for customers starts with thinking first about employees, for example by continuing to pay their employees a regular rate, even if they need to remain at home due to illness, or provide new tools, training, and support to enable employees to deliver superior customer experience in a new environment (Diebner et al., 2020).

Meet your customers where they are

In times of crises, customers' normal patterns of life demand a shift. When they must stay at home, retailers must meet their customers where they are and adapt their business models. Customers need different solutions on how they do their shopping (e.g., digital, at-home, and low-touch and even contactless options). It's likely that customers who have tried digital services will stick to them after a crisis is over. Moreover, companies who make this shift to digital and deliver superior experiences have an opportunity to increase adoption and maintain these customer relationships after the crisis (Diebner et al., 2020).

Reimagine customer experience

Normally changes in consumer preferences, habits, and business models outlast a crisis. Once customers are getting used to a new business model, some consumers will stick with it and permanently use it. In an economic downturn, cutting costs is necessary to survive. But customer experience should not be neglected as it can create substantial value. Often, the best ways to improve experience and efficiency at the same time are to increase digital self-service and to make smarter operational trade-offs, grounded in what matters most to customers. When a business model or service is changed or adopted, a customer-centric mindset must be considered, including migrating customers to self-serve channels, simplifying a product portfolio, or optimising the service-level. Moreover, omnichannel solutions are likely to increase, for example, buy online, pickup in the store (Diebner et al., 2020).

Build capabilities for a fast-changing environment

Offering customer-centric experiences, not only in a crisis, requires research to understand customers, their desires, needs, and habits. In times of a crisis, when market situations can change daily, traditional customer insight techniques, such as surveys, take too long (they normally take at least two to three weeks). This can be far too long to deliver useful insights. So other techniques must be used to generate insights, for example, to listen to employees or to adopt agile innovations and release them in their "minimum viable" state, rather than waiting to perfect them (Diebner et al., 2020).

Gamification

One way in which retailers have begun to enhance the online customer experience is through the application of game mechanics to online shopping, a process known as "gamification." Retailers have started to combine elements of play and common game mechanics such as points, badges, and other incentives in retail contexts to affect consumer behaviour in a desired way, especially enabling consumer engagement with online retailers.

An interesting development in the retail sector is, that retailers offer discount coupons to incentivize online shopping across its sales channels. For example, Alibaba provided their customers the chance to participate in on-platform games to get coupons they could redeem on their e-commerce website Tmall. Moreover, popular web services such as Facebook, Twitter, or eBay incorporate game elements to increase customer engagement with their sites. Increasingly, retailers are exploring the application of game techniques to create reward mechanisms and position online shopping as an entertainment activity for their customers.

The main drivers in gamification are the desire for competition, status, and achievement. Gamification actively uses various stimuli (softengi, 2019):

- **Rewards:** One of the most efficient methods in retail gamification is rewards. With prizes provided for accomplished tasks, customers get a positive feeling when receiving a reward, like a badge, points, levels, special discounts, account credits, free gifts, or free shipping.
- **Challenges:** Challenges are also an important tool in gamified applications as they allow retailers to encourage their customers to take the expected action. The challenge setup is usually tailor-made and directs the customers depending on the context, which helps you to define where you want your customer to go and how you want them to get there.
- **In-game currency:** The desire for material benefits is an effective factor when it comes to influencing customer behaviour. A virtual currency added to gamification applications can shape behaviour as well as increase customer retention and engagement. Moreover, a virtual world, where virtual currency has a significant role, normally encourages its users to cash out in the real world.
- **Virtual environment:** Creating a virtual environment or adding virtual elements to a gamified application can highly benefit retailers in capitalizing on users' engagement. Applying virtual environment, retailers can drive purchase, providing an online experience that customers will return to time after time. Augmented

reality (AR) and virtual reality (VR) technologies can also enhance retail shopping by making customer experience more engaging and more personal. For example, when shopping surrounding AR can improve the changing room experience, offering customers an opportunity to view an outfit from different angles.
- **In-store games:** Another powerful application of gamification is the introduction of games at shopping venues. Implementation of in-store games can increase the time spent in a store, generate new and returning customers, promote brand awareness and brand engagement.

The emergence of gamification has come in the context of increasing interest among researchers in consumer motivations when shopping online. The key question here has been the extent to which offline models of consumer behaviour can be seen as analogous to online models. While some studies have found that online consumers could be segmented in similar ways to offline consumers based on key behavioural traits (Ganesh et al. 2010), others make the case for additional behavioural categories in online shopping. Rohm and Swaminathan (2004), for example, identify the "variety-seeking shopper" who is stimulated by the extensive choices available on the internet. However, the overall thrust of research into online shopping has been around online shopping related to utilitarian and functional motives. For example, Rohm and Swaminathan found that the need for social interaction was not significant compared to the offline store environment; they suggest that "online shopping appeals to more functional as opposed to recreational shoppers" (2004, 755). This is consistent with Avcilar and Özsoy's findings that enjoyment is not a direct influence on online usage and rather online shoppers primarily perceive utilitarian, but not hedonic, benefits as sure gains from using the channel (2015).

It has been recognized that retail success in a multichannel market depends on delivering an effective customer experience, not simply focusing on price and product innovation. For retailers in sectors such as fashion this focus on utilitarian motivations is particularly challenging in sectors where online retailers face difficulties re-creating the more sensory experience of apparel shopping (Elliott et al., 2002). Since clothes are an experiential product, the lack of physical contact, uncertainty about product quality, or inability to provide the atmosphere experienced in-store have been deterrents to customers purchasing online (Hansen and Jensen, 2009). The adoption of gamification strategies by fashion retailers can therefore be a response to this challenge, and an attempt to build effective customer experiences online as well as offline.

Returning to the initial question of gamification, this raises additional questions on how games can be appropriately incorporated into the online shopping environment. One implication is that "game" elements need to be built from, and integrated within, the core utilitarian (useful) functions of the shopping task.

The following box illustrates several examples of the use of gamification elements by retailers that build upon the core shopping functions.

Gamification elements included in daily business

Online fashion retailers ASOS regularly "gamifies" the online shopping experience with competitions such as fashion bingo, matching celebrities with clothing, and Pinterest competitions to win prizes. Flash sales and leader boards to gain early bird exclusivity to sales are also strategies used to encourage customers to participate in retailers' fashion games. British fashion retailer Jack Wills also incorporates interactive games around Christmastime as customers can scan their gift guide calendar each day for a chance to win prizes.

Missguided, an online women's fashion retailer, runs frequent competition through their Facebook site. In addition to fashion retailers, grocery retailers such as Tesco encourage customers to participate and interact with each other in social spaces for the chance to win various prizes (Insley & Nunan, 2014)

1.2.1.2 Customer experience management and technology

According to the research company Nielsen and their report related to the retail development in years to come, the future of retail is in experience, entertainment, and the usage of technology. Stores engaging the customer's senses and providing a unique experience will only gain more and more importance and marketshare. The report also says that it is not enough to astonish the customer with spacious and flashy screens in the store. The experience the customer is facing within the store must be meaningful and relevant to be valuable and must be present during the entire shopping time (Nielsen, 2015). Take, for example, the luxury market, about 80% of retail luxury transactions are carried out in brick-and-mortar stores. Only brands that create in-store experiences will be able to increase store traffic and conversions; expand their customer base; and experience growth. Most important for evolving in-store experience to satisfy the desires of the new consumers is to invest in their frontline employees and provide training to build emotional connections with the consumers and an environment of storytelling and authentic engagement.

In the years to come there will be a constant growth in e-commerce. Therefore, retailers need to improve their omnichannel consumer experience. Many brands have already started implementing new digital and tech strategies, for example, using Instagram swipe up, polls, and stories that allow them to interact with their customers or using Amazon's Alexa to provide consumers with tutorials and drive-increased engagement. AR can be used to allow customers to try on glasses and lipstick shades through smart devices.

Another retail development in years to come is the usage of AI. AI is putting new tools into the hands of retailers, helping them deepen their engagement with customers, uncover business insights, and automate processes. AI-powered devices don't just compute, they can learn, make decisions and solve problems. The technology enables machines to use massive amounts of data to uncover new trends

and insights, making new markets accessible and businesses more efficient. AI applications in retail fall into three main categories (Coresight Research, 2019):
- computer vision that enables e-commerce image searches, robotics, etc.
- language processing that enables chatbots, text analytics, content creation, etc.
- data analytics that enables business intelligence, predictive analytics and forecasting, and search recommendations

AI helps retailers improve the customer experience by eliminating friction in the shopping process, deepening engagement with their customers or potential customers, and closing the information gap between online and offline (physical) stores without the need for additional staff. Chatbots enabled by AI can understand and respond to the majority of customer requests, from answering questions to complaint handling, quickly and efficiently. Another advantage of AI-enabled voice recognition technology is, that shoppers can complete many transactions without human assistance. Therefore, there are hardly any time constraints or waiting times for the customers (Coresight Research, 2019).

The following box illustrates some examples of providers of AI-based technologies suitable for retailers:

The Tmall Genie (see https://www.producthunt.com/posts/tmall-genie) is a smart speaker that functions much like the Amazon Echo. The Genie can answer shoppers' in-store questions and enable online shoppers to search for specific products via voice commands.

Another artificial intelligence (AI) solution to enhance the customer experience is offered by Point Inside (see https://www.pointinside.com/). The company is a provider of digital-mapping and indoor location-based services. There services are based on AI-powered chatbots that help shoppers find products through the retailer's app, and enables retailers to customize product and deal search. The retailer's in-store beacons guide shoppers within the retail spaces, so they can easily find the departments and products they are looking for.

Another successful example is Pegasystems (see https://www.pega.com/). The American-based company is the leader in software for customer engagement and operational excellence. Pegasystems offers customer engagement software that helps retailers acquire and retain customers, build loyalty with them, and upsell and cross-sell products. The company's software uses AI technology to combine real-time context with big data and analytics to create an one-to-one offer to each customer, even on social media.

Another advantage of AI is that this technology enables personalization solutions. The technology is applied to analyse data that can be used to create customer profiles. Retailers can compare those profiles to other, similar customer profiles to predict preferences, make recommendations and create personalized incentives and benefits for their customers. Personali (http://www.personali.com/platform/) is a company that uses AI (machine learning and algorithmic intelligence) and behavioural economics to analyse current and past behaviour patterns to segment shoppers based on purchase probability and willingness to pay (i.e., price elasticity). The company's solution generates targeted and tailored incentives to increase conversion.

To conclude with, the box below provides an example of a total retail experience in a brick-and-mortar store that also uses innovative technologies to enhance customer engagement and create long-term customer relations.

The American Girl stores – A total retail experience

Experiential retail is a concept that was already used by American Girl about twenty years ago, when in Chicago, Illinois, the first American Girl Place flagship store was opened, followed by locations in New York and Los Angeles and many other American cities. Before those brick-and-mortar locations came into existence, American Girl dolls started with a mail order-only business. The physical stores were the first chance customers had to walk into a physical location and purchase a doll. But American Girl stores offer a lot more. They offer a total retail experience, a life event for their 8- to 11-year- old American Girl doll owners. They were also designed as product showcases, bistros for themed dining, doll salons, a doll hospital, and exclusive inventory. American Girl Dolls Store locations offer many other special events throughout the year where you can do crafts, meet a favourite author, take a cooking class, or celebrate a birthday party. The American Girl Bistro offers a casual meal and dessert counter for their customers and their dolls. Special packages are also available in many stores, like the "Day at American Girl Place" package and "Late Night at American Girl Place" package. A Day at American Girl Place includes a meal in the café, special souvenirs, and a sitting at the photo studio. The Late Night at American Girl Place is an after-hours party for girls and her friends. Girls shop without other customers in the store, get a new hairdo for their dolls, and enjoy a meal together.

The newest flagship store at Rockefeller Plaza in New York is a 40,000-square-foot two-story location. It includes a doll hospital and salon, where damaged dolls can get better and healthier dolls can experiment with a fresh new look. The new store now makes it possible for girls to pick matching hairstyles with their dolls, get a manicure together, and even share the experience of getting their ears pierced. The store also offers American Girl fans the chance to design and build their own American Girl doll from several design combinations (face molds, skin tones and freckles, eye and hair colours, hair textures and new cuts and styles, as well as accessories). American Girl also hopes to improve its digital offering through the creation of a "Content Hub" – a location for customers to interact with and sample the extensive catalog of media products the brand produces to support its core toy line.

There is also an augmented reality (AR) experience for in-store shoppers, which is demarcated by signage within the store and compatible with a smartphone. Further digital experiences will follow.

For further information see:

https://www.americangirl.com/intro2ag/pages/store-experience.html

https://www.youtube.com/watch?v=lfjaUCzlX9c

1.3 STP marketing strategy

In saturated markets it is necessary for retail companies to define their target market. A target market consists of a set of buyers who share common needs or characteristics that the company decides to serve (Kotler & Bliemel, 2001). The more specifically a retailer can identify what differences exist among their customers, the more they will be able to appeal to these consumers (PwC, 2013). When choosing a target market, the appeal of the market segments, the company's objectives, and competencies have to be considered. A useful strategy for targeting the right customer with a suitable marketing strategy is called *STP marketing strategy*. An STP marketing strategy is composed of the three fundamental elements (Kotler & Bliemel, 2001):

- Segmenting: market segmentation by target groups to develop segment profiles by identifying bases for segmenting the market
- Targeting: choice of target groups according to attractiveness
- Positioning: a specific positioning and marketing mix for each market segment

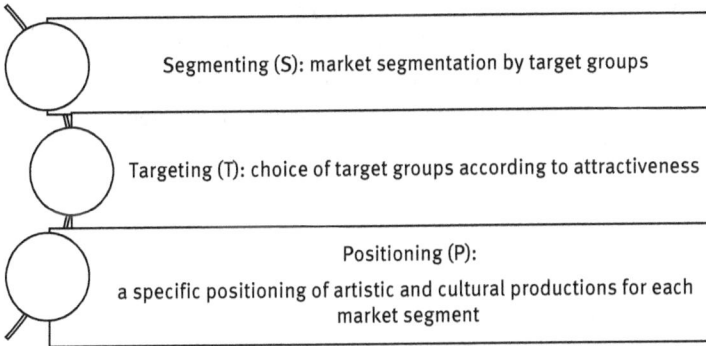

Segmenting (S): market segmentation by target groups

Targeting (T): choice of target groups according to attractiveness

Positioning (P):
a specific positioning of artistic and cultural productions for each market segment

Figure 1.11: STP marketing components.
Source: Kotler & Bliemel, 2001

1.3.1 Segmenting

Segmenting or market segmentation is the process of dividing consumers into different groups based on selected and distinguishing characteristics, which range from age, gender, etc., to psychographic factors like attitude, opinions, interest, and values. The member of these groups share similar characteristics and usually have one or more aspects common among them. The main aim behind market segmentation is that it helps retailers identify customers who are most likely to buy their products or consume their services and to create custom marketing mix for each segment and personalized marketing campaigns.

Gender is one of the simplest bases of market segmentation. The interests, needs, and wants of males and females differ at many levels, especially when it comes to cosmetics, clothing, or jewellery. Therefore, different marketing and communication strategies for male and females (i.e., gender marketing) is commonly used and extremely popular among marketers. Segmenting market according to the *age* group of the audience is a great strategy for personalized marketing. Most of the products in the market are not universal to be used by all the age groups, for example, cosmetics, sanitary products, clothing, etc. Income is another important segmentation criterion depending on the purchasing power of the target audience. *Income* is a key factor to decide whether to market the product as a need, want, or a luxury good. Marketers usually segment the market into three different groups: high income, mid-income, and low-income group. The *place of living* also affects the buying decision of customers. A person living high up in the mountains will have a need for different products than a person living in a big city. *Occupation* also influences the purchase decision of the target audience. There are many products, for example, clothing and shoes, which cater to an audience engaged in a specific occupation. *Product usage* also acts as a segmenting criterion. Users can be divided into heavy, medium, or light users of a product. The *lifestyle* of an individual, including interests, hobbies, religion, opinions, values, and other psychographic factors also affects the buying decision of a consumer.

Normally not only one criterion is used to segment the market, but a set of criteria, depending on the type of segmentation. The most common segmentation types that are used in retailing are:
- geographic segmentation
- demographic segmentation
- behavioural segmentation
- psychographic segmentation

Geographic segmentation divides the market based on geographical factors, like region, country, zip code, urban or rural area, etc. This segmentation type is commonly used for products that are used by people living in different regions and therefore having different requirements. For example, in many regions tap water is not drinkable, which inflates the demand for bottled water in these regions. People belonging to different regions may have different reasons to use the same product as well, for example, there are many beliefs when it comes to mourning, the colours of mourning are very different, from black in Europe to white at a Hindu funeral.

Demographic segmentation divides the market based on demographic variables like age, gender, marital status, family size, income, religion, occupation, nationality, etc. This is one of the most common segmentation practices among the marketers. Demographic segmentation is seen almost in every industry like automobiles, beauty products, mobile phones, apparels, etc., and is set on a premise that the customers' buying behaviour is hugely influenced by their demographics.

Behavioural segmentation is based on the target audience's behaviour, product usage and frequency, preferences, occasions, and decision-making. The segments are usually divided based on the knowledge and usage of the product, for example, those who know about the product, those who don't know about the product, former users, potential users, current users, frequent (heavy) users, light users, first time users, etc.

Psychographic segmentation divides the audience based on their personality, lifestyle, and attitudes. Personality is the combination of characteristics that form an

individual's distinctive character. It includes habits, traits, attitude, temperament, etc. Lifestyle is how a person lives their life, activities, opinions, and interests.
- Activities: how the consumer spends their time at work and leisure
- Interests: what the consumer places importance on their immediate surroundings
- Opinions: where the consumer stands on issues, society, and themself

All segmentation types have one thing in common: a market segment needs to be homogeneous. There should be something common among the individuals in the segment that the marketer can use for differentiation, one or more criteria which makes the segment unique. Marketers must also ensure that the individuals of the segment respond in a similar way to the stimulus. So, marketing segmentation criteria must have the following six characteristics (Kotler & Bliemel, 2001):
- Homogeneous: The consumers allocated to each segment should be similar in some relevant way, for instance, in terms of their needs and/or characteristics.
- Heterogeneous: Each consumer segment should be more or less unique, as compared to the other segments that have been constructed.
- Measurable: Some form of data should be available to measure the size of the market segment in order to evaluate the overall attractiveness of each segment.
- Substantial: The market segment should be large enough, in terms of sales and profitability.
- Accessible: The market segment should be reachable, particularly in terms of distribution and communication.
- Responsive: Each market segment should respond better to a distinct, target group-oriented marketing mix, rather than a generic mass market offering.

Market segmentation in retail clothing markets
Small clothing retailers, wholesalers, and manufacturers primarily focus on demographics, personalities and needs when segmenting their markets. This allows them to better reach nonbuying consumers and customers through advertising and other marketing efforts. There are several types of key market segments commonly used in national and international retail clothing markets based on the following segmentation criteria: gender, age, geographical characteristics, behaviour-related, and lifestyle characteristics (Suttle, 2018):

Gender-related segments
Smaller clothing retailers make frequent use of gender segments. For example, small, independent department stores may sell clothing lines for both men and women. These clothing lines may include casual and business attire for both genders. The clothing items the department store features is usually contingent upon the season. Men's shorts, for example, would primarily be sold in the spring and summer. A small clothing store may also specialize in a specific gender, selling men's suits or ladies' evening dresses.

Age-related segments
Age is another distinguishing characteristic that helps clothing retailers determine their target audiences. Many clothing retailers target teenage girls with their trendy new fashion lines, including jeans, T-shirts, and other apparel. They often promote these clothing lines in late July

and August, before the school year commences. The entire children's sector represents another viable buying group in apparel sales. Children's clothing retailers may also sell related items that appeal to children and their parents. Infants and toddlers represent additional age-related segments. Some small manufacturers and wholesalers may exclusively focus on the infant and toddler markets, as this segment is significant enough in size.

Geographic segments
Studies have shown that customer-clothing preferences vary in different regions or geographical areas. One determining factor is climate and weather conditions. People living in warmer climates wear shorts and swimwear for longer periods. Contrarily, the market for coats and jackets is greater in colder parts of the country. Clothing trends may also vary by geographic region. For example, retailers or manufacturers of the most extreme high fashion apparel may only sell their clothing in exclusive markets like big cities or cities famous for their fashion designers or celebrities (e.g., Paris, Milano, New York City, Los Angeles, etc.).

Behaviour-related segments
Consumers' choices in products, including apparel, may also be behaviour related. Some behaviours that marketers look at when segmenting customers include readiness to purchase, level of loyalty, frequency of interactions with the brand, occasion/timing and other factors. For example, customers may purchase a small manufacturer's clothing line for prestige. They may also shop at certain clothing stores for better quality, service, or other factors that are immensely important to them. Small clothing retailers may also appeal to the behaviour-related segment with holiday-related products. For example, clothing retailers may sell the popular colours of red and green during the holiday season.

Lifestyle segmentation
Lifestyle represents another market segment in which small clothing retailers base their product selections. For example, clothing manufacturers that produce clothing for hunters or military personnel sell camouflage and military fatigues, respectively, to meet their clients' lifestyle needs. Opinions may also play a role in what consumers purchase in this particular segment. For example, a coat manufacturer may need to produce faux fur coats instead of real fur coats for those who are more sensitive to animal welfare.

1.3.2 Targeting

The STP marketing component *targeting* deals with defining and selecting appropriate market segments. Because one of the biggest mistakes a retailer or marketer can make when starting a business is trying to appeal to everyone. Instead of trying to succeed by marketing to everyone, it is important to define the target audience. Knowing the target audience's needs, wants, and motivations is essential to tailoring products and services, but also marketing tools to meet their needs.

The attractiveness of the market segment plays a significant role in selecting the target market. But also, the objectives and competencies of the company are important. Several criteria should be considered to decide on the appropriate target group for the selection and evaluation of target segments. Therefore, it is useful to analyse the sector in respect to its attractiveness based on the following criteria (Kotler & Bliemel, 2001):

- size and growth of the segment
- structural attractiveness of the segment
- objectives and resources of the retailer

Social media platforms such as Facebook, Twitter, Xing, and LinkedIn are effective ways of surveying a target audience. Social media surveys are nowadays one of the most popular and simple ways of finding out more about a company's customers. Social media sites can help a company to engage and listen to their audiences and offer fully customizable forms that will help to expand the reach. These polls are equipped with analytical tools that will give information on a target audience's age, location, profession, interests and more (e.g., Android's 'N-Word' Poll Sparks Online Jeers).

Surveys are the perfect tool for a hands-on approach to staying up to date with what consumers are thinking and doing. It does not matter whether this is an online survey, an email survey or a telephone or face-to-face survey in the street, the most important part of conducting a survey is knowing what you want to learn from each question, and to keep questions short and easy to answer. Important questions that help to analyse a company's target audience, for example, are:

- How old are the current customers?
- Where do they live?
- Is the target audience primarily male or female?
- What is their average income?
- What is their profession?
- What are their activities, interests, and opinions?
- Do they have children or pets?

Analysing the target audience is important to direct a company's efforts towards the right audience. But another important step in STP marketing is to analyse a company's competitors. In detail, learning more about the competitors' services, products, and marketing efforts is essential to find out strategies to be different and which strengths are needed to be successful in the segment.

To summarize, targeting is an ongoing process that needs to be re-evaluated regularly to stay up to date with the target audience and a company's competitors and to find answers to the following questions (Kotler & Bliemel, 2001):

- Is this segment in decline or stagnant, or does it show high growth rates?
- How is the competition in the segment?
- How many suppliers are there per segment?
- Are there any changes or developments in a company's environment or among its stakeholders?

1.3.3 Positioning

In the literature there exist several positioning approaches. Berman & Evans (2013) define two main approaches: mass merchandising and niche retailing.

Mass merchandising is a positioning approach whereby retailers offer a discount or value-oriented image, a wide or deep merchandise selection, and large store facilities.

Niche retailing occurs when retailers identify specific customer segments and deploy unique strategies to address the desires of those segments rather than the mass market.

After audience and market segment are determined, the company must also differentiate itself from its competitors to reach an appropriate positioning on the market. Furthermore, the retailer must develop a target group-orientated marketing strategy for each segment. Kotler and Bliemel (2001) suggest using three approaches to target market coverage strategies:
– undifferentiated marketing (mass marketing)
– differentiated marketing
– concentrated or niche marketing

Undifferentiated marketing (mass marketing) means the total proceeding of a market for only one activity. It does not mean that there are no differences between individual segments. The retailer relies on the common needs of all customers and deliberately neglects differences that might exist. The main argument for this strategy is its cost-saving effects. Such savings can be passed on in the form of price benefits to customers. Indeed, it is cheaper to offer a product for all than many different products in smaller numbers for individual submarkets. The procurement, logistics, and storage costs and the marketing costs are correspondingly low. A disadvantage is that the different needs of different segments of the market are not considered (Kotler & Bliemel, 2001).

Differentiated marketing means that the retailer starts with the different needs of the individual segments and develops the different products according to those needs. Normally the turnover of a company is higher with differentiated marketing than undifferentiated marketing due to the fact that the potential of the individual submarkets is better exploited, and customers are usually willing to spend more money for special products. A disadvantage is that, in general, the costs are higher. The marketing costs rise significantly with the development of various products and special offers. Moreover, the higher organizational effort must be considered. One of the main advantages is that differentiated marketing normally leads to an increase in profitability because the company seeks out those segments that seem worthwhile for processing, nonattractive segments that are too small or too competitive, are not targeted.

Concentrated marketing (niche marketing) means that a company focuses exclusively on a part-segment of the market and does not process the other segments. The main advantage is that the company can develop a high level of expertise in its core segment. A disadvantage is the limited growth prospects and the overreliance up-on one product in one segment. Therefore, the strategy is mainly useful for small- and medium-sized enterprises. They can more easily use their corporate size in the segments, which are less attractive for larger companies due to the market size. Concentrated marketing may be chosen as a starting point for further growth in the future in other market segments. Properly applied, concentrated marketing can be very profitable for companies (Kotler & Bliemel, 2001).

Nowadays, retailers mainly run a combination of all the three marketing coverage strategies described above to avoid the disadvantages of each marketing coverage strategy and to avoid becoming transfixed in one segment with only one product. Sometimes it is necessary to tailor products, offers, and marketing programs to the needs and wants of specific individuals or local consumer groups. This practice is called micromarketing.

Micromarketing includes two different target group coverage strategies: local marketing and individual marketing (also named one-to-one marketing or customized marketing). *Local marketing* means that offers are tailored to the needs and wants of local consumer groups, for example, cities or even local stores, to respect local differences in demographics or lifestyles. *Individual marketing* is the opposite of mass marketing. By using this strategy offers and marketing programs are tailored to the desires and needs of individual, single customers. Customization has become extremely popular within the past years because most of the customers prefer interactive dialogue and marketing programs but also individual, tailor-made, and unique products. Consumers are empowered to design their individual products or services, which perfectly fit their individual preferences. So, customers get more involved in the product development and purchasing process, which results in more willingness to pay slightly higher prices and an increase in customer satisfaction.

It must be mentioned that by using micromarketing manufacturing and marketing costs are usually higher due to the fact that economies of scale are reduced. Nevertheless, in times of fragmented or saturated market situations this strategy helps to be more competitive and fulfil the needs and wants of individual and local customers. The box below provides an interesting example of how the apparel manufacturers and retailers make use of customization to create the right apparel size and shape and fulfil the need for personalized products.

3D body-scanning technology for creating the perfect fit
Designing the right ready-to-wear apparel size for all shapes has always been a challenge. Most apparel manufacturers decide the fit and sizing of their garments based on limited information. In the absence of accurate body measurement data, apparel manufacturers generally size their garments by using fit models in one or two standard sizes, and then scale prototypes proportionally

to all sizes based on these models. For a consumer, finding the right size for one's body shape is often challenging, as the retail industry has no standard sizing system for all brands. Different brands have different numerical sizes and definitions of small, medium, and large. The fit problem is particularly challenging for online shoppers because they can not try on garments before they purchase them. This has resulted in high return rates in e-commerce: the average return rate for online apparel purchases is 30%–40%. In some categories where fit is an important factor, such as women's dresses, the return rate is as high as 50%, according to industry sources. Therefore, 3D body-scanning technology could be the solution to these fitting challenges. The noncontact technology can be used to capture the shape of a human body via a laser light or a camera. The technology records the body's exact shape and size and creates a 3D digital model of the body within seconds. This 3D body-scanning technology can help apparel companies create garments with a more accurate fit by providing true measurements of customers of different shapes and sizes (Weinswig, 13 June 2017).

Looking beyond current industry practices, consumer-generated 3D body measurement data could help retailers optimize the size composition of their inventory and avoid excess markdowns. Retailers could use body measurement data collected by devices such as fitness scales and smartphones to make sizing decisions. Further interconnection between artificial-intelligence powered shopping devices, for example, Amazon's Echo, and body-shape-tracking devices are possible in the near future creating a holistic shopping experience (Weinswig, 13 June 2017).

1.3.3.1 Differentiation and competitive advantages

In the sense of a market-oriented retail management, it is necessary for the management to define strategic marketing goals and to concretize them by appropriate orientation of the sales policy instruments. In this way, the retailer determines its behaviour towards demanders and competitors. On the other hand, by the creation of a strategic successful positioning a differentiation with unique, unmistakable achievements (USP = unique selling propositions) can be achieved. Porter (1999) distinguishes three strategies with which competitive advantages can be created (see Figure 1.12):

- cost leadership
- differentiation strategy
- market segmentation strategy

A clear positioning and profiling in one of these strategies is a central basic decision to be able to stand up to the competition. While Porter (1999) speaks of the "loss of the middle," the unprofiled midfield, Bosshart (2003) calls this decision the "flight from the middle," since the standard segments in the middle no longer have the strength to differentiate themselves. This chapter deals with these three strategies according to Porter (1999) and shows the possibilities of finding a target-group oriented differentiation and profiling for a retailer.

Markets Where Company Competes

		Broad	Narrow
Source of	Costs	Cost Leadership	Cost Focus
Competitive Advantage	Differentiation	Differentiation Leadership	Differentiation Focus

Figure 1.12: Porter's generic strategies.
Source: own elaboration based on Porter, 1999

Strategy of cost leadership

When we have a look at the retail landscape in western countries, we see that "trading down" measures, and consequently low-price strategies, are an attempt to attract new customers and retain existing ones. Favoured by a general economic downturn, the last few years have seen an increase in the emergence and growth of discount-oriented types of retailing. They use aggressive "price wars" based on absolute performance efficiency as a dominant marketing instrument. This strategy of so-called *cost leadership* is referred to in retail as the "discount strategy."

Discounting as a corporate strategy is not limited to "cost leadership," however, it is limited to the "simplification of services" component. Cost leadership is characterised by a simplification of corporate structures and processes, by growth and efficiency orientation, and by an innovative business system. The simplification of services is reflected in simpler shopping for customers, the elimination of quality risks for customers, and customer integration. Discount-oriented company types can be found in almost all sectors.

Business types that use the strategy of cost leadership as a profiling strategy vis-à-vis competitors try to target price-oriented consumers in a targeted manner. The fact that this strategy can be successful is demonstrated by developments in the retail landscape in western countries in recent years. It should be noted, however, that not many companies have succeeded in achieving a unique position in the perception of consumers with their strategy of aggressive prices compared to their competitors. It will therefore be necessary to develop alternative strategies to position a retailer uniquely and successfully.

The successful cost leadership strategy of Walmart
Walmart, the largest retail store in the world, started its operations more than 50 years ago in 1962. The retailer employs over two million employees and operates more than 10,000 retail stores worldwide. It is present in over 50 countries worldwide. To manage such a large retail business, Walmart needs to effectively employ its core business strategies and principles. When you walk into a Walmart store, the first thing you will notice is that the prices are much lower than those of any other stores. There are two activities that drive the strategy of Walmart in lowering prices and its "everyday low price strategy" (EDLP): primary activities include all the activities such as supply chain management, operations, distribution, sales and marketing and

services, etc. Support activities include general administration, human resources management, research and development, technology, and system development (see Figure 1.13).

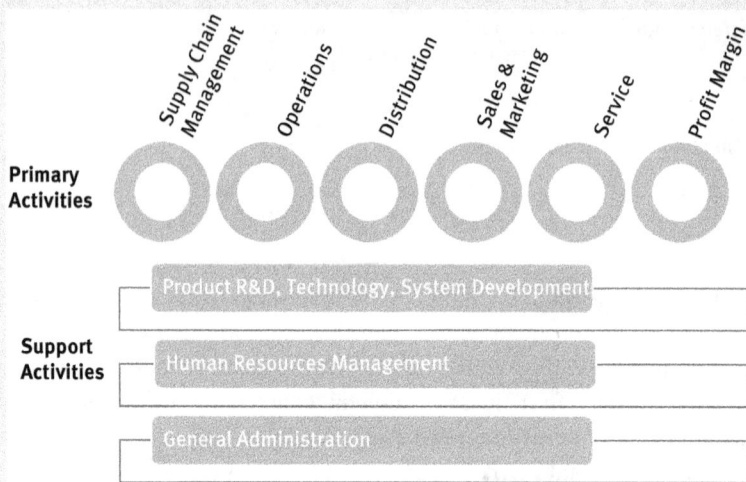

Figure 1.13: Cost leadership strategy of Walmart.
Source: Ko, 2011

When we focus on one of the main primary activities that help to reduce costs, we must consider efficiency in supply chain management. Walmart is incredibly successful in managing its supply chain. Walmart applies the most reliable supply chain management system, which is very efficient because almost all product data can be tracked to and from the manufacturer, warehouse, and the store shelf. Efficiency in supply chain system may save Walmart several million dollars as it can prevent losses from faulty product management (Ko, 2011).

Another primary activity that helps to reduce costs is efficiency in operations and distribution strategies. Walmart only has store locations that are outside of large cities and within 200 miles of existing stores. By bunching stores together in small areas, distribution costs are below average. Location is vital in any business undertaking. Business placement and geographical accessibility are key elements for customers. Walmart employs various operations and distribution strategies to ensure that all factors related to the place as a marketing mix element are efficient and effective. For example:

– A strong e-commerce platform that allows customers to purchase goods without having to visit a physical Walmart store (http://www.walmart.com).
– A well-planned network of distribution centres with more than 150 that make it easy for stores to collect their orders, as well as to deliver their products directly to consumers. Walmart transportation has a fleet of 6,100 tractors, 61,000 trailers, and more than 7,800 drivers. Each distribution centre is more than 1 million square feet in size and employs more than 600 personnel unloading and shipping over 200 trailers daily. Every distribution centre supports 90 to 100 stores in a 150 plus- mile radius (Walmart, 2019a).
– Branding and differentiation of their many Walmart outlets, such as Walmart Supercentres, Walmart Neighbourhood Market, Walmart Express Stores, and Walmart Discount Stores. Walmart Supercentre: Walmart began building supercentres in 1988 and are around 182,000 square feet employing about 300 associates. Walmart Supercentres offer a one-stop shopping

experience by combining a grocery store with fresh produce, bakery, deli, and dairy products with electronics, apparel, toys, and home furnishings. Most supercentres are open 24 hours, and may also include specialty shops such as banks, hair and nail salons, restaurants, or vision centres. Walmart Discount Store: smaller than a supercentre, discount stores employ about 200 associates and offer electronics, apparel, toys, home furnishings, health and beauty aids, hardware, etc., in about 106,000 square feet of open, brightly lit space. Walmart Neighbourhood Market: Walmart Neighbourhood Markets were designed in 1998 as a smaller-footprint option for communities in need of a pharmacy, affordable groceries, and merchandise. Each one is approximately 38,000 square feet and employs up to 95 associates. Walmart Neighbourhood Markets offer fresh produce, meat and dairy products, bakery and deli items, household supplies, health and beauty aids, and a pharmacy. *WalMart Express* are smaller outlets located in urban areas cities where physical space is at a premium.

Another important primary activity is a focus on profit margins. Walmart buys its products at very low prices, exchanges high purchase volumes for low cost while passing the savings onto its customers with its every-day low price strategy. The bargaining power of suppliers is weak. Many suppliers even give in to Walmart's pressure because they depend on the discount retailer for most of their sales. For most producers, Walmart is their largest account. Obviously, they would do what Walmart wanted them to do if they hoped to maintain their sales.

To conclude, Walmart's ability to continuously drive its costs lower while satisfying customers' needs makes it potential entrants very difficult to compete with Walmart. Therefore, those are the strategies that Walmart uses to sustain cost leadership position in the value chain market.

Differentiation strategy

According to Porter (1999), the differentiation strategy's main aim is to create something that is regarded as unique in the entire industry. This uniqueness must relate to something that appears useful and valuable to the consumer. The factors or elements used to differentiate the retailer can vary and be multifaceted. Many experts assume that personalized products create the highest customer loyalty, because then the product corresponds exactly to the wishes, desires, needs, and moods of the customer.

Moreover, experience orientation can also be used by retailers as a central differentiation factor. If one tries to justify which of the various differentiation factors promises the most success, a reference to the sociodemographic developments of our society is recommended. Here it must be mentioned that the change in values of the so-called hybrid consumer has led on the one hand to a desire for exclusive products and services and on the other hand, the increase in the number of single households, the professional emancipation of women and the high value of leisure time are leading to a redistribution of the time budget with a higher willingness to pay. Consequently, two strategies of differentiation are particularly promising: experience orientation and convenience orientation.

Experience orientation

Experience orientation be a consumer demand for products/services and a fundamental profiling possibility. Moreover, it is considered a successful marketing strategy because it has a positive effect on customer behaviour at the POP and can positively influence economic company data such as turnover, purchase amount per buyer or number of buyers. Starting points for the concretisation of experiences in retail stores can be manifold. Müller-Hagedorn (2003) divides these into four areas:

- related to objects: (e.g., by the possession of the purchased good)
- related to the phases of the purchasing process: (e.g., decision-making aids, information about the offer and advice, favourable purchasing conditions)
- to the human senses
- to psychological constructs: sensations, emotions, contentment

Heinemann (2013) tried to work out essential profiling factors in an empirical analysis based on centred performance factors such as assortment, service, price, communication policy, shop design, and presentation. One service area has crystallized as the most important, the design of the store. This includes performance dimensions such as:

- exterior design (facade, entrance, corporate design, lighting mood, etc.)
- atmosphere (experience-oriented sales room, customer guidance system, fascination points, exclusive programmes, etc.)
- decoration (unhindered access, no threshold fear, assortment decoration, deco-oriented ambience etc.)
- information presentation (special product information, new products, colour ambience, new product information in the [display] window, etc.)

The aim of an appealing store design is to create preferences for the retailer through a positive image based on shopping experiences. Several objectives should be reached:

- increased customer convenience and facilitation of shopping
- extension of the length of stay per customer in the shop
- frequency of visits should be increased
- emotional decision-making behaviour of consumers should be positively influenced (e.g., impulse buying)

In summary, retailers try to trigger pleasant sensations among consumers with experience-oriented sales concepts, so that the time spent in the shop is increased. As a result, this can lead to customer loyalty and increased sales. Action parameters for a supply-side experience orientation are: location, store design, assortment, personnel, discounting price policy, and corresponding design of the communication policy.

Convenience orientation

If one follows the developments of recent years in retail and gastronomy, one can see a trend towards systematic small-scale solutions with high supply and demand-side convenience orientation in addition to large-scale mixed-use centres, the so-called *convenience shops*. These are characterised by the fact that they usually combine retail, gastronomy, and services. One of their key success factors is customer orientation. They try to satisfy the need for convenience by differentiating themselves through low time requirements, no time restrictions when shopping, proximity to the customer and one-stop shopping from competitors. At assortment level, they offer products with a high manufacturing level and impulse products with a high turnover rate to meet short-term demand.

Convenience-oriented retail concepts include operating types such as petrol station shops, kiosks, neighbourhood shops, shops at a traffic junction (e.g., railway stations, airports), fast food restaurants and various other providers of convenience products such as bakeries or butchers. Some of these concepts represent a merger or cooperation between retailers and gastronomy. These include, for example, home delivery ("home delivery-services") from high level products to comprehensive complete services (e.g., event caterers).

The most important form of cooperation in the stationary sector is vertical integration. This manifests itself in the form of integrated shop systems, such as shop-in-shop shops (e.g., bookstores or textile shops with an integrated coffee bar concept) or standalone solutions such as fresh islands and meal markets of retail companies.

For the retail trade, this offers the possibility of differentiation by leasing existing areas to gastronomic cooperation partners. Retail concepts, on the other hand, could be implemented in catering establishments if they have locational advantages for the convenience sector.

Zara has successfully done a vertical integration
A popular example of vertical integration and its successful implementation is the Spanish apparel chain ZARA. The Spain headquartered company has done successful backward integration and operates through its own large retail stores across the world. The company manufactures the merchandise in its own units and design for the clothes also is done in-house. Due to such an integration the company is able to ensure a change of wardrobe and style based on season and has the fastest inventory turnover compared to its competitors who enable the company to keep an important competitive advantage (Educba, 2019).

However, not all vertical integration results in a successful story. Sometimes if not well integrated this strategy can result in serious ramification for a company and can even to lead its existence in danger. Vertical Integration makes sense when the company can perform the functions in the value chain in a better and efficient way resulting in optimization of cost and improvement in overall efficiency and quality which are otherwise outsourced to external players. A business choosing to opt for vertical integration must ensure that they take into consideration such factors and should not get affected by short-term gains arising out of forwarding or backward vertical integration but should see the long-term gains as well. The main point to remember while doing vertical integration is to ensure that those activities in the value chain are integrated, which the business can perform more efficiently and economically will result in a value accretive for business and its customers (Educba, 2019).

To conclude, vertical integration is an important milestone that companies try to attain to improve their profitability and achieve an advantage over their competitors and differentiate themselves from them and at the same time delivering better value for the customers. This is an important step in enhancing the efficiency in the value chain.

To meet the convenience needs of retail consumers it is recommended for retailers to have:

- a location close to the customer
- good accessibility and sufficient parking spaces
- a clear design of the shopping centre
- a wide range of convenience products (and take-away products) with the possibility of one-stop shopping
- as long as possible opening hours (no time restrictions)
- the possibility of self-service (low time requirement for purchasing)

A further possibility for differentiation of a company is to establish the respective type of business as a brand. This is dealt with in the following.

Business types as brands

In saturated markets it is important to give consumers a clear profile and positioning of the company or brand. With the help of brands, companies try above all to create orientation, market transparency, and a strong emotional bond (store branding). Experts are sure that the essential element of a brand to be competitive is to emotionally link the target group with the brand. A brand appears to be strong when a sufficiently large number of customers have positive attitudes towards the organisation, the ideas come close to the expectations of the customers, do not spread much, and at the same time stand out from those of competitors. In addition, brands can serve as a means of simplifying product selection, as a sign of quality, standard, and service and as an expression of a certain lifestyle. They therefore also fulfil the desire to present oneself to the public.

1.4 Consumer buying behaviour and the purchase decision process

Consumer buying behaviour refers to the buying behaviour of final consumers (individuals and households) who buy goods and services for personal consumption. Foscht, Swoboda, & Schramm-Klein (2015) define consumer behaviour as the behaviour of end consumers during the purchase and consumption of economic goods. In addition, consumer behaviour represents the process where individuals or groups select, purchase, use, or dispose their products with the goal to fulfil their personal needs (Solomon, 2015).

Research on consumer buying behaviour has the aim to answer the questions "why" and "how" a consumer buys certain goods and services and tries to analyse the consumer's purchase decision process. A consumer's purchase decision can be defined as "a process starting at the product perception and finally ends with the final product choice, conducted on an individual basis or in groups" (Foscht et al., 2015). The consumer purchase decision process can be divided into five stages (Solomon, 2015):
– need/problem recognition
– information search
– evaluation of alternatives
– purchase decision
– post-purchase behaviour

This purchase decision process differs according to how much time consumers have for making their decision and how important the final decision is for them. If they have enough time and the importance of the decision is high, then the consumer will put more effort into the purchase decision process and therefore search for all the alternatives, evaluate them in detail, and finally decide on the one the consumer thinks is the best option. In Chapter 1.4.2 the five stages of the consumer purchase decision process will be explained in more detail.

Consumer behaviour has changed over the last decades from a constant to a hybrid to a multioptional consumer behaviour. Today's consumers show a more complex and very often hybrid or contradictory shopping behaviour. The multioptional consumer is characterised by a combination of behaviour patterns and attitudes from convenience-oriented, price-sensitive, brand-conscious to quality-oriented, experience-oriented, variety-seeking, etc. Nevertheless, the consumers' purchasing behaviour can be broken down into four possible categories:
– complex purchasing behaviour
– variety-seeking purchasing behaviour
– dissonance-reducing purchasing behaviour
– habitual purchasing behaviour

Most customers fall into each of these categories at some point in their purchase decisions depending on occasion, timing, mood, shopping companions, price, or the product itself.

The *complex purchasing behaviour* is most evident when a customer is highly involved in the purchase and decision-making process, and there is a significant difference between the brands being considered. For example, the consumer shows a complex purchasing behaviour when he or she buys a new car. Differences, especially the price range, are evident between the various car brands. Therefore, when buying a car, the purchase process is quite complex.

The *variety-seeking purchasing behaviour* is evident when a customer is not very involved in the purchasing process, although there is significant difference between the products being offered by different brands. This purchasing behaviour is evident when buying low-involvement products, like a toothpaste. One day the customer decides to try and buy brand A and will stick with it for a while. But after some while, although the customer is satisfied with brand A, there is a special discount on brand B, the customer might switch to the other brand. So, the purchasing behaviour is rather inconsequential.

Dissonance-reducing purchasing behaviour is evident when a customer is facing a rather major purchase decision, but there is not that much difference between the products being offered. For example, when purchasing a new steel case chair for the office, a customer will base the decision on personal preference or price and will compare the products to be sure that this is the "right" product. Situations, customers experience a mental discomfort, especially in situations in which the decision of an individual clashes with new evidence perceived by that person. For example, a person purchases a dress in shop A and afterwards sees exactly this dress in shop B, but much cheaper. In this situation the customer experiences a so-called cognitive dissonance. When confronted with facts that contradict an individual's beliefs, ideals, and values, they will find a way to resolve the contradiction to reduce their discomfort.

Habitual purchasing behaviour is evident in purchases that don't require much involvement and when the product being offered doesn't vary much from brand to brand. In these cases, purchasing decision tends to come down to personal preference or habits and do not need much thinking effort. For example, when buying the daily newspaper or the daily coffee in the morning.

As we have seen above, consumer buying behaviour and the purchase decision process is multifarious. To understand the complex purchase decision process and buying behaviour of consumers, the following Subchapter 1.4.1 explains the most important approaches to examine the behaviour of consumers by pointing out selected consumer behaviour models.

The main purpose of consumer behaviour models is the attempt to explain in a simplified way the relationship between the different, interactive factors that influence consumer behaviour. Several models have been developed to describe consumer behaviour. The most frequently quoted of all consumer behaviour models is the Howard-Sheth model of buyer behaviour developed in 1969. This model points out the importance of various input factors to the consumer buying process and describes several paths to order these inputs before making a final decision. This model is based on the behaviouristic Stimuli-Organism-Response model by Mehrabian and Russell (1974). This model describes how consumers react to various stimuli in the environment by using three steps: stimuli (S), organism (O), and response

(R). In this model, stimuli (S), for example, marketing stimuli or environmental stimuli, are said to cause a reaction: approach or avoidance. This reaction or response (R) depends on the consumer's internal evaluations (O), on the so-called consumer's black box, the processes in the consumer's inside. The following chapter deals with these models in more detail.

1.4.1 Consumer behaviour models

The purpose of consumer behaviour models is to present a simplified version of the relationship between several factors that have an influence on a consumer's behaviour. Many different models have already been developed which attempt to explain consumer behaviour and the influencing factors with the intention of trying to influence this behaviour. Most of these models are based on the fundamental Stimuli (S)-Organism (O)-Response (R) that which will be explained in the following chapter. Within this book it is possible to review only the most important consumer behaviour model, especially for the retailing sector. For further information please refer to Kroeber-Riel & Weinberg (2013) or Foxall (2015).

This book widely concentrates on developments in saturated, volatile markets and focuses on agile strategies, new technologies and business models and adoptions to developments in consumer behaviour. Two models are widely used to identify the acceptance and adaption of new technologies by consumers: the Theory of Planned Behaviour (TPB) (Ajzen, 1991) and the Technology Acceptance Model (TAM) (Davis, 1989). Therefore, these two models will also be described within this chapter.

1.4.1.1 S-O-R model

Consumers' purchase decisions are influenced by many different factors. For marketers and retailers, it is essential to know why consumers buy certain products and why they avoid buying competitive products and what influences their decisions. The Stimuli (S)-Organism (O)-Response (R) model of consumer behaviour by Mehrabian and Russell (1974) examines the whole buying decision process of consumers. Figure 1.14 shows that marketing stimuli and other stimuli (economy, technology, politics, and culture) enter the consumer's so-called *black box*, the consumer's inside (characteristics of the buyer and the buyer's decision process) where all visible inputs cause an observable reaction or response to the stimuli. This reaction can be a product choice, a brand choice, a retailer choice, and/or the purchase time.

Marketers and retailers want to understand how and why certain stimuli are transferred into distinctive reactions in the consumer's inside. This can be achieved through different methods. The easiest way is to analyse direct observable and measurable variables. More complex would be to analyse intervening variables. These variables can be measured indirectly over indicators, for example, the consumer's

Input (Stimuli)	Black Box (Organism)	Output (Reaction)
Marketing Stimuli Product, Price, Place, Promotion **Other Stimuli** Economy, Technology, Politics, Culture	Characteristics of buyers Decision process	Product choice Brand choice Retailer choice Purchase time

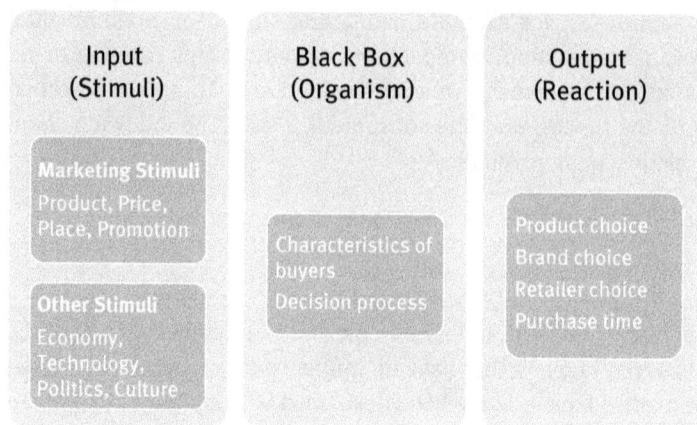

Figure 1.14: S-O-R model of consumer behaviour.
Source: Own elaboration based on Mehrabian and Russell, 1974

characteristics affecting the consumer behaviour in general and the decision process. The S-O-R model is a very basic and fundamental model that was used by many researchers as a starting point for their theoretical models and explanations for a certain reaction. Howard and Sheth (1969), for example, used this S-O-R model of consumer behaviour for developing a complex and comprehensive model for explaining the buying behaviour of individuals. This model is one of the most frequently quoted consumer behaviour models and is relevant for the retailing sector. Therefore, this model will be explained in detail in the following chapter.

1.4.1.2 Howard-Sheth model

The Howard-Sheth model of buying behaviour of final consumers (individuals and households) attempts to explain the consumer's rationality of choice of a product or service by considering several input and output variables that are subject to direct observation and perceptual and learning constructs, which can not be directly observed ("black box"). Figure 1.15 shows that the Howard-Sheth model consists of four main variable groups (Howard & Sheth, 1969):

- **Inputs (stimulus display):** there are three different types of stimuli arising either from marketing activities and/or the environment of the consumer:
    - *significant incentives:* contain physical characteristics and the attributes of a product, for example, price, quality, brand characteristics, service or accessibility
    - *symbolic incentives:* consists of verbal and visual characteristics of the product, for example, the form of a product or the effect of advertising
    - *social stimuli:* include social environment of the consumer: in detail the family, reference groups and social class (how people are classified socially).

- **Perceptual constructs:** Describe the process of obtaining and processing information, the attention to certain stimuli, sensitivity to certain messages, prejudice, etc.
- **Learning constructs:** Deal with trying to explain how the final consumer forms certain attitudes, opinions, and knowledge influencing the buying decisions. Here we also find the variables "satisfaction" (the product or service evaluation after the purchase) and "brand comprehension" (amount of brand information actually processed and stored in the consumer's mind).
- **Outputs:** Here we find the variables purchase, intention, attitude, brand comprehension, and attention. These variables are subject to direct observation because of internal processes. Examples are the intention to buy or not to buy a certain product, the disclosure of customer interest, or the most important output variable for a retailer – the actual purchase.

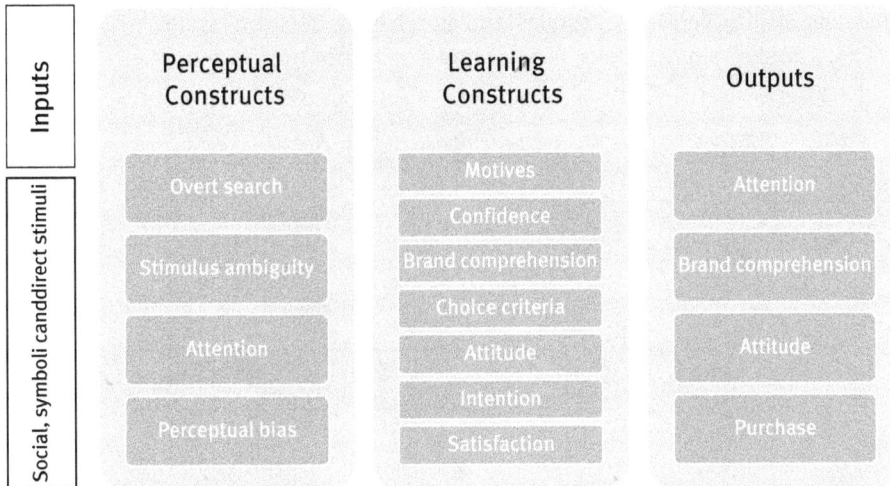

Figure 1.15: Howard-Sheth model of buying behaviour.
Source: Howard and Sheth, 1969

What has to be noticed is that this buying behaviour model does not present some important external variables that also have a significant impact on a consumer's buying decisions and therefore are relevant to mention. These external variables are: time pressure, financial status, personality traits, and culture. Howard and Sheth (1969) define those variables as follows:

Time pressure occurs when a consumer feels pressed for time because of environmental influences, it is necessary to allocate the time among alternative uses. A reallocation unfavourable to purchasing a product can occur and unfavourably affect the information search.

Financial status means the constraint a consumer may feel due to a lack of financial resources that results in creating a barrier to purchasing the most preferred product or brand.

Personality traits can be characterised by using the variables self-confidence, self-esteem, authoritarianism, and anxiety. Those variables have been researched to identify individual differences.

Culture is more comprehensive than the social environment of the consumer. It consists of patterns of behaviour, symbols, ideas, and their attached values.

1.4.1.3 Partial analytical lifestyle model after Engel, Blackwell, and Kollat

One of the most comprehensive theoretical approaches to explain consumer behaviour, mainly based on a consumer's lifestyle, was developed by Engel, Blackwell, and Kollat (1978). The authors have developed a partial analytical model in which the relationship between lifestyles and purchasing decisions (choice of product, brand, and shopping location) is presented (see Figure 1.16).

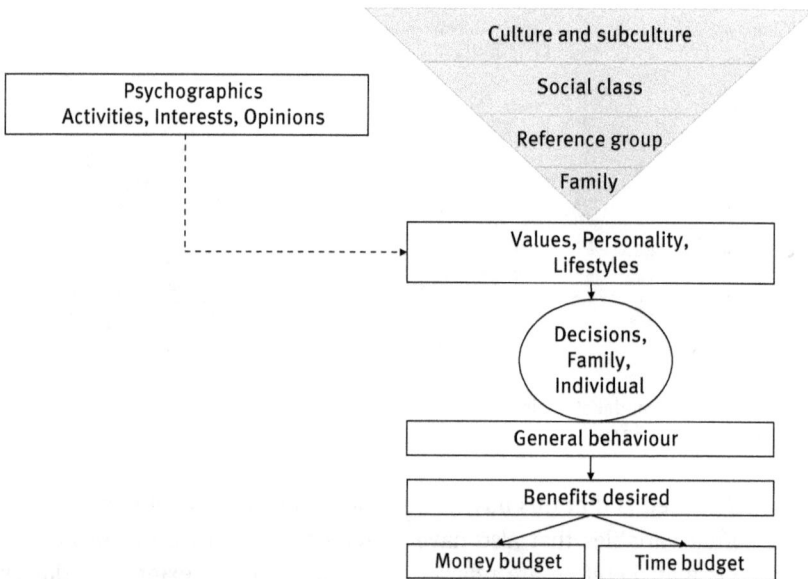

Figure 1.16: Lifestyle model after Engel, Blackwell, and Kollat.
Source: Engel, Blackwell, and Kollat 1978

This model summarizes the three constructs of values, personality, and lifestyles, which are measured by psychographic variables and AIO (i.e., activities, interests, opinions) statements. The three variables are influenced by the factors culture or subculture, social class, reference groups, and family. Values, personality, and lifestyles in turn influence the general behaviour of consumers, which ultimately influences consumer decisions. It should be noted that the model juxtaposes the three central variables of values, personality, and lifestyle without taking interdependencies into account and only considers temporal and financial restrictions as an influence on product choice. Furthermore, the model does not correspond to a real purchase and decision situation, as it does not show any feedback between the individual stages.

Since this model is too simplistic, experts tried to develop a comprehensive approach to explaining consumer behaviour regarding lifestyle theoretical modelling, which is described next.

1.4.1.4 Structural model of Carman's purchasing behaviour

The partial analytical structural model of Carman's purchasing behaviour (1978) focuses on the construct "Life Style." On the one hand, it offers an explanatory approach with regard to the influencing factors on the lifestyle of an individual, and on the other hand it also deals with the relationship between lifestyle and individual buying behaviour or buying decisions.

Carman's model (see Figure 1.17) is based on a differentiation into terminal and instrumental values. These individual values act as influencing factors, either directly or indirectly via feedback with social institutions and norms, on the lifestyle of the consumer, who in turn has a direct influence on brand perception and influences the subjectively desired product characteristics and services. According to Carman (1978), this is decisive for a certain attitude towards a product or brand (or a retailer) and behavioural intentions that ultimately lead to a purchase. On the other hand, exogenous forces such as environmental influences, socioeconomic factors, personality, an individual's life cycle and demographic factors affect a person's lifestyle.

Depending on the evaluation of the purchase decision made, feedback is given to the different levels of the model. This essentially involves a review and, if necessary, a change in attitudes and behavioural intentions. However, it can not be assumed that a single purchase decision will lead to a change in lifestyle or values. Thus, these hypothetical constructs could be considered largely stable.

In Carman's model of buying behaviour it can be stated that the values or value attitudes are hierarchically superior to the other variables influencing behaviour, such as brand perception or the desired product requirements, and influence the lifestyle, which plays a central role in his model. Further, it should be noted that the present model has not yet found an empirical foundation, since it is difficult to operationalize the complex relationships between the individual variables of the model. However, several empirical studies have already shown that the lifestyles of individual consumer groups are related to purchasing behaviour or buying decisions.

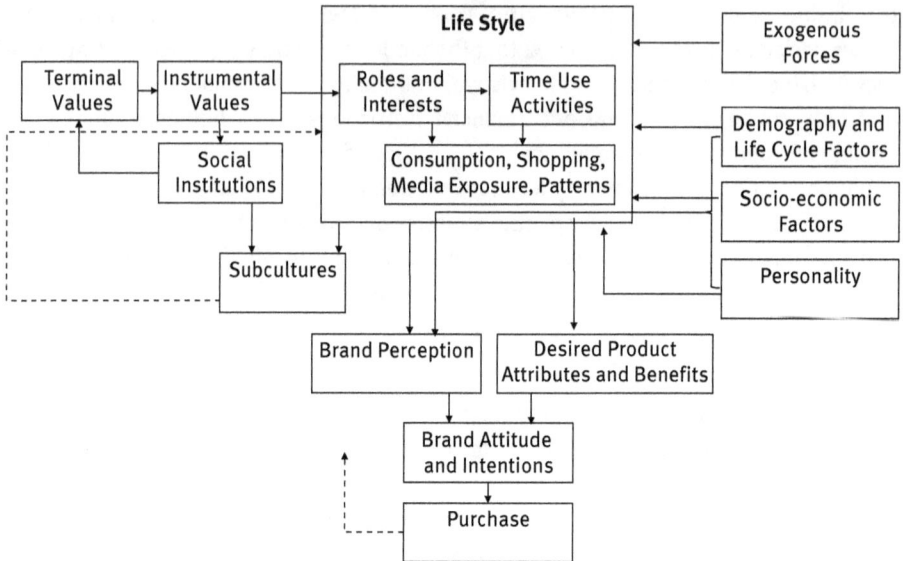

Figure 1.17: Structural model of Carman's purchasing behaviour.
Source: Carman,1978

1.4.1.5 The Theory of Planned Behaviour

The TPB was presented by Ajzen in 1991 (see Figure 1.19) as an extension of the Theory of Reasoned Action (TRA) by Ajzen and Fishbein, introduced in 1975 (Teo & Lee, 2010, 60). Both models are part of the multiattribute models. The TRA tries to explain a performed behaviour. The idea behind the theory is that behaviour is performed due to an intention to perform that behaviour. The intention is influenced by the subjective norm and the attitude towards the behaviour. The TRA thereby attempts to predict the possibility of the occurrence of a specific behaviour. Although it can be said that no behaviour can be predicted with a 100% certainty there are several studies that unveil that the intention to perform a behaviour makes a significant contribution to the actual performance. The intention is the motivational factor behind the behaviour. It indicates "how hard people are willing to try, of how much of an effort they are planning to exert, in order to perform the behaviour" (Ajzen, 1991, 80).

The main variables of the model are the subjective norm (SN) and the attitude towards the behaviour (AtB). The SN can be described as the assumption of the individual that people important to the individual are expecting the behaviour to be performed. In other words, that people close to the individual think that the behaviour should be performed by him or her (Schwenkert, 2006, 27–28; Teo & Lee, 2010, 61). This belief somehow conveys a sense of unconscious social pressure for the individual – the pressure to perform as the norm demands. Some researchers have found that the social norm does not have as much influence on the intention to perform a

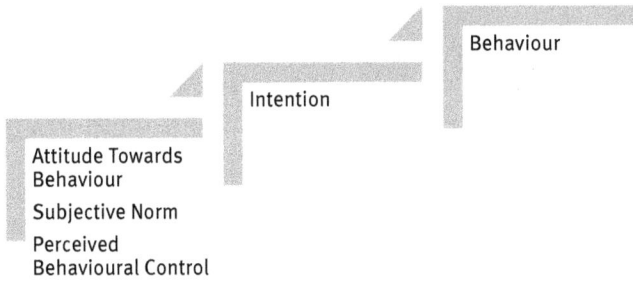

Figure 1.18: Theory of Planned Behaviour.
Source: Aijzen, 1991

specific behaviour as originally assumed. It has been found that the culture also tends to have an impact on the influence of the SN. People living in an individualistic culture tend to not be as influenced by social pressure as people living in a collectivistic culture. This may result in the fact that in collectivistic cultures the opinion of the group is incredibly important and therefore often followed. In individualistic cultures people are not that influenced by others, which may explain those differences in the impact of the SN.

The TRA involves another variable – the AtB. As the phrase already suggests, it does not describe the attitude towards an object, but the attitude towards the behaviour itself (Schwenkert, 2006, 27). The individual has a positive or negative feeling about the behaviour, which influences the intention to perform it, is influenced. The attitude towards a specific behaviour relates to one's inner beliefs about the consequences of executing it. Therefore, the possible consequences and outcomes of the behaviour are evaluated. If they are seen or predicted as positive the possibility of the intention to exert the behaviour is high, and so is the possibility of an actual performance (Teo & Lee, 2010, 61).

The TRA has been criticized as it only had an attitudinal and a normative component. This made it seem like customers' behaviours are only intentional and rational and as if they always have full control over their behaviour. But this idea of a solely rational acting consumer – the so-called homo economicus – shall be deemed obsolete (Kuß et al., 2020). The model does not offer an answer for impulsive behaviours and the affective component is entirely ignored. Moreover, attitudes can also be formed due to habits or unconscious processes, which is also not being illustrated in the model (Kroeber-Riel & Gröppel-Klein, 2013, 236).

As the TPB is an extension of the TRA, another variable has been added – the Perceived Behavioural Control (PBC). The PBC points out the "perceived ease or difficulty of performing the behaviour". By adding this variable Ajzen tried to include the element of uncertainty and to increase the ability to predict the behaviour. Studies show that the accuracy of prediction is higher than with the TRA but still the cognitive processes are in the foreground (Kroeber-Riel & Gröppel-Klein, 2013, 236).

1.4.1.6 Technology Acceptance Model by Davis et al.

The TAM is widely used to identify the acceptance and adaption of new technologies by consumers (Kim et al., 2008). Originally, the model was used to identify the acceptance of computers on the workplace. The TAM is also based on the TRA of Aijzen and Fishbein (see Figure 1.20). According to this model two factors are influencing the attitude towards the behaviour and thereby also the intention to perform that behaviour – the perceived ease of use and the perceived usefulness of the technology (Kim et al., 2008).

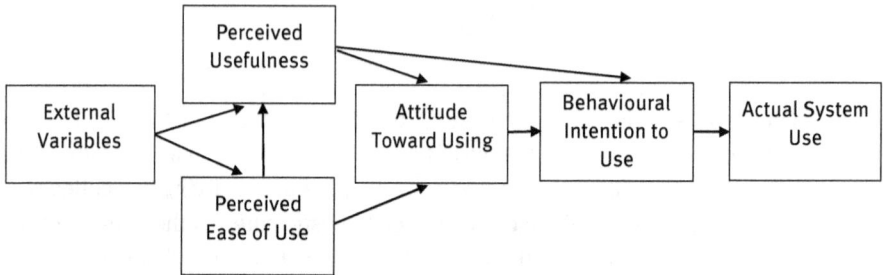

Figure 1.19: Technology Acceptance Model.
Source: Davis et al., 1989

The Perceived Ease of Use is described by Davis as "the degree to which a person believes that using a particular system would be free of effort" (Davis, 1989, 320). It seems natural that users will be more likely to use technologies that are perceived easier to use than others. The second determinant is the Perceived Usefulness which is defined as "the degree to which a person believes that using a particular system would enhance his or her job" (Davis, 1989, 320). Davis is expressing that users are more likely to adopt a technology if they believe that using the technology will help them to improve their job performance.

In further developed variations of the model the AtB has been eliminated and the intention to perform the behaviour is directly being influenced by the two main determinants Perceived Usefulness and Perceived Ease of Use (Schmaltz, 2009, 46). Moreover, additional extensions, like the belief factor Perceived Enjoyment, have been implemented. The Perceived Enjoyment is defined by Davis as the extent to which the activity of using the technology is perceived as enjoyable – apart from any performance consequences (Kim et al., 2008). The new determinant also had an influence on the overall structure of the model. Davis suggested that the Perceived Usefulness and Perceived Enjoyment would have a direct impact on the intention to perform the behaviour whereas the Perceived Ease of Use influences those two determinants (Kim et al., 2008). The Perceived Enjoyment is an important extension especially in this research as the original variables might not be enough to identify why users are or are not adopting mobile applications for purchasing fast fashion goods. Each user might adapt it for different reasons and the Perceived Enjoyment might be one important reason.

1.4.2 Purchase decision process

Before consumers make their final purchase decision, five stages of the purchase decision process have to be gone through, although sometimes consumers do not pass through each stage.

The five stages are (Engel, Blackwell, & Miniard, 1993):
– problem recognition
– information search
– evaluation of alternatives
– purchase decision
– post-purchase behaviour

Figure 1.21 gives a detailed overview of the consumers' purchase decision process.

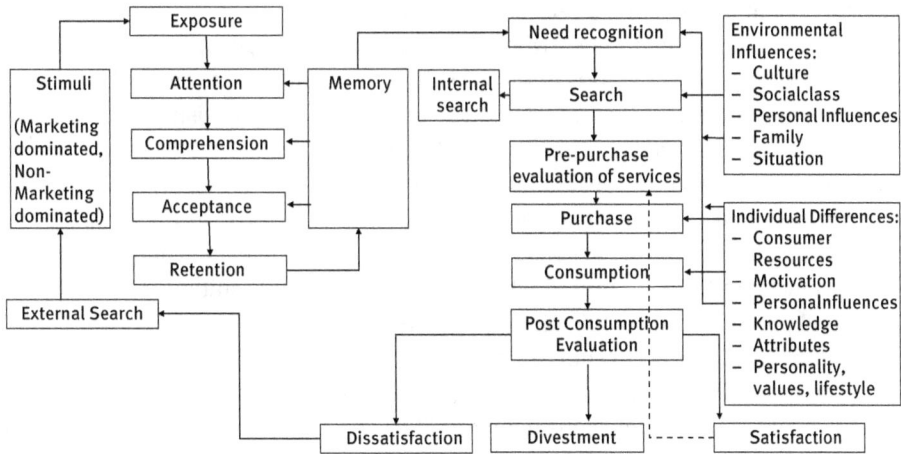

Figure 1.20: Consumer purchase decision process.
Source: Engel, Blackwell, & Miniard, 1993

In the first stage, the *problem recognition*, the purchase decision process starts as the consumer identifies a problem. This problem can be triggered by internal or external stimuli. Internal stimuli means that the consumer's needs, wants, and desires rise to a certain level until these needs and wants become a motivation to start a purchase process. An external stimuli would mean that the consumer identifies a problem externally, for example, if the person sees a friend with a new pair of sneakers and then desires to buy a new pair of sneakers for themselves (Kotler et al., 2009, 247).

When consumers have identified their problem, the second phase starts, the *information search*. Within this stage the consumer searches for information and tries to find a suitable solution for their problem to fulfil a need or desire. The information search can be done internally, by retrieving information from memory, or externally. The external information search includes the collection of information, all kind of different sources, online and offline. For example, by collecting information from family and friends, from visiting a shop and consulting the sales staff, from the internet, from leaflets or other promotional material. During this phase of information search, marketers have very little control over where and what customers are searching for. Although, by analysing search profiles and using search engine marketing (SEM), a form of internet marketing that involves the promotion of distinctive websites by increasing their visibility in search engine results primarily through paid advertising, these search processes can be influenced.

Depending on the urgency of a situation or a need, consumers will put more effort into searching relevant information to solve their needs. Individual differences, like personality traits, lifestyle, occupation, knowledge, and past experiences, etc, and environmental influences, like cultural background, current situation, social class, etc., have an influence on the amount of information searched for and the energy put into searching relevant information.

Here it must be mentioned, when consumers are satisfied with a certain brand or product, competitive brands or products find it very difficult to catch the customers' attention. On the other side, as soon as consumers get dissatisfied with a brand or a product, they are more open for alternatives and alternative products and brands will be taken into consideration (Blackwell, Miniard, & Engel, 2006, 75).

The next phase in the consumer's purchase decision process is the *evaluation of alternatives*. In this phase the consumer continues to evaluate and compare alternative products and brands to find which of them is the most suitable for his or her need and problem. During this phase preexisting evaluations from experiences that have been stored in the consumer's memory, are used, in addition to suitable evaluation criteria, like price, quality, packaging, colour, size, etc., for comparing the products that are taken into consideration (Blackwell et al., 2006, 80).

After finishing the evaluation of alternatives and deciding on the most suitable product or brand, the fourth stage, the *purchase decision* takes place. In this phase, intervening factors like unanticipated situational factors (e.g., like the functional, physical, financial, social, psychological, and time risk) and the attitudes and opinions of others are still considered, depending on how much the consumer wants to comply with this person's wishes and attitudes and to the amount of money that is invested (Kotler et al., 2009, 252–253). In the purchase decision phase other influencing factors, above all the packaging of the product plays, an especially important role. According to Silayoi and Speece (2007, 1496) consumers put their emphasize on the packaging especially in situations when they are undecided and do not know which product to choose. The packaging of a product is an essential communication tool, especially when the product is presented in a shop (online and offline). The packaging provides relevant information and gives the consumers an idea about the content and the quality of the product. Therefore, manufacturers and retailers need to know how consumers perceive a product's packaging and how consumers respond to it. Chapter 2.1.2 "Packaging" goes into more detail and explains the importance and the characteristics and features of the packaging of a product, along with the design elements like colour, information, material, size, innovative features, etc., which might stimulate the purchase decision.

The last stage in the purchase decision process, after conducting a purchase, is the *post-purchase behaviour*. The aim of every retailer should be that the customers are satisfied with the products. The more satisfied they are, the higher the possibility that they will buy the product again and recommend it to friends and family. Therefore, retailers must try to reduce dissatisfied consumers by using an effective CRM. For more details concerning CRM, see Chapter 2.6.2.

Another post-purchase behaviour represents the post-purchase use and disposal. Consumers can either keep the product and use it to serve the original purchase, convert it for a new purpose, or store it. Moreover, consumers can get rid of the product temporarily, where they rent it, or get rid of it permanently and sell the product to other consumers. These post-purchase uses or disposals are very important to know and analyse to understand the consumers and why they do the things they do (Kotler et al., 2009, 253–254) and how their needs and desires can be better served by retailers and marketers.

A key aspect that must be considered in the consumer's purchase decision process is to analyse how much effort the consumer puts into this decision process and the degree of consumer's involvement with a product or brand. In general, it can be said that if a product is purchased for the first time or if the outcome is important, for instance, the product is bought as a present for an important friend, consumers are more involved, and therefore put more effort into the purchase decision process.

To be more precise, the level of *involvement* is the degree of information processing and the amount of importance a consumer attaches to a product or brand while purchasing it. In other words, it shows how involved the customer is towards a product personally, socially, and economically. In general, we distinguish to two types of involvement (Kotler & Bliemel, 2001):
– low involvement
– high involvement

Low involvement means that the product intended to be purchased involves just a low level of risk and is normally not very expensive. Low involvement products are very often purchased automatically, for example, toothpaste or the daily morning coffee.

In contrast, high involvement products are products that involve a high level of risk and are charged a higher price. Examples of high involvement products are a new computer, a car, a new kitchen, etc. When a consumer is buying such a high involvement product, like a new computer, they will research about the different models, functions, price levels, etc., and decide on those models that fall in the planned budget before making a final purchase decision.

Several factors influence the level of involvement (Kotler & Bliemel, 2001):

– Personal factors: Needs, desires, importance of the product and the purchase decision, lifestyle (activities, opinions, interest), values, and beliefs
– Object factors: Differentiation of alternative products and brands, source of communication (e.g., word of mouth, TV commercial, newspaper ad, PR article, etc.), and the content of communication
– Situational factors: Purchase situation (time, location, shopping budget, stimuli at the POS, shopping companion, etc.), user of the product (present or for self-usage), and occasion

Depending on the factors described above, in different situations the same product can be a high involvement or a low involvement product. For example, when a consumer wants to buy biscuits for themselves during their lunch break, they will go to the nearest shop and buy their favourite biscuits. Nevertheless, when this person wants to buy biscuits as a present for a social friend, the purchase decision will take much longer, because several pros and cons will be weighed before making a final purchase decision.

1.4.2.1 The consumer shopper journey

With the emergence of new sales channels and innovative new ways of product and brand communication, this linear process of purchase decisions described in chapter XY must be reconsidered. A more sophisticated approach seems to be necessary to understand consumer decisions all along the customer journey and the key purchasing factors that influence their purchase decisions. This chapter illustrates how consumers make their purchase decisions in a digital world and retail market, and describes the consumer's purchase decision process as a circular journey.

Consumers have changed the way they research and buy products. For many years, consumer decision journeys and their touch points have been understood as a linear process, like a "funnel": consumers start with a number of potential brands in mind, marketing is then directed at them to reduce that number and move through the funnel, and at the end they emerge with the one brand they chose to purchase. Due to the explosion of product choices and digital channels, together with the emergence of increasingly well-informed consumers, retailers must find new ways to get their products and brands included in the initial consideration set of products (i.e., relevant set) that consumers develop as they begin their purchase decision journey.

An international cooperation between retail and manufacturer businesses, ECR (i.e., efficient consumer response) Austria, has developed a new process of the consumer shopper journey. This journey concentrates on the consumers' decision process concerning the purchase of FMCG. Figure 1.22 shows the stages of the consumer shopper journey in more detail (ECR Austria, 2014, 8).

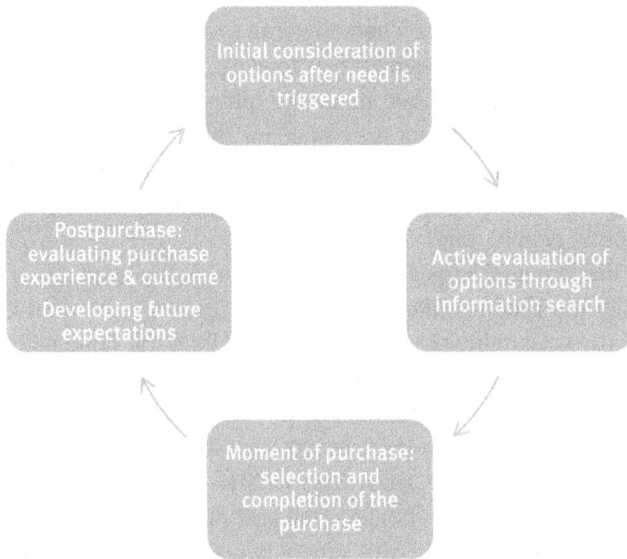

Figure 1.21: Consumer shopper journey.
Source: ECR Austria, 2014, 8

The purchasing process starts with the needs and habits of the consumers where a special consumption wish can be developed. Within the second stage, consumers are influenced by various touchpoints. This can be done through family and friends, or through advertising such as information from the internet or any other channel. These touchpoints can either arise the consumption wish, or it can be concretised or changed. Today's consumers come across a variety of online and physical branded touchpoints, and are frequently engaged with multiple touchpoints at the same time, for example, online price comparisons, social media platforms, traditional and digital advertising, brand ambassadors and influencers, peer reviews, physical stores, sales associates, etc. Research (McKinsey, 2009) has found that two-thirds of the touch points during the active-evaluation phase involve consumer-driven marketing activities, such as internet reviews and word-of-mouth recommendations from friends and family, as well as in-store interactions and recollections of past experiences. Only one-third of the touch points involve company-driven marketing, such as traditional advertising, direct marketing, sponsorship, in-store product experience, or salesperson contact.

Within this retail market of endless touchpoints retailers need to present and deliver a seamless, branded experience throughout. Plus, in the near future, with the developments of big data analytics and tools like machine learning and AI, retailers need to continue to advance personalization and customization because no two shoppers are alike. Therefore, no marketing campaigns should be alike.

In the third phase, the consumers decide where they can satisfy their needs and desires. By building up their "shopping mission" they consider whether they want to buy the product in their regular supermarket, in another physical retail outlet, or in an online setting. Sometimes, the search for the respective shop takes place even in the shopping centre. Once the consumers have entered the shop, lots of stimuli influence their purchasing behaviour like special offers, displays, shop layout, colour, music, temperature, other people, sales staff, etc.

Another thing that is fundamental represents the fact whether the good has already been decided or only the product category. When the respective product is not available in the store, the probability that another product from the same product category will be chosen is very high. After the consumers have bought the product, they make up their opinions about the product in the final stage. Afterwards, the process starts from the beginning again (ECR Austria, 2014, 8–9). So, the consumer shopping journey is an ongoing cycle, a circular journey.

The last phase in the consumer decision process, the post purchase phase, is of great importance, as consumer experiences with products and brands shape the consumer's opinion for every subsequent decision in this product category.

Concerning the consumer decision journey, it can be said that consumer behaviour has changed within the past years and has become more difficult. The percentage of traditional customers is decreasing, this means that marketers need to adjust to these changes and respond to the new customer journey (McKinsey, 2009). Depending on the respective consumer, the journeys can take more or less time, different sales channels and touchpoints might be visited, and the customer journey can last days or weeks (Maechler, Neher, & Park, 2016, 15). In previous years it has been easy for marketers to understand where customers were in the sales funnel, nowadays, with the extensive product assortment and the different communication channels, consumer behaviour is much more complicated. Therefore, marketers need to follow a more sophisticated approach to understand the well-informed and multioptional consumers (McKinsey, 2009).

Four kinds of activities can help marketers address the new realities of the consumer decision journey without wasting money and without pushing products and brands on customers rather than providing them with the information and experience they are searching for (McKinsey, 2009):
- prioritize objectives and spending
- tailor messaging

- invest in consumer-driven marketing
- integrate all customer-facing activities

Prioritize objectives and spending

In the past, most marketers focused just on one end of the marketing funnel, either building awareness or generating loyalty among current customers. Research has shown that marketers must be much more specific about the multiple touch points used to influence consumers as they move through all stages of the purchase decision process. Otherwise, they could miss opportunities not only to focus their marketing budgets on the most important touch points of the decision journey but also to target the right customers. For example, in the skin care industry, some brands are much stronger in the initial-consideration phase than in the active evaluation phase. Therefore, these retailers should concentrate their marketing efforts mainly in the initial-consideration phase, for example, in packaging and in-store promotional activities.

Tailor messaging

For many retailers tailored messaging is required to reach their customers, in whatever part of the consumer shopper journey offers the greatest revenue opportunity. A general message communicated across all stages must be tailored and replaced by one addressing weaknesses at a specific stage, for example, the initial consideration phase. The South Korean car manufacturer Hyundai is a very good example for reaching their customers with tailored messages and growing its market share. They built a marketing campaign around protecting consumers financially by allowing them to return their vehicles if they lose their jobs. This provocative message became a major factor in helping Hyundai break into the initial consideration set of many new consumers.

Invest in consumer-driven marketing

Companies nowadays must invest in communication campaigns and tools that let them interact with their consumers as they learn about brands. The main communication tool of consumer-driven marketing is the internet, which is very important during the active-evaluation phase as consumers seek information about products or brands, read reviews, blogs, and recommendations. Strong performance at this point in the decision journey requires a mind-set shift from buying media to developing information that attracts consumers: digital assets such as web sites about products, programs to foster word-of-mouth, and systems that customize advertising by viewing the context and the consumer. Marketers can influence online word-of-mouth by using tools that spot consumers' online conversations about products and brands, analyse their messages, and allow marketers to post their own comments.

Finally, content-management systems and online targeting engines let marketers create hundreds of variations on an advertisement, considering the context where it appears, the past behaviour of viewers, and a real-time inventory of what a company wants to promote. For instance, most airlines manage and optimize thousands of combinations of offers, prices, content, and formats to ensure that potential travellers see the most relevant opportunities to choose from (McKinsey, 2009).

Studies have shown that many consumers hold off on their final purchase decision until they are in a physical store. Merchandising and packaging have therefore become very important selling factors. Consumers want to look at a product in action and are highly influenced by visual dimensions. Up to 40%percent of them change their minds because of packaging, placement, or interactions with sales staff. For example, in skin care, some brands that are fairly unlikely to be in a consumer's initial-consideration set win at the POP with attractive packages and on-shelf messaging.

Sometimes it takes a combination of marketing approaches, for example, great packaging, a favourable shelf position, forceful fixtures, informative signage, etc., to attract consumers who enter a store with a strong attachment to their initial consideration set (McKinsey, 2009).

Integrating all customer-facing activities

In many companies several employees are responsible for specific customer-facing activities, for example, PR, CRM, promotional activities, social media activities, advertising, product development, market research, etc. But very often they don't coordinate their work or communicate with each other. All customer-facing activities must be integrated to be effective and reach the aim of customer engagement and loyalty.

A comprehensive view of all customer-facing activities also requires a broader role of the chief marketing officer (CMO) to realign marketing activities with other company-wide activities facing the consumer decision-making, with skills from advertising to public relations, product development, market research, and data management (McKinsey, 2009).

1.4.2.2 Changes in the consumer decision process

Within the past years, there have been significant developments in the consumer decision-making process, mainly due to developments in information and communication technologies, above all social media. Instead of C2B communication activities, consumers are switching more and more to customer-to-customer (C2C) communication. C2C communication focuses on including social media and customer forums into the consumer decision-making process. Customers build their opinion based on what their friends, followers, or influencers and bloggers think of, therefore, this C2C movement has a high potential in building or destroying brands (McKinsey & Company, 2015 4).

According to a study of McKinsey & Company (2016) 79% of the consumers trust online reviews to the same extent as personal recommendations.

Another change, which can be noted, is the fact that customers are less loyal than they were few years ago. Consequently, they are willing to switch between several brands if overpricing or poor customer service is perceived. Due to the fact that customers become less tolerant and inform themselves better, marketers and retailers face the challenge to react towards those changes. The digital technology, above all smart devices like mobile phone and tablet, provides the consumer with improved know-how about the products and services they want to buy. Consumers are getting more independent from retailers, their communication, and products. Instead of informing themselves in the shops consumers use their smart devices and inform themselves on online platforms, blogs, and forums (KPMG, 2017). Due to the fact that the competition among various brands in supermarkets is high nowadays, the decreasing loyalty of consumers represents a major challenge (McKinsey, 2009). As customers are very price sensitive, they are open to new brands or substitutes, which can satisfy their needs and desires. This often happens due to negative experiences, like a quality or price change or unsatisfied customer service. Another focus of this thesis represents the consumers' request to receive neutral information about the product they want to buy, this means that they do not only include the manufacturer's information, but also C2C communication, for example, influences their decision-making (KPMG, 2017).

For 79% of the 14- to 29-year-olds, opinions and experiences of other buyers play an essential role in their purchase decision-making. Comparing this to the 60 and older generation, only 52% consider experiences of other buyers as relevant for their own purchase decision. Concerning the influencing of products, 66% of those younger than the age of 30 want to have an influence on the product and assist in designing. Here we see an indicator that more and more of the younger consumers ask for personalization and creating their product how they want it. Regarding those ages 60 and older, only 50% have agreed that they would prefer to individualize their own products. Another change that can be seen, represents the loyalty and bond to the respective brand or company. The 60 and older age group are 63% very loyal and avoid switching between brands or companies, whereas only 51% of the 14- to 29-year-olds see that aspect as crucial.

Overall, it can be said that main changes exist between the different generations. The increase of millennials illustrates that they are more freedom oriented and smarter compared to previous generations. The special thing about this generation represents their tech-savviness, as they grew up with the internet, social media, and mobile as a standard, and can not imagine a life without these technical gadgets. This indicates that millennials differ in their expectations, attitudes, and behaviours to other generations. Due to this shifting demographic trend, the retail landscape changes. Therefore, businesses in today's economic environment must consider those facts and in a next step respond towards the modified consumer behaviour to follow a customer-centric approach (Nielsen, 2016b).

1.4.3 Different typologies of retail shoppers

The systematizing method of typology is characterised by the fact that, on the one hand, several features are used simultaneously to identify the object under investigation, for example, the shopper or consumer, and, on the other hand, an intrinsic overall impression is conveyed by meaningful selection and combination of these features. The main aim of every typology is to replace the multidimensional order from which it emanates with an equivalent reduced order. Therefore, it primarily serves to reduce the complexity of concrete facts, whereby a particular type represents more than the sum of its characteristics.

In marketing and retailing, typologies are mainly used in market and media research, mainly in the form of consumer behaviour typologies. The large number of buyer typologies currently on the market basically tries to meet the need for greater market transparency.

As various models indicate (e.g., Engel et al. 1978; Howard & Sheth 1969) consumer behaviour is overly complex. Consequently, a single characteristic alone is not sufficient to adequately define a target group. The combination of socioeconomic characteristics and psychographic characteristics with possession and consumption characteristics could therefore substantially improve the meaningfulness of characteristics in relation to a certain buying behaviour. Therefore, it seems sensible to combine and bundle individual characteristics. The result of combining several characteristics into "types" are typologies. Critically noted, typologies have a high degree of scope for interpretation and a high level of generalization ("stereotyping"). The inaccurate description of the type-forming characteristics and the simplifying use of short descriptions often lead to identification difficulties. Nevertheless, typologies are very helpful when it comes to segmenting consumers or consumer markets and targeting products and messages, for example, advertisements, social media marketing, newsletters, etc.

1.4.3.1 Generational differences

Many studies have shown that there are differences in the values, beliefs, and opinions between different generations of people. Those differences are also important for retailers to recognize and accommodate, especially when it comes to marketing mix decisions. Therefore, this chapter provides an overview of perceived differences between generations, especially regarding context, behaviour, and consumption. In the literature we find different perspectives on the range of dates for their births. Within this book the following categories are used:

- Baby boomers: 1940–1959
- Generation X: 1960–1979
- Millennials or Gen Y: 1980–1994
- Generation Z: 1995–2010

Experts (Francis & Hoefel, 2019) are sure that generational shifts could come to play a more important role in setting behaviour than socioeconomic differences do. Young people have become a potent influence on people of all ages and incomes, as well as on the way those people consume and relate to products and brands. In many countries, for example, Brazil, members of Gen Z already make up 20% of the country's population. Members of Gen Z are true digital natives because they have been exposed to the internet and to mobile systems from early on. Gen Z is a generation that is extremely comfortable with collecting and cross-referencing many sources of information and with integrating online and offline experiences. A survey investigating the behaviour of this generation and its influence on consumption patterns showed that Gen Z is mainly searching for truth. This search for truth can be explained in more detail by the following behaviour (Francis & Hoefel, 2019):
- Gen Zers value individual expression and avoid labels.
- Ge Zers mobilize themselves for a variety of causes, for example, environmental protection.
- Gen Zers believe profoundly in the efficacy of dialogue to solve conflicts and improve the world (e.g., "Friday for future"- movement).
- Gen Zers make decisions and relate to institutions in a highly analytical and pragmatic way.

In general, generations are shaped by the context in which they emerged. Baby boomers, born from 1940 to 1959, grew up in the post-World War II context. Their collectivistic behaviour can be described by consumption as an expression of ideology and idealism. Members of Gen X, born from 1960 to 1979, were raised in a context of political transition. Their behaviour can be described as materialistic, competitive, and individualistic. Brands and cars are status symbols for them and they mainly prefer to buy and consume luxury articles. Gen Y or millennials, born from 1980 to 1994, have been raised in an era of economic prosperity and focus on themselves. These persons are usually more idealistic, more confrontational, and less willing to accept other people's point of view. They love to consume experiences, visit festivals, and they like to travel. Generation Z has already been described above. In addition, members of this generation search for authenticity and uniqueness. They have a greater openness to understanding different kinds of people and other ethical groups. They don't want to define themselves through only one stereotype but rather for individuals to experiment with different ways of being themselves and to shape their individual identities over time (Francis & Hoefel, 2019). Therefore, businesses must rethink how they deliver value to the consumer, rebalance scale and mass production against personalization, and practice what they promise when they address marketing issues and work ethics. The generation shift will bring both challenges and equally attractive opportunities (see Figure 1.24).

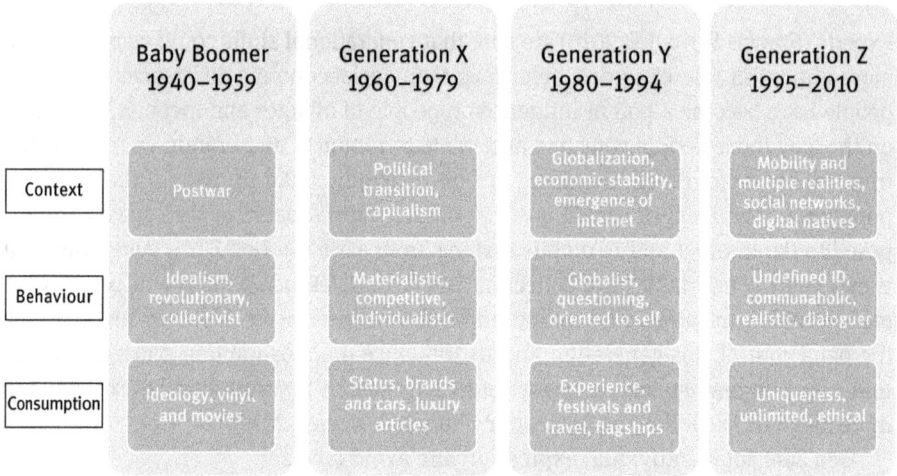

	Baby Boomer 1940–1959	Generation X 1960–1979	Generation Y 1980–1994	Generation Z 1995–2010
Context	Postwar	Political transition, capitalism	Globalization, economic stability, emergence of internet	Mobility and multiple realities, social networks, digital natives
Behaviour	Idealism, revolutionary, collectivist	Materialistic, competitive, individualistic	Globalist, questioning, oriented to self	Undefined ID, communaholic, realistic, dialoguer
Consumption	Ideology, vinyl, and movies	Status, brands and cars, luxury articles	Experience, festivals and travel, flagships	Uniqueness, unlimited, ethical

Figure 1.22: Overview and description of generations.
Source: Francis & Hoefel, 2019

When it comes to Gen Z, companies should be attuned to three implications (Francis & Hoefel, 2019):
– consumption as access rather than possession
– consumption as an expression of individual identity
– consumption as a matter of ethical concern

As collaborative consumption gains in importance, people are also starting to view it to generate additional income.

Car manufacturers, for example, are renting out their cars directly to consumers (see example in the box below), so rather than selling their cars, these companies can "sell" one car several times. Similarly, traditional consumer-goods companies create platforms of products, services, and experiences that aggregate or connect customers around brands by sharing ideas, suggestions, recommendations, etc. Therefore, companies historically defined by their products they sell can now rethink their value-creation models, leveraging more direct relationships with consumers and new business models and distribution channels. They will have the opportunity to adapt their businesses to this paradigm shift and potentially engage with new market segments.

DriveMyCar – Collaborative consumption

DriveMyCar is Australia's first and largest peer-to-peer car rental service, a peer-to-peer service that makes it possible for car owners to rent their car to other people. Owners earn money from their car and renters get access to a wider range of vehicles and save money compared to traditional car rentals, especially for long-term rental periods (DriveMyCar, 2020).

DriveMyCar screens people before they can book a car. The company verifies a renter's ID, performs a credit check, and collects the first payment and bond before a rental is confirmed. All vehicles are covered by insurance and 24/7 roadside assistance. Feedback from previous rentals is provided. The rental process involves a few simple steps (DriveMyCar, 2020):

For the owner the following steps must be done:
1. Upload details and photographs of the car available to rent.
2. Receive and accept booking requests. Arrange a handover time and location with the renter.
3. Complete an inspection report and take photographs to confirm condition of the car at the beginning of the rental.
4. Receive regular payments from DriveMyCar.
5. Arrange return with the renter and complete an inspection report.

For the renter the following steps must be done:
1. Search for suitable cars nearby and make a booking request.
2. DriveMyCar verifies your identity and performs a credit check.
3. Make initial payment including a bond via credit card. Rental fees include collision damage cover and 24/7 roadside assistance.
4. Arrange a handover time and location with the owner.
5. Return the car to the owner at the conclusion of the rental period.

The core of Gen Z is the idea of manifesting individual identity. Consumption therefore becomes a means of self-expression, for example, to buying or wearing brands to fit in with the norms of groups. Consumers across generations are willing to pay a premium for products that highlight their individuality. Moreover, 48% of Gen Z (but only 38% of consumers in other generations) said they value brands that don't classify items as male or female (Francis & Hoefel, 2019).

Although expectations of personalization are high, consumers across generations are not yet completely comfortable sharing their personal data with companies. Only 10% to 15% of them claim to not have any issues sharing personal data with companies. If there is a clear counterpart from companies to consumers, then the number of consumers willing to share personal information with companies goes up to 35% (Francis & Hoefel, 2019).

Gen Z consumers are mostly well educated about brands and the realities behind them. When they are not, they know how to access information and develop a point of view quickly. If a brand advertises diversity but lacks diversity within its own ranks, for example, that contradiction will be noticed. In fact, members of the other generations we surveyed share this mind-set. Seventy percent of our respondents say they try to purchase products from companies they consider ethical. Eighty percent say they remember at least one scandal or controversy involving a company. About

65% try to learn the origins of anything they buy – where it is made, what it is made from, and how it is made. About 80% refuse to buy goods from companies involved in scandals (Francis & Hoefel, 2019).

All this is relevant for businesses, since 63% of the consumers say that recommendations from friends are their most trusted source for learning about products and brands. The good news is that consumers, especially Gen Z, are tolerant of brands when they make mistakes, if the mistakes are corrected. This fact is more challenging for large companies, since most of our respondents believe that major brands are less ethical than small ones.

In conclusion it must be mentioned that some experts are of the opinion that all generations, no matter whether Gen X, Gen Y, or even baby boomers, have similar values. For example, family tops the list for all these generations. All these generations are similar in their values that matter most. For example (AMA, January 2019):

- **Everyone wants respect:** Everyone wants respect, but the generations don't define it the same way. Baby boomers talked about respect in terms of "giving my opinions the weight I believe they deserve," while Gen Y characterised respect as "listen to me, pay attention to what I have to say."
- **Leaders must be trustworthy:** Different generations do not have notably different expectations of their leaders, they all want leaders they can trust.
- **Nobody likes change:** Studies have shown that people from all generations are uncomfortable with change. Therefore, resistance to change has nothing to do with age, but it has to do with how much you stand to gain or lose because of the change.
- **Loyalty depends on context:** Research has shown that the amount of time an employee puts in each day has more to do with their level in the organization than with age. The higher the level, the more hours they normally work.
- **Everyone wants to learn:** Learning and development are issues that are important for all people regardless of their age. Everyone wants to learn and to ensure they have the training to do their job well.
- **Everyone likes feedback:** Studies have shown that everyone wants to know how they are doing and to learn how they can improve their performance.

1.4.3.2 Typologies

Retail marketing is often driven by the desire to attract more new customers and to create customer loyalty. New customers are necessary to keep a business profitable, but some other groups of customers are more likely to spend more money on a retailer's products than others. In the retail industry, retailers are constantly faced with the issue of trying to find new customers. Many of them are obsessed with making sure their advertising, displays, and promotions are aimed at attracting new customers. This focus on pursuing new customers is certainly necessary, but, at the same time, a retailer's focus should also be on 20% of its customers who currently are the "best" and most profitable customers.

Typology based on profitability
To better understand this idea described above, researchers suggest breaking down shoppers into five main types (Hunter, 2014) based on their profitability:
- Loyal customers: Represent 20% of a retailer's current customer base, but make up more than 50% of a retailer's total sales
- Discount customers: Shop a retailer's store frequently, but make their purchase decisions based on the price promotions and size of our markdowns
- Impulse customers: Do not have a particular item in mind when shopping. These customers go into a retailer's store to get inspired and purchase what seems appropriate at a particular time and occasion.
- Need-based customers: Go into a store because they have an intention to buy a particular item, for example, a snack during lunch break.
- Wandering customers: Do not have a particular need or desire in mind when they go into a store. These customers see the store visit as a social and leisure activity. They want a sense of experience and/or community.

When a retailer's aim is to grow their sales and profit, they need to focus the majority of their effort on the loyal customers and merchandise the store to leverage the impulse customers. The other three types of customers are also important, but a retailer must be careful not to misdirect their resources if they put too much emphasis on them. In the following, these five shopper types are described in more detail (Hunter, 2014):

Loyal customers: A retailer needs to communicate with loyal customers on a regular basis by mail, email, in the store, at events, etc. These customers are the ones who can and should influence a retailer's merchandising decisions. Nothing will make a loyal customer feel better than appreciating their input. Many times, the more a retailer does for them, the more they will recommend the retailer (or a brand or product) to others.

Discount customers: Discount customers help to ensure that a retailer's inventory is turning over and, as a result, this is a key contributor to cash flow. On the other hand, this group of customers can often end up costing a company money because they are more inclined to return products.

Impulse customers: Impulse customers is a segment that many retailers like to have. Many marketers and retailers target their promotional activities, for instance POS displays, towards this group because they will provide us with customer insight and knowledge.

Need-based customers: Need-based customers are driven by a specific need. When they enter the store, they will search for a product that fills their need as quickly as possible. If they do not find a suitable product, they will leave right away. They buy for a variety of reasons such as a specific occasion, a specific need, or an absolute price point. As difficult as it can be to satisfy these people, they can also become loyal customers. It is important to remember that need-based customers can easily be lost to a different retailer or the internet. To overcome this threat, positive personal interaction is required, for instance from the sales staff. If they are treated in a way not available from the web or another retail location, there is a strong chance of making them loyal customers. Therefore, need-based customers offer the greatest long-term potential, even surpassing the impulse customers.

Wandering customers: For many retailers, wandering customers is the largest segment in terms of traffic, but at the same time, they make up the smallest percentage of sales. The number of wandering customers is mainly driven by the location of the store. Although this consumer segment does not represent a large percentage of the total sales, they are very often opinion leaders and they spread through word of mouth. Since these customers are merely looking for interaction when shopping, they are also likely to communicate to others the experience they had in the store.

ECR Austria shopper types

ECR Austria, an initiative of manufacturers, retailers, logistics, electronics, and packaging service providers as well as market research and consulting companies to jointly reorganize the entire supply chain, have developed a pragmatic typology to classify individuals into shopper types.

Based on these results, better conclusions can be drawn about buying behaviour. Shopper insights from the path to purchase and the various shopping missions, insights from segmentation approaches, and the definition of different shopper types are the basis for successful shopper marketing concepts. Here are the five shopper types defined by ECR Austria (ECR Austria, 2014):

Bargain hunters

Twelve percent of all Austrian households are bargain hunters and they represent 11% of the total FMCG turnover (food, near-food, nonfood articles, which are also available in food retailers). The sociodemographic focus is on small urban households ages 50 and older. They make many small purchases, half of which are filled with special offers. Before shopping, they search the leaflets of retailers or daily newspapers for special offers. They have a lot of customer cards, but they don't use them more than normal – obviously only when it's necessary for the special offer. They use all types of promotions, but mostly all promotions in which an entire product group is in action. They shop around at different retailers and are willing to invest a lot of time. Of all shopper types, bargain hunters have the most fun while shopping.

The flexible ones

The flexible ones are predominantly young, urban, educated singles, and couples, possibly who already have children. They have above average education and earn a high income. They often eat out in restaurants, canteens, etc., or have a snack in between. They are pleasure oriented and like to spoil themselves with a good meal, whereby cooking should be easy and quick. They enjoy foreign, exotic dishes, but also like vegetarian food.

They are open-minded and modern and value good looks. They are very advertising affine, commercials or print advertisements consider them informative and useful. They are easy to reach in print media, via trade leaflets, and on the internet.

Their purchases are more spontaneous than planned. Usually, they go shopping on their way home from work. They spend more than average at supermarkets, drugstores, ethnic shops, and petrol stations. Flexible ones are brand oriented and prefer premium products. The share of fresh products in their total shopping basket is relatively low, probably because they often eat out anyway. Their expenditure on drugstore products, both for cosmetics & personal care and for laundry & home care products, is above average compared to other types.

They already buy new products, but the others don't even know there is anything new. They react spontaneously, emotionally at the POS and allow themselves to be steered more by their heart than their head. They love a large selection and it often happens that they buy more than they were supposed to. Flexible ones like to redeem coupons, but this is less reflected in their buying behaviour due to time pressure. Therefore, mobile couponing and mobile payment would be recommended for this very modern target group to make the payment process as efficient as possible.

The stockists

Twenty-three percent of Austrian households can be assigned to the shopper type of stockist. These shoppers are brand-oriented and prefer one-stop shopping. Of all shopper types, they have the lowest shopping frequency, but the highest receipt totals. They are loyal customers in classic grocery stores, where they not only buy the groceries but also the drugstore goods.

For even more target group-specific marketing, this shopper type can be divided into bulk buyers and comfortable ones:

– The bulk buyers are primarily classic extended families, some with children over the age of 14, who are already influencing the choice of products and brands. They usually travel to the consumer market by car and stock up there – often with bulk packs. They are very loyal to a shopping location and they also use loyalty cards.
– The most convenient ones are smaller households, including many single men. They are more likely to walk to the nearest supermarket to do their FMCG shopping. They are also loyal shoppers, probably because it is the most convenient and timesaving, or because in smaller rural towns there is little opportunity to visit several stores.

Premium buyers

The premium buyers are 23% of Austrian households. With their disproportionately high spending they have the highest sales significance of all shopper types at 30%. The premium buyers are predominantly older singles and couples. Many of them are already retired. They have a high income and also have or take time for shopping.

They are very demanding and attach importance to first-class quality. They pay attention to their health and cook more often than other households. High quality and fresh goods are particularly important to them. They also make high demands on environmental and ecological aspects and are willing to pay more money for organic and regional products, sustainability, fair trade, animal welfare, etc.

The premium buyers make many small purchases. They do so in a targeted and planned manner, many of them writing a shopping list. They are exceedingly difficult to address with advertising, because they are very critical and suspicious of advertising. Their preferred sales type, both for food and for drugstore goods, is the specialist trade. That is why they have above-average expenses at butchers, bakers, and other specialty shops. In their choice of products, they prefer premium products and trust well-tried brands. Special attention is paid to freshness, the organic share is above average. They consider organic products to be of high quality, healthier, and tastier.

Their behaviour pattern is very habitual. This means that they are difficult to convince with innovations, but they show high brand loyalty when they are convinced of a product. Premium buyers tend to make rational decisions and need a lot of information to do so. They are overly critical and want to control exactly what is contained in the products. They prefer natural products without flavor enhancers, preservatives, etc.

The premium buyers can be separated into demanding and organic buyers.
– The demanding buyers are even more likely to visit speciality trade and specialist shops. They have the highest total expenditure per household. Their shopping behaviour is even more habitual than that of organic buyers and they show a high degree of planning their shopping trip. In contrast to organic buyers, there is at least a certain use of print advertisement, for example, flyers.
– Organic shoppers are often single households, who tend to be younger than the demanding buyers. They are even more consistent in their shopping behaviour regarding fresh and organic products, regionality, but also in their aversion to advertising. They buy the organic brands in normal supermarkets or in organic supermarkets. Among the organic buyers there are also an above-average number of vegetarians.

In order to win premium buyers, a retailer has to focus on quality, organic, freshness, regionality, and sustainability. Price and promotion competition are not a useful way to reach this type of shopper. In contrast, a retailer can score with competence, expertise, and atmosphere. Moreover, security is also particularly important for them. Clear and comprehensive information, quality seals, test results, or advice from the staff would help to reach these shoppers.

Discount buyer

With 24% of Austrian households, discount buyers is the largest group. They mainly buy cheap private labels and spend the least of all types of buyers. Their significance for turnover is therefore extremely modest at 17%. The discount buyers are mostly younger multiperson households, the only thing that counts for these shoppers is a low price. For some it may indeed be a lack of interest, for others the financial situation does not allow high demands at all.

The discount buyers can still be separated into the focused discount buyers and the discount bill buyers. The focused discount buyers make a remarkably high proportion of their purchases at one retail chain, while the discount bill buyers divide their FMCG budget between different discounters.

To conclude, in the saturated retail market the competitive pressure has never been greater. To be successful, it will require patience and understanding in knowing the customers and their behaviour patterns that drive their purchase decision-making process. Using this understanding might help retailers to turn discount, impulse, need-based, and wandering customers into loyal customers to increase a retailer's total sales and profit (Hunter, 2014).

The typology of retail shoppers described above is just one example of an appropriate typology, which helps to divide the customers into homogenous groups or customer segments. Many of the existing typologies focus on specific industries or even retail fields, for instance, the automotive sector, the electronic appliance sector, the fast-moving consumer goods sector, the apparel sector, etc. The box below provides a good example of a typology for the apparel sector. Seven male and seven female outfit types are described here.

Male and female outfit types

The Outfit 9.0 survey by Spiegel Media (2018), developed jointly with the Sinus Sociovision Institute, is one of the largest media market survey of the German fashion market. The survey focuses on the needs, habits, and attitudes of consumers to products in the apparel and wristwatch sector (91 clothing brands and 62 wristwatch brands). The survey data was gathered online, the sample size is 5,182 participants. Therefore, this survey is providing the most comprehensive in-sights for the German apparel sector. The results of the survey are representative of 44 million German-speaking people between the ages of 14 and 69 who are accessible online.

This survey uses psychographic criteria (especially activities, interests, and opinions), preferred dress style, attitude towards fashion, clothes, selected brands and accessories for segmentation purposes, and to generate outfit types. In addition to these active criteria, passive criteria, for example, sociodemographic (age, family status, living conditions, education, occupation, income, etc.) and behaviouristic characteristics were used to describe the market segments. Seven different female and seven different male outfit types have been identified. These types vary in their attitude and behaviour towards fashion (Töpfer & Bug, 2015). The Outfit survey contains the Sinus Milieus as psychographic target group characteristics. Sinus Milieus is a target group segmentation based on an analysis of everyday life within our society and groups together individuals with similar attitudes (to work, family, leisure, expenditures, and consumption habits), lifestyles and basic values (Töpfer & Bug, 2015).

Figures 1.25 and 1.26 give an overview on the seven female and seven male outfit types.

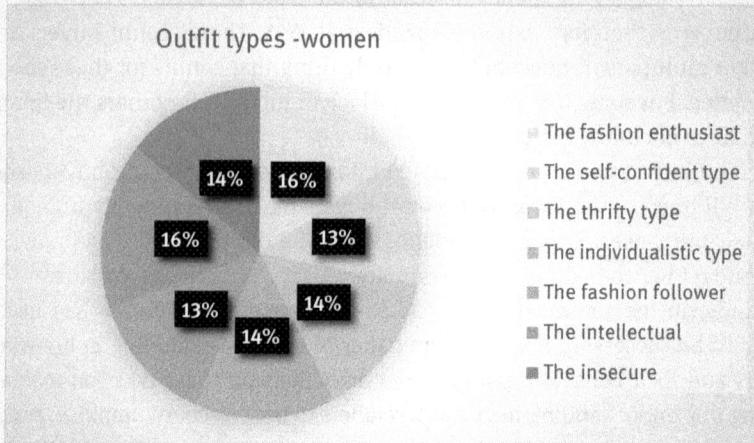

Figure 1.23: Female outfit types.
Source: Spiegel Media, 2018

The segmentation process, based on a factor analysis and a cluster analysis, resulted in the following seven female and seven male outfit types. For the women we see the fashion enthusiast, the self-confident type, the thrifty type, the individualistic type, the fashion follower, the intellectual, and the insecure.

Men can be divided into the fashionable type, the pragmatic type, the fashion conformist, the conservative, the disinterested type, the rebel, and the intellectual.

With regard to fashion, we see that attitudes and behaviour of men, especially the younger generation, are becoming more and more like that of their female counterparts. Both genders want to express their personality and their mood through their outfits and some of them, especially the individualistic female type and the male rebel, want to stand out from the rest.

The survey has shown that 79% of female participants, assess clothes shopping as self-rewarding, confidence boosting, and as a slightly self-indulgent experience. In contrast, less than half of the male participants see such a positive effect on their mood, the significance of clothing in general remains extremely high (Spiegel Media, 2018).

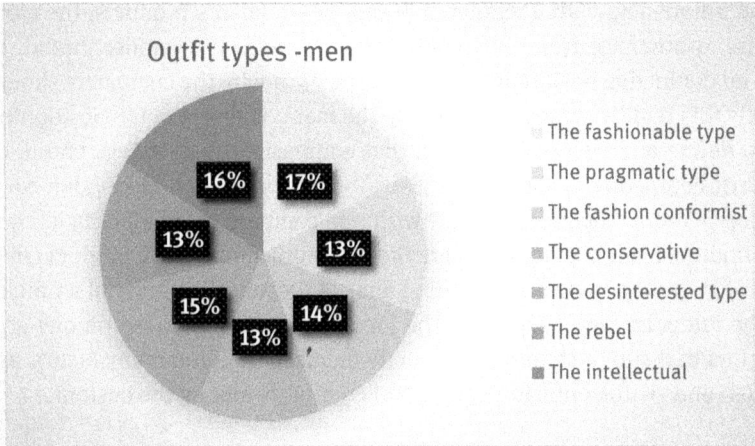

Figure 1.24: Male outfit types.
Source: Spiegel Media, 2018

Comparing women and men in matters of gender-specific apparel buying habits, men remain true to old habits to a greater extent than women. They tend to prefer their clothes practical and prefer additional functions, for instance breathable fabric or protection against ultraviolet rays. Also, women have become careful about spending their money on unnecessary things and look for the best quality for the best price. This so-called *smart shopper* is always looking for special offers (Spiegel Media, 2018).

What is more, the study has shown when buying clothes, consumers are becoming increasingly influenced by criteria such as social awareness and ecologically sound production. Almost one-third of respondents would like to know exactly where the garment in question comes from and how it was produced. Magazines and/or supplements or catalogues, in addition to the internet, are still by far the most important sources of information for decisions on what clothes to buy (Spiegel Media, 2018).

1.5 Retail branding and positioning

Retail branding and positioning has even become more important in recent years due to saturated market situations. Consumers nowadays are faced with thousands of products and brands to choose from. Many competitors may have similar offers and therefore it is so important to stand out and consistently deliver a positive, memorable experience and leave a long-lasting impression on the customers.

To start with a definition, *brand positioning* is the process of positioning a distinctive brand in the minds of customers. A strong brand positioning determines the marketing and competition strategy and builds a distinctive *brand value proposition,* a statement used by retailers and their brands to tell the customers why they should buy from them and not from their competitors. The more the customers associate positivity and uniqueness with a retailer, a brand, or a retailer's products, the more likely they are to purchase from this retailer or this brand. If a retailer, brand, or product has no distinctive positioning, there is no reason why the customers should choose exactly this retailer, brand, or product. The main objective of the positioning strategy is to define and occupy a position that emphasizes the retailer, brand, or product against competing products and gives the customer an added value compared with competitors. Therefore, to start with, the company must identify its own strengths to find the ideal positioning. Here the communication of the product characteristics is of great importance. Positioning aims at the active creation of a unique benefit for the intended target segment. The ideal positioning is based on one or a few more factors to distinguish and differentiate themselves. If too many factors are used, this often ends with confusion or a lack of credibility among the customers.

7-Step Brand Positioning Strategy Process

In order to create a brand positioning strategy, a retailer first has to identify the brand's uniqueness and has to figure out what differentiates the brand (or the company) from competitors. Literature defines seven key steps to effectively clarify a brand's (or retailer's) positioning in the market:
- Determine how your brand (or company) is currently positioning itself in the marketplace (e.g., by the help of a brand positioning map, see below)
- Identify your direct competitors
- Understand how each competitor is positioning their brand (or company)
- Compare your positioning to your competitors to identify your uniqueness (USP = unique selling proposition)
- Develop a distinct, unique and value-based positioning idea
- Create a brand positioning statement (will be described below)
- Test the efficacy of the brand positioning statement (see the 15 criteria below how the efficacy could be tested)

The first step in the brand positioning strategy process is to determine how the retailer's brand can be positioned in a particular market. A brand's position can be defined as the set of perceptions, impressions, ideas, and feelings that consumers associate with a certain product or brand compared with a competitor's products or brands. A main target for every retailer should be to create a position, with the help of the marketing mix, that gives their product or brand the greatest advantage in a particular market. In planning the ideal positioning, marketers or retailers create *brand positioning maps* (also referred to as perceptual maps) that show consumer perceptions of their brand compared to competing brands on attributes that are important to the consumer. In the example below (see Figure 1.27) we see four quadrants. On the x-axis we have the attribute "style/design" of car brands and on the y-axis, we have the attribute "price." So, the first quadrant shows car brands that are conservative and expensive (e.g., Mercedes, Jaguar, Lexus), the second quadrant contains brands that are conservative and cheap (e.g., Honda, Ford etc.). The third quadrant contains brands that can be described as sporty and cheap (e.g., Mazda, Toyota) and in the fourth quadrant are car brands positioned that are sporty and expensive (e.g., Audi, BMW, Porsche, etc.).

The usage of this strategic tool of the brand positioning map has several advantages:

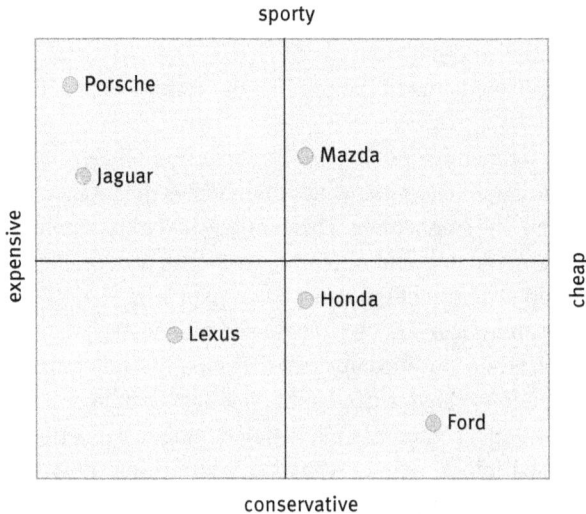

Figure 1.25: Example brand positioning map for car brands.
Source: inboundrocket, 2015

Competitive advantages of a retailer's brand can be identified by comparing your positioning to your competitors to identify the brand's uniqueness (USP, unique selling proposition). Consider in our example in Figure 1.27 the car brand Porsche, we can see that Porsche has a string competitive advantage as it is seen as the classiest and sportiest of the positioned cars in the consumers' minds.

Moreover, the positioning map identifies opportunities for new brands and helps to reposition existing brands. For example, an empty space near an attractive market segment would mean that there are potential market opportunities for a certain brand. In addition, brand positioning maps show how ideal positioning points can shift as a market matures. Consequently, a retailer must reposition its brand in order to retain or gain a competitive advantage.

The last steps in the brand positioning strategy process are to create a *brand positioning statement* and to test the efficacy of the brand positioning statement. A brand positioning statement can be defined as a one or two sentence declaration that communicates a brand's unique value proposition (i.e., USP) for its customers to differentiate itself from the main competitors. When formulating a positioning statement several key questions must be asked:

- Who is the target customer (attitudinal and demographic description of the target group)?
- Which need, desire, or opportunity is addressed (context of relevance for the customers)?
- What is the product category and the product name?
- What are the key benefits of the product or brand (most compelling emotional or rational benefit)?
- What are the primary competitive alternatives?
- What are primary differentiation elements of the product or brand?

In order to create a suitable and competitive positioning strategy, the retailer has to identify these unique characteristics and determine what differentiates the retailer, the retailer's products, or the brand from the competitors. This brand positioning statement is for internal use and guides the marketing and operating decisions of a retailer. A brand positioning statement should not be confused with a company's or brand's taglines or slogans. The terms *tagline and slogan* are very often used interchangeably, but they serve two different purposes. A slogan encompasses a company's mission and what the company stands for. Therefore, slogans can be much longer than taglines. A tagline is an external statement used in a company's marketing efforts. Insights from a positioning statement can be turned into a tagline. A tagline is very often next to a companys logo on an official advertisement, is catchy and evokes an image of the brand in the minds of the customers. In contrast, slogans should carry a brand's values and promises and are very often promoted under a brand's tagline. The box below provides examples of positioning statements in contrast to taglines or slogans.

Examples of Positioning Statements
Bodyshop: For people seeking wellness, the Body Shop offers the most natural bath and cosmetic products because we are the most environmentally friendly cosmetics company.

Home Depot: For do-it-yourselves, Home Depot offers the best prices because we are the largest building supply company.

Amazon.com (2001, when it almost exclusively sold books):

For World Wide Web users who enjoy books, Amazon.com is a retail bookseller that provides instant access to over 1.1 million books. Unlike traditional book retailers, Amazon.com provides a combination of extraordinary convenience, low prices, and comprehensive selection.

Examples of Taglines
McDonald's: I'm Lovin' It.
Apple: Think Different.
BMW: The ultimate driving machine.
L'Oreal: Because you're worth it.
Walmart: Always low prices. Always.
Nike: Just do it!
Coca-Cola: The real thing.
Target: Expect more. Pay less.

Examples of Slogans

Ikea: Home is the most important place in the world! (in German language: Wohnst Du noch oder lebst Du schon?).

MasterCard: There are some things money can't buy. For everything else, there's MasterCard.

M&M: Melts in Your Mouth, Not in Your Hands.

Kit Kat: Have a Break, Have a Kit Kat.

Red Bull: It Gives You Wiiiings!

Kelloggs Frosted Flakes: They're GR-R-R-reat!

The last steps in the brand positioning strategy process is to test and check the efficacy of the brand positioning statement. Literature defines several criteria for evaluating a brand's positioning strategy. The following questions should be asked:

- Does the brand positioning strategy differentiate my product or brand and withstand counterattack?
- Does it match customer perceptions and preferences?
- Does it have growth potential?
- Does the brand have a unique value proposition?
- Is it memorable, motivating, credible, and easy to understand?
- Is it consistent in all areas of your business?
- Is it difficult to copy?
- Is it positioned for long-term success?

Retail branding and differentiation

In the United States and Western Europe, many traditional grocery retailers are seeing their sales and margins fall. In developed markets, growth and profitability have fallen for many reasons: higher costs, falling productivity, and everyday low price policies. Traditional grocery retailers have to act, otherwise they'll be loose revenues to discount, online, and nongrocery retail channels (Kuijpers, Simmons, & van Wamelen, 2018).

This disruptive market situation can be mainly attributed to three major forces:

- consumers' changing habits and preferences
- intensifying competition
- new technologies

This disruptive market situation presents considerable challenges for retailers, especially in the grocery retail sector. Profitable growth has become difficult but is achievable by defining a distinctive value proposition and to differentiate oneself from the competition. The following differentiation strategies seem to be suitable for retailers, especially grocery retailers:

- convenience
- inspiration
- value for your money

Convenience

Convenience is partly about having store locations that are easy to get to, such as at train stations, office buildings, or in residential areas. But store location is only one aspect of convenience. Retailers have to make every part of the shopping trip more convenient, while maintaining standards of quality far above typical convenience stores. A grocery store's assortment might include grab-and-go items, prepared foods, frozen meals, and loose fruits and vegetables for shoppers looking for a quick snack during their lunch break. It might also provide self-service options, express check-outs, home delivery, and other in-store services, such as mail delivery service, tobacconist's shop, dry cleaning, or package pickup.

By reducing the number of products, supermarkets are able to cut prices, improve availability on its shelves, and improve orientation in the shop. The British multinational grocery chain Tesco, for example, has started to cut its range by up to a third of its products as shoppers are confused by having a choice of about 90,000 products for items during their weekly shopping trip. More details below.

Tesco cuts range by 30% to simplify shopping

The British multinational grocery chain Tesco has started pulling up to a third of their products off the shelves as it calls time on policy that left shoppers confused by having a choice of approximately 90,000 products for items during their weekly shopping trips The struggling supermarket chain, which has lost market share to low-cost, low-choice retailers such as Lidl, Aldi (Hofer), Penny, or Netto, has called in outside consultants to cut back about 30% of its products in an attempt to cut costs and make the weekly shopping simpler. Tesco stocks up to 90,000 different products (stock keeping units [SKUs]; every pack size and flavour of a certain product is a different SKU). As an example, with tomato ketchup, Tesco offers an array of 28 sauces while in Hofer there is just one ketchup in one size.

Experts say that the grocery industry had been guilty of self-serving innovation as big suppliers want to grow their businesses by bringing new products to the customers, while the employed buyers of supermarket chains, with financial targets, receive cash payments from the big suppliers for listing new products. But as a matter of fact, the average household buys only 400 products a year, with just 41 items in their weekly shop.

By stocking fewer products Tesco will be able to cut prices, make shopping easier and improve availability on its shelves. Tesco is expected to reduce the number of lines it stocks to between 65,000 and 70,000, looking at every product.

Hofer and Lidl, for example, are described as limited-range discounters because they stock fewer than 2,000 products. That dramatically far smaller number gives them a lot of buying power and makes the business much simpler to run and therefore they have a cost advantage, which means prices can be more competitive.

It depends on the strategic focus how many products a grocery store wants to carry. A superstore or hypermarket uses the huge assortment with up to 250,000 SKUs as their advantage of differentiation. Whereas a discounter with a smaller assortment and a limited range of SKUs offers its customers a cost advantage and a speedy, convenient shopping experience.

Wide ranges help the big grocery stores because they can demand payments from suppliers to put their products on their shelves.

Experts say that stocking fewer products is another way of saving money, because having less items makes it easier for staff to fill up the shelves. Consumers do want choices but there has to be a happy medium (Wood & Butler, 2015).

Inspiration

A retailer can differentiate itself by creating an inspiring and exciting shopping experience. Some grocery stores provide digital signage that offers extensive product information, including, for example, the origin of the products, ingredients list, nutritional information, etc. Others try to create an environment that feels like walking through a cookbook, with fully prepared meals on display or cooked directly in the shop, along with recipes and ingredients in the correct portions. A mix of education and entertainment can also create a shopping experience. For example, cooking classes taught by a celebrity chef, along with the recipes and ingredients to by in the shop.

Value for money

The third distinctive value proposition to differentiate oneself from competitors could be "Value for money." This strategy is mainly used by mass retailers and discounters. They provide cost advantage through cost leadership. To be competitive a traditional grocery retailer would need considerable scale and a low-cost operating model. This would require partnering with other retailers on sourcing, automation, or adopting a discount-store model. Therefore, a more likely path for a traditional grocery store would be to focus on either differentiation strategies, like convenience or inspiration.

To summarize, retailers must focus on their core strengths to be successful in the long run including, for example, broad product availability, better service and warranty programs, attractive CRM programs, etc.

1.5.1 Masstige positioning strategy

Now, we take as an illustrative example the global luxury fashion market and discuss positioning and diversification strategies of selected global luxury brands. Silverstein and Fiske (2003) assume that one of the biggest challenges for traditional luxury brands will be their brand extensions to enhance the brand at the high end and avoid negative influence on its brand essence at the low end. Without an appropriate and target-group oriented positioning a brand will be "stuck in the middle" and will not be successful in the long run.

Traditional luxury brands maintain a strict consistency between perceived prestige and price premiums, to preserve their brand exclusivity, whereas new luxury brand positioning strategies often combine a high perceived prestige with reasonable price premiums to attract middle-class consumers (Truong et al., 2009). Many new-luxury brands move upmarket to create a certain appeal and down-market to make their products more accessible. Still, they are careful to create and maintain a distinctive character for every price-level of their products by focusing on a common brand essence (Silverstein & Fiske, 2003). In the literature this positioning strategy is referred to as a "masstige" strategy (i.e., a combination of mass and class). Truong et al. (2009) view a masstige positioning strategy as "being very innovative and effective" due to combining a prestige positioning with a broad appeal but hardly any brand dilution. An appropriate example of a so-called *masstige* brand or new luxury brand is Michael Kors. The company sells mainly leather goods, like handbags and shoes, but also accessories and apparel at reasonable price premiums to target new consumers segments, especially the female younger age group. This brand has successfully differentiated itself from traditional luxury brands maintaining reasonable price premiums.

Most traditional brands, such as Gucci, are very careful when widening their product and price range in order to avoid a brand dilution. They do not want their products to be available to the mass market, focusing on an exclusive and prestigious branding strategy. But when traditional brands are losing market shares, masstige strategies may be an opportunity to be profitable by targeting new consumer groups.

According to the Brand Personality Model by Aaker (1996) different brands stand for certain characteristics that make a brand unique. Taking as an example the American brand Michael Kors, founded in 1981, this brand can be described best by the dimension excitement given descriptive attributes like modern, contemporary, trendy, young, cool, etc. In contrast, the brand Gucci has positioned itself with the dimension sophistication, including the attributes glamorous, good-looking, upper class, charming, feminine, and smooth.

In Figure 1.28 ratios calculated from average prices and average ratings of perceived prestige (using the Luxury Brand Index by Truong et al., 2009) based on the results of focus groups are shown resulting in a perceptual map. Three categories of brands are compared: traditional luxury brands (Gucci, Armani, Hugo Boss), new luxury brands (Calvin Klein, Polo, Ralph Lauren), and middle-range brands (Celio, H&M, Zara). Figure 1.28 shows that traditional brands are higher priced than new luxury brands whereas the latter are more expensive than middle-range brands. Comparing the perceived prestige, traditional luxury brands and new luxury brands are positioned relatively close having a much higher status than middle-range brands.

Each brand must have a distinctive and target-group oriented positioning. Without an appropriate positioning a brand will be "stuck in the middle" and will not be successful in the long run. Ansoff (1965) has developed a two-by-two matrix including four growth strategies, also known as product and market growth matrix. This matrix is mainly a marketing planning tool that assists companies in determining its product and market growth by focusing on whether the products are new or existing and whether the market is new or existing. The Ansoff Matrix has four alternatives of

High Status

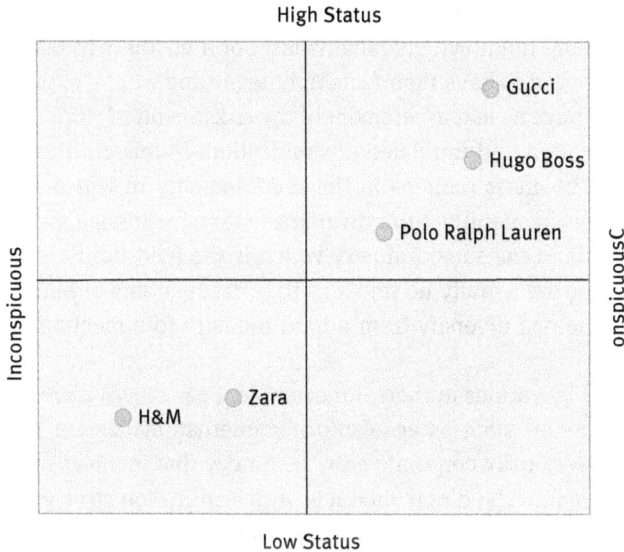

Figure 1.26: Positioning of selected luxury, masstige, and middle-range brands.
Source: Truong et al., 2009, 379

marketing strategies: market penetration, product development, market development, and diversification.

Market penetration: covers products that are prevailing in an existing market. In this strategy, there will be a further exploitation of the products without necessarily changing the product using promotional methods, more extensive distribution or encouraging the usage of the product.

Product development: new products are introduced into existing markets. This product development can differ from the introduction of a new product in an existing market to the modification of an existing product, by changing the design, style, flavour, or increasing the products performance or quality, etc.

Market development (market extension): existing products are introduced to new markets through further market segmentation to aid in identifying a new clientele base. There are various approaches to this strategy, which include: new geographical markets, new distribution channels, new product packaging, and different pricing policies. In new geographical markets, the business can expound by exporting their products to other new countries. It would also mean setting up other branches of the business in other areas where the business had not ventured yet.

Diversification: the company is selling new products to new markets. It is the riskiest strategy among the others as it involves two unknowns, new products being created and the business does not know the development problems that may occur in the process. There is also the fact that there is a new market being targeted, which will bring the problem of having unknown characteristics. For a business to take a step into diversification, they need to have their facts right regarding what it expects to gain from the strategy and have a clear assessment of the risks involved.

There is related diversification and unrelated diversification. In related diversification, this means that the business remains in the same industry in which it is familiar with. For example, a cake manufacturer diversifies into a fresh juice manufacturer. This diversification is in the same industry which is the food industry. In unrelated diversification, there are usually no previous industry relations or market experiences. For instance, one can diversify from a food industry to a mechanical industry.

This matrix was extended by various authors, for example, Egan (1998) included several important corporate issues such as acquisition or internationalization (see Table 11). Diversification is a very risky corporate growth strategy that involves moving simultaneously into new markets and new products. A diversification strategy in the luxury goods industry can help to extend a brand from a fashion brand to a lifestyle brand by offering a "total lifestyle concept" including various product groups and services in their portfolios.

Table 11: Egan's extension of the Ansoff Matrix (Proctor, 2000).

	Current Products	New Products
Current Markets	Penetration – organic – acquisition	Product augmentation
	Market expansion – increase usage – rejuvenate product life cycle	Product development – related – unrelated
New Markets	Market development – new uses – new users	Diversification – related – conglomerate
		Vertical integration
		Internationalization

The global luxury group Kering, for example, consists of several luxury brands in fashion, leather goods, jewellery, beauty, accessories, and services (Kering, 2017). Kering, and the former Gucci Group, mainly grow through acquisitions and internationalization. In 1999, the company started with the adoption of a multibrand strategy conducting several acquisitions and franchise deals, including the acquisition of Yves-Saint Laurent, Sergio Rossi, Stella McCartney, Alexander McQueen, and Di Modolo. Nowadays Kering has a very broad product range and a well-balanced portfolio of luxury brands from apparel and accessories to leather goods, fragrance, beauty, jewellery, etc., all in a high-end price range. Kering consists of several separated departments that are managed in an autonomous manner. The luxury fashion brand Gucci is also managed autonomously and has its own product divisions, including various new divisions like hotels, cafés, restaurants, museums, and eyewear, jewellery, beauty, apparel, children's collections, leather goods, and accessories. The brand has successfully moved from a fashion brand towards a lifestyle brand.

1.6 Sustainable retailing

The last few years have witnessed an increased interest in sustainable and ethical practices within the retail industry. Sustainability is emerging as a so-called megatrend and to stay competitive more and more companies start to use catchwords like "sustainable," "eco-friendly," "social," or "ethical" in their marketing communications. But this overdosing of sustainability claims has the effect that consumers very often mistrust such claims, especially when they can't verify the credibility. But if such "green" claims and sustainability issues are exaggerated, misleading, or not verifiable, companies might be accused of so-called greenwashing, which leads to a negative brand image or company's reputation.

In order to avoid "greenwashing," misleading marketing communications, and not proper use of "green" words, it is essential to define sustainable retailing in general and to identify key sustainable retail criteria in particular, which provide assurance for the customers that products are produced with social, ethical, and eco-friendly aspects in mind. Furthermore, consumers' confidence in retail companies can be enhanced by increasing transparency of production and manufacturing processes.

1.6.1 What is sustainability?

Sustainability means meeting our own needs without compromising the ability of future generations to meet their own needs. In addition to natural resources, social and economic resources should also be considered.

Sustainability is a holistic approach that considers three dimensions:
- ecological
- social
- economic dimensions

All three dimensions must be considered to find lasting prosperity.

The principle of sustainability encourages businesses and retailers, to make decisions with a view to the future rather than regarding the next quarter's profits and sales. When a company focuses on sustainability, sustainability goals must defined and efforts will be made to work towards them. A goal could be, for example, to cut CO_2 emissions by 5% within the next two years or to replace all company cars with electric cars within the next five years. Other sustainability goals could be lower energy usage, sourcing products from fair-trade organizations, ensuring physical waste is disposed of properly, transportation and logistics with as little carbon footprint as possible, etc. When the company achieves their sustainability goals, they can call themselves "green" or "sustainable."

When a large company such as Walmart commits to sustainability, producers and suppliers worldwide who supply Walmart must report on their business practices. This includes sourcing food but also clothing items and electronics from companies and countries that not only treat and pay their workers well but are committed to sustainability down the supply chain as well. If there are practices that are unsustainable, the suppliers must phase them out to continue to serve Walmart (Grant & Kenton, 2019).

Carbon negative by 2030 – The example of Microsoft

Microsoft has launched an ambitious climate protection program. By 2030 the company wants to be CO_2-negative and by 2050 it wants to have removed more CO_2 from the atmosphere than it has caused since its founding in 1975.

The latest goal can be described as one of the most ambitious in the company's history: Within ten years, the IT group is to become CO_2-negative, that is, to bind or compensate more CO_2 from the atmosphere than it emits.

In a second stage, the company wants to have reclaimed more CO_2 from the atmosphere by 2050 by reducing its own CO_2 emissions and supporting climate protection projects than it has directly or indirectly caused through its electricity consumption since its foundation in the year.

The crux of the matter: digitization and cloud services – two areas in which Microsoft is primarily involved – offer considerable CO_2 savings potential, but a great deal of energy is required for the development, provision, and operation of the services.

"Nobody can solve the Earth's climate problem alone, but as a global company we have a special responsibility to make our contribution," CEO Nadyella emphasizes.

Not all CO_2 is the same, which is completely irrelevant for the climate, but with Microsoft's climate plan, initiatives on three levels are required (Sempelmann, 2020):

- Level 1 (direct emissions): The emissions that arise from the company's own business activities.
- Level 2 (indirect emissions): The CO_2 that is produced in the production of the electricity and heat used in the company.
- Level 3 (involved emissions): All those CO_2 emissions that result from the company's activities. This includes CO_2 emissions from suppliers, from the extraction of raw materials for products, from materials used in the construction of company buildings or from employee business trips. It also includes the complete life cycle of a company's products at customer sites, for example, the electricity used for regular recharging.

In addition, Microsoft is launching a Climate Innovation Fund that will invest $1 billion worldwide over the next four years to develop new technologies that will solve the planet's carbon problem. The focus is on accelerating existing technology development through project financing and loans, but also on promoting innovation through equity investments in companies and loans.

In addition to the new fund, Microsoft will also continue to support climate protection projects through the "AI for Earth" program. In the last two years, 450 projects in more than 70 countries have already been supported.

The first measures have already been defined. By 2030, for example, the electricity used to operate the data centres and company buildings is to come from 100% renewable energy, and only electric cars are to be used as company vehicles.

In order to compensate for indirect emissions, Microsoft wants to extend the internal CO_2 tax to the entire supply and value-added chain and support suppliers in reducing their CO_2 footprint. In addition, Microsoft will provide users of Azure cloud services with a CO_2 calculator to calculate the emissions generated when using the cloud service.

Microsoft will also help its customers reduce their carbon footprint and publish an annual Environmental Sustainability Report to provide transparency on progress.

Microsoft's efforts will be complemented by, among other things, reforestation projects, measures to bind carbon in the soil, bioenergy in conjunction with CO_2 capture and storage, and direct CO_2 recovery from the air (Sempelmann, 2020).

1.6.2 Sustainable business practices

There are many ways a company can become sustainable and integrate sustainable practices in daily business. Some examples are by reducing waste, preventing pollution, adopting clean energy, conserving water, greening the planet by planting trees, using sustainable materials, making their products sustainable, or even reducing business trips by plane and by encouraging employees to take alternative, green transport instead of flying or limiting the need to travel at all by hosting video conferences.

For example, Patagonia is one of the most sustainable clothing brands in the sport and outdoor sector. Patagonia has been striving to be an environmentally friendly business for more than twenty years. One percent of their revenue goes to environmental organisations, and they organise workshops where consumers learn how to repair their own clothing and belongings, or the company offers to fix it for their customers. They also encourage sustainable travel by organising a yearly event in June, when their bicycle-loving employees come together. Moreover, the outdoor clothing brand plans to be completely CO_2 neutral by 2025 also having a fully sustainable production cycle by then. They will use solar energy and comply with strict standards in terms of production materials and the use of raw materials.

In the following subchapters you will find more details on sustainable business practices, in particular ecological sustainability, ethical performance in retailing and corporate social responsibility, collaborate consumption, and the idea of social supermarkets.

1.6.2.1 Ecological sustainability

Physical climate risk will affect everyone, directly or indirectly, also the retail sector. Responding to this climatically changes will require new ways risk of managing, due to physical and socioeconomic impacts of the climate change. An effective response to the socioeconomic impacts of physical climate risk would be to integrate climate risk into decision-making, accelerating the pace and scale of adaptation, and decarbonizing at scale to prevent a further risk. Thinking about information systems and cyber-risks has become integrated into corporate and public sector decision-making, climate change will also need to feature as a major factor in decisions (McKinsey, January 2020a).

For retailers, this will mean taking climate considerations into account when looking at capital allocation, development of products or services, or supply-chain management, etc. For example, large capital projects could be evaluated reflecting the full probability distribution of possible climate hazards at their location. This would include changes in that probability distribution over time and possible changes in cost of capital for exposed assets, as well as how climate risk could affect the broader market context and other implicit assumptions in the investment case. For cities, a climate focus will become essential for urban planning decisions. But developing a robust quantitative understanding of climate risk is complex. It requires the use of new tools, models, metrics, and analytics. Companies are already beginning to assess their exposure to climate risk, but much more needs to be done. Lack of understanding significantly increases risks and potential impacts across markets, and socioeconomic systems (McKinsey, January 2020a).

On the other hand, there are not only risks, but also opportunities from the changing climate, such as new places for agricultural production, or for sectors like tourism, as well as using new technologies and approaches to manage risk in a changing climate (McKinsey, January 2020a).

Changes in mind-set, operating model, and tools and processes will be needed to integrate climate risk into decision-making effectively. Today, decision-makers' experiences are based on a world of relative climate stability, with the changing climate, it will be important to understand and embrace the probabilistic nature of climate risk and be mindful of possible biases and outdated mental models. The systemic nature of climate risk requires a holistic approach to understand and identify the full range of possible direct and indirect impacts (McKinsey, January 2020a).

Most models do not consider geospatial dimensions. Direct impacts of climate change are local in nature. This requires an understanding of the exposure to risk via geospatial analysis. For example, companies will need to understand how their global asset footprint is exposed to different forms of current and evolving climate hazard in each one of their main locations and indeed in each of the main locations of their critical suppliers. Moreover, protecting people is crucial. Steps can range from prioritizing emergency response and preparedness to erecting cooling shelters and adjusting working hours for outdoor workers exposed to heat. For example, the Ahmedabad City Corporation developed the first heat action plan in India in response to the record-breaking 2010 heat wave that killed 300 people in a single day. The company has implemented programs to build the population's awareness of the dangers of extreme heat. These measures include establishing a seven-day probabilistic heatwave early warning system, developing a citywide cool-roofs albedo management program, and setting up teams to distribute cool water and rehydration tablets to vulnerable populations during heat waves (McKinsey, January 2020a).

Equally important will be to support socioeconomic development in ways that recognize the risk of a changing climate. Continuing to shift the basis of economic development from outdoor work to urban indoor environments in extreme heat-prone environments and factoring climate risk into urban planning. Scientists estimate that restricting warming to below 2.0 degrees would reduce the risk of initiating many serious feedback loops and restricting it to 1.5 degrees would reduce the risk of initiating most of them. Because warming is a function of cumulative emissions, there is a specific amount of CO_2 that can be emitted before reaching the 1.5-degree or 2.0-degree threshold (a so-called carbon budget). Scientists estimate that the remaining 2.0-degree carbon budget will be exceeded in approximately 5 years and the remaining 1.5-degree carbon budget in 12 years, given the current annual emissions trajectory. To halt further warming would require reaching net zero emissions (McKinsey, January 2020a).

To conclude, recognizing physical climate risk and integrating an understanding of this risk into decision-making is an imperative for individuals, businesses, communities, and countries. The next decade will be decisive, as decision- makers fundamentally rethink the infrastructure, assets, and systems of the future, and the world collectively sets a path to manage the risk from climate change (McKinsey, January 2020a).

Cradle-to-cradle vision

According to statistics, in the EU alone around three billion tonnes of high-quality materials end up in landfills and incinerators every year, and the trend is rising. The concept of the "cradle to cradle" wants to get to the root of this problem. It is the vision of a waste-free economy in which companies no longer use materials that are harmful to health or the environment and in which all substances are permanent nutrients for natural cycles or closed technical cycles. Compostable textiles, edible packaging, pure plastics, or metals can be used endlessly for the same purpose and are not to be thrown away.

The "cradle to cradle" concept was developed by the German chemistry professor, process engineer and ecovisionary Braungart and the US architect McDonough. Since then, they have sharply criticized the economy's efficiency orientation. Intelligent product design must be effective, do the right thing and achieve real environmental friendliness in all industries, product life cycles, and value chains. In some cases, companies have completely changed their business model, which means, for example, that they take back used products and recycle them "properly." Recycling is usually "downcycling," which turns a higher-value product into a lower-value product. Recycling according to the cradle-to-cradle principle means that the material can and will be reused again and again for the same product without any loss of quality because it is pure material (e.g., pure plastics, pure wood), for example, a backrest becomes a backrest, a carpet a carpet of the same quality. Some companies have changed from product manufacturers to providers of services, which has made the manufacture of the respective products largely superfluous. Some have expanded their range of services to include products, for example, a waste company has become a manufacturer of waste glass blanks from which drinking glasses can be made.

In the meantime, there are also companies that "up-cycle" used materials, for example, by making high-quality, modern garments from old textiles. The implementation of this approach is still at the beginning of a development but will increase in the near future.

However, dangerous substances can not be completely avoided. Without them, for example, the entire modern communication and data processing technology would not be possible. It is therefore crucial that toxins do not end up in the environment but remain in pure form in closed industrial cycles and do not pollute the outside world in any way. Even if there are recycling laws and waste separation in some countries, economic and social reality is still a long way from reusing all raw materials. Urban waste contains raw materials of the highest quality that mostly remain unused. One of the reasons for this is that many products are made of composite materials or mixtures, for example, plastic mixtures, which make genuine "recycling" more difficult. The cost is still higher than using fossil or freshly mined raw materials. In view of rising raw material costs and in some areas (partly artificially created) raw material shortages, the recovery of raw materials from urban waste under the term "urban mining" is becoming increasingly important. This could lead to approaches for further cradle-to-cradle business models.

The following box provides an example of the lighthouse project GreenPark based on the cradle-to-cradle criteria.

Lighthouse Project GreenPark
The Dutch province of Limburg has declared itself a model region and is developing an innovative industrial park called GreenPark Venlo as a lighthouse project on the site of the Floriade World Garden Exhibition, which took place in Venlo near the Dutch-German border in 2012. The buildings are based on cradle-to-cradle criteria, the site is to be completely independent of the national electricity and natural gas grid, and architectural eye-catchers are regarded as prime examples of sustainability and innovation. Since the end of the exhibition in October, a large part of the site has been further developed into a green business park. Companies will no longer be separated according to sectors, but the locations will be mixed in such a way that the companies benefit from each other. One company's waste heat will cover the other company's heat requirements, the other company's residual materials will supply the other company with raw materials, and product innovations will be developed jointly. The cities of Maastricht and Meerssen are basing their urban development project with the two-kilometre-long A2 tunnel on the concept to solve existing ecological, social, and economic problems.

In 2010 the Belgian Presidency of the Council set out to promote a cradle-to-cradle approach to resource management in the manufacturing sector. While New Zealand is discussing this, California also wants to become a cradle-to-cradle state.

Although many companies have changed their business models and many consumers have started to be attentive to which products they buy, there is still a long way to go. Politicians and companies should promote resource-efficient management. In detail, resource-economic advancement means that the same products or services are produced and offered with a fraction of the raw materials previously used. In order for this to be systematically put into practice in all sectors, however, politics, business, and society must change significantly.

A major challenge is the so-called *rebound effect*: although energy intensity is decreasing, energy consumption is increasing because of increased production and consumption. The rebound effect is particularly drastic when energy and raw materials become cheaper. Therefore, raw material prices would have to tell the "ecological truth," that is, the external costs (environmental pollution, social consequences) of raw material extraction would have to be integrated into the prices. The then rising prices of raw materials would result in a much better use of resources. There are enough tangible arguments for better resource use: scarcity of raw materials, distribution injustice, ecological and social problems of raw material extraction, as well as dependence on exports and increasing conflicts over resources (Nachhaltigkeit, 2019).

What is more, there is a growing concern for personal wellbeing and the environment. According to Euromonitor International's Lifestyles Survey 2019 (Euromonitor, 2020), 60% of global respondents agreed or strongly agreed that climate change is a worrying issue. Consequently, the percentage of respondents feeling good about buying ecologically or ethically sourced products grew to 28% in 2019.

Air pollution and climate change and the consequences, like the impact of rising sea levels, the increase in carbon dioxide emissions and global warming, are crucial drivers for politics and industries. In Mexico City, air pollution on some days is so high that schools are closed, and authorities advise against exercising outdoors. According to WHO, air particulates from dust, soot, smoke, and fumes increase the chance of lung cancer, while the American Heart Association suggests it as a possible risk factor for heart disease and stroke. The consequences of poor air quality also impact businesses and economic growth. By 2060, the annual number of lost working days due to poor air quality will reach 3.7 billion, up from 1.2 billion today.

Consequently, businesses are facing pressures to devise and implement solutions that save our planet and consumers from the effects of negative consequences of resource-wasting business practices. The following box provides examples of industry response to worldwide ecological issues.

Industry response to ecological issues

Cambridge Mask Co. (https://cambridgemask.com/) a start-up producing stylish and colourful face masks that protect consumers from the harmful effects of air pollution and airborne diseases. The face masks are equipped with filter technology for people walking or cycling in the city. Climate activists use these fashionable face masks in social media posts to increase air pollution awareness. Air pollution masks are gaining popularity with consumers as a tool to mitigate air pollution.

Elephant US Drunk Elephant (https://www.drunkelephant.com/) introduced D-Bronzi Anti-Pollution Sunshine Drops, a serum that protects the skin from the adverse effects of air pollution. The product directly caters to the needs of health-conscious consumers. It is free of drying alcohols, silicones, chemical screens, fragrances, and sodium laureth sulphate and contains antioxidants and natural ingredients. As consumers become more aware of air pollution, companies are creating products that can help shield their skin from the adverse effects.

Plume Labs SAS (https://plumelabs.com/en/) launched a mobile air quality measuring device. The sensor is linked to a smartphone app that provides a detailed analysis of the air pollutants in real time. It helps people avoid locations that are prone to high levels of air pollution. The device measures nitrogen dioxide, VOCs, and particular matter.

Pernod Ricard, the French alcohol manufacturer, sponsors a project to show their contribution to the global environment through credible projects and initiatives that make a difference. The Absolut Street Trees initiative involves artists painting giant murals in the city using Airlite paint, which purifies polluted air in a process similar to photosynthesis. When the paint is exposed to sunlight, the surrounding air is oxygenated through a chemical reaction. The project's creators say the murals should neutralize the equivalent of the pollution created by around 60,000 vehicles a year. The paint lasts about 10 years (Euromonitor, 2020).

1.6.2.2 Ethical performance in retailing

Since the 1980s, consumers are becoming increasingly aware of the social and environmental consequences of the products they purchase, especially in the grocery and apparel sector. Research has already been done on finding out why individuals show ethical behaviour and buy sustainable products. Consumers can be divided into several homogenous groups, Cervellon & Carey (2011) for example, found a typology of three different types of consumers:

- The health-conscious consumer purchases green products because of health benefits
- The environmentalist who purchases green products because of its environmental benefits and as a contribution to the protection of the earth
- The quality hunter trusts that the green products have superior ingredients, effect, and quality over regular products

In order to understand ethical consumption, it is important to define what the motivational factors are that primarily drive consumers to show ethical behaviour. Terlau &

Hirsch (2015) explored the ethical consumers even further and identified a set of motivations for ethical consumers when buying beauty products:

- Health motivation: sustainable and ethical beauty products are focused on having a positive effect on the consumer's health. It can be consumer's motivation because it does not possess harmful essences, fragments and all is made of natural ingredients. Some researchers believe that there is a strong connection between ethical purchase and health as a motivational factor. Those who agree are convinced that health is an important criterion that consumers tend to look for in sustainable products.
- Animal welfare motivation: consumers purchase an ethical product because ethical products are not tested on animals. Animals gain a fair recognition regarding ethical consumption. In one of the studies conducted by Carrigan and Atalla (2001) consumers expressed their sympathies towards animal rights, that is, in cosmetics – animal testing. In fact, more sympathy was dedicated towards animals than towards human rights.
- Motivation for environmental protection: ethical products are environmentally friendly, do not include chemicals, and their package is recyclable or from a natural material (wood, paper, or other) (Terlau & Hirsch, 2015).

Taking another example, the apparel sector. The fast fashion retail market experiences a rapid growth, although most of the consumers know about the criticism of sweatshop labour, environmental consequences of unethical production conditions, etc., by fast fashion companies (Fast fashion is a term used by fashion retailers for designs that move from catwalk quickly to capture current fashion trends. This philosophy of quick manufacturing at an affordable price is used in large retailers such as H&M, Zara, Primark, Topshop, etc.).

Consequently, consumers don't always show ethical behaviour when buying products and are not always willing to pay a price-premium for sustainable products. Potential causal factors behind this behaviour, attitudes, and perceptions towards sustainability and influencing factors for ethical consumer behaviour have been identified. Previous research has shown that consumers' beliefs about ethical products are based on their perceptions of a company in terms of the reputation in a certain market. Moreover, their beliefs influence their support for what they perceive as socially responsible and eco-friendly businesses. Consequently, consumer education is essential to raise consumers' awareness of ethical issues (Yulan Wang, Lo, & Shum, 2012).

McNeill and Moore (2015) found in their study that fashion consumers can be categorized in three different consumer groups. Each group has a different view regarding fast fashion and perceptions of fashion, and different fashion consumption behaviour. In general, ethical fashion purchase behaviour is determined by "their general level of concern for social and environmental well-being, their preconceptions towards sustainable fashion and their prior behaviour in relation to ethical consumption actions" (McNeill & Moore, 2015, S. 220). Other influencing factors are the influence of peer groups and the consumer's knowledge about sustainable fashion products and practices (Barnes & Lea-Greenwood, 2006). Self-enhancement and openness to experience personal values are also regarded as influencing factors when it comes to engagement in ethical fashion consumption (Manchiraju & Sadachar, 2014).

With our clothes we would like to make a statement. Most of the consumers want to wear fashionable clothes and sustainable clothing is very often perceived as less fashionable. Another conflict potential is the so-called *fashion obsolescence*. The fashion industry, especially the fast fashion sector, uses planned obsolescence as a business strategy so that the consumer feels a need to purchase new, fashionable products that replace the old ones. Fast fashion is often assessed as "disposable" fashion due to short product life cycles and to the fact that unfashionable items are commonly thrown away with the household waste. Emotionally durable designs ("slow" design) through customization of clothing (user-centred fashion), reuse, and upcycling of clothing and collaborative consumption might work against this fashion obsolescence.

Consumers are often missing a true added value that justifies the price premium of ethical products. Therefore, to make consumers care about ethical behaviour in general and purchase more sustainable products, marketing communication and consumer education are supposed to be the most successful tools that result in an ethical consumer behaviour. Most customers care about unethical behaviour, but this attitude does not always result in sustainable purchase decisions. Joergens (2006) states that personal needs motivate consumers primarily when they buy products and have priority over ethical issues. Although consumers have a gaining interest in ethical products, they are very often unable to make ethical judgements due to a lack of comprehensive information. Consumers only care about ethical issues that influence them directly.

Consequently, a truthful ethical label issued by a reliable and independent institution or organization, containing important ethical information, might be a helpful tool to facilitate customers' purchase decisions and to generate greater awareness. Awareness campaigns, in general, but also the increasing involvement of consumer activist groups and the availability of ethical products will help to encourage ethical consumer behaviour and change consumers' consumption (Teah & Chuah, 2015).

The box below shows a German initiative of how sustainable production in the apparel sector should be encouraged.

The Green Button to encourage sustainable production in the apparel sector
The Green Button is a government sustainability label awarded by the Federal Ministry for Economic Cooperation and Development (BMZ) in Germany to manufacturers who have passed the required examination procedure in sustainable textile production. The label combines social and ecological standards whose criteria and conditions are determined by the government, designed to help improve textile manufacturing is a seal.

There are a total of 46 demanding social and environmental criteria – from A for wastewater limit values to Z for prohibition of forced labour. What is special about the Green Button is that the company's entire supply relationships are checked. Individual showcase products are not enough because the goal is to make sustainability the standard throughout the textile sector.

With the Green Button sustainable textiles are made visible in the shops. Other objectives of the Green Button are:

- Objective: protection of people and nature throughout the supply chain
- Production stages: the Green Button aims to cover the entire textile production, from the cotton field to the hanger

How should these criteria be controlled along the entire supply chain?

This is done by independent auditors such as the TÜV. They monitor compliance with the criteria. If necessary, they also check the production sites, for example, in Romania or Bangladesh. The state German Accreditation Body, as "Prüfer der Prüfer," ensures that the controls are reliable and the auditors know what is important.

The fact that sustainable supply chains are possible is shown by the 50 participating companies. Even small start-ups can do it. In the age of digitalization, they can ensure compliance with social and environmental standards with appropriate effort throughout the supply chain check.

The Green Button is not only a "German seal," it also complies with EU and WTO law. The tests are based on international standards. Companies can therefore use the Green Button in other countries, also companies from abroad can apply for it (BMWE, 2019).

1.6.2.3 Corporate Social Responsibility

Corporate social responsibility (CSR) is a concept that provides companies with a basis for integrating social and environmental concerns into their business activities and interactions with particular interest groups on a voluntary basis. The application of CSR activities offers several primary benefits for retailers, for example, to systematically integrate and further develop the company's social commitment to its employees, the local community and the environment into its management, to maintain and expand the reputation of the company or to ensure the long-term viability of the company. The self-commitment of the company also includes legal, international, and official regulations as well as company-specific goals that go beyond these (WKO, 2019).

With the help of such a concept, the company can provide evidence to interested parties, like employees of the company, investors, residents, nongovernmental organisations (NGOs), consumers, authorities, etc.

Nowadays, large companies can hardly afford not to take CSR seriously. Some employ CSR specialists who formulate the company's moral code in writing also monitor its implementation. This often has an economically beneficial aspect if one knows how to use the resulting positive company image for marketing and PR. After all, everyone involved benefits from well implemented CSR. Some people accuse companies of saying that moral motives are rarely the driving force behind CSR. Rather, companies hoped that this would have an advertising effect, which would not least lead to an increase in turnover. Critics therefore often simply describe CSR as part of marketing. On the other hand, there is the widespread opinion that the actual intention behind CSR is not so important if its effect ultimately benefits people.

There are three areas of responsibility of CSR, each of which is named according to the nature of its public activity:

- The internal area of responsibility comprises all internal strategies and processes that do not reach the public, but which are essential for the ethical orientation of the company.
- The central area of responsibility includes all those fields that are publicly effective and have a direct effect on the environment, people, and society, but are still part of the normal working process.
- All actionist fields belong to the external area of responsibility, that is, a company becomes charitably active here (mostly financially) and interrupts or adapts its daily work if necessary.

Internal area of responsibility

The internal area of responsibility includes all internal processes that affect the corporate strategy itself. The internal area of responsibility is usually the responsibility of the executive management and influences important decisions, for example, which business partners to win, one's own responsibility on the market, fair and realistic growth planning, and healthy profitability. In the ideal case, the moral compass of the company plays an important role in decision-making: However, it is usually difficult to judge from the outside to what extent a company takes its internal area of responsibility seriously. However, a CSR management that is visible to the outside world is at least an indication that the internal strategy also takes moral principles into account.

Central area of responsibility

The central area of responsibility includes all those actions of a company whose effects on the environment and society can be measured directly. This includes CO_2 emissions and air pollution as well as working conditions for employees. This also includes responsible supply chain management, as cooperation with morally questionable companies ultimately supports their corporate policies. CSR in the middle area of responsibility is the most difficult to coordinate for many large corporations but has gained considerably in importance. This applies not only to the environment and society, but also to the own employees, stakeholders, and the company's reputation. For many companies, the customer is by far the most important stakeholder. If a company does not take its social responsibility towards its customers seriously, this is often due to poor CSR management (if any).

Other stakeholders are listed below:

- **Equity and debt capital providers:** Investors have a clear interest not only in the success of the company, but also in fair cooperation. Listed companies are threatened with considerable damage if their dealings with business partners and investors are morally questionable or dishonest.
- **Clients:** Companies that supply products should not deceive their customers. Especially in the case of consumer goods such as food, a company has the responsibility to correctly inform the customer about the preparation and composition of the product. The origin of the product or the building materials and raw materials used is also important to many customers.
- **Residents:** Companies located in cities have a responsibility towards local residents. The company should not have a negative impact on the quality of life of the residents. This applies, for example, to noise pollution and environmental pollution. In many countries, people still suffer from harsh living conditions because large factories ignore their social responsibility. In the worst case, companies cause drinking water pollution, unacceptable noise, air pollution, and damage to surrounding flora and fauna. If such injustices become public, the company is threatened not only with damage to its image, but also with problems with the law and environmental organisations.
- **Government organizations:** Companies must comply with the laws of the respective country. This also includes smooth and honest cooperation with government organizations. In production facilities, the quality standards and regulations specified by the legislator must be observed and not deceived during the corresponding controls.
- **Media:** Since corporate social responsibility is hardly subject to state control, the media often feel obliged to inform the public about corporate misconduct. However, good CSR management in principle involves an open and honest dialogue with the media. However, most journalists hardly report on the positive performance of companies, but concentrate more on the misconduct, because negative press sells better.

External area of responsibility

As part of their Corporate Social Responsibility (CSR), many companies not only concentrate on internal processes, but also assume social responsibility outside their own operations. Here are a few examples of what can be included in this external area of responsibility (which is often equated with the term "corporate citizenship"):

- **Donations:** Corporate Giving is the most popular means of actively living corporate responsibility. sometimes, these donations are linked to the sale of goods and are thus intended to contribute to higher sales figures, for example, by promising to donate part of the profit per product sold to a good cause. Many companies also take part in events such as marathons and fundraising galas in which they allow employees to participate.

– **Sponsorship:** Companies often also fulfil their social responsibility by sponsoring special initiatives or supporting associations that pursue charitable goals. In return, companies are positively mentioned by these institutions and benefit from being associated with them. Frequently, companies can also improve their reputation with local residents in this way, for example, by sponsoring city projects and regional events.

– **Social activities:** Companies are often willing to give employees time off if they want to carry out social activities. In the meantime, this is usually even regulated in employment contracts (e.g., and employees are granted half a working day per quarter). Many companies are therefore prepared to support and even pay for their employees' social activities (by recording these activities as working time).

So, we see from the details above that the dimensions of CSR are multifaceted. For example, a small local company acts in a socially responsible manner when it is involved in a particular location, for example, by providing financial aid for humanitarian institutions. A small financial injection for the local city park can also mean a positive CSR. Below you will find examples of socially responsible companies that have excelled in the field of corporate social responsibility.

Examples for socially responsible retailers
IKEA has committed to environmental and social initiatives
IKEA is one of the most recognized companies in the world when it comes to social responsibility and sustainability. In 2019, IKEA was ranked 2nd in Sweden's most Sustainable Brands Index. IKEA is always looking for better, socially responsible ways to create, sell, and recycle their products, and the company has committed to a variety of environmental and social initiatives. Two examples of such initiatives are IKEA's switch to a lighting range comprised entirely of energy-efficient LEDs and the IKEA Family Sell-Back program. With these campaigns, customers are educated on the benefits of switching to LED bulbs and encouraged to sell back unwanted furniture and home goods that may otherwise end up in landfills. Customers can return furniture products in every IKEA store to be recycled at no additional charge. They'll even do home pickup for a small fee (Foster, 2019).

Both programs demonstrate a commitment to not only their customer experience but their environmental footprint as a company. This aligns their values with those of their customers', creating a greater emotional relationship that will prompt customers to choose them over a competitor.

So, IKEA uses social responsibility to retain their customers by offering affordable, energy-efficient products customers can't find anywhere else. Customers can also take advantage of IKEA's recycling program that disposes of used products on the customer's behalf (Foster, 2019).

H&M provides sustainability reports and supplier details
H&M is one the greatest examples of social responsibility at work in the fashion industry. With an independent site, customers have access to sustainability reports and supplier details that clearly outline H&M's commitment to ethical and environmentally-conscious business practices.

Not only is H&M highly transparent about the way their products are made and their plans for a more sustainable future, but the brand has also launched a series of recycling initiatives that invite customers to get involved. Their H&M conscious line is built around products made entirely from recycled fabrics and organic cotton and features prominently on their website and in stores.

In addition to their commitment to environmentally friendly products, H&M also launched a garment collecting initiative to "close the fashion loop." Customers are encouraged to bring any unwanted clothes to an H&M store in exchange for 15% off their next purchase. Since the program launched·in 2013, the company has collected over 40,000 tonnes of used clothing that may have otherwise ended up in a landfill. So, H&M uses social responsibility as a customer retention tool by selling eco-friendly products that customers can feel good about. They also incentivize future purchases by offering discounts to those who recycle used garments in store.

Levi Strauss & Co.'s workers have launched a Workers' Well-Being initiative
Levi's is another company that focuses its efforts on CSR. Levi's approach is to reduce their environmental footprint by acting in human rights and environmental causes. Levi Strauss & Co.'s Worker Well-Being (WWB) initiative was launched in 2011. It aims to improve the lives of the women and men who make the company's products with factory-based programs that address issues related to health, financial security, and gender equality.

The initiative operates on the premise that when workers are healthy, satisfied with their job, and engaged at work, factory productivity will increase. Today, more than 219,000 apparel workers, working in 113 of our supplier's factories, have benefitted from these factory-based programs. More than 65% of the entire product volume is already made in factories that have WWB initiatives. At participating sites, managers begin by surveying workers to understand their most pressing needs. Factories then partner with local nonprofit organizations to implement programs that address the needs identified in the survey. To date, more than 90% of WWB sites offer health interventions and approximately 50% provide financial literacy workshops. For example, supplier factories in Bangladesh, India, and other countries offer on-site health trainings to female workers – covering critical topics such as nutrition, sanitation, and menstrual hygiene – in partnership with local nonprofit organizations.

Three quarters of participating factories report improvements in worker engagement, and over half report improved satisfaction and lower absenteeism (Almeida, 2020).

1.6.2.4 Slow versus fast fashion and collaborative consumption

The fashion industry in general and the textile and clothing life cycle consume more energy and water than do the product life cycles of any other industry (Black & Hilary, 2012). The combination of speeded-up fashion cycles, increased rates of consumption and falling prices of clothing has created growth in fashion waste. Perceived value of apparel has declined, and clothes have become a disposable commodity (Black & Hilary, 2012). In addition, overconsumption of fashion items has become a problem in terms of increased waste production and environmental issues and has been provoked by the emergence of "fast fashion," which is defined as trendy low-cost clothing items produced by international fashion companies that often involve unsustainable production processes (Shephard & Pookulangara, 2014).

Slow fashion is the counterpart to fast fashion. This fashion movement is a component of sustainable fashion consumption. Slow fashion items have a life span of several years and are normally of high quality. The main aim of slow fashion is not to present the latest fashion in the shortest possible time and on a regular basis, but to offer high-quality items that are sustainably produced and can be worn for a long period of time. All companies involved in a slow fashion value chain pay meticulous attention to sustainable production and logistics, as they are aware of the negative effects on the environment and on individuals. One of the main focuses is to avoid the use of any kind of toxins in the production of these sustainable fabrics.

Second-hand fashion is also part of the slow fashion movement, as it uses much less energy than the production of new clothing. Waste and over-consumption should be avoided. The procurement and resale of these fashion items is many times more energy-efficient than the production process of a new garment.

What is more, sharing has been around since human beings have lived together. Behind the concept of economic sharing there are various drivers. The main driver in the process of sharing goods and services between suppliers and consumers is the internet. The necessary framework conditions of the share economy are made possible by permanent access to the mobile devices.

In a so-called *sharing economy*, which stands for the business model that individuals rent or "share" things like their cars, homes, and personal time to other individuals (peer-to-peer), availability has a higher value than possessions. This peer-to-peer sharing initiatives offer opportunities and numerous possible applications for companies. Consumption is less desirable for many people as awareness of the environment and sustainability increases and possessions are perceived as a burden. The term sharing economy describes the economic transformation of the ownership of things to an economy of sharing or common benefit. Instead of sellers and buyers, the focus is on providers and users. Finished products are no longer sold. Through networks that are created, companies are operated jointly. Ownership is no longer the first priority for consumers either, but the pursuit of availability.

Over the last couple of years, due to these developments described above, a new "phenomenon" has emerged focusing on more sustainability within the retail sector: *collaborative consumption*. This "phenomenon" has disrupted various established industries around the globe, including the fashion industry. Consumers' attitudes towards ownership and consumption behaviour have changed during the last couple of years. Whereas consumption and materialistic values were praised throughout the 20th century, today, consumers prefer to pay for the short experience of using or accessing a product rather than owning it (Chen, 2009).

Consumers have started turning their backs on the traditional consumer-oriented paradigm and over-consumption and are progressively looking for ways that downshift or simplify their lives. Reasons for that mind shift are varied but may stem from bad experiences in the market or retail sector, societal, and cultural changes as well as an alteration of consumer's individual needs, values, and expectations.

Collaborative consumption is driven by a variety of factors including the global recession, anti-hyper-consumerism, cost-consciousness as well as awareness of the need for a waste-reducing and sustainable living (Gansky, 2010). One of the main drivers are technological advances, such as the internet and social media, which allow new ways of accessing and sharing. By using information technology, products and services can be reused, distributed and shared at the right time and location to the right customer (Gansky, 2010).

Within the fashion industry many collaborative consumption concepts and business models are developing, for example, clothing swaps, fashion leasing, and other sharing concepts, like charity shops or second-hand markets. Various product service systems offer the possibility of renting or lending luxury as well as fast fashion items for a limited period.

Rent the Runway – The Real Sustainable Fashion Movement
Rent the Runway (www.renttherunway.com) is an online service providing designer dress and accessory rentals, including jewellery, handbags, lingerie, tights, shapewear, and cosmetics. The platform's mission is to "make women feel empowered and self-confident every single day" and "to build a better future for fashion" (Rent the Runway, 2018).

Rent the Runway started in 2009 as a purely e-commerce company. Later it opened brick-and-mortar retail locations in large American cities, for example, New York City, Chicago, Washington, San Francisco, Los Angeles, etc. Customers can visit one of these stores, work with a personal stylist, and either take items directly with them or book dresses and accessories for future events.

As of October 2016, the firm has over 6 million customers, 975 employees, and the team is constantly adding new designers and expanding offerings. Today they partner with more than 550 designers, including well-known designer and luxury fashion brands, representing a myriad of different styles. Rent the Runway has also served as a launching pad for emerging talents all over the world.

The business concept is part of the "access economy" along with companies like Netflix and Spotify, which favour access over ownership. Here it must be mentioned that the average woman throws away 82 pounds of clothing per year. Therefore, renting clothes and accessories is a more sustainable way of being trendy and fashionable.

At the end of the season, we extend the life cycles of our garments through our sample sales and donations to organizations like Operation Prom.

The business model is like follows: Customers can rent one of the firm's designer clothing for a 4- or 8-day period for as low as 10% of the retail price through their traditional platform, RTR Reserve. Rent the Runway carries apparel in sizes 0 to 22, depending on the designer. Each dress rental includes a back-up size at no additional cost to ensure it fits. Customers can get a second dress style for an additional fee. Rental prices include the dry cleaning and care of the garments.

In March of 2016 the company launched Rent the Runway Unlimited, the first fashion subscription service to give women access to designer clothes and accessories for a flat monthly fee. Its customers select four pieces on the site and can keep each item for as long as they want or swap them out for new selections. The subscription costs $159 per month and shipping, dry cleaning, and insurance are included. In October 2017, the company announced a new, lower-priced tier of membership called RTR Update. Customers select four pieces and keep them for a month. Customers can select four new items and return their previous items at any time (Rent the Runway, 2018).

To summarize, collaborative consumption is a new approach to consumer access of goods and services based on an interdependent peer-to-peer model. The collaborative model is one in which consumers are much more frequently producers or providers as well, and individuals cooperate to serve the needs of a given community. The emphasis is on individual empowerment and the efficient use and distribution of resources rather than private ownership. Elements of the collaborative business model include bartering, sharing, gifting, lending, leasing, or renting.

This sharing economy initiatives are based on the ability and the preference for individuals to rent or borrow goods rather than buy and own them. The three primary drivers are:
- Economic driver: more efficient and resilient use of (financial) resources
- Environmental driver: more efficient, sustainable, and innovative use of natural resources
- Community driver: deeper social and personal connections among people and considerations for others

There are several requirements for the functioning of a sharing economy. One of the most important requirements is the trust between strangers because normally the individuals who are willing to share products or services don't know each other and have hardly any references. Moreover, there must exist a critical mass of users, companies, customers, producers or service providers or members. All these stakeholders should have in common the belief in the effective management of common resources. Finally, idling capacity must exist, otherwise a sharing economy business model would not work or make sense.

Literature differentiates between three sharing economy systems (Wagner, Kuhndt, Lagomarsino, & Mattar, 2015):
- Redistribution markets (redistributing things from where they are not needed to someone or somewhere they're needed); for example, Thebookswap (https://thebookswap.in/): a swapsite for books; ebay (https://www.ebay.com/): an online marketplace for buying and selling products
- Product service systems (allowing members to pay for the benefit of using a product without needing to own it outright); for example, Uber (http://www.uber.com): an app-based system that allows people to provide a driver service using their own cars;
- Collaborative Lifestyles platforms (allowing for the sharing and exchange of less tangible assets such as time, skills, money, experience, or space). The business models can be monetised or nonmonetised. For example, Airbnb (https://www.airbnb.at): allows people to rent out their homes, apartments, or rooms to travellers.

1.6.2.5 Social supermarkets as a sustainable retail format

Social supermarkets (SSMs) have developed as a unique retail format across several European countries. SSMs sell food and consumer products at low, symbolic prices to a restricted group of people living in or at risk of poverty. The products offered are mainly provided free of charge by partnership companies (e.g., manufacturers, retailers). While these products are consumable, they are not saleable anymore because of minor quality deficiencies, surplus production, or proximity to the expiration date. Therefore, availability of the products is limited to what is supplied. Social supermarkets are usually nonprofit organizations and operate with the support of volunteers or governmental support.

Social supermarkets are comparable to conventional supermarkets that operate in stationary outlets and primarily sell food and consumer products. The main difference of SSMs as compared to conventional supermarkets lies in a modified implementation of various retail marketing mix instruments, for example, the limited assortment and a significantly lower consumer price of approximately 50% to 70% less than regular market prices (Social supermarkets, 2019).

The target group of SSMs, as already mentioned above, is restricted to financially poor people, and access to the stores is controlled with the help of identification cards that are issued upon the presentation of an income statement. So, the main goals of SSMs are to support financially poor people, prevent the wastage of food, and provide job opportunities for long-term unemployed people. Therefore, SSMs are seen by the European Commission (2019a) as a simple and efficient solution beneficial to all stakeholders (Holweg & Lienbacher, 2016).

Social supermarkets have emerged to fill a gap in the grocery landscape providing a social safety net. In the short term, these initiatives provide a degree of choice and dignity to those people who are food insecure, helping them mainly to save money. They help in mitigating the effects of poverty and social vulnerability. Their impact on the increasing numbers of people turning to them can not be underestimated. Nevertheless, social supermarkets are at risk to survive due to the complexity and unpredictability of food surplus supply links, a heavy reliance on volunteers, and their financial viability. This raises questions about their sustainability and the positive outcomes they expect to achieve in supporting vulnerable people.

If social supermarkets become normalized, that may delay the solution to some of the deep structural problems in the food system and economy, which such initiatives emerged as a response to. Their vision is to reduce food waste, but they rely on a regular and a continuous supply of food surplus, which undercuts the prevention of food waste as a priority. Their social mission is to support people out of food poverty, but they work closely within a market system and a food industry that has faced criticism for creating greater inequalities through low-wage work. Their ability to provide healthy nutritious food is variable and often limited because of their dependence on food surplus supply of manufacturers and retailers (Saxena, 2018).

Examples of social supermarkets in Austria
Vinzi Markt
In Vinzi markets, all products that were previously simply discarded are sold at a maximum price of 30% of normal value.

This includes incorrectly packaged or labelled, slightly damaged, or other goods that are not suitable for conventional sales, but whose quality is nevertheless guaranteed. Also, goods shortly before the expiry date, which have previously been checked for their suitability for consumption by means of random sampling. Expired goods are marked as such. No sale of alcohol.

All financially needy citizens of Graz* who do not have an income of more than 950 Euro/month, or 1,450 Euro for two people, plus 150 Euro per child, are entitled to buy.

The shopping authorisation card is available in the shops during opening hours. A proof of income, the registration form and a photo ID are required. The identity card is limited to 1 year. There is also a shopping limit of 30 euros/week. This corresponds approximately to an actual value of goods of 120 to 150 Euros (Vinzi, 2019).

SOMA
The idea of the so-called SOMA markets was founded in 1999 and tries to support people with low income on the one hand and to counteract the waste of food on the other hand. With a shopping pass people can buy at the soma at their own conditions–usually the goods are offered at a price that should not exceed one third of the usual food discount price. The social market is not a competition to a supermarket, because despite the efforts to offer a certain variety of goods, no one is spared the trip to the regular supermarket. Basic foods with no or very long expiry date (e.g., sugar, pasta) rarely find their way to soma.

Goods that are damaged during transport are close to their sell-by date or come from overproduction, but are fully fit for consumption, are offered at low prices at soma. This redistribution of unused resources saves industry and trade high disposal costs and at the same time offers people at risk of poverty the opportunity to buy everyday necessities at a reasonable price (Caritas, 2019).

Several criteria and principles for a social market were developed and defined (SOMA, 2019):
- Only goods are offered that are produced by the cooperation partner in traditional distribution channels can no longer be sold.
- Goods are provided by the partner free of charge.
- The focus is on goods for daily use – there is no entitlement to full assortment.
- Alcohol and cigarettes are not traded.
- Goods are traded at symbolic prices (in the case of the social market) or free of charge to social institutions (in the case of LEO).
- The operator acts in a charitable way, profits are reinvested in social projects.
- The operator complies with the legal requirements for the food trade.
- The buyer is seen as a customer and not as a charity recipient.
- The goods are presented and placed accordingly.
- An identity card is issued after checking the income.
- Purchases are recorded and are limited to personal use.
- They are passed on to needy persons or social institutions with care services.

1.6.3 Sustainable marketing communication

This chapter discusses sustainable marketing communication in general and communication strategies to encourage ethical consumer behaviour. This chapter also takes up the issue of overstating "green" communication and the negative consequences.

Effective marketing communication and "greenwashing"

When consumers are asked what comes to their mind when they hear the term "ethical product," it is associated with "fair working conditions, a sustainable business model, organic and environmentally friendly materials or ingredients, certifications, and traceability". Therefore, these are important issues to be addressed in an effective marketing communication strategy.

Moreover, marketing communication is most effective when sustainable consumption issues are linked to values that are harmonious and congruent to the values the target group holds important, for instance, family health, attractiveness, or economic value (Martin & Schouten, 2014). The advertisements should include social and environmental messages about ethical fashion (Yulan Wang, Lo, & Shum, 2012).

The AMA (i.e., American Marketing Association) (AMA, 2019) defines "green marketing" as follows "Green marketing refers to the development and marketing of products that are presumed to be environmentally safe (i.e., designed to minimize negative effects on the physical environment or to improve its quality). This term may also be used to describe efforts to produce, promote, package, and reclaim products in a manner that is sensitive or responsive to ecological concerns." So, "green products," "ethical products," and "green marketing" are important issues when it comes to future developments and changes in our retail landscape.

But if such "green" claims and sustainability issues are exaggerated, misleading, or not verifiable, companies might be accused of so-called *greenwashing,* which leads to a negative brand image or company's reputation. Manchiraju and Sadachar (2014) suggest that companies should develop communication strategies that focus on self-enhancement values, such as hedonism, power, and achievement because these values are to intentions to engage in ethical consumer behaviour. They also suggest that older populations, especially females, should be targeted in ethical marketing campaigns, as women and baby boomers, for instance, are more likely to engage in ethical consumption. When it comes to the younger age group (e.g., Generation Y), which is normally very concerned with how they are perceived by their peers, targeting opinion leaders is likely to be efficient when it comes to changing a certain behaviour (McNeill & Moore, 2015). Social media is especially important for this age group. Therefore, social media campaigns with role models and opinion leaders, promoting ethical consumer behaviour, might increase interest in sustainable fashion.

Sustainable marketing communication must have certain aspects to be successful (Martin & Schouten, 2014):

- Accountability and transparency: a company should be openly accountable for its actions and expose business and marketing practices to outside observers
- Credibility: consumers should regard companies' claims as credible, for instance by third-party verification and reporting
- Consumer education: consumers should be well-informed about the need for sustainability, the consumption of green products and services, and its benefits and ethical business practices
- Value congruence: a marketing message has to be consistent with a target consumer's values by providing accurate information

To summarize, the relationship between consumer education (knowledge and awareness) and support from the supply side (designers, manufacturing, and retailing), but also from the government and other external stakeholders, are the most important aspects of establishing sustainable business and business practices.

The example in the box below provides information on sustainable brands and their ethical practices in the fashion retail sector. There already exist a lot of fashion companies that have a sustainable performance and others, mainly fast fashion companies, are constantly trying to improve their performance regarding sustainability.

Sustainable brands and ethical practices in the fashion industry

The fashion industry faces a lot of opportunities in regard to sustainable business practices, concerning environmental, social and ecological issues, but it also faces some barriers. Black (2008) identified the following barriers as the biggest ones: The fact that fashion is regarded as disposable and is turned into waste as soon as an item gets old or unfashionable and "the basic tenet of consumption for the sake of consumption" (Black, 2008, 63).

Opportunities are many and varied. Digitalization in general and new technologies will have an important impact on sustainable fashion. For instance, 3D body scanning and automated custom-fitting systems have the potential to move parts of clothing production from mass fashion to individualized fashion. It can be assumed that well-fitted clothing, well-aligned with personal tastes, give more enjoyment and have longer life cycles than ready-to-wear clothing.

Furthermore, mass customization is a promising way for creating more customer-centric products that perfectly fit customers' needs. Mass customization can provide environmental benefits in all phases of a product's life cycle (Piller & Steiner, 2008):

- During the manufacturing process: no storage of finished products is needed and there exists no overproduction
- During the use of the product: customized products provide better fulfilment of customer needs; products will be handled with greater care
- At the end of a product's life cycle: efficient recycling and reuse of product components due to a stronger customer-manufacturer relationship ("crade-to-cradle")

Literature research has shown that there do already exist various websites which help consumers to identify whether a brand is sustainable or not and to which degree. For instance, "The sustainable fashion directory" (http://sustainablefashiondirectory.com/about/) provides information on ethical practices by fashion companies so that consumers can shop responsibly, without spending a lot of their time doing research. Engagement of the customers is necessary to create a sustainable fashion industry. But, what is more, the supply side and the demand side have to work together on ethical issues within the whole value chain and make fashion more sustainable.

Competitive advantage for companies adopting sustainable practices

Fashion brands must develop competitive advantages to be successful in the long run. Competitive advantages could be generated by adopting various sustainable practices, for example by developing new sustainable business models or by introducing innovations in fabrics, like new methods of creating fabrics and enhanced fabric materials or smart fabrics.

Innovations in fabrics

Some retail and manufacturing companies, within the apparel industry, have already started to use sustainable fabric materials for producing their products. Their products are made of bio-based synthetic fibers from renewable resources (e.g., sugar cane, corn sugars, agricultural waste, etc.), instead of petroleum-based synthetic fibers, which leave a lower carbon footprint during the production process, and new materials like synthetic spider silk (Weinswig, September 2016). They also use water- and stain-resistant cotton fabrics, which help to reduce water and energy necessary for the washing process (Weinswig, September 2016).

Another innovation field are so-called *smart fabrics*. "Smart fabrics are textiles with embedded technology that enables clothing made from them either to perform functions that regular garments can not perform or to have special characteristics that regular clothing does not have" (Weinswig, November 2016). Innovative companies have developed nanofabrics and integrate silver nanoparticles into garments to make them stain-, odor-resistant, and waterproof. Another category is connected fabrics which have embedded digital, wearable technology (Weinswig, November 2016). Smart apparel offers the possibility to connect to other devices and collect and analyse data or offer additional features like music storage, file-playing features, charging batteries, tracking and tracing, etc.

All in all, smart apparel provides a huge potential and new business opportunities for the apparel industry, especially for sportswear and accessories manufacturer and retailers, although innovations in fabrics involve higher investment in R&D and generally higher production cost, which means that customers would have to pay a premium price for these products. Therefore, many of these innovations are not relevant to the mass market, at least not now (Weinswig, September 2016).

Another competitive advantage can be generated by developing new methods of creating fabrics. Examples are biomimicry, spray-on fabricant, enzyme-grown fabrics, or recycled materials.

The core idea behind biomimicry is that nature has already solved many of our problems and has developed sustainable solutions by emulating nature's time-tested patterns and strategies (Biomimicry Institute, 2016). For example, by mimicking the way colour is produced in the Morpho butterfly's wing, the fibre appears coloured without any dying. Iridescence in the butterfly's wing is formed through structural or physical colour, rather than chemical colour (Donna Sgro, 2012).

Spray-on fabricant creates an instant sprayable nonwoven fabric. This liquid suspension is applied via spray gun or aerosol on to any surface. The fabric is formed by the cross linking of fibers. It helps to create more customer-centric products that perfectly fit customers' needs and personalize the wardrobe (Fabrican Ltd., 2011).

New sustainable business models

Another competitive advantage for companies willing to adopt sustainable practices can be generated through innovative business models online apparel and accessory rentals, especially suitable for higher-end designer merchandise. These services allow customers to borrow fashion items for a limited period at lower costs than buying these items (Weinswig, September 2016). This business model is especially suitable for millennials (born between 1980 and 2000) because they put far more emphasis on corporate responsibility and sustainability in their purchase decisions than other generations (Weinswig, September 2016).

Online collaborative consumption for apparel and accessories helps to expand an item's life cycle, decreases waste production, declutters people's homes, and reduces, in general, over-consumption of fashion items.

Virtual fashion in general and digital prototyping is a business model that helps to reduce the amount of waste produced during the sampling stage of designing a fashion line and to promote a zero-waste fashion industry but also to reduce shipping transactions. Through virtual fashion platforms, for example, My Virtual Model, customers can make use of virtual models that can be personalized to look like the customer, and virtually try on clothes before they buy them (Calderin, 2009). One of the main advantages is that customers don't have to order clothes to try them on physically or to visit a brick-and-mortar store that helps to reduce the number of returns and the carbon footprint, and provides the advantage of customizing products (user-centric fashion).

Green marketing communication and social impact

Nowadays, incorporating sustainability into a retailer's communication plan is a fundamental element of the company's success. Studies have shown that consumers around the world are more likely to be loyal to a retailer that works with sustainable practices in daily business. Highlighting the retailer's sustainability effort, like lowering emissions, improved energy efficiency or equitable working environments, and being transparent to the public, can be profitable and the retailer can benefit by receiving positive PR and gaining new target groups.

Communication of sustainability efforts on the example of Unilever

Unilever heavily relies on metrics and reporting to communicate its sustainability efforts to the public. In fact, the packaged goods company's website (https://www.unilever.com/sustainable-living/our-strategy/un-sustainable-development-goals/) is filled with updates on its performance in real time. Interactive charts display economic, social, and environmental performance data. Stakeholders are given the opportunity to view Unilever's environmental impacts and data and share information via social media. In fact, stakeholders, including the Unilever Sustainable Living Plan Steering Team, external advisors, and consumers, can offer feedback about Unilever's efforts.

The company has recognised that the only business model for Unilever is one in which the planet and society thrive. That's why in 2010 the company launched the Unilever Sustainable Living Plan (USLP). It is the company's blueprint for sustainable growth, which responds to the challenges and opportunities of an increasingly resource-constrained and unequal world.

The company's vision for a new way of doing business is one that delivers growth by serving society and the planet. By inspiring every brand, in every country, to make a positive social impact and reduce the environmental footprint, the USLP harnesses the company's scale and influence to help bring about a better world (Unilever, 2019).

By being completely transparent, and updating reports on an ongoing basis, Unilever has been able to reach a broader audience, while capturing the trust of their current stakeholders and consumers. Their sophisticated and interactive website will set an example for other companies when looking to integrate their sustainable efforts and marketing communications.

Sustainability is a powerful tool in marketing communication, but it must be honest and rigorous with transparency and that is why many companies are not willing to go in this direction. Sustainability must focus on meeting the needs of the present without compromising the ability of future generations to meet their own needs. Moreover, most companies only change their daily business practices when consumers demand it, and that demand is increasing with younger generations. But consumers of all generations use green products the same way they do any other product, often wasteful. Consumers give their money to greener brands but still use the products wastefully. Like water bottles, easily recyclable, which normally tend to end up in landfills.

Market research has shown that 87% of consumers are concerned about the environment and would shop with that concern in mind, but only 33% said that they have already bought green products or were ready to do so. Especially the younger generation who demands more sustainable products. Many brands and retailers have tried to reduce their impact on the environment by making changes to products and suggestions to customers. With these actions, the brand changes and suggests greener practices to consumers, but the consumer is still left to act on their own. If the product and its packaging are produced in an eco-friendly manner, but consumers still send them to landfills, is the product actually green? Experts are sure to get consumers to change their behaviour, brands must present products and services in a different way, reframing a new, green action as essential and "normal" and it seem easy, obvious, and beneficial to the consumer. This so-called *intention-action gap* plays out in many ways in daily consumption. There's a small group of consumers who are fiercely green and will spend money on green products no matter what, but there's a larger group of consumers who avoid green products. So, the main objective must be to win the largest group of consumers, the people in the middle (about 60% of all consumers fall in this middle group). This middle group is more likely to be won over by ease, price, and quality. If a green product and its equivalent nongreen substitute have the same cost and quality, the average consumer will normally choose the greener product (AMA, 2019).

Now, most green products still aren't equal in price and quality. By advertising a product's sustainable values, marketers are reaching only the already existing green customers, people who are already consumers of these products. Many brands try to use alarmist tactics to reach the middle group, for example, by showing a polar bear on a shrinking block of ice to illustrate what happens if you don't buy this product. Normally the average consumer will turn away from fear-based marketing campaigns. Therefore, it is more effective if brands communicate in an easy-to-understand way, so the product benefits the middle group and gets people engaged. A customer that feels good buying a green product is likely to become a loyal customer. So, being green is a perception issue for retailers, brands, and consumers. Without knowing it, consumers likely ask themselves a question when they see a green product: "Is this something I can actually use, or is it just something I'll waste money on so I can feel good about myself?"

To summarize, if done correctly, retailers and brands can lead consumers to act greener, namely by "visible" evidence of the company expending effort on environmental efforts. Green innovations can mean more loyal customers, more money saved, and a better brand reputation and, above all, is promoting positive change in a consumption culture (AMA, 2019).

2 Marketing mix in retailing

The traditional marketing mix by McCarthy (1975) includes the elements product, price, place, and promotion. These four elements are not sufficient when it comes to a retailer's marketing mix because some more elements are important in a retail context. Therefore, three more elements must be included in a retailer's marketing mix: presentation, people and process.

All eight elements will be described in more detail in the following subchapters.

2.1 Product and innovation

The first "P" in a retailer's marketing mix is the element "product." This "P" deals with the actual things that are sold to the consumer, whether it is a physical product, or an intangible service. The company must consider what the customer is expecting and needing from the product, then look to meeting those needs and expectations.

When it comes to product and innovation, retailers are more innovation adopters than developers. They are more interested in selling products and services, while advanced technologies are mainly used to enhance the service delivering process. The retail industry can be viewed as a service-oriented industry subject to continuous innovations. As service-related processes, the involvement of consumers may increase the quality of provided service. For this reason, consumers' acceptance of innovations, especially new technologies, in terms of attitude, behavioural intention, and effective usage of the systems is a critical factor when it comes to technology selection and adoption.

This consumer behaviour can be explained by the Technology Acceptance Model (TAM) by Davis et al. (1989), which is widely used to identify the acceptance and adoption of new technologies by consumers. This model is described in detail in Chapter 1.4.1.6. According to this model two factors are influencing the attitude towards the behaviour and thereby also the intention to perform that behaviour – the perceived ease of use and the perceived usefulness of the technology. The perceived ease of use is described by Davis (1989) as "the degree to which a person believes that using a particular system would be free of effort." The perceived usefulness is defined as "the degree to which a person believes that using a particular system would enhance his or her job." Users are more likely adopting a technology if they believe that using the technology will help them to improve their job performance or in the retail setting, technology will provide an added value, like to save time or money, to provide entertainment, etc.

Main drivers for innovations in the retail sector are (Pantano, 2014):
- **Market orientation:** based on three main activities: understanding and predicting future consumers' needs and behaviours, distribution of gathered information

https://doi.org/10.1515/9783110543827-003

across departments, and organization wide responsiveness to such information. Market orientation focuses on consumers' behaviour, on competitors' strategies, and interfunctional coordination.

– **Entrepreneurial innovativeness:** refers to a company's ability to innovate and is linked to the capacity to adopt an innovation before the competitors do. Entrepreneurial innovativeness is also linked to the entrepreneur's personality in terms of openness to novelty and willingness to be the first adopter in a particular field.

– **Human capital:** retailer's size and entrepreneur's personality play an important role on the ability to innovate. For example, the role of an entrepreneur's innovativeness is marked especially in the case of small and medium-sized enterprises (SME), where the CEO and entrepreneur coincide in one person. Larger retailers have usually more financial resources if compared to SMEs, which have normally limited capacities when it comes to research and development or technical skills and are more focused on avoiding risks that may negatively affect their cash flow.

– **Organizational characteristics:** dynamic capabilities and ability of innovating, by including the capability to react to environmental change. The adjective "dynamic" refers to the ability to perceive environmental changes and to behave consequently, by renewing competencies, whereas the term "capabilities" emphasizes the role of strategic management in the process of integrating and reconfiguring internal and external organizational skills and competencies for the innovation objectives.

– **Progresses in technology:** continuous progresses in technology (a so-called technology push) as strong innovation drivers, mainly to enhance or simplify organizational processes.

There is a strong relationship between the product adoption process and the product life cycle (PLC). Both have a focus on new products. The product adoption process considers the "stage" that the consumer is in relation to the product (see Figure 2.1). In contrast, the product life cycle model indicates sales depending on the PLC stage. The product life cycle model proposes that four things are implied (Kotler & Armstrong, 2006):

– each product has a limited time of life,
– product sales depend on the particular stage in the product's life cycle
– product sales and profits vary at different stages
– each product requires different strategies regarding marketing, financial, manufacturing, human resources, etc. at each of these stages

The product life cycle is a frequently used, predictive instrument for forecasting marketing requirements and assisting in the planning of long-term product strategies. It was introduced to explain the expected life cycle of a particular product from the idea

to its obsolescence. Kotler and Armstrong (2006) divide the product life cycle into five
distinct stages (see Figure 2.1):
- product development
- introduction
- growth
- maturity
- decline

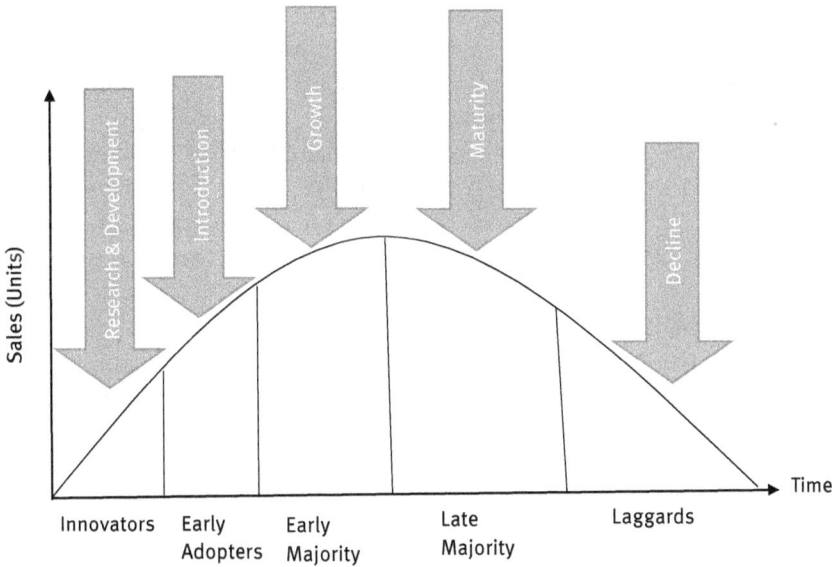

Figure 2.1: **Product adoption and the product life cycle.**
Source: Kotler & Bliemel, 2001

Kotler et al. (2001) assume that the objective of every new product is to meet customers' needs with a high quality at the lowest possible cost to generate the highest possible profit. However, during the first stage – the product development stage – sales
are low and revenues are negative since there are high investments in research and
development.

The product introduction stage includes the launch of product with its requirements to have maximum impact at the moment of sale. The main objective in this
stage is to build awareness of their products among potential customers. This is the
point when companies must focus on their marketing mix, especially on communication (P = promotion). During the next stage – the growth stage – product sales are
increasing, and it is the right time to focus on increasing the market share. Competitors try to copy or offer similar products. Consequently, product modifications are
necessary. Promotion and advertising continue, but not in the extent that was in the
introduction stage.

The next stage in the PLC is the maturity stage. In this stage the market becomes saturated which is characterised by the fact that competitors offer alternative products. Maturity stage is the period of the highest returns from the product. Sometimes it is difficult for a company to conceptualize the decline signals of a product. Usually a product decline is caused by decline in sales, change in trends, or consumer demands or unfavourable economic conditions. At this stage market becomes saturated and the company tries to keep loyal customers before it finally withdraws the product from the market. A withdrawal of the product is not always possible or useful. When the product is a so-called flagship product, a major product of the company that made the company well-known or is the most advanced in the product line (e.g., Apple's Mac and iPhone), a withdrawal of a product should not be done, also when the product is in the decline stage.

In the decline stage, sometimes already in the maturity stage, innovation could help to create new demand and extend or change a product's life cycle. These innovations can be large or small, radical or incremental, to products, processes, or services. The result should be that the retailers offer something new that adds value to customers and creates a new demand. Innovation is always built on creativity and sometimes on invention, resulting in the creation of new knowledge and learning within a company.

The following two boxes provide an example of a radical innovation and an example of an incremental innovation.

An *incremental innovation* would mean that small improvements to an existing product or product line are made to improve a product's competitive position and to include new features to better fulfil consumers' desires and needs. Whereas a *radical innovation* would mean that there is an invention that destroys or supplants an existing business model. We start with an example of an incremental innovation.

The world's oldest denim brand Levi's uses a new laser technology

The denim brand Levi's introduced a new technology, the Levi's F.L.X. technology, a laser-powered process, which allows consumers to customise and personalise a unique distressed finish on their pair of jeans. The denim stalwart's newest service is emblematic of the ever-changing denim industry, driven by innovation and a greater focus on sustainability as demand continues to grow. By giving consumers the opportunity to design exactly what they want, laser distressing could be used to create the thousands of finishes currently on offer through traditional methods like sanding. What's more, the environmentally friendly procedure steps in line with the industry's growing preference for sustainable practises, such as using recycled water and recycled fabrics. Traditionally, labourers use chemicals and sanding blocks to create fades and finishes on a pair of jeans. It's a process that can stretch over 20 separate steps and can involve large amounts of water and over 1,000 types of chemicals.

Levi's started with an invite-only Los Angeles customisation studio in August 2018 and rolled out in 2019 (see the video https://fashionista.com/news/levis-customization-studio-laser) where consumers can pick patterns of distressing (e.g., rips, fades, etc.) on an iPad. These unique finishes are then created on a blank pair of jeans with infrared lasers operated by a digital craftsman in the studio. The laser process takes less than three minutes, and after a final hour-long wash, the jeans are ready to be taken home. The company has been testing this technology behind-the-scenes for two years.

The advantage of this laser technology is that it cuts out much of the manual labour and nearly all of the chemicals. The technology also has major cost-saving potentials. Levi's currently offers 2,000 variations of denim finishes a year. If the company could make products on-demand, it could reduce the products it needs to carry at any given point, therefore reducing especially inventory risk.

More recently, denim makers have faced growing pressure to reduce their environmental footprint, as more brands and consumers demand sustainable fashion. Jeans require enormous amounts of water to produce (up to 1,800 gallons needed to grow and harvest the cotton for a single pair of jeans) with factories requiring water for various washing and dyeing stages. Denim brands such as Levi's and G-Star Raw have already made strides in reducing harmful water usage by nearly 100%. To summarize, Levi's new laser technology is way into the right direction of more sustainable production (Chen, 2018).

The next box provides an example for a radical innovation. As the world's population will continue to grow in the years to come, food production will also have to increase. High-tech food could revolutionize the worldwide food production.

High-tech food

According to UN estimates, the world population will grow to 9.8 billion people by 2050 and two thirds of them will live in cities. While food production must therefore be greatly increased, it is increasingly threatened by climate change, monocultures, and dependence on imports. One possible solution is closed high-tech food systems in which plants are cultivated under digitally controlled conditions that are resource-efficient and require less space, water, fertilizer, and pesticides (see topic "cell factories").

These systems are referred to as vertical farming when it comes to growing significant quantities of plants in multistorey buildings within the city. Breeding and harvesting will take place fully automatically, and they will be supplied with nutrients by a closed water cycle. Different systems will be used: In hydroponics, plants are grown in an inorganic substrate instead of in soil; in the current and more efficient variant, aeroponics, the exposed roots of the plants are wetted with water by atomizers. These plant breeding systems are already being combined with the breeding of fish: The term aquaponics covers the process that combines the breeding of fish in aquaculture with the cultivation of crops in hydroponics. As automated indoor agriculture, food systems combine decentralized approaches with digitization and automation, for example, when indoor salad farms are completely managed by robots and computers in the future. Further systems are intelligent floating farms and high-tech urban agriculture.[1] High-tech food systems can generally strengthen food sovereignty in cities, regions, and contexts that can not rely sufficiently on traditional agriculture due to environmental conditions or lack of space, and at the same time support decentralisation of food production. In the long run, it will be possible to produce more efficiently on a smaller scale; food production can be integrated closer to or even directly into urban centres. However, it is unclear to what extent these systems can contribute to the future world food supply. Furthermore, the actual environmental impacts (energy, water, and land consumption) are still unclear – as is comparability with conventionally produced food. In industrialized countries with differentiated agriculture, high agricultural know-how and advanced digitalization and automation, high-tech food systems offer the opportunity to develop a wide range of product and process innovations (ITA & AIT, 2019).

2.1.1 Merchandise management

Merchandising is the process of acquiring goods or services and making them available at the right place, at the right time, in the right quantity, and to a particular target group. Merchandising in retail involves many different processes, from sourcing, assortment, pricing, to communication with the customers. The main aim of each merchandising process is to maximize profitability through a better planning of sales and inventory (Ray, 2010). Merchandise management refers to the diverse activities that contribute to the sale of products and brands to the final consumers. Every retail store has its own line of merchandise to offer to the customers. The display of the merchandise plays an important role in attracting the customers to visit the store and to increase sales.

Merchandise management sets the guiding principles for all merchandise decisions that a retailer makes. Merchandise management elements, which must be reflected, include:
– target market desires
– retailer's institutional type
– market-place positioning
– defined value chain
– supplier capabilities
– costs
– competitors
– product trends

It is the key responsibility of the merchandiser to create an attractive display to pull the customers into the store. Effective merchandising techniques are very important in the retail sector due to the fact that consumers are more demanding and the level of competition among brands has increased. To be competitive and attractive for the consumers retailers must find the right merchandise mix. This merchandise mix is a combination of merchandise variety (depth), assortment (breadth), and quality and price points. The merchandise mix must meet the needs and wants of the consumers and is a good fit for the target market (Ogden & Ogden, 2005).

Variety means the number of product lines or categories (breadth) a retailer has to offer the customers. Breadth is a term that can also be used for expressing the number of different brands within a product line. Table 2.1 shows that breadth of merchandise (number of product lines/categories) can be described along a continuum of narrow to wide. A hypermarket, for instance, carrying thousands of different articles in general and hundreds of different product lines and categories has a broad variety. A small convenience store normally carries just a few different categories and product lines and therefore has a narrow variety.

Assortment (depth) stands for the number of SKUs that a retailer has to offer within each product line or category it carries. Each category could include different types of brands, colours, or sizes. Table 2.1 shows that depth of merchandise can be

Table 2.1: Assortment and variety decisions (Source: Berman & Evans, 2013).

Assortment Depth of merchandise (number of items per category)		Variety Breadth of merchandise (number of categories)
Narrow & deep + Specialist image + Focus brings effectiveness (e.g., training of personnel, supplier relations, . . .) − Narrow market − Dependent on success of category (influenced by factors out of control) − Greater marketing effort to reach into the catching area	**Wide & deep** + Broad market + High customer traffic + One stop shopping → loyalty + No reason to be disappointed − Complex inventory management − Items with low turnover → obsolete	
Narrow & shallow + Convenience / value focus + Least costly operation + High turnover of items − Neither attractive to customers looking for one-stop-shopping neither nor for expertise → disappointed customers − Weak image (unless otherwise created) − Loyalty at risk	**Wide & shallow** + Broad market + High customer traffic + One stop shopping → some loyalty + Less complex & costly to manage − Low variety → disappointed customers − Reduced loyalty − Weak image (unless otherwise created)	

described along a continuum of shallow to deep. Therefore, the merchandise ranges from wide and deep (e.g., the assortment in a department store) to narrow and shallow (e.g., the assortment provided by a specialty retailer).

The four assortment and variety decisions shown in Table 2.1 can be explained as follows:

- **Narrow and deep:** many types of products in one or just a few product lines. These retailers are called "category killers" because their focus brings effectiveness through their specialized selection, pricing, and market penetration. Therefore, they obtain a massive competitive advantage over other retailers. Examples for category killers are Toys "R" Us, Best Buy, or Staples.
- **Narrow and shallow:** means that the retailer carries just a few types of products in one or just a few product lines, for instance, convenience stores, a small retail outlet that offers a range of everyday items, or specialty stores, a small retail outlet that focuses on selling a special product range and associated products, like a tie shop or a chocolate shop.

- **Wide and deep:** stands for many different types of products in many different product lines or categories to reach a broad target market and high customer traffic in the store. A very good example for focusing on this merchandise mix are department stores, like Macy's, Harrods, or KaDeWe.
- **Wide and shallow:** means that the retailer offers a just a few types of products in several different product lines, like discount stores. This merchandise decision aims at targeting a broad market and high customer traffic in the store. Examples are the grocery discounter Aldi or the American multinational retailer Walmart.

Assortment is one of the top three criteria, along with location and price, in determining retail patronage. In earlier years, retailers assumed that larger product assortments better met consumer needs. Broad assortments should increase the probability that consumers can fulfill their needs and wants and find their ideal product. Moreover, a broad assortment offers flexibility for variety seekers. In recent years, the number of products offered in a regular supermarket escalated from 6,000 SKUs in the 1980s to over 30,000 SKUs in the early 1990s. However, broad assortments also have disadvantages. First, this large number of SKUs results in higher inventory costs and more out-of-stocks for retailers. Second, these higher inventory costs make it difficult for conventional supermarkets to compete against the price-oriented retail formats, such as discount stores or hypermarkets.

However, consumer assortment perceptions were found to not be a one-to-one function of the number of items offered, as consumers do not process assortment information in a great amount of detail. Instead, studies showed that consumers were not sensitive to an SKU reduction by 25%–50% in the popcorn category if the size of the shelf space was held constant and their favourite item was still available. In fact, consumer perceptions increased following a 25% SKU reduction if shelf space was held constant. This increase in assortment perception was due to popular SKUs being duplicated, which made it easier for consumers to find their favourite products. Another study has shown similar results. The leading five product categories (accounting for 80% of sales) were subjected to a 54% SKU reduction at two test stores, and assortment perceptions in the test stores were compared against those in two control stores. In-store intercepts with customers revealed no change in assortment perceptions, but customers did report that it was now easier to shop. In addition, overall sales increased by 8% in one of the test stores and by 2% in the other. Thus, substantial SKU reduction was shown to have positive consequences for the retailer without negatively affecting consumers' perceptions of the assortment (Broniarczyk & Hoyer, 2010).

To summarize, when it comes to finding answers on how consumers normally perceive a retailer's assortment, the following results can be concluded (Broniarczyk & Hoyer, 2010):
- In addition to several total items, assortment perception is based on the similarity of items, the shelf display size, and the availability of favourite products.

- Large SKU reductions will decrease assortment perceptions more when initial assortment is small than large.
- If most sales are driven be a few SKUs, reduction of low selling SKUs will have minimal impact on assortment perceptions.

Another challenge that retailers must face when deciding on their merchandise assortment is to find the right balance between their own brands (*retail brands* or *private labels*), and *national brands* (*manufacturers' brands*). The retailer's own brands or private labels offer the retailer many advantages, like control over product factors such as size, package design, production, and distribution, retailers have more control on decisions of their own brands and category gaps that have not been filled by national brands can be done. Private labels usually provide higher profit margins.

In contrast, national brands are usually heavily advertised through all different kinds of communication channels and are distributed through many different retail stores and retail chains.

Private labels are experiencing rapid growth, constantly increasing market share and rising popularity among all consumer groups. Therefore, they pose great threats to national brands. Consumers nowadays look for products that are comparable to national brands in terms of quality, but which are sold at a lower price.

The US private labels grocery market – A comparison with Europe
Private label's share of grocery sales is much lower in the United States than in European markets, especially the UK, Germany, and France. There are three reasons why private labels hold just a small market share of grocery sales in the US (Weinswig, 19 October 2017):

"1. Private Label's Share Is Distorted by Grocery Discounters
The presence of grocery discounters such as Aldi and Lidl has a meaningful impact on private label's share of a country's overall grocery market. Compared with a number of European countries, such as Germany, the UK, and France, the United States has a minor hard discount sector. Aldi had just a 1.3% market share in the United States in 2016, and Lidl entered the US market only in the summer of 2017. This relatively small presence of hard discounters depresses private label's share of the overall market in the United States. However, once grocery discounters are stripped out, the major European economies see relatively similar levels of private-label share as the US does.

2. Private-Label Development Reflects Sector Concentration
The grocery sector is unusually fragmented in the US, with only two retailers enjoying double-digit market share. Walmart is by far the market leader in US grocery, with a 26% share in 2016. Its closest competitor, Kroger, had a 10% share last year. This fragmentation limits the potential for tiered, innovative and well-known private labels that convince shoppers to switch from branded goods. In other markets, retailers with a very substantial market share have used their scale to develop sophisticated, tiered private-label ranges. The correlation between private-label market share and degree of concentration in grocery retailing appears to be consistent across countries.

3. Walmart Is a House of Brands
Market leader Walmart's long-standing strategy to be first and foremost a house of brands appears to have limited private-label development in the US market. The company's origins as a

general merchandiser, rather than as a food retailer, naturally led to its more brand-focused positioning relative to many competitors in the grocery sector.

David Cheesewright, President and CEO of Walmart International, said in June 2016:
If you started life as a food retailer, you view private label as the place you start, and brand is the thing that you only sell if you can't create a proper private label. Because if a sign says we save people money, then why would you want to sell something that costs more for the same quality? If you start in general merchandise, I think you tend to view things as a house of brands."

Kumar & Steenkamp (2007) distinguish between three different types of private label brands (PLB):
– generic brands
– copycat brands
– premium brands

These three types of PLBs can be described as follows (Kumar & Steenkamp, 2007):

Generic brands simply stand for a type of product and do not disclose the name of the manufacturer or brand owner. This type of brand is usually low-priced and of low quality targeted at price-sensitive consumers. Retailers add generic brands to their store brand portfolio to develop an undifferentiated product with the lowest price possible. Generic brands normally don't contribute substantially to a retailer's sales volumes or profits, therefore those brands are often placed on lower levels of the store shelves where they are less visible.

A *copycat brand* is an imitation of a manufacturer's brand, which uses a similar design or packaging, but states the name of the retailer. Retailers very often take advantage of manufacturers' innovative strategies and recreate their products. The advantages for retailers are that they can save substantial costs in research and development and marketing. Moreover, the copycat products can be sold at a significantly lower price than the original branded product, while still being able to maintain a good quality. In addition, retailers do not have the risk of product introduction to the market when copying an already existing manufacturer's brand. By adding copycat brands to their product portfolios, retailers considerably increase competition in the market and drive revenues and profit margins (Kumar & Steenkamp, 2007). Many retailers decide to use the retailer's name as a brand name for the copycat product, sometimes even using the same colour and design. When using this branding strategy, marketers must take into consideration the reputation of the retailer, which can have significant influence on the resulting perception of the identically named store brand (Sarkar, Sharma, & Kalro, 2015).

In contrast to generic and copycat brands, *premium brands* have a high level of quality and the potential to help retailers differentiate themselves from competitors. Premium brands in general and premium private labels are usually highly profitable for retailers due to the higher price levels and higher profit margins. Premium brands are often used in a retailer's brand portfolio to attract customers to visit and buy in their stores. There are two different types of premium brands (Kumar & Steenkamp,

2007): Premium-lite store brands and premium-price store brands. *Premium-lite store brands* have a high-quality level, unique features and are sold at reasonable prices. *Premium-price store brands* are of a superior quality level and therefore are sold at a higher price than manufacturers' brands.

Most retailers hold a brand portfolio with three different private label brands:
- low-budget brand
- medium-priced brand
- premium-priced brand

These are aimed at attracting a broad customer market, from the price-sensitive customers to the customers who are quality-sensitive. Another advantage of a broad brand portfolio, including private label brands with different price levels, retailers are more competitive, also in competition with hard discounters (Kumar & Steenkamp, 2007). Many manufacturers see themselves forced to partner with retailers and to produce private label brands for them, mainly because of competitive reasons. On the one hand, producing private label brands for a retailer can be beneficial for manufacturers in terms of economies of scale, production capacity, and coverage of fixed costs, but on the other hand, the produced private label brand very often cannibalizes with the manufacturer's own brands.

To summarize, manufacturers' brands should not be neglected in a retailer's merchandise management in general and brand portfolio as those brands can contribute to the image of a retailer, increase store loyalty, and attract new customers. Nevertheless, it is also important to have manufacturers' brands in a retailer's assortment to enhance product recognition (a brand can be visually recognizable from its packaging, logo, shape, or advertisement), helps to build brand loyalty and helps with product positioning because well-developed and promoted brands make product positioning efforts more effective and, last but not least, strong brands can lead to financial advantages through the concept of brand equity in which the brand itself becomes valuable (for more information see Chapter 4.5).

2.1.1.1 Types of merchandising

As we have already learned, merchandising is the practice and process of displaying and selling products to customers, no matter whether this is in-store or digital. Merchandising is used mainly to influence customers and to reach a retailer's profit and sales objectives. In practice, there exist several different types of merchandising. This chapter describes the most important types within the retail sector promotional merchandising, cross merchandising, visual merchandising, digital merchandising, and omnichannel merchandising.

Promotional merchandising

Promotional merchandising involves employing promotional products to help companies advertise their products and to build brand recognition. Each promotional product used in promotional merchandising is imprinted with information related to the company or a particular event. Depending on the objective of the promotion, imprints typically include the company name, logo, or a slogan. Promotional merchandising is mainly used to create a target-group oriented advertising campaign while providing the target group with a useful and functional item. Various products are available for use in promotional merchandising activities. They range from pens, other functional office items to clothing items.

A merchandiser has several possibilities to maximizes the sales of a product. A highly effective promotional merchandising measure is to make packaging more attractive, in detail to use promotional packaging. Packaging includes all the activities of designing and producing containers or wrappers for a product. In the retail sector consumers very often evaluate a product according to its packaging. Studies (Silayoi & Speece, 2004) have shown that from a consumer's point of view, the quality of a packaging reflects the quality of the product. This means, for example, that a low-quality packaging is interpretend that the product quality itself is also low. And a product kept in a nice container or wrapping will normally catch the attention of the customers.

The promotional products and packaging industries are very often accused of being responsible to contribute to pollution and excess waste. Therefore, we see a trend towards sustainable promotional products and biodegradable packaging options. For more information regarding packaging please refer to Chapter 2.1.2.

Cross merchandising

Another important merchandising types is cross merchandising. Cross merchandising refers to the display of opposite and unrelated products to sell them together with the objective of increasing sales and profits. Products from different categories are kept together at one place in the store so that the customers find a commonality among them and buy them together. Therefore, the retailer increases sales by linking products that are not related in any sense and belong to different categories. In addition, it helps the customers to know about the various options that would complement their product and helps save time.

Examples of cross merchandising are:
- Products that may act as substitutes, for example, dried fruits placed in the fresh fruit section.
- Products that are used together, for example, electronic devices and batteries, fashion jewelry with clothing.
- Popular products that are displayed in multiple places in a store.
- Themed products such as products that are needed to bake a strawberry cake, like flour, sugar, baking powder, strawberries, decoration, etc.

– Themed products such as products that are needed to bake a strawberry cake, like flour, sugar, baking powder, strawberries, decoration, etc.
– E-commerce products are displayed online as recommended when e-commerce sites have tracked them to be bought together.

Cross merchandising is often used by retailers to convince the customers to buy additional products apart from the products on a planned shopping list or give the customers an opportunity or an idea to buy something. Sometimes customers can't really decide what they need apart from the products they have already purchased, for example, when baking a cake. So cross merchandising is useful for the customers and helps the retailers to increase its sales.

Visual merchandising

Visual merchandising deals with all activities involved in presenting products to potential and existing customers. The main objective of visual merchandising is to attract potential buyers and increase sales and profits. In detail, visual merchandising encompasses activities of displaying (visualizing) the merchandise to influence the consumers' buying behaviour in an effective and emotional way (Biegel, 1997). Visual merchandising is a method to direct the customers' attention to specific products, stimulate unexpected purchases and impulse buying, and deliver an intended image of a product (Ebster & Garaus, 2015). For more details see Chapter 2.1.1.2 on visual merchandising.

Digital merchandising

Digital merchandising involves all promotional activities used to sell a product through an online channel. The main objective is to create a digital retail experience for the customers. Digital merchandising is also referred to as online merchandising.

Digital merchandising can include several different elements, like site performance, digital product displays, digital marketing, email marketing, etc. In the future, as already mentioned in Chapter 3.2.1, in-store and digital experiences will continue to merge. Many physical stores do already include digital elements and experiences in their stores, like info terminals, digital signage, smart mirrors, and other digital tools. Some retailers go over to the fact that there are only showrooms, which means that no physical merchandise is sold in these physical stores. Instead, sales staff help customers find the right product before asking the customer to place a digital order.

The following box provides an example of an interactive digital merchandising experience.

Samsung's experimental store is divided into interactive spaces
Samsung recently opened a retail outlet that is divided into various interactive spaces. While many stores already experience with digital displays, Samsung's outlet provides visitors with a wide variety of interactive experiences.

The new Samsung experience store is located within the company's main building in Seoul. The store features two different floors, each of which is divided into various interactive spaces. The first floor allows guests to test out current Samsung products and services. The second floor is aimed at educating guests about how new technology is impacting their lives and different industries. Each floor features different interactive displays. The multitired store is designed to showcase Samsung's current and future innovations.

Moreover, the interactive store is designed to impress visitors by allowing them to get up close and personal with new technology and helps consumers better understand how they can use new products in their everyday life (Trendhunter, 2019a).

Omnichannel merchandising

Omnichannel merchandising refers to creating a unified customer experience across all possible touchpoints of the customer journey. For retailers with offline and online stores, omnichannel merchandising involves creating a seamless customer experience so that the customer does have hardly any additional effort when switching from one channel to another. Omnichannel merchandising is often referred to as omnichannel retailing. The term is normally used to describe all the elements within a single customer journey, regardless of where each element takes place.

For example, a customer visits a physical store and finds a product which catches his or her attention. Without buying the product the customer leaves the store and tries to find the item via a Google search. The digital retailer sends a personalized behavioural email showing the customer offering a 5% discount. The customer accepts the offer and completes their purchase. This experience is a typical omnichannel merchandising experience because the customer moved from the physical store to the search engine, to the website, to their email, and then back to website.

Another example of the usage of omnichannel merchandising is provided in the box below.

The New Macy's Location Features Millennial-Focused Tech Displays
The newest Macy's retail space is a millennial-focused fashion boutique that features massive displays of real-time Instagram feeds. These elements show consumers what other shoppers are buying. By utilizing real-time social feeds, the retail space provides consumers with an overall immersive shopping experience.

The entirely revamped Macy's location in New York City features a new millennial-focused floor that is equipped with tech-savvy displays. The new floor utilizes the basement of Macy's flagship shop, which provides a less busy shopping experience for consumers. This floor is titled "One Below" and contains a variety of cost-conscious products which provides a retail environment that is ideal for the millennial consumer. With a heavy focus on interactive technology, the store features lounge areas with outlets built into seats and an interactive 35- by 5-foot Instagram board. Additionally, another section of the store features a selfie camera that allows shoppers to snap images using different backgrounds and to then post them to various social networks. With its real-time experience and social media interactions, Macy's can build stronger relationships with consumers who are highly motivated by social media (Trendhunter, 2019b).

2.1.1.2 Visual merchandising

In general, visual merchandising is the art and science of how to present products to potential and existing customers with the attention to attract potential buyers, prompt them to buy and eventually increase the sales. In simpler words, visual merchandising is the art of displaying the merchandise to influence the consumers' buying behaviour "Visual" means as to visualize a product for the customers and "merchandising" stands for sales promotion. Visual merchandising is used to optimize product presentation as well as their surroundings to connect to the customers in an effective and emotional way (Biegel, 1997). For retailers visual merchandising is an effective marketing tool to communicate with their customers through their product presentations. Visual merchandising is a method to direct the customers' attention to specific products, stimulate unexpected purchases and impulse buying, and deliver an intended image of a product (Ebster & Garaus, 2015).

Visual merchandising can be beneficial for retailers in many ways. It can:
- increase customer frequency and retention time
- arouse the customer's interest
- lead customers into the shop
- help to build a unique image and make the retail store distinct from others

To reach these objectives the retailer has to offer a positive ambience to the customers for them to enjoy the shopping in their store and to increase the customers' retention time. Moreover, the location of the products in the store has an important role in motivating the consumers to buy them. Proper space layout and location, professional lighting, the colour of the walls, the type of furniture, appropriate music and the fragrance in the store can help in increasing the sale of the products.

To extend the retention time of customers, paths must be optimized and fascination points must be installed. It also helps to boost sales by displaying product suggestions to stimulate impulsive purchases. Since successful brands do not communicate their products but their brand image, a unique POS presentation can be achieved with fresh ideas and lifestyle staging. Visual merchandising also provides orientation and encourage self-service by structuring store space logically and clear. When retailing low involvement products such as fast-moving consumer goods, it can also encourage people to self-service without needing the help of a shop employee (Spanke & Löbbel, 2012).

Visual merchandising encompasses a wide range of activities and includes various elements like the choice of fixtures and fittings used, methods of product presentations, the choice of the store layout, the usage of point-of-sale materials, the construction of window displays and the presentation of products in online channels (Varley, 2014).

Visual merchandising designs customer experiences that will encourage them to buy into a brand. Visual merchandisers try to attract customers by creating unique retail experiences using various elements, like window installations, store layouts, communication tools, live brand experiences or visual effects. The future of visual merchandising will be a "digital" one. Digital visual merchandising where technology is incorporated in window displays of physical store will become more important. Consumers will get used to augmented realities, virtual and mixed realities when purchasing products. There will be an increased demand for gamification elements included in online and offline sales channels to create online visual experiences.

Lighting

Lighting is a very important element in a retailer's visual merchandising strategy. Proper lighting increases the visibility of the products displayed in the store and affects the atmosphere in the store.

Studies have shown that there is a relation between lighting and ambiance. Lighting can influence emotions, the mood and cognition of the customers but also of the employees, and the atmosphere and spatial impressions. Studies indicate that there are more pleasant emotions when light levels are higher. Cool white light is supposed to be arousing. A combination of high illuminances and a large indirect lighting component results in higher feelings of dominance.

There are six categories of human impression that can be influenced by lighting design: perceptual clarity, spaciousness, relaxation, and tension, public or private space, pleasantness and spatial complexity. These impression dimensions can be related to lighting characteristics and several lighting design guidelines concluded.

For perceptual clarity, for example, bright and peripheral lighting must be applied. An impression of spaciousness can be achieved by using uniform and peripheral lighting. Pleasant and relaxing impressions are generated by peripheral, nonuniform lighting. And a private space can be achieved by nonuniform, dimmed lighting. In addition, rooms appear more spacious when higher ratios of indirect lighting are used, whereas rooms with high levels of indirect lighting are preferred over rooms with less indirect lighting (Custers, De Kort, & Ijsselsteijn, 2010).

To summarize, it can be concluded that lighting is able to influence the customers' impressions of a retail store.

Colours

Studies have shown that there exists a relation between colours used in a store, especially for walls, furniture, floor, carpet, etc., and mood of the customers. Therefore, every retailer must be extremely cautious about the colours used in the store (see Table 2.2).

Table 2.2: Colours and their effects (Source: Stream, 2017).

Colour	Effects
Red	Red is a powerful colour that attracts one's attention immediately. It is usually used to give the impression that time passes by and that you need to hurry up, especially used in fast food restaurants. Red also accelerates the pulse rate.
Blue	Blue is a very popular colour. It is one of the most calming colours. Its purpose is to make individuals clear their mind and give them the impression that there is plenty of time to reflect upon anything or to spend time in the store.
Yellow	Yellow is known as the colour of happiness. It is the strongest colour the human eye. It helps us calm, but also to get creative and even be more optimistic.
Green	The colour green is associated with freshness, peace, total relaxation and a general feeling of happiness and safety. It is a balanced and trustworthy colour, which is wanted for shoppers to feel like they are safe when buying products.
Black	Black is a paradoxical colour because on one hand it implies classiness, strength, and authority, but on the other hand it can be quite frightening. It can be also used to put in contrast the products that need to be sold.
White	White is associated with feelings of pureness, cleanliness, and perfection. It can give a classy and minimalistic look to a shop and make it look more respectable and even fancier. White needs to be handled carefully because large doses of white can produce a boring ambience. White walls can help to set a contrast.
Pink	Pink is the colour of love, nurturing and sexuality. It is primarily used for feminine products and gifts for women. It appears that the colour pink makes people think about cute things and makes shoppers want to buy presents for females, for example, their girls, girlfriends, wives, etc.
Gold, silver	Gold and silver are associated with money and richness. Silver is considered to be more modern and stylish than black. Both colours can induce a feeling of success, prestige, and abundance. They are mostly used to give prominence to certain objects or products.
Violet	Violet is a spiritual colour that makes people think about magic. It induces a mysterious atmosphere, it is the colour of nobility and wealth. It is often used for beauty and anti-aging products.

Colour can be everything to a successful store, if the palettes work well across the whole shop and complement other elements such as product displays and lighting.

We react fundamentally to colours because they help us make sense of our surroundings. Eighty percent of information reaches our brains via our eyes. It means that we are instinctively more comfortable when colours remind us of something familiar.

In children, by contrast, those colour associations are still being formed, which is why youngsters respond best to bright primary colours. Those bold colours are the colour of most toys, clothes, and children's books, and the colour schemes of the most successful kids' retailers.

We all share similar responses to colour, although some cultural variations exist. For example, white is the colour of marriage in western societies but is the colour of death in China. In Brazil, purple is the colour of death. Yellow is sacred to the Chinese but signifies sadness in Greece and jealousy in France. People from tropical countries respond most favourably to warm colours; people from northern climates prefer cooler colours.

Colour association also extends into food retailing. For example, most fast-food restaurants are decorated in vivid reds and oranges. These colours encourage us to eat quickly and leave. Luxurious brands, on the other hand, favour softer colours that appear more sophisticated. It has been already scientifically proven that every colour has a unique effect upon individuals and each one of them can be used to acquire a certain objective.

Regarding the employees, colours can have a huge impact upon them too – they can affect one's moods, performance, productivity and attitudes, and a study made in 2007 at The University of Texas stands to prove this. For instance, if yellow and orange will only transmit positive feelings and a lot of energy and enthusiasm and green and blue will generate a feeling of relaxation and loosening, light grey will do the exact opposite, it will create a dull atmosphere.

Vivid colours, such as red, will stimulate the employees and will bring upon them only beneficial things (physically and psychologically). It is important for an employer to have the people who are working for him in a good mood and willing to perform as good as possible.

And not only the employees will percept a well-decorated store or office as an ideal place where they can work, but shoppers will be impressed by a well-done design as well, whether they realize it at first or not (Stream, 2017).

Scent

Human physiology and psychology place great importance on the sense and links it quickly and deeply to positive memories so we can repeat those experiences. Studies have found that the usage of scent in a retail store can increase the intention to purchase by 80%. For example, the smell of fresh-brewed coffee at a petrol station can increase coffee sales by 300%. Scents have also been shown to persuade customers to stay in retail spaces longer, improve their sense of quality, and create a warm feeling of familiarity.

Well-received ambient scents can positively influence purchase behaviour if the scent seems to match the products in the store. The opposite is true if the scent doesn't seem to match the context of the shop; consumers may turn away from the retail space. Gender-designed scents seem to matter as well. A "feminine" scent in a woman's clothing store helps create positive purchase intention. Retail stores often use incorporate different scents in various areas of the stores, depending on the product focus, to avoid gender-designed scents and to attract every target group. Another important point in scent marketing is to keep the season in mind when creating scentscapes. In December, for example, cinnamon scents that remind consumers of Christmas while playing Christmas music produces positive consumer outcomes (Orvis, 2016).

Scent marketing by Singapore Airlines
The Asian airline Singapore Airlines is a pioneer in the practice of scent marketing. Singapore Airlines recognized over 30 years ago that stale air of a pressurized airline cabin isn't the best smelling space and was one of the first to develop a custom scent to spray into their hot towels. They started using a floral and citrus fragrance in the airline cabins, which become very popular. So, the airline gave the fragrance a particular name: Stefan Floridian Waters.
   In addition to improving the smell of the stale air, Singapore Airlines, and other airlines, aim to use fragrances in order to help customers to reduce anxiety, to improve customer experience in flight and to create long-lasting memories.

Music

According to Kotler (2001), in addition to helping stores attract and maintain a targeted customer group, visual merchandising elements have the potential to be more important for generating sales than the actual products on the shelves. Different aspects of sound and music can be used to trigger different customer behaviours.

Researchers have looked at the effect that music volume had on shoppers. They found that when the music was loud, shoppers tended to spend less time in the store. When the music was softer, shoppers tended to spend more time in the store. But music volume only affected the amount of time people spent in stores, not sales volume.

Tempo, the speed at which music is played, is another important determinant of human response to music. The tempo of a store's background music can influence both the pace of customer traffic flow, which means how fast people walk through the store, as well as the sales volume. Fast music makes people move more quickly through a store, buying less. Slow music makes people move more slowly through a store, and they end up buying more. Researchers found that, on average, sales volume was 38% higher on days when stores played slow background music.

Moreover, the mode of the music plays a role when it comes to increase sales volume. Customers do not buy as much when the music is slow and happy. A slow tempo and a minor, sad mode results in increased spending behaviour in a shopping environment.

Here, it must be mentioned elements that work in one store might not work in another, for example, what works in a supermarket might not work in a luxury fashion store.

In addition, the genre of the music has a significant effect on a store's overall ambiance and on sales. The genre of the music playing in the background does not influence the quantity of sales, but the quality of sales. For example, researchers found that shoppers in a wine store bought more wines that are expensive when the classical music was playing. Classical music also helps nonexperienced shoppers into thinking that wines are of a high quality and worth buying (Devaney, 2016).

Window display

The window display is an important brand image projection tool and can be used as a sales medium and as a communication tool (Okonkwo, 2007). To show the individuality of a brand it is very important to create brand-conform, but creative displays. Of all the elements incorporated within visual merchandising, window displays are often the most direct in attracting potential new customers. A window display is usually the first point of visual contact a consumer has with a store and the beginning of a potential retail experience.

Retailers need an effective window display to drive traffic into their stores. It's a unique form of advertising, which defines a store and gives the consumer an idea of what the brand is all about. They are an effective form of visual merchandising and often creative and different types of window displays create talking points among consumers and other retailers. With strategic planning and innovative designs, window displays can effectively create brand awareness.

There are many different types of window displays and the one used will often depend on the store. Each brand should have a different focus and approach, which will reflect in the style of display they use. The main types of window display include open, closed, semi-closed, elevated, corner, island, and shadowbox.

- **Open window displays** have side walls but no back wall, allowing the interior of the shop to be seen from the outside. These windows are viewed from both inside and outside the shop and therefore should be attractive from both sides.
- **Closed window display** is often found in department stores. They have a large glass front, a solid back wall and two solid sides, with a hidden door to access the window. These windows resemble a room and capture the customers' attention from just one point of view, from the front.
- **Semi-closed windows** are created to mix the advantages that a closed window display provides, and the inviting atmosphere that an open window display creates. This type of window display usually consists of a partial screen or graphic display, that covers the majority – but not the whole – of the window.
- **Elevated window displays** are commonly used in jewellery and cosmetic applications, particularly for higher value items. This type of elevated display is used to raise featured products enough to catch the customer's eye, usually combined with a graphic display or method of displaying the item itself to raise awareness.
- **Corner window displays** are created on the corner of stores. Retailers can create awareness of the items displayed as people walk around the outside of the store.

- **Island window displays** are usually found in large department or flagship stores, where retailers have a huge space to fill but also want to create a particular atmosphere and a focus on selected products or promotion articles.
- **Shadowbox displays** are used by retailers who are specialised in smaller items such as jewellery and accessories. These displays draw the attention of the consumer to the displayed products that would often be lost in a larger window display.

2.1.1.3 Category management

Studies have shown that 60% of shoppers decide on which brand and product to purchase when they are standing in front of a shelf. Therefore, when consumers are uncertain about their purchase choices, retailers have a significant opportunity to influence the purchase decision. Making a purchase decision at the shelf is very often a difficult task for the shopper. Retail stores are more crowded than ever, and contain up to 50,000 different SKUs (shop keeping units) and sometimes even more (e.g., in hypermarkets up to 200,000 different food and nonfood products).

In the retail sector conflicts regarding the renewal of annual cooperation agreements between retailers and manufacturer are sometimes inescapable, although it this cooperation is necessary to achieve mutual goals. These goals mainly refer to product costs, payment terms, listing fees, or product launching schedules. But there are many more goals which are just as important as these quantitative goals.

Category management has the potential to inspire new ideas. By understanding the core values of category management, manufacturers and retailers should be able to use common language to reach common goals and solutions with a win-win-situation for both, but also for the customers. Instead of spending time arguing, this time and energy can be used more efficiently to address more important issues, then focussing solely on revenues. A category management project should primarily focus on fulfilling customers' needs, increasing customers' satisfaction, and retaining target consumers. Category optimization and customer satisfaction can only be reached when both manufacturers and retailers work together to enhance customer satisfaction and increase category performance (Wang, 2014).

Going back to history one key reason for the introduction of category management was the retailers' desire for suppliers to add value to the retailer's business rather than just the supplier's own. For example, in a category containing the two brands A and B, the situation could be as follows: every time brand A promotes its products, the sales of brand B would go down by the amount that brand A would increase, resulting in no net gain for the retailer. The introduction of category management suggests that all actions undertaken, such as new promotions, new product launches, POS advertising, etc., should be beneficial not only to the supplier (in this case the supplier of brand A), but also to the retailer and the customer in the store. What is more, a close and friendly collaboration with the supplier means that the retailer can make use of the supplier's expertise about the market, brand or products, and the retailer could delegate certain tasks in developing the category to the supplier (Wang, 2014).

A *category* can be defined as products that meet a similar consumer need, or products that are interrelated or substitutable. Products that are placed together in the same category should be logistically manageable in store. For example, having room-temperature and chilled products together in the same category would be difficult to manage even though these products meet a similar consumer need or are interrelated.

Five steps in defining a category

Step 1: Defining the consumers' need, for example the customer wants to have breakfast.

Step 2: Which options provide similar solutions to meet the need? For breakfast there are various products which can fulfil this need, for example, bread, cereals, eggs, fruits, yoghurt, beverages, cake, biscuits, etc.

Step 3: Which products does the consumer see as substitutable or interrelated? Examples for substitutable products are bread or rolls, cereals or muesli, cake or biscuits, etc. Examples for interrelated products, which means products which are usually bought together, are coffee and milk, bread and butter, cake and cream, etc.

Step 4: Which products does the retailer see as interrelated and logistically manageable together? Customers would prefer coffee and milk stored together, but fresh milk has to be chilled. So, these products are interrelated but not logistically manageable together. Milk powder and coffee can be located next to each other in a store because these products have similar storage requirements.

Step 5: Which products (SKUs = stock-keeping units) should be put together in a certain category or subcategory? This step defines the category name, the category structure (subcategories and subsegments) and aligning the SKUs to the lowest structure within the category. For example, the category dairies, subcategory milk, subsegments low fat milk, full fat milk, goat milk, etc., with several SKUs, for example, low-fat milk 1litre, low-fat milk 500 millilitre, or low-fat milk 250 millilitre.

There are many ways to establish a consumer-centric category management project between a retailer and a supplier. To ensure a successful implementation, eight fundamental steps of category management have been defined (Wang, 2014):

- **Category definition**: stands for defining a distinct and manageable grouping of certain products that the retailer and manufacturer would like to optimize by increasing the understanding of the customers' needs.
- **Category role**: Outlines the distinctive role each category plays in retailing in accordance with the type of retail store, retail format and target group.
- **Category assessment**: This step assesses the potential of a certain category from various data sources, for example, shopper studies, retail indexes, market shares and sales and profit data.
- **Category scorecard**: Quantifies a mutual key performance indicator (KPI) target determined by the assessment result and specifies the project length and deadlines.
- **Category strategy**: This step provides the strategic direction to execute tactics, and ensure consistency among category roles, objectives, and category tactics.

Category strategy also provides guidelines to allocate resources appropriately. Some important category strategies are traffic building, profit generating, excitement creating, image creating.

- **Category tactics:** This step focuses on reaching the targets set in previous steps by using assortment, space management, pricing, and promotion tactics.
- **Category implementation and review**: These last two steps incorporate all parties in decision-making to ensure tasks and schedules are communicated and commonly understood. Quarterly reviews for key categories are produced to ensure long term success and to make sure the whole project runs smoothly towards the mutual objectives.

Chocolate shoppers and their purchase decisions – A category management example
In grocery retailer found that their chocolate category display made it difficult for customers to shop. This presented a challenge in converting traffic into actual sales. After cooperating with the manufacturer in a category management project, in addition to analysing market and sales data, this retailer realized that, in the special case of chocolate, customers' purchasing decisions can be segmented by different chocolate consuming occasions. The retailer segmented their chocolate category into three occasions: functional, emotional, and social. By implementing this category management project and arranging the POS chocolate display, survey results showed that customer satisfaction could be increased by 70%, and the overall category sales increased by 15%. By following the eight fundamental steps of category management and focussing on the common objective "fulfilling the customers' needs and desires," manufacturers and retailers can achieve their objectives and increase their revenues.

Some researchers and especially practitioners have criticized this eight-step process as being too comprehensive and time-consuming in today's fast-moving sales environment. Survey data has shown that only 9% of manufacturers stated they used the full eight-step process. Most of the companies use this standard process as a basis to develop their own more streamlined processes, tailored to their own products and categories, mostly based on only five central steps:

- reviewing the category
- targeting appropriate consumers
- planning merchandising activities
- implementing the strategic direction
- evaluating results

It is commonplace for a particular supplier in a certain category to be nominated by the retailer as the so-called *category captain*. This category captain is expected to have the closest relationship with the retailer and will also be expected to invest effort and financial assets into the strategic development of the category within the retailer. In return, the supplier normally has a more influential voice with the retailer when it comes to category management decisions, above all category tactics and category strategy. The category captain is usually the supplier with the largest turnover or the largest market share in a particular category.

In order to do the job effectively, the supplier is granted access to a greater wealth of data-sharing, for example, more access to internal databases. Unfortunately, in recent years it has happened that some suppliers have paid large amounts of money in exchange for the fact that they are category captain in a certain category and gain an influential voice with the retailer, which should be prevented by law.

Organization of assortment

Studies have found that the way assortments are organized can have a significant impact on how consumers make their purchase decisions. In addition, the way information about a product or brand is presented greatly influences the way consumers process information about the items. This due to the fact that individuals tend to be constructive processors who adapt their decision-making style to the way information is presented, for example, if information is organized by brand, consumers tend to process by brand. If information is organized by attribute, consumers are more likely to make comparisons across certain product attributes, like price, packaging, size, ingredients, etc. Researchers have identified various key aspects of assortment organization that can influence how consumers process assortment information and conduct their purchase decisions (Broniarczyk & Hoyer, 2010). In the following six aspects will be discussed (Broniarczyk & Hoyer, 2010):
- nature of the display
- organization by brand or by model
- ordering of brands
- display organization
- symmetrical versus asymmetrical assortments
- comparability with consumer knowledge structures

Nature of the display

Research has shown that the nature of the display influences consumer decisions. It is well-known that most consumers make their purchase decisions of daily commodities directly in a store. Consumer behaviour is influenced by various in-store attention-based factors. The most important factors are shelf position, number of facings, packaging, time pressure, price, display but also out-of-store memory-based factors (e.g., brand preferences and store image) (Chandon, Hutchinson, Bradlow, & Young, 2007).

Eye tracking research has shown that eye-catching or obtrusive product presentations lead to the fact that dwell time of fixations are much longer, and fixation counts higher. Apparently, there is no correlation between duration of visual attention and purchase decision. Furthermore, it must be mentioned that the average length of a fixation is longer if the shopper is inexperienced and if the purchase of a product was planned. Moreover, the longer the participants stay in a store the more products they buy, which means there is a correlation between the length of stay and number of products purchased.

Side- by-side displays, for example, favour brands with a lower price or with superior features because the display makes it easy to compare the brands. Brands with high prices are better served by separate displays that inhibit comparison, for example, an end-of-aisle display. Moreover, the location of the product in the display is important, even more important than the number of facings. Brands in the middle of a display are more likely to be compared and to influence perceptions of variety.

Organization by brand or by model

Another way to organize assortments is by brand or by model. In detail, a retailer could either group all the models of a particular brand together (e.g., Apple, Microsoft, etc.) or group all different types of models together (e.g., all low-priced models together, mid-priced models together, and high-priced models together). When options are organized by model, studies have shown that consumers are more likely to select the mid-priced and top-of-the line brands (with a tendency to avoid the cheapest brand).

A study of yogurt found that organizing the display by brand encouraged consumers to buy the same brand in different flavours. However, organizing by flavour caused consumers to think about flavour first and then buy different brands. Various a brand display encourages more brand loyalty, while an attribute-based display encourages brand switching and variety seeking (Broniarczyk & Hoyer, 2010).

Ordering of brands

Retailers can also determine the order in which brands and information are processed. This is very easily accomplished in online environments, by controlling which brands are presented first. In store this can be accomplished by the position of the brands in the display (right-to-left and left-to-right, as well as shelf level). Consumers can also develop internal ordering of products. Research has shown that such ordering of information can have a big impact on consumer evaluations.

For example, when consumers engage in limited information search, a declining order (best to worst) leads to the most positive evaluations. This occurs because consumers tend to see only the brands that are rated most positively. When a search is extensive, however, evaluations are more positive for an increasing order (worst to best). Exhaustive searching ensures that all the brands are processed (especially the most positive ones at the end). Thus, it is clear the retailers should consider the likely search patterns of their consumers in determining how the brands are ordered (Broniarczyk & Hoyer, 2010).

Display organization

At the extremes, assortments can be either well organized or rather disorganized. When the assortment is large, actual variety is easier to recognize when assortments are organized. With small assortments, however, organized assortments can make the lack of choice more salient. Further, if actual variety is increased in a disorganized manner, the disruptive impact on consumers will be less than if it was increased in an organized manner.

Symmetrical versus asymmetrical assortments

When assortments are asymmetrical (i.e., some items appear more or less frequently than others) it is easier for consumers to appreciate the variety in them than it is in a symmetrical assortment (where all items are presented equally Kahn). This occurs be- cause low-frequency items carry more information and are rare compared with those that are high in frequency and are therefore more redundant. This notion is consistent with Hoch et al.'s statement (1999) that uniqueness of items in an assortment is critical.

Comparability with consumer knowledge structures

Assortment displays (either in physical stores or online) have the potential to be very complex as they contain vast amounts of information. Consumers deal with this complexity by developing an "internal structure," which involves categorizing brands and information into knowledge structures called "schemas." For instance, when categorizing the product category of popcorn, consumer A may organize the options around different brands (Orville Redenbacher, Pop Secret, Jolly Time) whereas consumer B organizes the options around different flavours (butter, low fat, cheddar). In a series of studies, Morales et al. (2005) show that when a consumer's internal structure for the category matches the external structure of the shelf display the consumer is more likely to perceive greater variety and be more satisfied with his/her choice.

Product schemas become more established in memory and play a stronger role in information processing as consumers gain experience with a product category. Thus, if consumers are very familiar with the product category, the internal schema structure is likely to be strong and it is critical that the assortment organization be congruent with their prior knowledge. However, when familiarity with the product category is low, consumers will not have well-developed schemas and it is more important for the assortment structure to be congruent with their situational shopping goals (e.g., foods for a snack, foods to take to the beach).

To summarize, how assortments should be organized, the following guidelines provide useful information (Broniarczyk & Hoyer, 2010):

- Side-by-side displays facilitate brand comparisons whereas separate displays are better for higher price brands.

- Organizing by brand encourages consumers to buy by brand while organizing by model stimulates other attributes such as price.
- Evaluations tend to be more positive when brands are ordered from worst to best.
- Organized displays are better for large assortments but for small assortments, make the lack of choice apparent.
- Aligning assortment organization with consumer mental representation is important.
- Asymmetrical assortments make it easier for consumers to see variety.

2.1.2 Packaging

Due to the product diversity and product homogeneity, which exists nowadays, marketers and retailers are required to find differentiation from competitive products. One way for differentiation would be to adapt the packaging of the product. Moreover, consumers become more interested in environmental issues, so packaging producers need to switch to preferable and environmentally friendly materials like recyclable packaging material, sustainable printing ink and glues, etc., to meet the customers' expectations. What also must mentioned is that in the retail sector consumers normally have a low involvement when buying goods, especially FMCG (like toothpaste, dairy products, toilet paper, etc.). This means that they do not search extensively for information when they buy such products and if their preferred product is unavailable, they look for a substitute product, usually a product which has an appealing packaging.

Studies have shown that in the FMCG industry consumers mainly evaluate the products according to their packaging. From a consumer's point of view, the quality of the packaging reflects the quality of the product. This means that a low-quality packaging is interpreted that the product quality itself is also low. As opposed to this, high quality packaging results in high product quality perception (Silayoi & Speece, 2004).

When we try to define the term "packaging" the following definition seems to be appropriate: "Packaging is the activities of designing and producing containers or wrappers for a product" (Keller, 2013). From the perspective of both the retailer and the consumer, packaging must achieve several objectives (Keller, 2013):
- identify the brand
- convey descriptive and persuasive information
- facilitate product transportation and protection
- assist in at-home storage
- aid product consumption

When deciding on a particular packaging for a product, marketers need to make two decisions: choosing the aesthetic and functional components of a packaging.

Aesthetic components: cover considerations about the size, the shape, the material, colour, text, and graphics. Specialized package designers bring artistic techniques and scientific skills to package design to meet the marketing objectives for a brand. They decide on the optimal look and content of each element of the package and choose which elements (e.g., brand name, illustration, other graphical elements, etc.) should be dominant and how the elements should relate to each other. For an appealing "shelf impact" of the package at the POS several decisions must be made:
- The visual effect of the package at the point of the purchase must be considered. One of the most important visual design elements of the package is the colour.
- The size and shape of the package is important when it is essential for a product to have enough shelf space or to be placed in a particular shelf position.
- The material of the package must be considered when it comes to determining where the product should be placed, and which target group should be attracted.

Consumers have learned that certain products or brands always use a distinctive colour. For example, consumers are used to buy milk in a mostly white carton or a glass bottle. They know that the "colour code" of Coca Cola is red and that Milka chocolate bars are wrapped in a lilac package. Since 1995 colours can be registered as colour trademarks at the German Patent and Trademark Office and legally protected. For example, Tiffany Blue was first associated with upscale jewellery in 1845 when Charles Lewis Tiffany chose the egg shade of robin for the cover of the company's first catalogue, the so-called *Blue Book*. According to the company, he chose the colour because turquoise was a popular colour in gemstones at the time. Today the colour is not only protected by a colour trademark, but also has its own Pantone number: 1837, the year the company was founded.

Packaging colour can also affect the consumer's perception of a product. For example, when it comes to food products, the darker a colour shade is, the more intense consumers believe the product will taste. Or the shinier and glittering a packaging is, the more exclusive the product is. For more information concerning the effect of a particular colour, see chapter visual merchandising (Table 2.2).

Functional components: include the structural design of a packaging. Functional components increase the value of a product and the overall customer experience through product interaction with the packaging. For example, when a packaging includes measurement tools built into the packaging or when a packaging can be reused. Many suppliers have started to employ more recyclable materials to lower the use of paper and plastic and contribute to environmental protection.

Examples of functional packaging
Recyclable candy wrapping (Chocolate truffles in compostable foil)
The exterior of this candy wrapping is colourful and appealing, like many similar candy wrappings in the supermarkets. In this case the metallic foil can be planted in the ground and composted. In

about six weeks, the packaging will be gone. Recyclable candy wrappers do already exist, but there are unfortunately few facilitates that accept it for reuse (trendhunter, 2015).

The biodegradable coffee cup
The next innovative example is a plantable coffee cup. This product provides an environmental solution to the 146 billion to-go coffee cups that end up in landfills every year. The cup is embedded with California-native seeds right in its packaging material. Planting instructions are listed on the bottom of the container.

Even if the consumer decides not to plant the cup, the packaging is biodegradable. This means it will turn into compost and break down completely within 180 days. In this case, instead of becoming a new tree, the seeds will turn into nutrients for other plant life.

McBike- a transporting container for bicycles
As we see there is a growing number of cycling communities worldwide. Therefore, the Tribal Buenos Aires agency in Argentina decided to create a package to transport breakfast, lunch or dinner on the bikes. McBike is a food container from McDonald's that is designed specifically to fit onto bicycle handlebars. Each box contains a complete McDonald's meal including a burger, fries and a drink all packaged into one takeaway box that conveniently hangs from a bike handlebar. The cyclists can also order from the drive-thru lanes. This innovative packaging is a perfect solution for cyclists to buy and transport their food without having to stop and lock their bikes.

When customers are asked about their associations with a brand, one of the strongest association consumers have is the look of the packaging. Consequently, the package can become an important means of brand recognition and can help to build valuable brand associations. Due to the information overload in supermarkets, consumers often have difficulties to find their desired products. Packaging helps the consumers to find their desired products.

Moreover, packaging innovations can create a point-of-difference for customers, provide an added value and higher margins can be reached. New packages can also expand a market and reach new market segments. What is more, the right packaging can help products stand out from substitute products. Nowadays only very few product differences exist in some product categories (e.g., pasta, dairy products, cereals, etc.), the average supermarket shopper is exposed to up to 20,000 or more products during the shopping trip in normally less than 30 minutes. Therefore, packaging helps to differentiate the products and influences unplanned purchases (so-called impulse buying) created by functional or aesthetic elements of the packaging, or indirectly through the reinforcement of brand awareness and image (Keller, 2013).

One of the major packaging trends of recent years is to make both bigger (for consumption with family and friends) and smaller packaged versions (for single households or consumption on the go) of products and combi packs combined with price promotions (like "2 + 1 packs" or "buy one, get one for free!") to be attractive for new target groups or to make consumers buy more. Packaging trends and innovations are also influenced by new challenges around waste management and recyclability. Consequently, FMCG companies and retailers will require much closer collaboration with upstream players, packaging converters, recyclers, and customers to successfully deal with these new challenges. Moreover, successful packaging innovations will need to be at an affordable cost trade-off to gain scale and are used extensively in the retail market. For more information on the future of packaging see Chapter 2.1.2.2.

ARIVA model – Five dimensions of the haptic effect

The packaging of a product is supported by the haptic effect, with touching consumers try and observe the product choice in more detail. The haptic effect arises directly over touching and feeling, indirectly other sensations like pictures, noise or texts also may participate. The five dimensions of the so-called haptic effect consist of:

– attention
– recall
– integrity
– value
– action

These five dimensions of the haptic effect are known as the ARIVA model. This model can be used to support marketers in analysing and evaluating different packages. The haptic effect arises either in one or in all these dimensions and can increase the effect of the respective marketing action (Hartmann & Haupt, 2014). Every dimension in this model can influence the consumers' purchase decision and therefore should be considered by marketers beforehand.

Attention

Due to today's information overload, consumers do not react towards every single advertisement. As soon as consumers recognize an advertisement as such, it only takes them seconds whether they are interested in this advertisement or not. This leads to the fact that without attention and interest, the information will not be stored in their short-term memory. In order that an information turns into the long-term memory, attention is not enough. The consumers need to understand the advertising and be able to retrieve the message. Haptic messages aim an action, so consumers actively put their attention and interest towards the respective product. With regard to packaging, it is of high importance to consider if there exist certain materials, which attract the consumer more, so that he or she has the desire to explore the packaging (Hartmann & Haupt, 2014).

Recall

Studies have shown that haptic advertising material or messages are better recalled than ordinary advertisement material. In order for information to be stored from the individual's short-term memory in the long term-memory, the message needs to be repeated and consumers must be touched emotionally. The longer consumers look at an advertisement or touch a product packaging, the easier the message or the product can be retrieved. With haptics, different codes like consistency, material, design, size, or the volume of a product packaging can be sent to the consumer. The sensing code like the movement is saved in the consumers' memory, in addition to that, the more associations exist, the easier consumers can retrieve the respective information (Hartmann & Haupt, 2014).

Integrity
Consumers heavily rely on their sense of touch. Through touching they can examine whether a product or a packaging conforms with their expectations. At the point-of-sale consumers often touch (or smell) products (even if its toothpaste with a safety seal) to check the quality and the product expectations. If quality and expectations of the product conform with the advertising message the consumer perceives it as coherent. Therefore, the haptic effect increases the credibility and trust of a product (Hartmann & Haupt, 2014).

Value
During advertising, marketers try to convince consumers about the benefits of a product. If these benefits are presented with a high credibility, the perceived risk decreases. Moreover, touching gives consumers a sign of safety which means they can check if the product feels like it looks like and positive associations can be evoked. It is important to analyse if the haptic of a packaging can increase the contact time with the product and whether the packaging reflects the quality and values of the brand respectively of the product (Hartmann & Haupt, 2014).

Action
Due to the involvement and activation of the consumer, it can be said that touching reduces the purchase risk and encourages users to buy the desired product. This criterion is also highly relevant for packages – the main aim represents the fact that the packaging should be able to increase the desire to explore the product packaging and therefore the purchase action is done (Hartmann & Haupt, 2014).

2.1.2.1 Sustainability and packaging
Sustainability is combining with other important trends to drive major changes in the consumer packaging industry. FMCG companies and retailers are proactively making commitments to improve both the sustainability of their packaging and to rethink their packaging systems. In the years to come there will be significant impact on packaging converters and their value chain, which could threaten the survival of many in the industry. Nevertheless, for packaging converters the new landscape could offer significant growth especially then, when they proactively

embrace sustainability issues as consumer demands and regulatory requirements multiply (McKinsey, January 2020 c).

In the recent years, widespread usage of single-use packaging containers has resulted in a heavy burden on the environment, and the management of packaging waste is facing problems due to two unresolved challenges (McKinsey, January 2020 c):

- **Packaging recyclability**: large amounts of packaging produced today can not be recycled in existing recycling systems, especially when it comes to multimaterial packaging, which poses a significant challenge in recycling.
- **Packaging recycling and leakage**: recycling rates for plastic packaging are relatively low. In Europe, the plastic-packaging recycling rate is approximately 40%, compared to approximately 80% for paperboard, and 75%–80% for metal and glass. Global leakage or unmanaged dumps of all plastic material flows is estimated to be around 19%, and only 16% of all plastic waste is reprocessed to make new plastics. In fact, most of the global plastics waste goes into incineration (25%) and landfills (40%), which means that these materials are lost forever as a useful resource.

Nowadays, public awareness of packaging waste leakage, especially plastic waste, into the environment has significantly increased importance. The effects of ocean plastics pollution have stirred up consumers all around the world. That's why governments all over the world have started responding to public concerns regarding packaging waste, especially single-use packaging waste, and are implementing regulations to both minimize environmental waste and improve waste-management processes (McKinsey, January 2020 c). Plastic is a versatile material that has had a major impact on industrial production in the 20th century. The material's resistance to natural degradation processes makes the disposal of plastic a global environmental problem, especially for marine ecosystems. A few years ago, Japanese researchers discovered bacteria that could gradually decompose plastics and developed them further. In 2018, British and US scientists found an optimized enzyme variant that decomposes PET many times faster. Now they are trying to make the enzyme usable for the bioinspired recycling of plastics.

In the past years, FMCG companies and retailers have mostly focused on initiatives such as reducing weight and materials usage to enable them to lower their packaging costs. Almost all the top 100 FMCG companies (in terms of revenue) have made declarations and commitments to drive sustainability over the coming years, mainly focusing on three areas of activity:

- emphasis on full recyclability and a significant higher degree of recycled content
- reduction of total plastics usage
- the innovation and promotion of change in the use of packaging

At the same time, these sustainability-focused initiatives around innovation and the need for change in the use of packaging are combining with other major industry trends affecting the packaging industry, for example, cost pressures, e-commerce and digitalization and shifting consumer preferences. As a result, FMCG manufacturers and retailers are beginning to experiment with complete packaging redesigns and a fundamental rethinking of their delivery chains and delivery models (McKinsey, January 2020 c).

To summarize, there is no one-size-fits-all solution that converters can embrace as they work on strategies for sustainable packaging with their FMCG and retailer customers. There are complexities and trade-offs to consider if they are to navigate through these sustainability challenges to find the most effective way to growing and preserving value with application innovations (McKinsey, January 2020 c).

2.1.2.2 The future of packaging

Continuing pressures from manufacturers, wholesalers, retailers, government regulators and consumers are increasingly exerting pressure on the packaging industry. Packaging innovations and new packaging technologies have changed how we consume products, for example, by extending the shelf life of products, by improving packaging or product functionality, etc.

The future of packaging will above all also show a development to reduce plastic. At the moment we have a worldwide plastic problem. With the prediction that by 2050 the oceans will contain more plastic waste than fish, it's hardly surprising consumers are getting more and more concerned and, on the other hand, more environmentally aware. In March 2019, the European Parliament adopted a directive forbidding families of single use plastic products. Plastic straws, for example, represent a real ecological threat. Therefore, from 2021, the marketing of plastic straws will be forbidden in the whole European Union. This action is already being carried out in some major American cities such as Washington and Seattle. Many global players have already started to eliminate all plastic straws from its products, using alternative materials like paper as well as innovative designs to reduce littering.

Most people are already refusing to use plastic straws or single use shopping bags in favour of reusable items. Therefore, it's essential for retailers and manufacturers to keep up with the customers' opinion. In terms of innovations, biodegradable and recycled materials are becoming a mainstay for modern packaging solutions and are continually evolving to provide more effective, sustainable, and environmentally friendly packaging for all kinds of products.

With several sustainable solutions already available, more and more biodegradable alternatives like paper, hemp, starch, and cellulose, begin to replace plastic (Insider Trends, 2019).

So, what do laboratory leather, plastic-eating bacteria and super wood have in common? These new developments are based on principles derived from nature or inspired by biological materials, processes, and functions (i.e., Biomimicry). The spectrum of these so-called *bio-inspired* materials range from the use of natural components, such as fast-growing wood species, which are transformed into harder and more stable super wood in a novel chemical process and by exploiting nano-structures, to genetically modified bacteria that produce collagen as the starting material to produce laboratory leather.

The potential contribution of bioinspired materials to the transformation of a petroleum-based economy towards a sustainable bioeconomy is great. As a cross-sectional subject, materials research offers starting points in a wide variety of areas, ranging from medical biomaterials to organic packaging materials and synthetic food sources. Research on bioinspired materials for white biotechnology makes it possible to replace conventional materials with renewable resources on a large scale, thus making industrial processes cheaper and more ecological. The use of bioinspired materials could in future make a significant contribution to achieving the UN's sus-tainability goals for climate protection and sustainable consumption and production conditions.

The use of bioinspired materials has a long tradition, especially in medicine. This involves the targeted development and modification of materials regarding their functional properties. This paradigm shift towards "Designed Biomaterials" or "Smart Materials" will allow new ideas from biology to emerge alongside the classi-cal approaches from medicine and materials science (Ratner et al. 2013).

Superwood, for example, is a new material that is produced from soft wood in a two-stage process. In a first step, the wood is split by chemical treatment, the lignin and the hemicellulose are removed; then the treated wood is hot pressed. This causes the natural cell walls to break down and special nanofibers are formed from the cellu-lose (Song et al., 2018). The resulting material is like wood, but much harder and tougher. Due to its weight advantage over steel, super wood could be used in aircraft and automobile production or generally as a sustainable building material.

Although leather production is a traditional European craft and the natural raw material is available at low cost, leather is imported to a large extent from low-wage countries. The reason for this is the high environmental impact of the manufactur-ing process, which in Europe has led to strict regulations and a disadvantageous position in global competition. An alternative to conventional leather and the tradi-tional tanning process is leather grown in the laboratory. Laboratory leather is pro-duced using genetically modified yeast cells that produce liquid collagen, which is then shaped and finished in a simplified and environmentally friendly tanning pro-cess. Laboratory leather could on the one hand guarantee a constant quality and on the other hand would not relate to the high pollutant load of the traditional leather processing. Controlled processes ensure timely availability; it currently takes around two weeks to grow a cowhide-sized piece of laboratory leather. Innovations in the processing industry could result from the fact that various properties of the material, for example, mechanical properties such as stiffness, can be determined by the nutrients used in production (Haneef et al., 2017).

Mycelia (braids of fungal filaments) are very similar to plastics made of fossil polymers and resemble externally expanded polystyrene (EPS). They consist of biopolymers such as cellulose, chitin and proteins. Currently, substances from mycelia are mainly used in art (moonboots from mycelia at MoMA New York) and as packaging. So far, material produced from mycelia has been an expensive niche product. In the future, the bioinspired material is believed to have great potential, especially for use as a building material (ITA & AIT, 2019).

In the media, new bioinspired materials are associated with far-reaching promises for the future. Expectations of these materials range from the complete substitution of petroleum-based materials to the purification of the oceans from plastic parts. Little attention is paid to the potentially far-reaching consequences of the spread of bioinspired materials, which are intricately linked to the discourse on genetic engineering and nanotechnology (ITA & AIT, 2019).

Zero waste shopping as a change in the use of packaging material
Operators of a Zero Waste Shop try to offer as little as possible packed. They buy the goods in larger containers from the manufacturer or distributor and fill them into jars or special dispensers. Ideally, the customer brings his or her container, which is weighed at the cash desk, and afterwards filled with the goods, like muesli, rice, flour, etc., directly into the container. Some products, such as milk, or other dairy products, can be bought in returnable bottles. Products like sugar, pesto or honey are in glass bottles. Although not completely unpackaged, they can be reused or recycled.

If the consumer does not want to bring his or her own containers, a sack, bottle, paper bag or glass can be rented in the shop.

A Zero Waste Shop provides many advantages, above all less packaging which protects the environment. Moreover, costumers buy exactly what they need – avoiding food waste and probably saving money by not buying too much. Zero Waste Shopping is also good for your health because less packaging often goes hand in hand with less preservatives, less sugar, salt, palm fat, and what is not so good for the body and the environment (Zero Waste Austria Verein, 2019).

The Clean Kilo: Zero Waste Supermarket wants to take this green trend described above a step further and opened in 2019 several stores in Birmingham in the UK, as the country's biggest zero-waste supermarket.

2.2 Price

The next "P" in a retailer's marketing mix is *price*. Price is the one revenue-generating element of the traditional retail marketing mix and is among key benefits to build a strong brand. This chapter considers the different kinds of price perceptions that consumers might form, and different pricing strategies that a retailer might use to generate revenues and build a particular image.

The pricing strategy of a retailer will dictate what type of store the product will be sold in, for example, in a discount store or a specialty food store, etc. Moreover, the pricing strategy dictates how price sensitive a customer may be. There are many different factors which affect a retailer's pricing strategy, like:

- **Consumer behaviour**: one of the main issues affecting retail pricing is the price elasticity of demand. In detail, there is very often a relationship between consumer perceptions and price, which may influence the sensitivity of customers to price changes in terms of the quantities they will buy. For example, if there is just a small change in price, but a substantial change in the number of units bought consumers' demand is price elastic (Berman & Evans, 2013).
- **Governmental issues**: pricing strategy may be affected by local, state, or federal issues, mainly regarding price discrimination, unit pricing, minimum price levels, price fixing (vertical, horizontal) or price advertisement.
- **Environmental issues**: Environmental issues includes political, economic, sociocultural, technological, legal, natural, and demographic factors. The factors of the general environment are broad and nonspecific and the retailer usually has no or little control over these factors (noncontrollable factors). For example, natural factors include the availability of raw materials, changes in the cost of energy, environmental pollution, global warming, etc., which affect our daily lives but also a retailer's pricing strategy. Or, another example, important economic factors are inflation, interest rates, and the unemployment rate of a country or region. These factors affect the demand for products. During inflation, the company pays more for its resources and to cover the higher costs for it, they raise the prices for their products. Or, when unemployment is high, customers' buying power is low as fewer people are working and have many to spend.
- **Manufacturers and suppliers**: manufacturers and suppliers have a great influence on the final price customers must pay in a shop. Suppliers and manufacturers differ in their functions. Suppliers are the ones who supply the products and manufacturers are the ones who produce and manufacture the products. Manufacturers normally set their prices to retailers by estimating final retail prices first (which the end consumer must pay) and then in a next step they are subtracting potential retailer and wholesaler profit margins.
- **Competition**: When trying to adopt a product pricing strategy or determine the right price for a particular product, the market situation, especially the degree of competitive products, must be studied. The more intense the competition in the market is, the more flexible the pricing strategy must be. For more details see Chapter 2.2.1 competition-oriented pricing strategy.

Consumer behaviour

Studies (2013) have shown that consumers often rank brands according to price tiers in a category. Moreover, results demonstrate that there is also a relationship between price and quality. Within any price tier, there is a range of acceptable prices, called price bands, that indicate the flexibility and breadth retailers can use when pricing their products within a particular tier. In many categories, consumers infer the quality of a product based on its price and use perceived quality and price to arrive at an assessment of perceived value. Costs here are not restricted to the actual monetary price but may reflect opportunity costs of time, energy, and any psychological involvement in the decision that consumers might have. Consumer associations of perceived value are often an important factor in purchase decisions. Therefore, many retailers and marketers have adopted *value-based pricing strategies*, which means to sell the right product at the right price, to meet consumer demands.

In addition, retailers very often sell multiple brands in every price tier to better compete in multiple categories and reach a larger target group, so at one time they cover a wide range of prices in corresponding retail outlets. Customers are willing to accept different prices in different retail channels, for example, in specialty stores customers are willing to pay more for a certain product but is searching for price discounts and special promotions at a discount store. Since the last few years, we have seen the rise of the so-called *hybrid consumers*. This type of shopper loves shopping at both ends of the price tiers, frequenting hard discounters such as Hofer/Aldi for everyday groceries and buying premium brands at premium retail and specialty, when a product is socially or emotionally important for the customer (a so-called *high involvement product*).

Moreover, customers accept different prices in different retail channels. Therefore, retailers must think about introducing a so-called *omnichannel pricing strategy*, where prices vary between online and offline stores. The following box goes into more detail and provides findings of an interesting pricing study.

Retail customers may accept different prices in different channels
We find that for many retailers, prices increasingly vary between online and physical stores. Retailers tend to offer lower prices in the digital space, although there are exceptions. Understanding what customers value in each channel and how that affects what they are willing to pay is the key challenge for pricing teams today.

Customers weigh the convenience of immediate availability, the pleasure (or pain) of shopping in a physical store versus online, and a product's price. They often value different things in different shopping circumstances. Sophisticated pricing strategies need to take these customer-centric considerations into account.

To understand customer sensitivities to price differences, 2,400 customers in the United States (equally divided by gender and across key demographic cohorts) were surveyed, across three product categories: toothbrushes ($3), mid-priced sweaters ($30), and flat-screen TVs ($300). We showed people price differences of 5% and 20% for the same item online and offline – sometimes cheaper online, and sometimes cheaper in-store. We asked them whether these price differences were acceptable, and why or why not.

Across the board, people were fine with prices being higher in-store for the same item when they saw value in immediacy, physical proximity, and exclusive availability, although tolerance for the differential varied by how expensive the product was. Respondents expressed an understanding of the higher costs' retailers pay to stock items in physical stores.

Here are some of the details of the findings:

- Most people (59%) were comfortable with nonuniformity for a low-ticket item. Over two-thirds (68%) were comfortable with in-store being 5% more expensive for a $3 toothbrush, and 51% were still comfortable when in-store was 20% more expensive.
- For higher-priced items, people were more tolerant of price differences when the item was cheaper online. For a $30 sweater or a $300 TV, 37% and 38%, respectively, were tolerant of a price difference when the item was 20% cheaper online. Few – only 18% and 17%, respectively – were willing to accept that same item being 20% cheaper in-store.
- younger people were more accepting of price differences. Some 40% of those younger than 31 were comfortable with the differences, while just 20% of those older than 45 were.
- Women were more open to price differences in a mid-priced ($30) item. About 30% of women were comfortable with differences in mid-priced items while only 20% were comfortable with price differentials for low-end ($3) and high-end ($300) items. Men in our survey tended to be more accepting of differences across the board.

There retailers are advised to use an omnichannel pricing approach. This can be done in three ways:

First, pricing teams should focus on implementing price differential strategies. Deciding what prices to use for which channels starts with developing business rules that combine "hard facts" about price elasticity and competitive pricing, such as the impact of price change on demand by segment, with "soft facts" such as consumers' willingness to accept price differences by channel. Pricing teams need to put in place omnichannel pricing programs, actively monitor them, and continuously optimize prices based on what works and what doesn't.

Second, store employees must use the right words when talking about price differences. This new horizon of pricing requires a more active pricing communication strategy and an effective method to train staff. Too often, when asked why a price was different in the store versus what was appearing in the related mobile app, store employees avoided a straight explanation. Customers are often understanding about the higher costs for stocking an item in a physical store and the value of having immediate access to a product. When a customer has a question about a product and asks what the price is, regardless of whether the question is made in person, on the phone, or via chat, front-line staff need to be both aware of the price differences and equipped to explain its reason. The training should evolve based on what customers are asking and how effective in-store staff is in providing quality, on-brand answers.

Third, operational challenges in managing price differences by channel need to be worked out. If companies want to be to truly customer-centric, they should offer the option for a customer to return a product purchased online to a physical store because customers value to have different choices (Baker, BenMark, Chopra, Kohli, & Sajal, 2018).

To summarize, the price of a product has a complex meaning and can play various roles to consumers. Retailers need to understand all price perceptions that consumers have for a product or a brand, to uncover quality and value inferences, and to discover any price premiums that they can charge (Keller, 2013).

Manufacturers

In a traditional supply chain, manufacturers brand their products and sell them to the final consumer by using wholesalers and retailers. In turn, wholesalers and retailers sold only the manufacturers' brands. Manufacturers had the advantage to control the members of the distribution channel. In the past years, retailers have started selling their own brands, so-called private labels or store brands and give them more prominence in their retail outlets.

Manufacturer brands

Manufacturers brands are created by the producer and have a chosen brand name. The manufacturers have the responsibility for marketing the brand and normally have great advertising budgets. They usually have a large research and development division and invest a lot of money in development of new products or new, innovative features and investing in new technologies. Therefore, a manufacturer brand is normally more advanced and has more innovative features than private labels. Moreover, manufacturers must manage the distribution channels to reach the final consumers. This industry is characterised by relatively low margins, which explains a tendency towards consolidation and higher volumes.

The world's largest manufacturers are Nestlé, Procter & Gamble, PepsiCo, Unilever and Coca-Cola. The leading German manufacturers in the FMCG sector are Henkel, the Oetker Group and Beiersdorf. The main distribution structures for FMCG are large-format food retailers and complementary drugstores, especially in the near-food sector. In Germany, discounters and hypermarkets are the most important shopping outlets for everyday consumer goods. In general, food retailing is characterised by a high degree of concentration. In Germany, the four leading corporate groups share around 70% of the market. In Austria, only three leading companies share around 84% of the market. Most of the European countries have a similar market situation characterised by a high degree of concentration. Whereas, the specialist trade only plays a subordinate role overall, but has been able to maintain a certain importance in some areas, particularly in the food trades (e.g., bakeries and butchers' shops). Market concentration is much lower in other sectors, like the furniture sector or the apparel sector. In Austria, for example, the top three largest suppliers in the clothing industry, H&M, C&A and Peek&Cloppenburg, are claiming a market share of around 26% of the Austrian apparel market, which means that all other market participants share the remaining 74%.

In addition to the classic distribution of FMCG products in retail, the importance of e-commerce is also growing steadily in this consumer segment. The share of FMCG products in total online retail sales is constantly growing. Compared to other countries in the world, the potential of the online FMCG market in Europe has not yet been exhausted (Statista, 2019).

E-commerce during the Corona pandemic
The trend towards shopping on the internet has gained momentum during the Corona crisis. In June 2020, turnover in the online and mail-order business rose by almost a third in price-adjusted terms compared with the same month last year in Germany. Growth of this magnitude is unusual even in this very dynamic industry, it is due in large part to a special influence of the pandemic.

As many shops had to close at times during the Corona crisis and consumers feared infections, the already booming online trade received an additional boost. With a sales increase of more than 30% in June, the internet and mail order business grew much more strongly than the retail trade, which increased by 5.9%.

Revenues from furnishings, household appliances and building materials (up 14.6%) and food, beverages, and tobacco products (up 2.3%) also grew significantly, whereas business with textiles, clothing, shoes and leather goods, however, remained far below the previous year's level (minus 16%). The retail trade with goods of various kinds, including department stores, also suffered with losses of a good 11% (FAZ, 2020).

Private labels (store brands, retailer brands)

Private labels are created and owned by retailers, but they normally do not manufacture these brands, instead they outsource manufacturing. Private labels are usually of comparable quality with the manufacturers' brands but at a different price range depending on the branding strategy. Many customers find the prices of the manufacturer brands too high compared to those of private labels, whereas the quality is normally comparable. Customers have learned that the reason for lower prices of private labels is the lower cost due to the elimination of intermediaries and less advertising expenses and not because they are of lower quality. Now even premium brands in some categories are retailer brands. These private labels are given more prominence in the retail stores, thus enabling the transfer of power from manufacturers to retailers.

The power of low price of private labels have forced many manufacturer brands to introduce their own low-price alternatives. A major decision that manufacturers must face is whether to agree to supply private label products for retailers or not. An advantage could be to fill excess capacity and generate extra income. A disadvantage could be that the private label brand could cannibalize with the manufacturers brand and reduce sales and profit margins.

2.2.1 Different pricing strategies for retailers

In daily business retailers make use of different pricing strategies. This chapter explains the most important and frequently used strategies, demand-oriented pricing, cost-oriented pricing, competition-oriented pricing, one price for all, flexible pricing,

Demand-oriented pricing

Demand-oriented pricing uses the customer demand to set up the price in the market. Retailers can charge a higher price when the demand is high (in the case of services during the peak hours), whereas a lower price is charged when the demand for a product is low. Some of the methods used for demand-oriented pricing are:

- **Price skimming**: The retailers initially set a product at a high price and attracts customers less concerned with price than service, status, quality, and assortment. So, the retailer achieves high profit per product, but normally does not increase sales, and slowly the cost decreases. Initially the highest price which the consumers are willing to pay are charged. As the demand of the customers is satisfied and competition enters the market, the retailer lowers the price to attract more price-sensitive customers.
- **Psychological pricing**: The retailer prices the products with figures that end with 7 or 9, like 3,47 Euros or 99.99 Euros. These prices are perceived to be cheaper by the consumer than whole numbers, like 4 Euros or 100 Euros. So, these prices have a greater psychological impact of cost effectiveness.
- **Penetration pricing**: The retailers initially set a product at a low price to penetrate the market with a new product and to attract new customers or target-groups, also from competitors. Penetration pricing relies on the strategy of using low prices initially to make a wide number of customers aware of a new product. As soon as the retailers has built market share prices rise back to normal levels.
- **Prestige pricing (image pricing, premium pricing)**: When using this pricing strategy retailers assume that "expensive" is perceived by customer as "high quality," which means the quality of a product is determined by the price. Prestige pricing has a direct correlation with the brand and the perception of the customers over the image of the company. This strategy assumes that the customer will pay higher prices for the right image of a brand. The high price is also used as a marketing strategy by convincing the customer that their product or brand offers and added value. Basically, the retailer relies on the fact that the customers presummit that their product is of higher quality than those of their competitors because of the higher price.
- **Price bundling**: Offer a product or service together with the main product for a total special price.

Cost-oriented pricing (Mark-up Pricing)

Cost-oriented pricing, sometimes called mark-up pricing, is the most widely used pricing method in the retail sector. This is due to the fact that costs are an important component of pricing and no retailer can survive without being profitable and covering the costs. This cost-based approach means that the retailer adds a certain percentage to the actual costs, which is passed on to the final consumer in the form of a new price. However, this approach does not consider what the customer is willing to pay for a certain product.

In practice, the retailer defines as a main goal a particular gross margin that will generate a desirable profit. *Gross margin* can be explained as the difference between how much the product costs and the actual price for which it is sold to the final consumer. Gross margins (a certain percentage of net sales) vary among products and product categories and among retail type, for example, discounters have smaller gross margins than speciality stores.

> For example, a woman's dress costs 14.50€ and is sold for 49.99€. The mark-up is 35.49€. The mark-up may be designated as a percent of the selling price or as a percent of the cost of the product. In this example, the mark-up is 40.86% of cost (35.49€ /14.50€) or 70.99% of the retail price (35.49€/49.99€).

The reason why cost-oriented pricing is frequently used is that retailers don't have to forecast general business conditions or customer demand. Moreover, customers charge this pricing strategy as fair since the price they pay is related to the cost of producing the product.

Competition-oriented pricing

Competition-oriented pricing, also referred to as market-oriented pricing, is a strategy which bases the prices of the products on those of competitors without considering consumer demand or actual costs of the products. In addition, this pricing strategy considers the target market when setting the prices, considers the business objectives and considers how the difference between competitors' prices and the own prices will affect the customers. Competition-oriented pricing strategies have the disadvantage that the retailer sometimes does not realizes when prices need a changing due to market changes or a change in consumer needs and desires.

Competition-oriented pricing contains three different price levels, to set the prices below, at or above the market. First, prices can be set higher than those of competitors if the retailer's business objective is to market the products as high-end or exclusive products or to signalize that the products are of better quality than competitors' products. Second, the retailer can decide to set the prices below competitors' products. Reasons for choosing this strategy would be to be more competitive and more affordable. Third, prices can be set the same or similar to competitors. When choosing this strategy, the retailer has to offer an added value to be competitive, for example a special rewards program, a more attractive location, sustainable business practices, a better service level, etc.

When using competition-oriented pricing retailers must make sure that their prices cover at least their production costs and additional expenses. Moreover, the retailer must make sure that when providing an added value to be more competitive this should not cut into profits and reduce revenues.

Customary pricing and discount pricing

Customary pricing means that a retailer sets prices for the products and seeks to maintain those prices over an extended period, so that customers can take these prices for granted over long periods of time. Many discounters use this pricing strategy to win the trust of the customers. They very often use the so-called everyday low pricing strategy (EDLP) with the goal to establish set prices so their customers can take those prices for granted. Everyday low pricing has received increased attention as a means of determining price discounts and promotions over time. This strategy is also used to reduce the use of frequent short-term price reductions, instead they set low prices on a consistent basic rather than setting higher prices and frequently discounting them.

Discount pricing and price reductions are a frequently used tactic of retailing. Typically, pricing strategies based on discounts are designed to bring in more customer traffic that might offer the potential of purchasing higher-priced items at higher margins in addition to the price-reduced items. Discounts can take several forms:
- direct online price cuts
- coupons that could be used both online and at brick-and-mortar stores
- promotions offered during presale events
- platform discounts offered by e-commerce sites

The box below illustrates a prominent example of the successful use of the EDLP strategy.

Everyday Low Pricing at Walmart Inc

Walmart is the world's largest retailer founded in Arkansas, USA, in 1962 by Sam Walton. Walmart has gained significant success due to the everyday low pricing strategy. The retailer offers low prices to consumers throughout the year, instead of offering low prices during sales and promotion events. Walmart has built its reputation on being the company that offers consumers the lowest prices every day. Although this strategy results in slim margins, the retailer can generate significant profits from high sales volume. Today Walmart operates more than 8,500 stores and serves 200 million consumers around the world.

In early days, one of the key strategies was to concentrate just on small town locations. Walmart opened discount stores in small town and spread out its stores and filling an unserved market gap until Walmart saturated its market and competition came up.

Walmart always claimed to help their suppliers improve inventory management and efficiency as a win-win partnership. Another core competence of the major retailer is logistic management. Walmart very early demonstrated commitment to technology, being the earliest to adopt satellite technology connection the chain to one big network. Moreover, Walmart has been seeking for the continuing development by adoption, for example, of RFID technology.

In term of service and staff, Walmart knows how to motivate its staff. For example, the retailer has introduced the so-called *ten-foot rule*, which means any member of staff within ten feet of a customer must offer him or her assistance. Moreover, staff members are not plain employees but "associates." Being associate means that the employee is eligible for a share of the profits and stock options in the company. So, Walmart has reached to create a loyal and motivated workforce.

To summarize, Walmart has successfully introduced the Everyday Low Prices (EDLP) strategy to capture demand of consumers and brand reputation and trust of customers. Walmart has set up highly automated distribution centres, cutting down on delivery time and costs. The retailer's computerized inventory systems gave managers real-time information on their stocks, speeding up the re-ordering of goods. Another competitive advantage of Walmart is technology, being the earliest to adopt satellite technology connection the chain to one big network. Besides, Walmart has been seeking for the continuing development by adoption RFID in the system. Using the inventory management over the competitors and a lot of suppliers that deal with Walmart. Also, the main successful of Walmart is cost control. Walmart can control and avoid unnecessary cost very well, therefore Walmart can offer a low price than competitors to consumers because of economic of scale (UKessays, 2018).

Variable pricing (Yield management pricing)

Variable pricing is a pricing strategy in which the prices of a product or service coincide with fluctuations in costs or consumer demand. In detail, prices may vary based on region, sales location, date, time, age, or other factors. Variable pricing strategies adjust product prices to achieve an appropriate balance between sales volume and profit. So, variable pricing is a marketing strategy to sell products to consumers at different prices. The same product is sold at a varying price depending on the demand of the product at a certain time or certain region. The variable pricing strategy is a frequently used technique to generate profit.

Variable pricing is also frequently used in the airline and hotel business. It is commonly observed that the prices of air ticket vary depending on the season, date, and demand. The airlines change the prices of the tickets of the airplane when there is high demand, especially in the festive season, for example, Christmas, summer holidays or New Year's Eve. Similarly, in the hotel industry, the different prices of hotel rooms can be seen for the same type of room on different hotel booking platforms and the rooms near tourist attraction available at cheap prices during off season and the prices of the same rooms hiked up when there is high demand.

How Uber's dynamic pricing model works

Similar to the airline and hotel industry "Uber" is also known for using a variable pricing model. The price per kilometer rises when there is a rise in the demand for uber service. Companies use this technique to drive more profit during the demand period, and the low prices are offered to attract customers during the low demand period.

In detail, when you go to request a ride on a Saturday night, you might find that the price is different than the cost of the same trip a few days earlier. That's because of the dynamic pricing algorithm, which adjusts rates based on a number of variables, for example time and distance of the route, traffic and the current rider-to-driver demand. So, there is a temporary increase in price during particularly busy periods, these include Friday and Saturday nights, After-work rush hour, big events and festivals.

Once more drivers get on the road and ride requests are taken, the demand will become more manageable, and fares should revert to normal.

To summarize, dynamic pricing helps Uber to make sure there are always enough drivers to handle all the ride requests (Uber, 2019).

Leader pricing

Leader Pricing is also a frequently used pricing strategy in retail business. In detail, retailer sells selected items in a product family or assortment at less than usual profit margins, to introduce a new brand or product and to stimulate consumer interest in a particular product or brand, or to get lost customers back and increasing sales. Those products sold with leader pricing are very often sold at a loss, therefore, they are named loss leaders.

In general, the more competitive a market is, for example, in the grocery sector, the more likely the market players use loss-leader products, either in a particular category or throughout the store.

Multiple-unit pricing

Multiple-unit pricing is a pricing strategy used for frequently purchased products, often products for daily consumption, like sweets or dairy products, etc. When using this strategy, a single price is set for two or more units, such as two yoghurts for 99 cents rather than 50 cents per pot. Price-sensitive customers very often search for such promotions in the store because they want to save money. The main advantage for the retailer is to increase sales.

Price lining

When using a price lining strategy, the retailer offers a line of similar products at different price levels to reach a larger target group. In detail, a good, better, and best version of merchandise is offered at different price levels, from cheap to expensive- including a low-, medium- and high-end product. So, price lining also appeals to budget-conscious consumers because they have the feeling that they're getting a great bargain.

The retailer's main objective is, same as the other pricing strategies, to increase sales and generate more profit. Market research is needed to determine the right product mix and prices.

Apple uses price lining
An appropriate example of product line pricing provides Apple. For example, Apple offers different versions of iPads and iPhones, all at different price levels. On their website (https://www. apple.com/at/ipad/compare/) the offer and compare 16 different versions of iPads, from 12,9" iPad Pro for 1.099 € to the regular iPad for iPad 379 € or the iPad mini around 449 €. This is a great example of product line pricing because it includes the costs to make the versions, the different features included in each version, and how Apple is making several different versions of a similar product. Each of the products fits the demands of a certain consumer group. Some

consumers want to have the newest version and are willing to pay a premium price, whereas other customers just want to have an Apple iPad, but are not willing to pay a lot of money for the product. So, they accept an older version or less features offered at a lower price level.

2.2.2 Digital pricing strategies

Digital pricing strategies have become indispensable in aviation and getting more and more popular in retailing, online and offline retailing. Especially time-dynamic or personalized adjustment of prices bear great profit potential, which e-commerce retailers are often taking advantage of. Digital pricing strategies companies can achieve a significant increase in profitability through reduced inventory levels, value-added offers, and improved absorption of willingness to pay, without violating the perceived fairness principles of customers. Customers, on the other hand, can benefit from more conveniently distributed capacity utilization, better product availability and attractive prices, as digital pricing not only raises prices but can also lower them (Marketingverband, 2018). The time of the price adjustment can take two forms (Marketingverband, 2018):

- Periodically: Prices are adjusted and communicated on a period-oriented basis, for example, when annual product catalogs or newsletters are sent out.
- Frequently: Prices are adjusted and communicated at specific time points. The prices can be updated several times a day. The differentiation factors decide based on which influences the price points are calculated. Four dimensions are defined as an extension and concretization of differentiation factors:
  - Offer: corresponds to a quantitative price differentiation.
  - Internal: production and opportunity costs of the company.
  - Environment: all external or customer-related factors, such as weather, competition, exchange rates, etc.
  - Segment: prices considering the situationally different customer needs and target groups.

Amazon, for example, uses an algorithm-based tool for pricing the products that weighs several metrics to determine the best possible price for each product with the best return on investment (ROI). This is also called dynamic pricing. Studies have shown that most companies vary their prices dynamically on the internet. This strategic tool helps them to exploit the consumer's maximum willingness to pay for a particular product.

But there are also disadvantages when using such pricing strategies. Customers often react with dissatisfaction and complaining when they notice a price disadvantage due to dynamic pricing models. This dissatisfaction can have a long-term impact on the buyer-seller relationship as well as the company's reputation and profits. Therefore, price fairness perception is essential for dynamic pricing strategies.

The following box provides a very good example to learn from when it comes to retailers with innovative business models, in general, and effective revenue models, in particular. Facebook, launched in February 2004 by Mark Zuckerberg, is a great example to learn from as the company has more than a billion monthly active users worldwide having, in relation, just 5,000 employees. Facebook's mission is to make the world more open and connected. Facebook has a so-called advertising-based revenue model. The most common advertising revenue models are pay per click (PPC), pay per view (PPV), and pay per action (PPA). These three *advertising revenue models* are described briefly as follows:

– *Pay per click (PPC)* is the most popular revenue model. Advertisers pay each time a user clicks on an ad and is redirected to the advertiser's website. Advertisers do not pay for each ad view, but only when the ad is clicked on. For advertisers, this advertising model is called *cost per click (CPC)*.
– *Pay per view (PPV)* is also very common. With this model, the company gets paid for each ad view or page-view. For advertisers, this is called *cost per impression (CPI)*. An impression is the display of an ad to a user while viewing a web page. A single web page may contain multiple ads. In such cases, a single page view would result in one impression for each ad displayed. Advertisers normally prefer the first advertising model, cost per click, since they don't like to pay for an ad view also when the user ignores their ad.
– *Pay per action (PPA):* this advertising revenue model was added a few years ago to mitigate the risks of click fraud. Here the advertiser pays only if a customer has been delivered to a website and takes a further action, for instance buying a product or filling out a web form. For advertisers this model is called *cost per action (CPA)* or *cost per lead (CPL)*.
– In daily business there do exist several alternative payment models. The three advertising models described above are mainly used to assess the cost effectiveness and profitability of online advertising. PPV and CPI are the closest online advertising models to those offered in traditional, above the line media such as TV, radio, or print. Therefore, PPV and CPI provide a comparable measure to contrast internet advertising with traditional media.

Facebook's business and revenue model
Facebook's core consumer benefits are the following:
Connect and share with your friends: staying connected is the core feature of the business model.
Discover and learn: Facebook references public figures and organizations that interest them available through Facebook company pages.
Express yourself: Has become a fundamental need, especially for Generation Z. Facebook offers this possibility through its key features which it describes as the timeline, news feed, photos and videos and messaging through email, chat and text.

Stay connected everywhere: People can access Facebook through the website, mobile sites, smartphone apps, and featured phone products.

Facebook's revenue model
Facebook has an advertising-based revenue model using the payment model cost per click (CPC). Some of the features of Facebook ads include: targeting by age, gender, location, interests, and more. An alternative payment model is impression-based payment (CPM). It has to be mentioned that the most challenging time is the first years, when the website is unknown and page-views are low. Facebook has had several hundred million in funding when it started business in 2004 and has been profitable only after several years. Until the website gets a million page-views per month, revenue will be negligible, and advertisers won't be interested in the site. As a rule of thumb to get approximately 1 million Euros in revenue per year you would need 1 billion-page views in a year. Facebook has over 700 billion-page views per year, but also took several years to get there.

2.2.3 Future payment methods

Today customers very often take out their phones in physical stores to see how prices compare online and offline prices and competitors' prices. But this phenomenon of looking up how prices of the store itself compare in different channels is relatively new. It has become the subject of increased interest since customers have found out that many retailers are charging higher prices for products in stores than online due to higher overheads. Prices increasingly vary between online and physical stores. Retailers tend to offer lower prices in their online stores to generate traffic. Understanding what customers value in each channel and how that affects what they are willing to pay is the key challenge when defining a retailer's online and offline pricing strategies.

In addition, change in payments has been evident in daily business. From digital disruption, innovation to regulatory requirements and customer demands, traditional payments methods will have to change. Generation Z consumers are the retail and payments industry's future customer base. This group is projected to make up 40% of all consumers in developed countries by 2022. Gen Z consumers are so-called digital natives, which means that they have been raised with new information and communication technologies, especially social media. Gen Z consumers demand personalized and highly-relevant experiences. When it comes to payment methods, studies have shown that online banking is the most frequently used banking channel among all consumers whereas Gen Z tend to use mobile banking apps. This confirms a massive generation gap in accessing banking services that will continue to widen in the years to come (Accenture, 2017).

Intrigued by digital tools that manage payments, bills, expenses and personal finances, Gen Z consumers want their e-wallets to think for them. One example would be a wallet that automatically chooses the card that offers the best rewards or savings (Accenture, 2017). As Gen Z enters the workforce and their financial needs become more complex, they will reshape traditional payment methods and systems. They are likely to be the first generation to replace the physical wallet for the digital wallet (Accenture, 2017).

Mobile payments and E-Wallets

Mobile payments are payment processes performed via mobile devices that eliminate the need for a physical credit card payment infrastructure. The two most commonly used mobile payment technologies in retail business are near-field communication (NFC) and QR codes. Protecting customers' payment transactions is an important priority for businesses. Among the most secure payment tools available, near-field communication technology has emerged as the leading technology.

NFC is a technology that enables two devices to exchange data when they are within close proximity. The technology allows retailers to accept contactless payments from customers using a mobile wallet (e-wallet) stored on their smartphone. To complete a payment transaction, the consumer just must tap or wave the smartphone on the payment terminal (Worldpay, 2019). NFC technology presents various opportunities for conducting commerce that appeal to consumers and retailers alike. Tapping or waving a payment is easier and more convenient than a traditional card transaction. If the customers are assured of the security of NFC transactions, the technology holds the potential to fundamentally change and improve payments transactions (Worldpay, 2019). Popular payment services that rely on NFC technology are, for example, PayPal, Apple Pay, or Samsung Pay.

QR-based payment services are, for example, WeChat Pay or Alipay (used in China). QR-based payment services are used for products that have a QR code. Customer then scan the bar code that contains information (e.g., product or order information) and is then redirected to a payment page in the smart device's browser, mostly mobile phone, to complete the transaction. Quick response codes began to be used much more for payments when WeChat and Alipay in China started offering proprietary versions in late 2011. Outside of China, the usage of QR codes for payments has grown slowly in the past years. Still, several banks and payments industry players are reviewing their strategies to take full advantage of this payments alternative. Master Card, for example, has introduced Masterpass™ QR, a new payment solution that allows consumers to pay for goods and services using mobile phones at retail outlets. More details in the box below.

Master Card working with QR codes

Master Card started working on QR codes for payment acceptance in late 2011. The development has been driven especially by consumers wanting immediacy and more places to pay, and by retailers wanting to accept more payments, as well as by lower capital costs.

Key use cases vary depending on the market. Consumers in India frequently use QR codes for payment on delivery for online orders, for instance, while consumers in Vietnam use QR codes to pay for taxis. Consumers in Indonesia use QR codes for bill payments, since scanning the QR code on the bill and making a payment solves a pain point of having to walk somewhere to make a payment.

While there has been fraud in China around the QR code, the technology for the QR codes that Master Card uses is different. There are security elements in the QR code as well as a check digit, and merchants have credentials that are registered only to receive payments to them. If someone extracts payment credentials, false credentials that are not specific to the merchant could not be used. The basic transaction is also controlled by a mobile phone, authentication such as biometric identification is needed, and Master Card uses tools such as network rules and velocity parameters to prevent fraud. Master Card has introduced a new payment solution that allows consumers to pay for goods and services using mobile phones at merchant outlets, the so-called Masterpass™ QR. Masterpass QR is secure, smart and easy, providing a cost-effective alternative to cash payments, mainly used in African markets. Masterpass QR uses the customers' bank's mobile banking application to make payments securely from the bank account.

Merchant education is also very simple. Merchants simply need to display a QR code and have it scanned, then receive notification though an app or text message to confirm the payment. For consumers, the QR button is on the screen and usage is straightforward (The Asian banker, 2014).

E-wallets (mobile or digital wallets) are also used for mobile payments and are supported by NFC or QR technology. E-wallets enables the customers to store their credit card information in a mobile app instead of having to use the traditional plastic card. Users consider e-wallets as more convenient than traditional credit cards, as they provide a better user interface and can store coupons and loyalty card information.

Studies have shown that by 2022, just 17% of global payments will be made by cash. Instead, e-wallet usage will continue to rise, accounting for 28% of all payment transactions in 2022. The British have the third highest e-wallet usage in the world, with 5% of all POS transactions. Other European countries record the following figures: France (1%), Spain (3%) and The Netherlands (3%). The United States has the same e-wallet usage than Spain (3%).

Mobile wallets account for 36% of China's total POS transactions, six times more than nearest rivals India (6%) and the UAE (6%). Consumers in China use mobile wallets nine times more that the rest of the world. The figures show that mobile wallet usage is increasing, the global number of users is up by an average of 140 million. Whereas Apple Pay was used for just $15 million worth of transactions in 2015, by 2017, it had grown nearly six times in size, accounting for $86 million worth of payments (Bepari, 2019). Numerous businesses have already made it mandatory to deploy mobile wallets for the convenience of their customers. To attract and retain more consumers, mobile wallet providers, like Apple Pay, Ali Pay, or Samsung Pay have been providing attractive discounts and cashback offers that serve to encourage repeated purchases via e-wallet. Studies have shown that most mobile wallet users (35%) are in the 25–34 "millennial" age group, and that the majority (40%) are high earners, still growing in purchasing power (Bepari, 2019).

Mobile payments have become ubiquitous in the daily lives of Chinese urban consumers
Shoppers pay for everyday small expenditures by scanning QR codes at point-of-sale terminals with their smartphones – buying anything from breakfast at the local coffee shop or tickets for their metro commute, to access to a bike-sharing scheme or food delivery for dinner. Even street vendors selling everything from dumplings to mobile phone covers use QR codes to receive payment.

However, the popularity of mobile payments enables the proliferation of cybersecurity threats, as the hacking of personal data has become very appealing for cybercriminals looking at getting their hands-on users' financial details (Weinswig, September 2016).

China is a large and dynamic market for mobile payments. Market research has shown that third-party mobile payments, which means payments between a buyer and a seller processed through a third party that acts as an intermediary, such as Alipay or Tenpay, in China grew by 106% year on year to reach $13.6 trillion. In fact, China is the largest market in the world for mobile payments. The main drivers of mobile payment adoption in the Chinese market are the following (Weinswig, September 2016):

- **Ubiquity of mobile internet:** Completely 95% of Chinese internet users accessed the internet via their mobile phones in 2016.
- **Consumer preferences:** E-wallets are very popular among Chinese consumers in urban areas with a strong omnichannel retail presence. At the same time, China has a weak credit card culture that favours the adoption of alternative electronic payment solutions (such as mobile payments), which are considered safer and more convenient.
- **Infrastructure:** The mobile-phone industry and NFC terminals – the technology used most to process mobile payments – are relatively sophisticated in China, resulting in a mobile payment infrastructure that is more advanced compared to other countries.
- **Retailer adoption:** Most retailers in China offer mobile payment options, from large international chains such as Starbucks to small independents, such as street vendors. Retailers' adoption of mobile payment, which is in response to consumers' preference for this type of payment solution, contributes to the further penetration of mobile payment.

Ali Pay benefits from its first-mover advantage as it was the app that pioneered mobile payments in China when it was introduced in 2004 as a service to facilitate transactions on Alibaba's online marketplace Taobao. Combined, Alipay and Tenpay (China's dominant messaging app) make up 88.5% of the Chinese mobile payment market.

On the other hand, with so many people using e-wallets on their smartphones for everyday payments, mobile devices have become a leading target for hackers seeking to get data such as payment transfer details and passwords. Payment traps and user-privacy violations were the top cybersecurity threat in 2016, with 88.3% and 76.0%, respectively, of mobile internet users affected during the year. Smartphone users in China are largely exposed to cybersecurity threats. The financial impact of cybersecurity threats on internet users in China can be significant. According to a report, there were 20,623 reports of online fraud on the department's cybersecurity platform in 2016, with a total loss of $29.3 million and an average loss per victim from online fraud of $1,426.

In response to the rise of mobile cybersecurity threats, the Chinese government adopted the Cybersecurity Law. The legislation contains cybersecurity requirements such as measures aimed at the protection of personal data and individual privacy that organizations handling data must comply with (Weinswig, September 2016).

2.3 Place

Another "P" of the original marketing mix is *place*. Place deals with questions of channels of distribution and getting the product or service to the consumer. In detail, the place strategy is about how a retailer will distribute their products to the final consumers. The retailer must distribute the products to the customers at the right place, in the right quantity and at the right time. Efficient and effective distribution is important if the organisation wants to meet its overall marketing objectives. If a retailer underestimates demand, profitability can be affected. The place is where the retailer conducts business with its customers. The place can be a physical retail location or a nonphysical space like an online store. When selecting the "place" for the retail operation, it is important to conduct research to find out where the retailer's target group prefer to shop.

The example in the following box shows how retailers frequently use different "places" to sale their products to reach different target groups and therefore maximise sales and profit.

Walmart's retail divisions
Walmart has more than 10,000 retail outlets which are spread across 28 countries in the world, mainly the United States, and operates under 60 different banners. It sells their products both by brick-and-mortar stores (physical stores) and brick and click (e-commerce) formats, ranging from the Supercentres to the Walmart Express stores or Neighbourhood Markets (Walmart, 2019b):

Walmart Discount Stores
Since founder Sam Walton opened his first store in 1962, Walmart now has more than 1,000 discount stores in the United States. Walmart discount stores offer a variety of quality, value-priced general merchandise, and a pleasant, convenient shopping experience. The discount stores average 107,000 square feet employ about 225 associates and offer 120,000 different products. The stores feature wide, brightly lit aisles and shelves stocked with quality items including family apparel, automotive products, health and beauty aids, home furnishings, electronics, hardware, toys, sporting goods, lawn and garden items, pet supplies, jewellery, and housewares.

Walmart Supercentres
Developed in 1988 to meet the growing demand for one-stop shopping, Walmart Supercenters today number more than 2,300 nationwide and most are open 24 hours a day. Supercentres save customers time and money by combining full grocery lines and general merchandise under one roof at Walmart's pricing strategy everyday low prices. In addition to general merchandise, Supercentres feature bakery goods, deli foods, frozen foods, meat and dairy products, and fresh produce. Supercentres also are home to many specialty shops such as vision centres, Tire & Lube Expresses, Radio Grill, McDonald's, or Subway restaurants, portrait studios and one-hour photo centres, hair salons, banks, and employment agencies. Supercentres average 187,000 square feet, employ 350 associates on average, and offer 142,000 different products.

Walmart Neighbourhood Markets
Neighbourhood markets offer a convenient shopping experience for customers who need groceries, pharmaceuticals, and general merchandise. Generally, they are in markets with Walmart Supercentres, supplementing a strong food distribution network and providing added convenience while

maintaining Wamart's everyday low prices. First opened in 1998, the now more than 120 neighbourhood markets, averaging 42,000 square feet, feature a wide variety of products, including
fresh produce, deli foods, fresh meat and dairy items, health and beauty aids, one-hour photo
and traditional photo developing services, drive-through pharmacies, stationery and paper goods,
pet supplies, and household chemicals. Neighbourhood markets employ 95 associates on average
and offer about 29,000 items.

Sam's Club

The members-only warehouse club offers a broad selection of general merchandise and large-
volume items at value prices. Since 1983, Sam's Club has been the preferred choice for small businesses, families or anyone looking for great prices on name-brand products. Each day more than
584 Sam's Club locations, averaging 132,000 square feet, help small business owners and operators – such as offices, childcare, schools, restaurants, motels, vending companies, churches, con-
tractors, and beauty shops – stand to gain the most from Sam's Club, which offers a convenient
and cost-efficient warehouse for these businesses to purchase materials and supplies.

  Each Sam's Club employs an average of 160 to 175 associates and offers approximately 5,500
different products. A nominal membership fee ($35 annually for businesses/$40 annually for individuals) helps defray operating costs and keeps prices exceptionally low.

Researchers have identified several factors which influence the consumers store choice.
Convenience, variety of products, the product quality, prices, and store loyalty are the
main factors affecting consumers choice of retail stores. In general, the following eight
factors influence a customer's choice when it comes to selecting a store:
- general store characteristics (e.g., reputation, number of stores, brand name)
- physical characteristics (e.g., decoration, cleanliness, checkout services)
- convenience (e.g., time, location, parking)
- products (variety, dependability, quality)
- prices charged (e.g., value for money, offers, special sales)
- personnel (e.g., courteous, helpful, friendly)
- advertising (e.g., informative, aggressive, emotional, believable)
- peer groups perception of the store (e.g., well-known, liked, recommended)

Choosing an ideal place or location for a retail business is one the most important
decisions a retailer must make when opening an outlet. The best location for a
brick-and-mortar retail stores combines factors like visibility and affordability, but
also accessibility, which means to choose a location where many of a retailer's target customers live or work.

2.3.1 Choosing a store location

The selection of a store location is one of the most important strategic decisions in
retailing. When choosing a store location, the retailer must take enough time to analyse the areas which are available to choose from and that are appealing to the

retailer. Location decisions are very complex because high costs can be involved and there is little flexibility once a location is chosen. The choice of a store location requires extensive decision-making due to the number of factors, which must be considered, like population size and traits, the competition, transportation access, parking availability, nearby stores and area, property costs, the length of the agreement, legal restrictions, catchment area, etc. (Berman & Evans, 2013).

In general, there are three phases of choosing a location for a retail store:
– selection of the city
– choice of an area or type of location within a city
– identification of a specific site

Selection of the city

In choosing a city for the retail location several main factors must be considered. Apart from any strategic decisions, one of the most important factors is the size of the city's trading area, the size of the population and demographic characteristics of the population, like age distribution, the average educational and income level and composition of the household (e.g., How many household members? How many children?). Another important factors which must be considered are the total purchasing power of the city and the total retail trade potential. Moreover, the number and strengths of the competition must analysed when selecting the city.

Secondary data is normally available to generate data on the factors described above. For example, when it comes the characteristics of residents, like size, age, income level, etc., statistical institutions provide this information. Statista (https://www.statista.com/), for example, is a business data platform, which gives insights and facts across 600 industries and more than 50 countries, providing current market figures and forecasts for the most important consumer goods within a total of more than 200 markets. All key figures are based on extensive analyses of data from national and international statistical offices, associations, company reports and the trade press. In the United States the Census of Population (https://www.census.gov/) supplies important data, mainly on demographic characteristics.

Choice of an area or type of location within a city

Once the retailer has a general idea of what city is suitable for opening a store location, an area or type of location within that city must be selected. The retailer must evaluate alternate trading areas and decide on the most desirable one. Defining a trade area is an important step in choosing a store location. This step is so important because it defines the boundaries and helps retailers to identify opportunities to expand their own trade area in a further step.

A trade area is the geographic area from which most customers is generated. This often is the geographic area that represents 75% of current customers. Knowing the size and shape of each trade area is extremely important because its boundaries allow for measurement of the number of potential customers, their demographics, and their spending potential. This information provides valuable insight into a retailer's customer base and allows the retailer to calculate demand for stores, products, and services (Kures, Pinkovitz, & Ryan, 2011).

Trade areas often come in a variety of shapes and sizes and extend beyond city or neighbourhood boundaries, depending on a variety of factors including the population and its proximity to other competing business districts. These factors include (Kures, Pinkovitz, & Ryan, 2011):

- Population: Generally, the larger the population, the bigger the trade area is.
- Proximity of other competing business districts: There is a cut-off point where customers are drawn to the competing centre instead of the own.
- Mix of businesses: A critical mass of businesses pulls customers from a further distance than a more limited mix of businesses.
- Destination attractions: A significant destination business (e.g., a large discount department store) or community attraction can expand a trade area, drawing customers from a long distance.
- Traffic patterns: Each area has distinct traffic patterns strongly impacted by the network of streets, landforms, rivers, lakes, mountains, etc.

There are various means when it comes to defining a trade area. A frequently used theoretical mean is *Reilly's Law of Retail Gravitation*, which is based on the premise that consumers are attracted to larger communities to do their shopping, but the time and distance they must travel influence their willingness to shop in a particular city or trade area. In detail, consumers are more likely to travel shorter distances when possible. Additionally, customers are more likely to shop in larger communities as they typically offer more goods and services or special offers and lower prices (Kures, Pinkovitz, & Ryan, 2011).

Reilly's Law provides a mathematical formula that can be used to calculate hard numbers relating the distance people will travel. However, you can also combine a simple map and common sense to apply the concepts behind Reilly's Law to define general trade area boundaries. While theoretical, using Reilly's Law provides a general sense of the community's trade area. This method requires little effort and few resources. However, Reilly's Law does not capture possible variations in the trade area. Additionally, Reilly's Law is less appropriate if you are defining both convenience and destination shopping trade areas.

Reilly's law of retail gravitation applied on hypermarkets

Rosu (2013) found it his study when locating and planning a new location, strategies of geomarketing should be taken into consideration because "they offer a reliable foundation for expansion-planning decisions." A geomarketing approach is therefore indispensible to handle today's complex challenges.

Reilly's Law of Retail Gravitation provides a general sense a community's trade area. In this study Reilly's model offers an image of patronizing shopping area for a planned hypermarket.

The catchment areas of the existing hypermarkets (according to the Reilly model) cover only some neighbourhoods which are in the proximity; the customers located beyond the breaking points face themselves with the situation of having to choose between two or more possibilities. Those are residents of the neighbourhoods located in the South East and North West side of the city (residential neighbourhoods) and in the areas with the highest values of population density (Alexandru cel Bun-Dacia neighbourhoods). Therefore, a fifth hypermarket was considered in the analysis. The changes induced by a new shopping centre are visible especially in Alexandru cel Bun and Dacia neighbourhoods, which also correspond with a less patronized area. Another aspect that is worth mentioning is the change in what concerns the theoretical approximation of maximum possible customers of each hypermarket once a new shopping centre would be built (Rosu, 2013).

Types of trade areas

Trade areas business districts can be classified into two major categories (Kures, Pinkovitz, & Ryan, 2011):
- convenience trade area
- destination trade areas

Smaller communities normally encompass only one type of trade area, the so-called primary trade area. Whereas communities with over 10,000 residents normally have both a convenience and a destination trade area (secondary trading area).

A *convenience trade area* is based on the purchase of products and services needed on a regular basis, such as petrol, newspaper, groceries, sanitary products, etc. The purchases of those products are relatively frequent. Therefore, consumers find it more convenient to buy these products from shops located close to their home or workplace.

A *destination trade area* is based on the purchase of "major" products, very often nonfood products, like home appliance, apparel, gardening products, or products that are distinctive in a particular way, such as discounted products. People are willing to travel longer distances to do comparison shopping and purchase these kinds of items. A large discount department store's trade area can often be used to represent a community's destination trade area.

In addition to differing by types of goods and services, a business district differs in the types of customers who shop there. Three common market segments can be distinguished (Kures, Pinkovitz, & Ryan, 2011):
- **Local residents**: reside locally all the year round, therefore they provide the majority of spending potential for most retail shops.
- **Daytime employees**: either live in the trade area or commute from other communities. They have the potential to buy products within the trade area during the workday.
- **Tourists and second-home owners**: this market segment can offer a large amount of spending potential. While they are not permanent residents, tourists shop while visiting the area.

Several data must generated when it comes to analysing retail trading areas. Many different factors must be included to get a comprehensive basis for decision-making. The most important factors are the following:
- customer attraction power, also including concentration of customers and frequency of shopping
- nature of competition, including number, size and strength of competitors
- availability of access routes to the stores
- zoning and other regulations, like taxes, minimum wages, operating costs
- geographic direction of the city's expansion
- general appearance of the area, including saturation of the area
- sales and traffic growth prospects of the trade area
- availability of labour
- demographics, like age distribution, average educational level, average income, occupation, total size, average household size (including children)

Identification of a specific site

After choosing the city and deciding on the type of trade area, the retailer must decide on a specific site. The identification of a specific site mainly depends on the branch and on the size of the store. Stores depend often on the traffic created by large stores or a group of stores. In convenience trade areas stores depend on attracting customers from the existing flow of traffic. Whereas, in destination trade areas the site selection depends mainly on the customer's view of the goods the retailer offers. There are various factors that affect the site choice (Berman & Evans, 2013):
- flow of traffic (pedestrian traffic and vehicular traffic)
- general transportation and public transportation
- nature of neighbouring stores
- parking facilities
- characteristics of competitors
- saturation of area
- retail space/type of location

In general, retailers can sell three types of goods: convenience goods, shopping goods and specialty goods. The type has an influence on the distance the customers are willing to travel when they want to buy these goods. For example, *convenience goods*, like milk, bread, newspapers, candies, etc., which are low-priced, are frequently purchased goods that require little selling effort. These goods are bought by habit, and are sold in numerous stores, so competition is normally large. Quantity of traffic and accessibility is most important for retailers selling convenience goods.

Shopping goods, like apparel, household appliance, etc., usually have a higher unit price and are purchased infrequently. When buying theses goods customers normally compare prices and the item's features, so the purchase process requires more effort than when buying convenience goods. For retailers selling shopping goods, not the quantity (frequency) of traffic is important, but the quality of the traffic. Because certain kinds of shopping goods are purchased only by a particular consumer group. For example, a children's clothing store should be placed to a traffic generator like a department store. Whereas the location for a discount kids store should be easily accessible, ideally a highway location, and near similar stores because customers of shopping goods like to compare the goods in several stores. Moreover, shopping goods are very often bought together with complementary items, like apparel and shoes or household appliance and food products, therefore those shops should be located close to one another.

The third category is *specialty goods*. Specialty goods, like cars, expensive jewellery, exclusive perfume, etc., usually have a higher price, are bought infrequently, and require a special effort to buy these goods. Specialty goods are usually sold in isolated locations because customers are willing to travel longer distance to buy such goods. Therefore, specialty goods generate their own consumer traffic.

To summarize, a cluster of stores creates more customer traffic and creates a kind of "buying" atmosphere because customers are attracted by crowds and like their shopping trips to be social activities. Nevertheless, when choosing the ideal location for a store, retailers must branch off exactly the advantages and disadvantages of each location that is taken into consideration.

2.3.2 Store layout

A retail store layout is the strategic use of space to influence the customer's purchase decision, how he or she interacts with the merchandise and the POS experience (the so-called user experience).

In general, the retail store layout has two main elements, the store design, and the customer flow:
- **Store Design:** the planning of the store design includes numerous tasks and decisions, such as designing floor plans and the usage of space management, including decisions about the furniture, displays, fixtures, lighting, and (digital) signage.
- **Customer Flow:** deals with the way a customer navigates through a store. Understanding customer flow, the walking patterns and the customer's interaction with merchandise is critical to know for every retail manager. The customer flow has an influence on which goods are purchased and how the customer's shopping cart is composed. Retail management can track the customer flow by using analytics software and data from in-store video or other in-store localization solutions, like Bluetooth, beacon, laser, GPS, etc. The dominant tracking technology is based on the measurement of Wi-Fi radio frequency intensity from the customer's smartphone.

Another frequently used method is to detect the movement of the shoppers through video, some of the advanced video technologies also offer the possibility to recognize the mood of the shoppers or provide sociodemographical data.

Other in-store tracking solutions include Bluetooth technology which is based on the measurement of Bluetooth radio frequency intensity from the shopper's smartphones, or Bluetooth low-energy beacons that are based on a mobile application downloaded on the shopper's smartphones (a so-called store app). Another tracking solution provides laser technology. In this case sensors are placed at the entrance of a store, counting the number of customers entering the store, through laser detection.

The external retail store layout includes several important elements, including, for example, the retail building itself (size, architecture, location, etc.), the design of the entrance and exterior window displays, exterior space and building materials, etc.

In general, retailers can improve customer experience and increase long-term profitability with efficient store layouts. Experts (Ebster & Garaus, 2011) provide valuable insights how retail space can be maximised:

1. **Target the first floor**

   Studies have shown that customers prefer to navigate the floor of a retail store they initially entered. Walking up and down stairs or using elevators and escalators to navigate a store hurts the customer flow. In addition, planning for a single floor store design normally optimizes the customer experience. Therefore, if the retailer has more than one floor (multiple floors), the first floor should be used to feature products or high-margin merchandise.

2. **Identify the customer flow**

   Customer flow patterns vary depending on the type of retailer, the size of the store, and the target customer. Ebster (Ebster & Garaus, 2015) encourages retailers to use their observations to discover the problems and opportunities unique to their environment. The most effective method for understanding a retailer's existing customer flow and identifying areas of opportunity is video recording and heat mapping analysis. However, setting aside different times of the day to make in-store observations in person and recording notes is a step in the right direction for identifying customer flow patterns.

3. **Avoid the transition zone**

   After a retailer has identified how the customers navigate through the store, the transition zone area (so-called *decompression zone*), the space beyond the entrance to a store, must be in focus. Normally the customer needs this zone to transition so they can familiarise with the new environment. Experts recommend that nothing of value to the retailer, not high-margin merchandise, prominent signage, or brand information should be placed in this zone. Customers need time to adjust to new lighting, smells, music, or visual stimulation in the store (Ebster & Garaus, 2011).

Furthermore, an eye-tracking study has shown that in this entrance area also advertising ads and flyers receive hardly any attention. Special promotions or displays are noticed, but attention is poor. Fixation count and dwell time is the lowest compared to the other areas of interest. More attention receive end cap displays or promotional areas where, for example, customers could taste a new product.

4. **Design for clockwork navigation**

After passing the transition zone, the customers start walking through the store and running their errands. So, the retailer has to put the focus on how to leverage a customer's tendency to navigate the shop. The area just outside of the transition zone is where most retailers make a first impression. Studies have shown that customers normally turn right after entering a store and continue to navigate a store in a counterclockwise direction. Therefore, it is recommended to display high-margin merchandise and valuable information just to the right of the entrance (outside of the transition zone) (Ebster & Garaus, 2011).

Moreover, an eye-tracking study has shown that eye-catching or obtrusive product presentations lead to the fact that dwell time of fixations are much longer, and fixation counts higher. Apparently, there is no correlation between duration of visual attention and purchase decision. Furthermore, the average length of a fixation is longer if it is an inexperienced shopper and if the purchase of a product is planned.

The longer a customer stays in a shop the more products they normally buy. It can be concluded that there is a correlation between the length of stay and number of products purchased.

5. **Avoid narrow aisles and bottlenecks**

Many studies have shown that customers do not want to feel constricted in their shopping or at least not have the feeling of being oppressed. Therefore, it is important to design a sales room in such a way that tight spaces or bottlenecks along aisles or around fixtures and displays are avoided.

If a customer is touched, bumped, or otherwise interrupted when interacting with merchandise, they are likely to move on from the products or display or even exit the store. Therefore, retailers must make sure that the aisles in the store are broad enough and the walkways are accessible and spacious. These aisles send positive signals to shoppers and positively impact customer flow and merchandise interaction (Ebster & Garaus, 2011).

Once a retailer understands how the customers navigate the store, he has to make decisions how to influence the customers' purchase decisions. To create a shopping environment that emphasizes a desired purchasing behaviour, it is essential to make use of the floor space allocated to the merchandise and design the store layout in a favourable way. Several store layouts are currently used in the retail landscape to achieve a certain objective, depending on whether the retailer wants to influence image, increase sales of the products, or increase the time customers spend in the store. The most frequently used store layouts are (Smartsheet, 2020):

- straight store layout
- forced-path store layout
- grid store layout
- free-flow layout
- boutique store layout

Straight store layout

The straight store layout is the most frequently used store layout, especially in the grocery retail sector and here for convenience stores (see Figure 2.2). The straight store layout is efficient and simple to plan. The advantage is that it is the most economical store designs as it makes use of the walls and fixtures to create small spaces within the retail store. This straight design helps to pull customers also towards featured merchandise in the back of the store. POS displays and a mixture of materials and furniture keep customers excited and moving.

A disadvantage is that customers may find it difficult to see the whole assortment because customers might not quickly find the products they want to purchase.

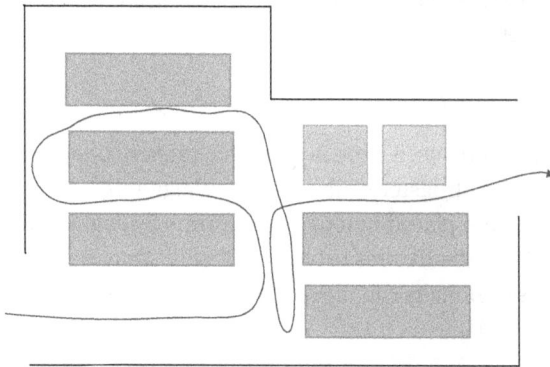

Figure 2.2: **Straight store layout.**
Source: Smartsheet, 2020

Forced-path store layout

The forced-path store layout aims to ensure that the customers are directed on a predetermined route through the retail store to be exposed to all the merchandise presented (see Figure 2.3). The Swedish furniture retailer IKEA is a suitable example for this design. The main advantage of this layout is that the customers see what the retailer has to offer and might buy products in passing that he or she wouldn't have planned to buy (Ebster & Garaus, 2011).

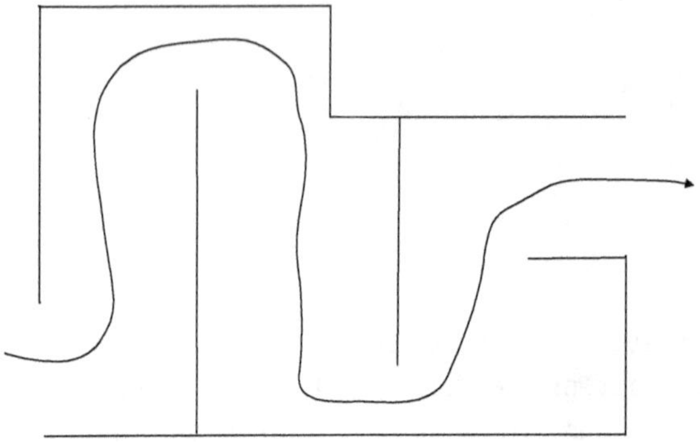

Figure 2.3: Forced-Path store layout.
Source: Smartsheet, 2020

This store layout has also disadvantages. One of the main disadvantages is that customers are often annoyed that they must go through the whole store before they can come to the checkout and pay for their products. Therefore, it is important to give the customer the opportunity to shorten his way. If a customer is short of time, he would otherwise avoid such stores.

Grid store layout

The grid store layout design is a frequently used store layout which is very often used in consumer markets, hypermarkets or drugstores like Müller, Walgreens, etc. (see Figure 2.4). The counters and fixtures are placed in long rows or runs throughout the store. Customers circulate up and down the fixtures usually willing to shop the entire store. One of the main advantages is customers can move quickly through an efficient

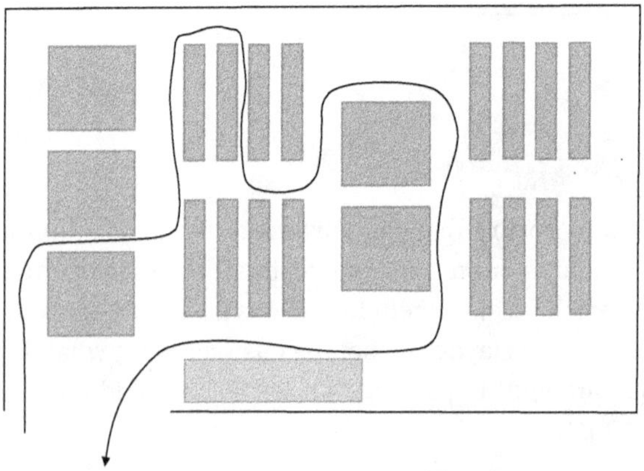

Figure 2.4: Grid store layout.
Source: Smartsheet, 2020

floor space using standard fixtures and displays. But a grid store layout can be confusing because it is normally difficult to see over the fixtures to find out where other merchandise is located. Therefore, Ebster (Ebster & Garaus, 2011) recommends effective signage to guide customers through the store and create a "cognitive map" of the store. "Gentle" customer guidance for orientation can be reached by creating key visuals, like a signage or an eye-catching advertisement, material, and colour changes (e.g., for different price ranges), integration of focal points and rest areas or different lighting concepts (e.g., to highlight items).

Loop store layout

A loop store layout uses a predefined path to lead customers from the entrance of the store to the checkout area (see Figure 2.5) with the objective to expose customers to every item displayed. With a loop floor plan, the central part of the store can be set up in a grid or free-flow layout (which will be discussed below) or even a mix of the two and surrounds customers with POS displays mainly in the centre of the store. A loop store layout is suitable for smaller retail stores, such toy stores, homewares, personal care, and specialty products, etc.

The advantage of this layout is that the whole merchandise is visible as well as the employees, and the retailer can make the most out of a limited display area. Retailers can also use a loop store layout to guide shoppers through their products in a certain order.

Nevertheless, a loop store layout does not make sense for every type of retailer. A loop design can feel overwhelming if products are stacked too high or too tightly and it is not suitable for convenience shopping trips, as customers must walk the entire store.

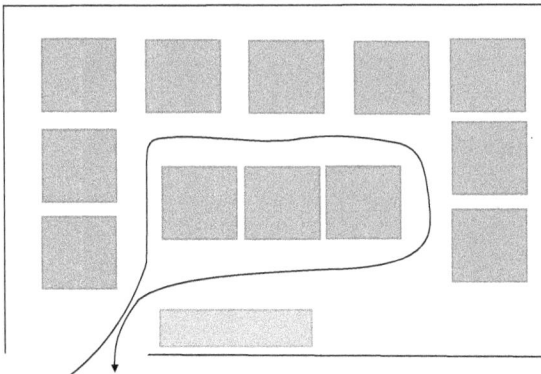

Figure 2.5: Loop store layout.
Source: Smartsheet, 2020

Therefore, Ebster (Ebster & Garaus, 2011) encourages a clear and visible loop for customer flow, for example, by making the floor path a standout colour, lighting the loop to guide the customer, or using a different floor material to mark the loop. The loop design must reward the customer with interesting visual displays and focal points on the way to the checkout area.

Free-flow store layout

A free-flow store layout is a layout that rejects typical design patterns and styles as there are no specific design rules, and customers have more liberty to interact with merchandise and navigate on their own (see Figure 2.6). In a free-flow store layout, the intent is not to lead the customer using predictable design patterns, displays, or signage. A free-flow store layout is frequently used by specialty retailers, like high-end apparel shop or children's clothes store, all stores with smaller inventories, etc., because it allows maximum creativity and is easily changed and updated. Fixtures and displays are placed at angles to encourage shoppers to slow down and explore highlighted merchandise. This store layout makes it easy to focus customers towards specific merchandise zones using eye-catching displays or colours.

Moreover, this layout allows stores to easily rotate or reconfigure product displays to feature new or seasonal items.

Free-flow store plans require a lot of creativity and careful planning. In that regard, they are more difficult to implement than a more structured retail store layout. Another disadvantage is the risk of confusing customers past the point of their preferred behaviour and disrupting customer flow (Ebster & Garaus, 2011).

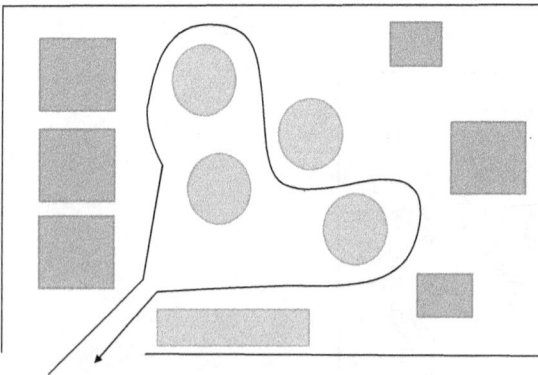

Figure 2.6: Free-flow store layout.
Source: Smartsheet, 2020

Boutique store layout

The boutique store layout, also called shop-in-the-shop layout, is the most widely used type of the free-flow store layout (see Figure 2.7). Merchandise is separated by category, and customers are encouraged to interact more intimately with like items in semi-separate areas created by walls, POS displays, and fixtures. Typically used by apparel retailers or gourmet markets, this layout stimulates customer curiosity in different brands or themes of merchandise within the overall category (Ebster & Garaus, 2011).

The boutique store layout also has disadvantages. One of the main disadvantages is customers might get confused by this free flow layout and the exploration of the different areas can distract from customer interaction with the merchandise. Moreover, the total display space for merchandise with is reduced.

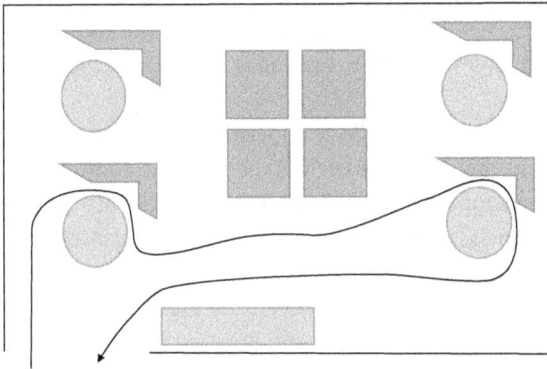

Figure 2.7: Boutique store layout.
Source: Smartsheet, 2020

To conclude, no matter which store layout a retailer chooses, it is important that stores have to create experiences and connect the customer experience with a mobile friendly retail strategy, as todays customers are increasingly dependent on their mobile devices and interacting with it, although during their shopping trips (e.g., checking prices or inventory availability, or using their device to find physical store location and opening hours). Retailers have to create a friendly, value proposition-focused customer journey and simplify the purchasing process.

The physical future store is well-arranged, transparent, open, generous with light colours and broad main aisles (min. 2.5 m). the entrance is friendly and open with a security system. The store provides in-store technology, in line with the overall store concept, like info terminals, digital shopping assistants, in-store TV, digital signage, self- scanning, and many more. For more details see Chapter 3.2.1.

2.3.3 Supply chain management and logistics

The supply chain in general has become an important issue for every retailer and organization during the last decade. Individual businesses no longer compete as independent and autonomous entities, but are obliged to form supply chains, and networks of multiple businesses and interrelationships, to assure smooth operations and flow of products. Supply chain management (SCM) is the management of multiple relationships across the entire supply chain. Supply chain management includes all business activities involved with the flow and transformation of goods and information of goods from raw materials to the final consumer. The flow of products and information can be both from the suppliers to the consumer and from the consumer to the suppliers or producers.

A supply chain consists of three or more individuals or organizations that are directly involved in this flow of materials, finished goods, finances, and information. Porter (1985) points out the importance of logistics and SCM as one of the core activities of a firm and as one of the main forces leading to increased profitability (Serdaris, Antoniadis, & Tomlekova, 2014).

Figure 2.8 illustrates the difference between SCM and logistics. It can be seen that *logistics* is just a part of the functions and activities of SCM that must be coordinated. Logistics activities concern both the supply and distribution channel and are interrelated with the rest activities and functions comprised by the supply chain of each firm. The logistics activities involved in SCM can be divided in key activities and support activities. Key Activities involve transportation, inventory management, customer service, information flows, and order management. Support activities of the SCM include warehousing, materials handling, purchasing, packaging, cooperation with production, and maintenance of information systems required for the smooth operation of the supply chain of the company. Support activities may differ across organizations depending on the industry they operate, the special characteristics of the products or services and the needs and desires of the consumers (Serdaris, Antoniadis, & Tomlekova, 2014).

Taking as an illustrative example the food supply chains, they face an increasing demand for high quality products and larger assortments that reaches final consumers that result to an increase for demand of logistics service. Moreover, that must be accomplished by keeping the cost as low as possible or even reducing it, to gain competitive advantage in international markets: Moreover, new issues have aroused concerning stakeholder's involvement with issues as food safety, environmental protection, animal welfare, corporate social responsibility and sustainable logistics strategies. Therefore, the main challenge that needs to be addressed to efficiently organize a food supply chain is this complexity in combination with cost efficiency of the logistics operations.

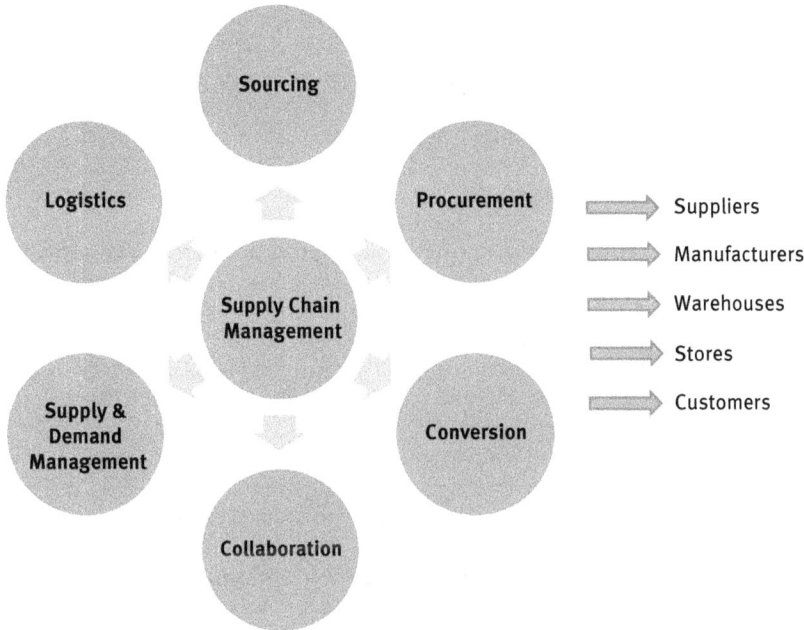

Figure 2.8: Model of functions and activities of Supply Chain Management.
Source: Mentzer et al., 1985

In 2018, China was the leading export country in the world, which accounted for 12% of the world's total export trade. With the outbreak of the coronavirus in January 2020 factories in China have been operating at partial capacity which has an enormous impact on supply chains globally. In the long term, companies are likely to accelerate supply chain diversification. Many retailers will localize their supply chains to minimize future risk and better meet consumer demand.

Disruptions to Global Supply Chain

Due to the coronavirus outbreak in China, many factories are still unable to operate at full capacity due to migrant workers being unable to travel from their hometowns. The government has also imposed quarantine regulations for factory workers from regions that belong to coronavirus outbreak clusters. They must isolate themselves for 14 days before they are permitted to return to work.

Factories that have resumed operations are facing component shortages, caused by intercity transportation restrictions. Consequently, supply chain breakdowns for companies that depend on China for manufacturing and components will occur.

China is the world's largest exporter of footwear and apparel. More than two thirds of total global shoe exports are from China. More than one third of clothing is from China. For example, Next, a UK-based apparel retailer, sources 20% of its clothes from China; Nike's contractor factories in China manufactured 23% of the brand's footwear; 21% of Gap's products were produced in factories in China; and 525 factories in China made around half of the clothes for Primark.

However, the coronavirus outbreak has caused delays in shipping the ordered apparel as factories are operating at partial capacity. Although retailers and brand owners could diversify their production line from China (to countries such as Cambodia, Vietnam, and their home countries) in order to minimize disruption, they would still rely on China for certain raw materials that would not be available due to the strict transportation bans that have been imposed by the government. The coronavirus outbreak has also disrupted fashion and trade shows, which might affect new brand and product launches as well as reduce brands' exposure within the industry.

Moreover, China is the leading supplier of smartphones globally, accounting for 24% of total shipments in 2019. Vendors in China manufacture components for leading brands such as Apple, Huawei, and Xiaomi. The coronavirus has enormous effects on the global smartphone industry. According to Apple's latest statement, "While all of these facilities have reopened, they are ramping up more slowly than we had anticipated." We expect that the launch of Apple's new iPhone, which was scheduled to occur in spring, will be delayed, and supply of the iPhone 11 and Air Pods will be temporarily constrained.

In order to learn from the impacts of the coronavirus, it is recommendable that retailers conduct risk assessments and stress tests to help them find alternative production lines. Several retailers have been diversifying their supply chains away from China since 2017 due to a wage rise in the country. Trade tensions between the United States and China also pushed companies to further evaluate their supply chains. Moreover, as the global emphasis on supply chain sustainability increases, more companies are considering localizing their supply chains, which will help them to reduce production lead times and enable them to respond quickly to consumer demand. In the long term, companies across different sectors may adopt fully automated production lines and supply chains by leveraging 5 G connectivity, artificial intelligence technologies, machine learning, and robotics. This would go a long way in minimizing risk during situations such as the coronavirus outbreak, as supply chains would not be dependent on manual labour (Coresight Research, 2020a).

The conceptual model illustrated in Figure 1.14 shows that a supply chain can be pictured as a pipeline showing directional supply chain flows: products, services, financial resources, the information associated with these flows, and the informational flows of demand and forecasts. The traditional business functions – marketing, sales, research and development, forecasting, production, procurement, logistics, information technology, finance, and customer service manager – accomplish these flows from the supplier's suppliers through the customer's customers to provide customer satisfaction, value, profitability, and a competitive advantage for the individual companies in the supply chain, and the supply chain as a whole. Interfunctional coordination includes an examination of the roles of trust, commitment, risk, and dependence on the viability of internal functional sharing and coordination. Intercorporate coordination includes functional shifting within the supply chain, the role of various types of third-party providers, how relationships between companies should be managed, and the viability of different supply chain structures. Finally, all these activities and functions phenomena vary in different global environments, which is relevant in a supply chain (Mentzer et al., 1985).

According to Kotler (2009), every supply chain should be structured in such a way that aims in:
- reaching the highest level of customer service
- ensuring the high quality of the distributed products or services
- achieving the minimum possible cost of management
- showing flexibility and adapting in the changes that the market dictates

The following example in the box below shows an example from the apparel industry and its efforts in rethinking their sourcing and their production models to enable sustainability and to support the adaptation of a circular economy in the apparel sector towards an *agile supply chain framework.*

The concept of agility means generally "readiness to change." From a business perspective, agility is defined as a strategy that is more responsive in a volatile marketplace, where this strategy is totally demand driven and based on the sensitivity to consumers' demands. Which means, as consumers buying patterns are changing, so does the whole supply chain management changes. The fundamental drivers of agile supply chain frameworks are speed, cost, and efficiency. An agile supply chain framework is based on four major elements that are as follows (Sher, 2016):
- **Virtual Integration:** In virtual integration information is shared among concerned departments for the real demand from market or end consumers. As demand information is gathered than it is collaborative planning among the various concerned departments that how to cater the demand from this market, and every department responds according to their capability and capacity to fulfil the demand. Virtual integration results in end-to-end visibility which is useful in identifying the bottlenecks and problems in the network.
- **Process Alignment:** In process alignment there are two major processes that are important: co-managed inventory and collaborative product design.
- **Co-managed inventory (CMI):** A business arrangement and collaboration between the supplier and the customer. Its main characteristics are that the consumable items are stored at the customer's premises. After the consumable item (s) are utilized fully, the item(s) are replaced by the seller with the consent and the knowledge of the customer. Co-managed inventory is similar to vendor managed inventory (VMI). Explaining vendor managed inventory, VMI is a business model set up between the buyer of the product and the supplier of the product. The customer provides information to the supplier about the product they need and the supplier takes the full responsibility for maintaining the decided level of inventory demanded at the buyer's premises.
- **Collaborative product design:** A highly iterative and interactive activity involving a group of people or departments who work together to handle the consumers' needs or wants.
- **Network Based:** A general understanding that every individual actor in the supply chain must put their efforts according with their core competencies to make

their efforts successful for the whole supply chain. This will reduce the burden on individual actors and increase the performance level of the entire supply chain framework.

– **Market Sensitive:** Normally a demand forecast is based on daily POS data. But sensing demand from past trends is an obsolete way to predict the demand in volatile markets. Therefore, it is recommendable to use daily feedback from market or sales terminals to forecast future demand. In addition, the success of a supply chain is very often based on the end consumer's feedback. Therefore, the final consumer should be involved in an agile supply chain network.

The concept of an agile supply chain framework has been recognized as a solution to increase the responsiveness of a supply chain in a changing environment. Today's supply chains compete on various strategies, but the most used one is agile strategy, because this strategy anticipates demand fluctuations in volatile markets. The agile strategy has become the mostly preferred strategy in present times. One of the main advantages is that excess inventory and potential shortages are eliminated by using this strategy. Agile supply chains are getting more accurate and up to date demand data by using an electronically connected network of retailers and all other drivers of the chain. To make a supply chain a robust chain, it is important to use state of the art planning applications, that supports the working teams in decision-making. Agile supply chain management is more information-centric rather than inventory centric. Through this strategy companies can retain the market and compete in volatile markets.

Furthermore, consumers are becoming increasingly aware of the environmental impact of traditional production modes. Consequently, the traditional supply chain setup is challenged, which leads to the fact that retailers are starting to rethink their sourcing and production models. The following example in the box below illustrates this situation and developments within the apparel sector.

> **Retailers are starting to rethink their sourcing and production models – An example from the apparel sector**
>
> In the last few years, many European and US mass-market apparel brands and retailers moved as much production to Asia as possible to gain a cost advantage, and afterwards moving from China to even more cost-efficient frontier markets. Today, the apparel industry goes more and more into the direction of adopting their cost advantage strategy towards an integrated sustainability strategy. Consequently, the traditional supply chain setup is now challenged, and brands and retailers are starting to rethink their sourcing and production models. Moves to increased nearshoring and more automated production models have the potential to enable sustainability and to support the adaptation of a circular economy in the apparel sector (see Figure 2.9) (Andersson, Berg, Hedrich, & Magnus, 2018).

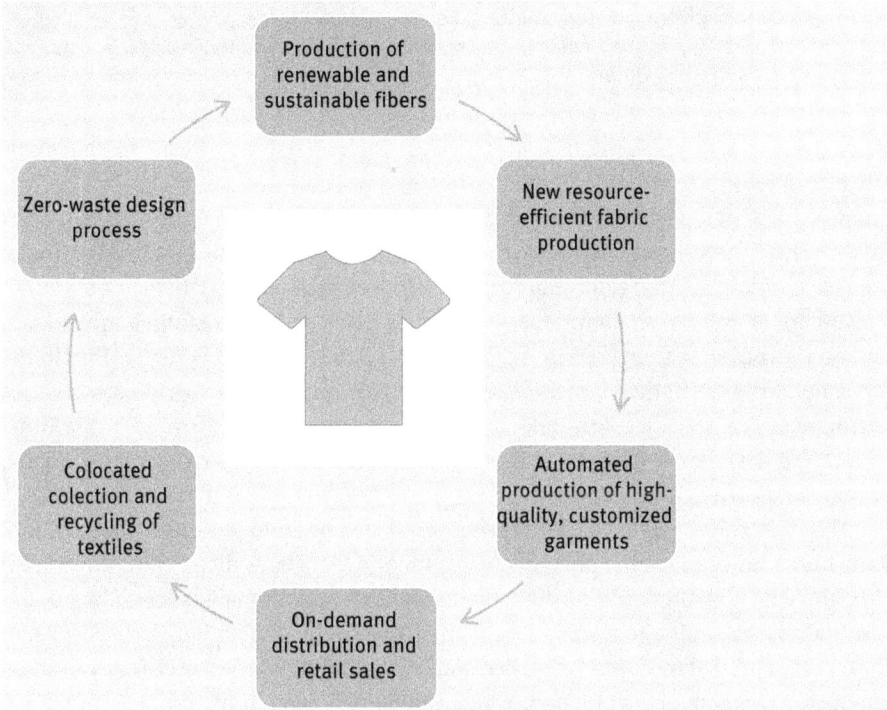

Figure 2.9: Circular business model in the apparel sector.
Source: Own elaboration based on Andersson, Berg, Hedrich, & Magnus, 2018

Consumers are becoming increasingly aware of the environmental impact of the traditional linear apparel production modes. Sustainability in general and more sustainable production modes are key purchasing factors for apparel consumers, also for the fast fashion (mass-market) consumers. Mass-market (fast fashion) apparel companies that embrace automation technologies to become faster and more sustainable will be successful in the years to come.

For many apparel companies, these new apparel production modes are very challenging, due to their labourious and linear production processes. Nevertheless, balanced investments in nearshoring, automation, and sustainability will be necessary, especially as the economics of nearshoring are starting to add up. Nearshoring can be economically viable, mostly due to savings in freight and duties. For instance, a US apparel company that moves production of basic jeans from either Bangladesh or China to Mexico can maintain or even slightly increase its margin, even without higher full-price sell-through. For Europe, unit costs remain significantly lower when sourcing from Bangladesh, but reshoring from China to Turkey is economically viable. Landed-cost prices for denim, for example, can be 3% lower when sourced from Turkey.

As the mass-market apparel sector is moving to a demand-focused, agile supply model, and as labour costs are rising, automation will be necessary in increasing labour efficiency and flexibility. Before being able to comprehend fully the prospect of automation for apparel production and its potential impact on nearshoring or onshoring, the apparel industry needs to have a deeper understanding of the technology landscape. To summarize, for certain apparel products, automation not only makes nearshoring more attractive for European and US apparel retailers and brands but also makes onshoring to the United States or even Germany economically viable (Andersson, Berg, Hedrich, & Magnus, 2018).

The last mile

From today's perspective, online orders are indispensable. A survey by Statistik Austria (2019) has shown that 62% of the Austrian population has ordered online in the last 12 months. A large proportion of these orders must be delivered and either consumers or online retailers must pay for this. According to studies around 228 million parcels were delivered in Austria in 2018, and the trend is rising. Due to rising wage costs and other factors, delivery is becoming increasingly expensive for companies. The so-called *last mile* accounts for a large share of these costs. It accounts for between a quarter and a third of total delivery costs (Arslan, Agatz, Kroon, & Zuidwijk, 2019).

The "last mile" refers to the last section of a journey to a planned destination. Particularly in recent years, business to customer (B2C) goods dispatch has increased strongly, which is ultimately attributable to the high growth in distance selling or online trading. According to a study by the Austrian Trade Association, Austrians spent € 7.6 billion on distance selling in 2017 (KMU Forschung Austria 2017). Many of these purchased goods must be shipped, which ultimately leads to the problem of the so-called *last mile*. Parcel delivery often takes place at times when nobody is present to receive the shipment. These unsuccessful deliveries are returned to the parcel depot until they can be delivered again. This has not only ecological (increased traffic volume) but also economic (congestion caused by delivery vans) and social (lower quality of life due to increased traffic volume) consequences (Allen et al., 2000).

But it is not only the high costs and the ecological issues that are a problem: customer satisfaction also suffers from the problem of the "last mile" and this is precisely what is becoming increasingly important, as it plays a key role in competition with other companies.

In order to increase customer satisfaction and to reduce costs, there are various approaches to solving the problem of the "last mile." Innovative concepts for dealing with this include, for example, customers picking up parcels at so-called parcel collection stations, or innovative delivery systems such as freight bicycles, V-feather vehicles, or drones (see Chapter 3.2 on future delivery methods). V-feather vehicles are electric cars with a modular design. The driver's cab can dock onto various freight modules (refrigerated wagons, hazardous goods, parcel wagons, etc.). Apart from the problem of the last mile, innovative solutions for packaging systems are also necessary, because until now the shipping packaging has been designed in such a way that it is deposited in the residual waste instead of being reused. There are already innovative approaches, such as the use of biodegradable packaging materials (see Chapter 3.2), but this has not yet become established. As delivery services will continue to increase in the future, there is scope for R&D and policy makers to develop innovative solutions to these challenges (ITA & AIT, 2019).

Future delivery methods

The world of delivery and transportation is changing, and with new technologies emerging, future delivery methods revolutionize the way products are delivered. Many companies start experimenting with new technologies to help streamline their delivery services. In this chapter we discuss the future of delivery services and selected delivery methods which have the potential to revolutionize the market or complement existing delivery methods.

Freight bicycles

The use of bicycles for goods transport is one of the most promising future delivery methods for short transport distances. Freight bicycles have made it onto the traffic agenda in many European cities and the potential for shifting from car to cargo bike is enormous. Studies have shown that every third or fourth delivery van trip can be switched to pedal power. An even higher potential for switching from car to a cargo bike for service providers and craftsmen. The highest potential is seen in private logistics: 77% of all car trips for goods transport (e.g., shopping) could be done by bicycle, bicycle trailer or cargo bike. In Copenhagen, for example, every fourth family does already have a cargo bike. To give a push in that direction some cities have promotion programs to purchase cargo bikes by private persons and companies (Cycle Competence Austria, 2017).

To combat the growing pressures of freight in major urban areas, some European and North American cities have responded by deploying alternative transport modes for delivering goods and have introduced electric-assisted (EA) cargo bikes. EA cargo bikes could provide a feasible technology to meet the increased demand for the movement of goods. According to studies, up to 50% of all light goods and 25% of all goods could be moved by bike. In addition, this study compared the delivery route cost trade-offs between box delivery trucks and electric-assisted (EA) cargo bikes that have the same route. It concludes that the delivery trucks are more cost-effective for greater distances from distribution centres and for large volume deliveries to one destination. Whereas EA cargo bikes may be well suited for traffic congested cities with designated bike paths and truck parking challenges (European Commission, 2019a).

V-feather vehicles

The demand for urban freight delivery is increasing across Europe. Despite the widespread focus on reducing CO_2 emissions in cities and adopting more sustainable modes of transportation, this need continues to be met using traditional delivery vans and trucks, which adds to existing congestion and pollution in urban centres. Therefore, industrial partners interested in finding a sustainable, flexible solution for urban last mile delivery, have started to develop a completely new modular electric light duty vehicle, from initial concept to working prototype.

The V-Feather vehicle is based on a modular building block concept that uses active, adaptive structural architecture. This means that it consists of multiple connected modules: a cab module where the driver sits, and one or more freight modules of different sizes and types. These can be added or removed over the course of the delivery route based on real-time requirements to increase capacity, improve agility, or transport special freight such as refrigerated goods. This enables better flexibility and cost reductions (European Commission, 2019a).

Drone-based delivery systems

The vision of a *drone-based delivery system* would be a realistic future delivery method but still must overcome regulatory and technical hurdles. Due to the great depth of intervention of this technological development––after all, the airspace surrounding us would change drastically and several questions arise: Are there ethical or safety concerns? Are there environmental risks? Can the technology be misused for criminal or terrorist purposes? Is there a potential for social conflict in view of different interests (e.g., noise, privacy, use of airspace)? Is the current regulation sufficient or must new rules be created? Experiments with delivery drones are also already underway in all the world. However, the scientific basis for political decisions is still largely lacking, and a public discourse on social cost-benefit considerations has not yet been conducted (ITA & AIT, 2019).

While the topic of drones was dominated by the military years ago, it has long since arrived in the civilian sphere and in the everyday lives of many. Millions of toy drones are in use worldwide. Pilot tests are being carried out in many areas to test the benefits of drones, for example in agriculture, in the humanitarian and medical fields, in the inspection of facilities, in surveying, in journalism, in tourism and not least in research, etc.

Finally, the major online retailers, some postal companies, and numerous start-ups around the world are working to deliver everyday goods through the air (the so-called *last mile*). The benefit for retailers and customers could be that their ordered goods can be delivered much faster and to places, which so far can not be supplied or only rarely for logistic reasons. For goods suppliers, this could mean new or geographically expanded markets and potentially a boost to their image. For delivery companies, the structure of personnel and travel costs would probably improve.

However, to realise this vision of a drone-based delivery service, many regulatory and technical hurdles would still have to be overcome, and it is likely that some aspects will also meet with resistance from the population. In order for deliveries "through the air" to be economically feasible, the drones must be able to fly autonomously, that is, without pilots on the ground. Several technical challenges have yet to be mastered. These range from weight, range, and weather problems to the optimization of sensor and avoidance technologies. In principle, it can be assumed that it is only a matter of time before these problems are solved, because many companies want to make progress here. In addition, the necessary infrastructure must also be provided on the ground, such as landing pads (ITA & AIT, 2019).

2.3.4 Distribution channels

In general, there are two types of distribution channels available to retailers: direct distribution and indirect distribution.
- **Direct distribution**: involves distributing direct from the manufacturer to the consumer which gives a manufacturer the complete control over their products.
- **Indirect distribution**: involves distributing a product using an intermediary, for example, a manufacturer selling to a wholesaler and then on to the retailer.

In the context of this book only indirect distribution will be discussed.

In daily business there exist three most frequently used distribution strategies: intensive, exclusive, and selective distribution:
- **Intensive distribution**: Used commonly to distribute low priced products or impulse purchases. For example, snacks such as chewing gum, chocolates, soft drinks, etc.
- **Exclusive distribution**: Involves limiting distribution to a single outlet. The product is usually highly priced and requires the intermediary to place much detail in its sell. Most of these products need detailed conseling. An example would be the sale of a car through exclusive dealers or the sale of a musical system for the living room.
- **Selective Ddstribution**: A small number of retail outlets are chosen to distribute the product. Selective distribution is common with products such as computers, household appliances, where consumers are willing to shop around and where manufacturers want a large geographical spread.

If a manufacturer decides to adopt an exclusive or selective distribution strategy, they should select reputable intermediaries, experienced in distributing similar products and an intermediary known to the target audience.

How can a distribution channel be described? To begin with, distribution is defined as the transportation of the product from the point of production or trans-shipment to the point or points where demand has been recorded, to satisfy the expectations of the production enterprise and the consumer (Binioris, 2008). The physical distribution is part of the supply chain, and its purpose is to deliver goods or services to the final consumers. More specifically to the demand points of the finished product in the right place and time, in the right quantity and at the lowest possible total cost (Blanchard, 2010).

- For the selection of the optimal physical distribution system, several questions must be answered (Binioris, 2008): What is the nature of the market and the customers to which the retailer aims at?
- What kinds of products will be traded?
- Do these types of products require special treatment?
- What are the distribution objectives for company?
- What is the cost of the distribution network?

Experts are sure that the most decisive factor that leads to the selection of an appropriate distribution channel is the nature of the product and whether it is functional with predictable demand (such as food) or innovative with unpredictable demand (such as high-tech electronic devices) and the general objectives of the company. The main objective is usually that the management of the distribution channel should be at the lowest possible cost.

When selecting a distribution channel several important considerations must be made (Serdaris, Antoniadis, & Tomlekova, 2014):
- planning financial resources to be used within the supply chain
- planning of the distribution networks and routes of which it is composed
- selection of partners within the distribution channel
- control of the system performance while ensuring that the products being distributed are of high quality and respond to consumers' needs and desires

The last point is important in this respect when ensuring the highest level of customer service, it is possible convert customers into loyal customers. Experts and companies are also thinking about future developments in this area. Some of these considerations are already reality while others are still dreaming of the future. The chapter below discusses recent innovations in distribution.

Innovation in distribution channels

Only a few years ago, devices with speech recognition could understand only simple commands such as "increase the volume." Now, smart devices can comprehend and follow complicated instructions such as "tell a joke." With AI-powered personal assistants, consumers can purchase products by just speaking with their devices, without having to log in and check out. Therefore, voice shopping is expected to be an important driving factor for e-commerce.

Speech recognition devices have already achieved a 95%-word accuracy rate and companies such as Google, Amazon, and Apple plan to design and manufacture even more products, especially smart speakers. The global market for smart speakers is predicted to grow from $4.5 billion in 2017 to $30 billion in 2024 (Coresight Research, 2018).

Further developments in AI technology are necessary for voice-activated online shopping. AI-enabled personal assistants can simplify the online shopping process (see Table 2.3). Using IPAs with voice recognition capabilities allows users to purchase items by simply speaking into their devices. For example, consumers can say "purchase XY brand toothpaste" and complete the transaction through the AI-enabled personal assistant. For items consumers are familiar with, voice shopping can reduce the friction in transaction and improve the shopping experience. The ability of these devices to interact with users differentiates them from traditional smartphones.

After Apple introduced Siri in October 2011, companies such as Google and Amazon followed and launched similar products. Google reported voice searches accounted for 20% of all mobile searches in the United States in 2016 and 50% of all mobile searches will be voice searches by 2020. The total number of smart speaker unit shipments worldwide reached 16.8 million in 2018 and the total number of smart speakers in use is growing to 225 million in 2020 (Coresight Research, 2018).

Table 2.3: Overview of the most important AI-enabled Personal Assistants (Coresight Research, 2018).

AI-enabled Personal Assistants	Launch Year	Description
Apple Siri	October 2011	Available only on Apple products
Samsung S Voice	May 2012	Superseded by Bixby (i.e., a virtual assistant developed by Samsung Electronics) in 2017
Google Now	July 2012	Superseded by Google Assistant (https://assistant.google.com/#?modal_active=none) in 2016
Microsoft Cortana	April 2014	Integrated into Microsoft Edge and Xbox
Amazon Alexa	November 2014	Was used in the Amazon Echo, now available also on iOS and Android
Sound Hound	June 2015	Does not have an own personality, available on iOS and Android
Facebook M	August 2015	Text-based personal assistant inside Facebook messenger
Xiaomi Xiao Ai	July 2017	Specifically tailored for Chinese markets
Alibaba AliGenie	July 2017	A China-based open platform IPA

Convenience is the primary driving factor behind the rise of voice-activated online shopping. However, a disadvantage is the lack of personal interaction consumers experience when selecting items, asking questions, or making purchases. Consumers normally like to interact and engage with other individuals, for example, sales staff, friends, or family, at some point in the buying process.

The AI-enabled shopping assistant learns about the customer's taste and interests while shopping online, and then uses this data to inform him or her about products he or she is likely to purchase, creating a virtual experience that's more like shopping in a virtual store.

Moreover, these devices need a fast and stable internet connection to the operation of these assistants. Experts are concerned that all wearable gadgets, smart consumer appliances, intelligent vehicles and connected infrastructure will cause localized pools of interference, and a continuous struggle for bandwidth. Factors like this may have a negative impact on the ability of speech recognition systems to access their databases and perform their primary function (Goddard, 2018).

2.4 Promotion

Promotion is another important element in a retailer's marketing mix. Decisions regarding promotion include what medium to use (TV, print, online, etc.), as well as when and where to promote. It is a marketing tool used by retailers mainly to increase sales and to help moving inventory. There are many different types of retail promotion, but not every kind of promotion works for every retailer or every store, so the type of retail promotion must be selected carefully and always related to the target group and to and the available budgetary resources.

One frequently used element of the promotional mix are *sales promotions*. The primary elements in the promotional mix are advertising, personal selling, direct marketing, and publicity/public relations. Sales promotion uses both media and nonmedia marketing communications for a predetermined, limited time to increase consumer demand, stimulate market demand or improve product availability. Examples include contests, coupons, freebies, loss leaders, POP displays, premiums, prizes, product samples, and rebates. Sales promotions can be directed at either the customer, sales staff, or distribution channel members (such as retailers in B2B markets). Sales promotions targeted at the consumer are called *consumer sales promotions* (in B2C markets). Sales promotions targeted at retailers and wholesale are called *trade sales promotions* (in B2B markets).

There are many different types of sales promotions including several communications activities, all with the main aim to provide an added value or an incentive to the customer to stimulate the attention, trial or purchase of a particular product or service. Examples of frequently used sales promotions in the retail sector are included in Table 2.4.

Table 2.4: Types of Sales Promotion.

Loyalty programs	Loyalty programs offer customers some form reward for spending money at a particular store. Most retailers use rewards cards, either a physical plastic card, the ATM card, or a loyalty card app on the smartphone. This type of sales promotion is aimed at creating customer loyalty and drive customers to make repeat purchases at this particular retailer's stores.
Free samples	Free samples mean that a customer is provided a sample of a particular product for free either in combination if another product is purchased or the product sample is given away free with a magazine or just for the fun of it. This type of sales promotion is very often used when introducing new consumer goods.
Contests	Contests are competitions held by retailers associated with the product that should be promoted. An example of a contest could be a breakfast cereals company offering the chance to win a small surprise inside the package of their products. The main objective of this type of sales promotion is to offer an additional incentive to purchases the product.
Coupons	Coupons are vouchers that allow consumers to purchase products at a discounted price. A common example of coupons would be discount vouchers distributed for buying food at a fast food chain to increase sales.
Discounts	A discount would mean that a product is temporarily offered at a lower price. For example, when a particular item is marked at "10% off." A retailer may use discounts to increase sales or to attract new customers.
Premium offers	Premium offers mean that a retailer offers a bonus second product when purchasing a particular product. This bonus may be given to the customer for free or at a discount and provides an extra incentive for purchasing a particular product.
Rebates	Rebates mean that a customer receives a refund of some of the purchase price at the time of purchase or with one of the next purchases. This type of sales promotion is used to offer to capture the consumer's attention and to offer an incentive to purchase their product over similar competing products. To claim a rebate customer very often must provide personal detail that can be used for further market research.
POP promotions	POP promotions are sales promotions that take place directly in a store, for examples a tasting promotion, a product demonstration, or a trial of the product.
Consumer sweepstakes	When participating at a sweepstake consumer must submit personal details for a draw. The names of the consumers are included in the winning contest. The lots are drawn, and the winners get prizes.
Free-standing insert	A coupon booklet is inserted into the local newspaper for delivery.

Table 2.4 (continued)

Checkout dispensers	On checkout the customer is given a coupon based on products purchased.
Mobile couponing	Coupons are available on a mobile phone. Consumers show the offer on a mobile phone to a salesperson for redemption.
Online interactive promotion game	Consumers play an interactive game associated with the promoted product.

As you see in Table 2.4 there are many different types of sales promotion. It is not easy for a retailer to decide on the right promotion tool. Literature suggests several steps a retailer can take to select the right one for his or her business. A retailer must:

- identify the type of sales promotion that fits and best suits the company or brand. Start by identifying the company's objectives. For example, Do you want to increase traffic? Do you want to make room for new inventory? Do you want to increase sales? If a retailer wants to increase traffic, for example, an attractive discount might be an appropriate promotion tool. If the objective is to move inventory, then you should offer extra value packs or multibuy promotions.
- identify the media channels (online and offline) to promote the products or brands and defined the right duration of the sale promotion (with a sense of "urgency"), always keeping in mind the objective of the sales promotion.
- avoid setting promotions with no end date, it is more effective to implement limited time offers to encourage customers to buy the product or brand or visit a retailer's store. Another effective communication strategy is to add countdowns telling people how little time they have left to take advantage of the promoted offer.
- create the promotion offers around a specific theme. Doing so will make it easier for people to see the necessity or urgency and to remember the promotion. For example, Valentine's day, Mother's day, start of school, etc.

One of the busiest shopping days of the year, mainly in the United States, is the so-called Black Friday. Black Friday is an informal name for the Friday following Thanksgiving Day in the United States, which is celebrated on the fourth Thursday of November. On this day many brick-and-mortar stores offer highly promoted sales. As brick-and-mortar stores do with Black Friday, online retailers usually offer special promotions, discounts, and sales on the so-called *Cyber Monday*. It is the second-biggest shopping day and the busiest day for online sales, at least in the United States.

Although Black Friday and Cyber Monday had its origins in the United States, it is now an international promotion concept all over the world, also in the European countries (see the following box for more details).

From Black Friday to Cyber Monday

The extended discount shopping period running from Black Friday (celebrated on the fourth Thursday of November) through Cyber Monday has become an established worldwide annual shopping event that has changed the way customers do their Christmas shopping. Black Friday has routinely been the busiest shopping day of the year in the United States since 2005. In Europe, just 19% of UK respondents had participated in Black Friday retail back in 2015, compared with an impressive 54% in 2017. Similarly, in Germany, with 9% of consumers getting involved in 2015; up to 43% in 2017. Anticipation in the other surveyed regions is also high, with 77% of respondents saying that they will consider making a purchase if the price is right. Asked to evaluate the top motivational factors for participating in Black Friday more than half of consumers said taking advantage of attractive discounts was their number-one reason, followed by the opportunity to encounter unique one-off promotions and making Christmas gift purchases (Anis, Elliott, & Koestler, 2018).

While many shoppers express enthusiasm about Black Friday, relatively few say they plan ahead and keep their options wide open with regard to which stores or products they will seek out. Digital and omnichannel purchasing behaviours dominate this shopping period. While European shoppers prefer to go digital, omnichannel is a popular option for shoppers everywhere. In the United States, 48% of respondents intend to shop both online and in stores. And it was a similar story for around a third of consumers in Canada (39%), Germany (32%), and the United Kingdom (30%).

Consumers intend to shop a variety of categories, and their channel preferences are changing. Clothing takes the top spot-on consumer shopping lists in all countries, followed by consumer electronics. While digital remains strongly ahead as the primary method consumers plan to use when shopping for consumer electronics, 50% of shoppers in Canada and 54% in the United States still favour offline shopping when it comes to selecting new clothes.

Movies, books, and music emerged as the third-most popular product category, selected by 33% of US and 39% of Canadian respondents, while 40% of consumers in Germany and 42% of UK shoppers plumped for beauty and fragrances.

When asked to evaluate what is motivating them to shop more online, the simplicity and convenience afforded was the top reason for shoppers in most age groups and in most countries. Mobile apps and mobile browsers proved a popular option, selected by 50% or more of consumers in all countries surveyed, with 75% of US and 61% of German shoppers using these channels. US shoppers (8%) are also using voice-activated digital assistants, such as Alexa and Siri, to buy their products on Black Friday. Black Friday has reached a preeminent position as one of the most significant revenue-generating opportunities on the retail calendar. Consumers set aside significant budgets (up to $1,000 and more) to fund their Black Friday shopping deals and have clear purchasing intentions when it comes to who they will be buying for and which product categories they will be prioritizing. But beyond that, they are adopting a much more spontaneous approach in relation to what items they will purchase, preferring instead to sit back and see which promotions and offers most entice them to spend (Anis, Elliott, & Koestler, 2018).

To summarize, today's multioptional consumers are leveraging every channel available, whether for researching deals, seeking out inspirations for gifts, or experiencing the excitement of the shopping event in person. Digital channels are increasingly dominant sales channels which makes it important for retailers to ensure they catch their target customers in the right channels and provide a seamless shopping experience as today's consumers move from one channel to another to complete their purchasing journeys (Anis, Elliott, & Koestler, 2018).

2.5 Presentation

Presentation in the retail mix refers to the physical environment of a retail store (brick and mortar) and the presentation of a retailer's website (i.e., nonstore retailing). Presentation of a retail store (i.e., brick and mortar) includes visual factors, like ambience, lighting, décor style, fixtures, etc., and access to products, car park, surrounding area, etc.

While presentation of a website (i.e., nonstore retailing) includes the virtual store ambience, easiness in access to customer, buying and selling, payment methods and comparison availability between product by other retailers.

2.5.1 Presentation of a physical retail store

Most consumers make their purchase decisions of daily commodities directly in a store. Studies have shown (POPAI, 2016) that 76% of consumers make their choice directly at the POS. These consumer decisions are influenced by many different factors, mostly in-store attention-based factors like shelf position, number of facings, packaging but also time pressure and out-of-store memory-based factors, like brand preferences and store image. There exist two different kinds of purchase decisions:
- Planned purchases can be defined as decisions that are entirely determined before entering a store. Purchase decisions may have been planned to the level of the brand (i.e., specifically planned) or to the level of the category (i.e., generally planned).
- Unplanned purchases are purchases that were not specifically planned before a shopping trip.

Customers' in-store decisions and unplanned purchases occur because stimuli encountered during a shopping trip, like point-of-purchase advertising or the physical product, lead consumers to believe or recall that they have a need for a distinctive product category or product. Several product and customer characteristics increase exposure and lead to positive reactions. These characteristics may be stable (i.e., relatively invariable over time) or transitory (i.e., variable across shopping trips). The retailer can directly influence transitory factors at the product-category level, for example, by using a store display or a coupon. Transitory customer characteristics, like shopping companion, store familiarity, etc., can also be influenced by a retailer and his marketing activities.

On the other side, there exist factors of customer activities that limit in-store decision-making (see Figure 2.10). Examples are the usage of a shopping list or restricting the number of aisles visited in a store. Unplanned purchases may result in negative outcomes, like overspending or buying unnecessary products. So, in some cases consumers take steps to limit the impact of stimuli on their purchase decision and use a shopping list to avoid unplanned purchases. Some consumers use the

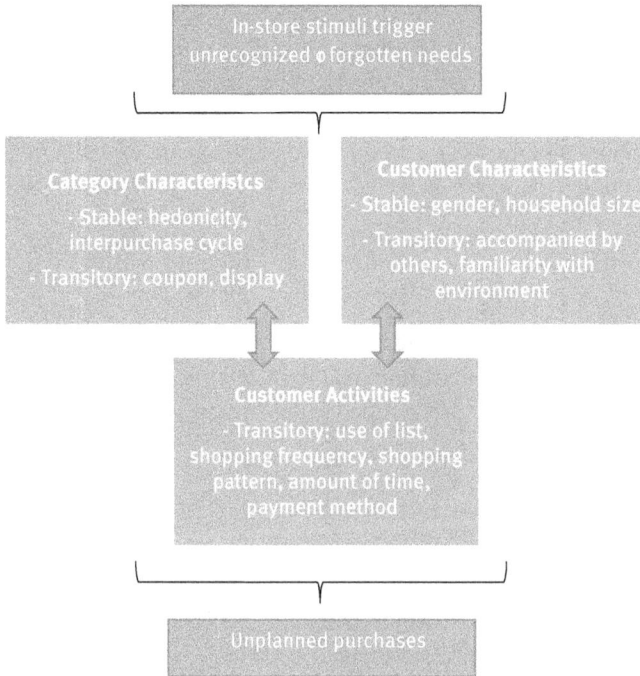

Figure 2.10: Factors influencing in-store decision-making.
Source: Inman, Winer, & Ferraro, 2009

shopping environment to their advantage and rely on in-store stimuli to influence their needs. Such customer activities are initiated by the customer and can vary across shopping trips (Inman, Winer, & Ferraro, 2009).

Research has shown that the in-store shopping experience of retail shoppers strongly influence the satisfaction of retail shoppers and determines the consumers' attitude towards the retailer, which in turn will influence the amount of money they spend over time. In detail, satisfaction with personal interaction, merchandise value and variety, and assortment impact positively the overall satisfaction and loyalty. This consequently means, if retailers want to realise the objective of store loyalty, they must ensure that the basic elements of competent staff, sufficient choice and merchandise value are in place (Terblanche & Boshoff, 2006).

Brand awareness, quality and price are just a few factors that influence a consumer's decision-making process and buying behaviour in a store. Product presentation is also a very important instrument in in-store marketing. Product presentation is so important because it is often the decisive incentive for an impulse purchase. Therefore, a meaningful placement of goods should influence the behaviour of consumers and a stimulus from an effective product presentation engage the attention of the customer (Hurth, 2006). The basic of *product placement* is the determination of the exact position a product is placed at the POS (Witzler & Pavelka, 2007). The central task is to decide where to place individual goods, product groups or product areas, on the sales floor, on shelves in which form and to what extent (Zielke, 2002). The way a product is presented is very important because the product has to stand out, otherwise the customer does not even notice it. The consumer only takes notice of product presentation if it is emotionally interesting. Emotionally uninteresting, or even neutral, subjects are usually not even noticed by the customer (Häusel, 2007) and consequently not purchased.

2.5.1.1 Neuromarketing elements at the POS

Nowadays retailers use more and more different forms of *neuromarketing elements* at the POS, in the store. Four important neuromarketing elements to attract the attention of the customer in the store will be described in further detail:
- product tastings
- decoration
- displays
- scent

Product tasting is an unwrapped product, which is usually presented by staff or a promoter in small units for the customer to consume directly in the shop (Frey, Hunstiger, & Dräger, 2011). An important fact is that almost 90% of all food products are flops because the customer has never tried them, but not because they so not like them (Underhill, 2012). Different tasting samples can engage the consumers directly in the food experience and stimulate them to buy the tasted product (Morrison & Mundell, 2012). They can also reduce uncertainty for customers. Furthermore, attitudes which are reached by tasting are stronger and safer than through advertising (Lotzkat, 2013). Any time products are displayed as a sample or tasted, it is important that these tastings can be seen by other consumers, to reach customer engagement and emotional connections. It is essential to stimulate desire and to move the consumer to purchase a distinctive product (Pradeep, 2010).

Decoration can help to attract consumers and entice them to stay longer in a store. Moreover, pleasant decoration creates a certain atmosphere and can make customers feel more comfortable and buy more products. The primary function of decoration is the usage of decoration as a promotion tool. Furthermore, decorations should be pointed and targeted at a certain customer group, should fit the whole store concept and retailer's image, and should be repeated at least once in the sales room. Moreover, decorations should follow a special schedule, which is often changed, for example daily products should change every week and seasonal products should be presented differently every season or even twice a season. Decoration is an important element and tool in customer experience management. The so-called surprise effect should be used intensively in decoration to create awareness and memorable customer experiences. An appealing form of decoration can raise the buying mood.

The *display,* POS display or POP display, is a special form of product presentation at the POS. It is possible to generate the customer's attention with a prominent design type and this encourages spontaneous purchases. A display in isolated form can also suggest a special offer because they are often used as a sales aid for sales. Mostly, displays are made from cardboard, plastic, wood, or metal. They are additional product shelving as well as the permanent place on the shelf). In practice, four different types of displays are distinguished (Schröder, 2012):

- Sale displays: can be floor displays standing out from other items or cash desk displays found near, on or next to a checkout counter. The main objective is to entice the customer into buying certain products, mostly products that are on a special offer. They can be related to a special event, either one going on in a shop, or a holiday-time sale.
- Pallet displays: are the largest displays, mainly cardboard display units. There advantages are the amount of product the display can carry and that it is viewable from all four sides.
- Presentation displays: are used especially for information materials.
- Permanent displays: are stocked with common items that may be there year-round, for example are batteries, candy, chewing gum, etc. These displays are also useful in places with limited floor space. They are usually made from cardboard, and/or covering over a plastic stand. These displays are easily replaceable and disposable.

Presentation displays normally have the highest impact in terms of total shoppers who looked at the display for a sufficient period, to make a conscious decision as to whether to engage with the promoted product or not. The highest conversion rate (i.e., total shoppers who bought the product/total shoppers who looked at the display) normally have pallet displays. The engagement ratio (i.e., total shoppers who interacted with the product/total shoppers who looked at the display) is highest with sale displays, especially cash desk displays.

The preferred locations for displays are checkout areas, contact points, service zones, aisles and near product magnets (high frequency products). An eye tracking study has shown that eye-catching or obtrusive product presentations or displays lead to the fact that dwell time of fixations (i.e., the actual length of time that a shopper spends on a viewing the object) are much longer and fixation counts (fixation, i.e., a period where the eyes are locked towards an object; fixations are excellent measures of visual attention) higher. Apparently, the average length of a fixation is longer when it was an inexperienced shopper and when the purchase of a product is planned or very important. What is more, the longer a shopper stays in a store the more products are normally bought, which means that there is a correlation between the length of stay in a store and number of products purchased. Consequently, in-store marketing should be used to make shoppers feel comfortable and make them stay longer in a store.

Digital POS displays are a trend

Since the overall customer experience in a store is viewed as a key competitive differentiator, most brick-and-mortar retailers are planning to make significant investments into their customer experience strategies in the next few years. Using innovative digital POS displays and mixing technology-enabled experiences in physical stores with internet or mobile sales components, is now a top-trend. These devices can now collect valuable information, ranging from how long people stand in front of the display to which items generate more interest. Consequently, digital POS displays offer retailers the opportunity to market exactly to their needs.

Digital POS displays can provide a real sensory and personalised experience, which will eventually encourage shoppers to complete a purchase, increase customer engagement and sales opportunities. Furthermore, as more data will be collected, retailers will also be able to come up with better store layouts and reduce inventory volumes to eliminate inefficiencies.

The first challenge is to find a target-group oriented combination of "smart" technologies that can help brick-and-mortar retailers develop a flexible yet consistent technology system in their stores. Some retailers have already started providing solutions for customers to have access to product information from their mobile devices, for example, by using QR Codes or Beacon technology. Other retailers have combined digital POS displays with mobile clientele applications to bring a completely new level of personalisation to the customer's shopping journey. Mobile clienteling applications help to engage shoppers with product information, comparisons and/or customer reviews. Individual customer purchasing preferences with individual purchase histories, wish lists, product recommendations, typical price points, etc., can be tracked.

Since retailers can use these applications to collect accurate data relating to shopper preferences, responses to marketing and communication activities and customer service history, they can create product, brand, and behavioural clusters to provide a more target-group oriented retail experience.

Providing a seamless omnichannel shopping experience across multiple channels is another critical trend across the retail industry. With digital POS displays, retailers can deliver in-store experiences and strategic messages that are consistent with their online and offline marketing communication. This means that brick-and-mortar retailers can use digital POS displays to offer an integrated shopping experience across multiple touch points that consumers encounter on their purchase journeys.

The following link provides an illustrative example of a digital POS display: https://www.you tube.com/watch?time_continue=32&v=axHa1_n1Azs

The sense of *smell* (scent) probably has the highest unconscious effect on customers because it reaches straightforward the customer's emotional centres in the brain (Häusel, 2006). The nose transmits its impulses directly to the limbic system. As previously mentioned, emotions and instincts are in the limbic system. It reacts in a split second to fragrance stimulus. How people rate odour and how they react, depends on the memories. Odour is never neutral, because they are interpreted emotionally and rated subjectively (Häusel, 2007).

Due to the stimulant effect of scents, providers of products and services in general and retailers can use scent as an ideal anchor point for an experience-oriented multisensual product presentation due to its ability to elicit emotions and experiences.

The potential that lies in the emotional effects goes far beyond other stimuli because of the incredibly early evolutionary origin of smell.

The main objective of "scent management" in the retail sector is to keep the customer in the store if possible. The longer a customer stays, the more he buys (Häusel, 2006). Scents are used both to increase sales, as previously mentioned, at the POS and in the context of multisensory branding to increase the value of a brand. Smells can trigger direct expectations of the consumer. For example, a customer assumes that if something smells good, it is not harmful (food), probably delicious in flavour and may cost more.

Having a unique scent in a store can differentiate the brand from others. When customers smell that scent outside of the store, this will trigger their senses and remind them of that brand and its products. Scents can also trigger emotional responses for example:

- lavender, basil, cinnamon orange: are relaxing, soothing, calming, and reduce anxiety
- peppermint, thyme, rosemary, grapefruit, eucalyptus: are enterprising, stimulating and increase arousal and productivity
- ginger, chocolate, cardamom, liquorice: create a certain feeling of romance
- vanilla: has a comforting and calming effect
- black pepper: is sexually stimulating

Distributing scents throughout the store such as vanilla, lavender, thyme, rosemary, grapefruit, and eucalyptus can be advantageous for the retailer. These scents calm, soothe, and comfort, therefore, stimulating the consumer to loiter in the store, leading to increased merchandise awareness and increased impulse purchasing.

The right scent can even make people cooperative. The effect of these scents is based on a simple scent association since all these smells are already associated with the products. Scents do not just brand store but they also evoke emotional response, as previously mentioned, people can become more cooperative. Furthermore, they can feel more relaxed, peppy, or nostalgic. Because of this strong impact on the mood of the customers, is it possible, for scents to have desired effects on shopping behaviour (Ebster & Garaus, 2011).

To summarize, the four neuromarketing elements described above – product tastings, decorations, displays and scent – attract the attention of the customer and may create multisensorial brand experiences. These brand experiences create psychological differentiation, an added value through entertainment and customer engagement which may attract new customer groups and, in the long run, may create customer loyalty. Emotional relationships with the customers help to reduce traditional media spending and enhance positive word-of-mouth and PR (public relations).

Moreover, simple and more rewarding customer experiences will enhance customer satisfaction and loyalty and lead to sustainable sales growth and profit. There are numerous opportunities how to add value to a product and create memorable shopping experience. Basic requirements for every retailer are innovative thinking and to courage employees to be different. What is more, it will be necessary to adapt to market changes, in particular demographic, societal, economic, and technological changes. To be successful in the long run, retailers must have a focus on the individual consumer by segmenting markets and by following a consumer-centric approach. They have to adjust their marketing efforts to consumer's needs, add value to their products and services and provide uncomplicated solutions that are easy to handle and to understand.

2.5.2 Presentation of a website

Visual appeal is an extremely important aspect of a company's website – particularly when it comes to building a lasting relationship and brand affinity with the shopper. At the same time, basics should not be neglected, above all that the website is findable, usable, and accessible. Consequently, a combination of functionality and visual appeal of a website is necessary to get the most out of a site. Within the restricted computer interface the online retailer should convey the feeling of being in a real store. Studies have shown that the effective manipulation of the layout, atmospherics and theatrics of a website is a strategic marketing tool that can contribute to the effectiveness and differentiation by determining consumers' internal states and their overall responses. These components can be found in the Online Store Environment Framework (OSEF) (Vrechopoulos, O'Keefe, Doukidis, & Siomkos, 2004), aiming at providing a comprehensive typology of the online store interface. This framework proposes that the online store environment consists of:
- virtual layout and design
- virtual atmospherics
- virtual theatrics
- virtual social presence

By considering these components e-tailers can entice consumers to visit their store, shape their attitudes towards the store, enhance their satisfaction, strengthen their purchase intention, or urge them to recommend the store to others.

Virtual layout and design
The layout of the online store defines, to a large extent, the consumer's navigation within the store. The most frequently used layouts when it comes to website design are the freeform layout, the grid layout, and the racetrack layout (Fazal Ijaz, Rhee, Lee, & Alfian, 2014):

The *freeform layout* is a retailer's primary choice when it comes to layout planning and design. The freeform layout increases the time consumers want to spend in the (virtual) store. It's easy to use structure, makes it easier for shoppers to browse and allow customers to move in any direction within the store. So, the customer enjoys considerable freedom to move in any direction within the store. Its ease to be used in small stores where customers wish to browse, amicable working for same type of merchandise, provision of flexibility and visual appeal to customer in intimate relaxed environment are some of the advantages of free form.

The *racetrack layout* is a layout that has a centre point that directs towards various sections of the store. The racetrack store layout helps the customer along specific paths to visit as many store sections as possible. This is because of the main aisle/corridor which facilitates customer movement through the store. The retailer who adopts this type of layout creates an entertaining and interesting shopping environment. This layout exposes shoppers to the greatest possible amount of merchandise by encouraging browsing and cross-shopping.

The *grid layout* encourages the customers to navigate the online store through a hierarchical structure from product category to product sub-category and lastly end product. It provides the home page button which facilitates users need to pass through a hub or use the back-forward bar to visit the product categories.

Vrechopoulos et al. (Vrechopoulos, O'Keefe, Doukidis, & Siomkos, 2004) found that consumers perceive the freeform layout as significantly more useful in finding their shopping list products within the online store. The grid layout is significantly easier to use than the freeform and the racetrack layout, while the freeform layout is, by a small margin, more entertaining. Finally, they report that the racetrack and the freeform layouts engage subjects for longer.

Virtual atmospherics

Colour is an atmospheric element that is very important on web sites. Studies have found that colours that induce more relaxed feeling states (i.e., cool colours) lead to greater perceived quickness of the download. Colour also affects users' evaluations of the web site, their likelihood of recommending the web site to others and consumers' evaluation of the store personality. In addition, when an expensive item is featured on a cool background colour, respondents indicate a higher likelihood of purchase. Additionally, highlighting and text display colour combinations affect visual preference and reading performance (Manganari, Siomkos, & Vrechopoulos, 2009).

Virtual theatrics

Virtual stores very often look like a "theatre" using images, graphics, animation, and icons. Complexity refers to the richness of elements in a setting and is often operationalised with the use of images, graphics, and animation. Simpler webpage backgrounds are in general more effective and appealing than more complex ones, and motion on a dynamic web interface demands greater user attention than a static web interface. New media can incorporate levels of vividness and interactivity which traditional media can not. Interactivity is the extent to which users can participate in modifying the form and content of a mediated environment in real time and vividness is the representational richness of a mediated environment. More vivid web sites provide consumers with more of the information available through direct contact with the product and result in more positive attitudes towards the web site than less vivid ones. Moreover, the duration of total search and brand examination is longer in a 3D interface than in the 2D interface. The 3D represents a highly vivid interface, while a 2D is a highly interactive interface. Along these lines, enhanced vividness of the message by means of colours, graphics, and animation is more likely to generate a favourable impact than comparable levels of interactivity.

Virtual social presence

Social presence refers to the degree to which the media allows a user to establish personal connection with the other users. These interactions may result in discovering products, aggregating, and sharing product information, and collaboratively making shopping decisions. Normally consumers have two distinct types of orientations when visiting a website: transactional and social.

The transactional orientation focuses on completing the shopping tasks, while the social orientation focuses on relationship building which tends to lead to new product discovery and the development of feelings of warmth and satisfaction through the online shopping process. The provision of customer reviews and personalized recommendations (e.g., on Amazon.com) has been shown to be a significant feature that improves the online shopping experience. Similarly, electronic word-of-mouth websites (e.g., epinion.com) where consumers can read the opinions and experiences of other consumers and provide their own comments and ratings on a wide range of products online, have become very popular. Although these technologies enhance the online shopping experience, the focus of these technologies should be primarily on shopping efficiency (Shen, 2012).

Customers today like the idea of websites that go beyond traditional consumer reviews and enable them to enjoy the social aspects of shopping online and establish a personal connection with other users.

2.6 People

People is the sixth element in the retail marketing mix and can be considered as an element of the extended marketing mix, compared to the four P's in the traditional marketing mix. People is mainly concerned with the people that are working for the retailer. These include customer service representatives, salespeople, and anyone else a consumer may deal with that represents a company, people who are involved in process of providing product or service to the customer. These people have responsibility about a product or service from pre-sale to post-sale activities. Therefore, it is very important to recruit and train the right people, because this is who the customers will be dealing with.

A human resource is a person within a company's workforce, with each individual lending his or her skills and talents to the company helping to reach the company's long-term and short-term objectives. Every person who is willing to trade his or her performance, knowledge, or time for compensation, to improve the company and its objectives, is a human resource. All these people must be hired, satisfied, motivated, engaged, developed, and retained. A human resources department is the department that manages a company's human resources.

Human resource management (HRM), and all processes and activities that belong here, has to be aligned with the retailer's business strategy, to work in keeping with all of its corporate objectives. Furthermore, HRM should be aware of employee interests within the organization – life-long learning should be an integral part and motivation measures, as well as measures to increase employee loyalty in the company and reduce fluctuation. HRM specialists must ensure the long-term performance of the retail organizations, the biggest challenge is to meet the future needs of the organization and its employees.

2.6.1 HRM

Nowadays issues like globalization, process management, "war for talents," corporate social sustainability, resource-friendly behaviour or value-based management dominate the current discussion of management in retail companies. There has been an increasing realization that people are one of the retailers' key assets. Retailing means working and serving customers in a direct, personal way. This calls for special strategies and activities from retailers to fulfil the demands of an increasing number of well-informed, demanding, and sophisticated consumers. In view of all the changes and developments in both national and international contexts, it is essential to have the right people, at the right time, in the right place to be successful in the long run.

Retailing is a labour-intensive sector. Therefore, retailers are continually challenged to reorganize and adapt their structures and activities to become more efficient. The necessity for part-time workers, because of long store opening hours and peaks in the trading day and week, requires a flexible framework to optimize labour processes. Future HRM must find a practical approach that will lead to the right balance of companies' and employees' needs in terms of payment and hours for the workforce, and service and price guarantees for their customers. Emotionally, the workforce needs orientation and vision in changing times. In the future, retailing must adapt and change towards a more formative and proactive style of HRM (Merkel, Jackson, & Pick, 2010)

New challenges in retail HRM

In recent years, the retail sector is facing major challenges in HRM, mainly due to demographic changes. Demography, especially in European countries, shows that the share of the older generation is increasing and that of the younger generation is decreasing. As a result, companies will see a change in the age structure of their workforce in the future, as it becomes increasingly older. At the same time, the acquisition of young employees will become more difficult because of the lower number of personnel available. This demographic change does already have an impact on the companies. Many companies complain that they are already experiencing a shortage of specialists and managers, but also skilled workers and apprentices. In addition, many companies show an aging workforce, whose positions need to be filled in the future. Literature and experts refer to this phenomenon as the so-called *war for talents*.

This stands for the "battle" between companies for the best talents – for the best employees which results in an increasing competitive environment in the context of recruiting and retaining "talents" from various educational institutions.

Since personnel is essential for the provision of corporate services, strategic personnel acquisition and retention is becoming increasingly important for companies. Therefore, companies are increasingly focusing on creating an employer brand with the aim of positioning themselves as an attractive employer, the so-called *employer of choice,* and differentiate it from other companies.

Many companies, especially retailers, have recognized that HRM is an essential component in achieving long-term success, and not just a means of recruiting employees. Areas such as the recruitment process, selection, induction, retention, performance monitoring and evaluations, staff training, development and motivation, decision-making, and resourcing for expansion will continue to demand the professionalism of HRM.

Retailing means working in a global context but simultaneously adjusting to local needs. Several retailers have identified internationalization as a huge opportunity for growth. A major task of the international HRM professional is to provide expertise in terms of interpretations of the local laws and working practices, to offer practical steps for successful operation of the international retailer.

A HR strategy must builds on the general business strategy of a company. The HR department has to be business partners for the company's management, providing strategic and practical operational solutions in the form of HR concepts or staffing solutions. So HRM plays a crucial role in assisting corporate management and understanding and adapting to local cultures.

In general, HRM of a retailer must fulfil two categories of tasks- strategic and operational tasks. Both categories will be described below:

Strategic tasks of HRM include:
- To assist the retailer's top management dealing with complex issues, like a competitive marketplace, changing environment, fierce competition, time management constraints, aging population, skills shortage, etc.
- Being up to date with continuously developing technology and being able to optimize its usage for the company, answering the question: How much technology can customers and staff handle in the store?
- Dealing with demographic changes, in detail an aging workforce in Western Europe but young and inexperienced employees in other areas of the world, such as Asia and the Middle East. This fact poses one of the hardest challenges for HR professionals when it comes to recruiting and training staff, build up a corporate culture with may assist to reduce fluctuation.
- Cross-cultural recruiting and training: All cultures have their own unique practices and emphases, so the HR departments must ensure that staff, regardless of their cultural background, is aware of company policies as well as sensitive to the local culture.

Operational tasks of HRM of include:
- Continuous training and development of employees to broaden their experience by the acquisition of new skills – skills that are required due to changing market conditions, for example knowledge of new information and communication technologies, knowledge of automatic processes, new methods in increase customer service and complaint management, etc.
- Ongoing search for suitable personnel and corresponding company presentation at job fairs, in educational institutions, in the media, push positive word-of-mouth, etc.
- HRM itself must change its role from being a pure "personnel" department to act as a strategic business partner for the company in that the department supports the management in all areas where it is necessary.

To summarize, today, HRM is exposed to changing market conditions, which it must adapt to to succeed in the long run in the "war for talents" and to bind its employees to the company. The following subchapter "Human Resource Management Process" will describe all the activities HRM has to perform, in greater detail.

2.6.1.1 HRM process
The HRM process involves several equally important activities. It starts with
- the recruitment and selection of new employees
- training of new employees
- training and retraining for existing employees
- compensating the employees (direct and indirect payments)

- supervising and
- motivating the employees.

Recruitment and selection of new employees

Employee recruitment and selection is one the most essential HR functions. It deals with analysing the job requirements and then finding the prospective candidates who are then encouraged and stimulated to apply for the job in the company. However, the retail industry is faced with difficulties in attracting highly educated people, but also skilled workers and apprentices. This development is described in the common literature as the so-called *war for talents*, that is, the "battle" for qualified young talents, stands for fewer and fewer young skilled workers on the labour market with a constant and even increasing demand for companies. The European economy is already facing this tension, and the situation is likely to become even worse in the coming years.

The recruitment process is a process of identifying the jobs vacancy, analysing the job requirements and specifications (like skills, qualifications, experience needed for the job, etc.), reviewing applications, screening, shortlisting, and selecting the right candidate. The so-called recruitment committee decides on the number and the type of applicants to be contacted. The aim of any organization must be to attract more candidates than needed as some of them might not be willing to join the company, or some might not qualify for the job position. The candidate required for the job is well specified in terms of the task and responsibilities involved in the vacant job along with the qualification and experience expected and needed.

To increase the efficiency of hiring, it is recommended that the HR team of an organization follows the five steps to ensure consistency and compliance in the recruitment process: recruitment planning, recruitment strategy (make or buy employees, types of recruitment, geographical area, recruitment sources), searching (using internal and external sources), screening (reviewing applications, conducting interviews, identifying top candidates), evaluation, and control.

The challenge for HRM is to show the attractiveness of the retail sector and ensure that appropriate training and careers are available, so that this sector can take a leading place in the competition for available talent and in the relevant set of job seekers. Retailers reacts to changing market conditions by employing more elderly people, by building up programs for part-time workers or offering a dual training programme, such as apprenticeship with a final exam (in Austria called Matura).

In detail, recruitment is divided into internal and external recruitment. Internal recruitment deals with the company's own existing employees and external recruitment focuses on the external labour market, that is, job seekers from outside. Both recruitment options have several advantages and disadvantages.

To begin with the advantages of *internal recruitment*, the following can be mentioned: the promotion of development and opportunities for advancement, and personnel strategy aspects, a shorter training period, increased employee loyalty, lower-cost procurement, and experience and knowledge about the employee.

However, there are also some disadvantages, such as the limited number of candidates to be reached, no additional knowledge is generated from outside, it is merely relocated and does not really increase the quality of the employees, the envy of colleagues and increased costs for further training (Schulz, 2014).

What is of advantageous in internal recruitment can be cited as a disadvantage in external recruitment and vice versa.

Advantages of *external recruitment* are a selection from a higher number of applicants, to avoid company blindness, no connections with previous decisions in the company and the personnel dependencies of the applicant. Disadvantages are the demotivation of existing employees and the resulting fluctuation, the increased costs for procurement, still no knowledge of the procedures and processes in the company, mostly higher salary demands and of course the costs and expenses for the entire application process (Schulz, 2014).

In order to address suitable job seekers, it is necessary to select the right recruitment instruments. For this purpose, an analysis is carried out in advance to determine how the potential candidate can best be reached. The following tools and measures are available for external recruitment (Schulz, 2014):

- classical job advertisements in print media
- regional and national newspapers and magazines
- job portals
- university recruitment
- lectures, advertising, bachelor, and master thesis supervision
- own homepage
- Personnel consultant/head-hunter
- Social network portals such as Xing, LinkedIn, etc.
- Employee networks
- Recommendations

In order to complete the recruitment process itself, it is necessary to make the right choices after a selection of measures and tools to reach potential employees. Personnel selection is to determine the extent to which the requirements of the field of activity match the qualifications and skills of the applicant. The most common and widespread form of analysis is the evaluation of previously received application documents. In this process, the formal parameters, education and training, professional experience, any evidence of certificates and references and any special knowledge are revealed or rather checked. So-called work samples or situation-related interviews (business cases) are another way of providing a basis for decisions on personnel selection. Work samples are simulations of the daily work routine that are relevant to the job. In contrast, a situation-related interview is more about how the employee reacts in certain work situations.

Furthermore, it is possible to identify the right candidate by means of ability, personality, and motivation tests. Identifying such potential is particularly important when it is not yet clear what tasks await the candidate in the future, so that he or she can be deployed in a more targeted manner if necessary.

Training of new employees, training, and retraining for existing employees

Training is the process of enhancing the skills, capabilities, and knowledge of employees for doing a particular job. Moreover, training is crucial for organizational development and success of any company, especially in retailing. It is advantageous for both employers and employees of an organization because it helps the employee to get job security and job satisfaction, there are fewer accidents, employees acquire new skills and become an asset for the company and, finally, training improves efficiency and the productivity of the employees.

Training is recommended when:
- new candidates join a company to familiarise them with the mission, vision, strategic, and operational goals, a company's rules and working conditions
- existing employees need to refresh and enhance their knowledge and working skills
- there are updating or amendments in technology, especially in the productional sector but also in retailing when there are computer impartments or other equipment is purchased
- when employees are trained for a higher-level job

In general, there are two different ways of training employees:
- **On the job training:** On the job training methods are those that are given to the employees within the everyday working of a concern. It is a simple and cost-effective training method. The in proficient as well as semi-proficient employees can be well trained by using such training method. The employees are trained in actual working scenario. The motto of such training is "learning by doing." Instances of such on the job training methods are job-rotation, coaching, temporary promotions, etc.
- **Off the job training:** Off the job training methods are those in which training is provided away from the actual working condition. It is generally used in case of new employees. Instances of off the job training methods are workshops, seminars, conferences, etc. Such method is costly and is effective if and only if large number of employees must be trained within a short time period. Off the job training is also called as vestibule training, that is, the employees are trained in a separate area (e.g., a hall, entrance, reception area, etc., known as a vestibule) where the actual working conditions are duplicated.

Compensating the employees

Compensating the employees include monetary and nonmonetary components which normally are the employee's basic salary and additional benefits. These additional benefits include indirect financial compensation and nonfinancial compensation. The compensation program of a retailer normally has three components:

- **Direct compensation:** employees are compensated by monetary reward, like wages, salaries, bonuses, and commissions.
- **Indirect compensation:** nonmonetary reward or additional benefits such as paid vacations, sick leave, holidays, medical insurance, children's care, etc.
- **Nonfinancial compensation:** is the satisfaction that an employee receives from the job.

Compensation is an important issue when it comes to attract high-quality candidates during the hiring process. Normally, a high salary and additional benefits which are suitable for the addressed candidates (e.g., flexible work time) can attract more top applicants to work in a particular company. Moreover, a well thought out compensation affects an employee's motivation, job satisfaction and work performance. For example, sales staff will work harder and give their best to achieve their targets to get the base salary and a bonus or commission. Finally, compensation also can retain high-quality employees. The company can give the benefits to them such as retirement packages to retain them and bind them to the company. In return, the company can save money in recruitment fees, time, and job training costs.

To summarize, a well thought out compensation system is one of the key factors for any successful retailer. The key objectives of an appropriate compensation program are:

- to attract high-quality applicants and generate positive word-of-mouth
- to motivate employees by giving bonuses or commissions to them
- to retain employees by giving additional benefits to them

Gender Pay Gap

The Gender Pay Gap Indicator is used to compare the gender pay gap within the EU. This is calculated uniformly for all EU member states and refers to the average gross hourly earnings of women and men in companies with ten or more employees in the private sector. Hourly earnings are used for better comparability, which means that part-time and full-time earnings can be compared independently of the respective working hours. The indicator measures the unadjusted pay gap, that is, without adjusting for gender differences in the employment structure of a country. The adjusted gender pay gap is calculated by removing structural differences. The survey takes place every four years in all member states.

In Austria, the gender pay gap in 2018 was 19.6%, well above the EU average of 15.7%. Nevertheless, the gender pay gap in Austria has improved significantly over the past 10 years. In 2008 it was still 25.1%. The high gender pay gap in Austria correlates with high employment and part-time work rates for women. By comparison, the gender pay gap and labour force participation are low in Italy or Romania. Nevertheless, a high employment rate does not necessarily lead to a high gender pay gap, as is the case in the Scandinavian member states. Sweden and Denmark both have a high employment rate but are below the EU average. The reasons for the differences are therefore manifold (Statistik Austria, 2019b).

When adjusting the gender pay gap some characteristics such as sector, occupation, educational level, age, length of service in the enterprise, full-time and part-time employment, type of employment contract, region and size of enterprise must be considered. The most important factors include the sector, occupation, level of employment and length of service in the company. Women are more likely to work in lower-paid service occupations and industries, while men are often in the higher-paid technical occupations and in managerial positions. In addition, part-time workers, which account for almost half of all women in employment, are paid less per hour. Despite all factors considered, more than half of the gender pay gap in Austria remains unexplained (Statistik Austria, 2019b).

As a result, the Austrian government, for example, has introduced some measures to achieve equal pay for equal work or work of equal value (Bundeskanzleramt, 2019):

1. the promotion of career prospects for girls and women in all professions, especially in technical and scientific professions
2. the removal of obstacles for women to take up full-time employment
3. initiatives to promote women in economic management and decision-making positions
4. measures to increase income transparency in Austria

Supervising the employees

Basically, supervision is the activity carried out by employees or managers of company to oversee the productivity and progress of employees who report directly to the supervisors. For example, first-level supervisors supervise entry-level employees. Depending on the size of the organization, middle-managers supervise first-level supervisors, chief executives supervise middle-managers, and so on. Supervision is a management activity and supervisors have a management role in the organization (Mc Namara, 2019).

Supervision of a group of employees includes several important management tasks (Mc Namara, 2019):

- conducting basic management skills, like decision-making, problem solving, planning, delegation, and reporting
- deciding what human resources are needed, ideally in terms of knowledge, skills and abilities regarding specified roles, jobs, and tasks
- organizing their department and teams
- noticing the need for and designing new job roles in the group and recruiting the necessary human resources
- training new employees or at least to initiate the training
- managing employee performance, like setting goals together with each employee, observing and giving feedback and other forms of guidance, addressing performance problems, but also giving notice to an employee and ensuring sufficient rewards

Supervising should be carried out according to carefully designed and approved personnel policies in a company. One of the key requirements is respect when monitoring and managing any group of employees. And finally, the supervisor should be an example and a role model who shows good behaviour and maintains an open communication culture.

Motivating the employees

The term "motivation" comes from Latin and expresses "to move." Motivation is a current condition; it is defined by the behaviour of a person towards a certain objective. Motivating employees is essential for every company to retain job satisfaction and bind the employees to a company. Insufficient levels of job satisfaction can cause withdrawal behaviours expressed in turnover, absenteeism, lateness, negative communication internally and externally and/or decision to retire. Therefore, employee retention in general, and job satisfaction, is a very important ongoing process in every company to retain the employees for the maximum period of time.

The motivation of the employees is inseparable from the quality of performance of an employee. Especially in times of saturated markets and the so-called *war for talents*, it is necessary to keep the motivation of the employees on a high level. So, HRM has to ensure that the workforce is motivated and trained to satisfy consumers' needs. Retailers must develop the employee value proposition. This means an attractive position with the fulfilment of employee needs and expectations and achievement of a good, unique image in terms of recruiting and keeping human capital.

- Below, some approaches are listed which might help to retain employees:
- creating a transparent and fair internal job market for the internal employees
- offering a perspective for the future and an attractive career path
- flexible models of working times, such as part-time working concepts, annualized hours contracts, and balancing of profession and family with the aid of sabbaticals
- ensuring adequate processes to achieve the employee's objectives and ambitions
- life-long learning and providing skills and training programs
- training the workforce in soft skills and mentoring to ensure proper alignment of their values with the company's values and beliefs
- initiation of an employee suggestion/inquiry system to improve the process of cooperation
- sharing a company's success with the employees, for example, by offering an incentive system at all staff levels, based on parameters that are achievable for the employees
- offering attractive fringe benefits, such as discounts for shopping at the employer's stores, company cars, equity programs, retirement arrangements, company kindergarten, employee trips or events, and other social benefits

With the help of the *overview model of motivated action* (Heckenhausen & Heckenhausen, 2018), the path from the original situation to the reaction and the consequences for the individual himself or herself is illustrated (see Figure 2.11). In the initial situation a person finds himself or herself guided by a need, an objective, or a motive. When this person encounters a situation, an interaction follows, which finally leads via the action further to the result and to the consequences (e.g., long-term objectives, self-evaluation, external evaluation, material benefits) for the individuum. The action and the result are intrinsically anchored, the motive to complete it thus comes from the activity itself. In contrast, the consequences are of an extrinsic nature.

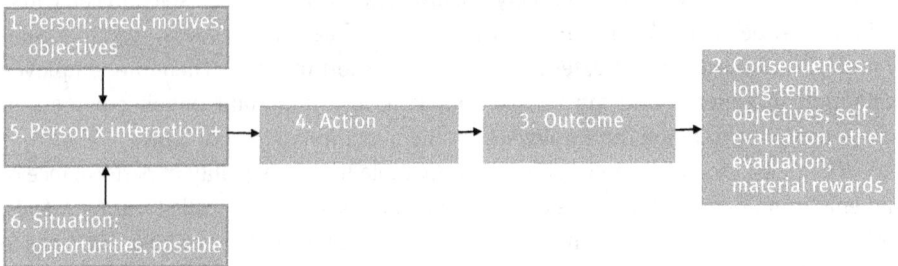

Figure 2.11: Overview model of motivated action.
Source: Heckenhausen & Heckenhausen, 2018

The sources of motivation can be divided into intrinsic and extrinsic motivation.

Intrinsic motivation: describes the first of the five sources of motivation. When people work for the sake of work and not for reward, we speak of intrinsic motivation. Thus, work itself is motivating enough for intrinsically motivated individuals because they enjoy what they are doing. In a way, internal motivations push people to behave explicitly, whereas external factors tend to attract them. This source of motivation of internal self-image is the basis for the ideal self, internal standards, values, and competencies. They are motivated to engage in behaviour that corresponds to their internal standards and from which they expect higher competencies (Barbuto Jr. & Scholl, 1999).

Extrinsic motivation: stands for external sources of motivation. Instrumental reward systems are extrinsically motivated and thus build on tangible results such as pay or promotion opportunities. These individuals enter tangible barter transactions. In this extrinsically motivated attitude, the external self-image, individuals seek to meet the expectations of others by changing their behaviour to the extent that they believe that it will provide the social feedback they desire in advance. People with external self-image aim to gain acceptance and improve their status within a group (Barbuto Jr. & Scholl, 1999).

In the *objective theory of Edwin A. Locke*, the basis for job motivation was created. In this theory, the interaction of productivity, goals and employees is made clear. The first discovery of Edwin A. Locke describes that goals which can be measured by indicators have a higher efficiency than those which are generally formulated. It is essential that employees are informed that there will be no negative consequences for them personally if ambitious goals are not achieved.

In order to enable the practical realization of goals, the theory of goals explicitly defines characteristics which must be given for a smooth realization of goals. Through goals, which are precisely described, the performance is increasingly strengthened. Through the participation of employees in the achievement of goals, a high degree of commitment to the goal is achieved. A goal is a level of performance that a person usually wants to achieve within a certain period. Setting goals is therefore primarily a process that creates discrepancies, as the goal creates constructive dissatisfaction with our current performance.

When people find that their performance is below the set goal, countless studies show that, given their commitment to the goal, they are likely to increase their efforts or change their strategy to achieve it. The core premise of goal setting theory is that goal-oriented action is an essential aspect of human life. Without goal-oriented action, people can not achieve the values that enable their survival and happiness. High goals lead to more effort, concentration, and endurance than moderately difficult or simple goals (Fischer, 2020).

Furthermore, a high goal requires self-satisfaction as well as the assessment of one's own success from a higher level of performance than the achievement of a simple goal. People with high self-efficacy set themselves high goals because they are not satisfied with less (Latham & Locke, 2006). The experience of success does not depend on the absolute level of performance that is achieved, but on performance in relation to one's own goals. If people exceed their goals, they experience success; if they do not achieve their goals, they experience dissatisfaction. When people perform well, they not only feel satisfied with their performance, but generalize this positive effect on the task. They like the task more than before. Challenging goals form a basis for increasing personal effectiveness. In addition to the achievement of goals, which leads to a person's sense of achievement, the achievement of challenging goals leads to operational recognition and associated benefits. Many companies use incentives as a motivating instrument to direct the energies of their employees towards organizational goals. Money alone is by no means enough to motivate people to perform well. Other incentives, such as participation in decision-making processes, changing behaviour to enrich jobs and organisational development, affect employees to varying degrees (Latham & Locke, 1979).

The so-called *Goal Setting Theory* by Locke and Latham (1979) is the most widely used theory dealing with the relationship between goals and performance motivated behaviour. In practice, the theory of Locke and Latham is of significant relevance. In business administration, a management technique known as "management by objectives" has been developed based on Locke and Latham's theory of objectives. To date, traces of the theory of objectives can be found in coaching as well as in psychotherapy. As a rule, employees will primarily identify with goals whose achievement they can personally influence. In this context, corporate goals are an exception to this principle. The higher up in the hierarchy of a company, the more employees contribute to the achievement of corporate goals (Fischer, 2020).

The achievement of goals may require different levels of effort from different employees. Future goals should be set in such a way that the degree of difficulty is significantly higher than the previous level, but it must be possible to achieve the goal. Goals that are clearly and unambiguously formulated lead to a predominantly increased performance than goals that are not achievable. Achieving goals may require different levels of effort from different employees. Future goals should be set in such a way that the degree of difficulty is clearly above the previous level, but it must be possible to achieve the goal. Goals which are clearly and unambiguously formulated lead to a predominantly higher performance than goals which are not specifically formulated. Compared with clearly defined goals, vaguely formulated goals are usually accompanied by a positive assessment of the output achieved, since no clear targets have been set (Fischer, 2020).

2.6.1.2 Internal and external employer branding

The employer brand represents the identity of a company as an employer. It includes a value system, behaviours and strategies that are designed to attract potential employees and motivate and retain existing employees, to position a company as the "employer of choice" among potential and existing employees. The employer brand is the result of *employer branding*. The process of employer branding is based on the positioning of a particular employer, which can be compared with the unique selling proposition (USP) in product marketing.

Employer branding is an instrument for taking up an advantageous position in the increasing competition among employees. In this context, classical marketing offers orientation, whereby brand management and HR management are combined within the framework of employer branding. It encompasses all activities used by companies to build a unique and differentiating employer brand. This represents the employer identity of a company and contributes to the perception of a company as an attractive employer (Stock-Homburg, 2013).

The employer and internal branding activities should precisely and consistently articulate what the organisation, based on its culture and values, can offer its employees and customers (potential and existing). Therefore, highlighting the need for an integrative framework across human resources and marketing activities is important for every retailer.

In the following, the functions are discussed from the perspective of employers and employees and the effects on different areas of the company.

Functions from an employer's perspective

The most important functions of the employer brand from the employer's point of view are preference formation, differentiation, and emotionalization, including their effects on different areas of the company.

Preference formation

The focus of employer branding is to create a preference among the target group for the company as an employer. This is intended to establish the company as the "employer of choice" among existing and potential employees. Since the search for the future employer starts with the comparison of the offers of known companies, it is important to get in touch with the target group before the job search begins and to create positive points of contact. Various measures are available for this purpose, such as information events at educational institutions, participation in trade fairs and presentation on websites. Since the employer brand conveys the values of the company, applicants can independently check whether their ideas, expectations and personal values fit the company. In addition to reducing recruitment costs, successful employer branding has a positive influence on employee loyalty and commitment.

Differentiation

In order for the employer brand to create a preference among potential and current employees, the company needs to differentiate itself from competitors. Therefore, another function of the employer brand is differentiation. The goal is to achieve a monopoly position with the target group through the employer brand policy and thus to generate the image of being the "Employer of Choice." If the same characteristics are not attributed to competitors or are attributed to them in a weaker form, differentiation is achieved. In order to fulfil this function, employer branding must convey the uniqueness of the company as an employer. On this basis, companies should succeed in differentiating themselves from others and in anchoring themselves as an attractive employer in the consciousness of potential and existing employees.

Emotionalization

Experts are sure that an emotionally charged brand generates brand loyalty. In terms of the employer brand, this means that employees are emotionally bound to the company. If employees feel emotionally connected to the corporate brand and thus to the company, this results in a high level of organisational commitment. Employees that identify themselves with a company, will remain loyal and the company's strategy and objectives will become their own. This increases the feeling of taking responsibility and commitment. Consequently, productivity and quality of work will increase.

Functions from the perspective of employees

The most important functions of an employer brand from the employee's perspective are orientation, trust, and identification. These three functions will be described below.

Orientation

A well-established employer brand helps to give potential employees orientation in their search and choice of a potential employer. As there is an oversupply of information on the job market, job seekers are confronted with too much information. An employer brand has the advantage that it bundles emotional and functional messages and transports information about the company. This information enables to compare their professional competence and values with those of the company. This provides orientation for employees and simplifies the decision-making process for an employer.

Trust

The choice for the right employer that has the greatest fit between the professional competence and values of the job seeker and the workplace and values that the company has to offer, has a medium to long-term effect on the job seeker and is therefore an important and time-consuming decision. There is usually too little information available to be able to judge a company as a potential employer. Therefore, job seekers must trust the information and promises that the company provides. An authentic employer brand message should reduce the risk of taking a wrong decision for applicants and, in the long run, the employee will trust the employer and be loyal to his or her employer.

Identification

As already mentioned above, an employer brand represents the values and the image of a company. Therefore, the employer brand helps job seekers to check whether their personal values and skills match those of the company. If this is the case, job seekers will apply and will be committed to the company because their values and skills are in line with those of the company, under the condition that the company-specific values that are communicated are credible and realisable.

2.6.1.3 Future of HRM

The most important drivers for the future of HRM are globalization, technology, and a workforce that fits the company's requirements. Managers must be able to make changes happen of their own volition and to support the company in its drive for sustained success. Managers must be able to empower their own staff, so that staff will really contribute to the changing needs of a company, since they will then be doing things because they understand them and for the right reasons, thinking and reflecting on the changes and their likely impact.

According to experts, men are more threatened than women, low-income earners and jobs in the health, care and social sectors are crisis resistant. That is what we also have seen during the corona pandemic.

AI and machine learning will change the labour market

Experts have a controversial opinion whether digitalization in general and the introduction of AI, machine learning, robotics, etc., will lead to the loss of many jobs, whether they will be replaced by new jobs and whether the gap between lower and upper incomes will widen even further. Some of the jobs that are already poorly paid will probably not be automated as quickly, while others, even in the high-wage sector, will most likely no longer be done by people but be machines. What experts are sure about is the fact that it will be jobs that do not require excessive skills, such as drivers, cleaners, etc., that will be most affected.

On the other side, well-paid jobs that require good training, will also be threatened by AI. Software and robotics can replace routine tasks and rule-based processes, but AI is smarter. While automation has so far rather threatened jobs in the lower income segment, AI is likely to replace well-paid specialists such as radiologists, legal experts, or opticians.

The less an employee earn on a job, the less AI will impact here, at least if human labour is cheaper than using AI technology. It is particularly dangerous for the top third of incomes. High managers or CEOs are still protected.

Nevertheless, according to the analysis, AI will have an impact on agriculture, construction, production, or mining, but also on jobs such as market analysts, sales managers, financial advisors, or computer programmers, all of whom are currently earning well. By contrast, jobs in the education, health, and social sectors, in the arts and entertainment sector, in retail or in gastronomy are initially "immune" to AI applications.

Women, who often work in the low-paid social and health sector, are much less at risk. And of course, the younger ones, who must work even longer, are at greater risk.

Highly paid jobs will break away, especially those for which predictions are important. But new jobs will also be created, especially in machine learning and AI specialists. The group of employees who feed and train AIs with data could grow even more. AI will have similar effects, but, as the authors admit, which will be the case, AI is more uncertain than other automation processes (Rötzer, 2019).

Generation Z in the workplace

Generation Z will soon surpass Millennials as the most populous generation in the world, with more than one-third of the world's population. In the United States, Gen Z constitutes more than a quarter of the population and, by 2020, will be the most diverse generation in the nation's history. Different than Millennials, this generation has an entirely unique perspective on careers and how to define success in life and in the workforce.

Given its experience growing up in the aftermath of the Great Recession, you might think Gen Z has emerged as a pragmatic, risk-averse, nonentrepreneurial group motivated by job security. Instead, a more nuanced picture emerged as we explored their career aspirations, career development, working styles, core values, behaviour and character, education, and stance on diversity (Deloitte, 2019).

While salary is the most important factor in deciding on a job, Generation Z values salary less than every other generation: If given the choice of accepting a better-paying but boring job versus work that was more interesting but didn't pay as well, Gen Z was fairly evenly split over the choice.

To attract Generation Z candidates, companies will need to highlight their efforts to be good global citizens. Moreover, companies must demonstrate their commitment to a broader set of societal challenges such as sustainability and climate change. In addition, companies must offer robust training and leadership programs, with a real and tangible focus on diversity (Deloitte, 2019).

What is more, studies have shown that 8 in 10 millennials and Generation Z workers are interested in working as freelancers part- or full-time, so they show a clear interest in the so-called *Gig Economy* (gig = "appearance"). Gig Economy refers to a part of the labour market where small orders are placed at short notice with independent self-employed, freelancers or marginally employed persons. An online platform often serves as an intermediary between the customer and the contractor, setting the framework conditions and withholding a commission from the operator (Zachary, 2019).

2.6.2 Customer relationship management

Due to globalization and products becoming more homogeneous and replaceable in the customer's eyes, it has become essential for companies do differentiate themselves and their products from competitors. A popular strategy nowadays for differentiation is to lie the focus on customer service and customer care and building long-term relationships with their customers.

Kotler et al. (2001) define CRM as the handling of information gained about their customers (see Figure 2.12). A company uses every single touchpoint to get information about their customers, for example customer service hotlines, website visits, satisfaction surveys, sales figures, etc., analyse, and centralize them. Figure 2.12 shows that CRM is a part of the more general Relationship Management. CRM focusses on the direct contact to the customer by introducing an individual relationship with the customer. It concentrates on the potential, current, and lost customer, and the information about each single point of contact whereas Customer Retention Marketing concentrates

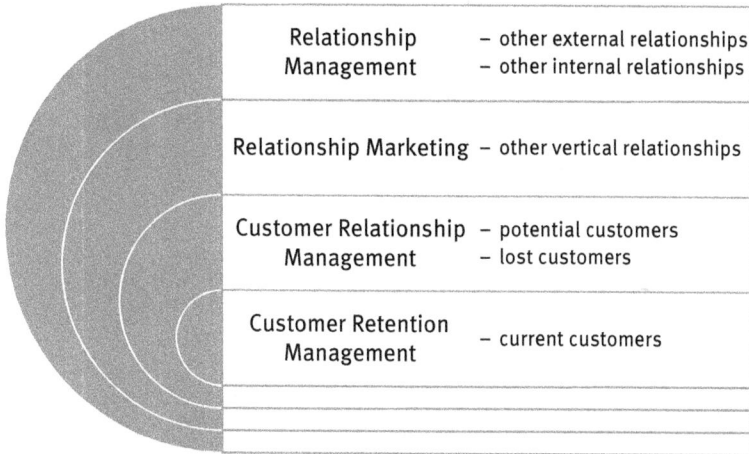

Figure 2.12: Definition of customer relationship management.
Source: Leusser, Hippner, & Wilde, 2011

just on current customers. Relationship management include relationship marketing, CRM, and customer retention marketing (Leusser, Hippner, & Wilde, 2011).

For customers it is important to communicate with one single and uniform business organization, no matter which sales or communication channel they use. Therefore, an efficient CRM helps companies to establish customer profiles which include all relevant information about the customers. Relevant information mainly consists of:
- demographic and socioeconomic data, for example, age, gender, date of birth, occupation, education, income, marital status, family size, religion, nationality, etc.
- buying behaviour, for example, user rates, loyalty status, attitudes, responses to a product, occasions, etc.
- psychological data, for example, social class, lifestyle, personality characteristics, etc.

With the customers' consent, companies can use this data for various analyses and marketing activities. It must be mentioned that keeping the customer in a close relationship to the company requires less effort than the acquisition of new customers (Leusser, Hippner, & Wilde, 2011).

Figure 2.13 shows the four most important objectives of CRM. The first objective is to achieve a higher quality of customer processing, especially one-to-one marketing and providing an added value for the customer. The second objective is an improvement of internal handling process, like workflows. The next objective is an improvement of the customer data management and data integration. The fourth objective is to attain an improved interface to the customer by creating customer profiles, keeping customer histories, and implementing an efficient complaint management. It is

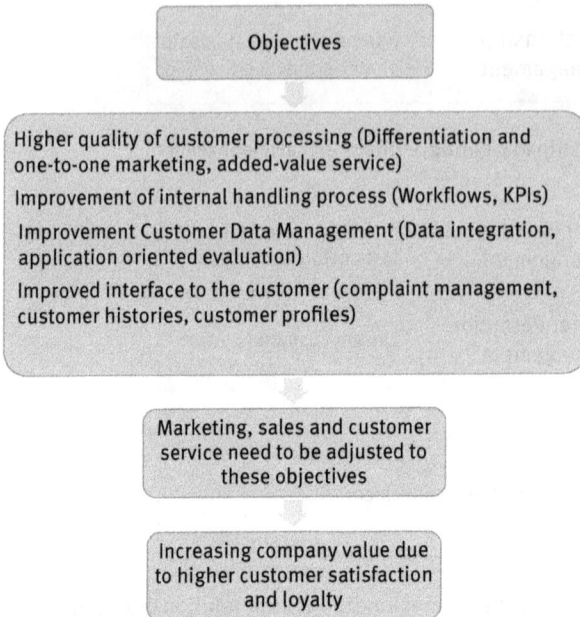

Figure 2.13: Objectives of CRM.
Source: Helmke, Uebel, & Dangelmaier, 2013

important to mention that marketing, sales, and customer service must be adjusted to these four objectives. Consequently, the fulfilment of these objectives may lead to an increase of the company value due to higher customer satisfaction and customer loyalty.

Losing a customer means for a company more than just losing a single sale. It means losing the entire stream of purchase which a customer would make over a lifetime of patronage (Kotler & Armstrong, 2006). This value is referred to as the so-called Customer Lifetime Value (CLV). The CLV is a prediction of all the value a business will derive from their entire relationship with a customer. The CLV helps a retailer to make important business decisions about sales, marketing, product development, and customer support, for example (Customer Lifetime Value, 2017):

- Marketing: How much should be spent to acquire a new customer?
- Product: How can products and services be offered to be tailored for the most valuable customers?
- Customer Support: How much should be spent to service and retain a customer?
- Sales: Which and what types of customers should sales representatives spend the most time for acquisition?

How to calculate the Customer Lifetime Value
The most straightforward way to calculate the CLV is to take the revenue earned from a customer and to subtract out the money spent on acquiring and serving the customer.
   To give an example:
   An average consumer spends 50 Euros every time he goes grocery shopping to a middle-sized supermarket. He/she normally visits the supermarket 50 times a years and remains in a certain area for about 10 years. Therefore, the calculated Customer Lifetime Value would be 25.000 Euros minus the money spent on acquiring and serving the customer that is a small fraction of the 25.000 Euros. If this customer has an unhappy experience and will switch to another supermarket, the retailer will lose 25.000 Euros in revenue, and even more, when this customer spreads negative word-of-mouth. Therefore, working to retain and grow customers is essential for a retailer's economic success.

CRM can be divided into three basic steps:
- customer acquisition
- customer retention
- customer development

Companies need to acquire strategies for every stage the clients go through to increase their value and keep them for a long time connected. Therefore, the most important part is to get the attention of the customer that takes place in phase one, *customer acquisition*. Even in successful companies' customers can switch to a competitor on the market and then these customers need to be replaced. This depends mainly on the size of the business, especially for small organizations or start-ups this process can be as important as the second phase *customer retention*. The second phase, the customer retention phase, concentrates on the maintenance of a group of customers, which are worth keeping for business activities. A company needs to evolve strategies to select those and maintain and increase the value, which is the focus of the third phase *customer development*. The importance to focus on each individual customer is given constantly but not every customer is worth to be kept for a long-term period. It is important for companies to find the exact strategies for being successful and customer orientated. Nowadays information technology-based CRM-systems show the total picture of a customer and help companies to understand the needs and desires of their customers to provide a better customer service and create a strong and long-lasting relationship with their customers (Buttle & Maklan, 2019).

2.6.2.1 Customer loyalty and customer satisfaction
The importance of consumer loyalty in business in general and retailing can hardly be over-emphasized. Singh and Sirdeshmukh (2000) even suggest that consumer loyalty is emerging as "the" marketplace currency of the 21st century. Developing a loyal consumer base is, however, easier said than done. In recent years retail competition has intensified, generally because of new technologies, more sophisticated

management practices and industry consolidation. Several issues such as the commoditization of products, time scarcity, greater choice

of stores and products, more mobile and better-informed consumers, all contrive to discourage strong loyalty to individual stores by consumers (Schriver, 1997). When we try to define the term customer loyalty, the following definition seems to be appropriate (Terblanche & Boshoff, 2006): "Consumer loyalty is the tangible and measurable outcome of attempts to sustain meaningful and profitable relationships with consumers."

The satisfaction of customers is considered a central prerequisite for their loyalty. However, recent observations from business practice increasingly refute this assumption. Here it becomes apparent that satisfied customers do indeed migrate, and that on the other hand dissatisfied customers remain loyal. In her work, Giering (2000) examines the factors that influence the strength of the relationship between customer satisfaction and customer loyalty. The author identifies and systematizes these moderating factors and empirically examines their influence on the relationship between customer satisfaction and customer loyalty. The results show that although customer satisfaction has a fundamentally positive influence on their loyalty, the strength of this influence depends on characteristics of the business relationship, the customer, the product, the provider, and the market environment.

In 1980 Oliver introduced the so-called Confirmation/Disconfirmation-Paradigm (C/D-Paradigm), an integrative frame explaining customer satisfaction. Oliver (1980) proposed a cognitive model that describes customer satisfaction as a function of expectation and expectancy disconfirmation.

Expectations (expected performance), perceived performance, disconfirmation, and satisfaction are the major variables within the C/D-Paradigm. In its original form the paradigm suggests that individuals compare the performance of a product to their preuse expected performance. The comparison results in a certain degree of disconfirmation, which determines if the individual is satisfied or dissatisfied. Various studies have examined the nature of the relationships between the variables extending the original C/D-Paradigm including direct relationships between perceived expectations and satisfaction as well as between perceived performance and satisfaction. Figure 2.14 illustrates the relationships between expected performance, perceived performance, disconfirmation, and satisfaction.

Satisfaction is the consequence of buying and using a product and comparing the costs and benefits. In a cognitive process, individuals compare their prior expectations with their perception of performance leading to satisfaction or dissatisfaction. In this context customer expectations have two functions. First, they can serve as comparative references, which refer to a comparison standard against which the actual experience of performance is assessed, leading to confirmation or disconfirmation. Disconfirmation can be defined as the difference between expected performance (expectations) and perceived performance. If an individual has high expectations but receives a product with poor performance, he or she is negatively disconfirmed. If the product

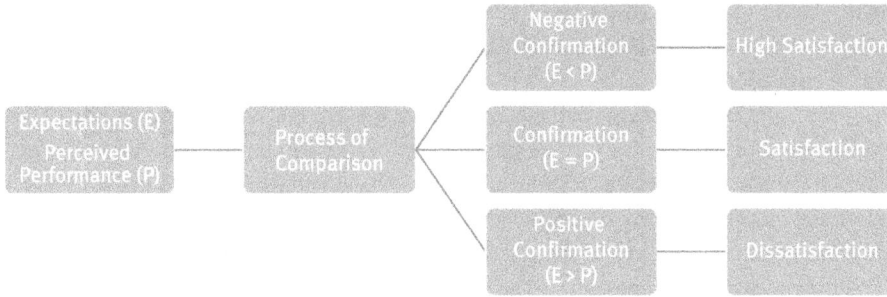

Figure 2.14: The confirmation/disconfirmation paradigm.
Source: Homburg, Giering, & Hentschel, 1999

performs just as expected the individual's expectations are confirmed and if the product performs better than expected, the individual is positively disconfirmed (Krüger, 2016). So, customer satisfaction can be seen as the result of a target-performance comparison.

This C/D paradigm has been the basis for today's research and papers on customer satisfaction. Homburg et al. (1999) explain the confirmation/disconfirmation paradigm in such a way that satisfaction occurs as the result of a complex information processing process, provided that the actual experienced satisfaction of a customer's needs correspond to or exceeds the customer's subjective previous expectations (Homburg, Giering, & Hentschel, 1999). In Figure 2.14 we see that the C/D paradigm can be divided into three phases.

In the first phase, a customer chooses from a selection of options for a product or service. The decision for a certain product is accompanied by an expectation about the performance of the product (target component). The subsequent use or consumption of the product represents the actual phase. The comparison of target and actual component results in the third phase, the comparison. It should be noted that the expectations of customers are highly subjective and individual and shaped by many different influencing factors. These include the service promise propagated by the company, communication by third parties (e.g., consumer centres) or the communicated experience of friends and family. A too large negative gap between target component and actual component results in dissonance and thus in customer dissatisfaction (Homburg, Giering, & Hentschel, 1999).

In the retail sector saturated markets, slow growth and intense competition have refocused retailers' attention on the need to retain their existing consumers as more and more retailers began to realise that acquiring a new consumer is much more expensive than keeping an existing one. Consequently, loyalty programs become more and more important to maintain a company's most valuable customers through long-term, interactive and value-added relationships. So many retailers have established loyalty programs through different mixtures of specialized services, newsletters, premiums, and incentives, often including extensive co-branding arrangements or brand alliances (Keller, 2013).

Literature differentiates between customer loyalty and customer retention. Customer retention stands for the demand-related and supplier-related view of a relationship, whereas customer loyalty describes the demand-related perspective of a relationship and can only be achieved through customer satisfaction. Customer loyalty management refers to activities on the supplier side and is defined as follows: "Customer loyalty management is the systematic analysis, planning, implementation and control of all measures aimed at the current customer base with the aim of ensuring that customers will maintain the business relationship in the future" (Bruhn & Homburg, 2017).

Connectivity and *commitment* are two strategies for companies to achieve customer loyalty. Commitment describes the strategy when the retailer creates a bond between a retailer and a customer trough setting so-called *obstacles* for their customers. These obstacles make it difficult for a customer to switch to a competitor or a competitor's product if the change involves, for example, a monetary effort, a search effort, negotiation costs or the loss of loyalty bonuses. To overcome economic barriers competitive retailers mostly use price policy measures such as price discounts or granting special conditions. Such obstacles are usually not in the interest of the customer but in the interest of the retailer (Kotler, Keller, & Bliemel, 2007).

Therefore, *connectivity* is more useful for building long-lasting customer relationships. Connectivity will be achieved when the customer is fully satisfied with the product or the retailer. If this strategy is successful, customers will not consider competitors or substitute products in their purchasing plans and it is almost impossible to entice customers away.

Furthermore, long-lasting customer relationships can be created through relationship marketing. Relationship marketing includes all measures of a company to know and appreciate its recipients better, to satisfy them and to cooperate with them. The establishment of long-term customer relationships with the use of targeted customer retention measures is becoming more important.

Bruhn and Homburg (2017) distinguish six steps in the customer retention strategy that form the basis for a successful *customer retention concept*:

- **What**: The initial key question refers to the object to which the customer should be bound. This can be a product, a service, a manufacturer, the sales representative, or a retailer.
- **Who**: The priority with which the various customer segments are to be addressed must be defined to increase customer loyalty. While so-called A-customers receive a more individual customer loyalty approach, C-customers are those with a particularly low customer benefit.

- **How**: The type of customer retention deals with the question of how customers are to be retained. A distinction must be made here within the situational, economic, social, technical-functional, contractual, and emotional bond.
- **With what**: As an additional strategy dimension, the definition of customer loyalty instruments follows, which – depending on the customer loyalty strategy defined in advance – can be positioned more precisely on the structure of dialogue and interaction as well as customer satisfaction or the structure of barriers to switching.
- **How often and when**: When and to what extent the selected instruments should be used (e.g., sending mailings or newsletters every two months or only once a year).
- **With whom**: It must also be clarified whether customer retention measures can be achieved more effectively by cooperating with partners, like additional manufacturers, intermediaries, or other retailers.

The main objective of customer retention management is to retain customers for a long period of time, as well as to systematically restore lost buyers. Strategic approaches to customer retention include determining the customer retention instruments that are used. The traditional instruments of the marketing mix are used for this purpose in a target group-oriented manner. Since the trust and familiarity of customers largely depends on personal contact with the company, reliable and competent employees are essential. Consequently, personnel policy is nevertheless essential for the successful management of customer loyalty (Bruhn & Homburg, 2017).

The following Table 2.5 shows important marketing instruments, which are frequently used in the retail sector to retain customers.

Table 2.5: Marketing instruments for customer retention (Bruhn & Homburg, 2017).

Marketing instruments	Examples
Product policy	Product design
	Definition of service and product quality
	Product programme
	Brand policy
Price policy	Discount and bonus systems: financial, natural advantage
	Contracts and guarantees (also voluntary commitment)
	Price differentiation strategies: spatial, temporal, etc.
	Financial incentive: reimbursement

Table 2.5 (continued)

Marketing instruments	Examples
Communication policy	Direct mail: direct approach to customers
	Customer magazines
	Loyalty cards: Link purchase data/persons
	Customer clubs
	Telemarketing: follow-up campaign, customer survey
Distributions policy	Sales organization
	Distribution channel design, for example, online, omnichannelling
Personnel policy	Personnel intensity
	Appearance
	Employee performance
	Employee competence and motivation

2.7 Process

The last P in the retail marketing mix is process. Process refers to the flow of activities or mechanism that take place when there is in an interaction between the customers and the businesses. Moreover, process deals with customer service, and a company's ability to offer a service, handle complaints, and foresee any issues before they actually happen. These clearly defined and efficient processes should garner customer confidence in the company's ability to handle any issues.

An example of a very simple process of a virtual service would be when a customer decides to take membership of a video service providers (e.g., Netflix, Amazon prime, etc.). The customer will download the application that was constituted as the first process, then the customer will register his or her account with it, which will constitute as another process. Marketers need to make sure that all these processes are controlled tightly and generate a positive customer experience.

An ideal process should be taking the least amount of time among all the available options and should cost less to the company will delivering and efficient output to the maximum of its capacity. The process delivers value to the marketing mix with the help of all the elements involved and can be changed depending on the feedback which is received (Hitesh, 2019).

There are several types of processes (Hitesh, 2019):

Technological processes: The process of creating tangible products is called technological process. The objectives to ensure that the customers feel the product to be theirs. The manufacturer should ensure that he creates the product that is wanted by the customers and should also make the products that he as a businessman would want to sell in the market. The balance between both would ensure that the technological process would run smoothly.

Electronic processes: Use of receipts or barcodes or forms or other methods of information about a particular product of a company that manufactures them is called an electronic process. This also includes the course which is used to scan with the help of an application using a mobile phone.

Direct activities: Direct activities, as the name suggests, is about the reactions of the customers regarding the process. How did they feel about the process that they just underwent through is known thereby making any changes if necessary, to make the process smoother? Direct activities ensure to add value to the interface of the customers as the customer experience is the service.

Indirect activities: When the interaction does not take place in person and it happens before or after the product has been bought is termed as an indirect activity. Indirect activities are also known as back-office activities. Indirect activities support the direct activities before and after they have been consumed.

There are various concepts which are related to processes, like workflow, business process reengineering, business process management or total quality management. All those connects will be describes below.

– **Workflow**: movement of information or tasks for material from one participant to the other is termed as workflow. This includes but is not limited to people and tools procedures that are involved in every step of the marketing mix process. The workflow may be sequential that is the consequent step is begin only when the prior step is completed or parallel that is multiple steps may occur at the same time. Single workflows may be combined in multiple ways to have an overall process.
– **Business process reengineering** (BPR): is a means to enhance or improve the effectiveness of the organization along with its productivity. It consists of starting right from the beginning or from scratch and creating a major business process along with the application of IT or information technology to achieve significant improvement of performances.
– **Business process management** (BPM): is defined as a discipline which has a mix of different business activities and their flows and which strives to support the vision and mission of business within and beyond many boundaries which one was people customers internal the employee's external stakeholders as well as external partners.
– **Total quality management** (TQM): is sought to improve the quality of the product. Six sigma method was used by Motorola to find out about total quality management. It consists of methods to improve the processes in the business and thereby reduce the problems in the output increase the output and thereby maximize the profits (Hitesh, 2019).

3 E-commerce, E-tailing, and digitalization

Researchers have developed various scenarios about future developments in the retail sector. No one knows exactly which of these scenarios will come true. But it is highly likely that in the future there will be a significant struggle for power and dominance between the retailer and the consumer.

Retailers will be willing to get even more out of their customers' database so that their customer-centric, targeted and personalized marketing activities ("one-to-one"-marketing) will deliver even more value. This consumer-oriented approach will also allow retailers to better understand and predict their customers' needs, wants, and requirements and therefore provide them with better and targeted customer service.

Concerning the e-commerce sector, it will be the most technologically oriented retailers who will dominate this sector as they have a deeper understanding of their customers. Moreover, all scenarios suggest that the competition in the retail sector, especially in the e-commerce sector, whether on global, national, or regional level, will become more intense. Therefore, all retailers will need to develop strategies for responding to enhanced consumer influence, mainly with initiatives such as: communication via social networking sites, growing and strengthening their brand, differentiating their product and service offerings, and working hard to ensure that their web sites provide consumers with an enjoyable and reliable shopping experience to create customer engagement.

Well-established retailers will also need to consider how they can integrate their online and offline channels more efficiently to provide customers with the very highest levels of service and create customer satisfaction and long-term relationships.

Digital technology can connect any retailer to any customer in the world who has access to the internet. The consumer can shop from anywhere via all manner of personal technology devices, like mobile phone, PC, smart devices, and futuristic accessories like wearables (PwC, 2013), smart electronic devices that can be worn on the body as implant or accessories. Having an outlook on future trends and developments, the so-called *experience economy* will change into the direction of a virtual experience economy with a focus on VR, AR, and mixed reality (MR) technologies.

E-commerce, in general, is a growing business, especially in the developing markets in the Asia-Pacific, Latin America, and Africa/Middle East regions. Online shopping is particularly popular in the Asia-Pacific, above all in China, due to rapid urbanization, high population density, low labour costs and booming smartphone ownership (The Nielsen Company, 2015). But e-commerce does not fit every product category, especially immediate-use item, for example, fresh or frozen food, are not very suitable for e-commerce. Stock-up categories, like personal care or household products, are very well suited. Also, specialty retailers can benefit from using e-commerce because they can offer online a greater product selection and can fulfil unique customer needs (The Nielsen Company, 2015).

https://doi.org/10.1515/9783110543827-004

Research has shown that digital natives (the millennials and Generation Z), who grew up with digital technology, are the most willing consumer group to use E-commerce options, like home delivery, in-store pickup, drive-through pickup, curb side pickup, virtual supermarket, or automatic subscriptions (The Nielsen Company, 2015).

Although most retailers know about the potential of e-commerce, e-tailing, and digitalization, some of them are actually more overwhelmed than exited and don't know how to make use of these digital developments. This applies to SME.

Therefore, this chapters aims at facilitating the decision-making processes and points out the most important issues which must be considered when "going digital."

3.1 Differences between E-tailing, E-commerce, and digitalization

E-tailing (electronic tailing) and e-commerce (electronic commerce) are two terms, which are very often used synonymously. The two terms do have similarities but there do exist more key differences. The most important key difference is that *e-tailing* describes the activity of selling of retail goods and services on the internet whereas *e-commerce* is the commercial transactions conducted by electronic means on the internet. So, e-tailing is a subcategory of e-commerce, and e-commerce is the umbrella term. When customers want to directly buy goods or services from a seller over the internet, they use e-tailing. They have a wide variety of choices and can compare product attributes and prices, which helps them save time and money. But still, some customers don't want to engage in e-tailing because of a lack of trust and privacy concerns. E-Commerce encompasses not only E-tailing, but many more terms and activities, like providing information to customers about company offers, online branding and marketing activities, B2B buying and selling and electronic data interchange, gathering, and using customer data through market research and online financial exchanges for currency exchanges or trading purposes (Difference Between, 2017).

Table 3.1 summarizes the most important differences between e-tailing and e-commerce.

Digitalization stands for the integration of digital technologies into the customer's everyday life by the digitization of everything that can be digitized. An example for digitization into everyday like is the Apple watch. Various technical features are integrated into an ordinary watch, like phone and internet capabilities and messaging (businessdictionary, 2017). Another example for digitalization is the so-called smart fridge. Food and beverages shopping can be easily organized by scanning the barcodes of the products with a scanner on the fridge door or by using a voice recognition technology. Automatically the fridge's content is monitored and necessary items are added to an online shopping list or directly ordered via e-tailing. There are many more applications of digital technologies, some of them are described in the following chapter.

Table 3.1: Differences between e-tailing and e-commerce (Difference between, 2017).

E-tailing versus e-commerce	
E-tailing is the activity of selling of retail goods on the internet. Customers can purchase goods and services through e-tailing.	E-commerce is the commercial transactions conducted by electronic means on the internet. E-commerce involves several services such as electronic funds transfer, internet marketing and online transaction processing.
Nature	
E-tailing is a narrow concept.	E-commerce is a broad concept in which e-tailing is a part of.
Markets	
The United States is the biggest market for e tailing in the world at present.	At present, China is the biggest market for e commerce.

Digitalization is deeply linked to a variety of other trends. The following sub-chapters will also give insights into the most current and influential trends based on digitalization and technology in general and innovative technologies.

When it comes to the world's leading e-commerce giants, these are the Chinese e-commerce company Alibaba Group and the US e-commerce leader Amazon. Taking the Top 3 the online marketplace (auction service) eBay also represents a leading company in the global e-commerce sector (Forbes, 2015). Table 3.2 shows that Amazon is the leading company when it comes to market capitalization, as one of the best measures of a company's size. Market capitalization refers to a company's total value and stands for a company's stock price times the number of shares outstanding. Alibaba is the market leader when it comes to the number of active buyers and leads the e-commerce market regarding the company's revenue.

Table 3.2: Top 3 e-commerce giants (Forbes, 2015).

	Amazon	Alibaba	Ebay
Market capitalization (billion $)	249,1	157,7	31,1
Active buyers	270 million	367 million	157 million
Business model	mix	marketplaces	marketplaces
Revenue ($)	95.8 million	13.1 billion	8.6 million

Comparing the two e-commerce giants Alibaba Group and Amazon we see that they are leaders of the two largest e-commerce markets in the world, China, and the United States. One basic difference between the two e-commerce companies is that

Alibaba only provides an online shopping marketplace where other retailers sell and does not sell directly to customers. In contrast, Amazon both sells merchandise that it owns to customers and operates a marketplace. The following box gives a brief outline on the history of the US e-commerce leader Amazon.

The following box provides a brief historical outline of the e-commerce leader Amazon.

A brief history of the e-commerce giant Amazon

Amazon.com was founded in 1995 when it sold its first book online. The company has come a long way since then. Its products and service offerings are numerous as well as their delivery channels. In 2000, Amazon launched its well-known marketplace platform, which allows third-party sellers to set up digital storefronts on the Amazon site. In return Amazon charges fees and provides marketing tools and logistics services to their sellers. Amazon's customer base is mainly online and all over the globe.

Amazon Web Services (AWS) was first launched in 2002 to "expose technology and product data from Amazon and its affiliates, enabling developers to build innovative and entrepreneurial applications on their own." After engineers at Amazon put forth a paper detailing a standardized and automated retail services infrastructure for the business, as well as to sell access to virtual services and storage as new revenue streams, AWS evolved into an independent service offering. In 2006, it was relaunched in the form of a suite of digital services including computing, storage, and database solutions.

Over its initial 10 years of operations, the e-commerce giant was very successful. To push this success further, Amazon introduced the so-called prime membership program in 2005. The program provides various shipping benefits to shoppers, such as same-day and next-day delivery (Weinswig, October 2017).

Amazon has already put several innovations on the market that enable even more efficiency and provide more touchpoints to reach its customers. Some of these innovations are (Weinswig, October 2017):

Amazon Echo: Amazon introduced a range of speakers under the name Echo in 2014. These speakers allow users to shop by voice commands as they house an artificial intelligence (AI)-powered digital assistant called Alexa.

Dash Button: Dash buttons were introduced in 2015. These buttons allow "one-click" ordering of products, especially regular household goods, from laundry detergent to pet food.

Prime Air: Amazon is experimenting with a drone delivery system that will allow deliveries in approximately 30 minutes.

Amazon Go: Amazon has introduced a new staffless convenience store concept that allows automatic, unmanned checkout. Shoppers can pick up a limited range of products, mainly convenience products, at the physical store by using a particular app.

Amazon's e-commerce platform is present in only a limited number of countries. The company has an established presence across North America and Europe and has been expanding across the Asia-Pacific region. In its early years, Amazon chose developed economies in which to launch its online bookstore and full e-commerce platform. This is the reason why its market share is higher in such countries, most likely attributed to its early launch in these countries, which have a higher disposable income per capita and were early adopters of internet shopping compared to the emerging markets.

The US is Amazon's largest market, accounting for 67% of its 2016 revenues ($135.9 billion global revenues), followed by Germany, Japan, and the UK. The remaining markets it operates in account for just 8% of total revenues. Currently, Amazon operates under its own name in four emerging markets: China, India, Brazil, and Mexico. It operates in the US under the name of Souq.com, a company that it recently acquired (Weinswig, October 2017).

To summarize, Amazon has been a constant innovator and with the multiple touchpoints the e-commerce giant has created to engage with its customers, it will continue to hold a leading position in the e-commerce sector.

When we try to figure out which factors are the most important ones when it comes to affecting the growth of electronic retailing, the two most important factors are (Weitz, 2010):
– the number of people with broadband access
– the degree to which electronic retailers make use of the benefits and address the limitations of electronic retailing

Broadband access

A substantial number of people worldwide have access to the internet and exactly those people are potential users of electronic retailing. According to the Internet World Stat, in 2018, 4.2 billion people worldwide had internet access- this means about 50% of the global population accessed the internet- and it estimated that this figure will increase especially in regions where the internet penetration rate is still low, for example, Africa and Asia, but also in the Middle East and Latin America/ Caribbean. The countries with the greatest access penetration rate in percentage of the population are North America (95%), Europe (85.2%). Oceania/Australia (68.9%) and Latin America (67.2%). Asia has the lowest penetration rate (49.0%), followed by Africa (36.1%) (Internet World Stat, 2018). Most global internet users are in East and South Asia, while China is the largest online market in the world. In 2016, China had over 721 million internet users, more than double the amount of third-ranked United States with nearly 290 million internet users (Statista, 2018).

Most of the people with internet access were classified as active at-home users and have broadband connections. Broadband's prevalence is important because consumers need such connections to have constant contact with the internet without a login process, downloads and multimedia (music, movies, etc.) are much faster and there are no automatic cutoffs.

Internet users often turn to their mobile devices to access the internet. Millennial or Generation Y internet users (i.e., people born in the early 1980s until the mid-1990s), for example, spent an average of 185 minutes on mobile internet services every day. Generation X (i.e., birth years ranging from the early-to-mid 1960s to the early 1980s) internet users' average daily use of mobile internet stood at 110 minutes that year.

Many companies have been profiting from the increased mobile usage by following a mobile-first strategy and optimizing their content for mobile devices. Some of the most popular mobile internet activities are using email, working, social networking, online search, online video, and online shopping. Instant messaging is also popular among mobile internet users worldwide. WhatsApp is the most popular mobile messaging app in the world with one billion monthly active users. Facebook Messenger closely follows with 900 million monthly active users. Facebook is the leading social network with 1.7 billion active users. Other popular social networks include Instagram, Twitter, and Tumblr, as well as mobile chat apps such as WhatsApp, Facebook Messenger, or We-Chat (Statista, 2018).

The constantly expanding e-commerce market is a huge attraction to internet users worldwide, as shown in the growth of e-commerce volume and consumer spending. Electronic retailing revenue is forecast to nearly double until 2020. Mobile retail is also one of the fastest growing online categories, considering global mobile e-commerce to generate about 669 billion US dollars in revenue in 2018. Mobile commerce is incredibly popular in Asia, especially in South Korea and China, where nearly half of the shoppers stated buying something online via phone (Statista, 2018).

Given this significant penetration of internet usage especially in industrial countries, the primary factor driving the growth of online retail sales will be the degree to which electronic retailers make use of the benefits but also consider the limitations.

Limitations of electronic retailing

Starting with the limitations of electronic retailing, the following limitations should be discussed (Weitz, 2010):
- security and privacy concerns
- browsing
- providing sufficient information

Security and privacy concerns. Perhaps the biggest challenge for online retailers is establishing and maintaining trust due to spams, fraud, identity theft, etc. However, reputable retailers have taken steps to offer secure connections and protect their internal data. Also, as consumers become more accustomed to placing orders over the internet, their concerns about security are diminishing. Although consumer security concerns are declining, online retailers face in- creasing losses owing to credit card fraud. It is estimated that credit card fraud will cost online US retailers more than $1 billion in 2004. Online retailers use a variety of fraud management techniques, including using in-house or commercially available screens, requesting card verification numbers, and checking orders with credit card authentication services (Weitz, 2010).

In addition, many customers are concerned about retailers violating their privacy when they collect private information about them, although detailed information about individual customers helps retailers to provide more benefits to their customers. Besides collecting transaction data when buying online, electronic retailers can collect information by placing cookies on shoppers' hard drives (Weitz, 2010). In May 2018, the European Union (EU) has introduced the *General Data Protection Regulation* with the main aim to protect natural persons in relation to the processing of personal data. In detail, businesses can only collect consumer information if they have a clearly defined purpose, such as completing the transaction. This purpose must be disclosed to the consumer from whom the information is being collected and the information can only be used for that specific purpose. If the business wants to use the information for another purpose, it must initiate a new collection process and the permission from the customer.

Browsing: Before consumers were offered the possibility to buy their products online, they were searching for products they needed and very often conducted unplanned purchases. When using an electronic channel, customers have a much more limited visual field than they have in a physical shop. Only a limited number of selected products can be featured on the first web page or on the subsequent web pages and unplanned purchases are rather limited. Electronic retailers work on addressing this limitation and suggest two solutions: either customising the main page, also with the help of cookies and other algorithm, to display just products of interest to the customer and improving the search function. The search function on web pages is very important because most shoppers use the search function to find the product they are looking for.

Providing sufficient information: During their customer journey, consumers normally need information to conduct their final purchase decision. Providing useful and helpful information is a challenging task for electronic retailers. They normally provide standard information through a list of frequently asked questions (FAQs) or standardized online solutions or contact details for further information. Customers demand timely information and do not want to wait until they receive an answer to their question. Therefore, two applications might help to solve this limitation: online chats, chat bots and automated self-service solutions. Chat bots are computer programs that mimic conversation with individuals using AI. They can transform the way a person interacts with the internet from a series of self-initiated tasks to a conversation (see the following box for examples).

Examples of Chatbots.
Imagine you would like to buy a new pullover online. First, you would go your favourite website, browsing and searching for a suitable pullover, in the right size, design, colour, prize, etc., and finally purchasing your favourite pullover. If this online fashion retailer has a chatbot, it would be much easier because you would simply ask the chatbot certain questions and it helps you to find what you are looking for. Instead of browsing a website, you will have a conversation with

chatbot, similar than in a physical store where you would ask the sales staff certain questions to help you finding a suitable pullover.

Buying textiles or other products is not the only thing a chatbot can be used for. There are many different chatbots in all kind of fields and businesses:

Weather bot: get the weather whenever you ask.

News bot: ask it to tell you whenever something interesting happens.

Life advice bot: to tell it problems and it helps to think of solutions.

Personal finance bot: helps to manage money better.

Scheduling bot: organizes a meeting with someone on the Messenger team at Facebook.

A friend bot: in China there is a bot called Xiaoice, built by Microsoft, that over 20 million people talk to.

Online chat provides customers with the opportunity to click a button at any time and conduct an instant messaging email conversation with a customer service representative. Other applications allow a consumer to initiate a voice conversation with a customer-service representative. These applications also enable electronic retailers to automatically send a proactive chat invitation to customers on the site. The timing of these invitations can be based on the time the visitor has been on the site, the specific page the customer is viewing, or a product on which the customer clicked.

Overcoming the Need for Sensory Information. When evaluating some types of merchandise, information about "look-and-see" attributes, such as grams of fat in a breakfast cereal or colour and style of a wool scarf, can be effectively communicated over the internet. However, "touch-and-feel" attributes are more difficult to communicate online. Owing to the problems of providing "touch-and-feel" information, apparel retailers experience returns rate of more than 20% on purchases made through an electronic channel and only 10% for purchases made in stores.

3D/Zoom Imaging. Electronic retailers are taking steps to overcome this limitation by converting "touch-and-feel" information into "look-and-see" information. Online customers now expect large, accurate product images. However, electronic retailers are going beyond offering the basic image to giving customers the opportunity to view merchandise from different angles and perspectives using 3D imaging and/or zoom technology. Although only a limited number of electronic retailers are employing these technologies for a few products, the use of these image-enhancing technologies has increased conversion rates (the percentage of consumers who buy the product after viewing it) and reduced returns.

However, these imaging technologies can frustrate consumers using dial-up connections because of the slow download times. Also, some of the technologies require plug-ins that must be downloaded and may not work effectively with all browsers. Finally, some retailers initially utilized these imaging technologies but have now removed them because visitors were not using them.

Virtual Models. To overcome the limitations experienced because apparel obviously can not be tried on, online apparel retailers have started to use virtual models. These virtual models enable consumers to see how selected merchandise looks on an image with similar proportions to themselves and then rotate the model so the "fit" can be evaluated from all angles. The virtual models are either selected from sets of "prebuilt" models or constructed based on the shopper's response to questions about their height, weight, and other dimensions.

For example, at Landsend.com, online shoppers choose a model that looks like them. The customer then dresses the model using a "click-and-drag" interface. Items are suggested while the customer "tries on" apparel. Land's End reports that customers using the virtual model feature are 28% more likely to make a purchase and spend 13% more on the average purchase. When JCPenney offered this feature on its website, more than 100,000 customers saved their model for future visits.

In a similar way to the imaging technologies discussed previously, the virtual model technology is complex and results in slow download speeds for consumers who have no broadband connections. Also, the present applications are not true fit predictors, but provide some information about how combinations of apparel and accessories look together and what apparel styles might flatter a specific figure. However, these applications are harbingers of future applications in which customers can have a personal, 3D, digitized body scan serve as an actual model rather than a virtual model. Also, the measurements for the body scan could be inputted along with information about the garment to a predictive model advising customers on how well a specific item fits using a five-star rating system and then suggesting the appropriate size.

Personalization. One of the attractive features of Laurie Waters' online shopping experience, previously described, was the personalized service offered by FRED. This personalization assisted Laurie in satisfying her need for a gift. Had FRED's services been offered by a retailer; the personalization would have engendered Laurie's loyalty to the retailer. When a retailer has a thorough understanding of her preferences and uses this it effectively to facilitate Laurie's shopping experience, she has little incentive to switch to other retailers lacking this capability.

Although not achieving the level of personalization offered by FRED, Amazon. com is clearly on the forefront in terms of personalizing its offering. Visitors are greeted by a personalized "store" featuring their name and recommending products based on their past purchases, click-stream data, or expressed preferences. Besides personalizing the websites, customers can elect to receive emails announcing the availability of new product in which they might be interested. However, an important issue related to personalization is that of privacy concerns.

Cash Purchases: The lack of credit cards inhibits teens and tweens, a sizable and fast-growing retail segment, from shopping online. However, several internet service providers let parents establish an account for children using a credit card to set the initial balance. The teenager logs onto the site using a password, browses the site's electronic retailer partners, selects desired merchandise, and puts it in an electronic shopping cart. The shopping site takes care of the payment. Using their own passwords, parents can check up on their teens' buying habits and balance.

Although online retailers are using technology to address the limitations of online shopping, the store channel continues offer superior benefits to an electronic channel, such as providing information about "touch-and-feel" product attributes and ability to get products immediately after purchasing them, and offering a stimulating, social experience. Thus, most analysts project that online retail sales will only be 4%–5% of total retail sales by 2010. However, retailer websites play a major influence on retail shopping behaviuor. A recent survey of a representative sample of internet users found that more than 40% of consumers shopping for consumer electronics, books, PCs and peripherals, clothing, and CDs visited a retailer's website and then shopped at its store. This synergy between electronic and store channels is one factor leading to the growth of multichannel retailing.

3.2 Innovative technologies in retail

Information technology and digitalization have changed the landscape of consumer behaviour and have empowered the consumers, also in the retail sector. The internet has evolved from a medium of enhancing brand awareness and disseminating information to an essential channel of retailing. More and more brands use the internet as a retail location, mostly choosing the e-retail strategic option of channel integration combining online and offline retailing activities (Okonkwo, 2007). Technology, in general, has fundamentally transformed the way retailers and the consumer packaged goods industry operate. Retailers are successful by leveraging technology to enhance the shopping experience and meet the customers evolving desires (The Nielsen Company, 2015). The most important objective of technology at the POS is to meet customers' needs, to provide an integrated experience and to come up with the desire of identification (Morschett, Zentes, Schu, & Steinhauer, 2013). Technology is also said to be the fundament for the trend of "everywhere-shopping," which means that consumers' buying behaviour become independent from time, location and the retailer's distribution channel (Schramm-Klein, Wagner, Neus, Swoboda, & Foscht, 2014).

The innovative store concept Amazon Go

In 2017 Amazon launched Amazon Go, an automated, checkout-free convenience store in Seattle, powered by technologies such as computer vision, sensor fusion and deep learning. Amazon Go is running the "world's most advanced shopping technology," bridging the digital and physical worlds, and creating convenience for the consumer.

To be able to shop at Amazon Go, shoppers need to download and log-in to the Amazon Go app, which provides them with a QR code they scan when entering the store. Shoppers are then allowed to pick up and return items freely from the shelves. Amazon's technology detects shoppers when they walk out of the store and charges their purchases to their Amazon account. There are no checkouts, cashiers, or physical payments. Amazon has released a video on YouTube to describe the Amazon Go technology (https://www.youtube.com/watch?v=NrmMk1Myrxc).

The Amazon Go technology has various advantages for Amazon and benefits for the customers, such as the following (Weinswig, 6 December 2016):

– More consumer data will lead to better shopping recommendations: Amazon is known for its ability to gather and use data to offer an ever-improving customer experience. When shopping for convenience purchases and food, people inherently shop differently than when doing so online. Therefore, a brick-and-mortar convenience store is a new consumer touchpoint for Amazon, and one that is inherently different from online shopping. Having access to data from the store will likely enable Amazon to provide even better shopping recommendations to its shoppers.
– A feed into Amazon's Web Services: The technology powering Amazon Go will likely become a commodity sooner rather than later, and Amazon can choose to offer it to other retailers as a complement to its Amazon Web Services, which include cloud-computing services, analytics, and marketplace platforms.

A play into health and wellness: As Amazon Go sells primarily meal-kits and ready-to-eat snacks, Amazon will in fact be collecting data on people's food consumption and nutrition habits. This as an interesting opportunity to develop original products or integrate data with existing wearables that track fitness and health to offer a convenient 360 wellness-monitoring solution.

Taking the example of the innovative store concept of Amazon Go described above, we see that retailers must integrate innovative technologies in their business strategies to adapt their strategies to varying market situations. By merging or acquiring, retailers try to stay profitable, but this strategy does not lead to fundamental changes the way retailers do business. Innovative technologies, above all virtual, augmented, and mixed realities, have an enormous amount of potential. Having an outlook on future trends and developments, the so-called *experience consumer* and the "experience economy" will change into the direction of a virtual experience economy with a focus on VR, AR and mixed reality technologies (Trendwatching, 2016). Those three technologies will be described in the following subchapters.

Augmented and virtual reality

Technologies for the generation of virtual and augmented realities are currently in a boom phase. The well-known technology companies (e.g., Microsoft, Apple, Google, Facebook, Amazon, etc.) are trying to position themselves in this new technology sector. The fields of application are extremely broad and cover almost every economic sector. Initial application examples already provide an insight into the potential of this new technology.

Studies (Tavolieri, 2019) have shown that over half of global consumers (51%) are already willing to use AR or VR technology to assess products. So, we see a high level of interest for adopting this emerging technology. By contrast, only 44% of consumers say they are willing to use self-service checkout, a much simpler technology. Consumers are similarly interested in driverless cars, drone delivery, custom 3D printed products or receiving personalized health advice from an AI driven appliance.

Many consumers are already relying on AI-driven appliances to simplify their lives, especially for personal use and domestic cleaning tasks. According to Euromonitor International's 2019 Lifestyles Survey (Euromonitor, 2020), 12% of respondents own or currently have regular access to in-home virtual assistant devices for personal use, for example, voice assistants, smart lighting system, etc. In addition, one-third of respondents own smart laundry or kitchen appliances, and there is still a rise in demand. Globally, 41% are willing to pay a premium for smart appliances and products while 26% feel comfortable sharing their data through smart home technology. Especially millennials and Generation X are particularly open to the usage of technologies, like VR, AR, or AI-driven robots, mainly for curated experiences.

Due to expert opinions, robots will replace tasks and repetition, not jobs and not humans. Instead, robots and humans will work and interact side by side. The industrial world will be the main driver in robot adoption as the world is faced with an ageing society and an increasing cost of labour.

The following box provides several examples how AI-driven robots can be used in daily life.

AI-driven robots

Ubtech Robotics Inc. is a humanoid robotic company that creates consumer-facing robots for science, technology, engineering, and mathematics. Ubtech launched a portable robotic toy, the Alpha Mini, which has several functions, like LCD eyes capable of voice interaction, facial recognition, and flexible movement. This AI-driven robot mainly entertains and accompanies children, because product functions are tailored to children (Euromonitor, 2020).

Another example is Brain Corp US, a platform that automates more than 100 of Walmart's commercial floor scrubbers across the country. The company provides the machines with autonomous navigation and data collection capabilities, all tied into a cloud-based reporting system. This technology allows store associates to map a route during a training ride then activate autonomous floor cleaning simply by pressing a button. The robot uses multiple sensors to scan its surroundings for people and obstacles (Euromonitor, 2020).

Or, the so-called *Furhat* robot is a social robot that can interact with people by speaking, listening and showing emotions. The robot can speak 40 languages and change its appearance to suit a variety of scenarios. The robot is trained to overcome emotional biases and improve decision-making efficiency (Euromonitor, 2020).

To summarize, AI-driven robots are on the rise and will in future be used in many industries and for many different purposes. A condition is, however, user-friendly interfaces which critical to increase robot adoption for daily usage.

Virtual realities (VR) refer to artificially created (virtual) environments, which are made accessible to human perception through vision and hearing through appropriate technologies. One also distinguishes between virtual realities, in which a completely artificial reality is created, and so-called augmented realities (AR), which are created by overlaying the actual reality with an artificially created, digital reality. The technologies used range from so-called *head-mounted displays,* that is, screens that are mounted (e.g., Oculus Rift, HTC Vive, PS-VR), "smart glasses" (e.g., google glass), to various forms of head-up displays and handheld devices such as smart phones (ITA & AIT, 2019).

Smartphones, with their rich basic equipment of various sensors are ideal for further dissemination of AR and VR technologies. This trend means that AR and VR technologies will be made available relatively quickly to a large part of society through the widespread use of handheld devices. It is estimated that VR's and AR's market potential in 2021 will be €92 billion at the converted rate, with AR's mobile application accounting for the lion's share at €70 billion (ITA & AIT, 2019).

The North Face VR experience.
The VR technology also offers many new opportunities for the retail industry. "The North Face" shop in South Korea is a very good example for a total retail experience. After trying on a new jacket, customers could take a virtual dog sled ride directly in the store, which should enhance their shopping experience. While wearing VR glasses consumers can experience the wearing comfort of the jacket in a winter landscape (to watch the video https://www.adweek.com/creativity/north-face-gave-these-shoppers-vr-experience-suddenly-got-awesomely-real-167900/).

Nowadays more and more retailers make use of virtual commerce – so-called *v-commerce*. Virtual commerce is a type of application, service, or product feature that assists retailers to implement strategies for e-commerce – the buying and selling of products and services through the internet. Retailers from different lines of businesses have already started to experiment with virtual and AR features. Starting with the apparel sector retailers try out virtual dressing rooms or use these innovative technologies to bring customers into the physical store with VR marketing campaigns. Grocery retailers must face the challenge that consumers will be able to shop for their weekly groceries all within a virtual space due to VR technology, similar to e-commerce or online shopping, but with the ability to virtually pick-up products and walk around a virtual retail store.

Luxury brand Valentino partners with Alibaba for a virtual retail experience
The Chinese multinational conglomerate holding company Alibaba, specialising in e-commerce, retail, internet, and technology, partners with the luxury brand Valentino and launched a 3D online virtual store on the e-commerce giant's luxury shopping experience, Tmall Luxury Pavilion, to provide premium and luxury brands with an exclusive and tailored experience to engage with high-end consumers (for more information see https://www.alizila.com/tmalls-luxury-pavilion-launches-new-loyalty-club/).
The online virtual store mirrors a physical Valentino pop-up store hosted in Beijing's fashionable Sanlitun District. The virtual reality (VR) store allows customers to explore the interior of a Valentino pop-up shop, letting them examine the pieces on display and purchase them if

desired. The experience aims to integrate the online and offline brand experience to create a unique luxury destination in a seamless way to engage their consumers (Long, 2019).

As China continues to become a major market for luxury brands from around the world, Alibaba is hoping to act as a conduit between Chinese customers and western brands. VR has become a hot selling point for luxury consumers in China. Over the past year, VR has continued to infuse every aspect of global luxury and fashion, including the runway.

AR describes the combination of real environment with virtual additional information, in forms of texts, images or virtual objects on smart devices, for example, mobile phone or tablet. With AR retailers are given endless possibilities, especially when it comes to omnichanneling (see Chapter 3.3). AR may enhance the shopping experience of single distribution channels by specifically designed apps (Schramm-Klein, Wagner, Neus, Swoboda, & Foscht, 2014). Haderlein (2012) differentiates between two concepts of AR with regards to the grocery retail sector:

- *Seeing through the camera*: The actual image of the camera is completed with digital information, which gives users additional inputs about a product in sight.
- *Marker-based AR*: Usually a marker is printed onto promotion materials like flyers. This marker can be placed into the camera field of mobile devices and creates 3D views with more information about the product.

Tesco's usage of augmented reality in the grocery sector

The UK-based supermarket chain Tesco is considered a pioneer regarding the usage of augmented reality (AR) in the grocery retail sector. AR has enabled Tesco to establish a high level of brand engagement with its consumers on their mobile devices by encouraging shoppers to "discover more." The company's smartphone app "Tesco Discover" gives customers the possibility to scan certain markers with the device's camera. The results are insights in exclusive contents and enhanced digital experiences. AR was implemented across Tesco magazines and other publishing, products and directly at the POS. By scanning Tesco product labels, magazines, and other instore POS elements the app enables the user to get more information about the products, interact with editorial features, purchase products, and engage with instore experiences. Other AR content include gamification elements like video games and other family friendly entertainment. For further information please watch this video about "Tesco Discover": https://www.enginecreative.co.uk/portfolio/augmented-reality-publishing-retail-strategy/#

As we have seen above virtual and AR has various advantages, for retailers and consumers, but at the same time, its application poses new challenges and problems (ITA & AIT, 2019):

AR raises the question of under what conditions and whether digital public space should be used for all kinds of applications (entertainment, advertising, art, etc.).

VR applications raise the question to what effects the technology will have on users and their psyche and self-perception.

Initial studies suggest that there are effects on the psyche and self-perception of users. Immersion, that is, the degree to which VR is perceived as real by human sensors, plays an important role here. With the increasing spread of these technologies, above all via smartphones, these and numerous other questions may already become relevant in the near future from an innovation and economic policy perspective as well as from a health and consumer protection policy perspective.

To summarize, almost all major companies in all branches currently have plans to be active in this area. The areas of application are multifaceted. In the industry sector, for example, VR and AR can be used to instruct people during maintenance work. In medicine surgery could be possible application. In schools those technologies could be used for interactive learning experiences and in the entertainment sector, VR and AR can be used to make a film or video game even more intense.

Mixed reality

Mixed reality is the term used to describe environments or systems that mix a user's natural perception with an artificial (computer-generated) perception. Besides the mainly computer-generated VR, these are especially systems of extended reality and extended virtuality. Therefore, mixed reality is the result of combining the physical world with the digital world. The combination of computer processing, human input, and environmental input sets the opportunity to create true mixed reality experiences. Boundaries in the physical world can influence application experiences, such as game play, in the digital world. Without environmental input, experiences can not blend between physical and digital realities.

For example, imagine going to a supermarket to do grocery shopping. In this context, extended reality could be spectacle lenses on the inside of which a computer projects the user's shopping list in such a way that the user has the impression that the shopping list is written on the wall of the supermarket. So, physical reality is here enriched with virtual information. As you can see, the experiences enabled between these two extremes is mixed reality: Starting with the physical world, placing a digital object, such as a hologram, as if it were really there.

So, innovative technologies used in retailing have the fundamental objectives to meet customers' needs and desires, and to provide an integrated experience to improve customer engagement. Two additional technologies can help to reach these fundamental objectives: AI and IoT.

Both technologies will be described below.

AI

Over the last few years, AI technology has entered nearly every industry, also the retail sector. Nevertheless, not every retailer is using AI mainly due to high costs or inaccessibility, only the largest players in the retail sector are very active in using this technology. AI is intelligence displayed by machines (machine intelligence). AI technology makes use of a big data set about something, runs it through AI algorithms and produces a simplified model which can provide answers similar to human beings. The AI answers depend on whatever the system has already learned about a certain matter. In the retail sector the dataset that AI learns from would be, for example, sales data linked to the customer data. AI technology provides many advantages for a retailer, the most important advantages are the following:

- AI helps the retailer to learn about the customers, their preferences and their behaviour and inform the retailer what the customers need and when they need it
- AI can help to generate additional revenue for the retailer by improving the customer experience by offering exactly what the customer wants and at an accepted price
- AI helps to improve customer engagement by building a personal selling relationship with the customers
- AI can be used to improve inventory turnover, optimize stock, and predict future sales and revenue

To summarize, when provided with sales data, AI technology can discover certain patterns in the shoppers' buying preferences. Based on information, AI can provide the retailer suggestions on which items to sell, where to locate these items in the store and which products to put next to each other.

But there is a lot more AI can do for retail businesses. Within the last few years many start-ups have developed AI personal assistants that specialize in specific tasks. These tasks range from scheduling meetings, acting as health coaches, or doing online recommending and purchasing to arranging accommodations. More and more consumers are adopting AI personal assistants as they are available on increasingly more smart devices, from smartphones, smart watches and even in automobiles, and it is possible to use them on Bluetooth speakers. Two well-known AI personal assistants are Apple Siri and Amazon Echo. *Apple Siri* introduced by Apple has a third-party integration, whereby users can send messages on WhatsApp, book a ride on Uber (car sharing and transportation company) and make payment by using Square Cash (mobile payment company). Apple has also integrated functions such HomeKit (home automation) and CarPlay (provides access to Apple apps such as Phone or Maps, and third-party apps such as Spotify), enabling users to control their home appliances or the climate control in their vehicles. Another popular AI personal assistant is *Amazon Alexa*. Amazon launched the Echo smart speaker in 2014 and released in 2016 the smaller Echo Dot and the portable Amazon Tap. Amazon Alexa already has over 3,000 skills and features, which are third-party developed capabilities ranging from controlling smart home devices to ordering food (Weinswig, 20 November 2016).

AI personal assistant Operator 2.0.
An example for an AI personal assistant for online purchasing is Operator 2.0. Operator 2.0 is a personal shopping assistant service powered by a human assistant with the help of AI. More detailed, it is a shopping network with curated product recommendations which can help the user to find a specific item or to receive personalized recommendations such as which dress to wear for a birthday party in winter. The startup was founded in 2014 and received $25 million in seven rounds of funding. Users can browse products in different categories, including home goods, fashion, beauty, and electronics. The main advantage of this AI personal assistant is that the user can get help from so-called chatbots (computer program that conducts a conversation via auditory or textual methods and simulates a human conversation) if they require it, which connects the user with human agents who are experts in a specific product category, who usually work on a commission basis and receive a commission for every item they sell.

To summarize, AI technology has many advantages for the retail sector. As already mentioned above, not every retailer is using AI mainly due to high costs or inaccessibility, only the largest players in the retail sector are very active in using this technology. But in the future, technology will become cheaper and more accessible, so usage will increase rapidly. What must be considered is that digital systems and devices that recognize, interpret, process, and respond to human emotions will raise new ethical questions as well as insurance and data protection issues when used context, like in working life, in traffic, in learning environments or in the field of mental illness. The question arises how the basic right to informational self-determination can be protected, especially regarding the use of data by third parties. AI technology also opens potential entry points for hackers, which can have serious consequences. For example, imagine hackers tricking the "autopilot" of an electric car causing a serious accident. So, it must be considered that such technologies, like AI technology, is not error-free and still leaves many questions open.

IoT

The IoT (network of things) takes place in many areas in our daily lives, for example, a smart, networked refrigerator, which independently orders food and drinks, or the remote access via smartphone to various devices, such as heating, surveillance cameras, lighting, etc. In robotics, networking could be used, for example, via cloud services to exchange collected data, "learning experiences" or algorithms. Interesting fields of application for the IoT arise above all in mobility. Many new cars already support the SIM card standard, and the trend is rising. This makes it possible to network vehicles with each other, but also with the manufacturer. Remote diagnostics, real-time navigation and various infotainment services can thus be made available and are intended to increase driving comfort and the driving experience. Further potential advantages result from the collection of data on mobility behaviour, which could be used for a more efficient transport system. In addition to increasing efficiency in the transport sector, the increasing networking of vehicles is also expected to increase road safety (ITA & AIT, 2019).

IoT retail technology can be divided into two core types, according to the main function of the connected devices:

– Technology that tracks inventory and/or consumer behaviour: This includes devices with RFID sensors that can track the location and movement of items in-store, as well as track consumer behaviour in-store.
– Technology that interacts with customers: This includes devices that make shoppers' experience easier and more engaging, such as smart mirrors that enable customers to virtually try on clothing.

IoT retail technology offers several advantages. Above all, there are three main advantages: the application of IoT technology helps retailers to make inventory management more efficient, measure store performance and improve the customer experience. Additional advantages are (ITA & AIT, 2019):

– **Optimization of store operations**: A major advantage of IoT in retail is the digitization of in-store inventory. In detail, inventory levels can be tracked, and items in-store can be located at any time to avoid misplaced stock. This improves store readiness, increases transparency and visibility of the operations, and makes it possible to run systems that improve efficiency, such as automated alerts for stock replenishment.
– **In-store analytics**: Data generated by tracking the movement of items in-store and consumer behaviour makes it possible to record metrics such as conversion rates and to make decisions to improve store performance such as increasing the visibility of the best-performing items. For example, using sensors to track the movement of items in-store can help retailers improve store layout by placing more popular items in high-traffic areas and increase sales.
– **Closer integration with the rest of the supply chain**: In-store inventory tracking through IoT enables closer integration with other stages of the supply chain such as distribution, supporting more efficient operations.
– **Improved consumer experience**: In-store connected technology increases customer engagement, for example by using smart mirrors that enable customers to virtually try on items or through NFC tags that send information about an item to a customer's digital device.
– **New revenue opportunities**: By increasing the opportunities for customers to connect and interact with retailers, IoT can help retailers grow revenues. For example, with the help of in-store digital screens or terminals, customers could order items or sizes, colours, etc., that are not in stock in a store.

Smart fridge makes daily life easier?
In 2012 LG launched the so-called *Smart Manager fridge* at a technology fair in Las Vegas and went on sale in 2013, priced around £2,000. The smart fridge has an LCD touchscreen, a camera and an internet connection which allows the fridge to download recipes and link to various online grocery shopping services. The idea behind this intelligent fridge is that it makes daily life, especially grocery shopping, due to the function that the fridge manages food shopping by scanning the barcodes of the products, or a shopping receipt, with a scanner on the fridge door, or by describing the desired product via voice recognition technology. The smart fridge has a computer which can monitor the content of the fridge and automatically add food products to the customer's online shopping account when stocks are running low. It can even suggest recipes based on the ingredients in the fridge and once a recipe is chosen, the fridge can switch on the oven to the correct temperature and set a timer via a wireless connection. The screen on the door then tells the customer exactly what to do.

A disadvantage of this smart fridge is that many customers don't want to communicate with their fridge or scan the barcodes of the food items, food is something personal and many customers don't want to make their fridge content open for the public. So, every customer must decide on his own whether such a smart fridge really makes the daily life easier.

3.2.1 In-store technologies and applications

Many researchers, but also retailers and consumers, ask themselves what the "store of the future" will look like. There will be robots to serve us, using built-in facial recognition technology to adjust each sales process to the customer's mood or even past spending preferences. There will be voice-activated personal assistants in the store for downloading the availability, colour and fit of any garment to a smart device, 3D printing stations in the store to print out the customer's favourite item, like pasta or cookie. There could be holographic product displays on the shop floor that change when a customer walks by. Customers could make all their purchases from their own home, using virtual fitting rooms via VR headsets. Drones will then drop deliveries at the customer's homes. Even if this description still sounds very futuristic, all those technological features do already exist and are currently tested. But experts do not see a rollout of all those features described because it depends on the consumer and which features they except and on what sort of shopping experience the consumer wants.

AR and VR technology, already described in the sup-chapters above, have the potential to bridge the gap between the physical store and customer's home, online and offline. By combining personal data with AI and machine learning, retailers will have the possibility to deliver a personalized experience, for example to figure out if a particular product seen in a physical store fits in the customer's home. Physical stores will still exist in the future, but AR and VR will help the physical store to offer brand experiences and a certain level of personalization (Tavolieri, 2019).

In-store augmentation technology such as navigation apps or electronic shelf beacons (i.e., a small Bluetooth radio transmitter) will create individualized experiences for consumers who prefer a physical retail experience, based on their personal data profiles. Smartphones, AR apps, and smart glasses will provide a custom store experience for everyone, which could include personalized advertising, content and product recommendations all aimed at helping consumers make more informed decisions (Tavolieri, 2019).

What is more, although 70% of high-end purchases are influenced by online interactions, physical stores will always play an important role, with 75% of sales still occurring in a physical location by 2025. What may change is a store's primary purpose (Paton, 2017). In the future, we will no longer speak of pure online or offline worlds, but both forms will increasingly merge, so that the customer no longer perceives them as separate shopping opportunities. For example, AR and VR technology will tear down the delineation between online and offline, enabling consumers to easily see and access extended product offerings in-store.

Experts are sure that in the next years, AR and VR technology will augment the customer's shopping journey in increasingly meaningful ways, starting from the way consumers discover, choose, share, buy and engage with brands. When connected with product data, this technology will reduce the premium on shelf space by enabling consumers to easily sort, navigate to and identify products like they might online. In-store merchandising and promotions will become increasingly personalized and complex, matching specific deals with the shopper's behaviours (Tavolieri, 2019). Connected services with an AI-based personal shopping assistant might also lead to an increased shopping experience. There are so many more in-store technologies and applications, which could help to generate an increased shopping experience and make shopping easier for customers. Table 3.3 describes the most important technologies and applications.

Table 3.3: In-store technologies and applications (Source: Weinswig, October 2017b).

Technology	Description	Application
Visible Light Communication (VLC)	Fluorescent lamps or LEDs transmit signals through visible light that can be received by a smartphone camera.	VLC is used to communicate with the customers in the store, for instance to find an item on their shopping list.
Beacon technology	Wireless transmitter technology that can communicate with a special software, including smartphone apps, by using Bluetooth signals.	Beacons are used to send their customers targeted messages, especially promotions, on their smartphones.
Near Field Communication (NFC)	This short-range wireless connectivity technology enables communication between devices.	Customers scan an NFC tag with an NFC-enabled smartphone and receive information about an item.

Table 3.3 (continued)

Technology	Description	Application
RFID	RFID technology uses radio waves to track items or to enable communication between devices.	RFID is mainly used for inventory management but also for in-store applications such as interactive screens (smart mirror) or RFID tags on products.
Smart Shelves	Electronic, connected shelves that use mainly RFID technology for inventory management or pricing tactics.	Mainly used for inventory management or price adjustments.
Smart Robots	Smart robots are autonomous mobile devices that can navigate through the store and complete simple tasks.	Smart robots are mainly used for inventory management, for instance checking the stock level or replenishment.
Interactive Mirror and Fitting Rooms	Connected interactive screens with technologies, especially product recognition or touch screens based on RFID technology.	Smart screens can detect what item the customer is trying on and can interact with the shopper, for instance making product recommendations.
Smart Packaging	Packaging with connected technology, mainly NFC but also RFID, used for product information or for monitoring the freshness of a product.	Smart packaging is mainly used to improve inventory management and customer engagement.
Smart Shopping Carts	Sensor-enabled carts can communicate with other in-store items, for instance smart-tagged items or smart shelves.	Smart shopping carts are used for navigation through the store or to locate items.

Electronic shelf labelling

Electronic price tags can be seen as the replacement of paper price tags. There is an endless list of advantages on both sides (Kalyanam, Lal, & Wolfram, 2010, 149). The most important factors are as follows: firstly, retailers no longer need to worry about human errors or mistakes in terms of price badging. Instead, the fully electronic system automatically adjusts prices whenever there are changes. Respective changes in pricing can finally result in significant savings of costs compared to the use of paper price tags. Nonetheless, the part of correct filling the shelves still requires human hands (Raman & Naik, 2010, 442). Secondly, this technology allows grocery retailers to change prices several times during the day. In other words, shops may charge different sums during the morning, the afternoon, or the evening. Special offers may also be promoted by flashing screens or badges. Despite of these aspects, by enabling dynamic pricing, customers' focus will be even more on prices.

In-store displays

Foscht, Swoboda and Schloffer (2012, 145) claim that modern humans have become resistant to stimuli from the environment, especially in urban regions. However, the importance of digital instore advertisements must not be underestimated. It also gives retailers the possibility to choose what ad to show at what time of the day. Until now, targeted promotions have mainly been used in online stores. This new technology offers the possibility to show ads in brick-and-mortar stores (Gedenk, Neslin, & Ailawadi, 2010, 405). The goal of instore displays is to increase sales by drawing as much attention as possible to specific products on a display, which is placed on certain areas at the POS. The trend is also mentioned as digital signage. Advertisements are not only shown on large screens, but also on data projectors. Another advantage is that traditional promotion materials like flyers do not longer need to be replaced manually by hand. Retailers may change the ads without spending much money on printing papers for all their stores. Eventually, videos and animated graphics can be displayed as well, which is expected to stand out even more (Morschett, Zentes, Schu, & Steinhauer, 2013, 237).

Self-checkout systems

Within the last decades, customers worldwide started to become familiar with self-service systems. In banks or airports these machines are used for many years now. Though, in grocery retailing self-checkout is a trend which is still at a very early stage (Litfin & Wolfram, 2010, 189). Haderlein (2012, 136) claims that the biggest advantage of self-checkout systems is the faster processing of consumer payments. For finishing the shopping, consumers need to scan their products on their own, without or with limited support from staff. In grocery retailing, these systems also allow customers to weigh fresh vegetables or fruits directly at the checkout without the necessity of doing this separately at the fresh-food corners. Usually, self-checkout systems require the shopper to pay with debit or bank card (Morschett, Zentes, Schu, & Steinhauer, 2013, 235). The advantages of self-checkout systems can be leveraged by combining the technology with the option for mobile payments (Morschett, Zentes, Schu, & Steinhauer, 2013, 231) or fingerprint-secured payments. Grewal et al. (2009, 4) found out that using self-service technology can have outstanding positive effects on the customer's shopping experience. However, retailers need to pay attention to the usage of these systems before implementing them, especially in retail sectors with fast moving consumer goods as part of the product range (Haderlein, 2012, 140).

RFID technology

RFID is wireless technology based on radio frequencies and allows retailers to mark their products with so-called RFID tags (Kovacs et al., 2012). RFID systems consist of two basic elements (Lux, 2012):

- The *tag*, which is also called transponder or smart label. The tag contains a small chip with an integrated antenna. It can be placed on products and packages. Information is stored digitally on the chip, including the electronic product code (EPC), which is similar to the EAN barcode. The tag is also able to store information about origin, a more detailed description of the product or details about the ingredients.
- The *scanner and writing device* which allows the retailer to read and edit information from and on the tag.

RFID technology has a variety of advantages for a retailer. For example, at the POS intelligent product shelves with RFID technology allow the retailer to receive continuous information about the stock and possible shortages (Verhoef & Sloot, 2010). Info stations with integrated readers give consumers the possibility to scan products to gather more information about a product, which may lead to reducing staff costs. Checkout systems with RFID technology may reduce the time at the cash desk by providing a certain gate the customer may pass with their shopping carts. Simultaneously, the checkout system sends information to the security system of the store, signalizing that the products in the shopping cart have been paid, which helps to prevent thefts (Verhoef & Sloot, 2010).

RFID technology provides a broad field of application in the retail sector, not only for retailers and consumers, but for all members along the entire supply chain, from the first labelling by producers to the checkout of supermarkets and could be expanded to the customers' homes, for example, an intelligent fridge.

To summarize, RFID technology can be used to optimize processes and efficiency and can help retailers to lower logistics, warehouse, and labour costs. In the future, it is highly likely that most retailers will use RFID technology, mainly due to cost reduction. But a prerequisite for a successful comprehensive implementation of RFID technology is the acceptance of the customers. Many customers have privacy concerns or are not willing to accept RFID tags on certain products, for example, fresh products like vegetables or meat that can not carry RFID chips without packaging (Verhoef & Sloot, 2010).

3.2.2 Blockchain technology

A blockchain is a decentral organized database that makes it possible to document, digitally represent and authenticate transactions between actors, for example private individuals, companies, and public institutions. The technology guarantees that the interactions have taken place exactly as documented and ensures that the documentation can not be changed. In addition to applications like crypto currencies (e.g., Bitcoins) blockchains are currently being developed for other applications in business and government: for title deeds, contracts, insurances, licenses, etc.

Blockchains have the potential to overcome monopolistic business models like Airbnb, ebay, and Uber and to connect providers and customers directly with each other. However, if Blockchain would become omnipresent as a technology, the everyday life of all citizens would be comprehensively depicted and clearly comprehensible for others. A person-based blockchain would mean that all actions would be stored in the biographical course. The potential for abuse is enormous but has not yet been addressed.

The best-known application of a blockchain algorithm is the Bitcoin crypto currency in the financial sector. A blockchain is a cryptographically linked chain of blocks. These blocks are created in a certain time interval and contain transactions that the participants of the system accept as executed, so that, for example, a block is considered accepted upon receipt and the underlying transaction becomes a component of the system. Since all participants have a copy of it, and the previous data sets are linked and stored with the following data sets, the sequence and the individual transactions are regarded as protected against subsequent manipulation. The promise is that technology can automate trust and thus make instances superfluous that create trust and thus generate costs.

The disruption potential of the blockchain results from the character of a peer-to-peer infrastructure that enables transactions without intermediaries. Since intermediaries in the financial sector are more important than in other sectors of the economy, the technology is most discussed in this area.

Blockchain technology has many potential applications, in many different areas, like supply-chain management, trade finance, insurance, cybersecurity, etc. Blockchain is a database, which is shared across several participants each having a computer. The idea behind this technology is that at any moment in time, simultaneously, each of these participants hold an identical copy of the blockchain database on their computer. Blockchain technology has three main characteristics (Carson, 2018):

- It is a cryptographically secure and very robust database. When data is read or written from the database, the user needs the correct cryptographic keys to do that: a public key, which is a basically the address and the database where information is stored, and a private key, which is the personal key, which prevents other people from updating the information.
- It is a digital database of transactions. Digitization is an important first step blockchain technology can be used.
- It is a database that is shared across either a public or a private network: the most famous public network is the Bitcoin blockchain. Everyone can become a node on the network with a computer, without any expressed permissions, and can leave whenever he or she wants without anyone else knowing who has joined or left the network.
- The essence of blockchain is a chain of blocks of information together. When those blocks are chained together, a perfect audit history is created, for instance

if property titles are recorded, a previous owner of the property and the current owner can be seen.
- The database can only be updated when the correct credentials are being applied and most participants in the network is verifying those credentials.

In general, there are six distinct categories of blockchain use cases illustrated in Figure 3.1: static registry, identity, smart contracts, dynamic registry, payment infrastructure and other use cases composed of the previous groups.

Static Registry	Identity	Smart Contracts	Dynamic Registry	Payments Infrastructure	Other
Distributed database for storing reference data	Distributed database with identity-related information	Set of conditions recordedon a blockcha in triggering automated, self-executingactions when these predefined condition saremet	Dynamic distributed database that updates assetsare exchanged on the digital platform	Dynamic distributed databasethat updates as cash or cryptocurrency payments are madea mong participants	Use case composed of several of the previous groups
	Particular case of staticregistry treatedasa separate group of usecasesdue to extensive set of identity-specific use cases				Standalone use case not fitting any of the previous categories
Example	**Example**	**Example**	**Example**	**Example**	**Example**
Food safety and origin	Voting	Insurance-claim payout	Drug supplychain	Cross-border peer-to-peer payment	Blockchain as a service
Patent	Identityfraud				

Figure 3.1: Blockchain use cases.
Source: Own elaboration based on Carson, 2018

In the following, several examples are listed to illustrate what is the strategic business value of the blockchain technology, especially for retailers (Carson, 2018):
- Trade finance will be much simpler because no intermediaries are necessary anymore. For example, the UN, delivering some of their aid to Syria, has used a blockchain-based solution. By using this technology, they've been able to authenticate individuals using biometric data and use that to ensure that the aid give is given to the right people. This is a very clean and secure way of taking out what would be traditionally money that would follow multiple steps with various intermediaries and transaction costs to get to the end users.
- Another example would be somebody who's certifying the quality of a supply chain, for example, organic foods and genetically modified foods. In that case, blockchain can provide details of the supply chain.

– The third example is cross-border payments. Up until very recently, it took three to five business days to complete a cross-border payment transaction, paying fees and commissions along the way. For international money-transfer organizations, this has been a very profitable revenue stream. The promise of same-day, seamless, low-cost, cross-border payments, instantaneous payments using blockchain, is a truly disruptive innovation.

For further information please see the TED talk video by Don Tapscott. He is the Executive Chairman of the Blockchain Research Institute, one of the world's leading authorities on the impact of technology in business and society. Video link:https://www.ted.com/talks/don_tapscott_how_the_blockchain_is_changing_money_and_business.

3.3 Multichannel, omnichannel, cross-channel, no-line channel

Most retailers today sell their products not only through one single channel but make use of various online and offline channels to reach their target customers. This distribution strategy is referred to as *multichannel retailing*. The term "multichannel retailing" is just a new way of referring to a very old retail issue. Over recent decades, nonfood retailers have combined the physical store format with catalogue sales. The concept of multichannel retailing used today refers mainly to the internet in general and to e-commerce. This may either be a new sales channel; it can be also used simply as an advertising medium (information platform on the internet or ordering platform and picking up the goods at a physical retailer) or it can be used as a sole distribution channel (e.g., Amazon, Alibaba, etc.).

The various channels can complement each other, or they can be used to gain a new customer segment that had been unavailable so far, mainly for reasons of positioning.

To summarize, multichannel retailing refers to a concept including all ways in which the consumer can contact a retailer, or a retailer can contact the consumer. This includes all physical (offline) and nonphysical (online) store formats and channels.

Table 3.4 illustrates significant retail branches and the overlapping of various store formats and channels which result in specific consumer behaviour. Consumers can purchase food and other products for their daily needs through various store formats, while also being able to purchase almost every product available through a range of different channels. For example, a DVD is available in a large supermarket, as well as in a specialist store or at a service station, whereas a notebook in a discount store is usually just available as a special sales promotion for a limited period. So, a particular channel can be used to meet a need, while another channel may be used to generate a certain need. The parallel usage of various online and offline store formats and channels is becoming increasingly complex for retailers but will be unavoidable to be competitive in the future.

Table 3.4: Main branches of retail and overlapping store formats. (Sonneck & Ott, 2014).

Main branches of retail:

Store formats/channels	Food	Clothing	Multimedia	Entertainment electronics/appliances	Household goods/Home textiles	Watches/Jewellery	Cosmetics/drugstore products	DIY
Discounter	x	x	x	x	x		x	x
Supermarket	x	x	x				x	
Shopping mall	x	x	x	x	x	x	x	x
Department store		x	x	x	x	x	x	x
Branch specialist store		x	x	x	x	x	x	x
Specialist trade store	x	x	x	x	x	x	x	x
Mail order		x	x	x	x	x	x	x
Newspaper stand	x		x					
Service station	x		x				x	
Tele-shopping		x	x	x	x	x	x	x
Internet shops		x	x	x	x	x	x	x
Internet auctions		x	x	x	x	x	x	x

Multichannel occurs when there is a combination of different sales channels that a customer can choose to use to obtain products from a retailer. Multichannel refers exclusively to the combination of physical stores (brick-and-mortar) and internet trade plus a possible additional sales channel, such as catalog shipping. This means that the customer has at least two sales channels available for buying the desired products.

Cross-Channel refers to all activities of a multichannel retailer that are geared towards harmonizing and/or integrating the various sales channels. Cross-channel and multichannel are often used synonymously, but they differ significantly. In multichannel retailing, the channels are served independently of each other. A purchasing process, for example, takes place completely in a single channel without establishing a connection to another channel or offering the possibility of continuing the process via another channel. Whereas, in cross-channel retailing, activities and messages are harmonized across all channels, giving customers a more consistent experience.

For retailers, cross-channel retailing has several advantages. On the one hand, it offers more potential for conversion, because although each of the channels has its own specific characteristics and must be used accordingly, synergies can be created and messages can be better disseminated in a coordinated manner. Through the interaction and automation of the channels, a dialogue is developed along the customer life cycle. Such a life cycle concept recognizes the individual characteristics of each customer and picks them up with customized messages on their preferred communication channel.

Omnichannel describes the simultaneous use of two or more sales channels, like using a mobile phone while shopping in a store. The term is also used to describe the consistency or harmonization between different sales channels. This means that a customer's data, configurations or settings stored on one channel are stored and considered on all other channels. So, omnichannel refers to the integration of all physical channels (offline) and digital channels (online) to provide a seamless and consistent customer experience.

In order to avoid customer confusion, multichannel retailing should no longer be separated into pure online and offline worlds. From the customer's point of view, online and offline channels must rather be merged into "no line" systems in which all sales channels are maximally networked and integrated.

No-line retailing means that offline, online and mobile retailing emerge while their exist an independence of the trading system from the communication channel. Multichannel systems are merging into each other against the background of omnichanneling. No-line retailing differs from conventional multichannel retailing in that all distribution channels are maximally networked and integrated in them. The provision of information is identical in all channels, as are prices and simplicity, but not the manner, of the purchasing process. In no-line retailing mobile commerce, which means the use of the smartphone for shopping purposes, enables retailers to adapt their offers to the individual shopping habits of their customers in line with their personal needs and wants, their situation and lifestyle. Moreover, the smart device is necessary to build a bridge between online and offline retailing to shop in the online or mobile channel parallel to their physical shopping (Heinemann, 2013).

For example, a no-line retailer can enable his customers to compare prices by scanning the EAN code and offer them the maximum possible spectrum of multichannel services via his system using the mobile shop, whereas a classic multichannel retailer, on the other hand, can certainly do without the mobile channel and the offer of mobile services. Key topics in no-line retailing are "RoPo" retailing (which stands for Researching online and purchasing offline), location-based services, and mobile commerce (Heinemann, 2013). Nowadays, traditional physical retailers are more and more confronted by new technologies already described above with new expectations of customers.

A worldwide survey has shown that one-quarter of customers already order grocery products online and more than half are willing to do so in the future. Growth of online shopping is mainly driven by the maturation of the so-called digital natives; the consumers how grew up with digital technology. Digital natives are members of the Generation Y (also named Millennials) and Generation Z (The Nielsen Company, 2015), people born between the early 1980s and the mid-1990s (Gen Y) and birth years that range from the mid-1990s to early 2000s (Gen Z). Consumers are no longer shopping entirely online or offline, but using whatever channel best suits their needs. Multichannel retailing offers the customers the possibility to buy their products when and where they like. Most important when following a multichannel strategy is to offer a seamless and consistent customer experience throughout all sales channels, into the direction of omnichannel retailing or no-line retailing. A new customer orientation towards multiple sales channels requires adapted marketing strategies that make products more visual- online and offline- and create holistic customer experiences.

Although buying online has become very popular within the last few years, traditional retail outlets, as already mentioned, will not be erased from the shopping landscape and won't become mainly showrooms in the future. Physical stores have strong key advantages over pure online retailers. When consumers are asked what makes shopping at a physical store attractive, the main reasons are:
- the ability to see
- touch and try products
- to get the product immediately without paying shipping fees
- the benefits of human interaction

Therefore, the physical store will remain the centrepiece of the consumer's purchase journey for many product categories, even though the number of consumers intending to shop more online within the next few years, will constantly increase (PwC, 2013). Virtual baskets are normally different from physical ones as some product categories are better suited for e-commerce than others. E-commerce is well suited to specialty retailing because it allows retailers to offer broader product selection and to fulfil unique customer needs (The Nielsen Company, 2015).

Top reasons to shop online are lower prices, ease of comparison, free shipping, and convenience (24/7, fast checkout). Physical stores still dominate the shopping experience, but e-commerce has a huge growth potential.

To summarize, online retailing is becoming more and more relevant for all industries. Companies that wait too long will therefore be at a competitive disadvantage.

What motivates traditional store-based retailers to engage in multichannel retailing

Traditional store-based retailers are nowadays placing more and more emphasis on electronic sales channels and are engaging in multichannel retailing. Reasons are as follows:
- the electronic sales channel gives them the potential to reach new markets and new target groups
- the electronic sales channel overcomes some limitations, like limited opening hours, security of shopping, providing more convenience, local conditions, parking problems, etc.
- the electronic channel enables retailers to gain valuable insights into their customers' shopping habits and makes it possible to analyse the acquired customer data and derive improvements
- the electronic sales channel is necessary when providing a multichannel sales experience which may lead to increased customer loyalty

Adding an electronic sales channel to the retailer's sales portfolio is particularly attractive for companies with strong brands but limited locations or sales and distribution network. For example, retailers such as Tiffany's that is widely known for offering unique, high-quality jewellery. Before they launched their electronic sales channel, their customers had to travel to England or major US cities to buy the desired merchandise.

Moreover, store-based retailers can use their existing physical sales channel to create awareness for an electronic sales channel by advertising the webshop in the store or on the shopping bags. Store-based retailers can also utilize their stores to lower the cost of fulfilling orders and processing returned merchandise. In this case, the physical store can be used for gathering merchandise for delivery to customers. In addition, the retailer can offer customers the opportunity to pick up and return merchandise at the physical stores and thus save the delivery charges (the so-called *click and collect* services: products are ordered online for pickup at a store or other location). Other possible options are in-store pickup, drive-through pickup, curbside pickup, virtual stores, and automated subscription.

One of the greatest constraints facing store-based retailers is their limited store size. The amount of merchandise that can be displayed and offered for sale in stores is limited. By combining physical stores with internet-enabled terminals, retailers can expand the merchandise assortment they offer and offer goods which are already sold out in the shop or also additional colours.

It has the mentioned that an electronic sales channel may lead to some cannibalization with the physical store, but it normally results in gaining additional consumers and consumers making more purchases from a retailer. Studies have shown that multichannel customers spend 30% more than customers who shop only in a physical store. Therefore, each retailer should think about offering more than one sales channel, to gain more customers and to increase sales and profit.

Studies have shown that when customers use multiple channels, the majority spend more at their favourite retailer (PwC, 2013). An essential condition is that the retailer first need to make it into the relevant set of preferred multichannel retailers. Cheap prices might help a company to enter the relevant set of favourite retailers, but price points are not always a critical factor in getting customers spend more. Four key drivers affect spend: fast and reliable delivery, exclusive or early access to products, a "return to store policy," and innovative marketing and innovative products (PwC, 2013). The use of online or mobile coupons and mobile shopping lists are the most popular forms of in-store digital engagement in use today (The Nielsen Company, 2015). A comprehensive digital strategy includes interaction at every touchpoint along the customer journey, starting with finding stores, checking prices, researching products, sharing content, and purchasing. Consumers are willing to use technology to simplify and improve this customer journey.

Recent studies show that 73% of consumers ages 25 to 34 ("Millennials") begin their shopping journey on a smartphone. Whether that's to check product reviews, search for similar recommendations or look up a better price, customers are influenced in many ways, making their journey highly unpredictable. Yet, 90% of sales still happen in the store. As a result, creating the perfect cross-channel experience for today's consumer is no simple task.

Consumers will choose the best, cheapest, and most convenient option available often. So, you must give them a reason to come to the store. When they are online, they expect personalization. We have the technology to bring that to the physical store experience. If people enable Bluetooth on their phones, physical retail can do a million things. Through alerts, AR, lighting, and music, physical retailers can take shoppers anywhere they want them to go and make it an experience. And that's the new key to brick-and-mortar retail: Make it an experience (Barrett, 2017).

To position themselves for success in a multichannel world, retailers must reassess the role of the physical store. The five-step approach STORE is recommended (Herring, Wachinger, & Wigley, 2014):
- starting with a clear vision for the future role of the store
- tailoring categories and formats accordingly
- optimizing the store portfolio using forward-looking analytics
- reinventing the in-store shopping experience
- executing systematically across channels

Shifting from a store-focused approach to a multichannel mindset requires retailers to change their traditional retail strategies and tactics. As consumers increasingly shop across channels, their expectations have changed. They expect price consistency across all sales channels and the ability to buy their products online and pick up them up in the physical store or at a pickup station or return products in a store. They demand a variety on payment options and an in-store shopping experience. The excess to comprehensive online information available to consumers raises the need for better in-store service and employee expertise.

The following box illustrates the five-step approach STORE (Herring, Wachinger, & Wigley, 2014) in more detail and gives examples how to manage the digital transformation process and meet customer expectations and in a multichannel world.

The five-step approach STORE (Herring, Wachinger, & Wigley, 2014):

1. Start by redefining the role of the store

Retailers must find out what their customers truly care about. They need to know which aspects of a store matter most to customers and what purposes a store serves for them:

- Convenience and proximity: the ease and speed of being able to visit a store and the immediate availability of products
- Efficiency: the store is a place that helps make better use of the time, for example, as a pickup location or place for returns when ordered online
- Inspiration: the store is a place to discover new products, give new ideas and surprise the customers
- Instant gratification: the store is a place to accelerate impulse buying and give customers credits for visiting the brick-and-mortar store
- Discovery of information: the store is a place to exchange knowledge and expertise
- Entertainment and social interaction: the store is a place for entertainment and leisure time, a place to hang out with friends or to spend time with family and kids
- Experiencing brands and products: the store is a place for brand-interaction and brand engagement, a place to touch, feel, and engage with products and brands

The agreed-upon roles of the store should dictate every decision about strategic retail management decisions, such as location, assortment, staffing and employee training, suppliers, logistics, etc.

2. Tailor categories and formats accordingly

Customer priorities and store economics should become critical inputs into ongoing category reviews, to ensure that assortments and space allocations are continually optimized for a multichannel world. Long-tail products (i.e., niche products) should no longer stored in a physical store, but in central warehouses being available to consumers only online, except emergency items (for instance, spare parts for fixing a leaky sink) and products that are part of a bigger basket and normally used together (e.g., baking ingredients and cake decoration).

Customer research has found that the frequency and purpose of customer visits, as well as average driving times, varied significantly by category. Only half of customers were willing to drive more than ten minutes to buy kitchen appliances in person, compared with almost 100% of customers buying a TV. Indeed, half of customers said they would never buy a TV without first seeing it, testing it, or comparing it with other models in a store. Therefore, retailers need different assortments in their stores, as well as different shop floor and service levels.

Some retailers are also adapting their store formats to the tastes and preferences of certain customer segments, for example, creating zones with segment-specific brands.

3. Optimize the portfolio using forward-looking analytics

Leading retailers regularly analyse correlations between sales performance and catchment data to identify promising locations for new stores and to figure out their top-performing stores; by examining factors such as population density, income, competitor presence, and average tenure of the sales staff. Retailers must always look ahead and understand the impact that channels have on one another.

The most forward-thinking retailers use analytical tools and techniques to reshape their entire store networks. They use financial and geospatial modelling to highlight not only where stores should be opened but also which should be closed, resized, or reformatted. Geospatial analysis is useful for creating an optimal mix of store formats by location type. In a populous city, for instance, the optimal mix for an apparel retailer might include one or more flagship stores with a long drive time, high-footfall destinations (such as stores in malls or on suburban main streets) with a medium drive time, and "in-fills" (such as seasonal shops or pop-up stores) to cater to small catchment populations.

4. Reinvent the in-store shopping experience
Creating the store of the future will mean overhauling the in-store customer journey, in part by using new technology to make the shopping experience as seamless and easy as possible. A multichannel mind-set must be embedded in the store design and in employees' new ways of working. Retailers could give store staff easy access to detailed product information so that they can provide knowledgeable customer service. Mobile devices that tell store employees where exactly in the store an item is located and how many units are in stock could enable them to better assist customers. Handheld payment points would allow customers to avoid long checkout lines. In-store terminals/kiosks could assist shoppers to place orders or customize their products.

Retailers should focus on what matters most to their customers and enable multichannel shopping while taking costs out of the things that customers do not care about.

5. Execute systematically across channels
Retailers should ask themselves: Does the organizational structure support the new multichannel network size and role? What would it take to shift the focus away from opening new stores towards making better use of existing space, introducing, and refreshing store concepts quickly, and scaling back on real estate? How can the online team become fully integrated with the stores? This integration is essential, as the store of the future should allow shoppers to move seamlessly across channels. Store staff should be well trained and comfortable in directing customers to the right products, both offline and online. The technology and systems staff members use should be connected to or aligned with the retailer's website, so that they will not have to spend precious time trying to reconcile different information. The web can support the stores as well – for example, by showing inventory levels for nearby stores.

Change of this scale is not easy and affects many functions across the organization. Pace and flexibility are critical. Retailers should test new ideas quickly, and they should pilot individual aspects of store design to figure out specifically what is working and what is not. To summarize, the future of retail will belong to those retailers that can satisfy the customers' needs and wants, whether they decide to buy their products offline and/or online.

Today, retailers concentrating on only one store format or on selling to a specific consumer channel are getting very rare. Important national and international retailers are all focusing on multichannel strategies and augment their portfolios with more channels or new store formats. Retailers have several options for building up further channels, it is necessary to make decisions on three levels to find the right strategy (Sonneck & Ott, 2010):
- Store format and channel segmentation: the first step is to identify the segments that have not been covered, or only partially, by the present store formats or

channels. If relevant, new, or restructured market segments can be used to implement a new store format or a new channel.

- Market positioning: means to find a unique positioning for a certain store format or channel, with the goal of achieving a distinctive profile for consumers and differentiation from the competition.
- Portfolio implementation: the implementation of a multichannel strategy follows a basic development of growth and expansion, reduction, or elimination of store formats, or retaining the same formats or channels. For example: the expansion of a store format can be attained by an increase in outlets or retaining means that an existing store format is used to attain the highest possible margin.

3.4 Opportunities and challenges

Online shopping will grow, but physical stores (brick-and-mortar stores) will still dominate the market due to several reasons. Physical stores fulfil immediate shopping needs without paying shipping fees. What is more, they offer the advantage of sensory experiences which are virtually not possible to replicate. Human interaction is also a very important advantage over online shopping or the thrill of unplanned discovery that a brick-and-mortar store can provide. When consumers are asked why the visit a physical retail store, the majority will answer that shopping is an enjoyable and engaging experience. Therefore a physical store has to focus on offering a great shopping experience to keep customers satisfied and keep them coming back, mainly through an innovative store design, executional excellence and exceptional service (The Nielsen Company, 2015) but also by offering technology-based in-store convenience options, for example, hand-held store scanner, self-checkout and convenient payment options, or in-store digital enablement options, for example, mobile coupons, mobile shopping lists, retailer loyalty program apps on a mobile phone, store Wi-Fi to receive additional information and offers, usage of in-store terminals to receive information or view extended product ranges, QR code scanning to get additional information on products or services. A Nielsen study (2015) has shown that today, just a small percentage of consumers are using technology-based in-store options, but most of them are willing to use some of these options in the near future.

Therefore, retailers have to understand how consumers are using technology in general and technology-based options and include digital touchpoints along the entire customer journey, for example by improving the in-store experience and offering in-store digital engagement options, such as mobile coupons, mobile shopping lists, loyalty program app on the mobile phone, in-store Wi-Fi availability to receive more information or offers, in-store computers to view extended product ranges available from the retailer online, scan QR codes to receive additional product information.

One of the most significant online shopping days in the world is the so-called *Singles' Day*. Find more information concerning the Singles' Day annual shopping event below in the box.

Singles' Day- the most significant online shopping day in the world.
November 11th is the so-called Singles' Day, the most significant online shopping day in the world, because sales totals exceed Black Friday and Cyber Monday sales in the United States. The Singles' Day annual shopping event was created by the Chinese e-tailer Alibaba in 2009, especially for single people who wanted to treat themselves by buying things they desired. Total gross merchandise volume (GMV) reached $25.3 billion in 2017 within 24 hours compared to US online sales totals for Black Friday ($3.0 billion) and Cyber Monday ($3.45 billion). Mobile penetration was 90% and Alibaba's logistics network processed 812 million packages on Singles' Day. A total of 140,000 brands and merchants participated in the global shopping event and Alibaba's payment system, Alipay, processed 1.48 billion transactions in the 24-hour period (Weinswig, November 2017).

The Single's Day record sales results in 2017 represented a major success for Alibaba's new retail strategy, which refers to the integration of online and offline retail, logistics and data across a single value chain. Alibaba offered a more integrated online/offline experience along with additional offline components and leveraged brands' offline locations to drive sales. The offline components enriched the overall experience for customers and improved engagement throughout their shopping journeys. Alibaba partnered with 1,000 brands to set up 100,000 smart stores in 31 cities in China. Customers at these stores could browse merchandise and then purchase items via Alibaba's e-commerce platforms by scanning QR codes on the items in the stores.

Singles' Day has evolved into the biggest online retail event in China, and it benefits many other industry players besides Alibaba. Retailers are using the occasion to promote their products regardless of whether they have a presence on Alibaba's platforms. Alibaba deployed artificial intelligence (AI) technology to personalize the customer experience on Singles' Day, analysing customer data such as shopped items, browsed items and time spent on site pages to create new, personalized shopping pages throughout the 24-hour period. This data-driven personalization drove additional product discovery during the festival and was highly effective in increasing spending by existing shoppers.

Not only is the number of online shoppers continuing to increase, but also the number of orders per online shopper. This increase in orders poses increasingly greater challenges for both shipping service providers and online retailers. From the customer's point of view, the parcel delivery process is included in the total value of the product delivered. In addition to shipment tracking, short-term address changes, and the selection of delivery windows, customers are increasingly looking to choose the shipping service provider. But it is not only online retailers and delivery companies that are increasingly reaching their limits; cities and communities are also facing new problems. They too are interested in the most efficient delivery possible, since landing zones, roads and, increasingly important, the environment can be relieved (Rumscheidt, 2019). In addition to all these challenges, traders are currently facing a new major challenge in the delivery of parcels. Studies have shown that fast delivery is crucial when it comes to online shopping.

If given the customer faster delivery options, consumers will be more loyal. For example, research has shown that 55% say that a two-hour delivery option would increase their loyalty and 61% say the same for same-day delivery. But when delivery moves out to three days or more, only 30% say this will increase their loyalty (Capgemini, 2019). In contrast, the minority of companies offer two-hour or even faster delivery. Therefore, making faster delivery options available is a significant opportunity for every retailer to differentiate themselves from their competitors and meet consumer expectations.

What is more, satisfied consumers are willing to pay higher delivery charges (price premiums) for fast delivery as a value-added service. Experts are sure that views on free delivery are changing. Many customers still expect free shipping when they purchase something, but this attitude and views on free delivery are changing, particularly among the younger generation, like Generation Y and Z, mainly from an environmental perspective.

The "last mile" of transportation still provides problems which have not been solved yet, particularly sizeable logistics and cost concerns. "Last mile" is a term used in supply chain management and transportation planning to describe the movement of a product or package from a hub to a destination. Some challenges of last mile delivery include minimizing cost, ensuring transparency, increasing efficiency, and improving infrastructure.

To solve these problems or challenges many retailers have already started to experiment with technology.

Technology driven innovations in last-mile delivery. Last-mile logistics leads the pack in terms of retail technology funding, with $1.3 billion in capital raised in Q2 2018. This is driven by the early adoption of new autonomous-delivery models in developed markets as well as an attractive business case founded on urban demand and the prevailing high labour costs for fulfilment.

7-Eleven was the first to successfully complete a Federal Aviation Administration approved drone delivery in July 2015. The retailer partnered with drone operator Flirty to make the delivery. Since then, several retailers – including Amazon – have piloted these.

Ford, Walmart, and delivery service postmates are collaborating to design a service for delivering groceries and other goods to Walmart customers using autonomous vehicles. It aims to use autonomous vehicles by 2021 to reduce the costs of last-mile delivery.

Self-service lockers allow customers to select any locker location as their parcel delivery address. They can then retrieve their orders by entering a unique pick-up code, removing the need for human involvement. Amazon was among the first to implement this, with Home Depot and Walmart among the major retailers to follow suit.

A service that gives couriers access to a person's vehicle, allowing them to leave deliveries inside. John Lewis has teamed up with Jaguar Land Rover's mobility and venture arm – InMotion – to trial delivery to shoppers' cars. Amazon has also launched this service in partnership with General Motors and Volvo.

A delivery service that allows couriers to enter a customer's home and leave packages. Waitrose is the first retail supermarket in Britain to offer this service. The Dutch supermarket chain, Albert Heijn, a subsidiary of Ahold Delhaize, is also experimenting with this service.

Walmart, for example, has introduced an innovative last-mile delivery service. Details are provided in the box below.

Walmart introduced an innovative last mile delivery service.

As Walmart expands its grocery delivery service, giving its customers the option to shop when and how they want, the company introduced a last-mile delivery option, Spark Delivery. Spark Delivery is a crowd-sourced delivery platform that allows Walmart to learn even more about the full last-mile delivery process. This delivery service uses an in-house delivery logistics technology platform that provides drivers with the ability to sign up for windows of time that work best for their schedule as well as grocery delivery order details, navigation assistance and more. Walmart's team of personal shoppers are an important component of the overall service as they do the shopping for the individual consumers. Spark Delivery engages the services of independent drivers who partner with Delivery Drivers, Inc, a nationwide firm who specializes in last-mile contractor management, to crowdsource deliveries in a way similar to Uber and Lyft's ride-hailing network. The main objective is to build out a more robust delivery network so Walmart can get online orders delivered even faster to customers' homes.

Delivery Drivers manages the recruiting and screening of the personal shoppers, as well as payment, accounting, and other services for drivers. Drivers are paid by the delivery. The drivers also have access to helpful services and information through Delivery Drivers, for example assistance in understanding order flow, group discounts, etc., and help each independent driver run their transportation business correctly. Deliveries will be handled like rides in a ride-hailing network, with algorithms determining how to best route drivers and orders to the final consumer.

Combined with third-party crowd-sourced delivery providers, Walmart is well on its way to bringing delivery to 100 metro areas covering 40% of US households. Today, the retailer's grocery delivery service is available in nearly 50 markets in the United States (Walmart, 2018).

Walmart's cooperation with third-party delivery providers is very important for the company's delivery strategy, at present and in the future.

—

Part Two: **Brand management**

An overview of Brand Management

Part Two focuses on brand management in the retail sector and looks at fundamental aspects of branding decisions and strategic brand management, especially in a retail environment. In detail, in the following two chapters it will be thematised how a brand differs from an unbranded product and states why brands are important, and which functions they perform. Furthermore, essential steps in a strategic brand management process will be explained. A focus will be placed on how to create a retail brand, how to position the brand and how to create brand loyalty.

Finally, there will be an emphasis on branding and digitalization. The increase in the number of smart devices and their daily use means for retailers that they must use new ways of communicating with their customers. So, branding concepts should be applied not only to a physical world but also to digital media and technology to develop and communicate brands through interactions with consumers on their digital devices and for personalized brand communication.

Nike's digital branding strategy

Many brands have started to use technology to enable their end-to-end business to create the best experience for their customers and build long-lasting relationships. They are using data to better understand consumer and their desires, needs, and wants.

Today's brands must be relevant, useful, and entertaining. They have to offer brand experiences and build relationships with their customers, not just selling their products.

For example, Nike, the world's largest supplier of athletic shoes and apparel and a major manufacturer of sports equipment, has introduced the Nike Run Club App (https://www.nike.com/at/nrc-app), an app that can track runs, provides online coaching and bringing people together that share the same interests. The app offers the consumers the possibility to interact with the brand, even when they're not buying a Nike product, through health tracking and workout instructions. One of the main advantages of the app is that customers form relationships with that brand Nike and in addition, it provides the company with valuable insights that enables it to enhance the customer experience.

Furthermore, the app gives the brand access to personal health information so it can help the consumer become more active and it meet their fitness goals. In addition, Nike better understands the needs and lifestyles of its consumers. Another advantage of using technology and digital channels is to increase direct-to-consumer sales. For example, Nike's Snkrs app (https://www.nike.com/snkrs-app) offers limited products to a small group of customers. SNKRS provides insider access to the latest launches of sneakers, exclusive events and releases of new products. The users of this app, the so-called *sneakerheads* are highly coveted and engaged customers, and Nike's most loyal customers (so-called brand addicts), which makes them a valuable source of customer insight that can drive innovation.

For more information visit http://www.nike.com.

– **Chapter 4 Strategic Brand Management** introduces brand management in general and explains how retail brands are created. Furthermore, the brand positioning process will be discussed with a focus on differentiation from competitors' brands.

https://doi.org/10.1515/9783110543827-005

Another essential issue when it comes to strategic brand management decisions is how positive feelings towards a brand can be generated, so that consumers purchase the same product or service repeatedly now and in the future from the same brand. That's why brand loyalty will also be discussed within Chapter 4. Finally, brand equity and brand value, which are measures that estimate how much a brand is worth, will be explained and discussed.

- **Chapter 5 Branding decisions** explains brand sponsorship, brand development and how brand communication contributes to build brand equity. There is a special emphasis on branding and digitalization.

- **Chapter 6 Brand communication** illustrates why brand communication is one of the most important tools when it comes to establishing a dialogue between a brand and a customer and build a relationship with the customer. The five most important brand communication tools will be explained: advertising and promotion, interactive marketing, events and experiences, sponsorship and mobile marketing. The chapter concludes with a short digression on the topic "brands and packaging".

- **Chapter 7 Branding and Digitalization** starts with providing definitions of digital branding and digital branding strategy. Furthermore, the importance of digital customer journeys and touchpoints, including digital communication, with a focus on the retail sector will be discussed. The chapter concludes with an outlook on future developments.

4 Strategic brand management

In a world of global markets, saturated market situations and fierce competition, brands are essential when it comes to creating value and to differentiation from competitors. Retailers and marketers have recognised that strong brands stand for revenue growth and improved returns to shareholders. Therefore, they focus their strategies on building powerful brands as they represent competitive advantage, value to the customer and to the company. Consequently, every brand must define its key strategy which distinguish the brand from competitors, and which is appropriate for its target group.

Within this chapter several aspects of strategic brand management, especially important for the retailing industry, will be discussed. A focus will be laid on how to define a branding strategy, how to position a brand, and how to create brand loyalty, brand equity and brand value. Moreover, a focus will be laid on the topic "brands and digitalization." Nowadays, digital channels and assets are used to communicate a brand's purpose or positioning as part of multichannel brand communication strategies. Digital capability is becoming more necessary for retailers that are seeking to build or enhance their brands through brand building programmes. Digital is a powerful tool for brands and with many brand-building benefits. For example, online consumer reviews are the second most trusted source with 70% indicating they trust these, when it comes to a final purchase decision.

The focus in every company should be about putting the customer or consumer at the centre of everything the company does. New communication and sales channels and technologies provide more ways of delivering engaging, consumer-centred brand experiences. When the right segmentation is used to communicate with the target consumer, brand value and loyalty will be built.

In summary, success in digital will comprise participating in a wide range of online activities integrated with offline brand events. An integrated approach is key rather than seeing digital as tactical, experimental, a way of providing great content and an easy way of measuring effectiveness. The overall aim should be to deliver an authentic and consistent total brand experience that is aligned with the brand's strategy, positioning, and purpose (Keller, 2013).

4.1 Definition of brand and brand management

Products and brands are among the basic factors for every company to achieve and maintain a competitive position in a market. The customers use a particular product or brand to make a purchase decision and to find a solution to their needs, wants and desires. A company can have several products under multiple brands or multiple products under one brand. For example, Apple is a brand and Apple has many

https://doi.org/10.1515/9783110543827-006

different products under this brand, like iPad, iWatch, Mac, etc. So, we can conclude that a brand and a product are not the same. Products must be manufactured, for example, in factories or grown in agricultural fields, whereas brands are created by marketers and built in the mind of the consumers.

The following chapter investigates the difference between a brand and a product in more detail.

4.1.1 Difference between a product and a brand

In the literature there are different views and explanations of how a brand can be defined. There is no general hand definition that describes the concept of brands entirely. The most commonly used definition for brands was coined form the American Marketing Association (AMA) and narrows down a *brand* as a name, term, design, symbol, or any other feature that identifies a seller's product or service as distinct from those of other sellers.

A brand is more than a product, a brand creates a difference between just a car and a Mercedes or Volkswagen. A brand is what people feel about a particular company and its products, services, or ideas. Branding is about creating emotions, telling a story, and creating a differentiation in the minds of the consumers. A brand creates an added value to the core value of a product. Whereas, a *product* is a commodity, merchandise or deliverable. Goods, services, ideas, or anything that offers a solution to a problem are products. A product has five levels of meaning (Keller, 2013):

- The core benefit level: includes the fundamental need or want that consumers satisfy by consuming the product.
- The generic product level: encompasses only the attributes or characteristics necessary for its functioning but with no distinguishing features.
- The expected product level: stands for the set of attributes or characteristics that consumers expect when they purchase a product.
- The augmented product level: includes additional product attributes, benefits, or related services that distinguish the product from competitors.
- The potential product level: encompasses all the augmentations and transformations that a product might undergo in the future.

In the retail sector most competition takes place at the augmented product level because most products are produced at an expected product level and product attributes are often very similar. So, marketers and retailers try to differentiate their products through packaging, price, advertising, or services, like delivery arrangements, and other services that customers value, but also through branding. There, a brand is more than a product because it can have dimensions that differentiate it in some way from other products designed to satisfy desires, needs and wants of consumers. These differences can be tangible (related to the product and its features) or intangible (more symbolic and emotional, and intangible, related to what the brand stands for (Keller, 2013).

The main points of difference between a brand and a product are given below (Marketing, 2019):

1. Market value

   Products have a base value, and they are generic. Brands are the added value to make a product perception better inside the minds of consumers. Studies have shown that people very often stereotype generic products as poor quality, cheaper or less effective than branded products. On average, a branded product is 30% more expensive than a generic product.

2. Consumer expectation

   Brands are more expensive because users expect more from a branded product than from a generic product. Branded products intend to provide a better experience for consumers. Users spend more to get more out of a particular product, so markets tend to have higher expectations from brands.

3. Emotional appeal

   Brands target the emotions of consumers. Strategies are focused on triggering and creating an emotional appeal among consumers to convince them.

4. Attraction for consumers

   Brands are designed to attract their consumers, create a unique positioning, and increase sales by creating a personality.

5. Trustworthiness and reliability

   Consumers like certainty, they need to be sure about a product before making a purchase. Brands offer evaluation of products so that consumers can trust. Products without a brand are anonymous, and it is hard for customers to trust them or become loyal to them.

6. Market identity

   Generic products are anonymous whereas brands have market identities. A brand represents the identity of products in a competitive market, and brands display the quality and reputation of products. Consumers tend to develop a specific preference for a particular brand or its product over time, and this creates a brand's identity and brand loyalty (see Table 4.1).

To summarize, the key to creating a brand is to be able to choose a name, logo, symbol, package design, or other characteristic that identifies a product and distinguishes it from others. These different components of a brand that identify and differentiate it are the so-called *brand elements*. Retailers very often create their own brands based on their store name or some other means. Brand names come in many different forms. Brand names can be based on people's names, like the grocery discounter Aldi (Albrecht Diskont) or based on places, or a combination between people's names and places. For example, IKEA, the world's largest furniture

Table 4.1: Differences between brands and products (Marketing, 2019).

Market value	
Brands add value to a product. The whole process of branding is about meaningful value addition.	Generic products have less face and market value in comparison to branded products.
Consumers expectations	
Brands must meet higher consumer expectations. In general, brands are more expensive due to higher consumer expectation.	Generic products are relatively cheaper, with fewer users' expectations.
Emotional appeal	
Brands gave an emotional relationship with consumers.	Products do not have a personalized relationship with customers.
Attraction for consumers	
Brands have a magnetic effect in attracting customers. Brands can be status symbols for consumers.	Many good products fail to capture consumers because of being anonymous. A product without a brand is unknown.
Trustworthiness and reliability	
People trust brands, and a strong brand can sometimes cover up for a weak product.	Consumers tend to trust anonymous products less.
Market identity	
Brands gave market identity, which provides them with more authority and reputation in a market.	Products have no market identity; therefore, they have less influence and reputation over competitors.

retailer, uses the name of the founder *I*ngvar *K*amprad and the name of the farm and the village where he grew up *E*lmtaryd and *A*gunnaryd.

A good and memorable brand name must have five characteristics (Watkins, 2014):

Suggestive: brand name evokes a positive brand experience. For example: the name of the online retailer Amazon is synonymous with enormous.

Meaningful: a good brand name must resonate with potential customers no matter when and where they encounter it and easy to understand, spell and remember.

Imagery: the name should be visually evocative to stay in the customers' minds. It's much easier for a customer to remember a name that can be associated with a memorable image in their minds, like English breakfast tea or Viennese Sacher cake.

Creativity: brand names are likeable when they provide potential for wordplay and verbal branding opportunities, like for example the brand names Eat the ball (bread), Hanky Panky, (underwear) or Chunky Monkey (ice cream).

Emotional: good brand names provide an emotional connection, involve the customers, and make them feel positive, for example Happy Day orange juice or Hipmunk (travel search site).

Brands can be seen as valuable intangible assets of a company, there amount of power and value they have in the marketplace varies from brand to brand. Brands, in general, are complex entities which exist only in the customers' minds. Blombäck & Axelsson (2007) state that a brand is based on the totality of the perception of a certain audience and holds a distinctive position in the customer's mind based on past experiences, associations and future expectations. With a certain brand, a customer connects experiences, attitudes, and feelings towards a company. Therefore, successful branding requires a holistic approach with strategic perspectives, the so-called *strategic brand management*. Brands ought to be managed in an impact-oriented way that derives out of the customers' perceptions. Strategic brand management deals with strengthening the perceptions of brands in the customers' minds (Baumgarth, 2010).

Brands perform several valuable functions, for both, for a company and for the consumer (Keller, 2013):

Functions for consumers
- identification of source of product
- assignment of responsibility to the product maker or provider
- risk reducer
- search cost reducer
- promise, bond, or pact with maker or provider of the product
- symbolic device
- quality signal

Functions for the companies
- means of identification to simplify handling or tracing
- means of legally protecting unique features
- signal of quality level to satisfied customers
- means of endowing products with unique associations
- source of competitive advantage
- source of financial returns

In general, a brand consists of three main elements: the brand identity, the core brand values and the brand design. All three elements are explained briefly as follows (Aaker, 1996):

Brand identity: by creating a brand identity, the company focuses to formulate a customer benefit and to show specific core competences of the brand. The brand identity then provides direction, purpose and meaning for the company´s brand. Within this process, the brand identity provides the benefit, characteristics, and emotions to the target group. In order to fit into different markets or product context, the brand identity needs to be adapted. The aim is to have a common set of associations, whereas some of them are in the core identity. A brand identity is fundamental to the strategic vision, and referred to as brand personality.

Core brand values: derive from the brand identity and its core competences. They can be described as the conception of what is desirable and how the brand wants to help the customer achieve his/her goals.

> **BMW brand values versus Mercedes-Benz brand values.**
> The brand promise of BMW is defined as the "sheer driving pleasure." As the driving force at BMW this is achieved by the combination of dynamic and sporting performance, constant innovations as well as appealing, contemporary designs. These values are reflected in their range of car models and sub brands which BMW offers their customers. The sub-brand "BMW i" substantiates innovation at BMW by offering sustainable mobility by combining electric drives, innovative technology, and material with a premium character. The sporty edge of BMW is represented by their high-performance sub brand "BMW M." In contrast, considering the brand values of Mercedes-Benz, the core of the brand is their leadership aspiration in the fields brand, product, and communication. This aspiration is represented in their leading message for brand communication: "The best or nothing." This ambition is manifested by the three-core brand values fascination, perfection, and responsibility. Each of these core brand values are then verified by three brand experiences each: the brand value "fascination" is justified via the experiences "refined sportiness," "distinctive style," and "trendsetting design."

Brand design: the brand design consists of the brand name and the trademark. The brand name serves as a linguistic synonymous for the brand, the trademark represents a typographic and/or graphically designed brand identification, the so-called logo. The process of applying a trademark to a certain product is called branding.

4.1.2 Definition of strategic brand management

In the literature there do exist many different definitions of the term "brand management." The most appropriate definition for this book is the following:

> Brand management is the process of maintaining, improving, and upholding a brand so that the name is associated with positive results. Brand management involves the design and implementation of marketing programs and activities to build, measure, and manage the brand equity.
> (Keller, Aperia, & Georgson, 2008)

Brand management covers the systematic planning, implementation and controlling of the chosen market position of a brand with the use of appropriate marketing instruments. The overall economic objective of managing a brand is to increase the value of the brand (brand value). This fundamental objective can be achieved by increasing the brand awareness and through securing a self-contained and distinctive brand image. A brand image is much stronger when the brand is perceived as emotional, unique, positive, and relevant for the customer. Strong brands are strategic assets for a company and ensure long term performance (Aaker, 1996).

Brand management is the procedure of improving, upholding, or maintaining a brand so that the name is related with optimistic and positive outcome. It also takes account of several essential aspects such as the cost, competition, in-store performance, and customer satisfaction. Appropriate brand management can lead in higher sales of the product related with that brand. For instance, if a client loves a specific brand of biscuits, she or he is more probable to purchase other product provided by the business such as chocolate and others.

Whereas *strategic brand management* involves the design and implementation of marketing programs and activities to build, measure, and manage brand equity. Keller (2013) defines the strategic brand management process as having four main steps:
- identifying and developing brand plans
- designing and implementing brand marketing programs
- measuring and interpreting brand performance
- growing and sustaining brand equity

Identifying and developing brand plans

Every strategic brand management process starts with finding a common understanding of what the brand stands for and how it should be positioned with respect to competitors. When developing a brand plan three questions must be considered.

Purpose: What is the purpose of the brand? What are the brand values? What are the value propositions around this purpose?

Potential: Which aims for the brand must be considered? Are there resources to achieve those aims or is it necessary to reassess the aims?

Promise: What is the promise to the final consumer and how is this promise going to be achieved? How will the brand purpose be made reality, considering the identified potential?

Designing and implementing brand marketing programs

Building brand equity requires properly positioning the brand in the minds of customers and achieving as much brand resonance as possible. In general, this knowledge building process will depend on three factors:
1. The initial choices of the brand elements making up the brand and how they are mixed and matched; The most common brand elements are brand names, URLs, logos, symbols, characters, packaging, and slogans. The best test of the brand-building contribution of a brand element is what consumers would think

about the product or service if they knew only its brand name or its associated logo or other element. Because different elements have different advantages, marketers often use a subset of all the possible brand elements or even all of them.

2. The marketing activities and supporting marketing programs and the way the brand is integrated into them, because the biggest contribution comes from marketing activities related to the brand.

3. Other associations indirectly transferred to or leveraged by the brand because of linking it to some other entity. For example, the brand may be linked to certain source factors, such as the company (through branding strategies), countries or other geographical regions (through identification of product origin, see the box below "The country-of-origin effect"), and channels of distribution (through channel strategy), as well as to other brands (through ingredients or co-branding, see the box below "Examples for ingredient branding"), characters (through licensing), spokespeople (through endorsements), sporting or cultural events (through sponsorship), or some other third-party sources (through awards or reviews).

The "country-of-origin effect"

The so-called *country-of-origin effect* is defined as the fact that the country of origin of a product influences the consumers' evaluation and thus their purchase decision. For example, German cars, Japanese electronics, and Italian fashion products are rated differently than Italian cars, German electronics, and Japanese fashion products. This is because the image of the countries interacts with the country-of-origin effect. This effect causes consumers to react differently to a product because the country of origin is perceived as the actual source of supply for that product.

Nowadays it is difficult to draw the correct distinction between the country of origin and the country of the product brand.

At this point, Usunier points out that in the country-of-origin effect, there is a shift of attention from the country of production to the country of the product brand. This is primarily about the consumer's need to recognize the origin of the brand. Positive associations between the country and the product or brand should be created (Usunier, 2011)

In summary, the following is stated: The country of origin of a product or a brand influences the product evaluation or purchase decision of the consumer and interacts with the country image. The country-of-origin effect can have cognitive, affective, and normative effects on a product or brand and there are a number of social and cultural factors that influence the effect.

A study regarding luxury brands and the country-of-origin effect was conducted in 2008. A cross-national sample was formed to understand how the country-of-origin effect works in different countries and in different product categories. The study compared 165 young people in eight different countries. Strong differences were observed between the countries regarding the concept of the country-of-origin effect. The respondents are usually very aware of the country of origin of the individual brands. For example, approximately 94% of the respondents correctly assigned the Gucci brand to Italy as their country of origin. The most important factors influencing the evaluation of luxury goods are the brand and the design. In addition, the brand has a greater influence on product evaluation and purchase decisions in all analysed product categories than the

country of origin. For luxury goods, the brand is much more important in the evaluation and purchase decision than the Country of Origin. The luxury brands are generally well-known to the respondents. Young people therefore clearly seem to be more interested in brands and their origin
than the country of origin of the product.

Examples for ingredient branding.
An ingredient brand is a brand which is not sold directly to the final consumer. It is a component
of a complete product that is available to consumers on the market. One of the most successful
examples of an ingredient brand is Gore-Tex® for clothing and shoes. Other examples of ingredient brands are: Tetrapack, Teflon, 3M, Lycra, Alcantara, Tencel, NutraSweet, etc.

Consumers trust ingredient brands when they have come to know them as guarantees for
high quality, trust, and satisfaction. Ingredient brands can even become a selling point for the
product itself. Ingredient branding is a very intensive form of brand cooperation, which must
succeed for the long term. It requires both sides to be vigilant: The owners of the ingredient
brand must monitor whether the final quality of the partner brand meets their standards. The
managers of the end user brand, in turn, must keep an eye on the brand fit (Brand Trust, 2019).

Even though ingredient brands are only sold indirectly, a large portion of their brand communication addresses end consumers: It ultimately must be understandable, visible, and tangible for
them – no matter how complex its performance may be. Also, the owners of ingredient brands communicate directly with retailers, so they can present their peak performances adequately. They must
concern themselves with the attractiveness and desirability of their brand (Brand Trust, 2019).

Measuring and interpreting brand performance

To manage brands profitably, managers must design and implement a brand equity
measurement system. A brand equity measurement system is a set of research procedures designed to provide timely, accurate, and actionable information for marketers so that they can make the best possible tactical decisions in the short run and
the best strategic decisions in the long run. Implementing such a system involves
three key steps: conducting brand audits, designing brand tracking studies, and establishing a brand equity management system.

The task of determining or evaluating a brand's positioning often benefits from
a brand audit. A brand audit is a comprehensive examination of a brand to assess
its health, uncover its sources of equity, and suggest ways to improve and leverage
that equity. A brand audit requires understanding sources of brand equity from the
perspective of both the company and the consumer (Keller, 2013).

Growing and sustaining brand equity

Maintaining and expanding on brand equity can be quite challenging. Brand equity
management activities take a broader and more diverse perspective of the brand's
equity – understanding how branding strategies should reflect corporate concerns
and be adjusted, if at all, over time or over geographical boundaries or multiple
market segments.

Effective brand management requires taking a long-term view of marketing decisions. A long-term perspective of brand management recognizes that any changes in the supporting marketing program for a brand may, by changing consumer knowledge, affect the success of future marketing programs. A long-term view also produces proactive strategies designed to maintain and enhance customer-based brand equity over time and reactive strategies to revitalize a brand that encounters some difficulties or problems.

Another important consideration in managing brand equity is recognizing and accounting for different types of consumers in developing branding and marketing programs. International factors and global branding strategies are particularly important in these decisions. In expanding a brand overseas, managers need to build equity by relying on specific knowledge about the experience and behaviours of those market segments (Keller, 2013).

4.2 Creating retail brands

Retail brands, brands that are owned and marketed by retailers, are omnipresent in daily life. Some are perceived consciously, others subconsciously. What they have in common is that successful brands are those with strong, emotionally-based connections with highly engaged consumers. Creating long-lasting and powerful relationships with their customers, for example, by creating experiences that are relevant, intimate, and fun, is one of the main objectives when it comes to creating strong retail brands.

In the retail market, the emphasis has shifted in the last couple of years from the retailer having all the control, setting the price and selling the products the retailer has on the shelves, to a more demanding customer who is in control. Nowadays the customer has multiple online and offline shops to choose from, so it has become harder for retailers to find a unique positioning and to differentiate themselves from competitors. The customer normally does not want to make just a transaction but prefers a personalised experience, that will engage and connect him or her to the brand.

Literature provides several helpful suggestions how effective retail brands can be developed. One of the first steps on the way to creating a strong retail brand is knowing the target audience. Deciding on an appropriate target audience will help to form a brand identity that is suitable and appealing for this group of consumers. The next step in creating a strong retail brand is to tell a brand's story and get the customers emotionally connected.

Studies have shown that customers are normally price-sensitive and quality-conscious when they buy FMCG. They are interested in the price of a product, the features and benefits the product has to offer. But a soon as they hear a story, they can relate to; they are willing to pay a higher price and get emotionally connected to the brand. In the technical language, this process is referred to as *storytelling*.

The following box provides an example for successful retail storytelling – the story about the American supermarket chain Trader Joe's.

Retail storytelling- about Trader Joe's story.

Retail storytelling is one of the most critical factors in creating a great experience for the customer. Stories that form an emotional connect with the customer are remembered for a long time. Storytelling makes the brand more human and relevant to its customer. It helps the brand form a deeper and lasting connect with the customer.

The American supermarket chain Trader Joe's is a very good example for successful retail storytelling. Here you find their story (Trader Joe's, 2020):

In 1958, Joe Coulombe took over a small chain of convenience stores around the LA area. These were called Pronto Markets, a kind of place where you could get anything from, say, a pack of gum to some pantyhose. After 10 years of running Pronto Markets, the convenience store formula just didn't continue to make sense. So, Joe, the classic entrepreneur, took note that the demographics were changing in the United States.

The first Trader Joe's store opened in 1967 in Pasadena, California. That store is still operating. The store had a nautical theme, and it was run by people who were described as "traders on the high seas." At the time, Joe had been reading a book called "White Shadows in the South Seas," and he'd been to the Disneyland Jungle Trip ride. To this day, Trader Joe's Crew Members consider themselves "traders on the culinary seas" and are known for their bright, tropical-patterned shirts and for generally being nice, helpful, and well informed.

In 1972, Joe introduced a total game changer for Trader Joe's . . . Granola. This was the first private label Trader Joe's product.

Focusing on private label (products with "Trader Joe's" name on them) simplified a lot of things and removed a lot of costs and the savings were passed on to the customers. For Trader Joe's the focus on value is vital, as they don't have sales, loyalty programs or membership fees. Instead, they buy direct from suppliers whenever possible and pass the savings on to the customers.

In 1988, when Joe retired, Trader Joe's had 19 stores. John Shields took over as CEO and saw the opportunity to transfer this grocery store concept across geographical boundaries. In 2001, Dan Bane assumed the role of Chairman and CEO and focused on making Trader Joe's a national chain of neighbourhood grocery stores. Today, the chain has over 500 stores in 42 states in the US (Trader Joe's, 2020).

When it comes to developing effective retail brands, it must be added that brands need to create an emotional connection to their customers – an emotional connection that is meaningful and engaging, an emotional connection by creating personalised experiences. Traditional bricks and mortar retailers have an advantage over online sellers when it comes to creating a more personalised experience. Physical retailers find it easier to tap all the five senses of their customers, creating so-called multisensory experiences. Physical retailers must make use of this advantage and create multisensory experiences for example by playing music, having product tastings, using pleasant lightning and temperature, creating an appealing atmosphere, and encouraging customers to touch, smell and feel the products.

When starting a brand, marketers oftentimes do not put enough thought into naming, preferring to go with something generic and universally accepted. However, the name of a brand is one of the first things that attracts the attention of a potential customer. The following box provides recommendations which brand names are most effective.

How to find an appropriate name for a retail brand
To begin with, brand names should be easy to remember and should be likeable, they must not relate to negative associations. These names must not have any confusing or negative meaning in other languages. Brand names should be easy to pronounce and to spell, and they should be easy to understand by any customer. The following suggestions can help to find a suitable name for a retail brand (brandlance, 2019):

First names
Giving human first names for retail brands is slowly becoming a popular trend. For example, the supermarket chain Trader Joe's or IKEA (I= Ingvar, the first name of the founder, K= Kamprad, the surname of the founder, E= Elmtaryd, place where the founder was raised, A= Agunnaryd, hometown), or H & M (Hennes & Mauritz).

Made-up words
Means to come up with a completely new name. Many well-known retail brands have made-up names. For example, BILLA (stands for BIlliger Laden = cheap shop) or EDEKA (abbreviation of the purchasing cooperative of the colonial goods traders) or Aldi (Albrecht Discount).

Two-word combinations
Two words can be combined to form one name for a retail brand. Very popular examples are Snapchat, a photo messaging app, or Soulfood, a name for a slow food supermarket chain.

Misspellings
Another option would be to just intentionally misspell a name. Nevertheless, this name should still be easy to be pronounced. Examples of such retail brand names are Publix, a grocery store chain, or Flickr, a photo messaging app.

Mainstream name
A simple and common name is also very effective and easy to understand and remember, like the retail chain Target, or Home Depot, the largest home improvement chain in the world.
   Another approach would be to use an automatic name generator to brainstorm some names. Here you find a link of a business name generator: https://namelix.com/.

Another important aspect when it comes to creating a retail brand is to have a strong personality behind the retail brand and its products. One way to make a brand more personal is to include customers into the development process. This approach has the advantage to find out what customers really want and what the product can do for them personally. In addition, this approach lays the foundation for a strong relationship between the retail brand and the customer.

   What is more, every retail brand must express what it is most passionate about. Before a brand is created that the target group trusts, the company must know what value the brand provides. A so-called mission statement, a formal summary of the aims and values of the brand, must be specified. A statement that is not only reflected in the branding, but also in marketing campaigns, and everything surrounding a successful retail brand.

Mission statements of popular brands.
A mission statement is a written declaration of a company's main purpose and focus. Figure 4.1 provides some examples of famous brands and how the define their mission. The mission statements are formulated so that they can inspire the employees of a company and the customers alike.

Figure 4.1: Mission Statements of famous brands.
Source: Dvornechuck, 2020

Finally, it must be mentioned that creating a successful brand is never a static process. Ideally, it should evolve along with changing customer preferences and emerging trends in the market. In addition, by watching a retailer's or a brand's competitors you can learn some valuable insights for the own brand.

The most valuable global retail brands 2019 are shown in Figure 4.2. In this research we see that the world's most valuable retail brands are worth $339 billion more than last year, a total of $1.4 trillion. Innovative use of technology and digitalisation such as AI, IoT, and data analytics has helped e-commerce deliver additional human benefits, which results in a 33% growth in brand value for the most powerful players in retail. The world's most valuable retail brand is Amazon ($315.5 billion), the e-commerce giant accounts for nearly a quarter (23%) of the total brand value of the top 75 retail brands.

The Chinese e-commerce giant Alibaba, the world's largest online and mobile commerce business, has increased its brand value by an additional 48% to $131.2 billion. The retail company has more innovations than Amazon and is disrupting its logistics model to better facilitate super-fast delivery.

Some online providers such as the German fashion platform Zalando (number 62 in the ranking), a new entrant to the ranking, also shows an enormous growth rate, mainly because of an intent focus on quality, simplicity, and service (BizCommunity, 2019).

While e-commerce is a key success driver, providing a great customer experience in store is also an important part when it comes to contributing to a retail brand's increased brand value. Nike, ranked fifth, launched experiential stores designed to provide closeness to their brands and a more personalised interaction with sales staff. Or, the discount supermarket Aldi (number 19 in the ranking), is shifting its highly standardised store formats towards more flexible and innovative models, including catering to the "customer on the go," that offer greater flexibility for the customer.

Retailer focusing on price also should relevant growth rates. For example, Amazon, Ikea (no. 15) and Aldi (no. 19) all continue to grow their brand values in 2019 with their low-price strategies through building a strong brand and offering a great customer experience. Consumer consciousness about the environmental cost of fast fashion impacts retailers in the apparel sector. For example, Zara (–10% to $22.6 billion) and H&M (–39% to $6.4 billion) were impacted by rising customer concern about the cost of producing, transporting, and selling disposable products (BizCommunity, 2019).

Rank 2019	Brand	Brand value 2019 ($bn)	Category	Rank 2018
1	Amazon	315.5	Retail	1
2	Alibaba	131.2	Retail	3
3	McDonald's	130.4	Fast Food	2
4	The Home Depot	53.5	Retail	5
5	Nike	47.4	Apparel	7
6	Louis Vuitton	47.2	Luxury	6
7	Starbucks	45.9	Fast Food	4
8	Chanel	37.0	Luxury	N/A
9	Walmart	36.8	Retail	8
10	Hermès	31.0	Luxury	9

Figure 4.2: The most valuable global retail brands 2019.
Source: BizCommunity, 2019

4.2.1 Brand concept

A brand concept is a general idea and an abstract meaning behind a brand working as its core and character that gives the consistency to the brand and creates a distinctive identity in the market and in the minds of the consumers. It can be briefly described as the first thing that comes to the minds of the customers when they hear or think about a particular brand (Bashin, 2019). A well-defined brand concept is the most important starting point for any brand. Having a well-defined and aligned brand concept is the fundament for defining a brand strategy and related elements discussed later in this book.

A brand concept should include several key elements (Bashin, 2019):

Brand Name: The first element which is very important is the name of a brand. This name should go along with the nature of the business, aims and objectives of the retailer, features, and attributes of the products or services offered. It is very important for the marketers and brand experts to find a name brand that is distinctive, unique, catchy, positive and easy to understand and remember. It should not be similar to the ones of competitor brands to avoid confusion and copyright issues.

Tagline: The second most important element of the brand concept is the tagline. The tagline is basically the slogan of the brand consisting of two to five words that reflect the brand attributes and features in a short and catchy manner. For example, the tagline of the popular sports brand Nike is "Just Do It." With this catchy tagline Nike complements the nature of its products: offering sportswear for a target group consisting of sports personalities, hobby athletes, and fitness enthusiasts.

Visual elements: The visual elements of a brand include the logo, typography, fonts, and colour palette. All these elements in a combination should be designed in an aesthetic and attractive way signifying the nature of the retailer and characteristics and strengths of the brand. For example, taking the Nike brand, the logo of the sportswear brand has the mascot of a right forward tick or a check sign in a curved manner signifying that the products of the brand are the best for fitness enthusiasts, hobby athletes and sports personalities to which modern, contemporary design is important and who attach importance to comfort and performance.

Language: The element of language is quite important for a brand concept as each brand should have a specific tonality and play of words depending on its objectives and types of products and services offered. The tone of a brand language can range from sincerity, authoritative, helpful, or customer centric. A brand might be described using various adjectives, including positive, negative, warm, caring, impersonal, confident, or service-oriented words. A company must choose the right combination of words and images to build up the tone for its branding messages. What is more, the tone of reflects the brand personality, helps the brand to connect with the target group, and makes the brand different from competitors' brands.

Messages: The brand concept should also include the most important messages and information that the brand wants to communicate with its stakeholders (e.g., employees, customers, producers, vendors, sponsors, investors, etc.). The so-called *messaging statement* of a retail brand encompasses the following elements: the mission statement, the vision statement, values, positioning statement, value proposition, the slogan, and the tagline (see Table 4.2).

Table 4.2: Example of a messaging statement of a retail brand.

Mission	To be a high-quality conglomerate, with a clear focus on each of our businesses and bridging the gap between online and offline retail.
Vision	To deliver superior value to our stakeholders, in particular customers, employees, vendors, shareholders, and sponsors and providing a digital advantage.
Values	Acting and taking decisions that are fair, responsible, and honest. Providing customer-oriented innovation. Striving to be the leading retail brand in the market.
Value proposition	Buy the things you desire at high-quality and an affordable price.
Tagline	Putting the customer first.
Slogan	A shop that has it all!

4.2.2 Brand identity

Brand identity can be defined as the characteristics of a brand, which in turn define the character of the brand values (Burmann, Blinda, & Nitschke, 2003). Consequently, it represents the self-image of the product or the company. Prerequisites for a strong brand identity are reciprocity, continuity, consistency, and individuality. Accordingly, an identity is created only by maintaining the corporate philosophy, through consistent communication and unique brand benefits (Meffert, Burmann, & Koers, 2002). The brand origin is the cornerstone of the identity of a brand. It deals with the questions:
- Where does the brand come from?
- Who created it?
- How did it originate?

This includes all geographical, cultural, and institutional aspects of the brand (Boldt, 2010). The basis of the brand identity not only gives the origin of a brand credibility, but also authenticity (Burmann, Blinda, & Nitschke, 2003). The relatively new concept behind brand positioning, namely the concept of brand identity, is suitable for creating an emotional, human-like positioning in the minds of the customers, which is important for luxury brands or brands that hardly differ due to their physical properties, what is especially the case in saturated markets.

The brand identity corresponds with the intra-company self-perception of a brand, which determines precisely how the brand should appear to external target groups (Aaker, 1996). In contrast to mass-market positioning, the brand identity is not the result of market research, but represents above all the companies' mission, vision and value proposition. The elements of brand identity can be roughly divided into two main components: The physical-functional and the abstract-emotional components (Esch, 2010). For more information, see Table 4.3.

Table 4.3: The Brand Identity Framework Source: Esch, 2010.

Physical-functional component	Abstract-emotional component
Brand attributes *What characteristics do I have?* Characteristics of products Characteristics of company and/or brand	**Brand tonality** *How I am?* Brand personality Brand relationship Brand vision/values, etc.
Example: Nike Air shoes with tuned air for superior stability and unmatched cushioning.	Example: Nike Air shoes for the most powerful athletes.
Brand benefits *What do I offer?* Functional benefits Psychosocial benefits	**Brand symbols** *How do I appear?* Brand design and symbolism Brand communication
Example: These shoes are of high quality and allow maximum comfort.	Example: Nike Air shoes use its distinctive cushioned sole and genuine leather.

The basis of all brand activities is the central value proposition of a brand, because only a big idea and creative implementation creates attention. The brand experience or the brand essence is representative of entrepreneurial skills and the central value proposition. The sum of all the additional benefits are the brand values which surround the core brand.

In addition, the support function of the brand essence generates people's experience of the brand. Therefore, without conviction on the emotional level, brands will be forgotten. For this reason, both core brand and brand values need to appeal to the target group so that a unique brand positioning arises. Based on an appropriate brand positioning, the value proposition or the core message will be developed.

The brand tonality in general and the brand personality can relate to the existence of the brand. It describes the sum of characteristics that are associated with a brand (Aaker, 2001). Furthermore, the component describes the communication style and can make the brand-consumer relationship positive. An equally fundamental component of the brand identity is the *brand vision*. This is a response to the future development of the brand in the form of a mission statement and serves as a motivational incentive for the company. Brand visions are not equivalent to brand goals, because they are long-term oriented. Brand objectives, however, are both time-limited and more precise. The final component is brand power. It is a combination of skills, values, and the personality of a brand, giving rise to competitive advantage (Meffert, Burmann, & Koers, 2002).

4.2.3 Brand awareness

Brand awareness can be defined as the extent to which customers are able to recall or recognize a brand under different conditions. The consumer's ability to recognize or recall a brand is central to purchasing decision-making, therefore marketers put the focus on brand awareness when it comes to brand management, communication management. Purchasing decision-making can not proceed unless a consumer is first aware of a product category and a brand within that category. It must be mentioned that awareness of a brand does not necessarily mean that the consumer must be able to recall a specific brand name, but they must be able to recall enough distinguishing characteristics.

In general, brand awareness consists of two components: brand recognition and brand recall (Keller, 2013):

- **Brand recognition** stands for the customer's ability to confirm prior exposure to the brand when given the brand as a cue. In other words, when the customer visits a store, will he or she be able to recognize the brand as one to which they have already been exposed.
- **Brand recall** is customer's ability to retrieve the brand from memory when given only the product category, the needs fulfilled by the category, or a purchase or usage situation as a cue. For example, a customer's recall of Kellogg's Corn Flakes will depend on his or her ability to retrieve the brand when thinking of the cereal category or of what he or she should eat for breakfast. This can happen either at the store when making the purchase or at home when deciding what to eat for breakfast.

If consumer decisions are made at the POP, where the brand name, logo, packaging, etc., will be physically present and visible, then brand recognition will be important.

If consumer decisions are mostly made in settings away from the POP, for example, at home, then brand recall will be more important. For this reason, creating brand recall is especially important for services or online brands, because in this case customers must actively seek the brand and therefore be able to retrieve it from memory when appropriate.

There are three main advantages of creating a high level of brand awareness: learning advantages, consideration advantages, and choice advantages.

– **Learning Advantages**: Brand awareness influences the formation and strength
  of the associations that make up the brand image. To create a brand image, marketers must first establish a brand node in memory of the consumers, the nature
  of which affects how easily the consumer learns and stores additional brand associations. The first step in building brand equity is to register the brand in the
  minds of consumers. If the right brand elements are chosen which are appropriate for the target group, the task becomes easier.
– **Consideration Advantages**: Consumers must consider the brand whenever they
  are making a purchase for which this brand could be acceptable or fulfilling a certain need or desire. Raising brand awareness increases the likelihood that the
  brand will be in the relevant set of brands, which will be considered for purchase.
  Research has shown that consumers are rarely loyal to only one brand but instead
  have a relevant set of brands they would consider buying and another set of
  brands they buy on a regular basis. Because consumers typically consider only a
  few brands for purchase, making sure that the brand is in the consideration set
  also makes other brands less likely to be considered or recalled.
– **Choice Advantages**: The third advantage of creating a high level of brand awareness is that it can affect choices among brands in the consideration set, even if
  there are essentially no other associations to those brands. For example, consumers have been shown to adopt a decision rule in some cases to buy only more
  familiar, well-established brands. In low-involvement decision settings, a minimum level of brand awareness may be sufficient for product choice, even in the
  absence of a well-formed attitude. One influential model of attitude change and
  persuasion, the *elaboration-likelihood model,* is consistent with the notion that
  consumers may make choices based on brand awareness considerations when
  they have low involvement. Low involvement results when consumers lack either
  purchase motivation (they don't care about the product or service) or purchase
  ability (they don't know anything else about the brands in a category).

This elaboration-likelihood model (ELM) of persuasion was developed by Richard
E. Petty and John Cacioppo in 1980. They (Petty & Cacioppo, 1984) intended to provide a general framework for organizing, categorizing, and understanding the basic
processes underlying the effectiveness of persuasive communications. In detail, the
model aims to explain different ways of processing stimuli, why they are used, and
their outcomes on attitude change, illustrated in Figure 4.2.

As we can see in Figure 4.3 the elaboration-likelihood model proposes two major
routes to persuasion: the central route and the peripheral route. Under the *central
route,* persuasion will likely result from a person's careful and thoughtful consideration
of the true merits of the information presented in support of an advocacy. The central
route involves a high level of message elaboration in which a great amount of cognition
about the arguments are generated by the individual receiving the message. The results
of attitude change will be relatively enduring, resistant, and predictive of behaviour.

Under the *peripheral route*, persuasion results from a person's association with positive or negative cues in the stimulus or making a simple inference about the merits of the advocated position. The cues received by the individual under the peripheral route are generally unrelated to the logical quality of the stimulus. These cues will involve factors such as the credibility or attractiveness of the sources of the message, or the production quality of the message. The likelihood of elaboration will be determined by an individual's motivation and ability to evaluate the argument being presented (Petty & Cacioppo, 1984).

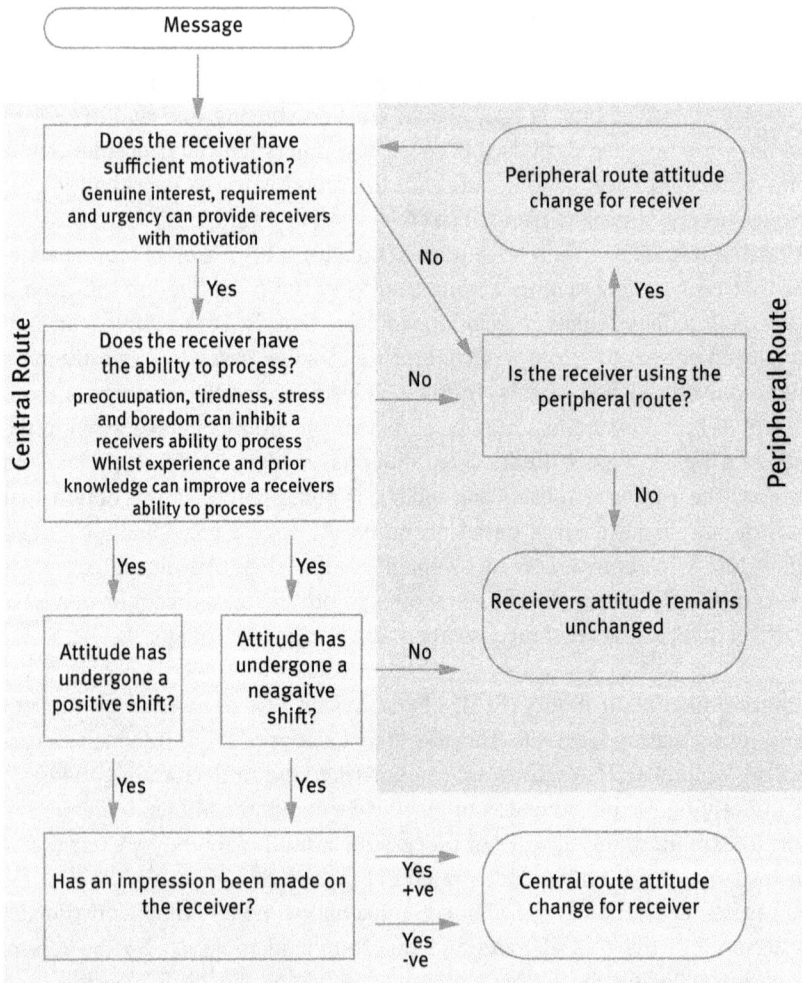

Figure 4.3: Elaboration-likelihood model.
Source: Petty & Cacioppo, 1984

Consumer purchase motivation versus consumer purchase ability.
Research has shown that consumers may make choices based on brand awareness considerations when they are low involved in a particular purchase situation. Low involvement results when consumers lack either purchase motivation or purchase ability.

Consumer purchase motivation: Although products and brands may be critically important to marketers or retailers, choosing a brand in many categories is not a vitally necessary decision for most consumers. For example, despite millions of euros spent in TV advertising over the years to persuade consumers of product differences, many consumers still don't know the differences between the brands or did not know which brand was best for their needs. A lack of perceived differences among brands in a category is likely to leave consumers unmotivated about the choice process.

As a result, increasing competition between car brands has intensified the importance of brand identity. As product standards continue to rise, the perceived image of a car brand plays a key role in purchase decision-making. The premium brands such as BMW, Porsche, Mercedes-Benz, etc., must develop attributes and values that reflect changing social values which influence buyers emotionally, to maintain their positions.

Consumer purchase ability: Consumers in some product categories just do not have the necessary knowledge or experience to judge product quality. For example, products with a high degree of technical sophistication, like telecommunications equipment with state-of-the-art features. But consumers may be unable to judge quality even in low-tech categories. Consider the college student who has not really had to cook or clean before, shopping grocery or cleaning products for the first time. Product quality is often highly ambiguous and difficult to judge without a great deal of prior experience and expertise. In such cases, consumers will use whatever shortcut or heuristic they can come up with to make their decisions in the best possible way. In many cases they simply choose the brand with which they are most familiar and aware or allow to influence them by word-of-mouth or online reviews.

Research has found out how brand awareness can be created and established. Creating brand awareness means increasing the familiarity of the brand through repeated exposure, although this is generally more effective for brand recognition than for brand recall. This means, the more a consumer "experiences" the brand by seeing it, hearing it, or thinking about it, the more likely he or she is to strongly register the brand in his or her mind.

Research has shown that anything that causes consumers to experience one of a brand's element – and here it does not matter whether it's a name, symbol, logo, the packaging, a slogan, a jingle, etc., also including communication activities – can increase a brand's awareness. The more brand elements are used and combined, for example, the name, the logo, and a jingle, the better to enhance awareness. What is more, repetition increases the recognizability of a brand and can also create linkages in memory to appropriate product categories.

When brand names become generic.
What do Tesa, Post-it, and Edding have in common? All are office supplies! What about Pampers, Labello, and Q-Tips? All belong to the field of hygiene. But what is more, they are more than just a name for a product – they are also generic brand names, that is, products that have become so successful that they now must be the name of a whole product category. Generic brand names normally develop, if a patent-legally and mark-legally protected product is introduced into the market without having competition. In this case, the brand becomes so market-dominant that consequently the consumers designate competitive products with the same name.

In linguistics, such terms that have managed the transformation from a proper brand name to a generic name are called deonyms – composed of the Greek words for "god(ness)" and "name." The field of deonyms is not limited to brand names: The verb "röntgen," for example, is derived from the discoverer of the rays named after him and is also a deonym.

Some more examples:
Handkerchief: "Tempo"
Transparent adhesive tape: "Sellotape" or "Tixo"
Lip balm: "Labello"
A portable music player: "Walkman"
Repellent against mosquitoes: "Autan"
Storage box made of plastic: "Tupperdose"

Brand associations are the basis for creating brand loyalty and favourable purchasing decisions. Aaker (1996) differentiates between several different types of associations, such as product and performance attributes, lifestyle, and personality or intangible attributes.

Brand associations facilitate the recall of a brand and help retailers to differentiate their brands from competitors. Consequently, brand associations constitute an essential source of competitive advantage. Furthermore, brand associations can evolve into beneficial attitudes and feelings that consumers have towards a brand, which in turn can motivate consumers to purchase a certain product.

Apart from brand awareness, it is also crucial to build a strong and consistent brand image. The following subchapter deals with this topic in more detail.

4.2.4 Brand image and brand imagery

The **brand image** is based on perceptions and associations that consumers link with certain brands (Aaker, 1991; Keller, 2013). Associations with a brand represent the meaning that the brand has for the consumer and can refer to certain features or characteristics of a product. For marketers, the main objective in terms of building brand image is to create and link unique, appropriate, and favourable associations to a brand to create a competitive positioning in the minds of the consumers (Keller, 2013). A brand image includes the impression of the brand which the external audience has. It is seen as a foreign image of the brand. Brand awareness is the basis for this.

Although they sound very similar, there is a difference between brand image and brand imagery. While *brand imagery* represents a brand's identity through aesthetic appearance (using images to visualize a brand), a brand image refers to how a brand is perceived on the outside and the reputation it has in general. Imagery can be used to help shape a brand's image, but a brand's image is impacted by many other factors too, such as values, actions, and communication activities.

Brand imagery depends on the extrinsic properties of the product or service, including the ways in which the brand attempts to meet customers' psychological or social needs. It is the way people think about a brand abstractly, rather than what they think the brand does. So, brand imagery refers to more intangible aspects of the brand, and consumers can form imagery associations directly from their own experience or indirectly through advertising or by some other source of information, such as word of mouth. Many kinds of intangibles can be linked to a brand, but the four main ones are (Keller, 2013):

User profiles: person (demographic such as age, gender, race, income; psychographic such as careers, attitudes towards life, social issues) or organisations (size and type, e.g., "caring")

Purchase and usage situations: channel type (department store, online, boutique); location (inside or outside home), activity during usage (formal or informal, dine-in or takeaway)

Personality and values: brand acts like a person, for example, modern, sophisticated, and angry. Consumers often choose brands that they perceive and aspire themselves to be like so the brand personality is consistent with their own self-concept; otherwise, consumers who are "self-monitors" will be sensitive to how others see them, so will more likely choose brands whose personalities fit the consumption situation

History, heritage and experiences: brands may use associations to relate to consumers' recollections of personal or shared experiences. Brands can become iconic by using these experiences to tap into consumers' hopes and dreams

Cadbury, Nivea, and Coca Cola brand imagery
The intangible association to Cadbury includes family experiences, cherish able memories. The product could be bought from supermarket on the insistence of parents or from department store or specialty store through impulse buying or for little pleasures. A popular brand with rich brand imagery in Europe is, for example, the skin care brand Nivea. This brand links many notable intangible associations to its brand, above all family and shared experiences/maternal, childhood memories and timelessness. The Coca-Cola imagery creates a feeling of freshness, modernity, activity, and the togetherness of family and friends on special occasions, to hold those relationships in life, which are of great importance.

Brand image is the most important factor when it comes to the sales figures of Coca Cola. The brand's identity should reflect the own unique equity and care essence which will ensure brand creativity and identity that is meaningful and sustainable in long term. Packaging changes have also affected sales and industry positioning, but in general, the public has tended not to be affected by new products. Coca-Cola's bottling system also allows the company to take advantage of infinite growth opportunities around the world.

The brand Coca Cola offers a unique set of associations in the mind of customers concerning what the brand stands for and the implied promises the brand makes. There is hardly any person around the world that hasn't heard the name Coca Cola. Ever since it beginning as world's leading name in cold drinks, Coca Cola has created a strong brand image irrespective of age, sex, and geographical locations. Millions of people around the world are consuming cold drinks or soft drinks as part of their daily meal. Coca Cola, ever since its inception has been the leader in soft drink market (cocacolabranding, 2016).

Another brand category that very often relies on brand intangibles are luxury brands. Luxury brands are great examples for creating a unique brand imagery as a key competitive advantage. Luxury brands often rely on an aspirational image that benefits from a "trickle-down" effect to a broader audience via communication instruments, above all PR and word-of-mouth. Important is that there is a good balance between accessibility and exclusivity. What is more, luxury brands can sometimes benefit from secondary associations with linked personalities, events, or countries (e.g., Made in Italy, or Italian fashion brand, etc).

More and more companies are attempting to tap into more consumer emotions with their brands. The following lists six important types of *brand-building feelings* (Keller, 2013):

- **Warmth**: The brand evokes soothing types of feelings and makes consumers feel a sense of calm or peacefulness. Consumers may feel sentimental, warm-hearted, or affectionate about the brand. Many heritage brands such as Louis Vuitton, Uncle Ben's rice, Nivea cream tap into feelings of warmth.
- **Fun**: Upbeat types of feelings make consumers feel amused, light-hearted, joyous, playful, cheerful, and so on. With its iconic characters and theme park rides, Disney is a brand often associated with fun.
- **Excitement**: The brand makes consumers feel energized and that they are experiencing something extraordinary. Brands that evoke excitement may generate a sense of elation, of "being alive," or being cool, string, provocative, popular, etc. Apple, for example, is a brand seen by many teens and young adults as exciting.
- **Security**: The brand produces a feeling of safety, comfort, and self-assurance. As a result of the brand, consumers do not experience worry or concerns that they might have otherwise felt. "Success is the sum of right decisions." (German Bank) or "He runs and runs and runs and runs and runs . . . " (Volkswagen) or "Money makes you happy if you make sure you have it when you need it." (Raiffeisen banks, Austria) are slogans that communicate security.
- **Social approval**: The brand gives consumers a belief that others look favourably on their appearance, status, or behaviour. This approval may be a result of direct acknowledgment of the consumer's use of the brand by others or may be

less overt and a result of attribution of product use to consumers. For example, the car brand Mercedes is a brand that is a signal of social approval.
- **Self-respect**: The brand makes consumers feel better about themselves; consumers feel a sense of pride, accomplishment, or fulfilment. Good examples are Haribo sweets with the slogan "Haribo makes children happy and adults as well" or Knorr foods "Food good, all good."

4.3 Brand positioning

Brand positioning is a very important strategic element when it comes to managing a brand. It is the main part of every marketing strategy. Brand positioning can be defined as the "act of designing the company's offer and image so that it occupies a distinct and valued place in the target customer's minds" (Keller, 2013). The term "positioning" means finding a proper place in the minds of consumers or a particular market segment. A proper brand positioning helps to guide the general marketing strategy by defining what the brand is all about, how it is different or similar to competitors' brands, and why consumers should purchase and use it. To find a proper positioning marketers and retailers need to find answers to the following three questions (Keller, 2013):
- Who is the target market or the target consumer?
- Who are the main competitors?
- How is the brand similar to or different from competitors' brands?

All these questions will be discussed in greater detail in the following subchapters.

4.3.1 Segmenting and targeting

Identifying a brand's target market is a fundamental strategic element in the brand positioning process because consumers normally have different perceptions and preferences for a certain brand. Therefore, each company must define and segment an appropriate market and, in a next step, choose a certain target market or target consumers.

A market is the set of all actual and potential buyers who have sufficient interest in, income for, and access to a product. Market segmentation is the subdividing of market into homogeneous sub-groups of customers (segments), where any subgroup may conceivably be selected as market target to be reached with a distinct marketing mix (Kotler & Armstrong, 2006).

Market segmentation is a process where two or more customers are grouped (segmented) to fulfil their needs and wants in a more efficient way. So, why is it so important to segment consumers into different "types," "segments," or "groups"? Market segmentation offers a company several advantages:

- Similar needs, wants and behaviour of the customers require similar marketing mixes
- The product or service can be better adjusted to the needs of a certain market segment
- A company's market budget can be allocated more precisely
- Competitors can be overcome more effectively
- The existing product can be modified, or a new product developed to satisfy the needs of the target market
- A brand's market can be defined more precisely

A retailer must consider that segmenting a market requires making a trade-off between costs and benefits. In particular, the more finely segmented the market, the more likely that the marketer or retailer will be able to implement marketing programs that meet the needs, wants and desires of the customers in any one segment. On the other side, a fine segmentation of the market means greater costs of reduced standardization.

There are several possibilities to conduct market segmentation of consumer markets. These *segmentation* bases can be classified into for main categories (Keller, 2013):
- Behavioural: user status, usage rate, usage occasion, brand loyalty, benefits sought
- Demographic: income, age, gender, race, family
- Psychographic: values, opinions, and attitudes, activities, and lifestyle
- Geographic: international, regional

Behavioural segmentation bases are often most valuable in understanding branding issues because they have clearly defined strategic implications. For example, defining a benefit segment according to the usage rate, for example, heavy users, medium users or light users, or usage occasion, for example, universal occasions, festive occasion, regular personal occasions, or rare personal occasions, makes it clear what should be the ideal point-of-difference or desired benefit with which to establish a certain positioning. Deciding on a brand's positioning requires above all determining a frame of reference and the optimal POP and POD brand associations. This frame of reference chosen must be competitive and will dictate the breadth of brand awareness and the situations and types of cues that should become associated with the brand. For more information on POP and POD brand association see Chapter 4.3.3.

Demographic segmentation bases are also used very frequently. The main advantage of demographic segmentation bases is that the demographics of traditional marketing instruments, like gender, age, income, family, educational level, etc., are generally well-known from various consumer studies. It must be mentioned, that with the growing importance of nontraditional media, above all social media and electronic word of mouth, this advantage has become less important.

Psychographic segmentation divides the consumers based on their personality, lifestyle, and attitudes. Personality is the combination of characteristics that form an individual's distinctive character. It includes habits, traits, attitude, temperament, etc. Lifestyle can be defined as the fact how a person lives his life, his activities, opinions, and interests. Its central constructs are defined as (also see Figure 4.4):

- Activities: how the consumer spends his time at work and leisure
- Interests: what the consumer places importance on his immediate surroundings
- Opinions: where the consumer stands on issues, society, and himself

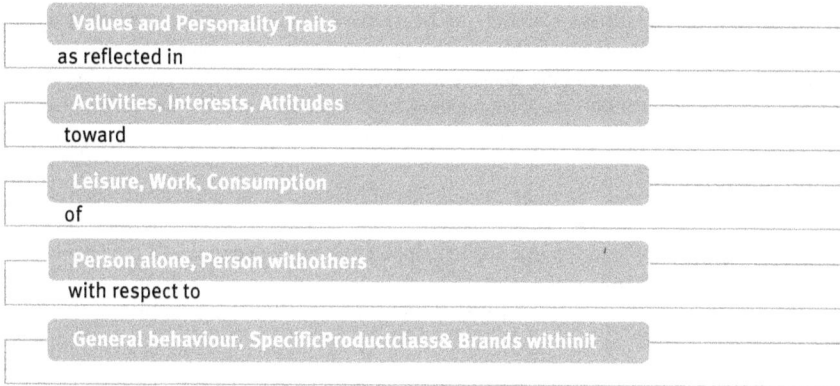

Values and Personality Traits
as reflected in

Activities, Interests, Attitudes
toward

Leisure, Work, Consumption
of

Person alone, Person with others
with respect to

General behaviour, Specific Product class & Brands within it

Figure 4.4: Lifestyle reference frame.
Source: Wind and Green (1974)

In sum these three central constructs (activities, interests, opinions) capture the main forms of human expressions of life, that is, observable activities, emotionally conditioned behaviour (interests) and opinions, linguistically formulated (verbalised) attitudes.

This classification of lifestyle characteristics offers a frame of reference for the methodical conception of model-theoretically based lifestyle research projects, which are adapted to the respective task and which should avoid the nonconsideration of essential aspects. The AIO dimensions are mutually interrelated and are modified according to the purpose and object of the empirical research.

One point of criticism of the approach is that its operationalization is limited to the dimensions "activities, interests and opinions," which means that other psychological constructs, such as values and personality traits, are not directly recorded. Moreover, it is difficult to target consumers within a population unless individuals participate in a particular psychographic survey. Nevertheless, this type of segmentation helps to understand consumers' unarticulated needs and motivations and empowers marketers to develop more compelling messaging.

Why psychographic segmentation is so valuable.
To see the value of psychographics, let's have a look at an illustrative example- the case of the family tech market.

Normally, families with different incomes, educational backgrounds, or with younger and older children, make different technology purchases. But their reasons for purchasing are much more tied to parent psychographics. In detail, parents who trust their children to make their own technology decisions (so-called *enablers*) tend to evaluate their technology purchases in terms of fun and entertainment value. Parents who focus on minimizing screen time (so-called *limiters*) tend to purchase software and devices that support their kids' literacy, math, or academic skills. Parents who actively guide and encourage their kids' technology use typically look for purchases that offer a balance of fun and educational value.

So, when we understand these kinds of psychographic differences, online marketing tools can help to make these insights actionable. Using psychographics allows marketers to do smarter keyword targeting, for example, for parents who are searching for "kids programming" and for parents who are searching for "kids videogames fun." Once we know the key differences in what customers care about, more compelling messaging can be directed towards these different customer groups.

To summarize, the internet has made these kinds of psychographic differences much more apparent and relevant to both consumers and marketers. Today's research, analytics, and ad targeting makes it possible to turn those psychographics into the foundation of a robust market research and marketing strategy. Thoughtful use of psychographics can help to develop not only the compelling messages but also the products and brands that specific customers want and desire (Samuel, 2016).

Geographic segmentation can refer to a defined geographic boundary (such as a city, ZIP code, country) or type of area (such as the size of city, urban/rural, radius around a certain location or type of climate). This segmentation type divides the market based on geographical factors, as already mentioned above, region, country, zip code, urban, rural area, etc. This segmentation type is commonly used for products or brands, which are used by people living in different regions and therefore having different need, desire, and requirements.

To give an example, in many regions tap water is not drinkable which inflates the demand for bottled water in these regions. Another example of geographic segmentation may be the luxury car company choosing to target customers who live in warm climates where vehicles don't need to be equipped for snowy weather.

Advantages of Geographic Segmentation:

- It's an effective approach for companies with large national or international markets because different consumers in different regions have different needs, wants, desire, requirements and cultural characteristics that can be targeted.
- It is also an effective approach for smaller companies with limited budgets. They can focus on a defined area and not expend marketing budget on approaches not suitable for their target geographic segment.

– It is an appropriate approach in areas where population density is very different. Consumers in an urban environment often have different needs and wants than people in suburban and rural environments. There are even cultural differences between these areas.
– And it's a relatively easy, fast, and cost-effective type of segmentation.

General criteria for market segmentation

Several criteria have been defined in the literature to assist marketers and retailers when it comes to segmentation and target market decisions: Market segments must be:
– Identifiable: the market segment must be easily identified.
– Size: is the market segment large enough to have adequate sales potential?
– Accessible: the market segment must be reachable by marketing instruments, especially distribution outlets and communication instruments must be available.
– Responsive: market segments should be responsive to target-group oriented marketing program.

By going beyond demographic-based segmentation, such as age, income, or gender, or grouping customers based on shared shopping habits and preferences, marketers and retailers can better develop products, brands and marketing campaigns that resonate with their customers. Many research institutes and marketing companies provide consumer segmentation studies analysing and focusing on all different kinds of segmentation criteria. Euromonitor International (2017), the world's leading independent provider of strategic market research, have segmented the global consumers into five global shopper types which seem to be appropriate for helping retailers better understand and appeal to cohesive consumer segments in their target market. This shopper type analysis focuses on shopping habits and shopping preferences to profile like-minded consumers.

Key traits of Euromonitor's five global shopper types.
While many companies often identify market segments using demographics alone, Euromonitor goes beyond standard demographic segmentation and has created distinct, personality and habit-driven consumer types at both the global and country level grounded in cluster analysis of the results of its Global Consumer Trends surveys which cover seven areas of consumer life: healthy living, eating and drinking, shopping, technology, green influences, spending, and personal traits and values across nine markets (Brazil, China, France, Germany, India, Japan, Russia, United Kingdom, and United States).

The five global shopper types and their characteristics are as follows (Euromonitor International, 2016):

Conspicuous Consumer (13%)
Brand-conscious
Highly influenced by ads
Tech-savvy
Very concerned about status

No-frills Saver (26%)
Extremely thrifty
Get in and out of stores as quickly as possible
Ignore advertising
Prefer brick-and-mortar

Thrifty Bargain-hunter (23%)
Look for great value
Enjoy shopping and researching deals
Ignore hype and status-based claims
Willing to buy private label

Social Experimenter (18%)
Will buy on impulse if they find the right product
Look to consumer reviews and peer recommendations
Enjoy treating themselves and others
Open to trying new brands

Thoughtful Planner (20%)
Think carefully before buying
Rely on peer recommendations
Loyal to trusted brands
Save rather than splurge

Filling the shopping cart when selecting a product in a retail outlet or online, those five shopper types prioritise different qualities and product features. Key considerations that factor into shopper decisions include flexibility, loyalty, and status, price and brand priorities, special features, and green considerations. When it comes to brand-consciousness the Euromonitor segmentation study shows the following results: conspicuous consumers, social experimenters, and thrifty bargain-hunters are especially prone to trying new products, especially those products that are on sale. Social experimenters and conspicuous consumers prefer to buy products with well-known brand names. Thrifty bargain-hunters like to buy unbranded products and private labels. No-frills savers and thoughtful planners prefer to always buy the same products and likely unbranded products.

Targeting in brand management

Targeting in brand management is a strategic approach that breaks a large market into smaller segments to focus on a specific group of customers within this market. It defines a segment of customers based on their unique characteristics and focuses on serving their needs, wants, desires or requirements. Instead of trying to address an entire market, a brand uses targeting to put the energy and budget into connecting with a defined group within a particular market.

Through market segmentation, we have already discussed the four main types of market segmentation above, brands get more specific about their target market. They can focus on a small group of customers who will be most likely to benefit from and enjoy the company's brands. Targeting in brand management is not just about getting the target group to select the own brand you over the competitor's brands. It's also about getting the customers to see the own brand as the sole provider of a solution to a specific problem, need or desire. So, a good brand has to clearly deliver a message and confirm the brand's credibility in the market. Moreover, a brand must connect a target group with a brand on an emotional level. It must deliver a certain promise, motivate the target group to make a purchase and, finally, create brand loyalty.

Targeting in brand management
For example, a brand that sells day planners may decide to focus just on a smaller, specific target group. Instead of selling the planners to the masses, the retailer may focus solely on selling planners to women, to female business owners. Or the retailer could focus on another market niche, to exclusively sell the planners to schoolteachers. Both examples are smaller, more specific target groups of the day planner's potential market.

4.3.2 Competitor

To find a proper brand positioning marketers and retailers need to identify who are the main competitors. Therefore, it is necessary to conduct a detailed competitor analysis.

A competitor analysis is a process that involves defining the main competitors of a product or brand, gathering information about them, and using that information to supplement the own branding strategy (Harvey, 2017).

A detailed competitor analysis has many advantages. One of the most important advantages is, that the company can learn how the biggest competitors in the market are positioning their brands, and to find out where there is still a positioning gap, which makes sense for the company.

A competitive analysis presumes that various factors have to be considered like the company's resources and capabilities, but also the future intentions of important competitors, to identify an appropriate target market where consumers can be profitably served.

When conducting a competitor analysis, a couple of standard questions must be asked and answered to gain valuable market insights:
- Who are the brand's main competitors and what are the products these competitors have to offer?
- Between which brands is the market divided and how much of a market share do they have?
- What are the marketing strategies of these competitors including their future intentions?
- What are the strengths and weaknesses of these competitors?
- What is the USP (unique selling proposition) of these competitive brands and how do they position themselves in a particular market?
- Which communications tools (online and offline) do they use to reach their target group and to create an advantageous brand image?

Here are some selected tools that can be used to monitor a brand's position online and offline:

Google alerts: is a content change detection and notification service, offered by the search engine company Google. The service can be used to find new results, such as web pages, newspaper articles, blogs, or scientific research, etc., that match the provided search terms, for example, about the own brand or competitive brands. Reports are generated and directly send by mail (Google Alerts, 2020).

BrandMention: is a simple to use social media search tool that aggregates user generated content from across the internet into a single stream of information. It's a social media monitoring tool that allows the user to track and measure what is said about a particular brand anywhere in the world. Moreover, it is an in-depth brand monitoring tool designed to track and engage in online conversations about a brand in real-time (BrandMentions, 2020).

SpyFu: is an effective tool that helps to track competitors and to identify which keywords the main competitors are targeting. This tool also helps to identify web sites which are the closest competitors and to watch for domains gaining on keywords. This can be useful when planning a content campaign online or launching a new website to be more visible. For more information see https://www.spyfu.com/seo/competitors (SpyFu, 2020).

4.3.3 Points-of-parity and points-of-difference brand association

Deciding on a brand positioning requires above all determining a frame of reference and the optimal points-of-parity (POP) and points-of-difference (POD) brand associations. This frame of reference chosen must be competitive and will dictate the breadth of brand awareness and the situations and types of cues that should become associated with brand. Once marketers have decided on the appropriate competitive frame of reference for positioning by defining the customer target market and the nature of competition, they can define the positioning itself. An appropriate positioning requires establishing the right POD and POP associations (Keller, 2013).

POD associations

Keller (2013) defines POD as attributes or benefits that consumers strongly associate with a brand, positively evaluate, and believe that they could not find to the same extent with a competitive brand. There do exist all kind of different brand associations. These brand associations can be classified into:
- functional, performance-related considerations
- abstract, imagery-related considerations

POD associations are so important because customers' brand choices often depend on the perceived attributes or benefits of a brand and the uniqueness of these brand associations.

Examples of POD associations.
The German discount supermarket chain ALDI sells its products at affordable prices maintaining top quality products. Aldi attracts customers who are looking out to purchase food and nonfood products at competitive prices.

The Swedish home furnishings and furniture retailer IKEA offers its products with most innovative designs at reasonable prices for the mass market. Ikea gains a POD through its appealing and easy to assemble product offerings, also making use of the reputation of Swedish products in general. Swedish products are well-known for good quality, safe and well-built products.

As already mentioned above POD associations may rely on *performance-related attributes*, like a robust packaging, or performance benefits, like a consumer-friendly, easy-to-open packaging. What is more, PODs come from imagery associations. This is obvious for luxury brands, like Gucci, Louis Vuitton, Chanel, etc. Many well-known brands attempt to create a POD on "overall superior quality" – this is obvious for luxury brands, like Gucci, Louis Vuitton, Chanel, etc. Other brands want to be associated with terms like affordable price, solid quality, "low-cost product."

PODs are normally defined in terms of consumer benefits. These benefits often have important underlying "proof points". These proof points can come in many different forms, like functional design concerns (e.g., a unique sealing system of a packaging, leading to the benefit of a longer shelf life) or key ingredients or key endorsements (recommended by nutrition experts, leading to the benefit of "healthier snacking").

POD associations may also rely on *imagery-related considerations*. Traditional luxury brands, for example, maintain a strict consistency between perceived prestige and price premiums, to preserve their brand exclusivity, whereas new luxury brand positioning strategies often combine a high perceived prestige with reasonable price premiums to attract middle-class consumers (Truong et al., 2009).

Many new-luxury brands move upmarket to create a certain appeal and downmarket to make their products more accessible. Still, they are careful to create and maintain a distinctive character for every price-level of their products by focusing on a common brand essence (Silverstein & Fiske, 2003). In the literature this positioning strategy is referred to as "masstige" strategy (a combination of mass and class). Truong et al. (2009) view a masstige positioning strategy as "being very innovative and effective" due to combining a prestige positioning with a broad appeal but hardly any brand dilution.

Most traditional brands, taking as an example Gucci, are very careful when widening their product and price range in order to avoid a brand dilution. They do not want that their products are available to the mass, focusing on an exclusive and prestigious branding strategy. But when traditional brands are losing market shares, masstige strategies may be seen as an opportunity to be profitable by targeting new consumer groups.

POP associations

POP associations are not necessarily unique to a particular brand but may in fact be shared with other brands.

There are three types of POP associations (Keller, 2013):
- category
- competitive
- correlational

Category POP are attributes or benefits that consumers view as essential or necessary within a certain product category. In other words, they represent necessary – but not sufficient – conditions for brand choice. Category POP may change over time due to developments, like technological advances, consumer trends, market developments, etc. These attributes or benefits exist minimally at the generic product level and are most likely at the expected product level. For example, customers expect a cinema to have a big screen and comfortable seats, as well as a range of snacks and drinks. Here it must be mentioned that individual attributes and benefits often have positive and negative aspects.

Competitive POP is designed to negate a competitor's point of difference. It provides a brand a suitable competitive positioning if it can give better or similar components as compared to the points of difference of its competitors. For a brand to attain a POP on a specific benefit or attribute, many consumers must trust that the brand is appropriate and trustworthy on that dimension.

> **McDonalds and the competitive parity problem**
> McDonald's had a competitive parity problem when it began losing customers concerned with healthy eating. So, they began to offer a healthier range of products, like grilled chicken sandwiches, a variety of salads, fruit salad, a choice of apples or cucumbers in the kids' Happy Meals, etc. The main objective of this change in product offering not to make McDonalds a place for healthy eating, but to create enough parity to reduce the number of customers who wouldn't even consider the brand (Aaker, 1996)

Correlational POP are potentially negative associations that arise from the existence of positive associations for the brand. One challenge for marketers is that many attributes or benefits that make up their POPs or PODs are inversely related. Giving an example, a long heritage can be seen as a positive attribute because it can suggest trust, experience, and expertise. On the other hand, it could be a negative attribute because it might imply being old-fashioned and not up to date. Or consumers might find it hard to believe a brand is "low in calories" and at the same time "full in taste." Therefore, marketers must find a trade-off.

To summarize, POP associations are important because they can undermine POD associations. For the brand to achieve a POP on a particular attribute or benefit, enough consumers must believe that the brand is "good enough" on that dimension. There is a so-called *range of tolerance or acceptance* with POPs. The brand does not have to be seen as literally equal to competitors, but consumers must feel that it does sufficiently well on that particular attribute or benefit. Assuming consumers feel that way, they may then be willing to base their evaluations and decisions on other factors potentially more favourable to the brand. POP is easier to achieve than POD, where the brand must demonstrate clear superiority. Often, the key to positioning is not so much achieving a POD as achieving necessary, competitive, and correlational POP (Keller, 2013).

To conclude, companies must think about how customers perceive their products or services. This is essential to know because it can help to figure how the brand is positioned from a customer's point of view and how to promote a product or service target group-oriented. One important fact is to know whether the product or service is a "necessity" for the customer or is perceived as "luxury" and adapt the marketing strategy accordingly. Today most consumer products and services are more luxury than necessity. Studies have shown that consumers feel a purchase is a real "necessity" only 30% of the time. In many cases, consumers could do without the product (Specialty retail, 2005).

Necessity: should be promoted as an affordable, desirable solution to a certain problem. Competence, caring, concern and product quality should be focused.

Luxury: should be promoted by pointing out how much better the customer's life will be after the purchase, for example, saving time, money or the product or service will make the customer look and feel better.

When promoting a product or service companies should focus on their ads and on their websites just on a few key advantages and keep it simple and streamlined. It is enough to list the top three advantages and provide the complete list of features when consumers really want it, for example on a second page on the website, or in a further sales conversation. Promoting a product or service in general, or a brand, effectively and reaching the right target group is not easy. Many companies think when they purchase an expensive series of TV ads, they would create product awareness and increase sales, but in many cases, the marketing message does not reach the right target group. Therefore, some common rules must be kept in mind (Specialty retail, 2005):

Today every customer is exposed to thousands of messages each day, from offline to online media. Most of these media messages are ignored and don't receive the customers' attention. Customers only pay attention to messages that speaks directly to their immediate needs, wants and desires. Therefore, it is essential to know whether a product is a necessity or a luxury to speak directly to the motivation for buying the product.

Marketing campaigns of a brand normally should not be targeted at a broad audience but should be narrowed down at an appropriate group of customers. Also, the media must be chosen well. TV, radio, and print can be used to sell products that are used by the mass market. For a more targeted and effective approach, specialized media forms should be used, for instance specialized magazines, topic-specific blogs, or neighbourhood editions of a paper.

4.4 Brand loyalty

Brand loyalty can be defined as a "measure of the attachment that a customer has to a brand" (Aaker, 2001) which generates positive attitudes and leads to a consistent repurchase.

According to Jacoby and Chestnut (1976) brand loyalty is "the biased, behavioural response, expressed over time, by some decision-making unit, with respect to one or more alternative brands out of a set of such brands, and is a function of psychological (decision-making, evaluative) processes." In this context, biased behavioural response means there is a certain tendency to buy the product of a certain brand.

Aaker (1991) divided brand loyalty into five categories, within the so-called *brand loyalty pyramid* (see Figure 4.5). The first level in this pyramid is called switcher, meaning those customers are not loyal to a brand. They are normally very price sensitive and consider every brand as adequate if the price fits the quality. The second level in this pyramid is considering satisfaction. Meaning if the customer has no reason to change, he will not change brands. However, if competitors offering perceived benefits for the customer, he or she will switch. The next category includes satisfied customers. They will perceive switching costs if they consider changing between brands. Switching costs can be loss of time, risks, or loss of money. The fourth level represents customers who really like the brand and based on experiences, perceived quality or emotions are attached to the brand. The last category contains customers who are really committed to the brand. They use the brand to express themselves, also use the brand as a status symbol or to show off in peer groups which is mostly important for the younger generations. They are proud to use the brand.

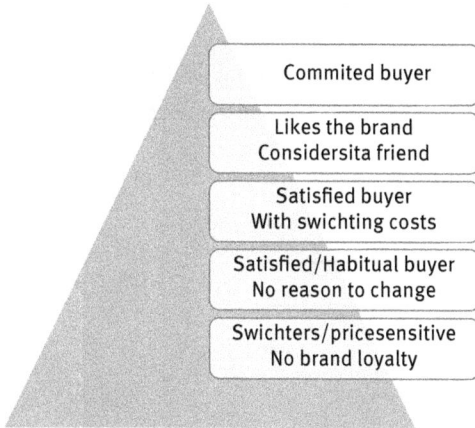

Figure 4.5: Brand loyalty pyramid.
Source: Own elaboration based on Aaker, 2001

The level of brand loyalty also shows to what extent a customer is willing to switch to competitor's brand. Therefore, increasing a customer's brand loyalty is a very important objective in a retailer's brand management strategy, due to several advantages (Aaker, 1996):

– Brand loyalty has a positive influence on a retailer's future sales and profits
– Establishing a loyal customer base can be cost saving as it is much cheaper to put effort into maintaining existing customers rather than to acquire new ones

Brand loyalty is strongly influenced by brand equity and associated factors of brand equity, especially brand associations and perceived quality. In order to generate loyalty to a certain brand, it is essential to investigate customer satisfaction and dissatisfaction with a brand among other factors, also past experiences with the brand. Another aspect that constitutes brand loyalty is the likelihood to recommend a certain brand to friends, family, relatives, or colleagues. In addition to measuring the level of satisfaction or dissatisfaction and the likelihood to recommend a brand, repurchase intention also plays an essential role (Aaker, 1996). So, brand loyalty is the key factor underlying customer-based brand equity, which is the differential effect that brand knowledge has on a customer's response to marketing efforts of that brand (Keller, 2013). A high level of brand loyalty demonstrates that customers value the brand and prefer the brand over competitive brands (Aaker, 1996). The next chapter will explain brand equity in more detail.

Dick and Basu (1994) state that loyalty can be divided into four categories. These categories are determined by high or low relative attitude and high or low repeat patronage.

Loyalty can't occur with low repeat patronage and low relative attitude (*no loyalty*), due to the "inability to communicate distinct advantages" or if there exist a lot of brands in a particular category which are very similar. Spurious loyal customers do not see differences between brands, however, buy the same brands due to a habitual buying behaviour (see Table 4.4).

Table 4.4: Categories of customer loyalty (Source: Dick and Basu, 1994).

		Repeat Patronage	
		High	Low
Relative Attitude	High	*Loyalty*	*Latent Loyalty*
	Low	*Spurious Loyalty*	*No Loyalty*

Latent loyalty is described as "a marketplace environment where nonattitudinal influences such as subjective norms and situational effects are at least equally if not more influential than attitudes in determining patronage behaviour." The last category is *loyalty* where customers perceive strong differences between brands.

Rowley and Dawes (2000, 538–546) took a closer look on no loyalty. In their study they argue that having a closer look on nonloyal customers is important to develop customer relationships. They categorize the customer behaviour *disloyalty* into four categories: disturbed, disenchanted, disengaged and disruptive. Disengaged loyal customers can be defined as customers who have not been customers before, however, this can change in the future, due to awareness of a particular product or brand or their needs and desire are changing. Disturbed loyal customers are existing and continuing customers, who are suffering a temporary perturbation in their loyalty status and are in the state of questioning previously assumptions about a brand. This can occur due to unfavourable experiences with the brand or attractive promotion or pricing campaign of a competitor. The third category are the so-called disenchant loyal customers. These are customers who used to be loyal, however, are not loyal anymore due to various, undefined reasons. The last type are disruptive loyal customers. This type of customers has strong negative attitudes and behaviours towards a particular brand and therefore would never buy this brand.

All four types of nonloyal customers are different in their behaviour. For these reasons marketers need to consider different communication and promotion strategies and tools to communicate efficiently with potential customers.

For marketers it is important to deal with the concept of brand loyalty because brand loyalty is a measure of the attachment that a customer has to a brand (Aaker, 1996). Brand loyalty brings a retailer many advantages, including repeat purchases and recommendations of the brand to other potential customers, especially friends and relatives. We have already learned in the chapters above that brands have a leading role in the consumer market. They are the interface between consumers and retailers, and consumers may develop loyalty to brands. Trust in a brand is essential and is a key factor in the development of brand loyalty.

Factors which influence trust in a brand include several brand characteristics, company characteristics and consumer-brand characteristics. Therefore, retailers should take careful consideration of brand factors in the development of trust in a brand. To win brand loyalty in today's consumer markets, marketers, and retailers must focus on building and maintaining trust in the consumer-brand relationship (Theng & Lee, 1999). Building brand trust is very complex, because a brand is just a symbol and therefore can't be trusted. We can only trust humans and human-dependent things. But there is trust that after the consumer makes the commitment, he or she is going to get the benefits which they expect. For more details on brand trust read the following subchapter.

4.4.1 Brand trust

The term "brand trust" can be defines as follows (Delgado-Ballester, 2012): "a feeling of security held by the consumer in his/her interaction with the brand, that it is based on the perceptions that the brand is reliable and responsible for the interests and welfare of the consumer."

This definition is consistent with the relevant components of research on trust. Brand trust involves a willingness to put oneself at risk, for example, through reliance on the promise of value that the brand represents. It is also defined by feelings of confidence and security. What is more, brand trust involves a general expectancy because it can not exist without some possibility of being in error. So, it is related to positive or non-negative outcomes. And it makes dispositional attributions to a brand, like being reliable, dependable, etc.

Another important characteristic of brand trust which can be found in the literature are beliefs about fiability and intentionality. Fiability deals with the perception that a brand can fulfil or satisfy consumer needs. It is related to the individual's belief that the brand accomplishes its value promise. Intentionality reflects an emotional security on the part of individuals. It describes the aspect of a belief that goes beyond the available evidence to make individuals feel that the brand will be responsible and caring in future problematic situations and circumstances with the consumption of the product (Delgado-Ballester, 2012).

So, a trustworthy brand places the consumer at the centre of the world and relies more on understanding real consumer needs and fulfilling them than the service or product. It is not merely responsive, but responsible (Bainbridge, 1997).

A survey found that 81% of 16,000 respondents, spanning eight different countries, described brand trust as a deciding factor in their purchasing decisions. Brand trust is a complex mix of trusting the brand's leadership team, employees,

policies and more. Literature describes brand trust as consisting of three elements (Rice, 2020):
- Competence: consumers believe the people who own the brand and run the brand have the skills to do the job and can meet or exceed expectations
- Benevolence: means that when the brand's leaders and employees make decisions, they take customer interests into account in a "tangible and legitimate way"
- Integrity: means the brand and its employees make statements that "match with reality" and tell the truth and keep their promises

When customers perceive a brand as all three elements, that's the highest form of trust. Trust does not only encompass the brand itself but also, for example, the management team, the look and feel of the stores, the employees and customer service, the products, the marketing campaign, the packaging, or the unstated expectations a customer has when buying a product from the brand. What is more, brand trust is very subjective. It's a belief that a company is going to deliver the promises that the customers are expecting (Rice, 2020).

> **Volkswagen and the diesel scandal.**
> Volkswagen is an illustrative example of a brand in which many customers lost their trust, due to the diesel scandal in 2016. The iconic automaker, which had nearly overtaken Toyota as the world's largest automaker, is now struggling to win back the trust of the customers. The sales figures in 2016 and 2017 indicate that customers no longer have full trust in the Volkswagen brand. No amount of advertising or compensation to diesel owners has been able to stem the decline in sales (Jennings, 2016).
>
> It appears that Volkswagen is a severely damaged brand that might never totally recover from this scandal. Management is undertaking a strategy review to find a new direction for the company. Possible changes at Volkswagen include selling off assets or brands, shrinking the company and shifting its focus from fossil fuel to electric-powered vehicles. News reports indicate that Volkswagen plans to invest $11 billion (€9.79 billion) in a factory that will produces batteries for electric vehicles.
>
> Such initiatives will help salvage Volkswagen's reputation, but it will take years; or even decades, for the company to regain lost market share and customer trust. There are now millions of consumers that distrust Volkswagen; and refuse to believe anything the company tells them. Some formerly loyal customers will never buy a Volkswagen again (Jennings, 2016).
>
> Marketers can learn several important lessons about branding from Volkswagen. Important lessons about branding to be learned from Volkswagen and the diesel scandal include (Jennings, 2016):
>
> "Ethics are everything. The most successful brands, such as Apple, have a reputation for highly ethical behaviour. Volkswagen had such a reputation before the scandal and lost it. Sales figures reveal that many customers view VW as an unethical company and refuse to buy its vehicles.
>
> Customer trust is the basis of a successful brand. Volkswagen's biggest problem is that customers no longer trust it. They look at the false claims about the diesel emissions; and wonder if they can believe anything the company or its people tell them. Trust is vital to an automaker because customers entrust their lives to its' products; every time they get behind the wheel."

Volkswagen teaches us that a successful brand must be built upon ethical behaviour and trust. Unethical behaviour, and the distrust it breeds, can destroy even the biggest and richest brands. Every marketer should take note of the situation at Volkswagen and learn the high cost of unethical business practices. The cost of repairing the long-term damage done to the brand by unethical behaviour will always exceed the short-term profits (Jennings, 2016).

As already mentioned above brand loyalty brings a retailer many advantages. Various studies have shown that brand loyalty increases the number of customers and sales. In addition, brand loyalty is also lowering the cost to acquire new customers and brand loyal customers are less sensitive to prices and price increases. Therefore, marketers need to give special attention to increase and obtain brand loyalty.

What is more, brand loyalty is viewed as a multidimensional construct. It is determined by several key influencing factors, like brand trust, the customer's perceived value of the brand, customer satisfaction and repeat purchase behaviour, but also commitment to the brand. Commitment, in particular, and repeated purchases of the brand are necessary basic requirements for brand loyalty followed by the influencing factors perceived value, satisfaction, and brand trust.

Trust in general is especially important in times of crisis. Individuals need support and something they can rely on. Therefore, in times of crisis a company should act in a way that customers can rely on the company, its brands, and products.

Brand trust in times of crisis on the example of COVID-19

Trust is an extremely important factor, especially in times of crisis. In the search for credible information, for example, during the Corona Pandemic about COVID-19, the own employer is an extremely trustworthy source. This is shown by the global "Edelman Trust Barometer 2020 Special Report: Trust and the Coronavirus," a study was conducted in ten countries all over the world. The most important results from the survey are as follows (currycom, 2020):

Communication from one's own employer has a high level of credibility: 63% of those surveyed stated that they trust information from their employer about the coronavirus. In contrast, 35% of those surveyed stated that they do not believe information published exclusively in social media.

What is more, established media, like TV channels and traditional print media, are the most widely used source of information. TV stations and traditional print media are used almost twice as much as the online sites of global and national health organizations. Younger people rely on social media to almost the same extent: 54% versus 56% for traditional media. In contrast, people over 55 years of age trust classic news offerings three times more. Overall, 74% say they are concerned about the spread of fake news and false information.

The results of this study also show that scientists and physicians are the most trustworthy voices: 6% to 83% of those surveyed say that they trust scientists and physicians the most. Persons from the personal environment trust 63% of the respondents. Eighty-five percent of respondents said they want to hear more information from scientists.

Consequently, governments and businesses need to work together, but they are not expected to solve the situation on their own. Rather, almost half of those surveyed would like to see a joint approach by politics and business. Seventy-eight percent of those surveyed expect business to act to protect employees and the local community. Seventy-nine percent see it as the duty of employers to adapt their procedures, create regulations for working outside of office premises, cancel nonrelevant events and prohibit business trips. In addition, 73% expect that personnel policies will be adjusted to ensure, among other things, that paid sick leave is granted and that employees at risk do not come to work.

Finally, employees want to be informed: 57% of employees want clarity about how many colleagues have become infected with the virus and whether this circumstance affects the company's ability to work (53%). Employees also want to be informed about the wider impact on the company – including advice on travel and what can be done to stop the virus spreading. They want to receive the information by email or newsletter (48%), by posting it on the company's website (33%), and by telephone/video conferencing (23%).

To conclude, trust is especially important in times of crisis. And here communication from one's own employer has the highest level of credibility.

Influence of involvement on consumers buying decisions

Buying decisions from consumers depend on their level of involvement with the brand. Brand loyalty can stem from whether the consumer is highly or lowly involved with the brand. High involvement consumers interact intensively with brands that are important to them or which involve a high level of risk or are charged a higher price. Whereas a low involvement buying decision means that the brand intended to be purchased involves just a low level of risk and is normally not very expensive.

Low involvement products or brands are very often purchased automatically, like for example a toothpaste or the daily morning coffee. Low involvement consumers take on the habitual buying behaviour or variety seeking behaviour. Habitual buying behaviour occurs when the consumer doesn't see large differences between brands, therefore don't search for information but buy the brand on the basis of advertising or intense promotion. Consequently, the limited amount of information processing and lack of cognitive effort a consumer must bring up when deciding on a particular product or brand can mean that these consumers stick with a brand simply because it is comfortable and less work. So habitual buying behaviour can subconsciously result in brand loyalty. The consumer isn't actively aware that he or she buys repeatedly a product from a particular brand, it is just in their habitual nature to do so.

In contrast, low involvement consumers very often also take on a so-called variety seeking behaviour who are using variety seeking behaviour. In this case the customer does not see important differences between brands and therefore switch a lot between brands. With these customers showing a variety-seeking behaviour it is almost impossible to make them loyal customers.

High Involvement consumers interact intensively with products or brands, searching for product attributes and engaging in product related activities, such as searching for more information on a brands background. This engagement makes consumers knowledgeable of a brands attributes, they have the feeling that they know the brand very well and are likely to shape behavioural brand loyalty.

4.4.2 Brand loyalty programs

Brand loyalty programs are an important tool when it comes to giving the consumer a reason to undertake a repeat purchase. Loyalty programs help to reward, encourage customers, and increase the likelihood of repeat purchase and have the advantage that they collect useful information about the buying and spending habits of the consumer. A great number of activities, tools, and instruments are used by marketers in order to increase brand loyalty, most frequently used are one-to-one marketing, events, sponsoring, rewards programs or social media marketing (Keller, 2013). Brand loyalty works best when marketers address the most important values of customers. In order to address these values marketers, have to study consumer buying behaviour, shopping tendencies and spending habits in great detail.

It is important for marketers to know, that customers can be loyal to several brands within a particular product category. There might be some customers who are exclusively loyal to one brand, however, most customers are loyal to several brands and switch between these brands mostly due to availability or price reasons. Therefore, consumers should feel a connection with the brand, ideally on an emotional level.

An empirical study tried to investigate how reward schemes of a loyalty program influence perceived value of a brand loyalty program and how value perception of the loyalty program affects customer loyalty. The results show that involvement moderates the effects of loyalty programs on customer loyalty. In high-involvement situations, direct rewards (e.g., a discount) are preferable to indirect rewards. In low-involvement situations, immediate rewards are more effective in building a program's value than delayed rewards. Moreover, under high-involvement conditions, value perception of the loyalty program influences brand loyalty both directly and indirectly through program loyalty. Under low-involvement conditions, there is no direct effect of value perception on brand loyalty (Yi & Jeon, 2003).

Direct rewards are the most popular form of rewards that refer to direct benefits and include economic benefits that are preferred by consumers because they are clear, fair, and easy to understand and to use. Studies have shown that consumers tend to prefer direct rewards that are specifically linked to the supplier. For example, consumers who buy cat food are more likely to appreciate discounts on future purchases of cat food.

Indirect rewards are usually presented in the form of additional services and privileges, which include intangible rewards such as privileged access to websites or newsletters for loyalty program members only. For example, for buying a product from a particular brand you can a discount when buying movie tickets. In order to take advantage of this discount, the customer normally needs to perform a number of additional actions to activate the reward, and this can also negatively affect the satisfaction of this kind of loyalty program.

There are many different loyalty programs, but not every loyalty program is suitable for every company or brand. It is therefore important to consider carefully which loyalty program has the best fir with the brand and the target group. Loyalty programs can come in various options. Frequently used options are:
- free merchandise
- valuable points which can be collected and exchanged for rewards
- coupons which can be redeemed
- special free services
- early access to new products

The aim of all these loyalty program options stays the same. They should encourage a customer to become a regular buyer of the product or brand.

Studies have shown that customers are registered in an average of 29 loyalty programs (offline and online programs), but only actively participate in 12 of them. Companies lose time and money by investing in loyalty programs which are not used, and customers no longer have any benefits even though they are loyal. Therefore, it is very important for every marketer and retailer to make the loyalty programs attractive to be used by the customers. Experts recommend several actions for successful loyalty programs:
- Loyalty programs must be as easy as possible, for example, by using a simple point system. This option may seem boring and old-fashioned, but it is still the most used method for loyalty programs, and it is also the method that is preferred by customers, due to several reasons: it is fair, transparent, and easy to understand. Customers earn points by conducting a purchase which they can later exchange for rewards. This can be a discount, a free product, or a special free service. Customers work towards a certain number of points to receive their reward.
- Loyalty programs should include a level system to stimulate more purchases and keep customers happy. Finding the right balance between achievable and desirable rewards is a challenge. This is where most companies have problems. One way to combat this problem is to implement a level system that rewards loyalty right at the start and encourages further purchases, for example, by presenting small rewards right at the beginning for participation in the bonus program. Then customers are encouraged to make more purchases by increasing the value of the rewards. A necessary condition is that these rewards must be attractive for the target group. In this way, customers are constantly reminded of their points and encouraged to continue conducting purchases.
- Charging a processing fee for the bonus benefits can be advantageous under certain circumstances. A one-time fee when registering for a loyalty program or annual fee may be appropriate, when it comes to customers using the program more often or not exiting so quickly. Giving an example: the e-commerce giant Amazon "waives" shipping costs for "prime" customers. The "Prime" offer is paid for annually by the customer and in return brings him or her several advantages.

The offer, with free shipping and faster delivery, causes high costs for the company, but also leads to prime customers spending twice as much money as normal customers.

- Gamification elements should be included in a loyalty program. A bonus program can be turned into a game to encourage customers to come back because of the entertainment factor and strengthen the connection with the brand and can improve the image of the brand or the company. However, this type of bonus program should be used with caution, because often contests and raffles feel to the customer as if there are no real chances of winning. The chances of winning should not be too low and the effort to participate should not be too high.

4.4.2.1 Loyalty cards and customer clubs

Today most retailers offer loyalty cards or/and customer clubs. A *loyalty card* is a kind of identity card that a regular customer of a company gets to take advantage of offers of the company. Loyalty cards are available in many different forms. The most common is the plastic version, but it is often used in combination with an app. Some companies do without the card completely and offer only an app. In standard customer card systems, the card is equipped with a barcode or QR code to identify the customer (Sielhorst, 2009).

A *customer club* is an initiative launched by a company to provide customized services to its customers. A distinction is made between customers and club members, as only members can take advantage of these special benefits. Members must join the club independently and of their own free will (Schneck, 2015). Sometimes they also must pay an annual membership fee.

The most important aims of loyalty cards and customer clubs are (Wiencke, 1994):

- customer retention, especially with regular customers
- acquisition of new customers
- development or optimization of a customer database (database marketing)
- increase in sales or market share
- to improve the image of the brand or the company

Loyalty cards

Today nearly every customer possesses at least one loyalty card. Most customers prefer loyalty cards because they can save money, receive attractive rewards, and enjoy collecting points (TNS, 2015). Loyalty cards can be used flexibly in the program design. The financial benefit for customers using loyalty cards has the advantage of cross- and up-selling in the provider's view, which in turn increases sales. Moreover, the card is also an advertising medium for companies. The more the opportunity is given to use the card, the more attention is drawn to the program and the company or brand associated with it. The positive correlation between the use of the benefits and the company can improve the company's image and increase the emotional bond between the customer and the company or brand (Lauer, 2011).

Moreover, the costs of customer care can also be reduced in the short term by using loyalty cards. On the one hand, the customer data collected with the card increases the possibility of a target group-oriented communication strategy with a higher probability of success in addressing customers in the areas relevant to them. On the other hand, the customer care costs can also be achieved through cost-saving behaviour, usually with the help of the customers. Potential for such cost-saving behaviour lies, for example, in changing the ordering process (internet instead of telephone) or in changing the invoice transmission (from the usual invoice with paper and printing costs, such as mailing, to an electronic invoice by email). The change-over of the payment method (from bank transfer to direct debit) is also much easier for companies to process and has no significant disadvantages for customers. For a change of the customer behaviour often only a small additional motivation is necessary, by offering additional bonus points or other one-time benefits (Lauer, 2011).

Disadvantages of customer cards from the provider's perspective are minimal compared to the advantages. Some of the disadvantages are the costs for the card production and distribution and the development of the internal company infrastructure (integration into the software, POS system, etc.).

The use and function of a typical customer card normally starts with the purchase of product or brand. As a reward for the specific behaviour, the customer receives bonus points, which can act as either discount or status points. These bonus points are collected by the customer up to the defined redemption threshold and then exchanged for certain bonus services. Saved discount points can then be used for one-time discounts on products or services offered. Status points can be exchanged for the acquisition of a special customer status (e.g., VIP club membership). These status values and the associated benefits must be defined in advance. In general, if these benefits create a positive experience for the customer and meets the customer's wishes and requirements, the probability that the customer will become a loyal customer is very high.

Rewe group launches jö loyalty card.
The German Rewe group launched in 2019 the largest cross-industry customer loyalty program in Austria, the so-called jö loyalty card. With just one customer card or with the jö app, club members can collect bonus points – so-called "Ös" – every time they shop in the more than 3,000 stores of the jö partner companies, which can then be redeemed at will. In addition to Billa, Merkur, Penny, Bipa, Adeg and Billa Reisen, Libro, Pagro, Interio as well as OMV and Bawag P.S.K. have been won as partners for the program. Thus, the jö Bonus Club bundles the strengths of eleven companies from different industries with immediate effect, whereby the network is to be continuously expanded. What is more, each jö partner offers individual collection possibilities. So, club members can collect for example one "Ö" per euro conversion in the stores or for two litres of fuel, further points receive one for vacation reservations with Billa

journeys as well as for conclusions of a contract with the Bawag P.S.K. In addition, there are naturally numerous possibilities of getting additional Ös.

The following advantages are offered (product report, 2019):

- jö shopping bonus: collected eyelets are directly converted into discounts when you buy. For 100 Ös at the cash desk there is a discount of 1 Euro
- exclusive benefits and promotions: special promotions or individual advantage vouchers, which – adapted to the personal shopping behaviour – are sent by mail or post and can also be called up via the app, for example, "–25% on a certain product" or "–15% on the purchase for 100 Ös"
- jö discount collectors: collected Ös can be redeemed at selected partners (currently at Billa, Merkur and Bipa) also for a one-time purchase discount in the following month
- jö bonus world: members receive special discounts for leisure and cultural activities. The bonus world can be accessed via the app
- do good: it is also possible to donate the collected Ös to Caritas or the Red Cross for a good cause

Customer club

In general, the customer club as an instrument in a company's loyalty program can be systematically distinguished from other customer-oriented instruments. Customer clubs are based on a communication and dialog concept. It is of great importance that, on the one hand, external communication is used for the purpose of acquiring new customers and that, on the other hand, a dialog takes place between existing members and the company. In this way, club members are rewarded at regular intervals with various offers and benefits (Wirtz, 2012).

Before a company starts to design a customer club, some preliminary decisions must be made. First, it is necessary to define the target group and the objectives of the customer club. The target group can be divided, for example, according to customer types (new or regular customers) or according to sociodemographic data (income, education, hobbies, etc.). The success of the measures subsequently also depends on the accuracy of this segmentation (Wirtz, 2012). The breadth of the target group also depends on the club's goals. For example, a wide target group width makes sense in the case of a goal where the focus is on collecting customer-related data. In contrast, a narrower target group width is advantageous for goals that focus on key customers (Hinterhuber & Matzler, 2002).

The so-called A-customers should be defined as the largest target group of a customer club. These are responsible for most sales and accordingly the connection to these customers is essential for a company. It is important to mention that other customers or possible new customers should not be neglected and excluded from the club under any circumstances, but in this case, relationship management with other measures is necessary. Since the customer club as a customer loyalty instrument can offer a high degree of flexibility, changes in the character, or even habits of the customers do not pose a problem (Hinterhuber & Matzler, 2002).

After the objectives and the target group of a customer club have been defined, the type of entry requirement must be chosen. There are two options how the club can be designed: open or closed. With an open concept, admission is not bound to any prerequisites, so that participation is open to all interested parties. In a closed customer club, however, there are certain admission requirements, such as all financial contributions for membership. This allows a more precise reaching of the target group and guarantees a high number of loyal customers in the club. The disadvantage of closed concepts, however, is that it is more difficult to acquire new customers because of doubts about the value of the club from the customer's point of view (Hartmann, Kreutzer, & Kuhfuß, 2004).

Basically, it can be said that the right choice of services that can offer a particularly high value of benefit to members is one of the most important decisions in the design process from the company's perspective. To design an appropriate combination of monetary (hard) and nonmonetary (soft) club benefits, the selection process normally must go through three steps (Hinterhuber & Matzler, 2002):

The first step is to create a raw format of a club service list that includes services relevant to the selected target group. This list is to be compiled independently of financial feasibility or similar. In the next step, a filtering of the list must be used, in which customers can express their opinions on the potential services – for example, in the form of a focus group discussion. At this point, it is also possible to use the customer's own imagination, so that new ideas and considerations can be considered when determining actual services. Finally, the list of reduced potential club services, also recommended by customers, is subjected to a more extensive market study. The goal of the survey is to create a ranking list and thus to have a temporary collection of benefit-oriented club services. With this three-level model, services with the highest, lower and nonexistent benefit value can be distinguished from each other from the customer's point of view. At this point, the club services from the highest and lower utility value groups can be compared and evaluated with factors such as costs, feasibility, and capacities of the company. In the evaluation it is important to note that services with a high-cost factor but with a high benefit for the customer should not be excluded immediately. Furthermore, when designing a customer club, it is not only necessary to consider the initial phase, but also the entire life cycle of the club. For this reason, recurring "refresher measures" are necessary over time to keep the excitement of the service offering high (Hinterhuber & Matzler, 2002).

Regular impulses by variation of services with very high but also lower utility value are the key to successful customer retention and loyalty of the club members (Hartmann, Kreutzer, & Kuhfuß, 2004). In addition, it makes sense to focus primarily on product-related services within the club (Hinterhuber & Matzler, 2002), as this can counteract developments and changes in the markets in many ways. The role of product-related services has generally increased due to the strong competitive situation on the market. Constant technological change and ever shorter product life cycles are the reason for the necessity of differentiation of a company in the market. In addition, the complexity and versatility of products is increasing more and more and therefore the customer expects appropriate consulting, maintenance, installation, etc.

Club communication is one of the components that are fundamental to an attractive customer club. As already mentioned, the basis of a customer club is a communication and dialogue concept. From this follows the fact that communication channels must be available on the one hand between the club and the members and likewise in the other direction, and between the individual members (Hartmann, Kreutzer, & Kuhfuß, 2004). Possible channels for internal communication with club members include a club magazine, newsletter, various events with integrated product presentations, club website, club app, customer hotline, etc. (Hinterhuber & Matzler, 2002).

On the one hand, regular contact and information transfer about current and future offers, basic and additional services of products is of great importance (Wirtz, 2012). On the other hand, the demand for content of general interest from the customers' point of view is also high (Hinterhuber & Matzler, 2002). The specialization of content to meet the needs of the target group should be a priority in club communication tools, such as club magazines (Wirtz, 2012).

In addition to the customers' emotional attachment and sense of belonging, monetary motives and advantages within the customer club are also relevant for success. For example, the integration of a loyalty program is a possible option. This is based on the granting of bonuses or discounts dependent on sales and/or purchase frequency. Thus, an incentive to buy or repurchase is created for the customer, as this type of reward acts on the extrinsic (externally influenced) motivation (Hartmann, Kreutzer, & Kuhfuß, 2004). Various nonproduct-related services, which are offered in addition to the core service of the products, can enhance the entire service spectrum of the club.

Collaboration with external cooperation partners helps to increase the diversity of the club's service offering, as the service program can be guaranteed to be consistently attractive from the customer's perspective. With the help of a cooperation, the range of services can be supplemented by additional nonproduct-related club services. In this way, the club-operating company can differentiate itself more effectively from the competition in the market. A cooperation can also offer advantages for the cooperation partner if the target group of the customer club is similar to the target group of the cooperating company. This gives the cooperation partner the opportunity to address the club's target group with their own products. Therefore, it is particularly important that the communication of the club members with the external partner is exclusively done through the club (Kotler & Armstrong, 2006).

One of the most successful reward programs in Europe is the Miles & More frequent flyer program. It is a combination of a customer club and a loyalty program in collaboration with external cooperation partners. For more details see the box below.

Miles & More frequent flyer and reward program

With more than 30 million participants, Miles & More is the largest frequent flyer and reward program in Europe. The Miles & More program was launched on January 1, 1993 with seven program partners and since September 2014 Miles & More GmbH has been operating as an independent company. As a wholly owned subsidiary of Deutsche Lufthansa AG, the company is based in Frankfurt am Main. Miles & More participants can earn and redeem miles with more than 300 partners. These include 40 airline partners, including the 28 Star Alliance airlines and around 270 nonaviation companies from the hotel, car rental, cruise, subscription and book, banking and insurance, telecommunications and electronics, shopping, and lifestyle sectors (Miles & More, 2020).

According to the operator, the average age of the participants is 46 years. 60% of the users are male, 40% female. In 2010, the participants collected a total of 198 billion miles. At the end of 2012, Lufthansa customers had 205 billion bonus miles. The company recorded their value internally at EUR 1.66 billion (deferred income). Around 20% to 30% of the miles are not used. The unit of account of the program is "miles." These are divided into Status Miles and Award Miles. Miles is personal. They are not transferable to other participants. Award miles expire after 36 months, unless the holder has a status, a (chargeable) Lufthansa credit card Gold or a (chargeable) Austrian Airlines Miles and More credit card Gold or Platinum or is under 18 years old and holds a Jetfriends card. From 1,500 miles for credit card transactions, holders of the Miles & More Credit Card Blue also have unlimited milestone validity (wikipedia, 2020).

Status miles are used to determine frequent flyer status. These can only be earned with purchased and departed flight tickets from Lufthansa, Swiss, Austrian, Germanwings and other Star Alliance partners. They expire at the end of a calendar year. The "HON Circle" miles are a special type of status miles. For these, the collection options are more restrictive than for normal status miles. If a customer collects 600,000 HON miles in two years, he or she will receive HON status as Lufthansa's highest frequent flyer status. As of September 1, 2012, these HON Miles can only be earned in Business and First Class. Select Miles are another form of Status Miles. The amount of accrued Select Miles is the same as that of accrued Status Miles, except that only flights operated by LH Group, Air Dolomiti, Croatia Airlines, LOT Polish Airlines and Luxair are considered. Depending on the frequent flyer status of the customer, there are rewards, such as WorldShop vouchers, lounge vouchers, Upgrade eVouchers or partner cards (possibility of awarding a status to a third party) as soon as certain thresholds are reached. Frequent Travellers reach the first Select award at 50,000 Select miles, Senators at 125,000 Select miles, and the first award for HON Circle members can be redeemed from 650,000 HON Circle miles. Award miles can be redeemed for flight and material awards. In addition to flights, miles can also be collected and redeemed at hotels, car rental companies, travel value and duty-free stores or Lufthansa's own WorldShop (a total of over 270 cooperation partners worldwide, as of 2017). They generally expire after three years at the end of the quarter. Award miles from status customers (Frequent Traveller, Senator, HON) or owners of a Lufthansa Miles & More Gold credit card do not expire. Owners of a Lufthansa Miles & More Credit Card Blue protect themselves against the expiry of award miles from a turnover of 3000 euros per year (wikipedia, 2020; Miles & More, 2020).

Miles are earned primarily through flights with Star Alliance airlines, but also through credit card sales. Other sources include bonuses for special customers, telephone services, bonuses for special flights, hotel bookings, purchases, and car rentals. The amount of mileage credit for flights depends very much on the booking class. For example, more miles are generally credited in higher classes than in lower ones. A distinction is also made between individual fares. The calculation is based on fixed mileage values without reference to the actual distance travelled.

For flights with partner airlines, sometimes – depending on the booking class – no miles are credited at all. The rule of crediting based on a factor multiplied by the distance flown has been in use since the introduction of the Frequent Flyer Program but changed on March 12, 2018. All flights booked on tickets issued by the Lufthansa Group from this date onwards will then be remunerated based on the ticket price and thus in direct relation to the costs and no longer based on the distance flown. However, the exact calculation of miles differs between Lufthansa Group airlines and partner airlines and depends on the status in the program. Members without status receive four times the ticket price (fare and international surcharge YQ). Status customers receive credit for four times the ticket price.

Redeem miles

The award miles can be used to book seat class upgrades (Economy → Premium Economy → Business → First Class) or award flights. Originally, these were the only possible uses. Economy guests can upgrade to both Premium Economy Class and Business Class. Otherwise, upgrades can only be made to the next higher class of service, that is, from Premium Economy to Business and from the latter class to First Class. Since the beginning of 2017, "Cash & Miles" for the first time gives participants in Germany the opportunity to use miles flexibly for their flight, thus reducing the amount of money they must pay. Since May 2008, it has also been possible to redeem for airport taxes and fees on intra-European flights, miles can also be donated, but these donations can not be directed to climate compensation projects and in the meantime can only be made to a Lufthansa-owned aid organization (wikipedia, 2020).

Another example of a an up-to-date customer club and loyalty program is "myMcDonalds" from the American fast food chain McDonald's. Please read the following box for more details.

McDonald's customer club – An example of a popular and modern customer club

The free customer club of McDonald's also called "myMcDonald's," is based on a point system whereby with each purchase points, so-called Ms, are credited to the account these points can then be exchanged for products. How many Ms the customer gets varies from product to product. This Bonus Club is accessible via the McDonalds app or a physical plastic card that can be obtained in a McDonald's store. To collect points the customer must scan the QR code on the map or on the start page of the app before making a purchase. Not every product is available when exchanging Ms points. From a list the customer can select products with a value of about 15 Ms to 30 Ms. In addition, there are always promotions where collected Ms can be exchanged for items that are not part of the traditional McDonald's assortment. At the beginning of March 2017, Bonus Club members could purchase a Playstation 4 for 150€ when they exchanged 350 Ms. This promotion was limited to 1,000 pieces and ran if stocks last.

Furthermore, there are coupons, independent of the point system, through which one could get certain menus or product combinations at a reduced price. These can be obtained in printed form at the cash desk or from various newspapers or, since 2016, can also be selected digitally via the customer club on the self-service panel, or from McDonald's also known as a kiosk. The Ms expires after 12 months and at the end of each quarter.

Advantages

A big advantage is that the system is mostly handled online, only the creation phase is more complex and then only the premiums and vouchers must be renewed again and again. The system therefore requires very little maintenance. Another advantage of this system is that it can attract customers very well because you don't have to spend money conditionally but can get complete meals for the points through the rewards. Of course, these must be earned first and then replenished.

In most restaurants, the order is placed mainly at the kiosk, so the club members can see the vouchers and rewards directly and therefore no additional information from McDonald's is necessary.

However, if McDonald's does want to send information to its customers, it has easy access to the email addresses of the customers through the customer club or can send notifications to the customers' cell phones via the myMcDonald's app. With the Mc Donald's App, the members will get exclusive deals, earn so-called McCafé drinks with McCafé Rewards and order ahead with Mobile Order & Pay (more information under https://www.mcdonalds.com/us/en-us/mobile-order-and-pay.html).

Disadvantages
If the customer uses the physical card to access the Customer Club and loses it, all the Ms which have already been collected are lost, unless the card is registered before. However, only the points of the first order are transferred from the new card and the old card is blocked.

4.4.2.2 Mobile online loyalty programs
In recent years, there has been a move away from traditional magnetic or plastic card, cards in the form of specially coded credit/debit cards or any other cards which are scanned at the checkout to ensure the customer's membership to online and mobile online loyalty programs. While these programs vary, the common element is a push towards eradication of a traditional card, in favour of an electronic version. Retailers have learned that most of a company's sales come from a minority of their customers. This small but important group of customers need to be retained, which can be done through loyalty programs. Technology has changed commerce and consumer habits, both having a profound effect on loyalty programs.

The main aim of a mobile online loyalty program is to retain existing customers and acquire new customers by convincing them to choose the specific retailer, brand, or product in the future. Comprehensive loyalty programs use direct marketing to foster communication by making use of targeted and effective customer addressing, as well as by increasing the contact frequency (Tomczak, Reinecke & Dittrich, 2010).

Mobile online loyalty cards can be an appropriate instrument to especially encourage the loyalty of the younger generation, Gen Y (1980 to 1994) and Gen Z consumers (1995 to 2010), mainly for two reasons. First, such loyalty programs give customers the feeling of being part of a particular group, which is an important need and desire for members of these age groups. Second, Gen Y and Z consumers want to be treated differently and more individually than others. Loyalty programs it is possible to meet these demands and needs which can have a positive impact on these generations' loyalty.

Nowadays, different apps such as "mobile-pocket" (https://www.mobile-pocket.com/de/) allow customers to additionally upload and store their various loyalty programs on their smartphones and call them up whenever they need them.

Retailers benefit from loyalty programs in many ways. It allows them to gain insights into their customers' shopping and purchasing behaviour and provides the retailer with valuable data, for example the customer's name, gender, address, household size, date, time and frequency of shopping visits, payment preferences, content and value of the shopping baskets, shopping preferences and patterns, any many more. The data gathered is used to segment shoppers and to establish target group-oriented marketing strategies, such as personalized newsletters, coupons, rewards, to address them appropriately (Kubu, 2016).

Location-based mobile marketing and bluetooth low energy beacons

Location-based services are services which send selective content to the customer's mobile device dependent on his/her current position in a store, in the streets or in a shopping centre. If mobile phones exist, companies have been able to collect various position data of mobile devices to establish movement profiles. The introduction of smartphones with its integrated GPS, Bluetooth-function, as well as Wi-Fi positioning system, allows a more detailed approach to directly address customers. By identifying the exact location of smartphone users, marketers can send them individual content which might influence their shopping behaviour and give them a reason to enter a particular store (Kubu, 2016).

Bluetooth low energy beacons (BLEBs) are senders, which are based on the energy efficient version of Bluetooth, the so-called Bluetooth low energy. Bluetooth is a radio standard technology, which allows users a cable-free connection for devices that are close to each other. What is more, BLEBs are small transmitters that are usually run by a battery and have a reach up to a few dozen meters although massive walls, different types of metal and liquids can reduce the reach to only a few meters. Additionally, the signals from other BLEBs or Wi-Fi can have a negative influence on the transmission as well. The main aim is that BLEBs send unique identification numbers which are received by smartphones with an activated Bluetooth function and required app installed. The app then reads the identification number and activates the specific function. Since each BLEB sends its own specific identification number, the distribution of more than one BLEB in a store enables instore navigation under circumstances where other technologies like GPS do not work. So, BLEBs can be used for different target group-oriented marketing activities, like various information and offers, and influence a customer's shopping behaviour. Consequently, retailers can contact the potential customer outside the store by sending him/her coupons, special offers or an invitation for a competition. Providing a personalized shopping experience is important to attract customers and opens new opportunities for brick-and-mortar stores (Kubu, 2016).

Customer club App

As already mentioned in the sub chapters above, the basis of a customer club concept is the targeted, personal, and individual approach to members to strengthen the relationship with the club, the brand, and the retailer, and create customer loyalty. In today's world, digital communication with customers has become very important.

With the introduction of host card emulation (HCE) and near field communication (NFC) technology for mobile applications, traditional contactless smart cards for loyalty programs are emulated in a smartphone. Google Wallet, for example, adopted these technologies for mobile off-line payment application. The major advantage of off-line over the on-line system is that the user's smartphone does not have to be online, and the transaction is very fast. In addition, multiple emulated cards can be stored in a smartphone to support multimerchant loyalty programs. Consequently, the user does not need to carry many physical cards anymore.

Here, the convenience of use is a major advantage over ordinary physical customer cards. As a customer, you usually have your smartphone with you, and you do not have to look for the right customer card when paying at the cash desk. For this purpose, easy operation of the app is essential, which can be ensured, for example, by using a QR code as an identifying feature of the mobile club card. In addition, the app can be used to manage and use mobile coupons, which can be stored and called up at any time or up to the validity date and redeemed directly via the smartphone. It is also possible to personalize coupons by giving members only coupons and various exclusive offers that are relevant to them personally. In addition, various location-based services can be integrated, such as the display of the location of the nearest branch in the user's vicinity (Bauer, Dirks, & Bryant, 2008).

AI and machine learning-powered loyalty programs

AI and machine learning has the potential to fundamentally revolutionize loyalty programs because loyalty is linked to customer experience and AI is becoming impressively accurate in predicting human behaviour and purchase patterns.

Historically, customer data collected through loyalty programs have been used to target customers with relevant messages. However, with the help of AI and machine learning brands can take these functions to predict customer behaviour and influence purchase patterns. For example, would it be possible to get real-time information of every customer who walks into a store along with insights on what they are most likely to purchase. Advanced AI algorithms can predict human actions long before the customer becomes aware of what he or she is going to buy.

Moreover, AI-powered insights provide the possibility to instantly give a retailer a segment of customers who are more likely to spend more once they move into the next level of the retailer's loyalty program. Prescriptive analytics can be applied to a wide range of retail scenarios to reduce churn, increase conversion rates, and improve overall customer experience. Over the years, retailers have faced a major dilemma when it comes to loyalty programs, how to increase revenues without negatively impacting the customer experience. AI and machine learning can help retailers with intelligent insights that can increase the overall sales and conversion rate while ensuring an attractive customer experience.

Blockchain loyalty program

Some companies, like Singapore Airlines, Rakuten, etc., have already started to launch blockchain-based loyalty programs to encourage customer engagement. Integrating a loyalty program into a blockchain essentially involves setting up an integrated open system. Blockchain-based loyalty programs allows brands to offer rewards across multiple products and services, thereby giving customers virtually unlimited options for reward redemption. Brands can easily track rewards across several engagement parameters like content consumption, beacons, or IoT product use.

Brands have often struggled with expanding their loyalty programs across affiliates and partners as it involves expensive system integrations. A blockchain loyalty program can significantly reduce development, integration, and security costs.

It also must be said that most enterprise blockchains are still in a "Proof-of-Concept" stages and are focused on generating more press releases than actual deployments. Brands will have to incur significant marketing spend in educating customers on how to use blockchain. Blockchain loyalty programs allow only limited access to personally identifiable information (PII) data due to limits on how much PII can be put on a shared network (Hamida, Brousmiche, Levard, & Thea, 2017).

In 2018 the SIA Group's KrisFlyer frequent-flyer programme launched KrisPay, a miles-based digital wallet which enables members to convert KrisFlyer miles into KrisPay miles instantly for everyday spending at partner merchants island-wide. This platform allows members to choose from using as little as 15 KrisPay miles (equivalent to about S$0.10) to pay for their purchases at partner merchants, either partially or in full.

KrisPay miles are accepted at more than 18 merchants spanning different categories of beauty services, food and beverage, petrol, and retail. More merchants will be added to the platform, in addition in-app promotions and more app features are provided to keep customers engaged with the brand.

KrisPay is available for download on the Apple and Google Play Store. Once it has been downloaded, members can easily turn their KrisFlyer miles into KrisPay miles using the app's instant top-up function. Once transferred, KrisPay miles have a validity of six months. To pay for purchases, members simply need to scan the KrisPay QR code at the merchant, and key in the amount they wish to pay with their KrisPay miles. More information under https://www.singapor eair.com/en_UK/es/ppsclub-krisflyer/use-miles/krispay.

4.4.2.3 Ethical reward programs

Ethical reward programs become more and more popular with brands and their customers because customers want to contribute to the common good. An ethical reward program is totally different from the others described above because the customer doesn't receive any direct compensation for his or her loyalty. An ethical reward program can be described as with every purchase made of a particular product or brand the company pledges to complete a charitable or ethical action.

This type of reward program does not won't work for every brand, but it's a great option for brands or retailers that have a strong focus on ethical issues. Studies have shown that nearly two-thirds of customers are willing to spend more money on a product or brand when they stand for an issue they care about. Many customers are also more motivated to buy a particular product to help others and "do something good" because than they feel that they have done something good to someone else which in turn legitimizes the purchase decision.

Austria's innovative social drink Sternderl.
The social drink Sternderl, refreshing with organic herbal syrup from Lower Austria, is not only a tasty drink but also helpful. The net proceeds of each drink sold benefit the Sterntalerhof children's hospice and its network partners. The Sterntalerhof in Austria gives children a today, whose tomorrow is written in the stars. In a protected and natural atmosphere, families with seriously, chronically, and terminally ill children are carefully accompanied on their way back into everyday life. Management is concerned about social cohesion in society, healthy nutrition for themselves and their families and a clean environment for all our children. Together with a branding agency they developed the social drink Stenderl. More information unter https://www.sternderl.org/.

The Raiffeisen tree – A climate protection program
For the Raiffeisenbank acting sustainably and taking responsibility in many areas means thinking about tomorrow today, so that future generations will also find an environment worth living in. To this end, the institute already offers not only innovative products and services for corporate and private customers, from sustainable investment instruments to the financing of climate-protection-relevant projects and professional advice on subsidies to active support in their implementation as a competent partner. The range extends from private homes to production plants, where ecological innovations and energy savings can make a significant contribution to CO_2 reduction and at the same time represent interesting economic investments.

The "Raiffeisen tree" is a further step towards living climate protection, which also creates habitats for animals and plants. For each newly opened account, the Raiffeisenbank provides a small tree, made of traditional old domestic varieties, which is planted in a guaranteed sustainably managed forest or corresponding open spaces – in cooperation with communities, farmers and foresters, has a positive influence on the local and global climate and "grows with it" throughout its life.

When retailers decide to use an ethical reward system, they must make sure that it is really appropriate for the customer base and their opinions and views. Giving an example, a bottled water companies (plastic bottles) pledge to donate money to water-well construction projects in developing countries. But in fact, due to the rise in concern over single-use plastic and the detrimental effect it has on the environment, the kind of customers who would feel motivated to support these pledges are no longer buying drinking water in plastic bottles.

4.4.2.4 Additional examples and outlook

To summarize, reward programs show customers that the retailers appreciate their loyalty, and it can boost customer retention rates by offering perks for repeat shoppers. When looking for ways to engage customers, grow the customer base and increase retention rates, especially as a new business, reward programs can provide many advantages. In the box below, you will find a few selected examples of successful reward programs.

Examples of successful reward programs
Adidas's Creators Club
With the launch of the new VIP rewards program, adidas' Creators Club intends to personalize the customer experience and creates a place where creators get rewarded. Customers can move through four different branded tiers: Challenger, Playmaker, Gamechanger, and Icon to unlock different experiential rewards. In the first tier, customers are given their unique creator ID which gives them the ability to integrate all of adidas' apps with their personal information. As customers earn more points and move through the levels, they unlock a slew of innovative exclusive rewards. As a Playmaker, customers gain access to member-specific products created with or for them.

In the higher tiers, Gamechangers and Icons can get free personalization on products and can even earn personalized training apps or nutrition plans. The main aim of the brand is to understand its customers and what matters most to them through their highly-personalized program (Donati, 2019).

Marriott Bonvoy
In 2019 Marriott International consolidated its three loyalty brands- Marriott Rewards, The Ritz-Carlton Rewards, and Starwood Preferred Guest (SPG) – into one ultimate travel program: the so-called Marriott Bonvoy. Customers can earn points at over 30 different brands and redeem them for an even larger variety of wins, such as free hotel rooms, flights, travel packages, gift cards, or exclusive events.

Marriott Bonvoy has even branded itself as being synonymous with "good travel." In an industry that relies on recommendations and reviews, Marriott Bonvoy makes it easy for their customers to connect with one another through their online brand community. In detail, Marriott Insiders is a forum for customers to connect with people across the world to ask questions, share travel tips, and talk about their experiences to inspire others.

With some of the most luxurious travel brands involved, Marriott Bonvoy has strategically created an exclusive rewards program to maintain their brand image. First, they offer a VIP program based on the number of stays, giving their customers a chance to work up towards Ambassador Elite status. In addition, they have created exclusivity through their so-called *Bonvoy Moments*. Here the customers can browse all sorts of experiential rewards from sporting events to cultural experiences and bid on them with their points. This innovative approach maintains the brand's exclusivity while giving customers the chance to decide how valuable specific rewards are to them.

Finally, brand loyalty is part of the final step of the so-called customer-based brand equity model (see Figure 4.6). This stage is one of the most important ones, as it has valuable impact on future activities of the company. It must be mentioned that all other stages of this brand equity model can enhance brand loyalty, like, for example, associations towards a brand, awareness, or perceived quality of a brand. To give an example, a customer can be loyal to a low-quality brand and dislike a high-quality brand due to individual reasons or become loyal due to increased awareness because of positive word of mouth. For more information, please see the following Chapter 4.5 on "brand equity and brand value."

4.5 Brand equity and brand value

Brand equity has grown in importance over the past years since branding in general has become more popular during the 20th century mainly due to saturated market situations in many European countries. Competing products have very often attributed which are very similar and where intangibles are important for differentiation and for guiding customers to make a decision. Therefore, the concept of building *brand equity* is based on the idea of differentiating products and brands from competitors' brands by means of distinctive brand associations, unique logos, brand names and packaging design to establish points of difference (Aaker, 1996). Strong brand equity allows retailers to introduce premium pricing and consequently to have higher profit margins. Moreover, it facilitates the process of brand extensions, a method of launching a new product by using an existing brand name on a new product in a different product category, if consumers are already familiar with a specific brand (Aaker, 2001).

Aaker (1996) defines brand equity as "a set of brand assets and liabilities linked to a brand, its name and symbol that add to or subtract from the value provided by a product or service to a firm and/or to that firm's customers." He provides the most comprehensive brand equity model which consists of five different assets that are the source of the value creation. Figure 4.6 shows Aaker's (1996) Customer-Based Brand Equity Framework. In this figure we see that brand equity consists of the following components:

- brand loyalty
- brand awareness
- perceived brand quality
- brand associations in addition to perceived quality
- brand assets

Customer-based brand equity occurs when the customer has a high level of awareness and familiarity with the brand and holds some strong and favourable brand associations in memory. Therefore, manufacturers and retailers need to strengthen

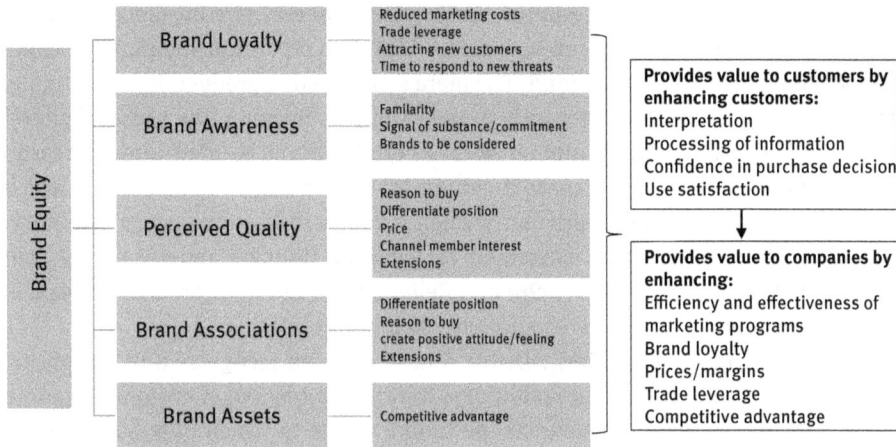

Figure 4.6: Customer-Based Brand Equity Framework.
Source: Aaker's (1996)

brand awareness first before building brand equity. In addition, they need to develop a strong and favourable brand image by establishing unique brand associations to be competitive (Keller, 2013).

Brand loyalty

The first major component of customer-based brand equity according to Aaker (1996) is brand loyalty. Brand loyalty was already described in detail in Chapter 4.4. Brand loyalty generates value mainly by reducing marketing costs because retaining existing customers is less costly than gaining new ones. Moreover, competitors normally find it very difficult to communicate to satisfied and loyal brand users and get customers excited about their brand, also if there exist low switching costs, because loyal customers have little motivation to learn about alternatives and switch to a competitor.

Brand awareness

Brand awareness is the second essential element of brand equity. Brand awareness can be defined as "the strength of a brand's presence in the consumer's mind" and "the ability of a potential buyer to recognize or recall that a brand is a member of a certain product category" (Aaker, 1996). Brand awareness plays an important role regarding brand positioning and building a competitive brand image. The main goal for marketers is that consumers consider their brands when making a purchasing decision, which means that a company wants its brands to be in the consumer's consideration set (Aaker, 2001). Brand awareness is the degree to which consumers can recognize and allocate certain brands under different circumstances. The degree of familiarity of a brand can be increased through repetition and multiple exposures to the product and the brand. The more elements of a product, like packaging, the name, or the logo, are constantly exposed to the consumer, the higher the level of brand awareness. Being familiar with a certain brand is often already reason enough for customers to purchase a certain brand instead of other brands, which they are not familiar with, particularly when it comes to low-involvement products (i.e., a common product that consumers buy without thinking about it much) (Keller, 2013). According to Aaker (1996) and Keller (2013), brand awareness consists of two different elements: brand recognition and brand recall.

Brand recognition defines whether a customer can recognize a brand among other products under different conditions. In other words, when customers go to a store, will they be able to recognize the brand as one to which they have already been exposed (Keller, 2013)? It is the lowest level of brand awareness and can be measured for instance by an aided recall test, where consumers receive a list of brand names and must specify, which brand they are familiar with.

Brand recall describes the degree to which customers can retrieve the brand from memory when given the product category, the needs fulfilled by the category, or a purchase or usage situation as a cue (Keller, 2013). For example, when they think of eating chocolate and they go to the store and buy their favourite brand, for example, Milka chocolate.

Perceived brand quality

Perceived brand quality is the consumer's judgment about a product's or brand's overall excellence or superiority. Perceived quality provides value by providing a reason to buy, differentiating the brand from competitors', attracting channel member interest, being the basis for line extensions, and being the reason for charging a higher price (Aaker, 1996).

Brand associations

Brand associations or brand image (also known as brand perception) is the most accepted component of brand equity. Brand associations can be anything what is linked in a customer's mind to a particular brand. Brand associations can include several information: from product attributes to customer benefits, users, lifestyles, product classes, competitors, etc. Brand associations help customers to retrieve information in memory and helps them to make purchase decisions. Brand associations can be the fundament for differentiation from competitive brands or a basis for brand extensions. These information in the customer's mind can be a reason to buy a certain brand and create positive feelings and emotions (Aaker, 1996).

Brand assets

Brand assets refer to patents, trademarks and distribution or distribution channels which can provide a strong competitive advantage for the company. For instance, a trademark protects a brand in general and brand equity from competitors who want to influence customers by using a similar name, colour, symbol, or packaging. A patent can prevent direct competition if strong and relevant to the purchase decision process. A distribution channel can be indirectly controlled by a brand as customers expect the brand to be available (Aaker, 2001).

To summarize, marketers nowadays face two fundamental questions: What do different brands mean to customers? How does the consumers' brand knowledge affect their response to marketing activities? Therefore, the challenge for marketers when it comes to building a strong brand is ensuring that customers have the right experiences with the branded product and their marketing activities so that the desired images, perceptions, beliefs, and emotions become linked to the brand (Ramanjaneyalu & Vishwanath, 2013).

The intangible benefits of brand equity – A comparison study on Coca Cola and Pepsi
When consumers report different opinions about branded and unbranded versions of identical products it must be the case that knowledge about the brand, created by various means, from past experiences, marketing activities to word of mouth, has somehow changed customers' product perceptions (Keller, 2013).

The easiest way to find out what brand equity means for a brand is to analyse the results of product sampling and comparison tests, especially a blind taste test. A soft drink tasting experiment with the two competitive brands Coca Cola and Pepsi showed whether one of these brands is superior or is it the consumers perceptions of a brand that one product is favoured. The results were as follows: In a blind taste test, consumers favoured Pepsi when compared with Coca Cola, but during an open test, in which the respondents know which brand they are consuming, people changed their mind and most of them had a preference for Coca Cola and liked the taste better. So, we see from this experiment that product features and product quality is not enough to be the preferred product or brand. It is important to create the right brand image and positioning of a product in the customers' minds (Ramanjaneyalu, G., & Vishwanath, 2013). This result shows that their do exists conclusive evidence that consumers' perceptions of product performance are highly dependent on their impressions of the brand that goes along with it (Keller, 2013).

5 Branding decisions

Branding consists of a set of complex branding decisions. Figure 5.1 provides an overview of the most important branding decisions which will also be discussed in the following subchapters. These four major branding decisions involve brand sponsorship, brand name selection, brand strategy decisions and brand repositioning.

Brand-Sponsor Decision: deals with the questions who should sponsor of the brand. A brand can be sponsored by the manufacturer or by the producer (also called manufacturer's brand or national or international brand) such as Apple, Microsoft, Kellogg's, etc. The distributor or retailer could also use its own brand, a so-called private label or private brand, which is very common in the grocery sector.

Brand-Name Decision: another key decision when bringing a new product to a market is the brand name selection. In general, there are two approaches to brand name selection. The first option is to have a brand name that is somehow reflective of the benefits and features of the product (e.g., Toys "R" Us). The second option would be to create an unusual, unique brand name, with the intention of building brand awareness and brand equity over time (e.g., Apple, Google, etc.).

Brand-Strategy Decision/Brand Development: deals with the question what branding strategies should be used by a company. The company must decide whether it should be new brand, a brand extension, or a line extension (introduction of additional items in the same product category under the same brand name) to provide the consumers more variety. The decision for a brand extension comes normally from the manufacturers' side to leverage the existing brand equity. Multibrands, which stands for the approach of a company to market several competitive brands of the same company under different brand names to be more competitive and increase the market share.

Brand-Repositioning: Research has shown that each brand must have a distinctive and target-group oriented positioning. Without an appropriate positioning, accompanied by an appealing communication strategy in line with the brand's identity, a brand will be "stuck in the middle" and will not be successful in the long run. Brand-Repositioning must be done, for example, in the case a competitor may launch a new brand close to the one carried by a particular company. Or a brand may need a repositioning when it is not effective anymore, to increase market share or attract a new target group.

5.1 Brand-sponsor decision

Brand-sponsor decisions deal with the questions how a brand should be structured. There are various options in structuring an overall brand. Firstly, a brand could be structured as a *manufacturer brand* (national or international brand) which is the

https://doi.org/10.1515/9783110543827-007

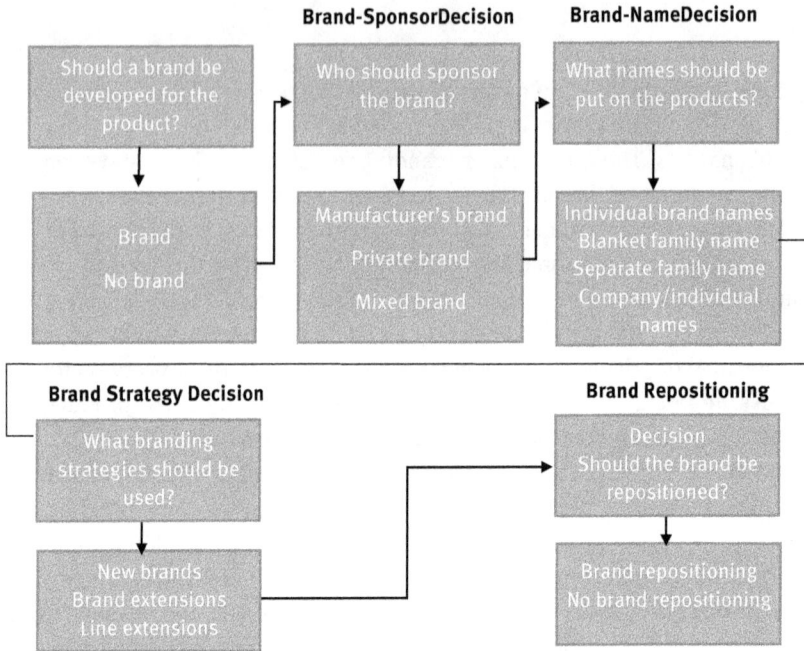

Figure 5.1: Branding decisions – An overview.
Source: drawpack, 2011

most common form, especially in the apparel and grocery sector. It is simply a brand that is owned by the manufacturer, such as Coca Cola, Nike, Volkswagen, Kellogg's, etc.

Secondly, a retailer could have products branded under his own name (or a generic name relative to them). This is called a *private brand* (or private label brand). Private brand means that this product or brand is only available in the stores of this retailer: Retailers, especially in the grocery sector, like to have products branded under their own name as this gives them a unique selling proposition for these products that can only be purchased at these stores. Moreover, private labels offer retailers control over product factors such as price, size, ingredients, package design, production, and distribution. Logos and taglines can be customised to the customers shopping experience. So, retailers have more control on decisions of these products. Moreover, category gaps that haven't been filled by manufacturers' brands can be done.

Another option how a brand can be structured is *brand licensing*. Brand licensing refers to using an existing brand on for a new product for a fee. For example, the funny animal cartoon character Mickey Mouse, created in 1928 by Walt Disney, was already licensed to many children's products throughout the world. In this case, a company would pay a license fee to Walt Disney's and then use their name, logo and cartoon character on products they sell. To the final consumer the product then appears to be a Walt Disney's brand. This means that the company gets the benefit of the brand's equity, without needing to build a new brand.

Co-branding is another brand-sponsor decision. Co-branding is when two brand names, that are unrelated and normally having different ownership, place their brands together on the same product. For example, McDonald's offers a soft ice-cream called McFlurry. This consists of creamy whipped soft vanilla ice cream and a flavouring additive (so-called topping) from another brand, like KitKat, Oreo cookies, Smarties, M&M's, Bounty, Mars, and many other toppings.

The final decision is whether a retailer wants to use an existing brand or wants to create a new brand. Here it must mentioned that creating a new brand is not only very expensive but also needs a lot of effort until a new brand is established. The advantage is that in the long run a new brand may create a significant asset for the company. Normally, many new products tend to be product line extensions and not new brands. However, when there is a significant new product being brought to market, there is often an incentive to create and build a new brand.

5.2 Brand-name decision

To start with, brand names have an impact in the marketplace, this is especially true for young brands when their brand equity is not high. The brand name helps to communicate what the brand stands for and may also communicate the main benefits or the most important features. For example, the brand name "Kentucky Fried Chicken" gives the consumer an idea about the features or benefit of the products offered- namely American fried chicken. Or the brand name "Vitamin water" tells the consumer that this drinking water contains vitamins. So even without knowing these brands or understanding these brands, the consumer could have a guess about what the brand is all about. Having a brand name that is reflective of the benefits of the product is an effective approach as it gives potential consumers the opportunity to gain some form of understanding of the product and its positioning in a particular market relatively quickly, from making an inference about the brand name.

In contrast, there are brand names that are not particularly tied to a product or to the original ownership of the brand, for example the brand "Apple." Apple is just a name and does not help communicate anything about what they do and offer. It is just a name which is unusual, distinctive, easy to communicate and easy to remember.

Therefore, one of the key decisions a company must make is whether the brand name should be reflective of the offering and benefits or simply be unusual, interesting and easy to remember. Distinctive brand names are often used by larger companies who have the capacity and resources to build strong and clear brands. When a brand name is quite unusual, it may attract the attention of interested consumers.

To conclude, no matter which approach a company decides on, it is necessary for brand equity to be built over time until the consumer has a clear understanding of what the brand stands for.

Principles for brand name selection

Once the decision is made on using a descriptive or an unusual brand name the following criteria should be used to screen potential candidates for the brand name (Marketing study guide, 2019):

- Distinctive: brand names need to be clear and different to other brands. They should be recognizable as a brand name, rather than a generic word.
- Easy to recall: a brand name should be simple, recognizable, and easy to remember. Making a brand name too complicated or too long is counterproductive.
- Avoid confusion: think about how the brand name may be used. Incorrectly chosen or confusing brand names can harm a product more than they are beneficial. Vicks, for example, a cleaning product from Procter & Gamble, is not a good name because the V is pronounced like F and therefore sounds dirtier than clean – for a cleaning product, this is certainly not the first choice for a brand.
- Translatable: for large companies that operate in an international market it must be considered how the brand name, and the slogan, can be translated and communicated. Misunderstood is the slogan of the beer producer "Beck's": It advertises with "Welcome to the Beck's experience." This slogan, which is called a claim in the advertising language, was translated correctly by just 18% of those questioned with "Welcome to the Beck's experience." Instead, other respondents believed it meant "Welcome to the experience of Beck's."
- Legal protection: brand names need to be trademarked and registered. Here it must be mentioned that some generalized names can not be registered, such as, "chocolate" candy bar as it is too generic.

In general, there are four strategies when it comes to finding a brand name (Kalpana, 2019):

- individual brand name
- blanket family name
- separate family name
- company name

Individual Branding: Under this strategy, different brand names are used for different products offered by a single company in the market. This helps in creating a unique image for every single product. Advantages of this strategy are that the positioning of these products is easier because the company can position each product differently. Moreover, the company can use a different marketing strategy for each product. A disadvantage of this strategy is that it is very costly. This strategy is normally used when a company sells several unconnected commodities which vary in price and quality and target different market segments. An example of a company that uses individual, branding is the Coca Cola Company. Each soft drink has a different name and a different logo, for example, Sprite, Fanta, Powerade, Diet Coke, Ciel, Fresca, etc.

Blanket Family Branding: Blanket family branding (also called umbrella branding) refers to the use of same brand name and identity for the whole product range of a company. Therefore, it involves creating huge brand equity for a single brand. Blanket family branding can be very challenging for a company because it needs to effectively coordinate among all individual brands of the company. But it also means that any single product of this company that carriers the same brand name is produced using the same quality standards. A famous example of umbrella branding is Apple. Under the Apple brand, we can find, for example, the IPhone, the IPad, Mac Book, Mac Air, the Apple watch, etc. All those products are easily recognized in the market because they enter with an established name.

Separate Family Brand Name: This strategy means that a company classifies its products in different families and gives each product family a separate brand name. The idea behind family branding is that a company can make a wide range of products both desirable and trustful by giving them all one recognizable or already well-known name. An advantage of family branding is that a company can use one advertising campaign to successfully market a range of products instead of just one at a time. Often, companies in the food sector use family branding to market their products. For example, the Austria dairy products brand NÖM makes and sells milk, butter, yoghurt, cheese, etc. all under one already well-known name. Some consumers are more likely to choose a product with a familiar name, especially when the company introduces a new product to the market.

Company Name Combined with Individual Name: Under this strategy, the advantages of corporate branding and individual branding are joined together. The basic idea behind this strategy is to create a stream-lined association context for the product line. It allows leveraging the family brand name while also creating a distinctive brand name that fit and distinguishes the product and its different product categories. Moreover, it can help to avoid confusion in the minds of the consumers. This strategy is quite popular, especially when launching a new product category by an established brand.

For example, KIA Motors, a multinational automotive manufacturer combines two brand names – the family brand name being KIA and a distinctive product brand name, like Sportage. The product brand name triggers better recall and associations in the mind of the consumers. The use of Kia is intentional and allows the company to leverage its brand equity. Current lineups are. For example, Kia Cadenza, Kia Carnival, Kia Ceed, Kia Picanto, etc.

5.3 Brand-strategy decision/brand development

Brand-strategy decisions deal with the questions: What branding strategies should be used? What strategies should be used when it comes to brand development?

In terms of brand development, a company has four main option:
- line extension
- brand extension
- multibrand strategy
- addition of new brands

Line extension

Line extension means that the company can extend an existing brand name to new products or product categories, for example, Red Bull energy drink, Red Bull Cola, Red Bull Lunaqua, Red Bull Racing, Red Bull Flugtage, and many others. Most new products consist of line extensions, especially in the food sector. What must be considered is that companies must be careful about overextending a product line as this could lead to customer confusion or dilution of the brand name.

Brand extension

Brand extension means that an existing brand name is extended to a new product category. For example, the chocolate company Milka has extended its brand name to include not only chocolate but also biscuits, cakes, chocolate drink, cereals, etc. The advantage of this brand development strategy is that as soon as the brand introduces a new product to the market, the consumers become attentive and curious faster. Moreover, the product acceptance is faster and advertising costs are lower. There are also disadvantages of brand extensions. In some cases, the brand name is not appropriate for the new product. For example, the automotive brand KIA would not fit to food products. What is more, if the new product is not accepted by the consumers or the consumers are not satisfied with the product, this could be harmful for the main brand name.

Multibrand strategy

A Multibrand strategy is defined as the approach of a company to market several similar and even competitive brands of the same company under the different brand names. The main aim of this strategy is to restrict the competition by offering various products with different features or at different price levels, and to increase the market share. It is also used as a means of occupying more shelf space in a retail outlet. The main disadvantage of this strategy is that the needs much more resources to serve all these brands.

Multibranding is normally used by larger companies to ensure that there is no internal competition among their brands and that they are positioned in a way that they attract different target groups.

Addition of new brands

Some companies may decide to add new brands as a means of defense against competitors or leverage its brand name to enter into a new product category and target a new market segment. It could also be an option when a company wants to replace a brand that is not attractive anymore, loses market share and there is a lack of market vitality. Here it must be mentioned, similar as with multibranding, the company must be mindful of the fact that the adding of too many new brands may result in wasting resources. In addition, it may also lead to consumer confusion and resistance as there may be too many brands with only a few differences, so the consumer is overwhelmed.

5.4 Brand repositioning

Another important branding decision is brand repositioning. When a company sees a decrease in sales over time and/or major changes occur in a particular market or within the company itself, they know it is time to implement changes within the company. Brand repositioning is when a company changes a brand's positioning within a particular market. This includes various important changes, especially changes in the marketing mix. But also, strategic decisions are involved. In detail, the company must decide whether the repositioning should focus on the consumer, other businesses, or the general market.

There is a difference between rebranding and brand repositioning. Brand repositioning is about changing the way that customers view the brand. This can be done in several ways like changing the communication strategy or other elements in the marketing mix or changing the personality of the brand. In contrast, rebranding involves changing the brand identity completely, such as by implementing a new logo or even changing the name of the brand.

When is it necessary or reasonable to reposition a brand: Above all, when a company wants to target a different audience with the brand because the audience that was initially targeted is no longer viable. This can happen due to several reasons:
- The brand has targeted a specific age group that has grown up and no longer using the product.
- Another audience would be more profitable.
- The brand has evolved over the years, by changing features or adding new products to the product line. For example, Apple had to reposition their brand from being a pure computer manufacturer to being a technology company that develops and

distributes computers, smartphones, and consumer electronics as well as operating systems and application software.
– Competition has changed over the years which makes it necessary to change the value proposition of the brand to avoid losing customers to competitors.
– There is a decline in the brand's sales figures. At this point, a brand repositioning must be made to prevent further decline in sales.

A company must be willing to invest in this change, because brand repositioning can be very expensive and bind a lot of resources. So, a brand repositioning process needs intense preparation and must be an investment in the future of the brand.

In addition to changing the look and feel of the brand, the whole strategy must be changed. Especially the way how the new audience is reached must be adjusted. For example, the communication strategy must change from traditional TV ads to social media if a younger generation should be reached. When the company decides to focus on the consumers, the main aim of the strategy is consumer engagement, which means consumers must be involved with the brand. To make this happen, companies must work to customize the products to fit consumer wants, needs, and desires. Another important aspect of repositioning a brand is to give the brand a unique identity that the consumer can easily understand.

To summarize, brand repositioning is about changing the customer's understanding of what the brand is and stands for.

Successful Brand Repositioning Example – Walmart
Walmart decided to use digital initiatives in its stores to reposition the brand and to keep up with times. In general, brick-and-mortar retailers faced challenging times when the internet turned into the source for all products, even lower cost consumer packaged goods. However, Walmart decided to focus on its brick-and-mortar locations and did not switch entirely to digital channels. Instead, Walmart tied the digital and physical channels together by focusing on convenience features for consumers such as (shopkick, 2020):

Store maps: The retailer offers an option to view location maps to find items at its stores easily. New maps are added regularly, as they have more than 4,600 locations to digitize. Through digital mapping, the brand improves the customer experience while limiting work for associates.

List building: Consumers can create an in-store shopping list to better budget their time and their grocery shopping and budget. They can gain information on product deals and discounts and easily locate in-stock items across various locations.

Third-party app partnerships: Partnering with third-party app developers like Shopkick allows Walmart to reach new audiences who don't typically use the retailer's own app. It also expands the kinds of apps the retailer can offer, as consumers may use several shopping apps while in the store or online.

Specialty department integration: Consumers can get details on Walmart photo centres, auto care centres, and pharmacies. They can also review availability for rug doctor rentals. This integration serves to cross-market these niche businesses within the store ecosystem.

To summarize, by using digital initiatives in-store customer experience could be enhanced and the brand was able to increase in same-store sales due to the enhanced omnichannel experience (shopkick, 2020).

6 Brand communication

Marketing communications, and brand communication, are the means by companies attend to inform, influence, and remind consumers about the products and brands they sell. So, brand communication is one of the most important tools when it comes to establish a dialogue between a brand and a customer, create brad satisfaction, brand loyalty and, in the long run, build a relationship with the customer (Keller, 2013).

Designing brand communication is a complex task also due to the rapidly changing media landscape and constantly new options in marketing communications. Several different models can be found in topic-specific literature to explain how communication works and describing in detail relationships between elements and effects of input and output factors. One of the basic models how communication works is Foulger's (2004) ecological model of communication.

As discussed in Chapter 1.4.1 consumers' response to a particular marketing or other internal or external stimuli is a particular reaction that is influenced by many different factors in the consumer's inside. For marketers and retailers, it is essential to know why consumers prefer certain products or brands and what influences their reactions and decisions. The Stimuli (S)- Organism (O)-Response (R) model of consumer behaviour by Mehrabian and Russell (1974) examines the whole buying decision process of consumers. Marketing stimuli and other stimuli (economy, technology, politics and culture) enter the consumer's so-called *black box* (characteristics of the buyer and the buyer decision process) where all visible inputs cause an observable reaction or response to the stimuli.

Foulger's (2004) ecological model of communication, based on this S-O-R-model, can be used to understand and analyse the main elements of the communication process of a communication message (see Figure 6.1).

Foulger (2004) describes in his model that the communication medium is the product of a set of interactions between its primary components, such as messages using languages within media. Creators (e.g., marketers, retailers, etc.) create and use messages that are constructed and consumed within the media. Consumers interpret these messages and give feedback, for instance through word-of-mouth, social media activities or conducting a purchase decision.

Social media is an increasingly relevant communication channel for many brands, especially for enhancing brand perceptions. As social media is developing, methods to present brands and communicate with the target audience are also evolving. Marketers and retailers are constantly looking for new ways to deliver their messages through their brands more effectively to the intended target audience. They constantly experiment with various stimuli and measure the effectiveness of those stimuli.

https://doi.org/10.1515/9783110543827-008

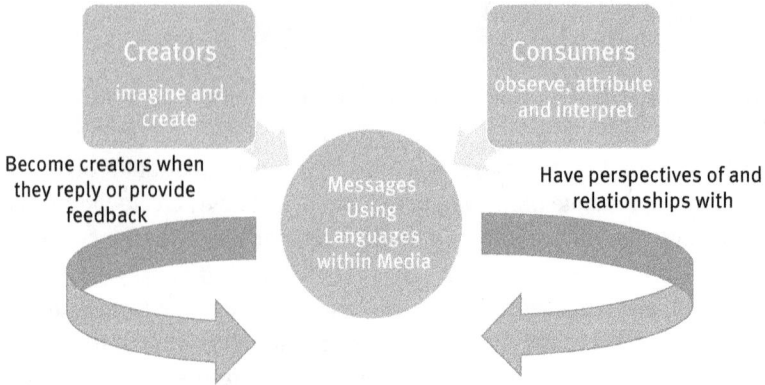

Figure 6.1: Ecological model of the communication process.
Source: Foulger, 2004

The easiest way is to find out why certain stimuli are transferred into distinctive reactions in the consumer's inside is to analyse direct observable and measurable variables. More complex would be to analyse intervening variables or indirect variables. These variables can be measured indirectly over indicators, or by psycho-physiology measurement methods. Physiological responses to a certain stimulus can be effectively measured via specific instruments that are able to read a person's bodily events, for example, the heart rate change or beats per minute via cardiovascular measures, electrodermal activity (EDA), brain waves (electroencephalography, EEG), muscle activity (electromyography, EMG) or the eye movements by using eye-tracking technology. The main advantage of eye-tracking research is that it provides direct measure of eye movements in a realistic stimulus-based setting that does not require the verbalization of any memory-based considerations (Chandon et al., 2007).

To summarize, Foulger's (2004) ecological model of communication transferred to a brand communication context suggests that retailers use particular messages that are interpreted by the customers who then show certain reactions. These reactions can be diverse, usually resulting in word-of-mouth, social media activities, or conducting a purchase.

There are several potential pitfalls in launching a new communication campaign, which won't result in successful communication, for example (Keller, Aperia, & Georgson, 2008):

1. A consumer may not be exposed to an ad because the media plan missed the mark.
2. A consumer may not notice an ad because of a boring or uninteresting creative strategy.
3. A consumer may not understand an ad because of a lack of product category knowledge or technical sophistication, or because of a lack of awareness and familiarity about the brand itself.

4. A consumer may fail to respond favourably and form a positive attitude because of irrelevant or unconvincing product claims.
5. A consumer may fail to form a purchase intention because of a lack of an immediate perceived need.
6. A consumer may fail to actually buy the product because he or she doesn't remember anything from the ad when confronted with the available brands in the store.

Consequently, marketers must make sure that these pitfalls will be eradicated or do not occur at all by carefully planning the brand communication. From an advertising standpoint, the ideal ad campaign would ensure that (Keller, Aperia, & Georgson, 2008):
- The right consumer is exposed to the right message at the right place and at the right time.
- The creative strategy for the communication campaign causes the consumer to notice and attend to the ad but does not distract from the intended message.
- The ad accurately reflects the consumer's level of understanding about the product and the brand.
- The ad correctly positions the brand in terms of desirable, realistic, and deliverable POD and POP.
- The ad creates strong brand associations to all these stored communication effects so that they can have an effect when consumers are considering making a purchase of a particular brand.

In the literature four elements are seen necessary to be included in an effective brand-building communication campaign (Keller, 2013):
- advertising and promotion
- interactive marketing
- events and experiences
- mobile marketing

All four elements will be discussed in further detail in the following subchapters.

6.1 Advertising and promotion

Advertising, in general, can be defined as any paid form of nonpersonal presentation and promotion of ideas, goods, or services by an identified sponsor. It is a popular means of creating strong, favourable, and unique brand associations, bringing forth positive judgments, emotions, and feelings. In contrast, advertising effects are often difficult to quantify and to predict (Keller, 2013).

Marketers must put a lot of effort into giving a brand the recognition they want it to have. So, advertising must be smart to be appealing and getting attention from the desired target group. Smart brand advertising must deliver clear messages, in particular a favourable brand identity (the character and personality of a brand including the colours, fonts, web presence, visual elements, and other stylistic choices). It should establish brand credibility (which means to inspire trust) and customer loyalty. It should help to engage with customers, on an intellectual and/or an emotional level (e.g., a mother is looking for cereals for her children; she will be attracted by the packaging but also by terms like "children love is," "makes every child happy," or information about the ingredients, etc.) and finally, advertising should motivate consumers to purchase a particular brand.

Marketers are faced with the challenge that they must decide which advertising medium best suits the target group and brand and which are also possible in terms of budget. Every advertising medium has different strengths and weaknesses and different roles in a brand's communication program. With the developments of new information and communication technologies and digital media, there are even more different advertisement media. Frequently used types of advertising are (LaMarco, 2018): display ads, social media ads, newspapers and magazines, outdoor advertising, radio and podcasts, direct mail, TV, video ads, product placement, event marketing, and email marketing.

Display ads

This includes digital and newspaper advertising. Digital ads are the updated version of newspaper advertising; it's the same concept but in 21st-century form. It means buying ad space on sites that are of interest to your target demographic. You can create text ads, which essentially look just like traditional print media ads, the floating banner above the site's contact and even wallpaper with your product or service on the site background.

The major difference between display ads and the ads you find in newspapers is the use of search engine optimization techniques to reach your target audiences more effectively when they search for you. These types of advertisements are typically also Pay Per Click, which means you bid on keywords most associated with your service or products and pay for your results to be at the top of the search engine search. Another one is Cost Per Thousand, which means to pay a flat rate to show up in search results 1,000 times.

Social media ads

TikTok, LinkedIn, YouTube, Twitter, Snapchat, Pinterest, Instagram, Facebook, and all other social media sites offer relatively inexpensive advertising possibilities. Paid social media ads are the kind of advertisement that focuses on reaching the target audience defined for the ad, payment is adjusted to how many see the ad and/or engage with it. Social media ads normally generate lots of word-of-mouth, especially within the younger ae group (Generation Y and Z). For example, the company posts an ad to a business Facebook page that offers a free product if followers click "like" and tag a friend.

TikTok has quickly grown to become the world's 7th most followed social platform and the 6th ranking app globally by monthly active users in 2019. It has a more sizable following than some of better-known platforms, like Snapchat, Instagram, or Twitter. TikTok is a short-form mobile video platform that provides content creators a chance to reach a large community. The nature of TikTok, featuring videos of 15 to 60 seconds, does limit the number of ad spots available. However, TikTok advertising isn't suitable for every brand and business. Forty-one percent of TikTok users are between the ages of 16 and 24, and roughly 50% of TikTok's global audience is under the age of 34. So, if a brand wants to attract another age group, there is probably no point in having a presence on this platform but use another one, like Facebook (especially for Generation X), LinkedIn, or Xing for business-related brands.

TikTok ads – Facts and examples

TikTok is one of world's most followed social platform, especially in the younger age group between 16 and 24. Therefore, brands that target the younger generation are well advised to place their ads on this platform – in several ad formats: TopView ads, brand takeover, in-feed ad, a branded hashtag challenge or branded effects (more information under https://www.tiktok.com/de/)

- TopView ads are 60-second videos that run immediately after opening the app. Their strategic placement guarantees that users will see whatever ad you run in this space and are an effective way of reaching the target audience.
- A brand takeover ad is shown on the app launch screen. These ads are fast- either a 3-second static image or a 3–5 second video without audio.
- An in-feed ad is similar to ads we see on Facebook or Instagram, except in this case they're embedded in the "For You" feed. This ad format can run up to 60 seconds of video with sound.
- A branded hashtag challenge is unique to TikTok and encourages user-generated content. Users are encouraged to create themed content that incorporates the branded hashtag. This content is then compiled in a hashtag challenge page. TikTok boasts an average engagement rate of 8.5% for this ad format and offers creative guidance to brands who want to participate.
- Branded effects are popular brand-sponsored visual effects similar to Instagram filters or the Snapchat lenses. Branded effects are placed on the first page of the effects panel and will remain there for three days.

This wide variety of ad formats allows a brand creative flexibility and room for experimentation. There are many brands that have already created powerful and engaging TikTok ads that have significantly increased their visibility on the platform. Here are a few selected examples (Johnson, Tara, 2020):

Guess Jeans

The #InMyDenim hashtag challenge was one of the first of its kind on TikTok in the United States and is still one of the best. The challenge encouraged users to post videos of themselves initially wearing shabby clothes, and then transforming into fashionable outfits that included Guess-branded denim products. The campaign lasted 6 days and included prominent TikTok personalities like @ourfire and @madisonwillow.

Kung Fu Tea

Kung Fu Tea's Boba Challenge is a perfect example for a hashtag challenge. The challenge is simple but entertaining and is unique to the brand's identity and product. The challenge is very easy to understand and to participate in it. The video looks like it could've come from friends, so viewers are drawn in almost immediately. A great example for a viral TikTok ad! Watch the video under https://www.youtube.com/watch?v=SDMi6jelwy4

Red Bull

The popular energy drink brand Red Bull also uses TikTok for its ads. TikTok's format of short, energetic videos suits the brand very well and engages both sports fans and viewers who just want to see something cool. Red Bull has earned over 4 million followers as a result.

You will find more information on mobile marketing in general and social media ads in Chapter 6.4.

Newspapers and magazines

These kinds of advertisements are traditional but no less effective. Combining this type of advertisement between local, national, and sometimes also international print media is a great marketing campaign strategy because many consumers still prefer to read their daily newspaper or love to settle down with a hard copy of a magazine. Most print media now also have a digital presence and can combine these types of advertisements with its virtual version.

Studies have shown that daily newspapers are still read by 30% of the population, although this number has been declining for years as more consumers go online to read daily news. On the other hand, although advertisers have some flexibility in designing and placing newspaper ads, poor reproduction quality and short shelf life can diminish some of the possible impact of newspaper advertising.

Although print advertising is particularly well suited to communicate product information, it can also effectively communicate user and usage imagery. Some brands attempt to communicate both product benefits and user or usage imagery in their print advertising, for example, car makers such as Mercedes, BMW, or Volkswagen, and or cosmetics makers such as Maybelline and Chanel.

Here, it must be mentioned that many readers only glance at the most visible elements of a print ad, making it critical that an ad communicate clearly, directly, and consistently in the ad illustration and headline. Finally, many consumers can easily overlook the brand name if it is not readily apparent. Therefore, ads in newspapers and magazines must follow three simple criteria: clarity, consistency, and branding (Keller, 2013).

Numerous studies have now shown that newspapers are perceived by readers as a quality product and that this image is also transferred to advertisements. Eye tracking can be used to find out where the reader looks at and follow the course of the reader's gaze. The method makes visible which areas and formats of advertisements receive the most attention. At the same time, brain activity can be measured by using brain computer interface. The results have shown that, on average, the reader looks at a newspaper ad for seven seconds. This is quite a long time, especially compared to other media. This long contact with the ad increases the chance that the reader will engage intensively with what he or she sees. The results of the study on brain activity support this thesis: the long period of viewing promotes a high level of mental activation in the reader. The reader is concentrated and is more likely to be stimulated. What is more, the central movement in newspaper reception takes place in the reader himself. It is not the articles that move on the page, as is the case in digital or audiovisual media, for example. Instead, the reader's senses, perception and emotions move, which makes newspaper reception a special experience.

It is the reading itself that triggers an active attitude, in contrast to moving image media, which tend to be consumed in passive mode. Reading focuses on the active search for information. This does not mean that moving image media can not have the same effect, they just must be used differently (Südkurier, 2016).

The size and the format of the advertisement also has an influence on the perception and quality of the contact. Readers process advertising messages more intensively if they are larger. Ads in 1/1 or larger format are on average viewed almost three times longer than smaller ads. The larger the ad, the more there is to see and understand. So, it seems logical that a longer viewing time is necessary and that this results in more attention. Overall, larger ads have a stronger effect: more than twice as many readers remember large-format ads than smaller ones and rate them better on average. Nevertheless, a generalization would be dangerous: Large ads only have a positive effect if they are attractively designed, and the advertising message is authentic. And even if large-format ads are characterised by a particularly high level of attention – the researched concentration in newspaper reading naturally also applies to smaller (Südkurier, 2016).

Outdoor advertising

Outdoor advertising is a huge industry. Studies have shown that 98% of consumers worldwide see at least one outdoor billboard advertising weekly and 68% of consumers claim their purchasing decisions are made while they are in a car or in another means of transport.

Outdoor advertising includes any type of advertising done outdoors with the objective to get people's attention. The most popular format is billboard advertising, but there is a wide range of other options, many of containing digital components.

Billboards have a long history, but they have been transformed over the years and now employ colourful, digitally produced graphics, backlighting, sounds, movement, and unusual images to attract consumers' attention. Now that billboards also have gone digital it's a huge way to make an effective advertising statement. This medium has improved in terms of effectiveness, technology, and provide a good opportunity for companies to combine their billboard strategies with mobile advertising. The most popular type of outdoor advertising are billboard-type poster ads. You can find them worldwide, everywhere in the streets. But there are also so-called transit ads on buses, subways, and other modes of public transport. Street furniture, like bus shelters, kiosks, and public areas, has also become a fast-growing area. Marketers can also buy ad space on billboard-laden trucks or taxi cabs to advertise via onboard television screens. They can buy space in stadiums and arenas, on garbage cans, bicycle racks, parking meters, airport luggage carousels, elevators, toilets, gasoline pumps, and many more public places. Promoting this way gives the brand an excellent brand recognition as these types of advertisements are seen everywhere daily and normally get consumers' attention (Keller, Aperia, & Georgson, 2008).

Outdoor advertising is also influenced by global digitization. The classic billboard-type poster ads will be replaced by digital screens in near future. This is not only more environmentally friendly, but also gives advertising companies much more scope for design and creativity. Moreover, outdoor advertising will be confronted with more personalization and individualization of advertising. The foundation for these major advances is the fact that almost everyone owns a smartphone today. The data, including GPS, can be used to tailor marketing measures to the respective target group and to measure the success of an advertising campaign (allbranded, 2020). Location-based personalised advertisements are also possible with Bluetooth beacons. These are small bluetooth radio transmitters, powered by batteries. Beacons are similar to a lighthouse in functionality. These small hardware devices incessantly transmit Bluetooth Low Energy (BLE) signals. The Bluetooth enabled smartphones are capable of scanning and displaying these signals. These beacons can be deployed in all kind of public (and also private) spaces, for example, on storefronts, real estate properties, amusement parks, events, etc., to broadcast contextually-relevant advertisements. The advantage is that customers receive only relevant marketing messages and are not bombarded with irrelevant deals and information that do not excite them.

Advantages of outdoor advertising
- A wide reach: depending on the location, outdoor advertising reaches thousands of potential buyers every day. Often even more than via social media channels.

- Acceptable costs: compared to TV or radio advertising, outdoor advertising costs significantly less, but is still far from being the most efficient way of advertising. For example, poster advertising usually costs between about 3 and 50 euros per day. As a rule, the agencies offer a 10-day minimum duration to have a certain amount of security in planning. The design and installation of the posters are included in the price in most cases.
- High acceptance by the population: imagine you watch a movie on TV and in an exciting moment the commercial starts. Many people feel annoyed by this and use this time to go to the toilet or get something from the kitchen. Advertising in public places, on the other hand, enjoys a much higher acceptance, most people do not feel annoyed by it.
- Increasing level of awareness: outdoor advertising is ideal for increasing brand awareness, as advertising on public spaces is seen by thousands of people every day, who consciously or unconsciously perceive the logo and other information about the brand.
- Privacy friendly advertising: outdoor advertising is one of the few types of advertising that in most cases does not collect personal data and does not set cookies (allbranded, 2020).

Disadvantages of outdoor advertising
- No protection against damage: advertising in public spaces is normally not protected against damage. Especially during elections, posters and banners of various parties suffer because their opponents deliberately damage them. But even stormy weather or hail can damage outdoor ads, like posters and banners.
- No conversion tracking: depending on the objective, it is important for companies to know how many deals or sales an advertising campaign has generated. Outdoor advertising excludes tracking because no one can say whether the increase in purchases was due to the ad.
- Not flexible: in contrast to digital advertising or advertising in social media, a poster, banner, display, or city light poster can not be changed once it has been attached to the public space. The disadvantage of this is that seasonal trends must be considered when planning and implementing advertising measures.
- Segmentation is not possible: outdoor advertising is one of the types of advertising where the target group can not be segmented according to selected criteria, like demographic, income levels or social factors.
- Banner blindness: people on the street are often overloaded with advertisements and other forms of information and visual impressions. Therefore, people's perception of ads is very selective and so it can happen that outdoor advertising is hardly noticed, regardless of the size and design of the advertising space (allbranded, 2020).

Radio and podcasts

Verbal promotion is a type of advertisement that can be repeated often as part of radio or podcast shows. You can have a traditional type of ad recorded to be played or there is also the chance of sponsorship. For marketers it is essential to narrow down the types of podcasts the target audience subscribes to or the station they most listen to for creating the kind of advertisement they will like and remember.

In general, radio is a pervasive advertising medium. To give an illustrative example, in 2019 the daily radio listening time in Austria was 201 minutes. Compared to the previous year, it has risen significantly and is now at about the same level as in 2011. Listening to the radio right after getting up, during breakfast and on the way to work is particularly popular. In detail, the ORF channels had a total daily reach of 63.2%. Hitradio Ö3 had a particularly high reach of 33.7%. In the same year, the domestic private stations had a significantly lower daily reach of 28.3%. The radio broadcasters' revenues in 2018 amounted to around EUR 97 million. What is more, most radio listeners have a favourite radio station. With over 600,000 social media fans, the radio station Hitradio Ö3 led the ranking of the most popular radio stations in Austria in 2017. However, when unpopular music titles or commercials are played, more than 35% of Austrian radio listeners change stations from time to time (statistia, 2020a).

One of the main advantages of radio ads is flexibility because stations are highly targeted, ads are relatively inexpensive to produce and place, and short closings allow for quick responses. As we have seen in the figures above, radio is a particularly effective medium in the morning and can effectively complement or reinforce TV ads. Radio also enables companies to achieve a balance between broad and localized market coverage.

One of the main disadvantages of radio, however, are the lack of visual image and the relatively passive nature of consumer processing that results. Therefore, radio ads are not suitable for every brand. But several brands, however, have effectively built brand equity with radio ads (Keller, 2013).

Direct mail and personal sales

Direct mailing campaigns or personal selling can offer a healthy return on investment especially for small businesses. The starting point is to identify the target market, then send an enticing offer out to all those prospects. Measuring the responses helps to see which type of customers are responding to this format. This is helpful for precision targeting with next mailing campaign.

Moreover, direct, or personal sales is still an important medium for advertising, especially for small businesses. A good salesperson can use his or her skills to persuade a customer to buy a product or a brand. If the salesperson is effective, the customer will continue to spread positive word-of-mouth about the brand through recommendations and referrals.

Although direct mailing campaigns are still very popular and effective. Especially direct communications through electronic or physical newsletters, catalogues, etc., allow marketers to explain new developments with their brands to consumers on an ongoing basis as well as allow consumers to provide feedback to marketers about their likes and dis- likes and specific needs and wants. By learning more about customers, marketers can finetune marketing programs to offer the right products to the right customers at the right time. Therefore, direct marketing is often seen as a key component in relationship marketing (Keller, 2013). So, one of the main advantages of direct marketing is that it makes it easier for marketers to establish relationships with its consumers. Furthermore, technological advances, changes in consumer behaviour, such as the increased demand for convenience, and the needs of marketers to avoid wasteful communications, contribute to the fact that this advertising medium is still very popular and is gladly used by marketers.

But there are also disadvantages. To implement an effective direct marketing program, marketers need to develop an up-to-date and informative list of current and potential future customers, put forth the right offer in the right manner, and track the effectiveness of the marketing program. To improve the effectiveness of direct marketing pro- grams, marketers normally make use of database marketing, to identify the most responsive customers for the purpose of developing a high quality, long-standing relationship of repeat business by developing predictive models which enable marketers to send desired messages at the right time in the right form to the right people.

Regardless of the means of direct marketing, database marketing can help create targeted communication and marketing programs tailored to the needs and wants of a specific target group. When customers place orders, send in a coupon, fill out a warranty card, or enter a sweepstakes, database marketers collect names and information about attitudes and behaviour, which they compile in a comprehensive database (Keller, 2013).

Television

Television is still a powerful advertising medium because it allows to reach a broad spectrum of customers on a multisensorial level. In 2019, television had by far the largest share (76%) of all moving image offerings used in Austria. However, digitization represents a challenge for classic television: By 2030, the minute volume of linear television is forecast to decline from 1.46 billion in 2019 to 1.38 billion minutes. At the same time, the predicted growth in the minute volume of nonlinear moving images represents a great potential. Nonlinear moving image refers to all video offerings that are not a running television program, for example, recorded television, media libraries, streaming providers or videos on social media platforms. In 2019, a total of 18,055 hours of television advertising were broadcast in Austria. Of these, 538 hours were accounted for by advertising on public radio (ORF) and 17,516 hours by advertising on private stations (Statista, 2020b).

In 2018, television viewing time in Germany was around 217 minutes per day, putting Germany in the middle of the European average: at 332 minutes per day, Serbia watched the longest television. Romania and Portugal followed in second and third place. Television was watched the shortest in German-speaking Switzerland and Norway.

According to the European Commission's Eurobarometer, in 2019 around 77% of the Europeans surveyed stated that they watched television daily or almost daily (Statista, 2020b).

From a brand equity perspective, TV advertising has two important strengths (Keller, 2013):
- it can be an effective means of demonstrating product attributes and explaining their corresponding consumer benefits
- it can be a compelling means for portraying user and usage imagery, brand personality, emotions, and other brand intangibles

On the other hand, television advertising also has disadvantages (Keller, 2013):
- In TV ads we often find distracting creative elements that can lead to the fact that consumers very often overlook product-related messages and even the brand itself.
- Moreover, the large number of ads and additional information through diverse media (information overload) results in consumers ignoring or forgetting ads.
- The widespread existence of digital video options gives the consumer the means to skip ads.
- The production and placement of TV ads is very expensive. In the box below you will find detailed information about costs and other facts.

TV advertisements-facts and figures from Austria and Germany.
Properly designed and executed TV ads can affect sales and profits of a brand. But studies have also shown that the end of an advertising block in TV, not even 10% of the viewers remember the brands advertised. Nevertheless, television is the second most important advertising medium, just behind print media. Some retailers, for example the world's largest retailer Wal Mart, advertises its products and brands via its own TV station, whose program is consumed by 100 million viewers every month (castelligasse, 2019).

The four largest US TV stations and major brand manufacturers, like Coca-Cola, Johnson & Johnson, Procter & Gamble, etc., founded the so-called Family Friendly Program Forum (FFPF). With this initiative the companies finance the main evening program, in return in the advertising insertions between 20:00 and 22:00 o'clock exclusively their own products are advertised.

Tables 6.1 and 6.2 show the costs in euros per second (plus fees and taxes) for broadcasting an advertising spot at a specific broadcasting time. Here it has to be mentioned, the more viewers watch a particular program, the greater its RANGE (indicated in %). This information is generated through the media analysis – the teletest. To give an example, if all Austrians were to watch a certain program at the same time, it would have a range of 100%.

The prices not only vary according to the time of day, but also depend on the day of the week and the calendar month (summer months are normally cheaper than winter months, December is the most expensive month, especially around Christmas).

The "most expensive" advertising time is that in the commercial breaks before the evening news program ZIB1 starts and the weather forecast starts. During this period, between 16.4% and 20.5% of all Austrians watch the advertising (castelligasse, 2019).

The thousand-contact price (TKP) also called Thousand Ad Impressions (TAI) or Cost-per-Mille (CPM) is a key figure from media planning. It indicates the amount of money that must be used for an advertising measure (such as TV commercials, online advertising or print advertising) to reach 1000 people of a target group by visual contact (on the radio listening contact). In the online sector, for example in banner advertising, an ad-impression is regarded as a contact.

This is obtained by dividing the broadcasting costs by the number of viewers and multiplying by 1000.

If you reach 317,000 viewers in one advertising block and pay a secondary rate of € 140,–, you have to pay 140,– times 30 = € 4,200,– net for 30 seconds of advertising time.

The TKP is calculated as follows: 4,200,– : 317,000 x 1,000 = 13.25

Table 6.1: TV advertising costs ORF 1 (Source: castelligasse, 2019).

Advertising block prices 2018/ORF 1				
Commercial break	Broadcast time	Day	Jul	Nov
Youth	15:55	Sun	130	225
Sports	18:05	Sun	140	265
Sitcom	19:15	Sun	100	240
Weather	19:53	Sun	160	275
Announcements	20:07	Sun	220	330

Table 6.2: TV advertising costs ARD (Source: castelligasse, 2019).

Advertising block prices 2018/ARD				
Commercial break	Broadcast time	Day	Jul	Nov
Brisant	17:56	Mo-Fr	5.760	12.480
Hubert + Staller	18:50	Wend	5.520	11.960
Tagesschau	19:59	Mo-Fr	24.480	53.040
Weather	17:47	Sat	4.200	9.100
Lotto	19:56	Sat	24.480	53.040

To summarize, in designing an effective TV advertisement the two main concerns in devising a proper advertising strategy are as follows (Keller, 2013):

– Defining the proper positioning to maximize brand equity: A TV ad should contribute to brand equity in some demonstrable way, for example, by enhancing awareness, strengthening a key association, or adding a new association, or eliciting a positive consumer response.

– Identifying the best creative strategy to communicate or convey the desired positioning: regardless of which creative approach marketers take, certain motivational devices can attract consumers' attention and raise their involvement with an ad. These devices include cute babies or puppies, popular songs or jingles, well-liked celebrities, provocative sex appeals, or even fear-inducing threats. But these attention-getting devices are often so effective that they distract the attention from the brand or its product claims. Therefore, the main challenge in arriving at the best creative strategy is to find out how to attract the attention of consumers but not distracting their attention to the wrong elements in an ad.

Video ads

This type of advertisement engages with the target customers on a digital level. Marketers create short videos and post them on social media or pay to have them run on an influencer's, YouTuber's or bloggers site. Video ads are a frequently used advertisement tool by luxury fashion brands. The reason video ads are so important for luxury brands is that it is a great passive medium and conveys the experience of luxury in a multisensorial way that few other mediums can while reaching a broad audience, also an online audience which is normally passive and dont "like and share" everything but watch videos which are entertaining and engaging.

For example, the luxury fashion brand uses video ads and films quite frequently to reach its target audience. The videos are always engaging and take up a contemporary issue and attends to send a message while presenting the new collection. For Christmas season 2020 Gucci used a retro office setting from the 90s and shows a holiday party set where the workplace becomes a mix of dance floor, nightclub, and bar. Watch the video under https://www.creativereview.co.uk/gucci-christmas-ad/

Product placement

Product placement is also known as advertising integration and describes the targeted presentation of branded products in various media. Product placements are commonly used in films and television, but also in video games or social networks, like Instagram, TikTok, YouTube, etc.

This kind of advertisement is frequently used by popular, strong brands with a sufficiently large advertising budget. Many major marketers pay fees up to 50,000–100,000 dollars or even higher so their products appear in movies or in TV shows, with the exact fee depending on the amount and nature of the brand exposure. Many brands such as Chase, Hilton, Heineken, Apple, Coca Cola, etc., pay large sums of money to be featured in popular TV series and shows. Marketers combine product placements with special promotions to publicize a brand's entertainment tie-ins and create "branded entertainment." For example, BMW complemented product placement in the James Bond film Goldeneye with an extensive direct mail and advertising campaign to help launch its Z3 roadster (Keller, Aperia, & Georgson, 2008).

Studies have shown that product placement, especially in social networks, is perceived by users as less disturbing than during watching a movie on TV or advertising banners on a website. On social media channels such as YouTube, TikTok, Snapchat, Facebook, Instagram, etc., so-called advertising integration takes place. This means that the advertised product or brand is part of a post or video. In order to operate effective product placement on a social media channel, companies are dependent on the support of so-called influencers, for example, YouTuber or bloggers, who have plenty of followers and therefore reach a large crowd of consumers. The company then selects the appropriate influencer based on reach, profiles, and statistics. Social media channels provide the possibility to reaching many people within a short period of time. Therefore, more and more companies try to use social media for their advertising purposes.

With more than 300 million members and more than 60 million published articles per day, Instagram is one of the largest social media platforms. Product Placement on Instagram is especially recommended for brands that want to promote products in the areas of fashion, beauty, lifestyle, or fitness. Instagram's versatility and visual focus is particularly attractive for fashion brands. Consumers prefer Instagram over other social networks, which is due to an active usage process. Moreover, interaction and engagement with the brand is much better than on Facebook, Twitter, or YouTube.

In 2017, Instagram published a study in which characteristics of luxury consumers using Instagram were characterised. The following characteristics were surveyed: on average 35 years, successful and motivated in their jobs and with a technical affinity. Luxury brands use Instagram to increase transparency and integrate the brand into a social environment. Moreover, consumers use Instagram as a source of inspiration. But not only the profile of the brand itself is used, but also the influencers as such are inspirations (Vinerean & Opreana, 2019). There are several approaches in which influencers can be classified, in the literature mainly the following subdivision can be found (John & Shyamala, 2019):

- **Celebrity influencer**: The Celebrity Influencer group is the origin of Influencer Marketing. Through success the reputation of the celebrities increased and thus a role model function developed. The reach guarantees a wide distribution of the brand. However, the identification factor could be a disadvantage. Consumers often can not identify themselves with celebrities, because the difference between the standards of living and lifestyle is a huge one.

- **Authority Influencer:** Authority influencers focus on the expert knowledge of one person. Through this, a base of followers can be built up. The targeted knowledge and experience in a niche area are the trademarks of these individuals. For consumers, the knowledge in a specific area is important and it increases the trustworthiness.
- **Social Media Sensations:** Social media sensations are the most natural form of influencers. Here products are presented by influencers, which have not been developed in any cooperation with brand. Influencers use the product and are associated with trust.
- **Micro-Influencer:** This group of influencers instructs influencers expert knowledge. However, the reach of these people is limited. This results in a relatively low price for companies. The main advantage of these influencers are the high authenticity and a strong connection to the consumers. Furthermore, the interaction is more intensive than with Authority or Celebrity Influencers.
- **Bloggers:** Bloggers present products, brands, service, etc., on their blog in their own and personal way and thus convey an everyday impression of these products or brands. Only they can determine which content is published on their blog and which products the followers will be associated with. Therefore, this form of product placement provides the possibility to reach potential customers indirectly via their Blog and to do consumer-oriented marketing.

Companies can integrate influencers into their social media strategy presenting the brand on their platforms. This can be either done by payment or the influencer will be given the products free of charge. In the latter case, the mentioning of the product by the influencer is on a voluntary basis. The selection of the right influencer is very important. Often the range is used as a measure to identify a suitable influencer. Because with a higher number of followers many people can be achieved at the same time. However, this indicator should not be the only benchmark for selecting an influencer. The process of selecting a suitable influencer can be considered appropriate if the influencer's values match those of the brand. The image of an influencer can be transferred to the brand and vice versa. The selection process is often very time-consuming, but when completed a beneficial long-term relationship can be established.

Event marketing

Event marketing refers to a target-group oriented and systematic planning of events, in particular sports and cultural events but also trade fairs, conferences, sales presentations, shareholder, or investor meetings, press conferences, etc., as an opinion-building tool to achieve corporate goals and build up a favourable brand reputation. Event marketing addresses potential customers very directly and personally and is a typical below-the-line marketing instrument. Marketing events are planned events that are intended to convey brand-related communication content to the addressees in an experience-oriented way. For example, paying to sponsor a sports team or a charity benefit falls under event marketing. These types of advertisements mean a large cross-section of people hear your brand name and associate it with that event. More information about event marketing can be found in chapter.

Email marketing

Email marketing is part of direct marketing and is based on working with digital messages. Email marketing is used to make customers aware of new products, brands or offers and to strengthen customer loyalty. The discipline of email marketing can be assigned to online marketing and to direct marketing and serves companies to further expand and consolidate existing customer contacts. As the name suggests, this part of the marketing mix works by sending emails (Gründerszene, 2019).

In general, a distinction can be made between two different types or approaches to email marketing. If, for example, the company specifically addresses a single person by sending the email, this is referred to as *one-to-one communication*. However, if an email is sent to any number of people, this is referred to as *one-to-many communication*. If this form of email marketing becomes outdated, one speaks of so-called spam, which is perceived by internet users as annoying and can also cause enormous economic damage.

The use of email marketing as part of effective customer contact and modern customer care is almost inevitable. The field of this marketing instrument is expanding more and more. Meanwhile even conferences for further education take place, where the newest trends and tools are presented. In the meantime, companies have a wide range of tools at their disposal to help them maintain customer contact and build brand reputation. Established tools are the classic newsletter and mailing. *Emailings* are the irregular sending of emails, which takes effect if, for example, there is a current campaign, or a new product or brand and the company wants to draw the attention of its customers to it. The situation is different with newsletter dispatch. The difference to emailings is that the *newsletter* is sent out to the customer base at regular intervals. The frequency varies. This can be done daily, once a week or even monthly. With the help of a newsletter, the company provides an overview of the most important activities or upcoming events, sale, and discount campaigns. An effective mailing or the newsletter contains sufficient call-to-action, which in this context are usually linked buttons with text or images or banners that redirect the subscriber to the company's landing page (Gründerszene, 2019).

If a company wants to use the possibilities of email marketing, there are a lot of guidelines that need to be observed to avoid being confronted with negative results. For example, an email may really only be sent to customers if they have given their express permission to do so or at least they are already existing customers and an interest in the content is obvious. In addition, care should also be taken to ensure that the structure and design are professional and clearly structured (Gründerszene, 2019).

As we have seen from the different advertisement media describes above, there are as many ways to utilize types of advertising as there are kinds of advertising. By diversifying the advertising approach in both traditional and digital worlds as well as focusing on a brand's target group will lead to a favourable and effective advertising campaign.

Although they do very different things, advertising and promotion often go hand-in-hand. In the following paragraph you will learn about the differences and promotion in more detail.

Promotion

Promotions are short-term incentives to encourage trial or usage of a product or brand. Like advertising, sales promotions can come in various forms. Whereas advertising typically provides consumers a reason to buy, sales promotions offer consumers an incentive to buy. Therefore, sales promotions are designed to change the behaviour of consumers so that they buy a brand for the first time, buy more of the brand, or buy the brand earlier or more often (Keller, Aperia, & Georgson, 2008).

Despite the time limit, sales promotion does not only pursue short-term goals. Although some promotions, for example price reductions, serve to increase sales in the short term, other promotions, like raffles, primarily aim to improve the image of the brand and increase sales in the long term. It should also be noted that the use of sales promotions does not only refer to the place where the customer purchases the brand, the so-called *POS*, but also at other places, such as in newspapers by advertising special offers.

Although sales promotion is increasingly characterised by communicative measures, in the marketing mix it can not only be assigned to communication policy. Rather, sales promotion is characterised by the fact that it has different elements of communication, pricing, distribution, and product policy. For example:
- Communication policy: newsletters, leaflets, inserts, advertisements, etc.
- Pricing policy: discounts, special offers, etc.
- Distribution policy: POS displays, wobblers, banners, secondary placements, etc.
- Product policy: product additions, promotional packages, etc.

Some marketers see promotions as a more effective means than advertising to influence the sales of a brand. Besides conveying a sense of urgency to consumers because of the limited time-period, carefully designed promotions can build brand equity through information or actual product experience that helps to create strong and unique brand associations.

On the other hand, there are also several disadvantages of sales promotions, such as decreased brand loyalty and increased brand switching, decreased quality perceptions, and increased price sensitivity. Perhaps most importantly, the widespread discounting arising from promotions may have led to the increased importance of price as a factor in consumer decisions, breaking down traditional brand loyalty patterns. Another disadvantage of sales promotions is that in some cases they may merely subsidize buyers who would have bought the brand anyway. Another drawback to sales promotions is that new consumers attracted to the brand may attribute their purchase to the promotion and not to the features of the brand per se and, as a result, may not repeat their purchase when the promotional offer is withdrawn (Keller, 2013).

Promotions have several possible objectives, above all to target new category users, existing category users, and/or existing brand users. Promotions are mainly designed to change the choices, quantity, or timing of consumers' product purchases. Literature distinguishes between (Keller, 2013):

– customer franchise building promotions: sales promotion activities that communicate distinctive brand attributes and contribute to the development and reinforcement of a brand's identity, for example, samples, demonstrations, information material, and

– noncustomer franchise building promotions: are methods which directly encourage consumers to buy a particular brand and, ideally, in a larger quantity, for example, price-off packs, premiums, sweepstakes, refund offers.

There are many different types of sales promotions including several communications activities, all with the main aim to provide an added value or an incentive to the customer to stimulate the attention, trial or purchase of a particular product or service. Examples of frequently used sales promotions can be found in Chapter 2.4 in Table 2.4.

6.2 Interactive marketing

The first decade of the 21st century has seen more and more companies integrating interactive marketing activities into their communication strategies. With the rapid development of information and communication technologies brand communication has found new options in marketing communications.

The main advantages of interactive online marketing are the low cost and the level of detail and degree of customization it offers. Interactive online marketing communications can accomplish almost any marketing communication objective and are especially valuable in terms of solid relationship building.

Studies have shown that 93% of marketers believe that interactive content is more effective in communication with its customers compared to static content. It also generates 4 to 5 times more page views and 2 times more conversions with the brand or product. With the aid of new technology and a growing list of interactive marketing tools, there are many ways how interactive marketing can be integrated in the marketing mix.

Literature suggests several elements that interactive marketing tools and campaigns must include:

- **Relevancy:** interactive content needs to be relevant to the targeted group of customers.
- **Entertaining:** successful interactive marketing must be entertaining and includes elements of fun and gamification. First, customers must be attracted with relevancy and second, they must be kept interested with appropriate interactions.
- **Design elements:** interactive marketing tools must have an appealing and professional design. This helps to build credibility and trust for the brand and company.
- **Virality:** interactive marketing campaigns must be engaging so that customers are willing to share the content. Therefore, it is important to build in virality and rewarding consumers for sharing the content and making it "viral."
- **Multichannel follow-up:** an interactive marketing campaign should also make sure that there is a follow-up across multiple channels with the customers that engage with the interactive content.
- **Customer Service:** interactive marketing must include "human" elements that provide the chance to interact with customers to humanize the relationship.

There are many different interactive marketing tools. The most frequently used tools in a retailing context are contests, quizzes, polls, calculators, emails, videos.

Contests

Contests are one of the longest standing forms of interactive marketing. The most successful companies and brands use contests as a holistic strategy, rather than a stand-alone promotion. Contests can be extremely relevant to a target audience if the are designed with the target group in mind. Contests are engaging and entertaining and customers normally like to participate when they think they can win something that may be beyond their budget, or that they wouldn't typically buy. Moreover, when it comes to customer service, a contest provides the possibility to collect all the information that is necessary to communicate with the customers.

Pennington's Lawn & Garden Envy Contests for Facebook Fans
Pennington's (https://www.penningtongarden.com/) most popular social media contest invited the eco brand's Facebook fans to battle for the best lawn or garden. The 'Lawn & Garden Envy' contest required Pennington's Facebook fans to post a photo of their garden while competing against other lawn enthusiasts. The winner with the greenest and most photogenic garden was named on Facebook and was the recipient of a $250 National Home Retailer gift card and an additional prize pack filled with Pennington's products.

In addition to submitting an image of their lawn, Facebook fans were also required to answer questions about their favourite home-grown dish and most beloved outdoor space. Appealing to its target group, baby boomer generation with an appreciation for gardening and home-cooked meals, Pennington reached a broad audience with this social media contest that was both memorable and engaging (trendhunter, 2017).

Quizzes

Quizzes are an extremely effective form of interactive marketing. According to studies, 90% of the most shared Facebook posts are quizzes. So, we see the power of this form of consumer engagement tool because consumers find quizzes entertaining and funny. This interactive marketing tool is built for virality, because most consumers like to share quizzes with friends, family, or like-minded people on social media.

Polls

Polls are also interactive marketing tools that engage and entertain consumers by providing feedback in the form of results. Consumers normally complete a poll because they want to find out the results or they want to see what other people have answered (e.g., https://nametests.com/). One benefit of a poll, compared to quizzes, is that it is quicker to complete and see the results immediately. Here, it must be mentioned that polls often lack in qualification because they are short and quick complete. So, they should only be used when quick responses from the target audience are the main aim of the usage. For example, marketers want to find out whether the target audience prefers logo A or logo B or to get a quick mood image or including a calculator that can provide accurate quotes to customers and excite people about the outcomes.

Interactive emails

The effectiveness of email marketing is still greatly underestimated by many brands, therefore interactive emails are a valuable tool when it comes to engaging with a brand's target audience. These emails can be designed by using autoresponders to follow up on an interactive marketing activity, like a quiz or poll. Or interactive emails can be created by using various interactive elements, like CSS-animated button for advertising emails, survey forms for event-driven emails and questionnaires, an image carousel to display some products on one screen, rollover effect to show products from different angles and their functions, videos to better present a new product or brand, to congratulate customers on holidays or to explain new users how to use a particular tool.

Walkthrough videos

Another popular interactive marketing tool are interactive videos which enable the user to choose their own way of getting active. Interactive videos increase engagement, create brand awareness and viewing time. Moreover, conversions from video content can be gained by providing gamified experience and personalization to the viewer. Interactive videos are also an effective tool for onboarding new customers or illustrating the benefits of a brand. If created with intent, interactive video can capture a viewer's attention as they are about to zone out and click away, by re-engaging them with a prompt to take action.

To summarize, interactive marketing campaigns can be beneficial for every brand, of all shapes and sizes. What is important, is to find the right content mix for the brand that will create relevancy, fun, and virality. Attention-getting online ads and videos can drive consumers to a brand's Web sites, where they can learn and experience more about the brand. Company-managed bulletin boards and blogs may then help create engagement.

6.3 Events and experiences

Events and experiences play an important role in brand management in general and brand communication. Brand building in the virtual world must be complemented with brand building in the real or physical world. Events and experiences can be designed in many different ways- from fantastic and impressing major international events to a simple local in-store product demonstration or sampling program. What they all have in common is that they aim at building brand engagement through attracting the consumers' senses and imagination and changing brand knowledge (Keller, 2013).

Formally, event marketing can be defined as public sponsorship of events or activities related to sports, art, entertainment, or social causes (Keller, 2013). Chapter 6.4 gives more information on sponsorship. Therefore, this chapter mainly concentrates on brand experiences.

Brand experiences are defined as subjective, internal consumer responses evoked by brand-related stimuli that are part of a brand's design and identity, packaging, communications, and environments (Brakus, Schmitt, & Zarantonello, 2009). So, brand experiences are the sum of consumers' perception of their experiences with the brand. Brand experiences must involve all five human senses to be engaging and effective because research has shown that the intensity of the brand experience increases with the number of senses engaged. Moreover, it has been found that consumers who once experienced pleasant feelings and emotions when engaging with a brand are likely to become loyal customers.

When experiencing a brand, consumers may have a certain brand image in mind. In this context, an "image" may be understood as the "cognitive representation of a real object" where the object is associated with personal values, beliefs, and experiences. Each time consumers experience the brand, the image of this brand may be refreshed or even changed. The brand image may also be regarded as construct consisting of both functional and emotional components. While functional components of a brand may be evaluated based on objective criteria, emotional brand image elements may be perceived differently from person to person (Cian & Cervai, 2011).

Even though research shows that visual perceptions of a product often prevail in the buying decision, other senses have been found to gain in importance at a later stage of the product experience. It has also been found that consumers largely rely on visual information when evaluating a product. Nevertheless, the relative importance of the senses varies considerably from one product group to another. When it comes to food items, for example, smell and taste play the dominant role. It has also been found that consumers report the most satisfying product experiences in relation to the daily usage of products based on pleasurable sensory experiences such as nice product design (vision, touch) or subtle tones (hearing). Negative product experiences have been related to repulsive sensations such as terrible smells or irritating noises or to unattractive product design (Fenko et al., 2010).

Brand experiences shall engage the five human senses to arouse feelings and provoke thinking, which shall eventually encourage consumers to act in favour of the brand. Positive brand experiences may create strong and positive brand associations. A sensory marketing approach may be adopted to get consumers involved in multisensory brand experiences. Brand-specific scents and sounds as well as distinct product shapes and characteristics may help to strengthen brand associations and may foster the creation of strong personal memories with the brand (Krishna, 2012, 333)

Tesco provides a digital brand experience.
In 2011 Tesco launched virtual grocery stores in public areas with high foot traffic, such as subway stations, where customers could use a mobile application, Homeplus, to scan an item's QR code and schedule its delivery. Using, for example, the walls of the Seonreung subway station in downtown Seoul, Tesco has displayed more than 500 of its most popular products with barcodes which customers can scan using the Homeplus app on their smartphones, then get it delivered to their homes. Tesco shoppers scanning products on their way to work can get a delivery that evening if the order is placed before 11.30am.

Instead of waiting for customers to visit their stores, Tesco innovated and brought a digital customer experience to them. By doing so, Tesco used their knowledge of local consumer behaviour and tech savviness to their advantage, and successfully adapted to these trends.

The Homeplus app was downloaded 900,000 times in less than one year, making it the most popular shopping app in South Korea. Online sales increased by 130%, and app users increased by 76%. As a result, Tesco became the country's top online retailer, with overseas sales bolstering the company amidst falling domestic profits (Creevy, 2011).

Research has found that 73% of people who took part in a brand's experiential marketing are more likely to purchase from the brand involved. Therefore, brand experiences can make a powerful way to engage consumers with a brand. Moreover, 91% of consumers share their most memorable experiences with others. When it comes to defining memorable experiences, the most popular responses were: Special family moments (24%), unforgettable trips (24%), live events (17%) and work-related achievements (11%), but only 7% of people mentioned the purchase of a new product as a memorable event. There is a shifting perception among consumers that favours doing things over having things. 80% of UK and US consumers find that physical experiences can build more lasting memories compared to physical products. Consequently, memorable experiences can help creating lasting memories and building trust (Litsa, 2019).

Consumers enjoy experiences that are fun and engaging. That's why such brand experiences can help consumers build a positive sentiment towards a brand. Most consumers want from brands to create experiences that entertain, engage, and educate them. Moreover, consumers are way more likely to share information about a new brand through a live experience than simply hearing about it through TV, word of mouth or social media. This means that brand that manages to create appealing experiences come with an advantage over the competitors (Litsa, 2019).

To conclude, brands that launch their own unique experiences gain an advantage when it comes to the final purchase decision and can create more memorable and engaging brand communication campaigns.

6.4 Sponsorship

Many marketers believe that a brand communication program including a sponsorship is what determines the success of the program. In general, sponsorship is a business relationship between a provider of funds, resources, or services and an individual, event or organization which offers in return some rights and associations that may be used for commercial advantage. So, sponsorship allows a company to demonstrate its affiliation to the target audience that it has chosen to associate with. The patrons or enthusiasts of the sport, event, organization, etc., that the business is sponsoring should be actual or potential customers of the business, and they should feel grateful to the sponsor (e.g., company or brand) for helping their favourite event, sport, organization, etc.

In general, the idea of sponsorship is to develop strong relationships between the company or brand and its customers due to their common ties with the sponsored event, sport, organization, etc. Main commercial sponsorship objectives include (Egan, 2020):

- Awareness: making a target audience aware of the brand
- Image building: associating the brand with a cause or an event
- Citizenship: developing bonds with a community
- Alteration of perceptions: changing people's attitude about the brand

- Motivating employees: building the reputation of the company and, in the case of charity sponsorship, actively encouraging the participation of staff
- Media attention: leveraging the news value of the sponsorship
- Shareholder reassurance: associating the organization with success or corporate responsibility, etc.

The main advantages of sponsorship are that it can be more cost-effective than advertising and can enable companies to target current and potential consumers more effectively. Moreover, ssponsorship provides an opportunity to create publicity in media. Worldwide events, such as important soccer games (like Soccer World Cup), provide the opportunity to gain global media coverage because people all over the world watch these games.

What is more, sponsorship can create entertainment opportunities for potential and current customers. Sponsorship of music, the performing arts, and sports events is particularly effective in this regard. Attendance at such events can be used to reward stakeholders of a company, like employees, customers, trade partners, etc.

Normally a large amount of money is involved in sponsoring activities and the possibilities to sponsor events is manifold. So, marketers must make strategic decisions about sponsoring activities, for example, which event to sponsor and in which manner. To provide an example, sponsoring an event or an organization which will help the community where the event is being organized or where the organization functions can foster a socially responsible, caring reputation for a company or brand. For example, a company could provide low-cost computers for schools or donations to a hospital or a special research program.

When more then one company or brand sponsors an event, it is important the logo or name is displayed at the site of the event. Where the brand can be consumed during the event, this provides an opportunity for customers to sample brands.

To summarize, there are several potential guidelines for choosing a suitable event which can be sponsored. First, the event must meet the marketing objectives and communication strategy defined for the brand. In particular. the audience delivered by the event must match the target audience of the brand. Moreover, the event must have sufficient awareness, possess the desired image, and be capable of creating the desired effects with that target market. Of particular concern is whether consumers make favourable attributions to the sponsor for its participation at the event.

A suitable event might be one whose audience closely matches the target audience of the brand, that generates much favourable attention, where there are not too many sponsors, and that reflects or enhances the brand or corporate image of the sponsor (Keller, 2013).

It is also important to measure the effects of a sponsorship activity, especially on brand equity. There are two basic approaches to measuring the effects of sponsorship activities:

- the supply-side method and
- the demand-side method

The *supply-side method* focuses on potential exposure to the brand by assessing the extent of media coverage. Supply-side methods attempt to approximate the amount of time or space devoted to the brand in media coverage of a particular event. For example, the number of seconds the brand is clearly visible on a television screen can be estimated, or the column inches of press clippings covering an event that mention the brand can be counted. Then this measure of potential impressions delivered by an event sponsorship can be translated into an equivalent value in adver- tising euros, according to the fees associated with advertising in the particular media (Keller, Aperia, & Georgson, 2008).

The *demand-side method* attempts to identify the effects that sponsorship has on a consumer's brand knowledge. Customer surveys can explore the ability of the event sponsorship to affect awareness, attitudes, or even sales. Marketers can identify and survey event spectators after the event to measure recall of the event's sponsor, as well as attitudes and intentions towards the sponsor because of the event. Internal tracking can be conducted to see how different aspects of the sales process are impacted (Keller, Aperia, & Georgson, 2008)

To conclude, event sponsorship has grown rapidly in recent years. Most event expenditures occur in the world of sports. Other categories are entertainment tours and attractions, causes, arts, festivals, fairs and annual events, and associations and membership organizations. Sponsorship provides a great means of improving a brand's image, prestige and credibility by supporting events that a brand's target audience finds attractive. Only large companies can afford to sponsor huge, worldwide events. However, smaller companies can gain favourable effects when sponsoring smaller events, like a soccer game or a school festival or participate at a clean-up of a town and show their visibility in the community, differentiating the company from competitors.

6.5 Mobile marketing

Another brand communication option has emerged in recent years and will play an even greater role in the future- mobile marketing. Mobile marketing is a multichannel, digital brand communication strategy aimed at reaching a target audience on their mobile devices, above all on their smartphones and tablets, via websites, email, SMS and MMS, social media, and apps. In recent years, more and more customers have shifted their attention to mobile communication searching for true omnichannel entertainment and engagement, preferring content that is highly personalized and relevant. Consumers use their mobile devices for information search, entertainment, and communication but also for shopping and payment.

Mobile marketing can be seen as a part of online marketing. Its main purpose is to establish a direct contact to the customer to transfer information- in both directions. Another objective of mobile marketing is to forward a potential or current customer to a company's or brand's website. Mobile Marketing comes in several functions and applications, such as mobile research, mobile games, mobile shopping, mobile information, mobile coupons, mobile customer loyalty programs, etc. Developments of new mobile devices over the last decade have created new ways of connecting with the customers. To give an example, information can be transmitted differently according to the customer's location by beacon technology. Location-based services use the smart device's GPS signal and delivers relevant information directly onto the smart device of the customer.

When it comes to mobile marketing, it mainly means keeping smart devices in mind and utilizing SMS/MMS marketing and mobile apps. Mobile marketing is an important element in a brand communication strategy, especially when it comes to building out any short-term or long-term communication plan. From email, to pay-per-click (PPC), search engine optimization (SEO), content marketing, and social media marketing, there is a mobile marketing channel to reach every part of a brand's target audience where they are most comfortable. For mobile marketing to be effective, it is important to curate a cohesive experience that customers expect (marketo, 2019).

Mobile marketing can be effective in driving brand value and demand for a brand by leveraging mobile devices to connect with more consumers in real time at any point in the customer life cycle. Mobile is growing steadily. According to research, mobile versus desktop usage stats show that the mobile-only audience will grow continually and that 79% of smartphone users have their phones on or near them all but two hours a day. Today, there are more mobile devices in the world (8.7 billion) than people (7.1 billion). U.N. data analysts have found that in the United States, 71.5% of citizens over the age of 13 have a smartphone, and 66.5% have smartphones globally. So, the main advantages of mobile marketing is that it is a unique communication option because content reaches the target audience in real time right where they are. Additionally, more and more sales are being initiated from mobile, so it's a vital part of any marketing strategy (marketo, 2019).

Smartphones present a unique brand communication opportunity for marketers because they can be in consumers' hands at the POS or even at the point of consumption. What must be considered are privacy and regulatory concerns surround mobile advertising. Opt-in advertising, where users agree to allow advertisers to use specific, individual information about time, location, and shopping preferences to send them targeted ads and promotion, will be the most frequently used option. Consumers are choosing to opt into different services and share their locations in return for coupons, discounts, and more relevant promotional material and brand communication (Keller, Aperia, & Georgson, 2008).

Online retailers are also recognizing the power of m-commerce, which stands for selling through mobile devices, by launching mobile apps and revamping online stores to handle mobile traffic more easily. Several years ago, the idea of mobile marketing was met with fear that marketers would alienate customers with annoying product pitches. But creative messages that pull willing consumers into dialogue with the brand have evolved into an appealing way to increase brand awareness, especially when it is part of a larger campaign in other media (Keller, Aperia, & Georgson, 2008).

Black Friday 2020 breaks records.
Black Friday is the Friday after Thanksgiving. Since Thanksgiving always falls on the fourth Thursday in November, the following Friday is considered the start of a traditional family weekend and the beginning of the Christmas shopping season. Black Friday is a retail sales event that focuses on discounts and is intended to encourage the purchase of products. In the meantime, the discount campaign has been adopted in many industrialized nations with a time schedule coincidence, especially on the internet.

For mobile shopping apps, it has been observed in recent years that the time at the end of November was the real highlight and exceeded the pre-Christmas December sales. 2020 was a special year. Stores were closed for months due to global corona restrictions, so digital retail was growing. There have been three major developments in the field of mobile shopping apps (Jeger, 2020):

- Increased demand: The pandemic led to a 35% increase in installed e-commerce apps between March and April 2020 alone, a period that exceeded the peak in the 4th quarter of 2019.
- Increased spending: Smartphone users spent on average 50% more in April 2020 than in November 2019.
- Aggressive marketing: Nonorganic installations (attributed to a media source) increased 56% between February and May 2020 as marketers invested in user acquisition, taking advantage of the fact that users spent more time at home during lockdown and later due to social distancing and health concerns.

In 2020, whether in Germany, France, the UK, or Russia, the sales increases were enormous, as shoppers installed retail apps during the event and made purchases through them. A 98% increase in sales in the UK, but Black Friday proved to be even more successful in France and Germany, where sales were up 196%, driving purchases in these countries. The organic installations had a significant impact on the revenue retailers generated through Black Friday and the number of buyers is increasing. Black Friday as an American invention has now become clearly established throughout Europe and creates shopping incentives, to make a bargain.

It has to be mentioned that the Corona pandemic has had and continues to have quite negative effects on the livelihoods of many consumers. While total revenues are likely to continue to rise compared to 2019, average spending per consumer will hardly change (if at all) from year to year. The economic slowdown resulting from the pandemic means a reduction in disposable income. At the same time, however, consumers have not had the opportunity to spend their money on things like travel, culture, sports and the like as they would have done in a "normal" year. Instead, there may be a greater need for shopping because of the willingness to "spoil" oneself in a difficult time.

For mobile marketers there was another fact to consider: At the beginning of the pandemic when marketers used their budgets for user acquisition CPIs were low. Many major brands held back during this uncertain period, and the reduced competition caused CPIs to drop in several European countries. As soon as these large retailers got going again, CPIs naturally started to rise again – in some cases to higher levels than before the pandemic.

The pre-Christmas shopping season is already fiercely competitive for marketers, and rising media costs mean that marketers must use data more than ever to generate high-quality revenue through intelligent targeting (Jeger, 2020).

As already mentioned above the Black Friday 2020 delivered new records. During the so-called *Black Week,* that is, the entire last week from Monday to Friday, sales rose by 60% compared to the previous year. The number of electronic devices sold rose by 3,554%, which means that Germans bought as many electronic products on that day as they usually did in an average month. Black Friday is popular in all age groups, for example, also the 66- to 75-year-olds made significantly more online purchases than last year.

6.5.1 Personalized communication

The rapid expansion of the internet and continued fragmentation of mass media have brought along the need for personalized marketing in general and personalized brand communication. To adapt to the increased consumer desire for personalization, marketers and retailers have developed several concepts. The two most important concepts, according to Keller (Keller, 2013) are experiential marketing and relationship marketing.

Experiential marketing was already discussed in chapter. Information on relationship marketing can be found in Chapter 6.5.2.

Personalization can be an important advantage for retailers. Targeted communication that is relevant and useful for the customers can create customer satisfaction, loyalty and drive revenue growth of 10% to 30%. The challenge is to personalize in a way that delivers genuine value and relevance for the customers, but also for the retailers. McKinsey (2017) found in a study five key points that customers said they value when it comes to personalized communications:

- To provide relevant recommendations the customers wouldn't have thought of themselves.
- To deliver information and brand communication when the customer is in a shopping mode.
- To remind the customers of things they wanted to buy but might not be keeping track of.
- To provide personalized communication and an omnichannel experience wherever the customer interacts with the brand.
- To share the brand value in a way that's meaningful to the customer.

One of the most frequently used personalization techniques is to remind shoppers of items they browsed but didn't purchase yet. Using a common digital-marketing feature called "retargeting," these reminders appear as ads on other websites the shopper visits or are delivered via email. This technique can also have disadvantages, because shoppers don't want to be constantly reminded of products they've already bought or searched for, especially if the ads appear either too soon, too frequently, or too late in the process.

Therefore, to provide something a customer might be interested in, companies need to use more sophisticated recommendation algorithms to offer complementary products instead of just the items the shopper has already browsed or bought. This might entail, for example, suggesting a fancy dress for someone who has just bought or searched for high heels. Another effective tactic is communicating in a way that people actually talk to each other (e.g., with the slogan "If you can't stop thinking about it, buy it").

What is more, it is important to send a message when the customer is in a shopping mode, which means that the company must reach the customers when they were either still thinking about shopping, or at a time when shopping for clothes made the most sense for their individual schedule. Previous order data can provide useful cues about activities such as purchasing time, purchasing items and other elements of purchasing behaviour.

A highly effective way to become relevant to shoppers is through tracking specific events and circumstances they are likely to want to know about. This might take the form of a reminder when someone may be running out of an item purchased earlier, when a desired item is back in stock or on sale, or when a new style is launched for a product or category the shopper has repeatedly bought. Retailers, however, should be careful to provide shoppers with a trigger for the targeted message because it can also lead to annoying a customer (Keller, 2013).

Studies have shown that customers want to be offered omnichannel experiences. In detail, they expect retailers to connect digital messages with offline experiences. This requires that companies collaborate between various areas of the organization, such as store operations, key account management, marketing managers, including PR, digital marketing, and analytics. Communications that seamlessly connect online and offline experiences, provide real value and engage customers, can make a customer feel a retailer really takes care of the needs and demands of its customers.

Loyalty programs and direct-purchase information can tell retailers what types of products an individual customer buys, how often he or she buys them, when they buy, and what product categories they never purchase. Many companies fail to take full advantage of all these data they collect which would be useful to personalize communications and promotional activities (like sending them coupons, vouchers, etc.) to their loyal customers. Customer offers are an important way to build customer loyalty. Personalizing them and even gamifying the experience is a highly effective way to encourage new purchasing behaviours (Keller, 2013). Technology is providing brands with more innovative ways of engaging with customers across every step of their customer journey. These ways should not be too complicated, tasks should be easy to understand, with the rewards being tangible and personal. Simple gamification examples include adding quizzes on a brand site to help shoppers find the perfect product or introducing a points-based system to an app. More sophisticated gamification solutions include VR and AR applications or interactive in-store displays.

Coca-Cola experiments with interactive in-store displays with Google AI.
Digital brand communication solutions are a perfect option for personalized communication with customers. Coca-Cola has launched in-store display systems that show personalised messages to approaching shoppers, based on data on their smartphones. The system is powered by Google Cloud technologies and works on any HDMI-ready display that serves as grocery store aisle "end caps," restaurant menu boards, and even interactive cinema posters. The system can also be used to offer custom branded videos and e-coupons to shoppers. The promotional content can range from brand campaigns to store-specific promotional offers, or even app-guided shopping lists. Moreover, proximity technology leverages built-in smartphone features and Google's wireless beacon technology, allowing a store to receive and interpret a nearby user's preferences and habits to deliver relevant content in real time.
A 250-store pilot with the Albertsons grocery chain delivered a one-month return on investment. They chain significantly increased category which means not only did the end-caps help sell more Coca-Cola products, also everything else on the carbonated soft drink could be increased in sales figures (Robin, 2017).

Studies have shown that customers see value as a function of how relevant and timely a message is in relation to how much it costs, which means how much personal information must be shared and how much personal effort it takes to get it. Moreover, trust in a brand can increase this value, that can grow or recede over time, depending on the customer's satisfaction with various interactions with the brand. So, marketers are constantly testing and learning to improve their communication and engagement with customers and to identify potential issues early. They can, for example, also evaluate the economic impact that negative activity, such as unsubscribes and app notification blocks, has on a customer's lifetime value. This allows them to appraise campaigns more accurately. For example, if one communication brings in twice the revenue but also elicits twice the unsubscribe rate as another communication, they will be able to determine which one is more valuable (Keller, Strategic Brand Management. Building, measuring and managing brand equity, 2013).

McKinsey has created a fully interconnected shopping experience which they call the "Modern Retail Collective," located in a huge shopping mall, the Mall of America located in Bloomington (Minnesota). The Modern Retail Collective is a collaborative venture between McKinsey, Mall of America, several retail brands, and technology providers like Microsoft. It's a physical multibrand store where retailers can test the latest technologies with actual customers. For more details see the box below.

Effective personalization can increase store revenues.
The rapid rise of e-commerce over the last few years will require changes in the retail sector. Experts are sure that the physical stores will not disappear from the market, but they have to change their strategies.

Change is always also a chance. And there is a great opportunity at the intersection of technology and analytics to transform the physical in-store experience for the customer, while making a step change improvement in profitability.

McKinsey's Retail Practice has created a fully interconnected shopping experience which they call the "Modern Retail Collective," located in the Mall of America. The Modern Retail Collective is a collaborative venture between McKinsey, Mall of America, several retail brands, and technology providers like Microsoft. It's a physical multibrand store where retailers can test the latest technologies with actual customers.

Experts are sure that online shopping will still rise but, nevertheless, most consumers still want a brick-and-mortar store, physical environments, where they can experiment with new types of in-store technologies.

The Modern Retail Collective is a safe space for brick-and-mortar businesses to test and learn, offering retailers the ability to experiment with little risk or disruption to their own stores and operations. To understand how digital tools affect store traffic, customer engagement, transactions, and productivity, the Collective helps retailers make sense of nonsensitive customer and operational data.

The Collective is mainly looking at product discovery: how can technology help in-store shoppers discover new products and get the same level of information that they would have online? One way is through interactive mobile hot spots. Through near-field communication technology, customers simply wave their phones over hot spots near a product they're interested in, and more product information and reviews appear on their screens. No app download is required. Interactive mobile hotspots provide in-store shoppers with online levels of detailed product information.

The store provides a mix of physically purchasable products along with additional digital options. The jewellery brand Kendra Scott, for example, offers top seller items for onsite purchase, as well as an endless aisle of custom designs that rely heavily on shoppers' interaction with actual stones, metals, and styles. Therefore, McKinsey, created digital displays that use radio frequency identification (RFID) technology to register a customer's choice of stone and design in the store itself. Purchases, then, are shipped directly to their home. Moreover, digital displays use RFID to enhance shopping experiences.

Elsewhere in the Collective, augmented-reality mirrors allow customers to interact with and virtually try-on merchandise. With an integrated social sharing component, customers can take selfies, share looks with friends, and make purchases of their favourite items.

From anywhere within the Collective, customers are able to check out quickly through a portable point-of-sale device. There's also a counter dedicated to Flexa, a platform for cryptocurrency payments, that helps educate shoppers on multicurrency wallets and offers retailers the opportunity to explore the future of lower cost and fraud-free payments.

Every four months, a new set of brands is featured in the store with new use cases to test. Examples could include looking at the impact of in-store technology on conversion, sales-associate productivity, inventory automation, post-purchase engagement, and more.

To conclude, the store's research shows that effective personalization can increase store revenues by up to 30%, and several next-gen technologies can improve store productivity by 10% to 20% (McKinsey, 2019).

To summarize, data and advanced analytic tools play a crucial role in understanding the shopper behaviour of consumers, but to rely only on these would clearly be not enough. Here we need the addition of qualitative listening tools in combination with ongoing shopper panels, ethnographic research, and observation, to get attitudinal feedback on the impact and effect of personalized communications. What is more, close monitoring of social media tools is useful to gain fast answers on the identification of potential problem areas.

6.5.2 Relationship marketing

Marketing strategies in general and communication strategies must exceed all expectations concerning the actual brand to create brand loyalty and maximize brand resonance. This broader set of activities is often referred to as *relationship marketing* and is based on the assumption that current customers, in contrast to potential customers, are the key success factor for a strong and profitable brand.

Relationship marketing aims at providing a more holistic, personalized brand experience to create stronger relationships with the customers. Relationship marketing provides many benefits for marketers and retailers. For instance, according to Keller (2013) acquiring new customers can cost five times as much as satisfying and retaining current customers. Moreover, the average company loses 10% of its customers every year. Therefore, to be profitable in the long run brand loyalty is fundamental.

Three main concepts can be helpful when it comes to relationship marketing (Keller, 2013):
- mass customization
- one-to-one marketing
- permission marketing

Mass customization can be defined as making products to fit the customer's exact needs, wants, desires and specifications. Products are adapted to meet a customer's needs which results in the fact that that no two products are the same. Due to technological innovations and digitalisation companies can offer customized products at affordable prices and within a short period of time without long waiting times. With the help of the internet customers can communicate their wishes directly to the manufacturer, without the need of an intermediary, which can assemble the personalized, unique product for an affordable price, comparable to that of a mass-market product. Mass customization provides many advantages, not only for the customer, but also for the retailer. One of the main advantages for retailers is that they can reduce their inventory, save warehouse space and costs and don't have to pay an intermediary.

It has to be mentioned that mass customization also has disadvantages. Above all, returns of products are more problematic for a customized product because of the personalized specifications of the product.

Today, many companies in all different lines of business make use of the mass customization business model. Almost all car and computer companies, such as Dell or BMW, have applied this concept for a long time. For example, for a car the customer can combine present elements and features like colour, the interior, the sports or luxury package, etc. But not all of those companies are successful. The following box provides an example of a very successful mass customization concept.

Mymuesli – A German mass customization success story
Mymuesli is a young German brand of breakfast cereals founded in 2007 and headquartered in Passau, Germany. It is the first company that enables customers to create their own personalized breakfast cereals according to their preferences and desires. The company was not among the first to apply the concept of mass customization to food, but they were the first to be successful. Mymuesli is a modular building system for organic cereals. The innovation of mymuesli was the mass customization, a low involvement, and their distribution via online channel. They didn't want to build an e-commerce start-up, but the online channel was the easiest way to reach an appropriate target group without investing too much capital. After two years of online market presence the company noticed that breakfast cereals, especially muesli, is a product that the customer wants to see, smell and taste. To give the customer these sensual experiences, Mymuesli decided to use offline distribution channels too. In 2009 the company opened their first store in Germany, five years later Mymuesli operates nationwide already twelve stores where the customers can see and taste the complete product range and even buy the products directly in the physical stores. For the company, the physical store has the advantage that they can speak directly to their customers and learn about their preferences. Today Mymuesli is a successful company with more than 300 employees and several million-euro turnovers.

One-to-one marketing stands for the tailoring of one or more marketing measures to each customer with the help of statistical methods and analytical tools, which can be summed up as "individualization instead of personalization." Instead of individual customer characteristics (such as income, age, profession, educational level, etc.), customer profiles are generated, to provide tailor-made or customized products.

One-to-one marketing is based on several fundamental strategies (Keller, Aperia, & Georgson, 2008):
– Focus on individual consumers through consumer databases – "We single out consumers."
– Respond to consumer dialogue via interactivity – "The consumer talks to us."
– Customize products and services – "We make something unique for him or her."

To summarize, one-to-one marketing means that different consumers are treated differently because of their different needs, wants and desires, and their different current and future value to the company and the brand. Peppers and Rogers stress the importance of devoting more marketing effort to the most valuable consumers.

Technological progress offers new and additional options for one-to-one marketing, for example:
- Cookies enable technical devices to personalize, possibly even the associated users, so that tracking can be used to determine how often a particular user visits a website or returns to it.
- Mobile devices enable regionally coordinated advertising measures, for example via Bluetooth, that is, for stores with a retail outlet, for example, the messages "Happy Hour" or "Buy now two for one," etc.
- Retargeting advertising as a successful form of display advertising, that is, a customer is interested in a product on an online site and subsequently receives targeted advertising for this product on his screen.

One-to-one marketing examples with personalized messages.
Hotel chains, for example RitzCarlton, normally use databases to store consumer preferences, so that if a customer makes a special request in one of its hotels, it is already known when he or she stays in another, like the softness of the sleeping pillow or the preference of the filling of the minibar.

We also find successful localized versions of one-to-one marketing in the retailing sector. After having ordered flowers at a local florist for Mother's Day, a customer might receive a reminder to inform the customer of the next Mother's Day to put a phone call for ordering a beautiful arrangement.

Permission marketing is a term that refers to consumers opting to receive marketing offers and announcements from a particular brand. This concept was coined by the marketing expert Seth Godin and is broken down into two schools: express-permission marketing and implied-permission marketing (Charmicheal, 2019):
- Express-permission marketing: means that the consumer provides his or her email address to receive marketing messages. For example, they might sign up for a newsletter. Express marketing is common type when creating new customer relationships.
- Implied-permission marketing: means that the company does already have an existing relationship with the consumer. This might include someone who's a current customer or only a frequent website visitor.

In contrast, nonpermission marketing is defined as any marketing offers sent to the individual without their consent. To give an example, the company receives a list of all visitors of a particular fair, and they use the list to send those people an email, this would be nonpermission marketing. With this approach, the privacy policy must be handled very carefully so that there is no violation here. Normally customers prefer permission marketing. Receiving permission to market to an individual and use his or her address or other personal information is a way to build trust, value, and brand loyalty with consumers. Sending nonpermission-based offers can result in consumer frustration and privacy violations.

Here are some examples of permission-based marketing activities:

- Promotions: a notification is sent to the subscribers, for example, during a promotional event, informing him or her about an exclusive offer.
- Newsletters: is used to keep the subscribers informed about the latest updates, changes to a product, new product releases and additional offers.
- Membership information: can be in form of an email or a letter and is exclusive for members of a particular customer (loyalty) club.

Permission marketing is a frequently used possibility to attract a consumer's attention. By eliciting such consumer cooperation, marketers might develop stronger relationships with consumers so that they desire to receive further communications in the future. Those relationships can only be developed if marketers respect consumers' wishes and requirements, and if consumers express a willingness to become more involved with the brand or the company.

To summarize, permission marketing is a way of developing a stronger relationship with a customer and leads in many cases also to the fact that the customer buys more or becomes attentive to a possibly offered product and buys or orders it. A disadvantage or a challenge of permission marketing is that it presumes that consumers have an idea what they really want to buy. In many cases, they only have a vague idea but no entrenched preferences or are not able to express their desires in a way that marketers know how they satisfy consumer objectives.

6.6 Brands and packaging

In the FMCG industry, the packaging of a product is a very important branding element. The packaging should act as a source of information and can be used as an important communication tool. The content on the packaging needs to be clearly identifiable and the function of the product must be stated precisely. Concerning the size, form, design, and material of the packaging these components should be chosen appropriate and suitable for the product. If the packaging is designed catchy and attractive, consumers will pay more attention towards the product and customers will be able to differentiate it from competitive products (Rommel, 2014), which is essential in saturated markets and when products have very similar features and no noticeable differences.

In general, it can be said that graphic symbols like pictures, colours and shapes are evaluated higher and are more memorable than verbal design elements on a packaging. Already children at the age of three can recognize without any difficulties which products represent chocolate or cookies, although they are not able to read the labelling of the packaging (Kastner, 2010). The colours used in a product packaging play a key role in consumer's purchasing decision. Each colour has a distinctive effect in the minds of the consumers. For example, products with white packaging convey simplicity, safety, and purity. Therefore, white is normally used for medical products. Blue, for example, has different meanings. A light sky-blue colour is considered more playful, while a dark navy blue is considered much more sophisticated and professional. In general, blue is the most liked colour, nevertheless this colour does not fit every product packaging. If you want a product to stand out on the shelf, it makes sense to use a bright colour, such as red. The more colour is added to a product's packaging, the less sophisticated the product will be judged. Nevertheless, colourful packaging is very popular for children's products, as they get the most attention in this target group.

The brand name helps the consumers to identify a product or brand and represents important verbal information on the packaging. Due to the high number of product offers in a supermarket, the brand name is a fundamental differentiation element on a packaging. What is more, the more consumers remember and talk about a brand the higher the chance that they actually use it. Brand names convey certain values and promises so that consumers can identify themselves with this brand. The name also ensures the quality and origin of the product. The logo represents the visual symbol of the brand and serves the consumer as an identification. With regard to logos it is of high importance that they can be easily remembered by their consumers and should help as a memory aid. With all their five senses consumers perceive the visual, hearable, tangible, smellable, and tastable product characteristics. Furthermore, they evaluate the product according to the functional benefit, the quality, and the usability (Kastner, 2010).

Claims or slogans should strengthen the product promise and should be remembered by the consumers very easily. It is of high importance that the slogan is rather short in order that consumers can retrieve the information without too much effort. In addition to that information of the producer must be displayed on the product packaging. Next to the producer's address hotlines can be stated in case there exist complaints, customers can contact the producer. Furthermore, information about the quantity such as ingredients and food additives represent other important design elements (Kastner, 2010).

Quality seals are a successful design element as the quality of a product can be pointed out. There exist different quality seals, like the individual quality promise, industry quality seals and governmental quality seals. The "Bio" quality seal, used in many product groups, has gained a lot of importance during the past years, as consumers focus more on a healthy lifestyle and are ready to pay more for organic products. Another important design element represents the batch number. In case of a manufacturing error the producer must be able to identify in which production line the defective product was. Furthermore, every product packaging comprises a barcode which is especially for the cashier desk of high importance as this code needs to be scanned for sales purposes. Sometimes bar codes are scanned by consumers to get price comparisons from online providers (Kastner, 2010).

Packaging trends.

Successful brands always find creative and innovative ways to express their brand attributes, deliver clear brand assets, generate a broad impact and differentiate themselves from competitors' products, and even the power to change consumer behaviour (White, 2020).

Here are some packaging trends for the years to come (White, 2020):

1. Sustainable packaging

Brand and packaging leaders are already offering edible wrappers for individually wrapped foods, and other zero-waste packaging concepts to promote packaging that's good for the individual and good for the environment.

Eco-friendly innovations include:
- edible plastic film fruit coverings
- potato-based wrappings for chocolate bars, sandwiches, bagels, and cookies
- compostable wine bottles
- seaweed-based packaging for coffee or tea sachets
- water-soluble packaging for all types of products, including sanitary products, detergents, personal care items, and even food

2. Transparency with consumers

In the last couple of years, companies have started to address the growing consumer demand for honesty and trustfulness about product ingredients and how products are made. Consequently, traditional packaging is being reinvented to embrace clear, and when appropriate, see-through cut-outs that show what's inside the packaging. By managing consumer expectations in the packaging itself, companies are removing the element of surprise. Studies have shown, when given a choice, consumers will choose transparent packaging over opaque packaging.

3. Sophistication

The global colour authority Pantone selected a rich deep blue as 2020 colour of the year. Companies are increasingly using strong, uncluttered messaging in simple, yet sophisticated bold colours and big type of letters to communicate trust and respect. So, in the years to come, we'll continue to see more one-word brand names combined by straightforward slogans, so consumers quickly understand product attributes and features at a glance.

4. Consistency

Occasionally it is important to refresh a brand's story and to ensure to convey it in the most compelling way, across all touchpoints, especially the packaging. New and innovative packaging structures that support consistent brand values across all product lines. To promote a healthy, better-for-you brand message, single-use harmful-to-the-planet plastic packaging should be replaced with compostable containers, for example to be used for greens to stand up on store shelves. The main objective should of each company should be that brand, packaging and company goals come together in one unified brand expression.

5. Tech-centric

Health-conscious consumers love their smart devices, and increased use of technology is putting pressure on companies to deliver "smart tech ready" packaging. The more economical it becomes to infuse radio-frequency identification (RFID) sensors in food and nonfood articles the more innovations will be possible in the near future.

The beverage industry is an early leader, where forward-thinking companies are introducing health drinks or herb- or CBD-infused products that "speak" directly to devices, enabling users to automatically track their beverage consumption via health apps. These smart packages can help consumers by sending alerts when they don't drink enough liquid.

There are thousands of products on the market all trying to get the customers' attention. Studies have shown that one-third of a consumer's decision-making is based solely on product packaging. Therefore, a brand's packaging has to stand out and look different from competitors. A brand's packaging can be an important marketing tool, especially when it comes to in-store advertising. Branded products can be easier recognized and help consumers to remember a product. Therefore, strong brands should not change too much and should remain true to their communication line.

7 Branding and digitalization

Digital marketing has emerged as a specialism over the last decade with its origins rooted in direct marketing. The increase in the number of personal devices and their use means brand marketers have many more ways of communicating directly and interactively with their target consumers or customers. Therefore, branding in general and its concepts and tools should be applied to digital media and technology to develop engaging and state of the art brands through interactions with consumers on their digital devices.

The following chapter explains digital branding in general, how a digital branding strategy can be developed, the elements that should be included, and how the effectiveness of such a strategy can be measured.

Moreover, the importance of digital customer journeys and touchpoints will be illustrated and explained. Marketers and retailers need to consider how they can stay in touch with their customers all along these customer journeys, in the sense of engaging them with the brands and creating long-term customer relationships. As we have seen in previous research, digital capability is becoming more necessary for businesses that are seeking to build or enhance their brands through brand building programmes. Therefore, retailers must make use of digital tools and elements and see them as powerful tools for brands with many brand-building benefits, especially when it comes to brand communication.

This chapter concludes with an outlook on future developments.

7.1 Definition of digital branding and digital branding strategy

When we try to find a definition for the term "digital branding" the following seems to be appropriate "digital channels and assets are used to communicate a brand's positioning or purpose as part of multichannel brand communication or engagement programmes" to establish brand recognition in the digital world. In detail, the main objectives of digital branding are not necessarily driving sales, but enhancing the brand awareness and the brand image, and in turn drives long-term customer loyalty.

A *branding strategy* is a comprehensive plan that focuses on the long-term development of a brand's purpose, consistency, and emotional impact. It defines how you differentiate a brand from the competition with a unique identity, a so-called USP (i.e., unique selling proposition).

Brand strategies are based on specific objectives, for example, to increase overall awareness, to build positive perception through interaction or to encourage brand loyalty and advocacy.

https://doi.org/10.1515/9783110543827-009

A *digital branding strategy* is part of an overall marketing plan. It focuses on all the components that help to drive growth in the form of leads and sales generated. This occurs mainly via online channels. While a branding strategy aims at positioning a brand, a digital branding strategy determines the tools and instruments to reach the objectives.

A digital branding strategy includes several important elements:
– website user experience
– SEO and content marketing
– social media marketing
– email marketing
– paid advertising (PPC)

What is more, digital branding is about creating and establishing a brand's story and presence in the digital realm. It's a comprehensive strategy for brand creation involving four key steps (Ostholthoff, 2017):
– building a digital brand story
– creativity in digital media and marketing
– digital channels and content distributed to channels based on consumer data and habits
– creating digital relationships

Building a digital brand story

A successful digital brand begins with a story that answers why the brand exists and why consumers should buy the brand, it should give the customers a reason for buying the brand. Experts are sure that customers don't get excited about a brand, but by the story behind the brand, and learning what makes the brand different from others. A brand's story should resonate emotionally, drive credibility and visibility and create so-called brand advocates who believe in the brand's story and its values (Ostholthoff, 2017).

Creativity in digital media and marketing

As marketing and branding continues to become more and more digital, marketing and media will intersect to the point where, we won't be able to recognize the difference. Digital branding pushes the boundaries of what we know to be marketing. Branding content needs to be engaging and add value to the customer. Creating a brand's own media hub that produces high-quality content could be an option when it comes to producing relevant content (Ostholthoff, 2017).

Digital channels and content distributed to channels based on consumer data and habits

Digital branding is dependent on data available to truly understand customers and their needs, wants, and desires. In detail, its necessary to know the customers social media behaviour, understanding the customers online journey, the channels they are engaging in and measuring their digital behaviour. The generated data shows when and where brands should post content to reach their target audience, while a creativity team effectively communicates the brand message to the potential and actual customers to generate as many impressions as possible (Ostholthoff, 2017).

Creating digital relationships

Digital branding includes establishing a brand identity online and building mutually beneficial relationships. All marketing efforts can be tracked and analysed by new digital key performance indicators (KPIs). The most important KPIs measure visibility, engagement, relationship, and opportunities (Ostholthoff, 2017).

- **Visibility**: Where does the brand rank on the Google search page? A brand's visibility to others drives purchasing decisions, and the higher a page ranks, the more likely customers will find the brand.
- **Engagement**: It is essential to know how much consumers engage with the content. So, it's important to measure how many times customers interact with a brand's site, keep track of bloggers who mention the brand on their site, and time how long people stay on each page of a brand's website.
- **Relationships**: This is a very important metric because human connections in a digital world are crucial and cheaper then to win new customers.
- **Opportunities**: It is important to identify what channels or sources yield the highest deal flow where a relationship can be monetized.
- **Sales**: Marketing efforts need to be converted into sales. Monitoring a brand's sales revenue is a great indicator to determine if a brand needs to come up with new strategies.

In the following box you find the most important KPIs when it comes to measure a brand's or a company's digital marketing performance.

> **The most important KPIs for Digital Marketing Performance.**
> **Click-Through Rate**
> Click-through rate (CTR) is a digital advertising metric that is calculated by dividing the total number of clicks an ad receives by the total number of impressions and then multiplying that by 100. This provides the percentage of the total clicks in relation to the number of times an ad was shown. Unlike CPM (cost per thousand impressions), CTR tells us how much impact the ad itself has had on prospects. Every click means a visit, and visits convert into the leads that can turn into customers.

Cost Per Click

Cost per click (CPC) is the amount charged by digital advertising platforms, for example Google AdWords or Facebook, each time a user clicks on an ad. CPC can be calculated by dividing the total expense of the campaign by the total number of clicks. This metric is useful to find out which digital media are offering the most convenient CPC-CAC (the customer acquisition cost ratio), which also ensures a good return on investment.

Cost Per Action (CPA)

This metric is important when it comes to finding a model that allows a brand to pay for certain actions only. These actions could be conversions, signups, forms filled out, or even purchases. Cost per action (CPA) refers to the total average cost of the desired action the brand wants the user to perform. It is calculated by dividing the total campaign cost by the number of actions completed.

Conversion Rate

The conversion rate is a fundamental digital advertising and marketing metric. It tells you how many of the leads generated by your advertising or digital marketing strategy actually became current customers. It is calculated by dividing the total number of prospects generated by the number of clients obtained from that same prospect database, and then multiplied by 100.

Knowing the conversion rate helps you find out whether the traffic and prospects generated by using a marketing or digital advertising campaigns was successful or not. It also tells you whether a company's segmenting was right, making an impact on the targeted audience, on the right media platform.

With the application of AI and machine learning it is possible to find the best target audience or demographic group for any ad and automatically manage the company's budget, guaranteeing to get a better cost per conversion (lower cost per sale or cost per lead).

The Percentage of Customers That Come from Your Digital Marketing Strategy

This ratio tells you the percentage of customers that have been generated by your online advertising or digital marketing activities. It's simple to calculate. You just need to identify how many customers were generated by your advertising or digital marketing efforts during a specific period and compare that with those that didn't come from your online marketing activities.

Return on Investment

The return on investment ROI is an important metrics when we want to know how effective an online advertising or digital marketing strategy is and if the efforts were profitable. The ROI is calculated as follows:

$$(\text{profits or incomes generated} - \text{investment costs})/\text{investment costs}$$

For example: After implementing a digital branding campaigns, you obtained 600 Euros of profit and you invested only 100 Euros. (600–100)/100 = 5

ROI: 5

This means that for every Euro invested, 5 Euros are gained back.

Customer Acquisition Cost (CAC)

The CAC is a metrics that tells us how much it costs you to acquire a new customer. The main objective is to ensure that the cost of customer acquisition is lower than the lifetime value of that client for the company. It is calculated by dividing the total digital marketing investment for a specific period by the number of clients acquired during that same period.

Customer Lifetime Value

The customer lifetime value (CLV) is the total amount of value a client generates during the time he or she remains a customer. Studies have shown that the likelihood of selling to a new customer is between 5 and 20%, and the probability of making a sale to a customer that has already made a purchased is 60 to 70%: Therefore, it is so important to retain existing customers.

By measuring the total profit that customer provides over the course of the whole customer relationship with a company or brand, we can work out exactly how valuable the customer is for this company or brand.

Churn Rate

This is the metric that tells you how many customers cancelled their payments or orderings. This metric only applies when clients are charged on a recurring basis. The easiest and most basic formula for calculating the churn rate is by dividing the number of lost clients during a period by the number of clients you had when that same period started.

For example, if 5 clients cancelled their payments and originally there have been 200, the churn rate is 2.5%.

Source: (Adext, 2019)

7.2 Importance of digital customer journeys and touchpoints

That retail branding also must move with the times is primarily due to the fact that the retailing industry is a highly competitive industry that stagnates after years of consolidation and growth. Business models that were successful in the past are no longer valid in their ability to meet consumer needs of tomorrow. Discount retailing is growing at higher rates than traditional distribution channels like supermarkets or hypermarkets. Particularly, large scale markets (e.g., hypermarkets) are challenged to keep their floor space economically justifiable. E-commerce is still small in terms of market share in many European countries but the demand for web-based solutions for shopping is evident and questions the existence of traditional business models in retailing. In detail, retailing companies with a wide network of physical stores need to redefine their business model according to a differentiation strategy. Excellent shop floor operations in combination with convenient e-commerce entry points for consumers are seen as the base for a promising business model. The principal that needs to be incorporated into every aspect of the business is to respect each customer individually and to create relevant touchpoints between customers, brands, and retailers. Digital touchpoints need to be developed and store solutions have to be implemented on micro-level according to their target groups.

In Figure 7.1 we see a typical customer journey, including physical touchpoints and digital touchpoints. Creating a holistic customer experience across all channels of communication is essential in a customer journey map. When creating a customer journey from the first step "awareness" to consideration until the purchase is made, the last step is equally important. Marketers need to consider how they can stay in touch with their customers, in the sense of creating long-term customer relationships. In the figure below, we see earned touchpoints and managed touchpoints. Earned touchpoints are touchpoints that a company achieves through well-done activities,

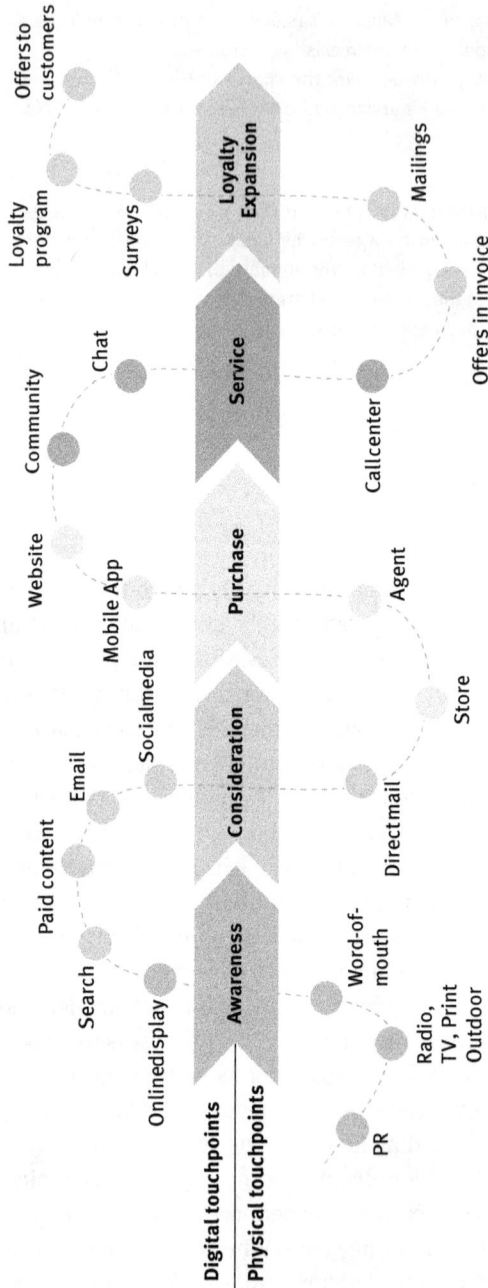

Figure 7.1: Digital customer journey and touchpoints.
Source: Bhargava, 2016

such as reviews or referrals, social media, 3rd party sites. Managed touchpoints are touchpoints that are managed by the company or marketers themselves. These are normally purchased touchpoints, such as radio, TV, billboards, Apps, Website, etc.

Information technology and digitalization has changed the landscape of consumer behaviour and has empowered the consumers in retailing. Okonkwo (2007) states that "the internet has evolved from a medium of enhancing brand awareness and disseminating information to an essential channel of retailing." More and more brands use the internet as a retail location, mostly choosing the e-retail strategic option of channel integration combining online and offline retailing activities but implementing e-retail just in a few markets leaving "an unfilled market gap in other regions" (Okonkwo, 2007).

The use and implementation of technology in the retail sector, but also in branding activities and concepts, are of essential value because customer experience can be enhanced, and business operations will be designed more efficiently. What is more, since the last couple of years, especially during the Corona pandemic, retailers are specifically struggling with recessions due to high fixed costs for store leases, high interest costs for store fixtures and renovation, and stagnating consumer markets, also characterised by uncertainty in general and uncertain prospects. Players, who are not holding top positions in their respective market in terms of market share, are particularly vulnerable to bankruptcy or liquidation, and are in part only kept alive with state support. This is especially the case for retailers that have increased their debt and retailers owned by private equity firms that were purchased during prior boom years due to their strong cash flow and property assets. In companies that are trading with perishable goods on a consumer basis and that are depending on opening hours, labour cost can not be reduced on short-term basis by shutting down plants on a temporary basis or through outsourcing production to suppliers with low-cost manufacturing facilities (Berman, 2013).

Furthermore, consumers have changed their behaviour during the past years and become more value conscious because of increasing consumer caution on their spending of disposable income. Market share among traditional supermarket operators are divided among price-oriented buyers, who will frequent discount shops, among convenience-oriented buyers, who will frequent convenience stores, specialty stores or e-commerce offers, and among quality-oriented buyers, who will frequent specialty independently owned food stores (Berman, 2013).

Consequently, retailers that develop a multichannel retail business model and that stays close to the needs and desires of their customers will be successful in the long run. E-commerce is one of the key factors that has changed the retail sector as business models were developed, which focused on online shoppers as their primary source of income. Consumer packaged goods and the location-based grocery retailing were rather untouched by the increasing consumer tendencies towards ecommerce. Due to the sensitivity of fresh food products, they are more difficult to be distributed via e-commerce sales channels. Nevertheless, major players, like

Amazon, successfully developed a business model how to sell and deliver consumer packaged goods by taking out the classic grocery retail store of the supply chain towards consumers. Therefore, grocery retail companies need to define their business strategy and develop core competencies in order not to get diluted by new market entrants. On the one hand the challenge will be to maintain consumer frequency in a wide network of physical stores and on the other hand add advantages from the ecommerce sector.

Therefore, marketers should focus on the customer journey and its touchpoints. Customer journeys are end-to-end business maps that offer a visualization of the customer experience. Right from the outreach to the target market, customer acquisition, adding value to the prospect, to conversion, the map defines it all keeping the experience in mind first. The aim behind creating a customer journey is to understand them better. What are your customers thinking when you approach them, what actions are they more likely to take, what are the thoughts that frequently come to them, what kind of concerns come up and when, what contact points are they comfortable sharing, and what their purchase triggers are (Bhargava, 2016)? Creating a journey to conversion keeping every little aspect of the customer in mind, helps brands achieve their objectives more effectively, especially in rapidly changing markets.

7.3 Digital communication in building brands

Digital capability is becoming more necessary for businesses that are seeking to build or enhance their brands through brand building programmes. Digital is a powerful tool for brands and with many brand-building benefits. Some of these benefits are listed below:
- Effective reach: Using digital channels, like social media platforms, online advertisements, search engine advertisements, chat sites, etc. for brand communication provides the possibility to promote the brand across several different platforms, allows a single brand message to be sent to various customers, yet personalized to each one.
- Virality: The great thing about digital branding is that brands are easily promoted through the activities of third parties, for example, likes, shares, recommendations, etc. The more opportunities marketers give the brand content to be different and unique, the better the chance that the brand message will be dispersed. Going viral can hardly be relied on, but a consistent digital brand communication is a good strategy to build a large online presence.
- Engagement: Digital brand communication allows customers to get involved with the brand and creates a unique customer experience. Some ways in which digital brand communication allows companies to interact with their customers include launching a clickable banner ad on certain sites or creating a GIF to be shared.

– Differentiation: In saturated markets where competition is fierce it is even more important having something that sets a brand apart from others. Digital branding can help to bring together all brand's strengths and successes. It can help to create an impression and to distinguish a brand from competitors.

Relationships: Creating a digital brand makes it easier for a brand to connect with the target audiences. Many digital platforms, like social media platforms, are simply designed for increased levels of connectivity. There are many new ways in which marketers can share a brand's message online which allow for feedback and direct interactions with the target audience.

The benefits of digital brand communication are supported by global consumer brand perception research conducted by Nielsen which showed the following results: 92% of consumers stating they trust earned media, such as word of mouth and recommendations from friends and family, above other forms of advertising. Online consumer reviews were the second most trusted source with 70% indicating they trust these sources of information. The reach of TV means this will remain the main way brand marketers communicate with their audience. Digital channels offer ways to connect with target consumers and create positive brand experiences that will help to build the brand's equity.

What is more, the refrain in many businesses is about putting the customer at the centre of every brand management activity. Changed buying behaviours, new channels and technologies provide more ways of delivering engaging, consumer-centred brand experiences. To be successful in digital brand communication means participating in a wide range of online activities integrated with offline brand events. An integrated approach can deliver an authentic and consistent total brand experience that is aligned with the brand's strategy, positioning, and purpose.

Competition among brands is steadily increasing as branding channels and messages proliferate. As consumers become more digitally empowered, brand messages lose their impact, and the likelihood of conversion, on average, decreases. The brands most likely to convert digitally jaded consumers into purchasers offer the strongest array of digital experiences. These successful players seem to be pulling away from less robust digital brands and gaining further momentum as they build up positive word of mouth on social media (Bughin, 2015).

More actively digital consumers are prone to abandon a brand midstream for several reasons. They are more likely to have joined Facebook, Instagram, Twitter, or product-evaluation platforms for conversations about the qualities of products or brands. The greater number of touchpoints before purchase increases the odds a consumer will encounter a deal breaker along the digital customer journey. What's more, companies have less control over more digitally seasoned consumers, who initiate their prepurchase interactions independently. And since the level and influence of advertising in the social-media space have yet to reach the levels common in offline channels, brand messages are less likely to influence decisions. Research

indicates that some companies have managed to navigate this competitive turbulence successfully. To understand the differentiating factors for that success, brands can be rated across four digital skills (Bughin, 2015):
- the ability to create brand awareness among an unusually high share of digitally savvy consumers
- to serve customers digitally during the purchase processes
- to generate an online customer experience deemed at least as good as the offline one
- to track the digital comments of customers about their experience and to use those comments to improve it

A related finding is that more thoroughly digitized brands also benefit from higher levels of positive word of mouth. The implication is that successful digitization creates additional momentum as winning companies benefit from free "earned" media, generated by recommendations and positive comments on social media. Polarization between digitally savvy companies and the traditional ones is already taking hold as feedback loops pile up benefits for companies early to adapt. Social-media recommendations that nudge customers to increase their purchases are becoming an important competitive asset. Positive consumer digital experiences also increase a brand's loyalty, raising the likelihood of repeat purchases.

To summarize, brands that have moved swiftly to master digital channels, to make use of digital brand communication, have the advantage to gain a deep understanding of customer preferences and behaviour, providing digital engagement through experiences, and improving offerings and communication via social media feedback.

Having an outlook on future trends and developments, the so-called experience economy will change into the direction of a virtual experience economy with a focus on VR, AR, and mixed reality technologies (Trendwatching, 2016). Information technology and digitalization have changed the marketing and retail landscape and consumer behaviour. Nowadays consumers are better educated, empowered and more demanding. They want products that emphasise their personality, combine advanced technology, elegant design and a certain sense of style, products that can be experienced with all their senses. Therefore, customer experience management will become more and more important in the years to come, especially when it comes to digital communication in building brands.

In the box below, we see an example of a successful strategy to align a digital marketing strategy with a company's retail growth strategy – a perfect way of responding to digital opportunities.

Tesco.com digital marketing strategy – An example.
An example of aligning the Tesco.com digital marketing strategy with the company's retail growth strategy is Tesco's online marketplace, as a way of responding to online opportunities. Within this online maketplace Tesco sells products from other retailers as part of its Tesco Direct offering. An important difference to other online marketplaces, for example, Amazon, marketplace sellers aren't

explicitly featured, instead, it's folded into search results for some products. This marketplace supports Tesco's core business strategy to support long-term growth (Chaffrey, 2012).

Tesco's marketing strategy has seven core principles for growth. Rather than creating a new strategy each year, Tesco has a series of common strategy elements. The original strategic principles were set out in 1997 when Tesco set out a strategy to grow the core business and diversify with new products and services in existing and new markets (Ansoff Matrix). Since then, this strategy enabled Tesco to grow by entering expanding markets in the UK – such as financial services, general merchandise and telecoms – and new markets abroad, initially in Europe and Asia and in the United States.

The seven main elements of the Tesco business strategy and how this strategy is aligned with Tesco's digital strategy is now explained briefly.

Growth strategy 1. To grow the UK core
The UK is still the largest core market for Tesco and a key driver of sales and profit. There are many opportunities for further growth. Tesco Direct and the online marketplace are aligned with this core – Tesco has seen the growth of Amazon and eBay marketplace and is responding to these.

Growth strategy 2. To be an outstanding international retailer in stores and online
This is Tesco's main objective since 1997. In 1997 international businesses generated 1.8% of the company's profits, today they represent 25%. The online channel is supporting this growth strategy.

Growth strategy 3. To be as strong in everything we sell as we are in food
The Tesco Direct and marketplace strategy also supports this objective.

Growth strategy 4. To grow retail services in all our markets
Nonfood services like Telecoms and Banking now account for 16% of Tesco's total sales although these are mainly implemented in the UK, they aim to grow these further.

Growth strategy 5. To put our responsibilities to the communities we serve at the heart of what we do
This objective is a response to negative perception about the brand in terms of corporate social responsibility. Tesco does run wider CSR initiatives such as the Tesco charity of the year.

Growth strategy 6. To be a creator of highly valued brands
Building brands gives Tesco more meaning with their customers. This relates to the retail brands such as the Tesco brand, but it also refers to product brands and pillar brands such as "Finest and Value." This strategic element relates to the development of sub-brands to fit specific market needs. Finding methods to add value to brands is at the heart of all effective digital strategies.

Growth strategy 7. To build our team so that we create more value.
Tesco refer to leaders to help build the team and achieve growth rather than building a team of all employees.

To summarize, a digital strategy must be shown to support the main business strategy of a company to get the recognition and resourcing it needs to be effective (Caffrey, 2015).

7.4 Future developments and outlook

The traditional retail industry and associated business models have gone through a significant phase of disruption. The rapid emergence of new technologies, e-commerce, and the evolution of social media platforms as a new sales channel continue to influence the whole sector. Three key factors have redefined the concept and principles of retail branding: the emergence and establishment of online (especially influenced by social media) as a significantly important sales channel and communication channel, branded experiences acquiring more importance and engagement than brands and the blurring of the physical and digital world in the customer journey. What is more, retail branding always followed the traditional principles of creating and establishing a differentiated brand positioning, bringing this positioning alive across all physical stores, and ensuring that the branding can positively influence brand image and brand equity. These principles have not really changed but have become more challenging and complex today to achieve the desired results (Roll, 2020).

Moreover, digital technologies inspired new visions for the future of stimulating engagement with retail customers while helping customers move along their shopping journey. The growth of online retail ecommerce sales has been steady in the last couple of years, still pegged at less than 10% in many countries. But there are great opportunities for integrating digital technologies in-store, particularly since they can support the consumer showrooming behaviour. So today, we are observing yet another technological shift in the retail experience. Mobile inspired customers are on the go make easy online transactions. These technology shifts have caused great disruption but have also led to innovation. The customer that is demanding the most from these technological shifts is the Millennial customer. They are telling us what to expect from upcoming generations. Today we are living in a challenging time for retail. The changes that digital technologies and innovations have created are providing retailers with opportunities to know their customers, create deeper relationships, and lower the friction of the connection through a seamless omnichannel (Spataro, 2014)

To conclude, consumer engagement with retail is constantly evolving and is being strongly influenced by technology. But one thing has remained constant – strong retail brands have survived disruptive changes in the past and will continue to do so. Continuous investment in building a brand identity and image, staying close to its purpose, moving with times, and establishing a core equity of the brand, are some of the key characteristics of a strong retail branding strategy (Roll, 2020).

List of References

Aaker, D. (1996). *Building Strong Brands*. New York: The Free Press.

Aaker, J. L. (2001). *Moderne Markenführung: Grundlagen Innovative Ansätze-Praktische Umsetzungen*. Wiesbaden: Gabler.

Accenture. (2017). *Accenture Driving the Future of Payment*. Accenture Consulting: https://www.accenture.com/_acnmedia/PDF-62/Accenture-Driving-the-Future-of-Payments-10-Mega-Trends.pdf#zoom=50

Adext. (2019). *Essential KPIs For Digital Marketing Strategy Performance*. https://blog.adext.com/kpis-digital-marketing-strategy/

Ajzen, I. (1991). The Theory of Planned Behavior. *Organizational Behavior and Human Decision Processes, 50*, 179–211.

Albertsons. (2018). *Traditions & History*. Albertsons: https://www.albertsons.com/our-company/traditions-history/

allbranded. (2020). *Aussenwerbung*. https://www.allbranded.de/Aussenwerbung/

Allen, T., Herst, D., Bruck, C., Sutton, M. (2000). *Consequences Associated With Work-to-Family Conflict: A Review and Agenda for Future Research*. Journal of occupational health psychology. 5, pp. 278-308

Allner, C. (11. November 2019). *Der Vertrieb muss digitalisiert werden*. Xing: http://www.xing-news.com/reader/news/articles/2777632?cce=em5e0cbb4d.%3AKVvG2SWhmY0xQcXIfb9GAW&link_position=digest&newsletter_id=53000&toolbar=true&xng_share_origin=email

Almeida, K. (8. January 2020). *Worker Well-Being: Surpassing 2020 Targets and Deepening Our Impact*. https://prod.levistrauss.levis.com/2020/01/08/worker-well-being-surpassing-2020-targets-and-deepening-our-impact/#:~:text=Levi%20Strauss%20%26%20Co.%E2%80%99s%20Worker%20Well-being%20%28WWB%29%20initiative%2C,related%20to%20health%2C%20financial%20securit

AMA. (24. January 2019). *The Myth of Generational Differences in the Workplace*. AMA Net: https://www.amanet.org/articles/the-myth-of-generational-differences-in-the-workplace/

AMA. (2019). *How Brands Can Help Consumers Green Up Their Act*. American Marketing Association: https://www.ama.org/marketing-news/how-brands-can-help-consumers-green-up-their-act/

Andersson, J., Berg, A., Hedrich, S., & Magnus, K.-H. (October 2018). *Is Apparel Manufacturing Coming Home?* Von McKinsey: https://www.mckinsey.com/industries/retail/our-insights/is-apparel-manufacturing-coming-home?cid=other-eml-alt-mip-mck-oth-1810&hlkid=1473c9c94bf747a4a519ee45c5ca2ea6&hctky=2889174&hdpid=4fee0838-da75-484b-934c-0f1ddde0e7b5

Anis, Y., Elliott, B., & Koestler, C. (November 2018). *Black Friday 2018: Consumers Are Eager, More Digital, and Willing to Spend*. McKinsey: https://www.mckinsey.com/business-functions/marketing-and-sales/our-insights/black-friday-2018-consumers-are-eager-more-digital-and-willing-to-spend?cid=other-eml-alt-mip-mck-1811&hlkid=5a61ae6f10544667b1bb82c00c9f6718&hctky=2889174&hdpid=45c15bcf-c0dc-45

Ansoff, I. (1965). *Checklist for Competitive and Competence Profiles*. New York: McGraw-Hill.

Arslan, A., Agatz, N., Kroon, L.; Zuidwijk, R. (2019). *Crowdsourced delivery—A dynamic pickup and delivery problem with ad hoc drivers*. Transportation Science, 1 (86), pp. 222-235

Aull, B., Kuijpers, D., Sawaya, A., & Vallöf, R. (19. March 2020). *What Food Retailers Should Do During the Coronavirus Crisis*. McKinsey: https://www.mckinsey.com/industries/retail/our-in sights/what-food-retailers-should-do-during-the-coronavirus-crisis?cid=other-eml-alt-mip-mck&hlkid=2743b8e3cdbf4665b4bea59667f9e720&hctky=2889174&hdpid=a49c7b8a-0bea-4a65-853c-92d7bd72e4a1

https://doi.org/10.1515/9783110543827-010

Ausick, P. (22. March 2014). *Walmart Now Has Six Types of Stores*. 247wallst: https://247wallst. com/retail/2014/03/22/walmart-now-has-six-types-of-stores/

Avcılar, M. & Özsoy, T. (2015). Determining the Effects of Perceived Utilitarian and Hedonic Value on Online Shopping Intentions. *International Journal of Marketing Studies*, *7*, 27–49.

Bainbridge, J. (23. October 1997). Who Wins the National Trust? *Marketing*, 21–23.

Baker, W., BenMark, G., Chopra, M., Kohli, S. (6. June 2018). Master the Challenges of Multichannel Pricing. *Sloan Review*, S. online. https://sloanreview.mit.edu/article/master-the-challenges-of-multichannel-pricing/

Barbuto Jr., J. E., & Scholl, R. W. (1999). Leaders' Motivation and Perception of Followers' Motivation as Predictors of Influence Tactics Used. *Psychological Reports*, *84*(1), 1087–1098.

Barnes, L., & Lea-Greenwood, G. (2006). Fast fashioning the supply chain: Shaping the research agenda. *Journal of Fashion Marketing and Management*, *10*, 259–271.

Barrett, J. (18. July 2017). *Experience: The Future of Instore Retail*. CMO: http://www.cmo.com/opin ion/articles/2017/7/5/experience-the-future-of-instore-retail.html#gs.8e5Pl4w

Barwitz, N., Körs, B., & Ramezani, S. (November 2017). *Putting the Right Price on Customer Interactions*. Mc Kinsey Quarterly: https://www.mckinsey.com/industries/healthcare-systems-and-services/our-insights/putting-the-right-price-on-customer-interactions?cid=other-eml-alt-mkq-mck-oth-1711

Bashin, H. (2019). *Brand Concept*. marketing91: https://www.marketing91.com/brand-concept/

Baumgarth, C. (2008). *Markenpolitik: Markenwirkungen, Markenführung, Markencontrolling*. Wiesbaden: Gabler.

Baumgarth, C. (2010). *B-to-B-Markenführung: Grundlagen–Konzepte–Best-Practice*. Wiesbaden: Gabler.

Bauer, H., Dirks, T., Bryant, M. (2008). *Erfolgsfaktoren des Mobile Marketing*. Wiesbaden: Springer.

BBC (November 2016). *Singles Day: How China's Alibaba wants to change shopping*. https://www. bbc.com/news/world-asia-china-37932751

Ben, E., Brousmiche, K.-L., Levard, H., & Thea, E. (2017). *Blockchain for Enterprise: Overview, Opportunities and Challenges*. Nice: ICWMC.

Bepari, S. (23. July 2019). *Mobile Wallet Usage Mapped: Brits Have the Third Highest E-Wallet Usage in the World*. Fintech News: https://www.fintechnews.org/the-number-of-mobile-wallet-users-grows-by-140-million-per-year/

Berman, B. R., & Evans, J. (2013). *Retail Management: A Strategic Approach*. Pearson: UK.

Bhargava, V. (8. November 2016). *Why Your Business Needs to Focus on the Customer Journey More Than Sales and How*. https://blog.exitbee.com/business-needs-focus-customer-journey-sales/

Biegel, B. (1997). *Visual Merchandising Deutscher Fachverlag*. Frankfurt am Main: Deutscher Fachverlag.

Binioris, A. (2008). *Logistics: Introduction in supply chain management*. Athens: Iatrikes Ekdoseis P.X. Passxalidis, Athens.

Biomimicry Institute (2016). *Biomimicry is the practice of looking to nature for inspiration to solve design problems in a regenerative way*. https://biomimicry.org/

BizCommunity. (14. May 2019). *The Most Valuable Global Retail Bbrands for 2019*. BizCommunity: https://www.bizcommunity.com/Article/1/168/190776.html

Black, S. (2008). *The Sustainable Fashion Handbook*. Thames and Hudson Ltd.

Black, S., & Hilary, A. (2012). *The Sustainable Fashion Handbook*. London: Thames & Hudson.

Blanchard, D. (2010). *Supply chain management: best practices*. New Jersey: John Wiley & Sons, Inc.

Blombäck, A., & Axelsson, B. (2007). The Role of Corporate Brand Image in the Selection of New Subcontractors. *Journal of Business & Industrial Marketing*, *22*(6), 418–430.

BMWE. (2019). *Grüner Knopf*. Bundesministerium für wirtschaftliche Zusammenarbeit und Entwicklung: https://www.gruener-knopf.de/presse.html

Boldt, S. (2010). *Markenführung der Zukunft: Experience Branding, 5-Sense-Branding, Responsible Branding, Brand Communities, Storytising und E-Branding*. Hamburg: Diplomica.

Bosshart, D. (2003). *Wohin entwickelt sich der Einzelhandel?* Presentation at REWE, Vienna, 12 June 2003.

Boudet, J., Gregg, B., Wong, J., & Schuler, G. (October 2017). *What Shoppers Really Want from personalized Marketing*. McKinsey: https://www.mckinsey.com/business-functions/marketing-and-sales/our-insights/what-shoppers-really-want-from-personalized-marketing?cid=other-eml-alt-mip-mck-oth-1710

Brakus, J. J., Schmitt, B. H., & Zarantonello, L. (2009). Brand Experience: What Is It? How Is It Measured? Does it Affect Loyalty? *Journal of Marketing*, *73*, 52–68.

Brand Trust. (2019). *Ingredient Brand*. Glossary: https://www.brand-trust.de/en/glossary/ingredient-brand.php

brandlance. (2019). *Cool Company Names*. barndlance: https://brandlance.com/cool-company-names.html/

BrandMentions. (2020). *Social Mention*. https://brandmentions.com/socialmention/#

Broniarczyk, S., & Hoyer, W. (2010). Retail Assortment: More Is Not Better. In M. Krafft, & M. Mantrala, *Retailing in the 21st Century* (225–238). Berlin: Springer.

Bruhn, M., & Homburg, C. (2017). *Handbuch Kundenbindungsmanagement: Strategie und Instrumente für ein erfolgreiches CRM*. Wiesbaden: Springer.

Bughin, J. (February 2015). *Brand success in an era of Digital Darwinism*. McKinsey: https://www.mckinsey.com/industries/technology-media-and-telecommunications/our-insights/brand-success-in-an-era-of-digital-darwinism

Bundeskanzleramt. (2019). *Einkommen und der Gender Pay Gap*. https://www.bundeskanzleramt.gv.at/agenda/frauen-undgleichstellung/gleichstellung-am-arbeitsmarkt/einkommen-und-der-genderpay-gap.html

Burmann, C., Blinda, L., & Nitschke, A. (2003). *Konzeptionelle Grundlagen des identitätsbasierten Markenmanagements*. Wiesbaden: Springer.

businessdictionary. (2017). *Digitalization*. businessdictionary: http://www.businessdictionary.com/definition/digitalization.html

Business-to-you. (2018). *Porter's Five Forces*. Business-to-you: https://www.business-to-you.com/porters-five-forces/

Buttle, F., & Maklan, S. (2019). *Customer Relationship Management*. Routledge.

Caffrey, A. (November 2015). *How to Integrate Sustainability into Marketing Communications*. Triple Pundit: https://www.triplepundit.com/story/2015/how-integrate-sustainability-marketing-communications/30571

Calderin, J. (2009). *Form, Fit and Fashion*. Rockport Publisher.

Capgemini. (January 2019). *Last Mile Delivery Challenge*. https://www.capgemini.com/wp-content/uploads/2019/01/Report-Digital--Last-Mile-Delivery-Challenge1.pdf

Caritas. (2019). *SOMA*. https://www.caritas-stpoelten.at/hilfe-angebote/menschen-mit-psychischen-erkrankungen/berufliche-integration/soma-krems/

Carman, J. M. (1978). Values and Consumptions Patterns: A Closed Loop. In Hunt, K., *Advances in Consumer Research*, (Vol. 5, 403–407). Chicago: Ann Arbor: Association for Consumer Research.

Carrigan, M., & Attalla, A. (2001). The myth of the ethical consumer – Do ethics matter in purchase behaviour? *Journal of Consumer Marketing*, *18*, 560–578.

Carson, B. (September 2018). *Blockchain Explained: What it Is and Isn't, and Why it Matters*. My Kinsey: https://www.mckinsey.com/business-functions/digital-mckinsey/our-insights/blockchain-explained-what-it-is-and-isnt-and-why-it-matters

castelligasse. (November 2019). *TV advertisements*. http://www.castelligasse.at/Werbetechnik/Werbetarife-TV.htm#:~:text=800%20Mio.%20TV-Zuseher.%20Fox%20hatte%20bereits%20im

%20Herbst,30-Sekunden-Spot%20kostete%20zwischen%203%2C8%20und%204%2C5% 20Mio.%20Dollar.

Cervellon, M.-C., & Carey, L. (2011). Consumers' Perceptions of "Green": Why and How Consumers Use Eco-Fashion and Green Beauty Products. *Critical Studies in Fashion and Beauty, 2*(1+ 2), 117–138.

Chaffrey, D. (June 2012). *Tesco.com Digital Marketing Strategy.* Tesco: https://www.smartinsights. com/digital-marketing-strategy/digital-strategy-development/tesco-marketing-strategy-in-2012/

Chandon, P., Hutchinson, J. W., Bradlow, E. T., & Young, S. H. (2007). Measuring the Value of Point-of-Purchase Marketing with Commercial Eye-Tracking Data. In M. Wedel, & R. Pieters, *Visual Marketing* (225–259). Lawrence Erlbaum.

Charmicheal, K. (2019). *What Is Permission Marketing & How Does it Work?* Von https://blog.hub spot.com/marketing/permission-marketing-automation

Chen, C. (8. August 2018). *Levi's Bets on Lasers; The World's Oldest Denim Brand Is Rolling Out a New Technology that Could Have Long-Term Implications for the Business.* BOF: https://www. businessoffashion.com/articles/news-analysis/levis-bets-on-lasers?utm_source=Subscriber s&utm_campaign=05890b2647-8-tips-for-mastering-the-in-store-experience&utm_medium= email&utm_term=0_d2191372b3-05890b2647-422496281

Chen, Y. (2009). Possession and Access: Consumer Desires and Value Perceptions Regarding Contemporary Art Collection and Exhibit Visits. *Journal of Consumer Research, 34,* 925–940.

Cian, L., & Cervai, S. (2011). The Multi-Sensory Sort (MuSeS): A New Projective Technique to Investigate and Improve the Brand Image. *Qualitative Market Research: An International Journal, 14*(2), 138–159.

Clement, J. (2007). Visual Influence on In-Store Buying Decisions: An Eye-Track Experiment on the Visual Influence of Packaging Design. *Journal of Marketing Management, 23*(9–10), 917–928.

cocacolabranding. (September 2016). *Coca Cola Emotional Branding Stratgey.* https://cocacolab randing.wordpress.com/2016/09/02/brand-meaning-imagery-and-performance/

Content Redefined. (2018). *Digital Branding.* https://www.contentrefined.com/digital-branding/

Coresight Research. (5. December 2018). *Voice Shopping: The Next Driving Force for E-Commerce?* Von Coresight Research: https://coresight.com/research/voice-shopping-the-next-driving-force-for-e-commerce/?utm_source=Primary+List&utm_campaign=32bcb9273d-DAILY+FEED% 3A+December+5+2018&utm_medium=email&utm_term=0_07f1d639d2-32bcb9273d-% 5BLIST_EMAIL_ID%5D&ct=t%28DAILY+FEED%3A+De

Coresight Research. (4. January 2019). *AI in Retail: Putting New Tools in the Hands of Retailers.* Coresight Research: https://coresight.com/research/ai-in-retail-putting-new-tools-in-the-hands-of-retailers/?utm_source=Primary+List&utm_campaign=efc6913f46-DAILY+FEED%3A +January+5+2019&utm_medium=email&utm_term=0_07f1d639d2-efc6913f46-%5BLIST_ EMAIL_ID%5D&ct=t%28DAILY+FEED%3

Coresight Research. (19. February 2020). *Coronavirus Briefing Outbreak Disrupts Global Supply Chain Particularly in Fashion.* Coresight Research: https://coresight.com/featured/ coronavirus-briefing-outbreak-disrupts-global-supply-chain-particularly-in-fashion/

Craven, M., Liu, L., Mysore, M., & Wilson, M. (March 2020b). *COVID-19: Implications for Business.* McKinsey: https://www.mckinsey.com/business-functions/risk/our-insights/covid-19-implications-for-business?cid=other-eml-nsl-mip-mck&hlkid=f3eec2cf6ea2444 c8702aa9cbcdf2bb1&hctky=2889174&hdpid=802e7585-5757-4ed6-9a6c-de278572bdf9

Creevy, J. (August 2011). *Tesco Opens Virtual Store in South Korea.* https://www.retail-week.com/ technology/tesco-opens-virtual-store-in-south-korea/5028571.article?authent=1

currycom. (March 2020). *Arbeitgeber als wichtige Informationsquelle.* https://www.currycom.com/ covid-19-arbeitgeber-als-wichtige-informationsquelle/

Custers, P. J., De Kort, Y., & Ijsselsteijn, W. A. (2010). Lighting in Retail Environments: Atmosphere perception in the real world. *Lighting Research & Technology, 42*, 331–343.

Customer Lifetime Value. (10. September 2017). *Calculate Your Customer Lifetime Value.* Customer Lifetime Value: http://www.customerlifetimevalue.co/

Cycle Competence Austria. (2017). *The Transport Revolution – Cargo Bikes on the Advance.* https://radkompetenz.at/en/1625/the-transport-revolution-cargo-bikes-on-the-advance/

Davis, F. D. (1989). Perceived usefulness, perceived ease of use, and user acceptance of information technology, *MIS Quarterly, 13*(3), 319–340.

Delgado-Ballester, E. (2012). *Development and Validation of a Brand Trust Scale.* Market management: https://markenmanagement.files.wordpress.com/2012/01/elena-delgado-ballester_development-and-validation-of-a-brand-trust-scale.pdf

Deloitte. (2017). *Global Powers of Retailing 2017.* Deloitte: https://www2.deloitte.com/content/dam/Deloitte/global/Documents/consumer-industrial-products/gx-cip-2017-global-powers-of-retailing.pdf

Deloitte. (2019). *Understanding Gen Z in the Workplace.* Articles: https://www2.deloitte.com/us/en/pages/consumer-business/articles/understanding-generation-z-in-the-workplace.html

Devaney, E. (7. January 2016). *Stores Are Using Music to Make You Spend More.* thinkgrowth: https://thinkgrowth.org/stores-are-using-music-to-make-you-spend-more-d6c85974b20b

Dick, A. S., & Basu, K. (1994). *Customer loyalty: Toward an integrated conceptual framework. Journal of the Academy of Marketing Science, 22*(2), 99–113.

Diebner, R., Silliman, E., Ungerman, K., & Vancauwenberghe, M. (April 2020). *Adapting Customer Experience in the Time of Coronavirus.* MyKinsey & Company: https://www.mckinsey.com/business-functions/marketing-and-sales/our-insights/adapting-customer-experience-in-the-time-of-coronavirus?cid=other-eml-alt-mip-mck&hlkid=d50bef124faa476c88600211ac015d3e&hctky=2889174&hdpid=19289b5b-5d9f-4245-a701-2aef6fe6388e

Difference Between. (24. July 2017). *Difference Between E Tailing and E Commerce.* Difference Between: http://www.differencebetween.com/difference-between-e-tailing-and-vs-e-commerce/

Donati, T. (2019). *Program Case Studies.* smile: https://blog.smile.io/top-10-customer-loyalty-programs-of-2019/

drawpack. (March 2011). *Branding Decisions Business Diagram.* https://www.slideshare.net/anicalena/branding-decisions-business-diagram

DriveMyCar. (2020). *About Us.* DriveMyCar: https://www.drivemycar.com.au/about-us

Dvornechuck, A. (2020). *Mission Statements.* ebaqdesign: https://www.ebaqdesign.com/blog/mission-statements

Ebster, C., & Garaus, M. (2011). *Store Design and Visual Merchandising: Creating Store Space That Encourages Buying.* Business Expert Press.

Ebster, K., & Garaus, M. (2015). *Räume, die zum Kauf verführen.* Wien: Facultas.

ECR Austria. (2014). *Consumer Shopper Journey: ECR Consumer Shopper Types.* ECR Austria: https://ecr-austria.at/whitepaper/ecr-austria-consumer-shopper-journey-ecr-consumer-shopper-types/

Educba. (2019). *Vertical Integration Examples.* Educba: https://www.educba.com/vertical-integration-example/

Egan, J. (2020). *Marketing Communications.* Sage.

Elliot, S. (2002). *Electronic Commerce: B2C Strategies and models.* Chichester: John Wiley & Sons Ltd.

Engel, J. F., Blackwell, R. D., & Miniard, P. W. (1978). *Consumer Behavior.* Fort Worth: Dryden Press.

Engel, J. F., Blackwell, R. D., & Miniard, P. W. (1993). *Consumer Behavior.* Fort Worth: Dryden Press.

Esch, F. R. (2010). *Strategie und Technik der Markenführung.* München: Vahlen.

Euromonitor. (2020). Euromonitor: http://go.euromonitor.com/rs/805-KOK-719/images/wpGCT2020-v0.5.pdf

Euromonitor International. (2016). *Euromonitor Consumer Shopper Types*. Euromonitor
International: http://go.euromonitor.com/rs/805-KOK-719/images/Euromonitor_Consumer-
Shopper-Types_Global.pdf

Euromonitor International. (2017). *About Us*. Euromonitor: http://www.euromonitor.com/about-us

European Commission. (2019a). *Are EA cargo bicycles the solution for urban freight*. https://
erticonetwork.com/are-electric-assisted-cargo-bicycles-the-solution-for-urban-freight/

European Commission. (2019b). *Horizon 2020*. European Commission: https://ec.europa.eu/
programmes/horizon2020/en/news/bringing-sustainable-freight-delivery-urban-centres

Fabrican Ltd. (2011). *Instant flowers! Manel Torres 2011 Fabrican*. http://www.fabricanltd.com/
components/instant-flowers-manel-torres-2011-fabrican/

FAZ. (31. July 2020). *Onlinehandel steigt um fast ein Drittel*. https://www.faz.net/aktuell/
wirtschaft/online-handel-steigt-um-fast-ein-drittel-in-corona-krise-16884012.html

Fazal Ijaz, M., Rhee, J., Lee, J.-H., & Alfian, G. (2014). Efficient Digital Signage Layout as a
Replacement to Virtual Store Layout. *International Journal of Information and Electronics
Engineering, 4*(4).

Fenko, A., Schifferstein, R., & Hekkert, P. (2009). *Shifts in sensory dominance between various
stages of user-product interactio*n. Applied ergonomics. 41. pp. 34-40.

Fischer, K. (2020). *Maßnahmen zur Steigerung der Motivation zur Absolvierung einer Lehre nach
Matura in Niederösterreich*. Krems: Masterarbeit an der IMC FH Krems.

Forbes. (2015). *A Comparative Look at the Valuation of Amazon, Alibaba and eBay*. Forbes: https://
www.forbes.com/sites/greatspeculations/2015/10/09/a-comparative-look-at-the-valuation-of-
amazon-alibaba-and-ebay/#3bc844691b6c

Forbes. (2017). *The World's Most Innovative Companies*. Forbes: https://www.forbes.com/
innovative-companies/list/#tab:rank_industry:Retailing

Foscht, T., Swoboda, B.; Schloffer, J. (2012). *Handelsmonitor 2011/2012: Herausforderung
Soziodemografie 2030plus*. Deutscher Fachverlag

Foscht, T., Swoboda, B., & Schramm-Klein, H. (2015). *Käuferverhalten. Grundlagen–Perspektiven–
Anwendungen*. Wiesbaden: Springer.

Foster, B. (April 2019). *Top 10 Examples of Social Responsibility as a Customer Retention Tool*.
smile.io: https://learn.smile.io/blog/top-10-examples-of-social-responsibility-as-a-customer-
retention-tool

Foulger, D. (2004). An Ecological Model of the Communication Process. Online under http://davis.
foulger.info/papers/ecologicalModelOfCommunication.htm

Foxall, G. (2015). *Consumer Behaviour – A Practial Guide*. New York: Routledge.

Francis, T., & Hoefel, F. (November 2019). -*'True Gen': Generation Z and its Implications for
Companies*. McKinsey: https://www.mckinsey.com/industries/consumer-packaged-goods/
our-insights/true-gen-generation-z-and-its-implications-for-companies

Frauenhofer IAO (2014): *Industrie 4.0 – Volkswirtschaftliches Potenzial für Deutschland*. https://
www.bitkom.org/Publikationen/2014/Studien/Studie-Industrie-4-0-Volkswirtschaftliches-
Potenzial-fuer-Deutschland/Studie-Industrie-40.pdf

Frey, U. D., Hunstiger, G., & Dräger, P. (2011). *Shopper-Marketing: Mit Shopper Insights zu
effektiver Markenführung bis an den POS*. Wiesbaden: Springer/Gabler.

Gabler, N. (2016). *The Magic in the Warehouse*. Fortune: http://fortune.com/costco-wholesale-
shopping/

Ganesh, J., Reynolds, K., Luckett, M., & Pomirleanu, N. (2010). *Online Shopper Motivations, and e-
Store Attributes: An Examination of Online Patronage Behavior and Shopper Typologies*.
Journal of Retailing, 3 (86), pp.106-115

Gansky, L. (2010). *The Mesh: Why the Future of Business Is Sharing*. London: Penguin Books Ltd.

Gedenk, K., Neslin, S., & Ailawadi, K. (2010). Sales Promotion. In M. Krafft, & M. Mantrala, *Retailing in the 21st Century*. Wiesbaden: Springer.

Giering, A. (2000). *Der Zusammenhang zwischen Kundenzufriedenheit und Kundenloyalität*. Wiesbaden: Springer.

Glowik, M., Smyczek, S., 2012: International Marketing Management – Strategies, Concepts and Cases in Europe; Oldenbourg

Goddard, W. (2018). *The Pros and Cons of Speech Recognition and Virtual Assistants*. IT chronicles: https://itchronicles.com/technology/the-pros-and-cons-of-speech-recognition-and-virtual-assistants/

Google Alerts. (2020). *Google Alerts*. https://www.google.at/alerts

Grant, M., & Kenton, W. (25. Juni 2019). *Sustainability*. Investopedia: https://www.investopedia.com/terms/s/sustainability.asp

Grewal, D., Levy, M., & Kumar, V. (2009). *Customer Experience Management in Retailing: An Organizing Framework*. Journal of Retailing, 3 (85), pp. 1-14

Gründerszene. (2019). *E-Mail Marketing*. Gründerszene: https://www.gruenderszene.de/lexikon/begriffe/e-mail-marketing

Haderlein, A. (2012). *Die digitale Zukunft des stationären Handels*. München: mi-Wirtschaftsbuch.

Hamida, E. B., Brousmiche, K., Levard, H., & Thea, E. (2017). Blockchain for Enterprise: Overview, Opportunities and Challenges. *Thirteenth International Conference on Wireless and Mobile Communications*. Nizza.

Haneef, M., Ceseracciu, L., Canale, C., Bayer, I. S., Heredia-Guerrero, J. A., & Athanassiou, A. (2017). *Advanced Materials From Fungal Mycelium: Fabrication and Tuning of Physical Properties*, Scientific Reports, 7, 41292

Hansen, T. & Jensen, J. (2009). Shopping orientation and online clothing purchases: The role of gender and purchase situation. *European Journal of Marketing*, 43, 1154–1170.

Hartmann, O., Haupt, S. (2014). *Touch - der Haptik-Effekt im multisensorischen Marketing*. Freiburg: Haufe

Hartmann, W., Kreutzer, R. T., & Kuhfuß, H. (2004). *Kundenclubs & More*. Wiesbaden: Gabler.

Harvey, S. (2017). *How to Conduct a Competitor Analysis and Create a New Template for Success*. fabrikbrands: https://fabrikbrands.com/how-to-conduct-competitor-analysis/

Häusel, H.-G. (2006). *Neuromarketing. Erkenntnisse der Hirnforschung für Markenführung, Werbung und Verkauf*. München: Haufe.

Häusel, H.-G. (2007). Neuromarketing – Der direkte Weg ins Konsumentenhirn. In H.-G. Häusel, *Neuromarketing – Erkenntnisse der Hirnforschung für Markenführung, Werbung und Verkauf* (7–15). Planegg/München.

Heckenhausen, J., & Heckenhausen, H. (2018). *Motivation und Handeln*. Deutschland: Springer Verlag.

Heinemann, G. (2013). *No-Line-Handel–Höchste Evolutionsstufe im Multi-Channeling*. Wiesbaden: Springer/Gabler. Heinemann, G. (2013): No-Line-Handel–Höchste Evolutionsstufe im Multi-Channeling. Wiesbaden. Springer Gabler.

Helmke, S., Uebel, M., & Dangelmaier, W. (2013). Inhalte des CRM-Ansatzes. In S. Helmke, M. Uebel, & W. Dangelmaier, *Effektives Customer Relationship Management – Instrumente – Einfuehrungskonzepte – Organisation* (3–22). Wiesbaden: Springer Gabler.

Herring, L., Wachinger, T., & Wigley, C. (December 2014). *Making Stores Matter in a Multichannel World*. McKinsey: https://www.mckinsey.com/industries/retail/our-insights/making-stores-matter-in-a-multichannel-world

Hinterhuber, H. H., & Matzler, K. (2002). *Kundenorientierte Unternehmensführung*. Wiesbaden: Gabler.

Hitesh, B. (18. April 2019). *Process in Marketing Mix–Concepts & Types of Processes*. marketing91: https://www.marketing91.com/process-in-marketing-mix/

Holweg, C., & Lienbacher, E. (2016). *Social Supermarkets in Europe – Investigations from a retailing perspective in selected European countries.*

Homburg, C., Giering, A., & Hentschel, F. (1999). Der Zusammenhang zwischen Kundenzufriedenheit und Kundenbindung. *Die Betriebswirtschaft, 59*(2), 174–195.

Home Delivery. (2019). *Balanced scorecard for furniture appliance large household good retailers.* Home delivery explained: https://home-delivery.org/2019/03/02/balanced-scorecard-for-furniture-appliance-large-household-good-retailers/

Howard, J. A., & Sheth, J. (1969). *Theory of Buyer Behaviour.* UK: John Wiley & Sons.

Hunter, M. (31. July 2014). *The 5 Types of Shoppers.* business know-how: https://www.business knowhow.com/marketing/shoppertypes.htm

Hurth, J. (2006). *Angewandte Handelspsychologie.* Stuttgart: W. Kohlhammer GmbH.

Hyde, R. (30. March 2018). *How Wal-Mart Model Wins with "Everyday Low Prices."* Von investopedia: https://www.investopedia.com/articles/personal-finance/011815/how-walmart-model-wins-everyday-low-prices.asp

inboundrocket. (2015). *Brand Position Map Example.* Inboundrocket: https://i2.wp.com/inboun drocket.co/wp-content/uploads/2015/12/Brand_Position_Map_example.png?resize=1330% 2C748&ssl=1

Inman, J., Winer, R., & Ferraro, R. (2009). The Interplay Among Category Characteristics, Customer Characteristics, and Customer Activities on In-Store Decision Making. *Journal of Marketing.*

Insider Trends. (11. September 2019). *The Future of Packaging: Where the Industry Is Headed in 2020 and Beyond.* https://www.insider-trends.com/the-future-of-packaging-where-the-industry-is-headed-in-2020-and-beyond/

Insley, V., & Nunan, D. (May 2014). Gamification and the Online Retail Experience. *International Journal of Retail & Distribution Management, 42*(5), 340–350.

ITA & AIT. (2019). *Foresight und Technikfolgenabschätzung: Monitoring von Zukunftsthemen für das österreichische Parlament.* Wien: Österreichische Akademie der Wissenschaften.

Jacoby, J., Chestnut, R. (1976). *Time 'Costs' and Information-Seeking Behavior*: Purdue Papers in Consumer Psychology, 155:

Jaishankar, G., Reynolds, K. E., Luckett, M. & Pomirleanu, N. (2010). Online Shopper Motivations, and e-Store Attributes: An Examination of Online Patronage Behavior and Shopper Typologies, *Journal of Retailing, 86*(1), 106–115.

Jeger, B. (25. November 2020). *Therefore the Black Friday 2020 Will Break Records.* https://www.marketing-boerse.de/fachartikel/details/2048-deshalb-wird-der-black-friday-2020-rekorde-brechen/173027

Jennings, D. (2016). *Is Volkswagen a Damaged Brand?* Von https://empresa-journal.com/2016/06/20/volkswagen-damaged-brand/

Joergens, C. (2006). Ethical fashion: Myth or future trend? *Journal of Fashion Marketing and Management, 10*, 360–371.

John, M., & Shyamala, K. (December 2019). The role of social media influencers in digital marketing era - an analytical study. *Journal of the Gujarat Research Society.*

Johnson, Tara. (10. June 2020). *8 Exceptional TikTok Ad Examples to Gain Inspiration for Your Next Campaign.* tinuiti: https://tinuiti.com/blog/paid-social/tiktok-examples-of-ads/

Jurevicius, O. (27. May 2013). *Porter's Five Forces.* Strategic management insight: https://strategicmanagementinsight.com/tools/porters-five-forces.html

Jurevicius, O. (19. August 2014). *GE McKinsey Matrix.* Strategic Management Insights: https://strategicmanagementinsight.com/tools/ge-mckinsey-matrix.html

Kalpana, R. (2019). *Four Important Strategies for Creating a Brand Name.* Businessmanagement ideas: https://www.businessmanagementideas.com/brand-name/4-important-strategies-for-creating-a-brand-name/2280

Kalyanam, K., Lal, R., & Wolfram, G. (2010). Future Store Technologies and their Impact on Grocery Retailing. In M. Krafft, & M. Mantrala, *Retailing in the 21st Century*. Wiesbaden: Springer.

Kantar Retail. (2016). *Brands Top 25 Most Valuable Global Retail Brands*. Retail Top 25: http://www. kantarretail.com/wp-content/uploads/2016/12/BZ_RETAIL_Top_25_201617.pdf

Kaplan, R., & Norton, D. (1992). *The Balanced Scorecard – Measures that Drive Performance*. Harvard Business Review: https://hbr.org/1992/01/the-balanced-scorecard-measures-that-drive-performance-2

Kaplan, R., & Norton, D. (1993). *Putting the Balanced Scorecard to Work*. Harvard Business Review: https://hbr.org/1993/09/putting-the-balanced-scorecard-to-work

Kastner, S. (2010). Quadratisch. Praktiksch. Gut–Textgestaltung von Verpackungen. In C. Vaih-Baur, & S. Kastner, *Verpackungsmarketing. Fallbeispiele. Trends. Technologien* (111–131). Frankfurt am Main: Deutscher Fachverlag.

Kaufman, R. (2012). Loyal customers, one box at a time. *Inc, 34*(3), 112.

Keller, K. L. (2013). *Strategic Brand Management. Building, Measuring and Managing Brand Equity*. UK: Pearson.

Keller, K. L., Aperia, T., & Georgson, M. (2008). *Strategic Brand Management: A European Perspective*. UK: Pearson.

Kering. (2017). *About Kering*. Kering: http://www.kering.com/en/group/about-kering

Kim, C., & Mauborgne, R. (2019). *Tools*. Blue Ocean Strategy: https://www.blueoceanstrategy.com/tools/

Kim, D.J., Ferrin, D. L., Rao, H. R. (2008). *A trust-based consumer decision-making model in electronic commerce: The role of trust, perceived risk, and their antecedents*. Decis. Support Syst., 44 (2008), pp. 544-564

Kim, Y.-K., Sullivan, P. & Forney, J. (2007). *Experiential Retailing: Concepts and Strategies that Sell*. Fairchild.

Kinney, L. (September 2011). *The Future of Product Innovation for Retailer*. Retail customer experience: https://www.retailcustomerexperience.com/articles/the-future-of-product-innovation-for-retailers/

knexus. (12. October 2017). *5 Key Factors Driving the Direct Consumer Model*. knexus: https://www.knexusgroup.com/show/blog/5-key-factors-driving-direct-consumer-model/

Ko, W. (11. October 2011). *The Successful Cost Leadership Strategies of WalMart*. winaungko: https://winaungko.blogspot.com/

Köhler, F. W. (1990). Die Dynamik der Betriebsformen des Handels: Bestandsaufnahme und Modellerweiterung. *Marketing ZFP, 1. Quartal*, 59–64.

Kotler, P., & Armstrong, G. (2006). *Principles of Marketing*. New Jersey: Pearson/Prentice Hall.

Kotler, P., & Bliemel, F. (2001). *Marketing-Management: Analyse, Planung und Verwirklichung*. Stuttgart: Schäffer-Poeschel.

Kotler, P., Keller, K. L., Brady, M., Goodman, M., & Hansen, T. (2009). *Marketing Management*. Pearson Education.

Kovacs, N., Bienert, R., Oehlmann, H., Schuermann, J., Schmidt, E., & Walk, E. (2012). *RFID – Standardisierung im Überblick*. Berlin: Beuth Verlag.

KPMG (2017). Global Online Consumer Report. Online under https://assets.kpmg/content/dam/kpmg/xx/pdf/2017/01/the-truth-about-online-consumers.pdf

Krishna, A. (2012). An integrative review of sensory marketing: Engaging the senses to affect perception, judgment and behavior. Journal of Consumer Psychology, 22 (3), pp. 332-351.

Kroeber-Riel, W., & Gröppel-Klein, A. (2013). *Konsumentenverhalten*. München: Vahlen.

Kroger. (2018). Kroger: https://www.kroger.com/

Krüger, M. (2016). *The Influence of Culture and Personality on Customer Satisfaction, International Management Studies*. Wiesbaden: Springer.

Kubu, M. (2016). *Bluetooth low energy beacons*. Krems: Masterarbeit, IMC FH Krems.

Kuijpers, D., Simmons, V., & van Wamelen, J. (November 2018). *Reviving Grocery Retail: Six imperatives*. McKinsey: https://www.mckinsey.com/industries/retail/our-insights/reviving-grocery-retail-six-imperatives

Kumar, N., & Steenkamp, J. B. (2007). *Private Label Strategy: How to Meet the Store Brand Challenge*. Boston: Harvard Business School Press.

Kures, M., Pinkovitz, B., & Ryan, B. (March 2011). *Trade Area Analysis*. https://fyi.extension.wisc.edu/downtown-market-analysis/understanding-the-market/trade-area-analysis/

Kuß, A., & Kleinaltenkamp, M. (2020). *Marketing-Einführung*. Gabler Verlag.

LaMarco, N. (21. November 2018). *10 Kinds of Aadvertising*. bizfluent: https://bizfluent.com/info-8369170-pros-cons-infomercials.html

Latham, G., & Locke, E. (1979). *Organizational Dynamics, 8*(2), 68–80.

Latham, G., & Locke, E. (2006). Enhancing the Benefits and Overcoming the Pitfalls of Goal Setting. *Organizational Dynamics, 35*(4), 332–340.

Lauer, T. (2011). *Bonusprogramme. Rabattsysteme für Kunden erfolgreich gestalten*. Berlin: Springer.

Leusser, W., Hippner, H., & Wilde, K. D. (2011). CRM–Grundlagen, Konzepte und Prozesse. In H. Hippner, B. Hubrich, & K. D. Wilde, *Grundlagen des CRM* (15–56). Wiesbaden: Gabler.

Litfin, T., Wolfram, G. (2006). *New Automated Checkout Systems*. In: Krafft, Manfred & Mantrala, Murali. (2006). Retailing in the 21st Century: Current and Future Trends.pp. 143-157

Litsa, T. (30. April 2019). *Experiential Marketing: What Makes a Brand Experience Stand Out?* Von https://www.clickz.com/experiential-marketing-what-makes-a-brand-experience-stand-out/235587/

Long, D. (April 2019). *Valentino Partners with Alibaba New Retail Experience*. The drum: https://www.thedrum.com/news/2018/04/23/valentino-partners-with-alibaba-new-retail-experience

Lotzkat, L. (2013). *Konkurrenzvorteile am Point-of-Sale: Möglichkeiten der Erfassung, Bewertung und Folgenabschätzung*. Wiesbaden: Springer.

Lux, W. (2012). *Innovationen im Handel*. Berlin: Springer Gabler.

Maechler, N., Neher, K., & Park, R. (2016). *From touchpoints to journeys: Seeing the world as customers do*. http://www.mckinsey.com/business-functions/marketing-and-sales/our-insights/from-touchpoints-to-journeys-seeing-the-world-as-customers-do

Manchiraju, S., & Sadachar, A. (2014). Personal Values and Ethical Fashion Consumption. *Journal of Fashion Marketing and Management, 18*.

Manganari, E., Siomkos, G., & Vrechopoulos, A. (2009). Store atmosphere in web retailing. *European Journal of Marketing, 43*(9/10).

McNeill, L., & Moore, R. (2015). Sustainable fashion consumption and the fast fashion conundrum: fashionable consumers and attitudes to sustainability in clothing choice. *International Journal of Consumer Studies, 39*, 212–222.

Marketing. (28. July 2019). *Brands vs. Products*. termscompared: https://www.termscompared.com/difference-between-brand-and-product/

Marketing study guide. (2019). *Brand Name Selection*. https://www.marketingstudyguide.com/brand-name-selection/

Marketingverband. (September 2018). https://www.marketingverband.de/fileadmin/Whitepaper_Pricing_final_Web.pdf

marketo. (2019). *Mobile Marketing*. https://www.marketo.com/mobile-marketing/

Martin, D., & Schouten, J. (2014). *Sustainable Marketing* (Pearson New International Edition). London: Pearson Education.

Mascarenhas, O., Kesavan, R. & Bernacchi, M. (2006). Lasting customer loyalty: A total customer experience approach. *Journal of Consumer Marketing, 23*, 397–405.

MBA Crystal Ball. (January 2019). *Introduction to Strategy*. https://www.mbacrystalball.com/blog/strategy/

Mc Namara, C. (2019). *Free Basic Guide to Leadership and Supervision*. https://managementhelp.org/management/guidebook.htm#anchor227239

McCarthy, J. E. (1975). *Basic Marketing: A Managerial Approach*. Richard D. Irwin.

McKinsey. (June 2009). *The Consumer Decision Journey*. McKinsey: https://www.mckinsey.com/business-functions/marketing-and-sales/our-insights/the-consumer-decision-journey

McKinsey (2016). *Enduring Ideas: The 7S-Framework*. https://www.mckinsey.com/business-functions/strategy-and-corporate-finance/our-insights/enduring-ideas-the-7-s-framework

McKinsey (2017). What shoppers really want from personalized marketing. Online under https://www.mckinsey.com/business-functions/marketing-and-sales/our-insights/what-shoppers-really-want-from-personalized-marketing

McKinsey. (November 2019). *How McKinsey Is Revitalizing Brick and Mortar*. McKinsey: https://www.mckinsey.com/about-us/new-at-mckinsey-blog/how-mckinsey-is-revitalizing-brick-and-mortar

McKinsey. (January 2020a). *Climate Risk and Response. Physical Hazards and Socioeconomic Impacts*. McKinsey: https://www.mckinsey.com/~/media/McKinsey/Business%20Functions/Sustainability/Our%20Insights/Climate%20risk%20and%20response%20Physical%20hazards%20and%20socioeconomic%20impacts/MGI-Climate-risk-and-response-final.ashx

McKinsey. (26. October 2020b). *Consumer Sentiment and Behavior Continue to Reflect the Uncertainty of the COVID-19 Crisis*. Our insights: https://www.mckinsey.com/business-functions/marketing-and-sales/our-insights/a-global-view-of-how-consumer-behavior-is-changing-amid-covid-19?cid=other-eml-alt-mip-mck&hdpid=9e710493-2f3e-48a8-a802-ca5619957b07&hctky=2889174&hlkid=3d27368b904949f2bea1d815

McKinsey. (January 2020c). *The Drive Toward Sustainability in Packaging – Beyond the Quick Wins*. McKinsey: https://www.mckinsey.com/industries/paper-forest-products-and-packaging/our-insights/the-drive-toward-sustainability-in-packaging-beyond-the-quick-wins?cid=other-eml-alt-mip-mck&hlkid=0ecb2099afd44e7492c58f5e1b3e25ec&hctky=2889174&hdpid=b9b2e61b-29dd-4263

McKinsey & Company. (December 2015). *The Consumer Sector in 2030: Trends and questions to consider*. http://www.mckinsey.com/industries/consumer-packaged-goods/our-insights/the-consumer-sector-in-2030-trends-and-questions-to-consider

McNair, M. P. (1931). Trends in Large-Scale Retailing. *Harvard Business Review*, *10*(1), 30–39.

Meffert, H., Burmann, C., & Koers, M. (2002). *Markenmanagement: Grundfragen der identitätsorientierten Markenführung*. Wiesbaden: Gabler.

Mehrabian, A., & Russell, J. A. (1974). *An Approach to Environmental Psychology*. US: MIT Press.

Mentzer, J. T., V. DeWitt, K. S., Keebler, S., Min, N. W., Nix, & Smith, C. D. (1985). Defining Supply Chain Management. *Journal of Business Logistics*, *22*(2), 2001.

Merkel, J., Jackson, P., & Pick, D. (2010). New Challenges in Retail Human Resource Management. In M. Krafft, & M. K. Mantrala, *Retailing in the 21st Century: Current and Future Trends* (257–270). Berlin: Springer.

Miles & More. (2020). *Vielfliegerprogramm*. https://www.miles-and-more.com/at/de.html

Morales, M., Mundy, P., Crowson, M., Neal-Beevers, A., & Delgado, Ch. (2005). *Individual differences in infant attention skills, joint attention, and emotion regulation behaviour*. International Journal of Behavioral Development, 29, pp. 259-263.

Morrison, M., & Mundell, M. (2012). Connecting, engaging and exciting shoppers. In M. Stâhlberg, & V. Maila, *Shopper Marketing – How to Increase Purchase Decisions at the Point of Sale* (81–86). London: Kogan Page Limited.

Morschett, D., Zentes, J., Schu, M., & Steinhauer, R. (2013). *Mega-Trends 2020+ HandelsMonitor*. Frankfurt am Main: Deutscher Fachverlag.

msn. (11. December 2019). *Wirtschaftsforscher für Rücksendegebühr im Onlinehandel*. msn: https://www.msn.com/de-at/finanzen/top-stories/wirtschaftsforscher-für-rücksende-gebühr-im-onlinehandel/ar-AAK0AVD?ocid=spartanntp

Müller-Hagedorn, L. (2003). *Einführung in das Marketing*. Köln: Schaeffer-Poeschel

Nachhaltigkeit. (2019). *Cradle to Cradle Vision*. Lexikon der Nachhaltigkeit: https://www.nachhaltig keit.info/artikel/1_3_f_cradle_to_cradle_vision_1544.htm

National Retail Federation. (2016). *Top 100 Retailers*. resources: https://nrf.com/resources/annual-retailer-lists/top-100-retailers/stores-top-retailers-2016

Nielsen. (2015). *The future of grocery*. https://www.nielsen.com/wp-content/uploads/sites/3/2019/04/nielsen-global-e-commerce-new-retail-report-april-2015.pdf

Nielsen. (2016b). *The science behind what's next*. https://sites.nielsen.com/yearinreview/2016/as sets/pdfs/Nielsen_AnnualReport_2016.pdf

Nieschlag, R. (1954). *Die Dynamik der Betriebsformen im Handel*. Essen: Schriftenreihe Rheinisch-Westfälisches Institut für Wirtschaftsforschung.

Obfuscata. (2019). *SWOT analysis*. http://www.obfuscata.com/swot-analysis-examples-4382.html

Ogden, J. R., & Ogden, D. T. (2005). *Retailing. Integrated Retail Managment*. USA: Houghton Mifflin Company.

Okonkwo, U. (2007). *Luxury Fashion Branding*. New York: Palgrave Macmillan.

Oliver, R. (1980). A Cognitive Model of the Antecedents and Consequences of Satisfaction Decisions. *Journal of Marketing Research, 17*(4).

Orvis, G. (11. August 2016). *The Science of Smell: How Retailers Can Use Scent Marketing to Influence Shoppers*. Shopify: https://www.shopify.com/retail/the-science-of-smell-how-retailers-can-use-scent-marketing-to-make-more-sales

Ostholthoff, H. (2017). *4 Ways to Master the Art of Digital Branding*. https://www.huffpost.com/entry/4-ways-to-master-the-art_b_9377440?guccounter=1&guce_referrer=aHR0cHM6Ly9l bi53aWtpcGVkaWEub3JnLw&guce_referrer_sig=AQAAAHBZ8BQRfAANWzGmeDtz5jhDpc9 juUVmXKImuboKzkeRUBsInZcs3-uyed1mfSyGXx11mkzWVovJCYJDHHEVfHfn5F-CIUeFUe1nA1mH4

Pantano, E. (June 2014). Innovation Drivers in Retail Industry. *International Journal of Information Management, 34*(3), 344–350.

Paton, E. (12. April 2017). *Imagining the Retail Store of the Future*. New York Times: https://www.nytimes.com/2017/04/12/fashion/store-of-the-future.html

Petty, R. E., & Cacioppo, J. T. (1984). Source Factors and the Elaboration Likelihood Model of Persuasion. *Advances in Consumer Research, 11*, 668.

Phau, I., Teah, M. & Chuah, J. (2015). Consumer attitudes towards luxury fashion apparel made in sweatshops. *Journal of Fashion Marketing and Management: An International Journal, 19*, 169–187.

Piller, F. & Steiner, F. (2008). *Mass customization: A strategy for sustainability in the fashion industry*. In: Black, S. (2008). The sustainable fashion handbook. London: Thames & Hudson, p. 287-288.

Podreciks, A., Uhlenbrock, N., & Ungerman, K. (July 2018). *Who's Shopping Where the Power of Geospatial Analytics in Omnichannel Retail*. McKinsey: https://www.mckinsey.com/industries/retail/our-insights/whos-shopping-where-the-power-of-geospatial-analytics-in-omnichannel-retail?cid=other-eml-alt-mip-mck-oth-1808&hlkid=2698e134eb574f3eac7886712fc11 be0&hctky=2889174&hdpid=23e1e18a-4ad5-4223-a4d0-9b69e

POPAI. (2016). *Mass Merchant Shopper Engagement Study*. https://view.publitas.com/popai/mass-merchant-shopper-engagement-study

Porter, M. E. (1999). *Wettbewerbsstrategie. Methoden zur Analyse von Branchen und Konkurrenten*. Frankfurt am Main et al.: Campus-Verlag.

Pradeep, A. K. (2010). *The buying brain: Secrets for Selling to the Subconscious Mind*. Hoboken/New Jersey: John Wiley & Sons, Inc.

Proctor, T. (2000). *Strategic Marketing: An Introduction*. New York: Routledge.

product report. (2019). *jö Bonus Club Kundenkarte*. produt report: https://productreport.at/joe-bonus-club-kundenkarte

producthunt. (2017). *operator 2.0*. posts: https://www.producthunt.com/posts/operator-2-0

Publix. (2018). *About*. Publix: http://corporate.publix.com/about-publix

PwC. (January 2013). *Demystifying the Online Shopper: 10 Myths of Multichannel Retailing*. pwc: http://www.pwc.com/multichannelsurvey

Qian, A. (18. April 2017). *Perficient*. Optimizing analytics in retail with geospatial data: https://blogs.perficient.com/2017/04/18/optimizing-analytics-in-retail-with-geospatial-data/

Raman K., Naik P.A. (2010). *Integrated Marketing Communications in Retailing*. In: Krafft M., Mantrala M. (eds) Retailing in the 21st Century. Heidelberg: Springer.

Ramanjaneyalu, N., G., C., & Vishwanath, K. (December 2013). Blind Taste Test of Soft-drinks – A Comparison Study on Coke and Pepsi. *International Journal of Application or Innovation in Engineering & Management, 2*(12), 244–247.

Ratner, B. D., Hoffman, A. S., Schoen, F. J. et al. (2013). *Biomaterials Science. An Introduction to Materials in Medicine*, 3rd ed.: Academic Press.

Ray, R. (2010). *Supply Chain Management in Retailing*. New Dehli: Tata McGraw Hill.

Rent the Runway. (December 2018). *Sustainable fashion*. Rent the Runway: https://www.renttherunway.com/sustainable-fashion

Reuters. (2018). *Company Profile*. Reuters: https://www.reuters.com/finance/stocks/company-profile/BBY.N

Rice, M. (August 2020). *What Is Brand Trust?* Von https://builtin.com/marketing/brand-trust

Robin. (May 2017). *Coca-Cola Pioneers Personalised Displays In-Store with Google AI*. http://www.netimperative.com/2017/05/10/coca-cola-pioneers-personalised-displays-store-google-ai/

Rohm, A. J. & Swaminathan, V. (2004). A typology of online shoppers based on shopping motivations, *Journal of Business Research, 57*(7), 748–757.

Roll, M. (2020). *Retail Branding in the new digital age*. Online under https://martinroll.com/resources/articles/marketing/retail-branding-in-the-new-digital-age/

Rommel, C. (2014). Grundlagen der Packungsgestaltung. In M. Kassmann, *Grundlagen der Verpackung. Leitfaden für die fächerübergreifende Verpackungsausbildung* (273–296). Berlin: Beuth.

Rosu, L. (October 2013). Geomarketing – A New Approach in Decision Making. *LUCRĂRILE SEMINARULUI GEOGRAFIC DIMITRIE CANTEMIR*(36).

Rötzer, F. (22. November 2019). *KI: Schlechte Aussichten für gut bezahlte Jobs mit Hochschulabschlüssen*. Heise: https://www.heise.de/tp/features/KI-Schlechte-Aussichten-fuer-gut-bezahlte-Jobs-mit-Hochschulabschluessen-4593558.html?wt_mc=nl.tp-aktuell.woechentlich

Rowley, J., Dawes, J. (2000). *Disloyalty: A closer look at non-loyals*. Journal of Consumer Marketing, 17 (6). pp. 538-547.

Rumscheidt, S. (2019). *Die letzte Meile als Herausforderung für den Handel*. ifo Schnelldienst, ifo Institute - Leibniz Institute for Economic Research at the University of Munich, 72(01), pp. 46-49

Samuel, A. (11. March 2016). *Psychographics Are Just as Important for Marketers as Demographics*. Harvard Business Review: https://hbr.org/2016/03/psychographics-are-just-as-important-for-marketers-as-demographics

Sarkar, S., Sharma, D., & Kalro, A. D. (2015). The Effect of Naming Strategy and Packaging on Perceived Quality and Purchase Intention of Private Label Brand. In F. Martínez-López, J. Gázqzez-Abad, & R. Sethuraman, *Advances in National Brand and Private Label Marketing* (103–112). Wiesbaden: Springer.

Saxena, L. (August 2018). *How social supermarkets are filling a gap in austerity Britain.* Independent: https://www.independent.co.uk/life-style/food-and-drink/features/social-super markets-filling-gap-austerity-britain-food-poverty-waste-welfare-reforms-a8466481.html

Schramm-Klein, H., Wagner, G., Neus, F., Swoboda, B., & Foscht, T. (2014). *HandelsMonitor: (R)Evolution des Mehrkanalhandels: Von Multi-Channel über Cross-Channel zu Omni-Channel-Retailing.* Frankfurt: Deutscher Fachverlag.

Schulz, L. (2014). *Das Geheimnis erfolgreicher Personalbeschaffung.* Wiesbaden: Springer.

Schütze, R. (1992). *Kundenzufriedenheit in Geschäftsbeziehungen.* Wiesbaden: Gabler.

Schwenkert, F. E. (2006). *Grundlagen der Untersuchung.* In: Käuferverhalten bei legalen Musikdownloads. Deutscher Universitätsverlag, Wiesbaden.

Sempelmann, P. (11. November 2019). *Industrie 4.0: Adidas Speedfactories wandern nach Asien.* Trend: https://www.trend.at/wirtschaft/industrie-adidas-speedfactories-asien-11210912?utm_source=Newsletter&utm_medium=email&utm_campaign=trend-Newsletter+-+2019-11-11&utm_content=https%3A%2F%2Fwww.trend.at%2Fwirtschaft%2Findustrie-adidas-speedfactories-asien-11

Sempelmann, P. (January 2020). *Microsoft schaltet den CO2-Rückwärtsgang ein.* Trend: https://www.trend.at/wirtschaft/microsoft-co2-rueckwaertsgang-11310875?utm_source=Newsletter&utm_medium=email&utm_campaign=trend-Newsletter+-+2020-01-17&utm_content=https%3A%2F%2Fwww.trend.at%2Fwirtschaft%2Fmicrosoft-co2-rueckwaertsgang-11310875

Serdaris, P., Antoniadis, I., & Tomlekova, N. (2014). Supply Chain Management: A View of the Distribution Channel. *Bulgarian Journal of Agricultural Science, 20*(2), 480–486.

Sgro, D. (2012). *Advanced theory and context.* https://claire-tid1330-blog-blog.tumblr.com/post/74427570651/morphotex

Shen, Y. (2012). Social Comparison, Social Presence, and Enjoyment in the Acceptance of Social Shopping Websites. *Journal of Electronic Commerce Research, 13*(3).

Shephard, A., & Pookulangara, S. (2014). The Slow Fashion Process: Rethinking Strategy for Fast Fashion Retailers. In T.-M. Choi, *Fast Fashion Systems: Theories and Application* (9–19). London: Taylor & Francis Group.

Sher, M. (2015. November 2016). *The Agile Supply Chain Management: What Is it and Why Should You Care!* Von Medium: https://medium.com/supply-chain-hubspot/the-agile-supply-chain-management-what-is-it-and-why-should-you-care-966ad9829d19

shopkick. (2020). *Successful Brand Repositioning Examples Designed to Reach a Greater Consumer Audience.* shopkick: https://www.shopkick.com/partners/blog/successful-brand-reposition ing-examples-designed-to-reach-a-greater-consumer-audience-slp-fc/

Sielhorst, T. (2009). *Marketingziel Kundenbindung: Die Kundenkarte im Einzelhandel.* Igel Verlag.

Silayoi, P., & Speece, M. (2004). Packaging and purchase decisions: An exploratory study on the impact of involvement level and time pressure. *British Food Journal, 106.*

Silayoi, P., & Speece, M. (2007). The Importance of Packaging Attributes: A Conjoint Analysis Approach. *European Journal of Marketing, 41*, 1495–1517.

Silverstein, M. J., & Fiske, N., 2003. Luxury for the Masses. *Harvard Business Review*, April, 48–59.

Singh, J., Sirdeshmukh, D. (2000). *Agency and trust mechanisms in consumer satisfaction and loyalty judgments.* Journal of the Academic Marketing Society, 28, pp. 150–167

Smartsheet. (2020). *The Essential Guide to Retail Store Layouts that Shape the Customer Experience.* smartsheet: https://www.smartsheet.com/store-layout

Social supermarkets. (2019). http://socialsupermarkets.org/

softengi. (2019). *Gamification in the Retail: Turning Shopping into a Game.* softengi: https://softengi.com/blog/gamification-in-the-retail-turning-shopping-into-a-game/

Solomon, M. R. (2015). *Consumer Behaviour. Buying, Having and Being.* Essex: Pearson.

SOMA. (2019). *Eine Idee, die hilft.* http://www.sozialmarkt.at/index.php?id=5

Song, J., Chen, C., Zhu, S., Zhu, M., et al. (2018). *Processing bulk natural wood into a high-performance structural material.* Nature, 554, p. 224.

Sonneck, P., & Ott, C. S. (2010). Future Trends in Multi-Channel Retailing. In M. Krafft, & M. Mantrala, *Retailing in the 21st Century* (175–192). Berlin: Springer.

Spanke, M., & Löbbel, S. (2012). *Erfolgreiches Visual Merchandising.* Frankfurt am Main: Deutscher Fachverlag.

Spataro, T. (2014). The digital future for retail. Online under https://www.smartinsights.com/ecommerce/multichannel-retail-strategy/digital-future-retail

Specialty retail. (fall 2005). *Are You Selling Necessity or Luxury?* Von http://specialtyretail.com/issue/are-you-selling-necessity-or-luxury/

Spiegel Media (2018). *Outfit 9.0.* https://www.spiegelgruppe.de/news/pressemitteilungen/detail/spiegel-studie-outfit-90-sozialvertraegliche-produktion-gewinnt-an-bedeutung

SpyFu. (2020). *Get Deep Keyword Research with a Few Easy Searches.* SpyFu: https://www.spyfu.com/keyword/overview

Statista. (2018). *Internet Usage Worldwide.* Statista: https://www.statista.com/topics/1145/internet-usage-worldwide/

Statista. (23. July 2019). *Statistiken zu FMCG.* Statista: https://de.statista.com/themen/574/fmcg/

statista. (3. February 2020a). *Statistiken zum Fernsehmarkt in Österreich.* statista: https://de.statista.com/themen/4275/fernsehen-in-oesterreich/

statistia. (4. February 2020b). *Tägliche Radionutzung in Österreich.* https://de.statista.com/statistik/daten/studie/315028/umfrage/taegliche-radionutzung-in-oesterreich/

Statistik Austria. (October 2019). *62% der 16- bis 74-Jährigen shoppen online.* http://www.statistik.at/web_de/presse/121982.html

Statistik Austria. (2019). *Einkommen.* https://www.statistik.at/web_de/statistiken/menschen_und_gesellschaft/soziales/gender-statistik/einkommen/index.htm

Stock-Homburg, H. (2013). *Handbuch Strategisches Personalmanagement.* Wiesbaden: Gabler.

Stotz, W., & Wedel-Klein, A. (2013). *Employer Branding: Mit Strategie zum bevorzugten Arbeitgeber.* München: Oldenbourg.

Strategic management insight. (1. May 2013). *BCG Growth-Sahre Matrix.* Strategic management insight: https://www.strategicmanagementinsight.com/tools/bcg-matrix-growth-share.html

Stream, Z. (3. July 2017). *The importance of Colors for Retail Stores.* Zenmerchandiser: https://zenmerchandiser.com/visual/the-importance-of-colors-for-retail-stores/

Südkurier. (Novemer 2016). *Eyetracking-Studie: So intensiv werden Zeitungsanzeigen wahrgenommen.* Südkurier Medienhaus: https://blog.suedkurier-medienhaus.de/werbung-printonline/eyetracking-studie-so-intensiv-werden-zeitungsanzeigen-wahrgenommen/

Suttle, R. (29. June 2018). *List of Market Segments for the Retail Clothing Market.* smallbusiness: https://smallbusiness.chron.com/list-market-segments-retail-clothing-market-32446.html

Taube, J., & Warnaby, G. (2017). How Brand Interaction in Pop-Up Shops Influences Consumers' Perceptions of Luxury Fashion Retailers. *Journal of Fashion Marketing and Management: An International Journal, 21*(3), 385–399.

Tavolieri, J. (September 2019). *AR and VR Will Drive Omnichannel 2.0.* Nielsen: https://www.nielsen.com/us/en/insights/article/2020/ar-and-vr-will-drive-omnichannel-2-0/?utm_source=sfmc&utm_medium=email&utm_campaign=newswire&utm_content=1-15-2020

Teo, T., & Lee, C. B. (2010). Explaining the intention to use technology among student teachers: An application of the Theory of Planned Behavior (TPB). *Campus-Wide Information Systems, 27*(2), 60–67.

Terblanche, N. S., & Boshoff, C. (2006). The Relationship Between a Satisfactory In-Store Shopping Experience and Retailer Loyalty. *South Africam Journal of Business Management, 37*(2), 33–43.

Terlau, W., & Hirsch, D. (2015). Sustainable Consumption and the Attitude-Behaviour-Gap Phenomenon – Causes and Measurements towards a Sustainable Development. *Int. J. Food System Dynamics*, *6*(3), 159–174.

The Asian Banker. (13. October 2014). *QR Code Payment System – A Game Changer?* Von The Asian Banker: http://www.theasianbanker.com/updates-and-articles/qr-code-payment-system,-a-game-changer

The Clean Kilo. (2020). *Shop*. https://www.thecleankilo.co.uk/shop

The Nielsen Company. (April 2015). *The Future of Grocery*. reports: http://www.nielsen.com/us/en/insights/reports/2015/the-future-of-grocery.html

The Reseller Network. (2018). *Types of Retailers*. The Reseller Network: https://www.the-reseller-network.com/content/88/types-of-retailers/

Theng, L., & Lee, S. H. (1999). Consumers' Trust in a Brand and the Link to Brand. *Journal of Market Focused Management*(4), 341–370.

TNS. (2015). *Anzahl der Karten im Portemonnaie*. statista: TNS EMNID Medien-und Sozialforschung GmbH. (18. 11 2015). http://de.statista.com/statistik/daten/studie/159304/umfrage/anzahl-der-karten-im-portemonnaie/

Tomczak, T., Reinecke, S., & Dittrich, S. (2010). *Kundenbindung durch Kundenkarten und -clubs*. Retrieved from https://www.alexandria.unisg.ch/60392/1/Handbuch%20Kundenbindungsmanagement2.pdf

Trader Joe's. (2020). *Our Story*. Trader Joe's: https://www.traderjoes.com/our-story

trendhunter. (12. September 2015). *Alter Eco's Chocolate Truffles Are Packaged in Compostable Foil*. https://www.trendhunter.com/trends/candy-wrappers

trendhunter. (19. June 2015). *'McBike' Is a Carryout Container Designed to Hook onto Handlebars*. https://www.trendhunter.com/trends/mcbike

trendhunter. (2. March 2015). *This Eco-Friendly Plantable Coffee Cup Turns into Compost as Well*. https://www.trendhunter.com/trends/plantable-coffee-cup

trendhunter. (2017). *Penningtons*. https://www.trendhunter.com/trends/penningtons

Trendhunter. (2019a). *Interactive spaces*. https://www.trendhunter.com/trends/interactive-spaces

Trendhunter. (2019b). S*Ted Baker Shoreditch*. https://www.trendhunter.com/trends/ted-baker-shoreditch

Trendwatching. (2016). *5 consumer trends for 2016*. Von http://trendwatching.com/trends/5-trends-for-2016/ abgerufen

Trendwatching. (2017). *5 Consumer Trends for 2016*. http://trendwatching.com/trends/5-trends-for-2016/

Tröpfer, M., & Bug, P. (2015). *Classical Consumer Lifestyle Segmentation Methods*. https://publikationen.reutlingen-university.de/frontdoor/deliver/index/docId/1370/file/1370.pdf

Truong, Y., McColl, R., & Kitchen, P. J. (2009). New Luxury Brand Positioning and the Emergence of Masstige Brands. *Journal of Brand Management*, *16*, 375–382.

Uber. (2019). *How Ubers Dynamic Pricing Model Works*. Uber: https://www.uber.com/en-GB/blog/uber-dynamic-pricing/

UKessays. (17. July 2018). *Walmarts everyday low prices strategy*. UKessays: https://www.ukessays.com/essays/management/wal-marts-every-day-low-prices-in-china-management-essay.php

Underhill, P. (2012). *Warum kaufen wir? – Die Psychologie des Konsums*. Frankfurt am Main: Campus Verlag GmbH.

Unilever. (2019). *UN Sustainable Development Goals*. Unilever: https://www.unilever.com/sustainable-living/our-strategy/un-sustainable-development-goals/

Usunier, J.-C. (2011). *The shift from manufacturing to brand origin: Suggestions for improving COO relevance*. International Marketing Review, 28, pp. 486-496.

Varley, R. (2014). *Retail Product Management: Buying and Merchandising*. New York: Routledge.

Verhoef, P., Lemon, K., Parasuraman, A. P., Roggeveen, A., Tsiros, M. & Schlesinger, L. (2009). Customer Experience Creation: Determinants, Dynamics and Management Strategies. Journal of Retailing, 85, 31–41.

Verhoef, P., & Sloot, L. (2010). Out-of-stock. In M. Krafft, & M. Mantrala, *Retailing in the 21st Century*. New York: Springer Heidelberg.

Vinerean, S., & Opreana, A. (2019). Social Media Marketing Efforts of Luxury Brands on Instagram. *Expert Journal of Marketing*, 144–152.

Vinzi. (2019). *About us*. https://www.vinzi.at/

Vrechopoulos, A., O'Keefe, R., Doukidis, G., & Siomkos, G. (2004). Virtual Store Layout: An Experimental Comparison in the Context of Grocery Retail. *Journal of Retailing, 80*(1), 13–22.

Wagner, T., Kuhndt, M., Lagomarsino, J., & Mattar, H. (2015). *Listening to Sharing Economy Initiatives*. http://projects.mcrit.com/foresightlibrary/attachments/article/1045/Listening_to_ Sharing_Economy_Initiatives.pdf#:~:text=The%20Sharing%20Economy%20initiatives% 20mainly%20focus%20their%20operations,and%20has%20a%20lower%20concentration% 20of%20underutilised

Walmart. (9. May 2018). *Walmart Tests New Last Mile Grocery Delivery Service*. https://corporate. walmart.com/newsroom/2018/09/05/https://corporate.walmart.com/newsroom/2018/09/ 05/walmart-tests-new-last-mile-grocery-delivery-service

Walmart. (2019a). *Our Business*. Walmart: https://corporate.walmart.com/our-story/our-business

Walmart. (2019b). *Our Retail Divisions*. Walmart: https://corporate.walmart.com/newsroom/2005/ 01/06/our-retail-divisions

Wang, S. (2014). *Category Management*. Nielsen: http://www.nielsen.com/content/dam/ nielsenglobal/tw/docs/category-management-2014en.pdf

Watkins, A. (2014). *Helly, My Name Is Awesome – How to Create Brand Names that Stick*. San Francisco: Berrett-Koehler.

Weinswig, D. (20. November 2016). *AI Personal Assistants: How Will They Change Our Lives?* Von Fung Global Retail & Technolgy: http://www.deborahweinswig.com/wp-content/uploads/ 2016/11/AI-Personal-Assistant-October-27-2016.pdf

Weinswig, D. (September 2016). *China's Mobile Payments*. Fung Global Retail & Tech: https://www. fungglobalretailtech.com/research/cybersecurity-china-mobile-payment-market-risk-chinese-consumers-great/?ct=t(DAILY_FEED_SEP_1_20169_1_2016) &mc_cid=a4f3116fda&mc_eid=0d34aa9f41

Weinswig, D. (6. December 2016). *What Is Amazon Go, and What it Means for Amazon and its Competitors*. Fung Global Retail & Technology: https://fgrtresources-rm31c3pfhm5geadr1. netdna-ssl.com/wp-content/uploads/2016/12/Amazon-Go-Flash-Report-December-6-2016.

Weinswig, D. (13. June 2017). *3D Body-Scanning Technology for Creating the Perfect Fit*. Fung Global Reatil & Technology: https://www.fungglobalretailtech.com/research/3d-body-scanning-tech nology-creating-perfect-fit/

Weinswig, D. (August 2017). *Alibaba Group: From Strength to Strength – An Overview of the Business Units of the World's Largest E-Commerce Company*. Fung Global Reatil & Tech: https://www.fungglobalretailtech.com/wp-content/uploads/2017/08/Alibaba-Group-From-Strength-to-Strength-August-4-2017.pdf?mc_cid=499350d674&mc_eid=0d34aa9f41

Weinswig, D. (19. October 2017). *Deep Dive: Private Label in US Grocery – Five Drivers of Growth*. Fung Global Retail & Tech: https://www.fungglobalretailtech.com/research/deep-dive-private-label-us-grocery-five-drivers-growth/?utm_source=Primary+List&utm_campaign=193851b8fb-DAILY_FEED_NOV_9_201611_9_2016&utm_medium=email&utm_term=0_07f1d639d2-193851b8fb-258116117&ct=t(DAILY_FEE

Weinswig, D. (October 2017). *Deep Dive: The Amazon Invasion – A Timeline of the E-Commerce Giant's Global Conquest*. Fung Global Retail & Tech: https://www.fungglobalretailtech.com/

research/deep-dive-amazon-invasion-timeline-e-commerce-giants-global-conquest/?ct=t (DAILY_FEED_SEP_1_20169_1_2016)&mc_cid=754dc658a3&mc_eid=84200c1fca

Weinswig, D. (October 2017). *Deep Dive: The Future Customer Experience- AI and IoT in Retail*. Fung Global Retail & Tech: https://www.fungglobalretailtech.com/research/deep-dive-future-cus tomer-experience-ai-iot-retail/?utm_source=Primary+List&utm_campaign=102bd0deed-Week end_Feed_DEC_3_2016_Infographics12_2_2016&utm_medium=email&utm_term=0_ 07f1d639d2-102bd0deed-258116117&mc_

Weinswig, D. (16. January 2017). *Millenial Lifestyles Drive Growth in Apparel Rental*. am 18. January 2017 von Fung Global Retail & Technology: https://fgrtresources-rm31c3pfhm5geadr1.netdna-ssl.com/wp-content/uploads/2017/01/Millennial-Lifestyles-Drive-Growth-in-Apparel-Rental-January-16-2017.pdf

Weinswig, D. (November 2017). *Singles' Day 2017 Wrap-Up: New Retail Helps Boost Singles' Day Sales to Record High*. Fung Global Retail & Tech: https://www.fungglobalretailtech.com/news/ singles-day-2017-wrap-new-retail-helps-boost-singles-day-sales-record-high/?ct=t (DAILY_FEED_SEP_1_20169_1_2016)&mc_cid=ce8b00db0c&mc_eid=84200c1fca

Weitz, B. A. (2010). Electronic Retailing. In M. Krafft, & M. K. Mantrala, *Retailing in the 21st Century* (309–324). Berlin: Springer.

White, J. (3. March 2020). *5 Branding and Packaging Trends 2020*. https://www.packagingdigest. com/packaging-design/5-branding-and-packaging-trends-2020

Wiencke, W. (1994). *Cards & Clubs: der Kundenclub als Dialogmarkteing-Instrument*. Düsseldorf.

wikipedia. (July 2020). *Miles & More*. https://de.wikipedia.org/wiki/Miles_%26_More

Wind, J. & Green, P. (1974). *Some Conceptual, Measurement, and Analytical Problems in Life Style Research*. Chicago: American Marketing Association.

Wirtz, B. W. (2012). *Direktmarketing-Management. Wi*. Wiesbaden: Springer.

Witzler, T., & Pavelka, W. (2007). *Erfolg im Handel - Ein Praxishandbuch für Verkäufer und Produktmanager*. Wien: Facultas.

WKO. (2019). *Was ist CSR?* Von WKO: https://www.wko.at/branchen/information-consulting/ unternehmensberatung-buchhaltung-informationstechnologie/csr/Was_ist_CSR_.html

Wood, Z., & Butler, S. (30. January 2015). *Tesco Cuts range by 30% to simplify shopping*. The Guardian: https://www.theguardian.com/business/2015/jan/30/tesco-cuts-range-products

Worldpay. (30. July 2019). *How Secure are NFC terminals?* Von Worldpay: https://www.worldpay. com/en-us/insights-hub/article/how-secure-are-nfc-terminals

Yi, Y., & Jeon, H. (2003). Effects of Loyalty Programs on Value Perception, Program Loyalty, and Brand Loyalty. *American Behavioral Scientist, 31*(3), 1511–1516.

Yulan Wang, B. S., Lo, C. K., & Shum, M. (2012). The Impact of Ethical Fashion on Consumer Purchase Behaviour. *Journal of Fashion Marketing and Management, 16*(2), 234–245.

Zachary, T. (2019). *HR Trends in 2020: The Future of Human Resource Management*. https://www. selecthub.com/hris/future-of-hr-software-trends/

Zentes J., Morschett D., Schramm-Klein H. (2011) Retail Formats – General Merchandise. In: Strategic Retail Management. Gabler Verlag.

Zero Waste Austria Verein. (2019). *Zero Waste Shops*. https://www.zerowasteaustria.at/ zero-waste-shops.html#

Zielke, S. (2002). *Kundenorientierte Warenplatzierung – Modelle und Methoden für das Category Management*. Stuttgart: Kohlhammer.

List of Figures

https://doi.org/10.1515/9783110543827-011

List of Tables

https://doi.org/10.1515/9783110543827-012

List of Tables

https://doi.org/10.1515/9783110543827-012

Index

https://doi.org/10.1515/9783110543827-013

www.ingramcontent.com/pod-product-compliance
Lightning Source LLC
Chambersburg PA
CBHW070149240326
41598CB00082BA/6875

9 783110 543834